1000 YEARS OF ANNOYING THE FRENCH

Stephen Clarke

BLACK SWAN

TRANSWORLD PUBLISHERS
61–63 Uxbridge Road, London W5 5SA
www.transworldbooks.co.uk

Transworld is part of the Penguin Random House group of companies
whose addresses can be found at global.penguinrandomhouse.com

Penguin
Random House
UK

First published in Great Britain in 2010 by Bantam Press
an imprint of Transworld Publishers
Black Swan edition published 2011
Black Swan edition reissued 2015

A CIP catalogue record for this book
is available from the British Library.

ISBNs
9780552779937 B format
9781784160401 A format

Typeset in 11/13pt Giovanni Book by Falcon Oast Graphic Art Ltd.
Printed in the UK by Clays Ltd, St Ives plc

Penguin Random House is committed to a sustainable
future for our business, our readers and our planet. This book
is made from Forest Stewardship Council® certified paper.

MIX
Paper from
responsible sources
FSC® C018179

1 3 5 7 9 10 8 6 4 2

To the Crimée Crew for their thousand years of patience, and especially to N., who helped me through every battle.

Merci to my editor Selina Walker for her sense of history in reminding me constantly of my deadline.

And to everyone at Susanna Lea's agency for their role in making this whole *histoire* possible.

'The English, by nature, always want to fight their neighbours for no reason, which is why they all die badly.'

From the *Journal d'un Bourgeois de Paris*, written during the Hundred Years War

'We have been, we are, and I trust we always will be, detested by the French.'

The Duke of Wellington

'The war of wars, the combats of combats, is England against France; all the rest are mere episodes.'

Jules Michelet, nineteenth-century French historian

'The French are a logical people, which is one reason why the English dislike them so intensely. The other is that they own France, a country which we have always judged to be much too good for them.'

Robert Morley, British actor

A selection of English synonyms for 'annoy'

Provoke, infuriate, anger, incense, arouse, offend, affront, outrage, aggrieve, wound, hurt, sting, embitter, irritate, aggravate, exasperate, peeve, miff, ruffle, rile, rankle, enrage, infuriate, madden, drive crazy/mad/insane, get up the back/on the tits of, bust the balls of, piss off.

All of these have been done to France, and more . . .

Contents

Introduction to the 2015 Edition

There are many important anniversaries in Anglo-French history, as you might expect from two nations who fought non-stop for about nine centuries and who have spent much of the time since the Entente Cordiale aiming snubs and slurs at each other.

But 2015 sees two of the greatest anniversaries – it is two hundred years since Waterloo, the battle that ended Napoleon Bonaparte's career, and six hundred since Agincourt, when the flower of French aristocracy was cut down by a bunch of lower-class British archers. Both will be commemorated with re-enactments and, with Napoleon enjoying a wave of nostalgia, France will probably be trying for victory at Waterloo this time. Even more than their other defeats against *les Anglais*, Waterloo is still very hard to digest.

There has also been a lot of new Anglo-French activity since *1000 Years of Annoying the French* was first published in 2010. We mischievous English-speakers have certainly not given up our old habits. Our addiction to annoying the French lives on, and this new 2015 edition gives me the chance to write about some of our most recent exploits.

There was the Dominique Strauss-Kahn case, for

example, in which the Americans proved how flawed their justice system is by actually treating a member of the French political elite *like a normal suspect*. What were they thinking of?

Britain and France also continued to demonstrate why the *Entente* is no more than *Cordiale*, even during the supposedly friendly 2012 London Olympics. We Brits seemed to decide to devote the Games almost entirely to the cause of baiting and humiliating the French, who responded with true Olympic spirit by accusing us of cheating. It was Waterloo in sports kit.

Meanwhile, annoying the French has become such a popular sport in the British and American media that France's politicians have actually adopted some new English vocabulary – '*le French-bashing*'. And they've complained about it so often that they can even pronounce it properly.

For this 2015 edition of *1000 Years of Annoying the French*, I have also looked back into the past, hunting out some historical cases of French-baiting that I didn't include first time round: there is, for example, the outrageous French claim that they wrote 'God Save the King'; the story of Napoleon's cruelly confiscated chamber pot; and British attempts to discredit Pierre and Marie Curie's discovery of radium.

My only regret is that I won't be around in a few centuries' time to put together *1500 Years of Annoying the French*. The way things are going, there will be no shortage of new material.

Stephen Clarke, February 2015

Introduction

One of the most frequent questions I get asked when doing readings and talks is: why is there such a love–hate relationship between the French and the Brits?

The love is easy to explain: despite what we might say in public, we find each other irresistibly sexy. The hate is more of a problem. For a start, it's mistrust rather than hatred. But why is it even there, in these days of Entente Cordiale and European peace?

Like everyone else, I always knew that the mistrust had something to do with 1066, Agincourt, Waterloo and all that, but I wondered why it persisted. After all, most of our battles were too far in the past to have much effect on the present, surely? So I decided to delve into that past and come up with a more accurate answer.

And having written this book, I finally understand where the never-ending tensions come from. The fact is that our history isn't history at all. It's here and now.

William Faulkner was talking about the Southern USA when he said that 'the past is never dead. In fact, it's not even past.' But exactly the same thing can be said about the French and the Brits; no matter what we try to do in the present, the past will always march up and slap us in the face.

To give the simplest of examples: if you are lucky enough to be invited to an Anglo-French function at the British Ambassador's residence in Paris, go in to the first anteroom and what do you see? A gigantic portrait of the Duke of Wellington, the man who effectively ended the career of France's greatest general, Napoleon Bonaparte. Essentially, a two-century-old defeat is brandished in the face of every French visitor to Britain's diplomatic headquarters . . . in France's own capital city.

This is not tactless or provocative – relations couldn't be better between the British Embassy and their French hosts – it's simply *there*. Just as the battle between the sexes will never end (we hope), neither will the millennium-old rivalry between the French and anyone who happens to be born speaking English.

And the most interesting thing for me was that while researching this book, I found that our versions of the same events are like two completely different stories. The French see history through tricolour-tinted glasses and blame the Brits (and after about 1800, the Americans) for pretty well every misfortune that has ever befallen France. Sometimes they're right – we have done some nasty things to the French in the past – but often they're hilariously wrong, and I have tried to set the record straight.

I realize that any book that gives a balanced view of history is going to irritate French people a lot. So I'm really sorry, France, but the 1000 years of being annoyed by 'les Anglo-Saxons' aren't over yet . . .

Stephen Clarke, January 2010

France, featuring the key places of historical interest –
famous and otherwise – mentioned in this book.

1

When Is a Frenchman Not a Frenchman?

The French are very proud of the fact that they were the last people to invade the British Isles. Hitler didn't make it beyond Calais, the Spanish Armada was swept into the North Sea, and even France's own Napoleon never managed to land more than a few bedraggled soldiers on British soil. William the Conqueror, on the other hand, not only invaded England, he grabbed the whole country and turned it into a French colony.

However, as with so many things in the French version of history, this is not quite correct. Or, to be more precise, it is almost completely wrong.

For a start, a Dutchman, William of Orange, successfully invaded Britain in 1688. But because this was a bloodless take-over, it could be argued that it was less an invasion than the response to a plea from the Brits to come and save them from themselves.

More importantly, though, if you look at the facts of the Norman Conquest in 1066, it becomes clear that France's claim to have launched the last successful cross-Channel invasion is completely unfounded. It seems rather harsh to begin this book by undermining one of the core ideas in France's collective historical psyche, but it has to be done . . .

My kingdom for a Norse

Before 1066, the issue troubling the inhabitants of what is now Britain was not 'Will I get a decent pension?' or 'How much is my house worth?' It was more along the lines of 'When will a horde of axe-wielding murderers come charging across the horizon to rape the women and steal the cattle (or in the case of certain Viking tribes the other way round)?'

If people didn't starve to death because of famine or pillage, if they managed to get the harvest in and have time to eat it, life was good. And to give themselves a reasonable chance of enjoying this luxury, what they needed most was a strong king. Someone who would tax them half to death but who might just keep them alive long enough to pay the taxes – a lot like modern governments, in fact.

In the ninth century, Britain had just such a king: Alfred. By maintaining a permanent fleet and a highly trained army, Alfred managed to keep England – or the portion he governed, up as far as the Midlands – free of Viking raiders. In fact, Alfred earned the title 'the Great' because of the way he transformed these raids on Britain from violent treasure hunts into suicide missions.

The upshot was that the Vikings, understandably frustrated at losing a sizeable chunk of their income, decided to sail a few miles further south and pillage France, where much easier pickings were to be had. So easy, in fact, that the Vikings set up bases on the French coast from which to raid inland – sort of pillaging resorts. Soon, the whole region was so unstable that the King of France was forced to pacify the invaders by ceding a large slab of territory to these 'men of the north'. And in the year 911 the region officially became the country of the Norsemen, or Normandy.

In short, Normandy owed its existence to an Englishman who deflected invaders away from Britain and over to France. An auspicious start.

In those days, the domain governed by the French King was little more than a collection of easily defendable duchies in the northeast of what we now call France, and the ruler was a puppet who could barely hold on to his own lands, never mind invade anyone else's. In fact, these kings didn't even call themselves French until more than a hundred years after William the Conqueror, when in 1181 Philippe Auguste first took the title 'Rex Franciae' (King of France) as opposed to 'Rex Francorum' (King of the Franks).

And when one of these Kings of the Franks did try to bring the troublesome Normans under his umbrella, it was with disastrous results. In 942, the Duke of Normandy, the formidable-sounding William Long Sword, was assassinated and succeeded by a mere ten-year-old called Richard. Sensing weakness, King Louis IV of the Franks decided to attack southern Normandy and capture Rouen, the major river port between Paris and the coast. But young Richard was not alone – he was supported by powerful clansmen with names like Bernard the Dane, Harald the Viking and Sigtrygg the King of the Sea, and the invasion ended in Frankish tears. Louis was captured and only released in exchange for hostages – one of Louis's sons and a bishop. In short, the Normans were issuing a clear warning that they had zero fellow feeling with the Franks, Burgundians, Lorraines or anyone else in the country that would one day become France. They wanted to be left alone.

All of which leads to a rather obvious conclusion: despite what a modern Parisian might tell you, the

Normans weren't French at all. Calling a tenth- or eleventh-century Norman a Frenchman would have been a bit like telling a Glaswegian he's English, and we all know how dangerous that can be.

In fact, the Normans thought of the Franks as a bunch of limp Parisians who acted as if they owned the continent and needed to be kicked back home if they strayed too far from their snobbish little city. (An attitude, incidentally, that hasn't changed much since the tenth century.)

And the feeling was mutual – the Franks looked down on the Norman dukes as dangerous Nordic barbarians who lived only for hunting and war, and who practised heathen-style polygamy, living with hordes of mistresses and illegitimate children.

The Franks were perfectly right, and it was into this context that William was born.

William was a bastard

It is still possible to visit the Conqueror's birthplace today, in a small Norman town called Falaise (the French word for cliff). William's castle, or, as the locals call it, le Château de Guillaume le Conquérant, dominates the whole area from a rocky knoll opposite the grey stone cliff in question.

At the centre of a walled enclosure stands a freshly renovated Norman keep, a proud angular tower made of the creamy-white Caen stone that William and his descendants exported all over their territories, both in Britain and on the continent. Norman castle-builders insisted on working with Caen stone because it was easy to carve, yet resistant to the onslaught of weather and missiles (plus, presumably, they had shares in the quarries back home).

However sure of itself le Château de Guillaume le Conquérant might look today, though, it suffers from something of an identity crisis, because it isn't actually the castle where William was born. In fact, in 1120 William's son Henry came to Falaise, knocked down the old chateau and rebuilt one of his own. None of the original structure survives.

It seems strange – Henry becomes King of England and Duke of Normandy, and the first thing he does is return to his father's birthplace and demolish it. It's almost as though he wanted to deny his origins, as if there might be some shame associated with William's birth. And it's true – the Conqueror did have spectacularly low-class roots.

William wasn't known as 'the Conqueror' at first, of course. But he did acquire his other nickname pretty well immediately – 'William the Bastard'. His unmarried parents were Robert, the younger brother of the incumbent Duke of Normandy, and a beautiful girl from Falaise whose name differs according to which history book you read. In French sources, she has been called Herleva, Harlotta, Herlette, Arlot, Allaieve and Bellon.*

The story of how the young maiden met Robert also varies. In 1026 or 1027, she was either washing animal skins in the river or dancing, or maybe both, when Robert rode through the village of Falaise on his way to the castle. He caught sight of the lovely girl (let's call her Herleva for simplicity's sake) and instantly started to plan what his contemporaries called a 'Danish marriage', or, as we might say today, a shag.

According to later Anglo-Saxon legends, probably invented to irritate the Normans, Robert kidnapped Herleva. To be fair, though, he did go and inform her father, a local tanner, what he was doing. The father tried

---

* Frenchmen don't always remember a girl's name, just her looks.

to insist on marriage, which Robert refused, mainly because Herleva wasn't posh enough – tanners were amongst the lowest of the low. Leather was tanned using a combination of urine, animal fat, brains and dung (dogs' muck worked very well, apparently), which meant that leatherworkers were even more malodorous than cesspit-cleaners.

Marriage was no real problem, though. Norman nobles didn't need to wed their conquests, so Herleva was washed of the leathery smell and laid out on Robert's bed in his creamy-white chateau to become his *frilla*, or local mistress.

Shortly after this, Robert's elder brother, Duke Richard of Normandy, attacked Falaise and took the castle. (It was the kind of thing warlike Normans often used to do to their brothers.) Feeling pleased with himself, Richard returned to his headquarters in Rouen, where he promptly died in mysterious circumstances, which was another thing Normans did, especially if they annoyed ambitious men like Robert.

With characteristic modesty, Robert dubbed himself Duke Robert the Magnificent and reclaimed his castle at Falaise. And it was there, in late 1027 or early 1028, that Herleva bore him a son. The French know the baby as Guillaume, but even French historians admit that the newborn's real name would have been something much closer to the English William, and the Bayeux Tapestry gives him the decidedly northern-sounding name of Willelm.

From a very young age, circumstances combined to prepare the little Bastard for his future role as conqueror of England. In 1035, Robert, who never married, proclaimed William his successor, a choice which in no way shocked or disconcerted the Normans. As the French historian Paul Zumthor says in his biography of

Guillaume: 'nowhere else in Christian Europe could a bastard have acceded to the throne'.* The boy William was sent to live with a cousin, and began to be groomed as a fighting duke.

He soon gained a reputation as a very serious young man, his only real pleasures being hunting and the occasional juggling show. He never got drunk at table, consuming a maximum of three glasses of wine (more evidence that he wasn't French), and had little or no sense of humour. He was, however, really excellent at hurting people, and reserved his most murderous rages for anyone who made a joke about his humble origins.

When he was twenty-four, William decided to consolidate his political position by making a good match. Not content with an old-fashioned 'Danish marriage', he decided to wed Mathilde (as the French call her, or Maheut, which was probably her original name), daughter of the Count of Flanders and a granddaughter of the incumbent King of the Franks.

Mathilde wasn't so keen, however, and made it public that she didn't want to marry a bastard. But William wasn't the type to let anyone get away with insulting his mum, so he leapt straight on his horse and galloped from Normandy to Lille, almost 400 kilometres away, crossing the Seine valley, splashing through the marshlands of the Somme and penetrating deep into the potentially dangerous territory of the King of the Franks. After several days in the saddle, and no doubt without stopping to freshen up or buy flowers, William bounded into the Count of Flanders's castle, threw Mathilde to the ground and, as Paul Zumthor puts it, 'tore her robe with his spurs', which is probably *not* a metaphor for 'asked her

* Although, of course, various European countries have been ruled by a fair number of bastards since.

27

really nicely to marry him'. Apparently, the haughty young lady 'recognized that she had met her master' and agreed to the wedding.

Her father probably had something to do with this sudden change of opinion, too. When a Norman rode into your territory and had his way with your daughter, it was a heavy hint – similar things could, if necessary, happen to the rest of your domains. And William himself was the living embodiment of his political clout. At a muscular five feet ten, he was a giant for his time, a veteran of several military campaigns, and quite obviously a man with a future. Not a bad candidate for a son-in-law.

There was just one hitch to the pair getting hitched. What William had forgotten, or chosen to ignore, was that he and his new fiancée were cousins, and the Church opposed their union. Never one to back down from a fight, William decided to go ahead anyway, and the couple were married sometime between 1051 and 1053.

The relationship was a tumultuous one. As we've seen, William was famous for flying into sudden furies, and in Mathilde he had apparently met his match, even though many sources say she was only about four feet four inches tall. The couple would often have flaming rows, and it is said that during one of these, William dragged Mathilde through the streets of Caen by her hair to show everyone who was boss. Despite the occasional descent into domestic violence, though, their marriage was deemed a great success. William was pretty well the only ruler of his time who sired no bastards and who was faithful to his wife,* and during their thirty-year union, the couple had ten children: six girls and four boys.

This devotion to creating a dynasty, coupled with

---

* Definitely not French, then.

William's obsession with getting his own way, did not bode well for the Anglo-Saxon rulers who were now sitting pretty in England.

A tapestry of illusions

If we know so much about William's reasons for invading England and ousting King Harold, it is because the Bayeux Tapestry paints such a detailed picture of historical events.

The 70-metre-long embroidery, with its vivid tableaux recounting events leading up to the Conquest and ending with Harold's death at Hastings, is a stunningly beautiful work of art, and anyone with the slightest interest in history, culture, needlework or just plain human endeavour should go and see it. Its survival is a miracle – in 1792, during the French Revolution, it was almost cut up to cover ammunition wagons, and in the Second World War Goebbels did his best to steal it. It is the only embroidery of its type and age to have lasted so long.

Its only failing is that it is definitely not a record of the historical facts.

A modern parallel might be ex-President Bush commissioning a film about Iraq. Make sure, he would say, that it starts with footage of Saddam's weapons of mass destruction. What do you mean there never was any footage? Make some! Then we want plenty of tanks and explosions – I like explosions. Torturing prisoners? No, we don't need any of that depressing stuff. Oh, and at the end, it's me who catches Saddam, OK?

This, anyhow, is what the Bayeux Tapestry was assumed to be. But what makes it so fascinating is that it didn't quite turn out that way.

For one thing, the job of putting the Conquest into pictures was given to Anglo-Saxon seamstresses, who

'Here they made a meal' – William the Conqueror's men land in England, and the first thing they do is have a barbecue. But they weren't French. Refined eating was just one of the habits these Norsemen had picked up while living on the Continent.

were famous throughout Europe for the quality of their embroidery, and seem to have taken the opportunity to add in lots of jokes. To make things even more complicated, the story itself would appear to have been told by someone who wanted to undermine everything William had done.

The best way to get to the root of all this is to try and unpick the tangled threads of the tapestry, and compare the Franco-Norman propaganda that has come down through history with another, perhaps more credible, telling of events. Let's take things step by step . . .

Step 1: The Duke who would be King

By the 1050s, William, now Duke of Normandy, had fought off Breton and Frankish invaders and quelled Norman rebels. Possibly inspired by the mistake that his late uncle Richard had made in capturing Falaise Castle and then letting his brother come and murder him, William had developed a simple but effective strategy for dealing with enemies. Instead of bashing down their portcullises, claiming their chateaux as his own, and then going home to be poisoned or otherwise assassinated, William would pursue aggressors or anyone he felt like attacking until he either killed them or seized all their riches and rendered them totally powerless. Pretty soon, word had got round that it was not a good idea to annoy William unless you were sure of being able to take him out, which was a slim possibility given that he had a personal army of highly trained knights and was himself a fearsome fighter.

William was also intensely ambitious, and had long had his eye on England. Under the Anglo-Saxons, it had become a rich, stable country, but things had changed since Alfred the Great's day: the Scandinavians were raiding again, and the King of England, Edward the

Confessor, was weak and under the thumb of warring earls. There was room for a strong man like William to step in and seize power.

Moreover, William knew that he might not have to do much fighting. King Edward was married to the daughter of one of the warring Anglo-Saxon earls, but he had taken a vow of chastity, and he had no direct heir. Edward was William's father's cousin, so in theory William had a claim to the English throne. In addition, Edward owed a debt of sorts to Normandy, because he had taken refuge there during the reign of King Cnut.* And just as Brits who have lived in France come home with a taste for almost-raw steak and unpasteurized cheese, Edward had a fondness for all things Norman, and surrounded himself with Norman courtiers. All in all, it was a situation that the ambitious William couldn't afford to ignore.

William duly went to visit his royal cousin Edward, and, according to Norman chroniclers, the trip confirmed his feelings about England: 'When William saw what a green and pleasant land it was, he thought he would very much like to be its king.' Yes, a cynic might add, green, pleasant and full of treasure, valuable farmland and taxpayers.

It was during this state visit that Edward is supposed to have appointed the young Norman as his official successor to the English throne. And if you go to the vast former monastery in Bayeux that now houses the tapestry, you will be informed categorically that this was the case: William was the only rightful claimant to Edward's crown, because Edward himself had said so.

---

* Canute, as history books used to call him, was King of England from 1016 to 1035. A Dane, he left his mark on his adopted country by inventing the typically English habit of sitting on a beach in a deckchair and not noticing when the tide comes in.

This is an opinion that was first recorded in the 1070s by the chronicler William of Poitiers, a friend of the Conqueror whose account of the Conquest is about as reliable as a biography of Genghis Khan published by Mongolians R Us Books. And it is this version of events that the modern-day Normans in Bayeux would still have us believe.

But it's a false premise, because, according to eleventh-century Anglo-Saxon law, the successor to the English throne had to be approved by a 'wise men's council' of bishops and earls, known as the Witangemot. Edward had no right to pass on his crown. His promise, if it really existed, was probably part of a deal – he no doubt wanted to buy William's support if he had to go to war to hang on to his crown. Edward, a Norman on his mother's side, was unpopular with his Anglo-Saxon subjects. As well as his Norman courtiers, he had brought in Norman sheriffs to rule parts of England – foreign noblemen who spoke no Anglo-Saxon and didn't have a clue about local customs. The Anglo-Saxon earls, who ruled over vast swathes of the English countryside, were in a semi-constant state of rebellion against the presence of these foreign lawmakers, and were also jostling for position to take over the throne.

The most powerful of the earls, Godwin of Wessex, had his eyes set firmly on the seat of power. He had married his daughter Edith to Edward, and was understandably annoyed that the union produced no princes. It was even rumoured that Edward had taken his vow of celibacy just to frustrate Godwin.

Godwin was virulently anti-Norman. In 1051, a group of Normans got into a fight in Dover and – having far less experience than the English of town-centre brawling after the pubs closed – came off worse. Several of the Normans were killed, and King Edward ordered Godwin to go and punish the townsfolk for being so inhospitable to his foreign friends. Godwin not only refused but thought that this Norman-bashing sounded fun, and declared war on Edward's continental cronies. He marched an army to London, where he received a hero's welcome from the people, and suddenly it was much less fashionable in England to be a Norman.

Godwin demanded that the foreign courtiers be sent home, and Edward was forced to comply. One can imagine the poor King sitting forlornly in his palace, deprived of his Norman playmates, begging his minstrels to play 'Je ne regrette rien'. Not surprisingly, it was around this time that he supposedly pledged the throne to William.

There was one consolation for Edward, though. Godwin had a dashing young son – the handsome, blond Harold Godwinson – and Edward liked handsome young men. (There are other theories about his lack of children, aside from his piety.) So, in the early 1060s, apparently forgetting his earlier promise to William, Edward elected Harold his new favourite. The brave, warlike young Anglo-Saxon, popular not only with the King but also with the Witangemot and the people, began to look like a very probable candidate for the throne of England.

On the other side of the Channel, however, someone wasn't happy . . .

Step 2: A hostage is just a guest who can't go home yet
For a man whose family had spent years saying rude things about the Normans, Harold Godwinson now did a remarkably rash thing. In 1064, accompanied by only a few companions and his hunting dogs, he came to Normandy. It was a bit like Martin Luther King turning up at a Ku Klux Klan barbecue. And the question is, why would a man from such a politically

astute and active family do such a brainless thing?

At the Bayeux Tapestry museum, you will be told one possible answer. The museum's audio-sets are an invaluable aid to interpreting the tapestry for anyone who can't read the Latin inscriptions and isn't an expert in early medieval iconography. The story of the Conquest is told by an Englishman with the sort of old-fashioned radio voice that used to tell people in the middle of World War Two that 'if Jerry pokes his nose across the *Chennel*, we'll give him a jolly good *threshing*.' You can't help but believe him as he informs you that Harold came to Normandy with a message from the ageing King Edward the Confessor, confirming that he wanted William as his successor after all.

But if you lift the audio-set away from your ear for a second and cut off the hypnotic voice, you might start to question why on earth Harold would do such a thing, when he himself was a likely candidate for the English throne.

There was another possible motive for his trip. It has been suggested that Harold crossed the Channel on a mission to retrieve two members of his family who had been kidnapped by Normans in 1051 and held hostage on the continent ever since. This is of course much more credible. If Harold became King of England and thereby provoked the covetous William, the two unfortunate Godwins languishing in Norman dungeons were bound to get their rations, or worse things, cut.

So the first tableau in the tapestry could well represent Harold getting permission from King Edward to go and reclaim the prisoners, and not Edward ordering him to go and deliver the humiliating, anti-Godwin confirmation of William's claim to the English throne.

Either way, as bad luck would have it, Harold's ship blew off course and he landed in Ponthieu (part of the

Duchy of Normandy), in an area ruled by a notorious hostage-taker called Count Wido. Harold's unexpected arrival made the Count a very merry Wido indeed, and he immediately seized the rich Anglo-Saxon.

Unluckily for Wido, his superior in the feudal system, William, heard about the windfall and decreed that the hostage was his. Which was true – as Duke of Normandy, William's rights included ownership of anything that washed up on the beach, including numerous whale carcasses, which were a valuable source of oils and ivory.*

As a prisoner of his Norman rival, Harold might well have feared for his life, but he was probably in little danger of receiving a sword stroke as a welcoming gift. William didn't usually kill his well-born enemies unless they were no longer useful to him or made a joke about the leather industry. He preferred to make them swear an oath of feudal fealty, which meant that they were obliged, on pain of death and/or eternal barbecuing in the fires of hell, to give him a percentage of everything they earned and help him defend his territory should the need arise. In short, he butchered the poor enemies and milked the rich ones.

With Harold, there was even more to be won – an oath of allegiance would sideline the Godwin family as contenders for the English Crown, because they would have to step aside for their superior, William. In the tapestry, you can almost hear the Norman chuckling as an abashed Harold swears eternal loyalty to William. According to Saxon sources, Harold didn't know as he gave his oath that holy relics were hidden under the

* When William later went off to conquer England, he created an even smellier job than leather-making: guarding the beached whales until he came home.

table, turning the simple promise into a sacred vow. But to William and the Normans, Harold's ignorance wouldn't have mattered. People were very literal about their religion in those days. If you swore on a saint's funny bone that you would do something, you had to do it, otherwise a plague of monster fleas would crawl inside your army's chainmail. In Norman eyes, Harold's oath was binding, with God as a witness.

William tightened the screws even further by betrothing Harold to his daughter Aélis, even though she was already formally engaged to a local nobleman – thus proving that all Norman oaths were binding, but some were more binding than others.

With Harold now inextricably bound over to submit to William's claim to the English throne, he was finally allowed to sail home to England. The tapestry shows Harold hunched apologetically as he tells his tale to King Edward, who points at him accusingly, as if to say, 'What, you went to Normandy and you didn't bring me any Camembert?'

The audio commentary talks about Harold's 'humiliation', but if Harold's mission really was to tell William he was going to be king, where is the humiliation? He had delivered his message and even sworn allegiance to the future King William. The trip took a bit longer than expected, and he forgot to bring presents, but it went exactly as planned.

On the other hand, Harold had every reason to be bowed if he had failed in his mission to fetch his relatives – not only had he returned alone, he'd also got himself tricked into swearing homage to William when Edward was grooming him, Harold, as successor to the throne.

We will never know the truth, but one thing is certain – when Edward the Confessor died on 5 January 1066, Harold accepted the Witangemot's nomination and became the legally appointed King of England. Across the Channel, William's self-congratulatory chuckles turned into threats of legal action. Harold had sworn allegiance, in front of witnesses and on a saint's funny bone, and could not therefore claim the throne ahead of him. The Normans immediately began to accuse the new King of oath-breaking, feudalism's most heinous crime.

Harold didn't need to hire expensive lawyers to dream up a credible defence, though – what hostage is going to refuse to take an oath to a man who is holding him hostage? And what jurisdiction did this Norman foreigner have in England?

Sensing perhaps that Harold might have a case, Duke William of Normandy even went so far as to plead for support from the Holy Church. (Yes, the same Holy Church whose ruling he had ignored when he wanted to marry his cousin.) As a reward for this new-found piety, the Pope sent William a consecrated banner that figures prominently in the tapestry, much like a sponsor's logo on a Formula One racer's overalls: 'This invasion is brought to you by God', or a message to that effect.

Also very visible in the tapestry is what looks like a kite in the shape of a fried egg. This is Halley's Comet, which appeared at the end of April 1066, and was of course claimed by the Normans as a sign from God that Harold was an evil oath-breaker and had to be ousted by the righteous, God-fearing William, who was, as it happened, just setting off to do the ousting.

These same omen-seekers conveniently ignored the storm that blew the Norman invasion fleet back to France and forced them to take refuge for two weeks before attempting another Channel crossing. And when the fleet finally landed in Hastings on 28 September 1066, there was another potentially bad omen – as William strode to shore, he fell flat on his face, and had to calm his superstitious troops' fear by saying, 'I have seized England in my two hands.'

The tapestry is curiously anti-Norman when it describes the landing. A gang of builders spend as much time brawling as they do constructing William's first stockade. There are also poignant depictions of Norman pillaging – soldiers rustle cattle, a shepherd boy tries to fend off huge knights who are stealing his sheep, and a house burns as a woman pleads for mercy.

Knowing a little about William the Conqueror, it is hard to believe he ever saw these images on the tapestry. But perhaps he simply skipped the first half of the story, because the battle scenes were just about to begin . . .

Step 3: Bring out the weapons of mass destruction
Never let it be said that the English are bad losers, or that we offer feeble excuses to explain away our defeats. When we lost to Argentina in the 1986 World Cup, for example, it really was because Maradona cheated by scoring a goal with his fist. The TV pictures prove it, otherwise we would never complain.

However, the Battle of Hastings, on 14 October 1066, is a bit of an exception, because the Normans would never have won if Harold had been able to field a full-strength team. He had so many star performers out of action, either wounded or dead, that it was always going to be an uphill battle.*

In the two weeks prior to Hastings, Harold had marched his army from London to Yorkshire to face the invasion force of another rival to the throne, the ferocious Viking Harald Hardrada.

Harold met Harald at Stamford Bridge on 25

---

* Although Harold's army held the higher ground, so for them Hastings was actually a downhill battle.

September by the river Derwent near York. The battle, it is said, got off to a bad start for the English when a single Viking stubbornly blocked the entrance to the bridge, killing forty or so of Harold's troops as they tried to cross. Eventually, an English soldier paddled downriver in a barrel, stopped under the bridge, and, thrusting his spear upwards between the planks, spiked the Viking in the groin. Not very sporting, perhaps, but technically the guy was holding up play.

The ensuing battle was horrifically bloody, and cost the lives of many of Harold's best men, but at the end of it, he had effectively smashed the enemy once and for all. Chroniclers record that the fleeing Viking survivors filled only two dozen of the 300 longships that they had arrived in.

After all this exertion, Harold's remaining troops then had to march south again – yet another week's hard slog – to face William, who was living the good life, robbing helpless Sussex peasants and having beach barbecues with the fruits of his pillaging, as well as the meat and vegetables.

The Normans had another advantage over Harold's exhausted army. The Bayeux Tapestry devotes about a quarter of its 70 metres to pictures of Norman knights charging around the Hastings district on their horses. Harold's soldiers fought on foot. The only horses they possessed were little Shetland-type ponies used as beasts of burden, which would have been no use in battle except to distract an enemy by making him laugh. The Normans, on the other hand, were trained in cavalry warfare, and arrived with shiploads of sleek battle horses that had had plenty of time to get over their seasickness.

The tapestry also makes much of the shower of arrows that hailed down on Harold, one of them eventually finding its mark and killing him. A frieze covering the best part of four panels shows a long line of Norman archers supporting the cavalry with their fire, while small groups of brave Anglo-Saxons, sometimes without armour or shields, defend their hilltop. The Anglo-Saxons didn't generally use archers en masse – they believed in the concept of man against man, axe against axe, two warriors face to face in mortal combat.* William would have none of this – it was much less tiring and risky to pincushion the Anglo-Saxons with arrows and then trample the survivors under the hooves of his cavalry.

In short, the Battle of Hastings was like two boxers meeting to contest the European Heavyweight crown, when one of them has just been forced to run a marathon and go fifteen rounds with the World Champion while the other was lounging about at the pool and doing some light sparring against schoolboys. And no sooner have the boxers climbed into the ring than one of them pulls out a grenade launcher and blows his opponent to smithereens.

Not, of course, that one would want to use all this as an excuse for an English defeat.

As it was, against all the odds, Harold came astonishingly close to winning the battle. His men may have been tired, but they were determined to kick these new invaders off their land. The Norman chronicler Wace says that when the fighting began, the Normans called out, 'God be with us!' to which the Saxons replied, 'Get out!' Though, being Anglo-Saxons, their actual words were probably a lot more colourful.

At first, things didn't go William's way. He had numerical superiority – around 8,000 troops compared

---

* Except for the very rare occasion when one of them was forced to spear an unsuspecting enemy from under a bridge, of course.

to Harold's 7,500 – but the Anglo-Saxons had secured an advantageous position on a hilltop. The first wave of Norman arrows plunked harmlessly into a wall of shields, and the follow-up infantry attack was bounced back down the hill, suffering horrendous casualties. Even the first cavalry charge failed, with the Norman horses shying away from the howling mob of axe-wielding Anglo-Saxons. William's own mount was felled under him, and as soon as he got to his feet he had to lift his helmet and show his face to stop his men giving in to panic.

It was at this point that, according to pro-Norman legend, William pulled off his master-stroke. Seeing that large numbers of Anglo-Saxons had charged down the hill after the retreating cavalrymen, the Norman is said to have staged a fake, full-scale withdrawal, tempting even more of his enemies to break ranks and leave the hilltop. As soon as the Anglo-Saxons were exposed on open ground, the cavalry turned and cut them down.

There is, however, a slightly more credible explanation for what happened. True, a large number of Harold's men did career down the hill, hacking away at fleeing Normans, and they did a great deal of damage. One section of William's army, mostly made up of Bretons, retreated in disarray, forcing their Norman colleagues to withdraw in parallel to stop the Anglo-Saxons wheeling around and surrounding them. And this seems to have given William an idea. With so many Anglo-Saxons running about on the lower ground, the battery of shields on the hilltop was thinner; also, Harold's personal bodyguard, the formidable housecarls, bunched together behind this front line, were more exposed. So William told his archers to fire higher, over the shields and into the housecarls. He also got his infantry and cavalry to charge again, and this time they broke through.

The faithful housecarls were slaughtered to a man, and Harold himself fell, either blinded by an arrow or cut down by Norman swords. Beside the famous picture of the knight with an arrow in the eye, the tapestry informs us that 'Harold Rex Interfectus Est' – 'Harold the King is killed'.

Which is bizarre. It is highly doubtful that William would have used that wording, or ordered someone else to use it for him. Chroniclers of the time were notoriously partisan – a more likely Norman commentary would have been something along the lines of: 'The treacherous usurper Harold meets the end he deserves, the Lord thrusting an arrow through his most tender parts as a punishment for trying to rob the noble William of his just title.' This would have been a bit too long for inclusion in the tapestry, of course, but at the very least, William, who had always considered himself as the rightful king and Harold as a usurper, would have ordered the 'Rex' to be omitted or removed.

Yet more evidence that someone was trying to annoy William personally, or the Normans in general.

Step 4: The call of booty
Another feature of the tapestry is that it refers to the invaders not as 'Normanni' but as 'Franci'. This confusion was nothing new. Long before William's invasion, Earl Godwin had warned that Edward the Confessor's 'French' cronies had too much influence at court. The epithet was, however, both geographically and ethnically misleading, and Godwin and co. were probably just being dismissively vague, rather like the present-day French when they want to moan about something that the English-speaking world has done. Forgetting the existence of Celts, African-Americans and many other branches of the Anglophone world, the French will

blame 'les Anglo-Saxons' for whatever is irking them.*

When the tapestry talks about 'Franci', though, the name is slightly more accurate, because William's invading army was not made up entirely of his faithful Norman clansmen. While planning his Conquest, William had sent out the word that there was lots of booty to be had. This promise attracted a mixed band of Normans, Bretons, Boulonnais, Angevins (people from Boulogne and Anjou) and other 'French' mercenaries, all thirsty for money and sex with English women – in short, much the same motives that have always brought young Frenchmen over to London.

This does not mean, however, that it was a 'French' invasion. For a start, neither the Normans nor the Bretons were Franks – they were Vikings and Celts. William's reputation as a provider of booty (and bootie) was so solid that fighters even came from as far away as the Norman colony in Italy to join him. And, most importantly, it was not the King of the Franks (then Philippe I) who launched the Norman Conquest. The Duke of Normandy was, in strict feudal terms, Philippe I's vassal, meaning that William owed allegiance to him. But William was very much his own man and the attack on England was, politically, a purely Norman one, aimed at extending William's personal power across the Channel and grabbing land for himself and his kinsmen. Close associates of his provided ships and soldiers in exchange for promises of land, and some of the funding came from Norman bishops and abbots, who realized that, should William succeed, there might be the odd silk cassock and/or brand-new cathedral in it for them. Every

* For the French, the half-Kenyan, part-Irish Barack Obama also became 'Anglo-Saxon' the minute he was elected President of the USA.

successful sword stroke at Hastings would have sounded to William's backers like a loud 'ker-ching'.

After the battle, as the plunderers moved around the battlefield chopping off limbs and heads so that they could strip the dead (and the not-quite-dead-until-someone-chopped-their-head-off) of their valuable chainmail, Normans and non-Normans alike knew that the fun was only just beginning. Before them lay the whole 'green and pleasant land' that William had salivated over all those years before, waiting to be picked clean.

The first thing the victorious William did was ride a few miles east to the port of Romney. One of his ships had blown off course and landed there, and the Norman invaders had all been killed, so William thought it only fair to massacre the townspeople.

He then headed inland to Winchester (King Alfred's old capital) to loot the royal treasury, before turning north, to Berkhamsted, presumably just to give that town the only bit of excitement that it would ever experience. It was here that William took the surrender of the teenage Anglo-Saxon pretender to the throne, Edgar the Atheling (meaning noble). Sadly for Berkhamsted, though, William declined to accept the crown there, and demanded to be enthroned in London.

All the while, William's men were plundering as they went, plunging the south of England into a chaos that it had forgotten since before Alfred the Great's day. This was partly revenge on Harold's old homeland of Wessex, but also a show of strength for the Anglo-Saxon earls in London, who were wondering how to react. Should they try to raise an army and resist, or swear allegiance to William and hang on to at least some of their possessions?

When William reached the outskirts of London, the locals demonstrated to the earls what they thought should be done – the men of Southwark attacked the invaders, annoying William so much that he burned the whole town and went off to ravage the surrounding countryside, destroying the recently harvested crops, killing peasants, and depriving Londoners of their main source of food.

William's show of force seems to have shown the Anglo-Saxon earls which side their bread was buttered on (in fact, Normandy was now their only source of butter), and they voted to recognize William's claim to the throne.

The new King of England was crowned on Christmas Day 1066, in Westminster Abbey. The venue was a political choice – the church had been built by Edward the Confessor, and it was here that the usurper Harold had been crowned just months before.

The ceremony must have been a bit like a shotgun wedding, with William surrounded by his soldiers while the gloomy Anglo-Saxons were forced to look on and witness the solemn handover of power. And as the crown was placed on William's head, it was somehow inevitable that violence should break out. Not from rebels trying to break up the celebrations, though; when the new King received a congratulatory cheer from his followers, the Norman guards outside the abbey heard the raised voices and assumed that there was a riot going on. They began a pre-emptive attack on the crowd that had gathered in the abbey grounds, and before they realized their mistake, many Londoners were killed and several buildings were burnt. It was just a taste of things to come for England.

Astutely detecting an air of instability in his new realm, William built the Tower of London – first a wooden stockade and then, when the famous white Caen stone arrived, the basis of the present castle. One can imagine the Anglo-Saxon bitterness when William refused to use English materials, despite the reassurances of London builders that 'if you want a white castle, you can't do better than this Dover chalk, mate. Look at them cliffs – solid as, well, rock, innit?'

As well as building his stronghold in London, William sent his army on a tour of England, not to get themselves acquainted with the local folk dances, but to let the Anglo-Saxons know that they now had new masters. This the Normans did by building castles in pretty well every major town in the country, usually demolishing whole neighbourhoods to make room for fortresses within the town walls. In Lincoln, for example, 166 houses were destroyed, in Cambridge 27, Gloucester 16, and so on. There is no record of William applying for planning permission.

The home-wrecking was not confined to brownfield sites, either. Deciding that the New Forest needed a bit of a makeover, William evicted 2,000 people from its villages, so that the 75,000-acre expanse of woodland would form a giant hunting playground, empty of all human construction. Similar operations were carried out in forests all over England, and terrible punishments were imposed on Anglo-Saxons who dared to replace their destroyed or stolen crops by eating one of the new King's royal deer, hares or hedgehogs – the penalty for poaching any animals was castration or amputation of hands and feet.

In the meantime, while his men were out demolishing houses and ethnically cleansing forests, William himself was busy doing admin, having taken on the exhausting task of confiscating some 1,422 manors that had previously belonged to Edward the Confessor and the Godwin family, as well as all the land in England that his men had completely ravaged, presumably on the grounds that its owners had let it fall into disrepair.

He was also amassing hoards of gold, jewels, cloth and other treasures, so that when he nipped back to Normandy in 1067 to see his wife and count his beached whales, even the snooty Parisians who saw William and his entourage were, in Zumthor's words, 'dazzled by the beauty of their clothing, which was embroidered with gold'.

William was careful to repay his investors – especially God. On the site of the Battle of Hastings, he built an abbey to give thanks for his victory, bluntly dubbing it Battle so that the Anglo-Saxons would never forget why it was there. And if you drive around Normandy today, you cannot fail to notice how many small towns have immense abbeys and cathedrals, all paid for with English money.

William's brother, Odo, was the Bishop of Bayeux. He can be seen in the tapestry, riding into battle brandishing a heavy mace instead of a spear or sword – churchmen were only allowed to bash enemies' brains out, not stab them, which would apparently have been ungodly. Thanks to Odo's willingness to smash skulls in the service of his brother and the Lord, he amassed a fortune which would, in today's money, have been worth an estimated £55 billion. He lavished much of this wealth on himself, but also a fair portion on a state-of-the-art cathedral that rises up from the centre of the small Norman market town of Bayeux like a gold brick on a pile of pebbles.

Other Norman churchmen received lesser, albeit substantial, windfalls. Jesus might once have said something about rich men having less chance of getting into heaven than a camel had of passing through the eye of a needle, but the Norman Church didn't need to worry about that – they now had enough cash to make giant needles.

Step 5: From Hastings to Domesday

The new King William had a lot less time than modern royals to go to nightclubs and do charity work – he had to charge up and down the country telling the English to behave themselves. In 1067 alone, there were revolts in Northumbria, Hereford, Exeter and the vital port of Dover, which was very nearly recaptured from the Normans.

This rebellion in Dover was led by one Eustace of Boulogne, who had fought in William's army at Hastings and then changed sides, probably hoping to rally Anglo-Saxon support for his own claim to the English throne – he was a former brother-in-law of Edward the Confessor. William forgave Eustace and allowed him to return to the Norman fold, because he needed all the allies he could get – in 1069, for example, Harold's mother Gytha and his widow Edith, who were still a bit peeved about those 1,422 manors they'd lost, invaded Devon, and it took all of the Franco-Norman forces in the southwest to repel them.

The North also did its bit to annoy William. In January 1069, the citizens of Durham killed the Norman occupiers (who had recently done a fair amount of massacring themselves). A few days later, York did the same thing, forcing William to come all the way up to Yorkshire in person to chase off the rebels and oversee the building of a new castle.

In September of the same year, a Danish force sailed up the Humber, supporting the claim of Edgar the Atheling to the English throne. Edgar and the Danes took York, with the unwitting aid of the Norman occupiers, who accidentally destroyed much of the city and their own forces when they set fire to the houses around the castle in an attempt to deprive the attackers of wood for siege machines.

William's words when he heard that his own men had burnt the brand-new castle he'd had built are not recorded, but suffice it to say that he was very angry at these developments, so much so that the poor messengers who brought him the news of events in York were, as the French historian Paul Zumthor puts it, 'mutilated'. Given that William frequently went in for punishments like castration, hand removal and blinding, it's not pleasant to imagine what this might mean.

The King rode north again to sort out his new York problem. However, once he'd done this, he then had to go and deal with another revolt in Stafford, and as soon as his back was turned, there was another uprising in York, forcing William to gallop up there a third time, only to find that the rebels had done a disappearing act.

By now, William was very, *very* angry at these Anglo-Saxons who – just like Harold – kept breaking their oaths of allegiance to him, and he gave orders for a war crime that would today be punished by having the perpetrator locked away for several years in a comfortable prison complex in The Hague.

William told his army to kill and destroy everyone and everything in a band of territory running from Lancaster to York, from the North Sea to the Irish Sea, an area 180 kilometres by 70 kilometres. Exact records of the number of dead and displaced are hard to find, but chroniclers tell of whole villages preferring to hide in the forest and starve to death rather than face the swords of the Conqueror's stormtroopers. The destruction was so massive and complete that the north of England remained a total wasteland for fifty years.*

With so many people swearing oaths and then betray-

* And culturally – snooty southerners allege – for several centuries longer.

ing him, William's land-grabbing was getting terribly complicated. Disputes over who owned what, and who owed the rent from which lands to whom, became so frequent that in 1085, William summoned his best lawyers and accountants to an investment counselling conference in Gloucester. Even though almost everyone in England owed him a percentage of their income, he was really keen to know who they were and exactly what they earned, so that they couldn't cheat him.

The answer the advisers came up with was that he should make a list of every bit of property, including human slaves – the serfs – in England. The resulting Domesday Book was as nerdy and completist as a trainspotter's travel diaries.

In early 1086, surveyors were sent out, and when they had finished collecting their data, the information was double-checked by more surveyors. As well as being a register of everyone's land, belongings and wealth, it also set the information out in feudal order, listing every fiscal debt, from the smallest landowners and absentee lords right up to King William himself.

The book's name, given to it in the twelfth century, points to the sheer scale and importance of the project. There was so much information in there that people compared it to the Book of Life, the catalogue of deeds that God would consult when deciding everyone's fate on Judgement Day.

And all this for a man who almost certainly couldn't read. Perhaps William got a kick out of the sheer size of his pile of account books. Or maybe, now that he was almost sixty, he enjoyed having excerpts read to him at bedtime, to bring back memories of his younger conquering days.

'Wait a minute. Bury St Edmunds, where's that?'

'You ransacked it on your way to Stafford, sire.'

'Ah yes. And where's this Chester you mentioned?'

'You ransacked it on your way to Lancaster, sire,' etc., etc.

The surveyors probably did their best to conceal the fact that there were gaps in the data, especially regarding property in London and the far North, which were troublesome areas where surveyors didn't like to ask too many questions.

'Didn't I ransack a place called Durham? Why is that not in the book?'

'Durham, sire? Oh no, no such town. Are you sure you read the signpost correctly? Or did you perhaps order the town to be completely obliterated?'

Another omission is even more revealing. Wine was the favourite drink of the Normans and especially of their Frankish colleagues, and forty-six vineyards are listed in the survey. However, according to the Domesday Book, only one of them (at Rayleigh Castle in Essex) was yielding a harvest. As William might have said, 'Mon arse.' Wine stocks were clearly not being listed by the Domesday surveyors, who seem to have been accepting liquid bribes to leave them out of the listings.

In any case, William didn't have much time to enjoy his bedtime storybook, because he died in September 1087, soon after the survey was completed. And he did so in a way befitting a King of England – while bashing the French.

King Philippe I of the Franks had attacked Vexin, the part of Normandy that lies just northwest of Paris, and when William sent out messengers warning him to back off, Philippe, feeling confident now that the Conqueror was old and rather plump, replied, 'When is the fat man going to have his baby?'

Despite his twenty-one years on the English throne, William still hadn't acquired a sense of humour, especially where jokes about himself were concerned, so he decided to go and burn something French. His troops were storming the town of Mantes, just outside Paris, and William was enjoying a canter through its charred streets when, legend has it, his horse trod on a fallen beam, and he tumbled to the ground, causing himself serious internal injury.

It took him six weeks of terrible abdominal suffering to die, the pain no doubt made worse by the fact that his French doctors kept turning him over and trying to stuff plants up his backside – the aerodynamic, easy-to-insert suppository had not yet been invented.

The *Anglo-Saxon Chronicle*, the year-by-year historical annals written by Anglo-Saxon scribes, has a lot of fun with William's obituary. A long insulting poem lists the hardship the Conqueror imposed in England:

> His people he did bleed
> Not from any need
> Into avarice he did fall
> And loved greed above all.

The monk writing the *Chronicle* even brings heavenly wrath to bear against William, saying that he died after destroying Mantes 'and all the holy churches in the city'. The chronicler laments that 'two holy men who served God were burnt to death', and then describes with some relish how William subsequently suffered horribly and died, so that 'he who had been a powerful king and lord of many lands now held no more than seven feet of earth'. It is the unmistakable sound of an English last laugh being had.

And the English probably weren't the only ones sniggering . . .

William is victim of an elaborate stitch-up

The French often refer to the Bayeux Tapestry as 'la tapisserie de la Reine Mathilde', implying that the work was overseen by William's wife. This is almost certainly wrong, though, and the name probably resulted from a kind of sexist assumption that embroidery must emanate from a woman rather than a butch man. Some say that it was commissioned by William's brother Odo, largely on the basis that he and his close followers feature in the action and that the tapestry was first rediscovered in Odo's abbey at Bayeux – though this last argument is a little like saying that a pharaoh's sarcophagus was made in England because it is in the British Museum.

As we have already seen, the tapestry is open to a less pro-William interpretation than the one given by the present-day Normans in Bayeux – there is the reference to Harold as 'Rex', for example, and the heartrending scenes of Norman pillaging when they first land in England. As well as this, the tapestry shows Harold as a brave man, rescuing Normans from drowning near the Mont-Saint-Michel while he was William's hostage, and depicts his coronation being performed by an archbishop, thereby giving it divine approval.

It has been suggested that this pro-Harold sentiment was put there by the Anglo-Saxon seamstresses, but there is strong evidence that the anti-Norman propaganda in the tapestry went much deeper than this.

One of the many books about the true origins of this mysterious work of art, Andrew Bridgeford's *1066: The Hidden History of the Bayeux Tapestry*, argues convincingly that the whole idea of the embroidery was to mount a subtle attack on William and the Normans. Bridgeford suggests that the tapestry was in fact commissioned by a disgruntled Frenchman called Eustace of Boulogne – the man mentioned above for leading an anti-William rebellion in Dover. Eustace had far more royal European blood in him than the ex-Viking William – he was a descendant of Charlemagne, the legendary King of the Franks who had reigned over much of France, Germany and Italy, and had also been married to Godgifu, the sister of King Edward the Confessor. In theory, Eustace was therefore a prime candidate for the English throne, and was no doubt peeved that William had got his hands on it.

This, Bridgeford says, might explain why the tapestry's captions refer to the invaders as 'Franci' – not only did Eustace want to underline the fact that William had non-Norman troops but he was also pointing the finger at his own Frankish ancestry. And talking of pointing fingers, the tapestry also depicts Eustace at the heart of the action during the Battle of Hastings, when he points to William as the Conqueror raises his helmet to show that he is still alive. Bridgeford suggests that this ingenious piece of pictorial sabotage was organized by Kentish monks (near Dover, where Eustace led his rebellion), and presented to Odo as a gift, supposedly flattering him and his royal brother, but in reality undermining their claim to be the rightful lords of England.

If this is true – and we will never be completely sure – the tapestry is like a bitter French laugh echoing down through the centuries. Only one fact is indisputable: William himself never got the joke, otherwise Eustace, the monks and the seamstresses would have been forced to eat the tapestry before having the lengths of cloth forcibly pulled out of their backsides and set on fire. William was that kind of guy.

Parlez-vous English?

Not everyone in eleventh-century England was completely anti-William. Even the sulking Anglo-Saxon chronicler had to admit that his reign hadn't been all bad. 'One must not forget the peace that he brought to this land,' he says, 'so that all men of property might travel safely throughout the kingdom.' By building castles to keep the Anglo-Saxons under control, and having his troops on more or less permanent alert, William had imposed stability on the country, or at least on those parts of it that he didn't trash completely. Once the initial massacring was over, life expectancy rose in England. True, taxes were high, especially for farmers unfortunate enough to have an absentee landlord as greedy as William's brother Odo. But as we saw earlier, it was quite a relief to know that you might just survive long enough to bring in your harvest, even if you were going to give most of the income to a fat Norman bishop. And in the long term, England as a nation was a definite winner, because the Norman Conquest kick-started the culture that the French now mistakenly call 'Anglo-Saxon'.

As of 1066, the invaders' French-based dialect became the official language of conquered England, and it would be spoken by the Kings of England and all the ruling classes for the next 300 years or so. But the Anglo-Saxon peasants were too numerous and uneducated to have a new language imposed on them, and in any case the average Anglo-Saxon only ever used Franco-Norman words in order to sell his wares to a nobleman or beg a soldier not to castrate him for killing a hedgehog.

For their part, the conquerors generally refused or failed to learn the losers' language (William tried and gave up). Amongst themselves the invaders developed a Franco-Norman pidgin that was a blend of their various regional dialects – a new patois that dispensed with many of the fiddly grammatical complexities that 'pure' French, the language of the Franks, would keep for centuries longer.

Gradually, as we will see in later chapters, Anglo-Saxon

and Franco-Norman came into closer contact, and the linguistic survival techniques on both sides led to the emergence of a supple, adaptable language in which you could invent or half-borrow words and didn't have to worry so much about whether your sentences had the right verb endings or respected certain strict rules of word order and style (as this sentence proves). The result was the earliest form of what would become English.

All of which goes to show that the Norman Conquest was as important linguistically as the moment when the first amphibians crawled out of the swamp and on to land. Anyone who has ever got bogged down in the mire of modern-day French grammar will appreciate how liberating English is. Jealous of our freedom, French grammarians will tell you that English is an impure, bastard language. They're right, and the hilarious thing is, it owes its creation to William, a Norman bastard born on what is today French soil.

The beginning of the end (of the beginning)

All in all, then, far from being the triumph of France over England, the Norman Conquest was really bad news for the French. William's invasion smashed the old Anglo-Saxon order, but founded a new nation that would outgrow its initial status as a Norman colony and become a fiercely independent force in Europe. What's more, in doing so, William had deprived a deserving Frankish (French) candidate, Eustace of Boulogne, of the English throne.

As William lay dying in agony from wounds sustained in an anti-Parisian war, he would probably have gained some solace if he'd known that, in creating England, he had sown the seeds of a whole millennium of pain for the French.

France in the 12th Century

London
Calais
HOLY ROMAN EMPIRE
English Channel
Rouen
Reims
NORMANDY
Paris
Seine
BRITTANY
Orléans
FRENCH KING'S DOMINIONS
ANJOU
Fontevraud
Chinon
Loire
HENRY II'S DOMINIONS IN FRANCE
Châlus
AQUITAINE
Bordeaux
GASCONY
Toulouse
Mediterranean

Thanks to his Anglo-French parents, King Henry II of England already possessed Anjou and Normandy. And after he wooed away the French King's landowning wife, Eleanor of Aquitaine, England could officially lord it over more than half of France.

2

French-bashing in Its Infancy

In the 250 years between the death of William the Conqueror and the Hundred Years War there were, predictably, quite a few historic events. After all, two and a half centuries is about the time that separates the invention of the bicycle and the atomic bomb (yes, just because we're going forward in time, it doesn't mean we're progressing).

There was, for example, the signing of the Magna Carta, the murder of Thomas Becket, and the exploits of legendary heroes like Richard the Lionheart, Robert the Bruce and Robin Hood (the latter being just that, of course – a legend).

Above all, however, this was the time it took for England, which in 1087 was just a Norman colony, to develop to the point where it was nationalistic and powerful enough to turn the tables and attack not only its old colonial masters, but the whole of France.

It was a long process, because for most of that time England's monarchs acted rather like a teenager from London who has lucked into inheriting the lairdship of a Scottish island – free whisky, cute castle, it's just a shame about the terrible weather and all these incomprehensible locals. Indeed, several Anglo-Norman kings thought of themselves as Dukes of Normandy with a second home in London, and almost all of them saw England and its peasants as little more than a source of funding for their hobbies, which varied from the boringly normal like hunting and wenching to more exotic pastimes such as crusading in the Med (Richard the Lionheart), architectural follies (Henry III) and thatching houses (Edward II).

But every king* between 1087 and 1327 contributed, in his own way, to England's limbering up for the Hundred Years War, even though in some cases they seemed to do it completely by accident . . .

Fighting for the right to party

Things got off to a slow start because William I's successor was such a waste of time.

On the Conqueror's death, his eldest son, Robert, received the Norman homeland. England, meanwhile, was bequeathed to the second surviving son, William II, or Rufus as he was called because of his red face. Yes, England was only a poor second prize in the family lottery.

William Rufus suffered from chronic spoilt-child-with-a-famous-name syndrome, and was a sort of medieval Paris Hilton, sharing – it is alleged – her taste for make-up, dresses and yappy little dogs. He spent most of his short reign (1087–1100) partying in various English castles and over-taxing his people to pay for his lavish lifestyle. He was so unpopular that when he was 'accidentally' hit by an arrow through the lung and left to

* Queens were illegal in England until Mary Tudor in 1553.

die where he fell, no one even bothered to investigate. It was perhaps fitting that Rufus died while hunting in the New Forest, the tract of land ethnically cleansed of Anglo-Saxons by his father.

The arrow that killed Rufus was rumoured to have been fired on the orders of his younger brother Henry, whose only inheritance in William the Conqueror's will had been some money with which to buy land. Henry was on Rufus's fatal hunting trip, and departed hurriedly for no apparent reason shortly before the 'accident' happened.

With the English throne vacant, and big brother Robert away on a crusade, Henry immediately stepped in as King Henry I. He was an altogether different ruler. Like Rufus, he enjoyed partying, and is said to have fathered about twenty-five illegitimate children, but he also had a measured political mind – his nickname was 'Beauclerc', or 'Good Scholar'. He saw the importance of uniting the two main peoples in England, and married an Anglo-Saxon, Eadgyth (usually modernized as Edith), a descendant of Alfred the Great and the sister of Edgar the Atheling, the man whom William the Conqueror had prevented from taking over the English Crown after the Battle of Hastings. Interestingly, their wedding took place on 11 November 1100, a date no doubt chosen to give a kind of numerological resonance to the union in those superstitious times.

When England's Norman nobility complained about Eadgyth's unpronounceable name,* Henry I simply changed it to his mother's Anglo-Norman name, Mathilde.

Henry promised to right all the wrongs of his brother's

* They didn't care that it was also unspellable, because almost none of them could write.

61

reign, and imprisoned Rufus's chief minister, a rich Norman bishop called Ranulf Flambard ('Ranulf the Hothead') who had been in charge of collecting revenue, a task he accomplished brilliantly by selling positions of power in the Church. But Flambard became the first prisoner to escape from the new Tower of London, and fled to Normandy to join Duke Robert, who was back from his crusade and wondering how to seize the throne of England from his uppity little brother Henry.

Robert, whose nickname was 'Curthose' ('Short Trousers'), because of his stumpy legs, was as hotheaded as Flambard, and had spent much of his adult life warring against his father William the Conqueror. The two had even met face to face in battle, with the son flooring his ageing father but sparing his life at the last moment. Egged on by Flambard, in 1101 Robert led a new Norman invasion of England, landing a small army at Portsmouth. However, the English barons who had promised to help him didn't turn up, because Henry I was becoming a popular king – one of his most astute reforms being a guarantee not to overtax his barons. In the end, the two brothers met in peace, and Robert agreed to renounce his claim in return for a regular income and some of the land Henry owned in Normandy.

But Henry didn't trust his big brother to respect the agreement, and, proving that England now felt strong enough to take on all-comers, he invaded Normandy. And it went surprisingly smoothly. Henry captured Bayeux and Caen in 1105, returned to England briefly to settle a dispute about whether he or the Pope should nominate English bishops, and then resumed his campaign the following year, finally meeting Robert in battle beside the castle of Tinchebray near Caen on 28 September 1106. Henry defeated the

Normans in an hour, and took Robert prisoner.

England had successfully conquered Normandy, exactly forty years to the day after William the Conqueror had landed on English soil – another numerological omen.

Henry I was now as powerful as his father had been, and to make sure he stayed that way, he put his elder brother out of action for good. Robert was thrown into prison, ironically in two Norman castles – at Devizes in Wiltshire and then Cardiff. And, after a failed escape attempt, Henry had Robert's eyes burnt out, and kept him in captivity for the rest of his life. Fondness for close relatives didn't seem to figure in those Anglo-Norman genes.

Fishy goings-on in Normandy

By 1135, King Henry I was an old man in his mid-sixties and thinking about his succession. In the autumn of that year, he went to Normandy to visit his daughter Mathilde, who had made an excellent strategic marriage to a Frenchman, Geoffrey, Count of Anjou, who reigned over the lands immediately to the southwest of Henry's domains in Normandy. Despite the recent births of two grandchildren, relations between father, daughter and son-in-law were strained, perhaps because the King had explained that although Mathilde was his only legitimate heir to the throne of England, she could not inherit the titles because she was an *heiress*, and at that time the essential qualification to become an English ruler was to possess a penis.

Anyway, after a hard day's hunting, Henry returned to Mathilde and Geoffrey's place, le Château de Lyons (at Lyons-la-Forêt in Normandy, not the city of Lyon in central France), where he sat down to one of his favourite meals, a plate of grilled lampreys. These are hideous eel-like creatures with sucker mouths surrounded by pointed teeth that they use to pierce the stomach of their prey and suck its innards out. They are now almost extinct thanks to their preference for unpolluted river water, but in medieval times they were a delicacy, and the city of Gloucester used to give a lamprey pie to the monarch every Christmas. Henry loved them despite their ugliness, and on 1 December 1135 he is said to have consumed such a 'surfeit of lampreys' that he died of over-eating.

Interestingly, though, the usual French version of the story is that he ate 'lamproies avariées' – lampreys that had gone bad. The French don't seem to be able to accept that you can eat too much of a good thing. Given the violence of the times, though, one might also ask whether Henry's meal hadn't contained a hidden ingredient – a little dose of poison, perhaps.

As soon as her father was dead, Mathilde sounded out the English barons as to whether she could overcome the problem of her gender and succeed to the throne, either alone or as a regent for her son. Some of the barons had sworn allegiance to her, but in the end her marriage to an Angevin, seen by many as a rival to the Normans, counted against her, and the throne was given to one of Henry's nephews, a French grandson of William the Conqueror's – Stephen, Count of Blois and Boulogne.

Despite his name, Stephen was not exactly a great ruler. In fact, he managed to lose not only the English link with Normandy, but also his own English throne. He just didn't have enough of that Conqueror blood in him, it seems. On the contrary, Stephen's father, Etienne-Henri, was a well-known coward. He had deserted the crusader army during the siege of Antioch in 1098, infuriating his wife so much that she sent him straight back to the Middle East, where he was killed in 1102. Not a great role model for a medieval king.

And unfortunately for Stephen, Mathilde and her husband, Geoffrey of Anjou, weren't going to give up without a fight. In 1139 Geoffrey began a systematic campaign of attrition against Normandy, while Mathilde brought an army of Angevins to invade England, basing herself in Gloucester – capital of the lamprey.

A terrible struggle between the lady from Anjou and the man from Blois broke out on British soil. The war between Mathilde and Stephen was known bluntly as the Anarchy, and gave the *Anglo-Saxon Chronicle* (which was in its final throes) one of its last chances to have a rant at foreigners. In its entry for 1139, the *Chronicle* laments that both factions of French powerbrokers kidnapped England's 'peasant men and women, and put them in prison for their gold and silver, and tortured them with unutterable torture'. Well, the chronicler says it was un-utterable, but he manages to utter quite a lot about it:

> They hanged them by the thumbs, or by the head, and hung fires on their feet; they put knotted strings about their heads, and writhed [twisted] them so that it went to the brain . . . Some they put in a chest that was short, and narrow, and shallow, and put sharp stones therein, and pressed the man therein, so that they broke all his limbs . . . I neither can nor may tell all the wounds or all the tortures which they inflicted on wretched men in this land.

As well as the everyday terror, there were pitched battles: in 1141, Stephen lost the Battle of Lincoln and was taken prisoner. Mathilde had herself crowned 'Angliae Normanniaeque domina', 'Lady of the English and the Normans', but was then defeated by an army led by Stephen's wife, who made things even more confusing by also being called Mathilde (though she tacked on an 'of Boulogne' to differentiate herself).

In the end, with the wavering allegiances of the English barons only adding to the anarchy, the two factions were forced to come to an agreement: Stephen would continue to reign, and on his death the throne would pass to Mathilde's son Henry.* It was a fragile, unsatisfactory solution for all concerned, and as G. M. Trevelyan says in his *Shortened History of England*, 'it was one of England's great good fortunes that he [Stephen] died next year.'

Stealing a French king's wife – not good for international relations

By birth, the future Henry II was already heir to the powerful territory of Anjou in France, via his father Geoffrey, as well as the Duchy of Normandy and the Crown of England. And at the age of nineteen he added even more land to his portfolio by marrying Eleanor of Aquitaine. Thanks again to the 'do you have a lump in your tights?' clause in rulership application forms, he thereby became duke of the extensive, and very rich, French territories of Aquitaine and Gascony, an area stretching from Bordeaux to the Spanish border.

This union was not only profitable – it was also a major anti-French political coup. Until only a few weeks earlier, Eleanor had been Queen of France, the wife of Louis VII. She had had the marriage annulled because Louis had produced no male heirs and, she felt, was not liable to, because, as she subtly expressed it, 'he is a monk

---

* This is Mathilde, daughter of Henry I, and her son Henry, grandson of Henry I. Yes, lots of Mathildes and Henrys, but we saw what happened when they tried something different and went for a Stephen.

rather than a husband'. As soon as the annulment came through, the thirty-year-old Eleanor proposed to the teenaged Henry, who – she rightly predicted – had great prospects. She was apparently a tall, beautiful, well-educated woman who knew what she wanted and knew how to get it – and she'd already tried out Henry's family pedigree by sleeping with his father.

As a result, in 1154, when King Stephen died and Henry (now twenty-one) was able to print an extra line – King of England – on his already crowded business card, he ruled over more 'French' land than Louis VII. If you look at a map of France at the time, the territories governed by Henry and Eleanor form a huge, solid slab covering the whole western half of the country, taking in almost all the north coast and stretching right down across the centre of France, only just excluding Paris. By comparison, Louis VII's territories hang like a stringy frog's leg across the map, from just west of Calais, down through Paris and to the Med. It is very clear who ruled France in those days, and it wasn't the French King.

Not that Henry II did much French-bashing. He didn't need to. Given the extent of his land-holdings, he was literally able to sit back and lord it over the French. In any case, Henry II's reign was much less about war than peace. He was the first of England's Plantagenet kings, named after the sprig of broom flowers (in French, *genêt*) that his father, Geoffrey of Anjou, wore in his hat. And as such, Henry was the founder of a dynasty that would rule England for the next 330 years. He couldn't know that, of course, but even so he reigned like a man laying down great foundations.

He tamed the volatile barons in both England and his French territories by taking money from the noblemen in lieu of military service, thereby enabling him to pay for reliable mercenaries. He introduced trial by jury, which meant that at least some crimes would be judged by hearing evidence rather than by making the accused walk barefoot over red-hot plough shares and declaring them guilty if they got blisters. Perhaps remembering the story of his grandfather and the lampreys, Henry also gained a reputation for being generous to the hungry, redistributing a tenth of all the food delivered to his castles.

A shame, then, that the French gained one of their greatest – but least known – victories in history by tarnishing good King Henry's name.

The murder in the cathedral

The one great blemish on Henry II's record book is the murder of Thomas Becket, his own Archbishop of Canterbury. In Henry's defence, though, it must be stressed that he wasn't entirely to blame. What is not said often enough is that, in part at least, it was France's fault.

The circumstances of the murder are a familiar story. In 1170, Henry complains loudly about Becket refusing to respect royal authority. Four of the King's courtiers take the complaint as a hint, and go to Canterbury, where they hack off the top of Thomas's skull and spread his brains over the cathedral floor.

However, what few people know is that Thomas Becket had spent the previous two years in exile in France, having left England to avoid signing an agreement that would have weakened the Church's influence. And while in France, Thomas was a guest of Louis VII, the lousy lover who had been scorned by Eleanor, Henry's wife. One can imagine Louis spending the long medieval evenings by his fireside telling Thomas how right he was to stand up to the ungodly English wife-stealer. All of which might explain why, when Thomas eventually returned to England, he was defiant enough to continue his political stand against Henry.

Thomas was so sure of himself that he even provoked his own murder. Initially, Henry's knights entered the cathedral unarmed, and simply wanted the archbishop to come with them and explain himself to King Henry. It was only when Thomas told them to go and get knighted that they went outside again to fetch their swords.

In short, if Thomas Becket hadn't spent two years learning the art of French petulance, he might have died in bed and Henry II might be remembered only as one of England's greatest kings rather than a priest-killer.

In fact, the murder was to cost Henry more than his reputation – it was one of the things that caused his ultimate downfall.

He and Eleanor had eight children, including five sons. But their relations were famously strained. Both were dynastically minded, and they were constantly jostling for position within their joint empire. Eleanor seems to have encouraged her native Aquitaine to remain independent of King Henry's authority, while Henry attacked cities like Toulouse that already belonged to Eleanor's family. Eleanor was piqued even more by the decidedly un-monkish Henry's infidelities, including a liaison with his own son Richard's fiancée. And although she usually turned a blind eye to his philandering, Eleanor refused to ignore Rosamund Clifford, the beautiful young mistress whom Henry dubbed 'rosa mundi' (the 'rose of the world'); as soon as Rosamund arrived on the scene, Eleanor's child-bearing stopped.

It is said that by flaunting this relationship, Henry was trying to goad Eleanor into annulling their marriage, in which case he would have made her an abbess and in-herited all her lands. But not only did she resist the provocation, she actively encouraged Henry's own sons to begin hacking away at his empire with their princely swords.

Suddenly, the King of England was under attack from France – by his own sons. The biggest troublemaker was his second son (but the oldest surviving one), who was also called Henry. The Young King, as he was known, bore an old grudge against his father. He had spent most of his childhood as the foster son of Thomas Becket, and is said to have declared that Thomas showed him more fatherly affection in a day than King Henry had in a lifetime – he was therefore mightily upset about Becket's murder.

Young Henry was married to Marguerite de France, the daughter of King Louis VII by a second marriage. This union had been a tactical move by Henry II to increase his influence in France, but now rebounded on him, because in 1173 Young Henry went to live with Louis (who was also, remember, his mother's ex-husband) in Paris, where he began to plot a rebellion.

At first, he was helped by his mother Eleanor, who was based in Aquitaine at the time. She sent two of her younger sons, Richard (the future Lionheart) and Geoffrey, to join the plotters, and would have gone to Paris herself if Henry (that's her husband, King Henry II) hadn't objected to this dubious reunion with her ex-husband and had her taken prisoner.

The French-led revolt went ahead, with Louis and Young Henry storming Normandy from the south, while various French counts attacked from the east. King Henry II, though, had come prepared. Instead of relying on the fragile loyalty of all the noblemen in his vast domains, he had hired a mercenary army of so-called Brabançons – fierce, unconventional fighters originally from Brabant on the Dutch–Belgian border, who had been used by King Stephen in England to inflict some of the worst atrocities of the Anarchy. They trounced the French attackers and sent the surviving rebels skulking back to Paris, where the weak Louis VII announced that he had had enough of all this messy rebelling.

But Henry II's success was short-lived. He had such a great empire, and so many eligible, ambitious sons, that he became like the ageing lion at the head of a pride – the young males were forever snapping at his heels, looking for signs of weakness, and were encouraged in this by the senior lioness, Eleanor. Both Young Henry and Richard kept up their demands for land, squabbling all the while between themselves about who was going to inherit what, and King Henry II was doomed to watch his family disintegrate.

Young Henry died of dysentery after a failed attempt to take another of his father's possessions, the town of Limoges in central France. Soon afterwards, his brother Geoffrey, who had taken permanent refuge in Paris after the failed revolt, was killed there in a jousting tournament.

Only John remained faithful and by his father's side, although he wasn't much of a consolation – in the end, it was John who finished Henry off.

In the summer of 1189, Richard heard that his father wanted to give Aquitaine to John. Furious at the idea of losing such a profitable chunk of his rightful inheritance as the oldest surviving son, Richard launched yet another of his patricidal rebellions in Anjou. And this time he found the only true chink in Henry's armour – he persuaded young John to betray his father.

Henry II's chaplain, a Welsh-Norman chronicler called Gerald of Wales, describes a painting in one of the rooms at the royal castle of Winchester. It depicted an eagle being pecked by three chicks, while another, smaller one looked on. And when asked the meaning of the bizarre scene, Henry is said to have explained that the chicks were his four sons, and that the youngest 'whom I now hold in dear affection, will one day cause me more grievous and more mortal pain than all the others'. Whether this is a true story or a parable after the event, it was now chillingly apt.

Henry went out to Anjou to defend himself, but Richard and his allies (who included Louis VII's son, Philippe Auguste) were running rampant, and Henry eventually decided to give in to all their demands. In any case, by now John's betrayal had almost broken the old King's heart.

Mere days after giving in to his sons and their French allies, Henry II died at Chinon Castle (where he had once imprisoned his wife Eleanor) on 6 July 1189. It is said that he died of grief, and that when Richard rather hypocritically came to pay his respects to the body, Henry's nose started to bleed, as if to show his errant son how many headaches he had caused.

Not that Richard was the emotional type – he had himself crowned Duke of Normandy, and then headed straight to London to be enthroned as King of England.

For sale: one capital city, full of antiques

Richard I (the Lionheart) is remembered as a great English king, but in fact he spent only seven months of his ten-year reign in the country he was supposed to be ruling. He preferred to rampage abroad, and was usually to be found defending the inhabitants of the Eastern Mediterranean against any kind of religious freedom they might aspire to, or kicking potential usurpers out of the immense French landholdings that he inherited from his parents – Richard was not only King of England but also Duke of Normandy, Aquitaine and Gascony,

Count of Anjou and Nantes, and Lord of Brittany.

He held little affection for England, and even said that he would have 'sold London if he could have found a buyer', to pay for his crusades.

It was while Richard was off crusading that his younger brother John continued the family tradition of anti-sibling plotting, thereby making himself the villain of countless Robin Hood films, along with his co-baddie the Sheriff of Nottingham. Or so legend would have us believe. Because despite the assurances of tourist boards everywhere from Hadrian's Wall to Wiltshire, it seems unlikely that Robin Hood ever existed. Or, at least, that the one-and-only Robin Hood as we know him existed – it was a very common name in the Middle Ages, Robin being a diminutive of Robert and Hood an alternative version of Wood. Robin Hood may also have been a collective term for outlaws that had been inspired by a real case, just as the word 'hooligan' comes from Houlihan, the name of a disreputable family in 1890s London.

Folk ballads telling of a Robin Hood's heroic exploits date back to the thirteenth century, and are mostly about resisting authority – not a surprising theme at a time when the common people were being worked almost literally to death by rich landowners, and could be hanged by a lord just because he felt like it. In a ballad called the *Gest of Robyn Hood*, written down at the end of the fifteenth century but apparently much older, 'Robyn' identifies his targets to his friend 'Litell Johnn' like this:

> These bisshoppes and these archebishoppes,
> Ye shall them bete and bynde;
> The hye sherif of Notyngham,
> Hym holde ye in your mynde.

Bishops, archbishops and the sheriff: the pillars of medieval authority, begging to get knocked down.

The Robin in these ballads doesn't always give to the poor; in one of them, he lends a knight some money to repay a debt to an abbot. And in the early sources, there is almost no mention of Robin supporting King Richard against his brother John – this seems to have been added later to give Robin a higher cause than local wealth re-distribution. In fact, to the average Englishman Richard was more of a financial burden than a king; in 1193 he was taken hostage by one of his many enemies, Henry VI of the Holy Roman Empire, who put in a ransom demand for 150,000 marks (about three times the English Crown's annual income). The money was raised by massive across-the-board tax increases for the English, probably made worse by John, who offered 80,000 marks as a bribe to keep Richard in prison.

Richard's release and return to save England from John's mismanagement usually come as the dramatic ending to Robin Hood's tale, but in fact Richard didn't hang around long to show his gratitude to his English subjects – the call of war, and of French-bashing, was too strong. Looking to take advantage of the Lionheart's spell behind bars, Richard's old ally Philippe Auguste, now King Philippe II of France, was trying to seize English-held lands in Normandy and Anjou. So Richard immediately grabbed all the money he could lay his hands on and left England yet again, never to return.

The war with Philippe Auguste was apparently made worse by an intense personal animosity between the two men. It was rumoured that he and Richard had been lovers back in the days of their alliance against Henry II. That ardour had cooled, but the two had gone on a joint crusade in the Holy Land, and, as with so many exes, holidaying together had only made things worse. At the siege of the city of Acre in 1191, Richard took an active part in the fighting despite being seriously ill with scurvy, and was even reported firing a crossbow at the walls while lying on a stretcher. Philippe Auguste, meanwhile, was laid up with dysentery and stayed out of the action, provoking Richard into making some deeply wounding remarks about shirkers.

So Richard now devoted the remaining five years of his life to fighting France's land-grabbing king. And he was so successful that, after the Battle of Gisors in northern France, in September 1198, he made the ultimate statement of his, and England's, independence from the old feudal allegiance to the King of France. Until then, as a duke or count of French territories, Richard, like all English monarchs, had theoretically been a feudal vassal of Philippe Auguste. But now Richard adopted the royal motto that has survived to this day, 'Dieu et mon droit' ('God and my right') – a neat explanation, in French so Philippe Auguste would get the message, that an English king owed allegiance to no one but God. And even then he had his rights.

It was, however, France that finally killed Richard.

In March 1199, he was putting down a revolt by a minor French nobleman in his territory of Aquitaine, and was leading a routine siege of Châlus Castle, which was defended by only a few knights, one of whom was using a frying pan as a shield. Richard was feeling so confident of victory that he went wandering around the moat one evening without his chainmail, daring the castle's defenders to shoot at him. Unfortunately, the one with the frying pan did just that, hitting Richard in the neck with a crossbow bolt. The wound became infected after an incompetent surgeon* tried to pull

---

* France had not yet developed its excellent health service.

the arrow out, and Richard was soon on his deathbed.

Legend has it that as the Lionheart lay dying, he had the offending French crossbowman brought to him for forgiveness. The soldier turned out to be a boy, probably called Pierre Basile, who told Richard that he had fired his arrow in revenge because the English had killed his father and brother. According to English versions of the story, Richard was so touched that he blessed the boy and gave him a large cash present.

Certain French sources allege that Richard treacherously had the archer killed, but this is an anti-English falsehood. What actually happened, it seems, is that immediately after Richard's death on 6 April 1199, the leader of his mercenaries (who was himself French, by the way) had all Châlus Castle's defenders brutally executed by hanging them from the ramparts. And he saved the cruellest punishment for young Pierre Basile, who was skinned alive, no doubt as punishment for shooting the hired soldiers' rich employer.

But then French historians will say anything to tarnish an English king's reputation.

A fond, and strangely peaceful, family reunion

In death, as in life, Richard spread himself thinly. His entrails were buried in the chapel of the castle where he died, at Châlus; his heart was taken to Rouen in Normandy; his brain was buried in Charroux Abbey in Aquitaine, and the rest of him went to take part in a touching, but rather surprising family reunion.

The Royal Abbey of Fontevraud, in the heart of Anjou, was founded in 1101, and resembles a castle as much as a religious community. It has forbidding outer walls, a gothic central courtyard that looks more like a jousting arena than a cloister, and a tower with a cluster of turrets like organ pipes (though they are in fact pointed chimneys). At its heart is a huge church, which is as pristine white as the rest of the buildings except for a few touches of colour in the middle of the nave that are fenced off to preserve the last flecks of paint from the ravages of history.

These are the decorated tombs of an unlikely collection of people. Here, lying side by side, their heads resting peacefully on stone pillows, are the effigies of Henry II and his estranged wife Eleanor of Aquitaine. And at their feet, apparently content for once to be in a position of inferiority, is their son Richard the Lionheart.

If there is an atmosphere of intense peace about the unlikely trio, it is probably because their bodies are no longer buried here – their mortal remains disappeared when the abbey was looted during the French Revolution. But it seems almost miraculous that they should ever have been reunited at Fontevraud, just a few kilometres from Chinon Castle, where Henry II died after losing a battle to Richard, and where Eleanor was locked up by her errant husband. The area can't have conjured up many warm family memories.

They are all here because Eleanor seems to have decided that family comes first. Henry II had nominated the abbey as the Plantagenets' royal mausoleum, and Eleanor, who outlived her husband by fifteen years and spent most of her final years at the abbey, respected his wishes. Although she seems to have had the last laugh – her effigy is several centimetres higher than his.

The only mystery is why John isn't beside his brother Richard; there is a fourth tomb in the nave at Fontevraud, but it is that of John's French wife Isabelle. The reason for John's exclusion from the communal forgiveness seems to be that by the time he died, Fontevraud, along with the rest of Anjou and almost all of England's other territories in France, had been lost. And guess whose fault that was . . .

Bad King John, the accidental hero

John was a truly awful King of England. He was mocked by his contemporaries as 'Lackland' and 'Softsword' – the latter a reference to his military incompetence, but clearly also a medieval joke about his private parts. In fact, John had only one redeeming feature as far as Anglo-French history is concerned – he was very adept at annoying France.

Within months of his accession, he became embroiled in a French love triangle that would delight modern tabloids. In 1200 he met the above-mentioned Isabelle, daughter of the Count of Angoulême, and, smitten by her beauty (and her large landholdings), he had her abducted and married her, despite the fact that she was only twelve years old and was already betrothed to a French nobleman.

At the time, abduction of under-age girls was not an uncommon seduction technique, but the cheated suitor complained to the French King, Richard's old (alleged) lover and enemy, Philippe Auguste, who summoned John to answer for himself. John refused, on the grounds that, as King of England, he was his own master and answerable to no one – *Dieu et mon droit, n'est-ce pas?*

Philippe Auguste countered that, despite any clever mottos that Richard might have dreamt up, the King of France was still John's feudal lord in Aquitaine, and therefore had authority over him. He duly stripped John of all his French lands except Gascony, which he didn't want because it was home to the troublesome Basques and too far from Paris to be kept under control.

This confiscation weakened John so much that the

French even felt emboldened to invade his traditional family stronghold of Normandy. At a stroke, Henry II's and Richard the Lionheart's empire, which had draped across the west of France like an immense red English curtain, was more or less reduced to England and Biarritz.

Next, John got into a standoff with the Church about who had the right to choose the Archbishop of Canterbury – the same old row that had provoked John's father Henry II into having Thomas Becket's brains bashed out. The Pope brought God into the argument by excommunicating John and declaring Philippe Auguste of France the true, divinely blessed King of England. In a fit of self-preservation, in 1213 John backed down, and even agreed to make the Pope the feudal lord of England, offering to pay a rent to Rome. A humiliating defeat, but it turned into an anti-French victory because it took all the wind out of Philippe Auguste's sails – he had been amassing an army on the Channel coast to come and stake his claim on England, and now had no excuse to invade. At the same time, by a huge stroke of luck, an English fleet encountered and destroyed the French navy, rubbing salt water into Philippe Auguste's wound.

With uncharacteristic, and unwise, boldness, John followed up these lucky breaks by attacking France. But his army was beaten in summer 1214 at the Battle of La Roche-aux-Moines in Anjou (where John distinguished himself by running away from the fighting) and again at the Battle of Bouvines, in the far north of France, after which John was forced to accept unfavourable peace terms, effectively renouncing any remaining claim he had to Normandy and Brittany.

Sadly for King John, it seems to have been too early in history for an Englishman to know that once you have successfully annoyed a Frenchman, it is much more satisfying to leave him to sulk about it rather than giving him a chance to get back at you.

The English get a French king

The consequence of this series of humiliations and misjudgements was that John's own barons distrusted him so much that they made him sign the Magna Carta, which essentially protected the barons themselves from injustice at the hands of any future ruler as bad as John.

To make things doubly safe, the barons also invited the French crown prince Louis to come and usurp the English throne – for a short while in 1216, he was actually Louis I of England. A heinous betrayal by the English barons, one might think, but a perfectly logical one. Many of them held lands both in England and Normandy, and therefore felt no exclusive allegiance to either side of the Channel. In fact, they probably reasoned that a French king who ruled over Normandy and England was just as good a feudal lord as an English king – he might even be better if he avoided getting himself into costly wars and demanded less tax.

However, in October 1216, when John died of dysentery while fleeing from the French invaders, the barons made a pro-English choice, switching their allegiance away from Louis and on to John's son, whom they crowned Henry III. This might well have been because Henry was only nine years old at the time, and therefore easy to dominate – you could make him cut taxes just by taking away his toy horse. But it was also a decision that isolated England from France, and forced the most powerful Englishmen, who had previously thought of themselves primarily as Norman expats, to get their head around the notion that, after 150 years on English soil, their families might actually be staying there.

This growing Englishness became all the more tangible when Henry III came of age in 1227 and began to reign without a regent. He invited a horde of foreign advisers to his court, including members of his French mother's side of his family, and made things worse after his marriage to a twelve-year-old countess called Eleanor of Provence; the child bride arrived with an entourage of interfering Franco-Italian cousins, whose prominence at the English court made Eleanor so unpopular that Londoners once tried to sink her barge as she was cruising down the Thames.

The Bishop of Lincoln, Robert Grosseteste,* disapproved of the situation so much that he criticized King Henry publicly, complaining that these French courtiers were 'foreigners and the worst enemies of England. They do not even understand the English language.'

The French, never ones to stay out of an argument, added fuel to this increasingly heated nationalistic debate. In 1244, King Louis IX of France (the son of the Prince Louis who had been invited to rule England) declared that 'it is impossible for a man who lives in my country but has lands in England to serve two masters. He must either bow to my authority or to that of the English King.'

The split from France was almost complete.

England takes its punishment where it hurts

Fortunately for France, England was not yet ready to attack it, because Kings Edward I and II, whose reigns lasted from 1272 to 1327, expended most of their energies persecuting the Scots and the Welsh. And they

* This was an Anglo-Norman name meaning 'Bighead', and nothing to do with large testicles.

received some painful wounds in reply, including the massacre of the English army at Bannockburn in 1314. However, this mauling at the hands of the Scots and the Welsh had two positive consequences that would come back to haunt the French.

First of all, the English found out to their cost that the Welsh were experts with the murderous longbow. This was a very different animal to the bow that had (possibly) killed Harold at the Battle of Hastings. The Welsh bows were five or six feet long – usually taller than the men firing them – and could shoot heavy, iron-tipped arrows 250 yards with deadly accuracy. It was like the difference between musket balls and sniper bullets. It took a lifetime of practice and forearm strength to pull back the string of a six-foot longbow, and, thanks to this defeat against the Welsh, English village greens were soon echoing to the swish-plunk of arrows hitting targets. It was a sound that would soon have French knights trembling in their armour.

Secondly, at Bannockburn, Edward II's army of 20,000 knights was decimated by Robert the Bruce's small force of Scottish footsoldiers because the English tried to charge in full armour across boggy ground. They learned from their mistake, and were to lure the French into exactly the same trap on two historic occasions in the next century.

Edward II was not a popular king. As well as his skill at losing battles, he was openly gay, which – despite William Rufus's pioneering work 120 years earlier, and Richard the Lionheart's alleged follow-up – was not yet fashionable amongst the English upper classes.

In the end, Edward's own wife, a French princess whose temper had earned her the nickname 'Isabelle the she-wolf of France', arranged to have him deposed and murdered in 1327, in gruesome circumstances. It was reported at the time that Edward, imprisoned in Berkeley Castle near Gloucester, was pinned to a bed while a horn or metal tube was shoved into his rectum. If this were not bad enough, a red-hot piece of metal was then inserted into the tube, burning Edward's innards and killing him.

While this was being done to him (if it was – other reports say he was suffocated), England was at a depressing low. The nation was impoverished because of a series of bad harvests and its rulers' fruitless attempts to oppress their Celtic neighbours. It had also lost yet another of its holdings in France, Gascony, which had been grabbed by the French without a struggle. All in all, Edward II's horrific death could be seen as a symbol of England getting its recent past shoved up its rear end.

The country therefore felt a deep desire to get back on its feet and regain its self-esteem. England was primed and ready for the Hundred Years War, the longest single conflict in British history. And its opponents of choice were the French.

3

The Hundred Years War: A Huge Mistake

Featuring the Black Prince, Henry V and lots of dead French people . . .

Most people who write about the Hundred Years War are at pains to point out that it is an obvious miscalculation: a conflict that lasts from 1337 to 1453 is clearly not a Hundred Years War. And the most disappointing thing is that it was given its name by the Victorians, who were generally excellent at maths because of all the measuring they had to do for the maps of their expanding empire.

In fact, though, the mistake goes far deeper than that, because the name is an almost deliberate piece of white-washing. For a start, it wasn't a single war; it was a whole series of conflicts that flared up and died down as the kings of England got up the energy and the cash to fight. And although the dates we remember today commemorate famous battles – Crécy in 1346 and Agincourt in 1415 – it is wrong to imagine that the Hundred Years War was fought out by armies of knights and archers battling for king and country on the field of glory.

This is because, apart from a few outbreaks of chivalrous combat, the 'war' was quite simply 120-odd years of terror inflicted on French civilians by gangs of out-of-control English bandits, claiming to defend their king's rights but actually hard at work enriching themselves and massacring as many people as they could in the process.

For more than a century, no town in the northern half of France was safe from siege, and peasants could not work in their fields without posting lookouts on hilltops and belfries or in trees. If a dust cloud was sighted, the farmers would instantly down tools and run, because they knew that any man caught alive by the English would be either held to ransom if he was rich enough, or killed out of hand if not, usually after being hideously tortured to reveal where his meagre savings were buried. For women captives, all the above was equally valid, except that they would also be gang-raped. It wasn't so much a Hundred Years War as a Century of Genocide, sanctioned by the King (and therefore, in feudal minds, by God).

The French-language Wikipedia entry for *La guerre de Cent Ans* summarizes the war by saying: 'Date 1337–1453. Outcome: French victory.' But that is a bit like saying 'Black Death 1349–51. Outcome: Human victory.' It ignores rather a large amount of suffering – and in the case of the Hundred Years War, most of it was French.

Annoying the French for fun and profit

The question is: why would the English inflict such a campaign of death and destruction on their neighbours? And the answer, as usual in such cases, is: because they could. Or, more exactly, because they couldn't do it anywhere else. To the east, the Flemish were allies. The Scots and the Welsh to the north and west had proved to be impossibly tough nuts to crack, and the pickings weren't especially rich. France, on the other hand, was like a widow on a Caribbean cruise: rich, available and convenient.

In the early 1300s, in comparison to England, France was a very wealthy nation. Its farmland was about the most productive in Europe, and the country was criss-crossed by trade routes from the Mediterranean and the Orient. Consequently, its population was growing in both size and sophistication – while the English were still chewing on turnips, the French were getting snobbish about how much pepper should go in the *soupe à l'oignon*.

What's more, King Philippe VI was the undisputed ruler of almost the whole of France. Seen from the English side of the Channel, his was a privileged position but a dangerous one. To give the soon-to-be-declared war another metaphor, it was a bit like a gang of English lager louts spotting a French playboy lying on the beach. There he is, his Rolex glinting in the sun, his eyes protected by super-hip Ray-Bans, his ears plugged into a limited-edition iPod. Even his swimming shorts are straight out of *Vogue Homme*. The temptation to go and pour beer (or worse) on his face is irresistible. This, plus the chance to steal all his valuable designer gear and dent his too-perfect teeth. And then go back and give him cigarette burns until he reveals his credit-card PIN number. In short, the war was going to be cruel, racist and criminal. But, most of all, it was going to be fun.

England's new king, Edward III, was not exactly a lager lout, but he was a fifteen-year-old emerging from a disturbed childhood. As we saw in Chapter 2, his father was probably burnt to death by a red-hot suppository, and Edward knew that it was with the connivance of his mother, Queen Isabelle. The young Prince must also have guessed that he had only been saved from a similar fate because his existence enabled Isabelle to rule England with a regent – her lover, an earl called Roger Mortimer. But when Isabelle got pregnant by Mortimer, Edward probably felt the hot metal closing in on his backside, so one night in October 1330 he broke down his mother's bedroom door with an axe, dragged Mortimer off to be hanged, drawn and quartered, and locked Isabelle away in Norfolk, where she is said to have had a miscarriage. Whether she was 'aided' in this by one of Edward's supporters is not clear, but suffice it to say that the King subsequently had one less potential rival for the throne.

England was now ruled by a teenage survivor who was looking for action. One of the first things he did was head north and burn large tracts of lowland Scotland, letting off some steam about Bannockburn. He also led an army of archers in a victorious battle against a few Scottish spearmen at Halidon Hill, near Berwick, in 1333, and returned to London to be hailed as 'the new King Arthur'. He had tasted not only victory but revenge.

It was at this point that King Philippe VI of France made the huge mistake of irritating the newly blooded young ruler.

In May 1334, Philippe invited the ten-year-old king of Scotland, David II, to take refuge from the English in France, and warned Edward III to stop bullying wee Davie. This was a provocative warning, because in giving it Philippe was repeating the old French taunt that the King of England was a feudal vassal of the King of France. Richard the Lionheart's claim that an English king had no superior except Dieu still hadn't convinced the French at all. And as if this wasn't bad enough, the Bishop of Rouen gave a sermon gleefully announcing that a

6,000-strong French army was getting ready to go and defend Scotland against English incursions.

So King Edward did what any red-blooded Englishman would have done: he claimed the throne of France.

All queens are illegal, but some are less illegal than others

Edward's mother Isabelle had already tried to claim France for herself in 1328. She was the sister of the recently deceased French King Charles IV, who had died leaving a baby girl as his only heir. Isabelle therefore argued that she was the natural candidate for succession. However, the assembly gathered to debate the succession refused Isabelle's claim because, as a contemporary chronicler, Jean Froissart, recorded, 'the realm of France was so noble that it must not fall into a woman's hands.'

In the event, the vacant throne was grabbed by Philippe VI, a 35-year-old champion jouster with a large army – the sort who quite often used to win arguments about who was going to be a medieval ruler. And Edward III seems to have forgotten about his mother's claim to the French crown until 1334, when Philippe made the mistake of declaring that he was a Scotland supporter.

Trouble was further stirred up by the presence at Edward's court of a scheming French nobleman, a fifty-year-old bon vivant called Robert d'Artois. Robert was King Philippe VI's brother-in-law, and had fled to England after – it was rumoured – poisoning his aunt to try and steal her inheritance. If true, this was small beer for the times, but Robert was sentenced to death and exiled. When Philippe VI announced that anyone who harboured Robert would be considered his mortal enemy, Edward took him in, made him an earl and gave him three castles. A clear statement if ever there was one.

A classic brother-in-law, and French to boot, Robert could not resist whinging about Philippe and egging Edward on to claim his 'rightful inheritance'. According to a poem of the time, 'Les Voeux du héron' – 'The Vows of the Heron' – Robert brought matters to a head at a banquet in 1338, during which he accused Edward III of being a coward for not invading France, and cajoled the influential dinner guests into promising that they would help Edward win the French throne. Robert did this by taking an oath over a cooked heron (a timid bird that symbolized cowardice),* and getting the other participants to invent variations on the vow – a fashionable dinner-party game in the early fourteenth century.

Before you could say who wants to pull the heron wishbone, Edward had announced his intention to go and grab the French Crown, and even designed himself a new coat of arms – a combination of England's rampant lions and the French fleur-de-lis. The new Anglo-French banner, which would have come with matching shield, helmet, doublet and squire's uniform, was the rudest, most provocative insult that Edward could have conceived, a bit like sleeping with a modern Frenchman's wife and putting the video on YouTube. With one bit of fashion design, Edward had just made it likely that the coming war was going to be very brutal indeed.

How to get funding for your conflict

Edward III was no longer a disturbed adolescent. In his mid-twenties, he was by all accounts a well-bred and

* And whose diet is, of course, frogs. Although in the fourteenth century 'frog' was not yet an insult applied to the French – it was usually aimed at the marsh-living Dutch.

learned man, who could even write. His first language was Anglo-Norman, as it was for all his class, but he was able to speak English like a native (which, of course, he was), and could understand Latin, German and Flemish. He also had, as one contemporary put it, 'the face of a god', and used it to maximum effect, enticing countless women with a shake of his long blond locks, a royal smile, and no doubt the odd Flemish joke.

He didn't limit his charms to sexual encounters either, and as soon as his mind was set on war, he embarked on a spectacularly successful career as a royal conman, wheedling a war chest out of a whole series of rich bankers and merchants in Italy, Holland and England, almost all of whom later went bankrupt when he failed to pay them back.

Edward also pawned not only his own English crown, but the one he had had made, rather optimistically, for when he would be crowned King of France.

Philippe VI, on the other hand, had severe problems getting funding for his war. Even in those days, the French liked nothing better than ignoring laws, and many of them refused to pay taxes. Philippe had to resort to slapping a duty on salt and debasing his currency, calling in silver coins and reissuing them in cheap metal. In the end, he was forced to top up his war chest by borrowing a million gold florins from the Pope.*

Philippe used his funding to raise an army of some 60,000 heavy cavalry, many of them aristocrats in search of a reputation as knights. Edward did more or less the opposite, and wrote to England's constables and bailiffs instructing them to send him the most suitable

* The Church in those days seems to have taken a much more liberal line on those Ten Commandments that deal with killing people and coveting your neighbour's chattels.

candidates for warfare aged between sixteen and sixty. As well as selecting the best longbowmen, most of these local officials also took the opportunity to pack off their thieves and murderers.

So while France's noblest knights strapped on their armour and tested each other on the rules of chivalry, thousands of English criminals were swapping hints on the best way to stab toffs.

Giving massacre a bad name

If any excuse is needed for the horrors that were about to be inflicted on France, it should be stressed that the French started it.

In 1337 they began to raid the English coast, and over the following year, Rye, Hastings, Portsmouth, Southampton, the Isle of Wight and Plymouth were all attacked and looted. English merchant vessels were captured, and French ships even sailed into the Thames Estuary. Rumours of a massive French invasion began to circulate, and it was said that captured Kentish fishermen were being tortured and paraded through the streets of Calais.

The English quickly realized that this raiding business was a good idea, and Norman and Breton ports began to get a taste of their own medicine. Sometimes, the English raiders were even able to steal back plunder that had recently been taken from their own towns. Soon, no ship in the Channel was safe. The Cornish port of Fowey had a band of pirates who roamed the coasts of England and France, and even attacked English ships. Though, as Cornishmen, they no doubt regarded the English as foreign, too.

Then came the invasion proper. In September 1339, Edward III attacked France with a force of around 15,000 men, many of whom were Dutch and German mercenaries paid for by his borrowed money. Philippe VI was waiting for them at a place called La Flamengrie in northeastern France with an army of 35,000. Even though Philippe had numerical superiority, he offered to make a sporting occasion of the battle by proposing a sort of tournament between France's *paladins* – its noblest knights – and the best men in the English army. This may well have been a jibe at Edward, who had been one of the *paladins* until Philippe confiscated his French lands.

Edward was spoiling for a fight – not just because he was that kind of guy but also because his Dutch and German mercenaries were complaining about not having enough food and threatening to go home. So he agreed to meet Philippe however he wanted, in a massive clash of two armies or a more chivalrous face-off between individual knights. In the end, though, Philippe simply didn't turn up.

Cowardly, perhaps, but effective. Like an English pensioner hit by the rising euro, Edward quite simply could not afford to stay in France, and had to withdraw. He was so short of money that he even had to leave his wife Philippa in Ghent as security for loans. His invasion – the attack that was supposed to sweep him to Paris and win the French throne – had lasted a month and got him no further than the outskirts of Calais.

However, in terms of the war to come, the mission had not been a total loss, because Edward and his troops had created a brand-new concept, and in a brilliant piece of double-speak they had given it a French name to hide the fact that it was an English invention.

The French word *chevauchée* had previously meant a harmless horse-ride, a refreshing trot in the country, but Edward III now gave it a much less innocent meaning. As his men marched through France, he ordered them to destroy everything in their path. He even boasted about it in a letter to his son, the Black Prince, noting matter-of-factly that he advanced with 'our people burning and destroying to the breadth of twelve or fourteen leagues of country', and that the area around the city of Cambrai was 'laid waste, of corn and cattle and other goods'. He didn't mention that this involved torching whole towns and forcing the population to flee or be put to death.

A similar technique had been used in England by William the Conqueror, mainly as a punitive action to put down rebellion. But this was how Edward planned to wage his *whole war*, in an attempt to make France so sick of the carnage that they would capitulate. It was almost exactly the same argument that would be used to justify bombing Hiroshima and Nagasaki in 1945. If nuclear warheads had existed in the fourteenth century, the only thing that would have kept Edward from using them would have been the loss of profitable hostages and the danger that the French throne would be too radioactive for him to sit on.

French tactics are a joke

Edward III was obviously a cruel man, but one thing you could not fault was his determination. Because no sooner had he returned to England than he persuaded Parliament to vote him a tax on wool, corn and lamb, and – to prove that he wasn't anti-rural – a straight one-ninth share of every townsman's property. He used the money to get his wife out of hock and prepare a new anti-French campaign. And this time he would meet with spectacular success.

Aware that Philippe was preparing an invasion fleet, Edward decided to hit the enemy at sea. In June 1340, he led around 200 ships, most of them converted merchant vessels, out of Suffolk and across the Channel.

On paper, this was pure folly. Edward's ships were converted cargo vessels, whereas the French had rented highly manoeuvrable Genoese war galleys that were equipped with rams and catapults and captained by an old Genoese sea-dog usually known as Barbanera, or Blackbeard. These, along with shiploads of French men-at-arms,* were now anchored in a large natural harbour at Sluys, in modern-day Holland, tied up side by side in a defensive battle line to prevent boarders.

Edward's plan was simple: he would sail straight at them and board, using his armoured troops. Men in medieval armour clambering over the gunwales of a ship? A less optimistic leader might have thought that this was not very practical. However, Edward did not know that he had one massive factor in his favour, a French weakness that lives on to this day.

Philippe VI's fleet may have had a great Genoese sea-captain on hand to lead it, but Barbanera was outranked by the two Frenchmen in charge, Hugues Quiéret and Nicolas Béhuchet, neither of whom were seamen. One of them, Béhuchet, was a former tax collector. And when Barbanera advised them to leave harbour and take to the open sea, where his nimble galleys would be able to dance around the sluggish English fleet and sink it, the two Frenchmen refused.

This is a very French trait. Today, if a big manufacturing company is in trouble, it will parachute in a graduate of one of France's *grandes écoles*, someone who has studied business theory and maths for ten years but never actually been inside a factory. The important thing to the French is not experience, it is leadership – or, more

---

* The medieval French term for men-at-arms, *gent d'armes*, is the origin of the word *gendarme*.

exactly, French-style leadership, which mainly involves ignoring advice from anyone with lots of experience but no French *grande école* on their CV.

So Quiéret and Béhuchet kept their fleet at anchor while Edward sailed slowly but surely into harbour and discovered to his surprise that the supposedly defensive French line left the end ships vulnerable to boarding from the side. What was more, the other ships, being tied up alongside, could not sail to their aid.

While the two French admirals consulted the manual on what to do in such cases, the English troops were able to clamber along the row of vessels, from one ship to the next, first wreaking havoc with a bombardment of arrows (British longbowmen were seeing their first major action abroad) and then storming the surviving French soldiers, taking the rich ones prisoner and throwing the rest overboard, where their armour did not help them swim to safety. Any lightly clad Frenchmen who made it to shore were promptly hacked to death by the Flemish locals.

Barbanera, the Genoese veteran, quickly realized that this was going to be a disaster of titanic proportions (even though the *Titanic* would not sink for another 572 years), and rowed his galleys swiftly away so that his men could live to fight for paymasters who might actually listen to his advice.

Overwhelmed, the French leaders, Quiéret and Béhuchet, tried to apply what they had learned of the theory of medieval war by surrendering and being held for ransom, but it was not to be their lucky day. Quiéret had his head lopped off, and Béhuchet was taken to Edward III's flagship and strung up, so that the sight of his swinging corpse would demoralize the remaining French troops. Edward might have needed ransoms, but he was fighting total war – so total that even the ship containing his wife and her attendants had taken part in the battle, resulting in the death of a lady-in-waiting. It was the last time the Queen was going to accept one of Edward's invitations to 'take a spin on my yacht'.

The result of the encounter was that the French invasion fleet was almost totally destroyed, and France lost tens of thousands of its troops. King Philippe VI's courtiers were so nervous about giving him the bad news that it was left to the court jester to tell him in joke form.

'Our knights are far braver than the English,' the jester said.

'Why is that?' Philippe asked.

'Because the English don't dare to jump into the sea in full armour.'

Like many French jokes, it had to be explained, and didn't get much of a laugh.

Crécy, a battle caused by the loss of some bacon

It was yet another French traitor who spurred Edward on to fight the next phase in the war – a little spot of collaboration that would result in an even more disastrous defeat for Philippe VI.

Geoffroy d'Harcourt was a Norman knight who had sworn an oath to fight for Philippe VI. However, when Geoffroy decided to marry a rich Norman heiress with the very rural name of Jeanne Bacon, he found that he had a serious rival – a powerful friend of King Philippe's called Guillaume Bertrand. Predictably, Philippe declared that Jeanne should marry Guillaume (no one asked Jeanne what she wanted), so Geoffroy started a small-scale private war against the Bertrand family. It probably got no further than burning a few farms and murdering some cows and peasants, but the Bertrands complained to the King, who confiscated Geoffroy's land and had four of his best friends beheaded.

Understandably peeved, Geoffroy went to England and offered his services to Edward III. More than this, he brought valuable intelligence. According to the chronicler Froissart, Geoffroy told Edward that:

> the country of Normandy is one of the richest countries in the world . . . and if you land there, no one will resist you . . . There you will find great towns that are not walled, so that your men will make so much booty that they will still be rich twenty years later.

Edward didn't even pause to ask what the local women looked like – he got together as many ships and men as he could and, on 5 July 1346, they all sailed for Normandy, landing a week later at La Hague, near Cherbourg, which (no doubt in commemoration of the event) France has more recently chosen as the site of a nuclear reprocessing plant.

Edward's army *chevauchéed* its bloody way across country, with Geoffroy d'Harcourt himself leading a raiding party of 500 men to do some personal plundering. At Caen, the inhabitants tried to defend themselves by climbing on to their rooftops and throwing down anything they could lay their hands on at the invaders. This so infuriated Edward that he ordered his men to burn the whole town and kill all the inhabitants. After three days of destruction and 3,000 deaths, the army had gathered so much booty that they had to send it downriver to the coast on barges. Soon, ships laden with jewellery, gold and silver plate, furs, richly embroidered clothing and, of course, hostages were sailing back to England.

The French allege that Edward now planned to head for Paris and unseat Philippe VI. If this is true, then his mission failed. But it seems more likely that the English King just wanted to goad the battle-shy Frenchman into fighting. So, after burning the Parisian suburbs of Saint-Cloud and Saint-Germain-en-Laye (both of which, ironically, are now strongholds of the British ex-pat community), Edward turned northeast again and made for Ponthieu, a territory that Philippe had recently confiscated from him. And after crossing the river Somme, the Brits stopped near a small town called Crécy.

Today, the site of the battle of Crécy probably looks much like it did in 1346, apart from a modern house built in one corner of the field, a bit of deforestation, and a small concrete toilet block by the car park. The windmill that stood at the crest of the muddy slope has been replaced by a wooden observation tower, from the top of which you can see . . . well, more sloping mud. Not that one should scoff at the mud – those are some of the most famous clods in English history.

At the foot of the observation tower there is a rather battered plaque that gives the visitor a short, quintessentially French, description of the battle. It is, basically, a list of excuses for losing – 'the [French] troops were blinded by the sun, which was shining again',* it says, and compares the French cavalry, who had had a long ride to the battlefield, with 'the [English] bowmen who were refreshed and well prepared'. The mass slaughter of France's noblest knights is mentioned almost in passing – 'the French cavalry encountered difficulties and was then defeated'. Yes, being hit by probably the most concentrated shower of arrows ever seen in Europe was just a 'difficulty'.

Down in Crécy itself, there is a wonderful little museum in the former village school, with an exhibition in two converted classrooms just opposite a line of five

* I love that 'again', as if God had turned on the sun just to annoy the French.

outside toilets – four loos with small doors for the children, one with a more discreet full-length door for the teachers.

The guide unlocked each room for my visit – it was a sunny afternoon in the February mid-term break, but no French people seemed to be interested in a history outing – and told me that until 2004 there was no mention of the battle in the museum. It was an archaeological display featuring shards of pottery and lumps of rust that had been excavated from the castle mound. This was the only history that interested the people of the village, apart from the fact that Crécy had been the site of the first launch pads for Nazi V1 doodlebugs. Perhaps the British bombing that knocked out the V1s had blasted the medieval battle from their minds.

Things changed, however, when the charity that runs the museum was taken over by an Englishman, who thought that a small commemoration of Edward III's victory might be appropriate. And it is the Brits who have provided most of the exhibits – Crécy is a mecca for pretty well every archery club in England and when they come, often in period costume, they bring artefacts with them. Some they donate to the museum, others they leave rather undiplomatically on the battlefield – a metal-tipped arrow, an exact replica of those used in 1346, was recently found embedded near the observation tower, with 'For Saint George and England' carved into its shaft. It was removed 'for safety reasons'.

And the most impressive exhibit in the museum is the case containing similar replicas of the arrows. One thing is for sure – it can't have been much fun being a French knight on the receiving end of one of these monsters. The shafts are a yard in length, as thick as a thumb, and tipped with metal spikes as long as an index finger. Some have straight, four-sided arrowheads – the 'bodkins' that were used to pierce armour – and others have wicked barbs that would slice into a horse's flesh and send the charger careering away, mad with pain.

At Crécy, there were around 7,000 English longbowmen, who could fire ten arrows a minute with deadly accuracy. In the first sixty seconds of battle, some 70,000 arrows would have fallen on Philippe VI's front line of troops. It's hardly surprising that things got off to a bad start for him.

French roads can be hell in August

Before going into the gory details of the battle, it might be a good idea to take in a little more background information.

Edward III, whose troops had just finished their highly profitable *chevauchée* across the north of France, chose where the battle would take place, and quite understandably picked the best location for himself. His camp was at the top of a long slope, protected on one side by a river and on the other by a thick band of forest.

Edward had a force of between 11,000 and 16,000 men, consisting of the aforementioned archers (both English and Welsh), around 2,000 armoured foot-soldiers, 1,500 or so knifemen (that is, dagger-wielding murderers) and a few hundred knights on horseback. His army was much smaller than Philippe's, but well trained, well positioned and, perhaps most important of all, blooded.

The French had a massive force, with some 15,000 Genoese crossbowmen, 20,000 men-at-arms, several thousand knights on horseback, and untold numbers of peasants wielding rocks, scythes and anything they could find that would enable them to take revenge for the havoc wreaked on their farmland. Philippe also brought along musicians – mainly trumpeters and drummers – to scare the enemy. Even then, French music was known to terrify the English.

It is true that Edward had time to prepare. He organized his troops in an attacking V formation, with men-at-arms in the centre and two wings of archers. The archers went out and dug small holes in the field, designed to put the horses off their stride, or even make them fall over. They also littered the ground with caltraps, large four-sided metal spikes designed to pierce hooves or footsoldiers' boots. Divisions of the English army were commanded by veterans, including the Norman deserter, Geoffroy d'Harcourt, who was given the task of protecting Edward's son, the sixteen-year-old Black Prince, about to see his first major action.

After they had made their preparations, Edward III had wine and meat distributed to the troops (fresh supplies had been 'liberated' nearby), and then let them rest. The morning of Saturday, 26 August 1346 was, admittedly, quite a relaxing one for the Brits.

The French, on the other hand, were characteristically late for the battle, and when Philippe VI got to Crécy, most of his army still hadn't arrived. One of his advisers told him that there was no point fighting that day, because the troops would be tired and, besides, it had been raining and some of the knights had water trickling down inside their armour and it was just too, too un-comfortable. Philippe, who, as we have seen, was never averse to avoiding a battle if he could do so, gave the order to make camp.

What Philippe didn't realize, because summer holidays hadn't yet been invented, was that the last week-end in August is absolute hell on French roads. Hordes of knights, footsoldiers and peasants were surging along all lanes leading to Crécy, and began to cause such a logjam that the front line of Philippe's army, the Genoese cross-bowmen, had no choice but to advance to avoid the crush.

These poor Italians (who obviously hadn't been warned by their compatriot, the sailor Barbanera, about bad French organization) were the first victims of Edward's arrow storm, and have been feeling the brunt of French resentment ever since.

They marched across rain-soaked terrain, straight uphill towards the longbowmen, having to stand still for up to a minute every time they wanted to reload their cumbersome crossbows. What's more, during their long trek to the battlefield, the Genoese had left their shields on the baggage carts in the rear, and hadn't been able to go back and fetch them. The English and Welsh longbow-men saw the first wave of attackers lumbering forwards and simply slaughtered them, their arrows tearing through leather jerkins, piercing helmets and slicing holes in faces.

The Genoese were mercenaries, and, just like Barbanera at the Battle of Sluys, seem to have had a collective bout of 'sod this job'. They turned and fled – or tried to. There was nowhere to flee, because they were being followed by massed ranks of French cavalry.

Some French sources forgive the Genoese – one chronicle goes as far as to say that they were handicapped because their crossbow strings had gone limp in the rain – but most are unforgiving. They report the fury of Philippe VI's brother, Charles de Valois, who, seeing this unchivalrous retreat, ordered his cavalry to 'stomp the rabble'. Some even accuse the Genoese of turning on the French, drawing knives and trying to cut horses' sinews and knights' throats. One thing is for certain, though: Edward's archers were now firing at will on a helpless mob of panicking crossbowmen, stumbling horses and indignantly snorting French nobles. Philippe's royal brother Charles himself rode at the cross-bowmen, got tangled up in the mound of bodies and was probably killed within minutes of entering the battle.

Fired up with pride, shoved in the back by the arriving mob, and urged on by tuneless music, the French knights just kept on coming. In complete disarray they rode or marched into the hailstorm of arrows, which, according to the chronicler Froissart, was so dense that it blacked out the evening sun.

Edward and his army must have wondered what was going on. At least the townspeople of Caen had thrown a few stones and rooftiles at them. These knights, the 'flower of France', were simply queuing up to be slaughtered.

The Black Prince and some white feathers

One of the most famous stories to emerge from the battle tells of a blind knight who insisted on charging to his death. King John of Bohemia, an ally of Philippe, had lost his sight owing to an eye infection caught while fighting in Lithuania, but didn't want to miss out on the excitement at Crécy. So he ordered his men to tie his horse's reins to theirs and pull him in the direction of the English lines. What he hoped to do if he got there is anyone's guess – ask the archers to shout out and give him a sporting chance of hitting them, perhaps. In any case, John's group somehow made it to the top of the slope, where they were all cut down by English men-at-arms.

The French charged up that hill over a dozen times, and even their own chronicler, Froissart, remarks on their total lack of discipline. Only when darkness fell did Philippe accept defeat and, sporting a wound that some

Medieval illustrators were never very reliable on exact troop numbers or perspective, but the general gist is right: British archers start wreaking havoc at Crécy in 1346.

sources place on his neck, others on his thigh (*cou* and *cuisse* are fairly similar words, after all), rode away to a nearby chateau, where he called out for the gateman to open up to the 'unfortunate King of France'. This, believe it or not, was a joke, because up until then he had been known as Philippe the Fortunate. Like his jester six years earlier, Philippe probably didn't get a laugh.

It wasn't until the following morning that the English discovered the full extent of their victory. Exhausted, they had slept in their battle formations, and awoke to find the whole valley full of fog. It can't have been a silent night – the wounded men and horses must have been groaning pretty loudly – but even Edward was shocked when his scouts reported back that the field was a huge mass of dead Frenchmen (with some Genoese at the bottom of the pile).

Edward quickly sent out more men to identify the dead. This was the cue for the knifemen to make sure that anyone not rich enough to hold for ransom, or too severely wounded to be taken prisoner, was actually dead. To do this, they used a long, thin blade called a misericorde or 'mercy-giver', which could be thrust between armour plates, into unprotected armpits or through visor slits, to pierce a knight's heart or brain.

The Black Prince went to view the carnage after his first battle, and was shown blind King John and the clutch of Bohemian bodies, still bound together in death. He was so moved that he stole (or perhaps should one say adopted) John's three-white-feather crest and his motto, 'Ich dien' – 'I serve'.*

By the end of the body count, the English had tallied

* This is of course the Prince of Wales's motto to this day, though subsequent princes have not adopted John of Bohemia's custom of fighting while tied up and blind. Except at private parties, of course.

up 1,542 dead French noblemen and an estimated 10,000 other ranks.

The 10,000 didn't bother the French so much, but the list of defunct aristocrats included various Henris and Louis and Charles, who were the crème de la crème de la crème of France. And the most shocking thing to the French was that almost all of them had been killed by archers or knifemen, what one chronicler bluntly calls 'gent de nulle valeur' – people of nil value. It was as if the French rugby fifteen had just lost to half a dozen boozed-up *Big Issue* sellers. Predictably, everyone blamed the team coach, Philippe VI. And his disastrous season was only just beginning . . .

A quick stop for some burghers

Whatever their name might suggest, the Burghers of Calais are not items on a cross-Channel ferry menu. They are French heroes, created just after Crécy. However, as with so many of France's heroes, including the soon-to-appear Joan of Arc, there is a French version of the story, and a true one.

The French version is that in 1347 these six citizens of Calais saved their town from the English. The truth is that they lost it.

The French would also have us believe that the burghers offered themselves up to Edward III for execution in exchange for a promise that the town would be spared. What no one mentions is that these same burghers, rich representatives of Calais's upper classes, had already sacrificed hundreds of the town's poor to try and save themselves.

At the risk of annoying French readers of this book, let's take a look at the facts.

After Crécy, Edward III decided not to capitalize on his

victory by marching on Paris. He didn't have enough men to mount a full-scale occupation of even the north-west of France. So he headed for the coast, and reached the nearest port, Calais, a week after the battle.

He hoped to capture the town easily, but it was well fortified and protected by marshland. All attempts to breach the outer walls failed. Edward duly laid siege, and even built a large, covered camp that gradually turned into a town, with a market where the locals could sell the produce that the English hadn't already plundered.

So determined was Edward to win the strategic harbour that he concentrated all his efforts on it, per-suading Parliament to give him more money to fund reinforcements. By the spring of 1347, he had some 30,000 men camped around Calais, and had even con-structed a line of fortifications facing outwards in case Philippe VI mustered enough troops to come and save the town.

An English fleet was moored offshore to prevent supplies coming in by sea, and by June the citizens of Calais were starving. In desperation, the community leaders, including the famous burghers, took the decision to expel 500 citizens who were considered lost causes. Most of these were the elderly and children, and inevitably all of them were poor. In a siege, what food there is gravitates upwards through the social classes to the people who can pay for it, so paupers are the first to suffer.

Until then, King Edward had been lenient, and had let non-combatants through his lines to avoid starvation, but by this time, nine months into the siege, his attitude had hardened, and he refused to let the 500 escape – he demanded total surrender or nothing at all. The towns-people wouldn't allow the 500 back in, so they were left to starve outside the town walls, watched, no doubt, by the six burghers as they chewed on slices of sautéed poodle.

In July, King Philippe VI of France finally decided that it might be a good idea to relieve his strategic port, so he marched an army to within a mile of the English fortifications, and challenged Edward to come out and fight. However, Edward knew that he was in a far stronger position, and that the town could not hold out much longer. So he simply dared Philippe to attack.

True to form, Philippe ordered his men to withdraw and, it is said, blocked his ears to the cries of the townspeople as he abandoned them to their fate. The surviving troops in the town took down the French flag – Philippe's personal coat of arms – and threw it over the wall in disgust.

The very next day, the commander of the Calais garrison, a knight called Jean de Vienne, shouted out a message that he was ready to surrender. Edward agreed, but warned that prisoners would be ransomed or killed, just as they were in battle. That is, the rich would survive and the poor would be slaughtered. Finally, an English knight called Sir Walter Mauny persuaded Edward to accept the lives of just six burghers.

One of the town's oldest and richest citizens, Eustache de Saint-Pierre, offered himself first, and was followed by five more volunteers. Obeying King Edward's instructions, they removed their fine clothing and came out of the town wearing only shirt and breeches (that is, in their underwear), and with a noose hanging from their neck. This is how they are depicted in the famous group statue by the nineteenth-century sculptor Auguste Rodin – as emaciated, haunted victims bravely going out to meet their deaths. And it is true that having heard of the *chevauchées*, the burghers no doubt expected to die, their only hope being that their value as hostages might just save their lives.

Most versions of the story say that Edward's Queen, Philippa, who was pregnant, begged him not to kill the burghers and bring bad luck on their unborn child. It is also said that Sir Walter Mauny warned him that the cold-blooded execution of rich prisoners who would otherwise have been kept alive as hostages would set a bad precedent, and might lead to future English deaths.

Either way, Edward did not carry out his threat. He banished all the town's wealthy citizens, and gave their houses and positions of power to Englishmen whom he summoned across the Channel. All of which goes to show that, however determined the French are to regard their Burghers of Calais as patriotic heroes, the truth is that they were part of a catastrophic defeat at the hands of the English, and that they only became symbols of self-sacrifice after trying to save themselves by kicking the poor out to die.

Rodin seemed to understand something of this. When the town of Calais commissioned the statue in 1884 he broke with tradition and instead of portraying the burghers in heroic pose, showed them in defeat. He also decreed that his statue should stand at ground level and not be elevated on a plinth. Needless to say, Calais ignored this demand, and erected the sculpture in front of its town hall on an ornate stone base.

The English, though, had the last laugh. In 1911, the British government bought one of the twelve casts of Rodin's statue and erected it in Victoria Tower Gardens in London, close to the Houses of Parliament. To this day, any British parliamentarian who goes out for a breath of fresh air in the park will come face to face with an image of abject French submission.

The Black Death – not such a bad thing for England (in the long run)

As if things weren't already bad enough for Philippe VI, in 1348 the Black Death arrived in France.

This Asian disease entered the country via Italy, and spread north, being hailed as yet another sign that God had turned against the French. The death toll in Avignon was so high that the Pope (who was based there, not in Rome) consecrated the river Rhone so that corpses could be flung into the water instead of being buried, and allowed people to give their last confessions to non-clergymen and 'even to a woman'. Extreme measures indeed.

To try and halt the plague's progress through France, King Philippe imposed harsh punishments for blasphemy. First-time offenders would lose a lip, and repeat offences would cost them the second lip and then their tongue. Meanwhile, the inhabitants of Strasbourg blamed the Jews and massacred the city's 2,000-strong community. None of this cured the disease, of course, and within a year the whole of France was infected.

Quite naturally the English felt pretty smug that God was putting the boot in on their enemies – until, that is, the pestilence crossed the Channel.

Population estimates in the fourteenth century tend to be very approximate, but it is thought that around one in three Western Europeans died in the space of three years. Densely populated cities suffered worst, and around half of London's 70,000 inhabitants died. In the similarly sized city of Paris, the death toll was 50,000 or so.

Chroniclers of the time on both sides of the Channel talk about abandoned villages, silenced cities, and (something that would have alarmed modern-day Brits) a slump in property prices – no one needed to buy because survivors could just move into an abandoned house. Meanwhile, previously valuable buildings like windmills were worth almost nothing because there was no grain to grind, and no city dwellers wanting to turn them into weekend homes.

In short, it was a disaster for all humankind, in which everyone suffered equally. Except that, by a quirk of fate, the Black Death worked in England's favour against the French. Or to be more accurate, it worked in *English*'s favour against *French*, because the epidemic sounded the (black) death knell for the Norman language in England.

There were various reasons for this. First, with the population decimated, the feudal system in England was doomed. There were villages without lords, and lords without serfs, meaning that the workmen who had survived were in such high demand that they could abscond and find work elsewhere as free men. Parliament tried to impose wage caps and forbid emancipation of the serfs, but this only led to open revolt. The landowning Anglo-Norman nobility's glass ceiling of wealth, power and privilege wasn't yet smashed, but it was showing deep cracks, as the formerly downtrodden Anglo-Saxon underclass expanded upwards as a real middle class. And as they travelled, they imposed their language – the bastardized mingling of Anglo-Saxon and Norman that we call English – throughout the nation.

This linguistic trend was intensified because the Anglo-Norman monks, who had formerly lived like lords of the manor in their monasteries, died out in massive numbers during the plague, having been inadvertently targeted by victims who came to them in hope of a miracle, or at least to receive the last rites. Now these Norman- and Latin-speaking monks were replaced by English-speakers, who were much humbler than their predecessors, and undertook an educational mission, teaching ordinary folk to read and write – in English.

All of which explains why the period just after the Black Death marks the final triumph of English in England. In 1362, Parliament was opened for the first time with a speech in English. In the same year, it was decreed that court cases should be heard in English because Norman French was no longer understood by enough people. This was apparently an overstatement, but such pro-English exaggerations were obviously in fashion, because two English diplomats of the time were reported to have refused to speak French on the grounds that it was 'as unintelligible to them as Hebrew'.

English, with its Anglo-Saxon roots and its hybrid Anglo-Saxon–Norman grammar, which had been growing like a fungus beneath the boots of the Anglo-Norman nobles, was finally gaining respect as more than a crude dialect used by peasants to grunt at each other. By 1385, the scholar John Trevisa was writing that 'in alle the gramere scoles of Engelond, children leveth Frensche and lerneth in Englische.' (Note the similarity of his spelling to that of modern English schoolchildren.) He even went so far as so say that English children knew as much French 'as their left heel'. (Again, just like modern kids.)

As we saw above, King Edward III knew English, and everyone was pleasantly surprised that he spoke it so fluently – he was apparently very good at swearing, having discovered right from the start that English was a much better language than French for cussing. By tacking on the Anglo-Saxon preposition 'off', English can turn pretty well any aggressive or rude-sounding word into an insult, and has both (harsh-sounding) Anglo-Saxon and (usually corrupted) Norman-French words to play with. French is just too Latin-based and grammatically prudish to achieve this.

Edward might have been fluent in English, but he had

learned it as a second language, and his first language was a French quite similar to that spoken by his enemy King Philippe. It was also still the chic way to express oneself at court, as Edward demonstrated with the famous 'dropped garter' incident in 1348.

During a ball at Windsor, the Countess of Salisbury's garter fell off while she was dancing with King Edward. He picked it up and attached it to his own leg, lapsing into French when he saw his courtiers raising an eyebrow – 'Honi soit qui mal y pense,' he blurted out, which might be roughly translated as 'Shame on anyone who thinks I did that because I'm after a bit of nookie.' The phrase was adopted as the motto for his newly founded Order of the Garter, and now figures on the British monarch's coat of arms, above 'Dieu et mon droit'.

However, by the time Henry V was giving his rousing speech before the Battle of Agincourt only sixty-seven years later, English would be the King's first language, and no translations of his pronouncements would be necessary.

In short, the tiny fleas that brought the Black Death to Europe also released England from the stranglehold of its foreign official language. Appropriate, really, because 'flea' is an Anglo-Saxon word.

War delayed owing to sudden illness

Naturally enough, the Black Death put something of a damper on the Hundred Years War. Ambitious conquest plans were shelved, and the action during the plague consisted mainly of sorties by enterprising English knights who took small armies on cross-Channel *chevauchées* to see if there was anything left to steal.

Edward III himself had also started something of a stock market for hostages, and anyone returning from

France with a valuable prisoner stood a good chance of selling him (or her – the French were outraged that abbesses were also being kidnapped) to the King. Edward would then contact the relatives of the rich captive and extort the full price.

Meanwhile, bands of English deserters took the concept of the *chevauchée* one step further by occupying French castles. Here they started extortion rackets, forcing everyone in the area to pay for 'protection' in wine, livestock or money, and bringing complete terror to the already desolate French countryside.

These bands of robbers gave themselves the innocent-sounding name of *routiers*,* or 'road travellers', and their idea was taken up with gusto by other mercenaries. Soon, gangs of deserters from Gascony, Brittany, Spain and Germany were adding to the chaos. Interestingly, though, the French didn't care which nationality was persecuting them – they referred to all the *routiers* as '*anglais*'. They also called the English 'les goddams', presumably because of their shocking habit of swearing while massacring people.

Henry V, much more than a funny haircut

The war was dragging its heels when Edward III died at the ripe old age of sixty-four in 1377, and was only kept going because so many Englishmen wanted the chance to hop across the Channel and make their fortune. Soldiering was as profitable a profession as modern-day football, with the added advantage that the opponents were likely to be hopelessly unfit peasants.

---

* This should not be confused with the modern word for trucker, and it is generally safe to go in roadside restaurants with a 'Routiers' sign outside.

But England was suffering internal revolt, and King Richard II, the Black Prince's son (the Black Prince had died, probably of cancer, before he could inherit the throne), sued for peace with France. In 1396, Richard even made an alliance with the French by marrying the new King Charles VI's six-year-old daughter Isabelle. In 1398 he went one stage further and accepted a truce with France. Frustrated Englishmen began to moan that Richard II was a closet Francophile, and this was one of the contributory factors to his being deposed in 1399 and (so it was rumoured) poisoned in early 1400 – in those days, you stopped annoying the French at your peril.

The French themselves were not all in favour of appeasement, and might not have accepted the truce if King Charles VI hadn't been a complete lunatic. He would often run around his castles howling like a wolf, and was convinced he was made of glass and that people wanted to smash him. In a fit of madness, he once killed four of his own courtiers.

This weakness at the top split France into two families warring for power – the Burgundians, led by Charles VI's cousin Jean de Bourgogne, and the Armagnacs under Louis, Charles's brother. Soon, both factions were committing atrocities that even outdid the *chevauchées*. The Armagnacs created a new terror, the *écorcheurs* (literally 'men who will skin you alive'), that they inflicted on their own countrymen for a good thirty years.

The only real winners of this long period of in-fighting were the English, who sold their support to first one faction and then the other, promising to intervene but switching loyalties when they were offered more money and territory by the opposing side. And the biggest benefactor of all was a new English king, Henry V, who in 1414 made a treaty with the Armagnacs that at one stroke earned him the regions of Poitou, Angoulême and Périgord in the southwest of France, thereby restoring at least partly England's old fortunes in that corner of the world.

Henry V, who was only twenty-six when he succeeded to the throne, was surrounded by very eligible male relatives, and needed to prove that he was a strong monarch. He was a born fighter, and wore his hair in the military pudding-bowl style of a helmet-wearing knight rather than the flowing regal locks of his recent ancestors. It is said that he was tall and so strong that he could walk in armour as though he was wearing a light cloak – no doubt because he had been put into battledress at an early age. While away persecuting Wales in his teens, he had been hit in the face by an arrow (they were still excellent shots, those Welsh archers), and was scarred for life – which is one of the reasons why his most famous portraits are all in profile.

Unfortunately for the French, Henry was fanatically religious, and convinced that God wanted him to be King of France. He was also the first non-gay ruler of England since William the Conqueror not to have a string of mistresses – another bad omen for his enemies across the Channel.

What's more, the French just kept offering themselves up for punishment. In 1414, the two warring factions, the Burgundians and Armagnacs, came to England asking for Henry's help. Henry replied by demanding the hand of a French princess in marriage, and, while he was at it, the French Crown. When this was refused, he retorted by saying that he had no option but to prepare for war – omitting to mention that he had been recruiting troops and having cannons made for the past year.

He had also been planning the details of his invasion carefully, and, like the Allied armies in 1944, chose to invade France via Normandy rather than the obvious route through Calais. On a sunny Sunday in August 1415, his fleet of 1,500 ships, carrying over 10,000 fighters, as well as horses, cattle and cannons, left the Solent. It must have been a colourful spectacle, with the knights' banners fluttering in the breeze and Henry's own ship, the 540-ton *Trinité Royale* (why he didn't give it an English name is not clear), sporting a provocative royal standard similar to the one created by Edward III, combining the English lions with the French fleur-de-lis.

The mood amongst the soldiers was optimistic, especially when swans came to swim alongside Henry's ship – a good sign, because his personal banner featured, in heraldic terminology, 'a swan with wings displayed argent'.

Henry's destination was the mouth of the river Seine, at Harfleur. He landed there on around 14 August, and legend has it that, in another parallel with William the Conqueror, on disembarking Henry tripped and fell to his knees. Like William, he reacted quickly, adopting the praying position, and a choir on board his ship began singing (no doubt to cover up the royal mutterings of 'Oh no, I've got sand in my armour').

The fleet was so big that it took two whole days to unload the ships.* Only when all his men had disembarked did Henry give them the bad news – this was to be no *chevauchée*. Looting, massacring and wholesale rape were forbidden. The English groan of disappointment was apparently heard as far away as Paris.

Henry immediately set about besieging Harfleur, and was annoyed to find that the Normans had learned a thing or two since Edward III's unopposed raids. They

---

* Stories that say this was because of a French dockers' strike are untrue.

had built impregnable defences around the town, and the siege of this small port, guarded by only a few hundred troops, dragged on with the English losing alarming numbers of men, not just from cannon fire and crossbow bolts, but also because of disease. It is said that the water was contaminated, and the chronicler John Capgrave wrote that 'many men died of fruit eating'. French summer fruits were clearly too exotic for the meat-and-turnip Englishmen, and they started to die, suffering what one contemporary picturesquely called 'a bloody flux', probably dysentery.

It wasn't until 22 September that the town finally surrendered, and the English were able to go in and grab rich hostages. Henry spared the poor, valueless citizens of the town, and even let some of them stay there, although he gave all the posh houses to Englishmen.

The problem for Henry was that after a month in Normandy, about a third of his army was dead, a large number had to be sent home on sick leave, and several hundred would have to stay and defend Harfleur. He was forced to abandon his plan to attack Paris, and decided instead to make a dash for the English stronghold of Calais, expecting no trouble on the way because his predecessors there had made such a good job of devastating the countryside and emptying it of opposition.

However, Henry's plan hit two major obstacles: the first was torrential rain that slowed his progress across country; the second was King Charles VI of France, still nominally in charge of his country. Charles had been informed by escapees from the siege of Harfleur that Henry's invading force had shrunk to manageable proportions, and he quickly raised an army that headed out of Paris to cut off the English retreat. Other Frenchmen were at work harrying King Harry's men as they marched northeast, and the Brits were horrified to find that one river crossing after the other was either destroyed or blocked. They had to fight at every bridge and ford, and make an unplanned 70-kilometre detour inland before they could skirmish their way across the Somme.

And then, just as English supplies, troop numbers and morale were at their lowest, the huge French army appeared. Shakespeare puts their number at 60,000 ('three score thousand'), though he was almost certainly exaggerating to talk up Henry's achievement; there were probably only 20,000 or 30,000 Frenchmen. Nevertheless, this was at least four times more than Henry's band of exhausted fugitives.

French messengers came to Henry telling him, rather needlessly, that they intended to fight him and 'take revenge for his conduct'. But instead of pleading that, for once, he had spared commoners' lives (not an argument that would have interested the snooty French nobility), Henry typically replied, 'be all things according to the will of God.'

His men camped that night in a rain-sodden field, probably unmindful of the fact that rain-sodden fields had brought the English good luck at nearby Crécy fifty years earlier. As they sat in the mud, they could see the French camps stretching away to the horizon, their fires blazing, the smells of expertly barbecued French sausages wafting over to torment the Englishmen, who had been living off wet bread, rotten fruit and dysentery bacteria for the past week. In their hearts, Henry and his men prepared to die.

Agincourt, lost in the mists of time – and geography

The first time I visited Agincourt, I had to give a wry grin at the French attempt to eliminate all memory of their second most famous military defeat ever.* It was even more flagrant than Crécy. It wasn't just that the museum was confined to two little rooms in an old schoolhouse. There was nothing at all.

Hardly surprising, really, because I was in the wrong place. I'd dropped into the village of Agincourt while on my way to Nancy in the east of France. And, as we all now know thanks to Bernard Cornwell's novel of the same name, the battle was at Azincourt with a 'z', almost 500 kilometres away, near Calais.

This is probably the most annoying thing of all to the French. Not only do we pronounce the battles incorrectly (Crécy should be 'Cray-see' and Waterloo 'Watt-air-loh'), with Agincourt ('Ah-zan-coor') we even get the spelling wrong.

But when Henry fought the battle, he didn't know exactly where he was, and only asked *after* he'd won. (Understandably – if he'd lost, he'd either have been dead or desperate to forget about the place.) Someone knew the name of the closest castle – Azincourt – and, because there weren't any road signs around, this was recorded wrongly as Agincourt. Strictly speaking, however, the battle shouldn't be called that anyway, because Henry's army was actually positioned at the nearby hamlet of Maisoncelle. But this doesn't matter either, because the English would only have got that wrong, and called it Maisonette or Maidenhead.

The museum in the village of Azincourt is a marked contrast to the little converted school at Crécy. It is an

---

* After Waterloo, of course. They don't really remember Crécy or Trafalgar; they think that Napoleon's failure to get to Moscow was a strategic withdrawal; and they don't regard the Nazi Occupation as a defeat – it was more of a waiting period until Charles de Gaulle was ready to come back and seal victory.

impressive, modern glass-and-timber building, its curved roof held up by beams in the shape of an English long-bow. Inside, visitors are given audio guides with sensors that activate headphones whenever you pass in front of interactive screens. It feels as though you're walking around listening to the voices of the dead. And the story they tell is much the same as at Crécy – it's all about French excuses.

Talking heads (literally – the displays include mannequins with television sets on their shoulders) tell you that the French knights had been in the saddle all night long, that it had been raining and horses had churned up the soil, and that the ranks of unmounted French men-at-arms were so tightly packed that they couldn't swing their weapons. You can press your face into helmets to see how poor the visibility was for these advancing French men-at arms. You can even lift swords and a mace to see how heavy they were. Meanwhile, Shakespeare's monologue,* in which a defiant Henry urges his men to fight for England and St Crispin, is recited by a gloomy, toad-like actor who looks as though he's about to die of grief.

The question is, how on earth did the French turn certain victory into a national disaster? The 'flower of France', which had had a few years to grow back since Crécy, was out in full bloom, and the knights there were so confident of winning that their only worry was that there wouldn't be enough Englishmen for each of them to kill. It really ought to have been a French walkover.

---

* Contrary to popular belief, Henry doesn't give his 'once more unto the breach, dear friends' speech before Agincourt. As the breach image suggests, he's talking at the siege of Harfleur, and referring to holes in the town walls. This is why he mentions that if they fail, they will 'close up the wall with our English dead'.

Resigned to defeat, Henry freed all his hostages and sent them over to the French with a last-minute plea to give him free passage to Calais in exchange for the return of Harfleur. He even offered to pay for any damage his men had done in France. Needless to say, the French refused.

In Shakespeare's *Henry V*, the King wanders around the English camp in disguise bantering with his soldiers, giving them what Shakespeare beautifully calls 'a little touch of Harry in the night'. In fact, though, the King forbade any noise in the English camp that night, probably hoping to limit defeatist talk, and threatened to cut off the ears of anyone who spoke except to give confession to the chaplains.

Next morning, Henry's chaplains said Mass three times (better safe than sorry), and the English took up their battle positions, in a similar formation to that at Crécy, with men-at-arms on foot in the centre and two projecting wings of archers. Shakespeare gives King Henry a rousing pre-battle speech that includes the famous lines about his small army being 'we few, we happy few, we band of brothers'. This is also where he says that 'gentlemen in England now a-bed/Shall think themselves accursed they were not here'. In reality, though, the King reminded his men that he was in France to claim his rightful inheritance (meaning that God supported England's side of the legal argument), and, according to the chronicler Jean Le Fevre, tried to motivate his archers to fight to the death by warning them that the French had threatened to cut off the fingers of any archer they caught. It is doubtful that they believed this, as everyone knew that low-born prisoners were killed out of hand, but it probably got a laugh and encouraged the bowmen to make rude signs at the French knights.

This is often cited as the moment when the

two-fingered salute was born, but in fact the theory that it was originally an anti-French gesture is probably unfounded. The connection between the French threat to disable the archers and the V-sign was apparently only made in the 1970s, and did not become really current until the 1990s, during a hate campaign against the European Union in general and France in particular. Desmond Morris's book *Manwatching*, published in 1979, comes to no conclusions about the origins of the gesture, and Morris seems to think that the two fingers might represent a vagina. In any case, fifteenth-century chronicles say that Henry warned his men that they would lose three fingers, not two, so the archers would probably have been giving a W-sign, not a Vs-up.

However they gesticulated, what Henry's men were doing was goading the enemy into an attack. He was probably praying that the French would commit the same error as at Crécy and come charging up the muddy hill. But they had learned some lessons from history, and waited calmly, hoping that the doomed Englishmen would come off their high ground and get the foregone conclusion over with.

This waiting game, though, turned out to be a fatal mistake.

The 'flower of France' gets trampled in the mud

At around nine o'clock on the morning of 25 October 1415, St Crispin's Day, Henry got tired of hanging about and ordered his archers to advance. They did so, in full view of the French, trudging slowly downhill in the mud, hauling their longbows, arrows, and long wooden stakes forward until they were only about 250 metres from the enemy.

This would have been an ideal time for the French to

attack, because the archers had no armour or shields and were encumbered by their stakes – their only protection was helmets made out of boiled leather. According to one observer, a French soldier called Jehan de Wavrin, the English even 'stopped several times to catch their breath'. However, perhaps because of the debacle at Crécy, the French had kept their crossbowmen at the rear, and missed the chance to snipe at the English. What was more, lots of French knights, over-confident of victory later in the day, had gone off for a ride.

Now within longbow range, the English archers erected a protective row of angled stakes and, at their leisure, fired a Crécy-style hailstorm of arrows at the front line of French knights. The horsemen weren't at full strength for the above-mentioned reason, but, faced with the choice between having their horses killed under them and getting an arrow through the top of their helmets, they charged.

Unbelievably, from then on, the battle was more or less a repeat of Crécy. The French cavalry rode forwards and were either felled by arrows or got themselves impaled on wooden stakes. Injured horses threw their riders, who lay helpless in the mud, weighed down by their armour and unable to get up. The fallen men's lives were spared temporarily because the unmounted French men-at-arms were now lumbering forward, and the English archers had to stay behind their stakes and keep firing.

The soil at Agincourt is heavy and sticky. I have tried walking a few steps across the battlefield in light shoes and my feet almost immediately doubled in size. Add heavy armour to the gooey equation and for those French men-at-arms it must have been like wading through shin-deep quicksand. Their mobility was further hampered by being packed in a tight formation to limit their vulnerability to a frontal barrage; seeing this, the English archers on the wings simply advanced and began firing into the two flanks of the French column.

By the time the men-at-arms reached the English, they were completely exhausted and almost blind – because of the constant threat from the arrows, they had to keep their visors down and could only see through two narrow slits.

A few of them managed to dent the English front line of men-at-arms between the wings of bowmen, but Henry ordered his archers to down bows and join in the hand-to-hand fighting. The densely packed column of Frenchmen now found themselves confronted with mobile fighters who could jump out of range of their swinging maces and deliver deadly stabs to the armpits and thighs, or simply trip the armoured men over.

Soon, just as at Crécy, the muddy field was piled high with dead or flailing Frenchmen lying on their backs like wounded tortoises. As always, the noblest survivors were pulled away to become hostages, the less privileged being finished off where they lay with a misericorde through the eye, heart or throat.

A few highly aristocratic Frenchmen were particularly unlucky. The leader of the men-of-arms, the duc d'Alençon, got as far as a face-to-face encounter with Henry himself, who lost a fleuret of his crown in the fight. But the Duke was quickly surrounded, and he took off his helmet and offered his glove in surrender, the traditional gestures of a beaten knight. Unfortunately for him, an Englishman saw an easy target and stove in the Duke's head with an axe.

Similarly, the duc de Brabant, arriving late and not wanting to miss the battle, did not take the time to put on his coat of arms. He rushed into the attack dressed as a herald, and when he was beaten in combat and attempted to surrender, he was killed, just as a simple herald would have been.

Not that being taken prisoner would have saved him, because what shocks the French most about the Battle of Agincourt or Azincourt is not so much the way in which three successive waves of their men went waddling helplessly through the mud to their deaths in an almost exact repetition of the errors at Crécy, but the fate of the prisoners.

Estimates vary as to the number of hostages taken in the first couple of hours of the battle, but French sources put it as high as 1,500. Having surrendered, they were under oath not to rejoin the fighting, and were probably confident of going home again as soon as their relatives had taxed the local peasantry enough to pay the ransom.

However, the lord of a nearby chateau, a man called Ysambart d'Azincourt, had noticed the ruckus going on down the road, and went out with a horde of some 600 locals to have a go at the undefended English baggage carts, which were carrying the plunder that Henry's men had dragged from Harfleur. Seeing an attack at his rear, and fearing that the French hostages, if freed, would rejoin the battle, Henry ordered each man to execute his prisoners.

This order didn't go down well with the soldiers who had nabbed such valuable human booty, so Henry was forced to send 200 of his most bloodthirsty and lower-class archers to do the job. Before long, the unarmed, and often trussed-up, French gentlemen were being beaten, stabbed or burnt to death.

Even today, outrage about this massacre can be felt in every French source relating to the battle, although one could argue that this is a bit rich coming from a country that indulged in the wholesale public guillotining of its own aristocracy at the end of the eighteenth century. It's true, killing the prisoners was a savage act by a supposedly chivalrous king, and contrary to all the rules of fifteenth-century warfare, but it was done while the battle was still hanging in the balance. Although things were definitely going in Henry's favour, there were still enough French soldiers in the area to attack the English from the rear or the flank and win a victory. Or, perhaps more sensibly, wait until Henry's army moved on – as they would have to do, being sorely short of food – and then pick them off in skirmishes all the way to Calais.

But French chroniclers say that the survivors were 'sickened at the bloodshed' (scared of getting thrown into the mud and spiked, one could argue), and the remaining knights decided not to attack. Many turned and went home – one of them, Jean, Duke of Brittany, doing a bit of unpatriotic pillaging of northern France with his Breton soldiers as he went.

Henry's troops rested the night at Maisoncelle and then went out to the battlefield next morning to 'clear up'. As usual, the dead were stripped of their valuable weapons and jewellery and the wounded were asked whether they were in *Who's Who*, and, if not, sent to join the list of the dead.

In all, the French had lost some 10,000 men, including – yet again – the 'flower of France' (they seem to have had several bouquets of these aristocratic petals). This compares to English losses of around 300, with just ten or so noble names amongst them.

Only when the English had left the area did the French come out of the woods. The retinues of the aristocratic dead found their masters and took the bodies back home for burial. The rest of the casualties were stripped naked by the local peasants and left to rot. It was not until several days later, on the orders of a nobleman who had lost several members of his family, that a mass grave was dug and, according to contemporary accounts, 5,800 bodies were buried, with a thick hedge of thorns planted around the site so that dogs and wolves would not dig up the bones.

Henry and his exhausted men, meanwhile, dragged themselves the 80 kilometres to Calais, where many of the soldiers managed to lose all their booty paying extortionate prices for food and drink. Henry himself claimed the most valuable prisoners and got them on board ships bound for England.

Despite a raging storm, all his ships arrived home safely, and Henry's conviction that God was on his side must have been stronger than ever. How else could he explain the way in which such a total, disabling victory over the cream of the French army had been won by a tired-out band of lower-class English dysentery-sufferers?

What Henry didn't know was that England was soon to come up against an equally low-class French opponent, a fervent believer who would reverse the tide of recent history . . .

4

Joan of Arc: A Martyr to French Propaganda

Concerning Lady Joan, whom they call the Virgin, on this day a sermon was preached at Rouen, while she was on a scaffold so that everyone could see very clearly that she was in male clothing, and there she was told the great and powerful ills that she had brought down on Christendom ... and several great, enormous sins that she did commit, and cause to be committed, and how she caused ordinary people to commit idolatry because by her false hypocrisy they followed her as a holy virgin.

A typically biased English view of Joan of Arc, aka 'The Witch of Orléans', one might assume.

But the above is actually a translation of a French text, the *Journal d'un Bourgeois de Paris*, a contemporary record of life and current opinion in the city between 1405 and 1449. And while the anonymous author wasn't a fan of Joan's, he wasn't just some pro-English collaborator, either. Elsewhere, he is shocked that the English 'burn those they can't ransom, rape nuns and eat meat on a Friday', and writes scathingly that 'the English, by nature, always want to fight their neighbours for no reason, which is why they always die badly'.

The modern French opinion of Joan of Arc couldn't be more different. She is credited with winning the Hundred Years War by 'booting the English out of France', and is revered as a military heroine – the French navy has a helicopter carrier called *Jeanne d'Arc*, and during the Second World War she was the reason for the Free French adding the Cross of Lorraine (her home region) to their flag. Her status as an icon is so strong that she inspired one of the first movies ever made: a film by the Lumière brothers that dates back to 1899. (Though it must have been hard making a silent movie about a girl who hears voices.)

Most of all, Joan is seen as a martyr at the hands of '*les Anglais*', a saint who was burnt at the stake in Rouen in 1431 by the tyrannical English invaders. During the Second World War this viewpoint was exploited in propaganda by the pro-Nazi Vichy government – when the Allies were bombing strategic Nazi sites in Normandy, posters were put up in Rouen, saying, 'they always return to the scene of their crimes.'

But, as is so often the case, the French have a completely skewed view of history where Joan is concerned. If you look at the less romanticized contemporary opinions of her, you will find that not only did Joan fail to boot the English out of France (how could she if she'd already been burnt by them in Rouen?), but by the end of her life she was regarded as something of a pest by her own king and his military leaders. And, to cap it all, she wasn't a victim of English tyranny at all – she was, in fact, betrayed and tried by Frenchmen.

So, Joan of Arc, a martyr? Yes – to French propaganda.

Joan's mission: to save the Dolphin

Joan was not, as the French usually think, a poor shepherd girl. She was born in about 1412 into a relatively well-off peasant family. Her father, Jacques, was a landowner, with some 20 hectares (about 50 acres) to his name, and a prominent member of the community in the village of Domrémy in northeastern France, on the borders of Lorraine and Champagne. The d'Arc family apparently gave generous gifts to the needy, so they must have been comparatively rich.

Joan was, however, something very rare for the times: a low-born girl who wanted to act to save her country. And by the time she heard the first patriotic voices in her head, in 1425, France was in dire need of a saviour.

After Agincourt, King Henry V of England had taken a lesson from his archers, and dealt a death-blow to the French while they were down. He had colonized Normandy much as William the Conqueror had done to England, bleeding it dry of money and anything saleable. He had more or less tricked the lunatic King Charles VI of France into a treaty that declared Charles's own son, the Dauphin,* ineligible to rule France, and guaranteed that Henry V and his heirs would inherit the French throne on Charles VI's death. To cement the deal, Henry married Charles's daughter, Catherine, and for their honeymoon the warlike English king took his new bride on a siege.

Henry then fired the flames of the civil war raging in

---

* From 1349 right up until 1830, male heirs to the throne were called 'dolphins', not because of any swimming ability, but because their coat of arms sported frisky-looking aquatic mammals alongside the fleur-de-lis. This was because in 1349 King Philippe VI of France had been allowed to annex the French region of Dauphiné on condition that royal male heirs be known as 'Dauphins'. The dolphins on the coat of arms were therefore a royal French pun.

France by allying with Duke Philip 'the Good' of Burgundy against the Armagnac faction (supporters of the disinherited Dauphin). Soon Anglo-Burgundian armies were occupying Paris and pillaging and besieging the whole of France north of the Loire. Henry V himself joined in the fighting, but contracted dysentery during the siege of the town of Meaux just east of Paris, and died in 1422, aged only thirty-five. Henry's son duly became King Henry VI of England and France, and upheld the family tradition of pillaging and besieging France.

One of the villages plundered by the Anglo-Burgundians around this time was Domrémy, home of the d'Arc family. All the villagers' cattle were stolen, the church was burnt, and Joan's family had to flee to the nearby town of Neufchâteau to escape a hideous death. And it was during this exile in 1425 that the thirteen-year-old Joan heard voices telling her to liberate France and put the Dauphin on the throne.

This call to arms came, she later said, from Saints Michael, Margaret and Catherine – an interesting choice of saints (if she chose them, that is, and didn't actually receive a visit), because both Margaret and Catherine were martyred for refusing to marry pagan men and were usually depicted carrying swords to lop off the heads or other offending bits of unwanted male suitors. Michael, meanwhile, although an archangel, was always depicted in armour. An angel in battledress might seem something of a contradiction to modern minds, but in medieval times it was a symbol of divine-led resistance.

After three years of being urged on by the voices, Joan finally left home with one of her brothers to undertake her holy mission. That's not what she told her parents, however – a typical sixteen-year-old, she said she was just going over to see a cousin who was about to have a baby.

In her own mind, however, Joan was very sure of her

motives. She had been brought up by a fervently religious mother who had been on several pilgrimages, and she must have believed that the voices really were visitations from God rather than her own brain telling her she was fed up with living under constant threat from Anglo-Burgundian looters.

Joan marched straight off to see the local *capitaine* (a sort of sheriff), a nobleman called Robert de Baudricourt, and announced that she had been sent by God to save France. Unsurprisingly, he told his servants to beat 'the mad girl' and send her home. She was, after all, just a female peasant, and was not expected to have more brains or initiative than the animals on her daddy's farm.

However, Joan did not give up. She seems to have possessed the natural charisma of someone who is utterly convinced that their cause is just, and her claim to be on a divine mission struck a chord with the people of her region who were desperate for a sign that someone up there was thinking of them. Word of Joan's voices spread rapidly, and it was said that she was the embodiment of a prophecy made by a mystic called Marie d'Avignon that a 'virgin girl from the borders of Lorraine' would come to save France. (Which was a prophecy that Joan would have known about, by the way.)

Hope, which had been extinguished for a hundred years by war and plague, began to glimmer again in French hearts, all of it focused on the small girl with big ideas. Baudricourt finally gave in to pressure from Joan's supporters and offered her an armed escort as far as Chinon, over 500 kilometres away, where the Dauphin was based.

By now, Joan's fame was spreading, and soldiers flocked to join the procession. The adolescent girl was turning into a liberation movement; every supporter she gained made her even more certain that God was on her side. News of her imminent arrival reached the Dauphin, who wasn't sure he wanted 'help' from someone who heard voices – his father, remember, was a raving lunatic. So for two whole days he kept her waiting outside the castle walls.

At this time, Chinon was undergoing a renaissance. Back in the 1150s, Henry II of England had chosen it as a royal capital, and transformed its simple fortress into a magnificent chateau that dwarfed the small market town on the bank of the river Vienne below. In the intervening centuries, the castle had lost some of its glory, and had been used by at least one French king as a dungeon. But Charles VII's arrival, with his retinue of troops and courtiers, had changed all that, and by 1429 Chinon was fluttering with royal banners again, abuzz with its own importance.

Making the uppity peasant girl wait was a tactic to impress on her that Charles was the star around here, not her. Joan didn't take long to make her mark, though. As soon as she was given permission to enter the castle, one of her first 'miracles' occurred – she was crossing the drawbridge when a guard taunted her: 'Is that the famous virgin? By God, let me have her for one night, and she won't be a virgin any more,' he scoffed.

Joan must have been used to this kind of 'wit', because she retorted with something along the lines of: 'It might be dangerous to take the Lord's name in vain when you're so close to death.'

The man later fell in the moat and died. 'A prophecy come true!' cried Joan's supporters. 'Which one of those religious nuts pushed me?' gurgled the dying guard.

Believers in Joan's saintliness cite her first meeting with the Dauphin as more proof that she really had been given divine insight. Wanting to test her, the Dauphin arranged for Joan to come to a crowded reception room, where she was greeted by an impostor claiming to be the

Prince. Without a second's hesitation, Joan ignored the fake Dauphin and turned to the true one, who had been standing amongst his courtiers, and embraced his knees before calling him 'sweet king'.

A miracle? Maybe. But it is said that Joan saw the Dauphin before their first public meeting. And even if this were a perfidious English rumour, she had almost certainly been briefed on what the Dauphin looked like, and he was reputed to be short and knock-kneed, with small squinty eyes and a receding chin. Given that most of his courtiers would have been chosen for their looks, he probably wasn't that hard to pick out.

To test whether Joan really was the girl in Marie d'Avignon's prophecy, and sent by God rather than the devil, the Dauphin had her questioned by a committee of clergymen, and asked a group of respectable ladies to confirm her virginity. She passed both exams, and, with religious sincerity and sexual inexperience apparently being considered excellent qualifications for a career in the military, she was given a suit of armour and an army of 4,000 men and sent to Orléans, which had been under siege by the English for six arduous months.

Again, doubters on Joan's own side put obstacles in her way. Although the English were camped on the north bank of the Loire, she was sent by French commanders to the south bank. It was explained to her that it would be useful if her men escorted boats carrying supplies down the Loire and into Orléans – the siege wasn't a total blockade, more of a long, continuous attack. Although initially furious at being prevented from having a go at the English, Joan finally relented, and her convoy entered the city to a rapturous welcome – and not just because her arrival meant that there would be wine on the table again. Accompanied by all the local nobility, she went on a torchlight parade through the streets and was hailed by the crowds as their saviour. The celebrations weren't spoilt when one of the torches set her pennant alight. On the contrary, when she swiftly put out the flames, it was heralded as another miracle.

The result of all this was that when Joan, in her white armour, attacked the English troops occupying a small fortified building outside the city walls, not only were her own men fired up with the certainty that victory had been promised to them by God and his visiting saints, but the English, who had heard about Joan, were completely terrified. In their minds, either she really was guided by angels or she was a witch sent by the devil.

When the spooked Englishmen ran for it, Joan's reputation soared even higher. And from now on, Joan's mere presence at a siege or battle was enough to send the *Anglais* into rapid retreat; four victories were won in the space of a week, including the lifting of the siege on Orléans. Suddenly, even the most sceptical French commanders wanted Joan as a mascot.

All of this was fuel to the fire of Joan's devotion to her cause, and she dictated a letter to the Dauphin informing him bluntly that she was going to have him crowned King of France in Reims. Despite the fact that the city is the capital of champagne production, and therefore a good spot for a post-coronation party, the Dauphin hesitated. He was probably afraid of being overshadowed by Joan, or of becoming politically vulnerable if she was eventually discredited. No worries – Joan wrote to Reims telling its citizens to get the cathedral ready. And finally, under pressure from the hordes of believers arriving to join Joan's army, the Dauphin agreed.

His coronation took place on 17 July 1429, admittedly not with the real crown – that was in the cathedral of Saint-Denis, near Paris, which was in English hands. But even so, this was an outcome that the Prince could never have dreamt of just a few weeks before. Here he was, King Charles VII of France, official rival to the false English monarch, on the crest of a wave of public support, his armies winning battle after battle against the invaders.

The only shadow on this glowing picture, he seems to have decided, was the little commoner in her silly white armour, grinning at him from beside his new throne as if she owned him.

Burning Joan's bridges

As soon as the coronation was over, Joan began ordering the new king to march on Paris and oust the English and the Duke of Burgundy. Charles was not at all sure about this – it was a massive undertaking compared to the isolated battles that Joan had fought so far, and, in case she hadn't been told, an army would need paying and feeding, possibly for the duration of a long siege.

Charles negotiated a two-week truce with Burgundy, and was furious when Joan wrote an open letter to the citizens of Reims declaring that 'I am not happy with this truce, and do not know whether I will keep it.'

From here on, things went rapidly downhill for Joan. She did manage to cajole Charles into marching on Paris, but he was secretly negotiating with Burgundy all the way there, while many of Joan's underfed, unpaid troops deserted. Joan attacked the gates of Paris, but she was wounded in the thigh by an arrow and carried, under protest, from the battlefield. To stop her returning, Charles ordered a bridge to be burnt.

Joan didn't give up, though, and in May 1430 Charles sent her to Compiègne near Paris, which (he told her) would be a good base for an attack on the capital. On the way, she stopped at a town called Soissons, intending to billet there. But the people of Soissons had suffered at

French hands before – soldiers 'relieving' the town from English occupation had raped and killed many of the innocent inhabitants. The townspeople refused to open their gates to Joan, and her army was forced to sleep in a field. Again, many of them deserted. Her spell had clearly been broken.

She arrived at Compiègne with only a couple of hundred men to find a Burgundian army of several thousand camped nearby. Anyone else might have guessed that Charles had sent her on a hopeless mission. Typically, though, Joan attacked, and, when she was predictably chased off, galloped towards the safety of the town. The townspeople, though, raised the drawbridge and cut off her retreat. Just like Charles, they were telling her *merci* but *non merci*.

She tried to fight her way to freedom, but was taken prisoner after an archer (a Frenchman from Picardy in the north) pulled her off her horse. As a commoner, Joan would normally have had her throat cut, but she was spared. She was, after all, a friend of the new king, who was sure to pay a huge ransom for her. Wasn't he?

The French abandon Joan to her fate

It would be too harsh to say that the ex-Dauphin, crowned Charles VII thanks to Joan and her army of followers, was a typical male, and dumped her as soon as he had got what he wanted. But it does seem to be close to the truth. From the time of Joan's capture to her execution a year later, Charles did not raise a little finger to help her.

And, contrary to what most French people believe, the suffering he abandoned her to was inflicted by Frenchmen, not Englishmen (though the *Anglais* would do some of the dirtiest work towards the end).

At first Joan was held prisoner by the local leader of the Burgundians, Jean de Luxembourg, who, despite his name, was a Frenchman, born in Picardy. Jean must have expected to receive generous ransom offers for Joan. *Au contraire*, one of the first responses he received was a declaration by the (French) Archbishop of Reims, Regnault de Chartres, saying that a shepherd boy had been discovered in Languedoc who would be replacing Joan as a holy messenger.

Next came a demand from the Inquisitor of France, Martin Billori, that Joan be handed over to the clergy for trial on the grounds that she had committed 'great scandals against divine honour and our holy faith' and had caused 'the perdition of several simple Christians'. Here was a Frenchman who wanted to burn Joan for heresy, and she was only saved from this fate because the Inquisitor failed to offer a ransom.

Meanwhile, another French clergyman, Pierre Cauchon, the Bishop of Beauvais near Paris, was begging Duke Philip of Burgundy to let him try Joan (in the legal sense, that is). When he got no answer, he started to harass the Duke of Bedford, Henry VI of England's regent, arguing that Joan 'belonged' to the English, and ought to be tried for heresy by them. Or rather, that he, Cauchon, should be allowed to do it on their behalf.

Bedford was not fond of Joan, who had cost him the city of Orléans and had also been sending him poison-pen letters, boasting that she 'had been sent by the King of Heaven to throw you out of France', and threatening him that if he didn't go home to England, he would 'be hearing from the Virgin, and the meeting will cause you much pain'.

Bedford duly handed over 10,000 *livres tournois* (pounds) – about 10 per cent of his annual income – as a ransom, and Joan was trussed up and handed over to the English. The future patron saint of France had been sold by a Frenchman to the enemy.

However, the English were only to be her prison guards, not her prosecutors. Cauchon was so keen to be Joan's inquisitor that he put in a rushed application to get jurisdiction in the diocese of Rouen, where the trial was to take place. He then appointed a second judge, a friend of his who was hostile to Joan: a man called Jean le Maître, who had the alarming title of 'Vicar to the Inquisitor of Heretical Perversity'.

The charges against Joan were many and varied; there were seventy of them, including witchcraft, blasphemy, fighting a battle on a Sunday and, most heinous of all, wearing men's clothes – and pretty well all of them carried the death sentence. Even though she was only a teenager, and convinced that she had been given her instructions by God, Joan must have understood the situation well enough to know that she stood no chance of being acquitted.

Nevertheless, she put up a spirited defence at the hearings, which went on for months. Professors of theology were shipped in from Paris University to try and catch her out with cunningly worded trick questions. For example, Joan was asked whether she thought she had obtained the grace of God. A 'yes' would have been blasphemy because only God knows who is in a state of grace, whereas a 'no' would have been a confession that she had committed mortal sins. But Joan answered: 'If not, I pray God puts me there, if so, that he keeps me there.' It was the perfect reply, the ecclesiastic equivalent of an untrained kid avoiding a punch from an Olympic boxing champion, and then flooring him with the riposte.

Joan also dodged leading questions about whether she had not only heard voices and seen angels, but also smelt and touched them. One might assume that this would be a logical extension of her visions, but saying yes would have been a confession of idolatry and a mortal sin; as far as divine visitations went, it was a case of 'look – and listen – but don't touch.' In the event, though, Joan was so careful with her answers, so devout and pious in her opinions, that it even looked for a time as though she might escape death.

Sadly for her, however, the French love an intellectual debate, and the one subject her judges wouldn't drop was her male clothing, even though she said that she had worn it to fight a holy war. Back then, it just wasn't the done thing for women to wear armour. It was as shocking as, say, a modern army being led by a transvestite in a dress.*

In medieval times, it was a mortal sin for women to cut their hair short, put on a helmet and fight – their role in war was restricted to being raped and/or murdered.

Some have suggested that Joan liked wearing men's clothing because she was a lesbian. One theory I have heard is that she had large breasts and was sick of male harassment. Whatever Joan's original reason, by the time of the trial she was so scared of being raped by her (English) prison guards that she refused to exchange her trousers for a skirt. Bizarrely to modern minds, the guards seem to have been too scared to touch her while she was dressed as a man in case she was a witch or a she-devil.

Joan's judges knew about her fears, and used the knowledge to trap her – they offered to spare her life and have her transferred away from her guards to a religious prison if she would only confess her sins and put on a dress. Joan, who still believed that God would ultimately

---

* Although in some Scandinavian countries that is probably quite acceptable.

boot the English out of France and install her good friend Charles VII on the throne as the unchallenged king, accepted the plea bargain, no doubt thinking that she would be freed as soon as the political pendulum swung Charles's way again.

A ceremony – probably the one mentioned in the *Journal d'un Bourgeois de Paris* – was held in a Rouen cemetery at which Joan, wearing a dress for the first time in at least two years, publicly signed a confession, or rather drew a cross because there was no prison education system and she hadn't learned to write.

But yet again, the French betrayed her. As soon as she had signed, she was taken back to her old prison with its rapacious guards. Terrified, she put her trousers back on, to the delight of her judges, who declared her a 'relapsed heretic' and condemned her to be burnt at the stake in Rouen's market square.

On 30 May 1431, her head shaven, Joan was made to walk through the streets past a jeering (French) mob, and when she arrived at the place of execution, her judges denied her the comfort of a crucifix to take to her death. It was an English soldier who put two sticks from the bonfire together to make her an improvised cross.

The French joke to this day about Joan being 'the only thing the English have ever cooked properly'. This probably refers to the fact that, after the fire had burnt out, the executioner raked through the ashes to expose her charred body and prove to the crowd that she was indeed female – the *Bourgeois de Paris* says that 'the fire was pulled back and everyone saw her naked, and all the secrets that a woman must have . . . When they had seen all they wanted, the executioner lit the fire again and the pitiful carcass was completely consumed by the flames.'

So yes, the English are guilty as charged of killing Joan of Arc. They burned her, and then burned her again to

A rare view of Joan of Arc out of armour. She was burned in Rouen in 1431, and despite French jokes about her being 'the only thing the Brits ever cooked properly', she was in fact captured, tried and condemned by Frenchmen.

make sure. But the people who made sure she ended up tied to the stake were Frenchmen, who were collaborating with the English invaders. In short, *les Français* got *les Anglais* to do their dirty work, and have spent the last 500-odd years in denial. And there's a lot to deny, because the bare truth of the matter is that France martyred its own future patron saint *for wearing trousers*. Which, it could be argued, is taking the famous French fashion sense just a step too far.

France is beaten up, but not beaten

From there on, the Hundred Years War more or less petered out, with the English gradually giving up the fight.

The French had finally got the measure of English archers, and had mastered a new weapon, the cannon. The English possessed these, but they had previously been used to make noise more than anything – as early as Crécy, cannon blasts were said to have scared French horses (another excuse). But by the mid-1400s, the French had learned how to aim their artillery, and anyone trying to besiege a town in France was likely to have their camp bombarded with hot lead. This understandably put English opportunists, in search of a bit of easy booty, off their pillaging, and after a golden century of profit the *chevauchées* started to lose money. It was a *chevauchée* crunch.

Furthermore, the infighting between the Burgundians and Armagnacs that had weakened France was ended when Duke Philip of Burgundy saw the tide turning and wriggled out of his alliance with the English, claiming that, on second thoughts, Henry VI of England might not be the rightful heir to the throne of France after all. In 1435, Duke Philip signed a new treaty with Charles VII, effectively reuniting France. Charles decreed that, from now on, anyone who even mentioned the words Burgundian or Armagnac was to have a hole burnt in their tongue with a hot iron. Fifteen years of French collaboration with the enemy officially no longer existed.

The English tried a rearguard action, and a certain Sir John Falstof, the man who inspired Shakespeare's Falstaff, tried to get support for the creation of an annual *chevauchée* season from June to November. His plan was that two armies of 750 men each should be sent across the Channel to spend the summer and autumn burning houses, crops, animals and peasants, thereby reducing as much of France as possible to famine. But by now *chevauchées* were totally *passées*, and the idea found no takers.

Charles VII's armies took Paris and Normandy, and then England's traditional stronghold in Aquitaine. On 19 October 1453, Bordeaux capitulated, and the English had finally been booted out of France – not by Joan of Arc herself, but as she had predicted.

And as soon as the war was over, the French started sweeping more bad memories under the carpet. To Charles VII's annoyance, people kept harking on about Joan of Arc, many of them claiming that she was still alive. Joan's own brothers were travelling around France with a woman claiming to be Joan, and collecting 'contributions' to her cause. Charles VII's argument that 'if she's alive, what are you all moaning about?' cut no ice, and after years of putting off the inevitable, he granted Joan a posthumous retrial.

The new hearing was just as fixed as the first, but this time it was biased in Joan's favour. The judges included Joan's own confessor, as well as enemies of the bishops and professors involved in the original case. Joan's mother made a heartfelt declaration of her daughter's innocence (written for her by clerics), and even managed to faint in the witness box. No one mentioned the touchy cross-dressing issue, Joan's voices were declared authentic because she herself believed they were true, and in 1456, twenty-five years after her death, the guilty verdict was overturned. Not that that helped Joan much.

Continuing the sweeping-embarrassing-evidence-under-the-carpet theme, the records of the original trial were publicly burnt on the spot where Joan herself had perished.

This did not mean, though, that Joan was immediately hailed as a saint; on the contrary, Charles was hoping that her memory would be expunged as completely as the written proof of her mistrial. He subsequently did everything he could to prevent her becoming an icon and to stop pilgrimages to Rouen and Orléans. It was even forbidden to display images of her.*

The most important thing for the French King was not an amnestied female heretic, but that he was now sitting unopposed on the throne. The official version of the war was that Crécy and Agincourt were mere glitches in the overall scheme of things, and, after a few lucky breaks in the first half of the fighting, the English had been humiliatingly booted out of France by King Charles VII. All on his own. OK, then, maybe with a little help from his bosom buddy Joan who had been treacherously murdered by the 'goddams'.

And what did the English think of all this? Well, the ordinary people of England would have scoffed at Joan's retrial and supposed innocence. Right up to Shakespeare's time and beyond, they thought she was a

---

* Joan would have to wait more than four centuries before she came in useful to France again. To read about the arguments surrounding her canonization, see Chapter 26.

witch, a she-devil used as a kind of ungodly secret weapon by the hated French enemy.

Defeat made a real dent in English national pride, of course, but many would have shrugged their shoulders at the war's final score. The gains during the conflict, had, after all, been enormous. Huge numbers of Englishmen had made money – from archers sharing in ransoms to merchants in second-hand French armour ('one previous owner, few arrow holes in breastplate') – and pretty well every stately home and castle built in England between 1330 and 1450 was at least partly financed by money extorted from France.

On the less material side, the Hundred Years War had served to give England a real sense of identity. Its monarchs had at last begun to speak English as their native language, and at Crécy and Agincourt the Brits had won victories that were branded for ever into folk memory.

And after all, what the French were conveniently forgetting during their 'total victory' celebrations in 1453 was that England still possessed Calais, one of the most strategically important towns in France.

5

Calais: The *Last* Last Bit of English Territory in France

For over 200 years, from its capture by Edward III in 1347 to its eventual fall to the French in 1558, the port of Calais was, all commentators agree, a thorn in France's side – although most people with a thorn in their side would pull it out, dab a little antiseptic cream on the wound and forget about it. Calais was much worse than a thorn. It was a veritable boil on the backside of France, a festering, incurable excrescence that for two centuries prevented the French sitting comfortably, sitting on their laurels, and many similar metaphors.

Despite all their claims of total victory in the Hundred Years War, the occupation of Calais enraged the French, and not just because the English insisted on misspelling its name as 'Caleys', 'Calleys', or even 'Kales'.

In 1394, during a lull in the Hundred Years War, a French poet called Eustache Deschamps published a ballad lambasting King Charles VI for being at peace with England, ending every verse with the lament, 'You will never have peace/Until they give back Calais.' (It was very convenient for him that in French *paix* and Calais rhyme with *anglais*.)

The English weren't going to let France get away with a unilateral attack of poetry, and had their own rhyme carved over the town gates, in French so that enemy spies were sure to understand: 'Never shall the Frenchmen Calais win/Until iron and lead like cork shall swim.'

It is a rhyme that seems to pre-empt Shakespeare, whose Weird Sisters tell Macbeth that he will be King until Great Birnam Wood climbs Dunsinane Hill to attack him. Macbeth, of course, feels safe because trees can't walk – until he is attacked by soldiers who have camouflaged themselves with branches cut from the forest. In the same way, residents of Calais would have to hope that they weren't tempting fate.

Pretty well every French king tried his own method of reconquering the town: Charles V unleashed constant quickfire attacks on the fortifications; Louis XI captured outlying towns and chipped away at the area controlled by the English; and Louis XII married an English princess in the hope that she'd put in a good word for him in London, a tactic that proved fatal – Louis was fifty-two, Mary was Henry VIII's eighteen-year-old sister, and a teenage English girl was just too energetic for an ageing Frenchman. Louis died in bed, having, it was said, 'exceeded his strength'.

But none of these attempts had any lasting effect, because the English were too determined to cling on to their tiny colony. They didn't even think of it as a colony – it was regarded as an integral part of England. Calais was represented in Parliament, and was home at one time or another to some very famous people. Geoffrey Chaucer worked there as a royal messenger in the 1360s. Dick Whittington of pantomime fame was simultaneously mayor of Calais and London in 1407. Kings Henry VII and VIII used to nip over to eat, drink and be merry. And for high-society girls like Anne Boleyn, it was *the* exotic getaway spot (the Caribbean had not yet been opened up for tourism).

Highly valuable staplers

Edward III made it clear right from the start that the English occupation was meant to be a long one – his instructions to his men after the siege of 1346–7 were to take possession of the town, imprison all the knights there, and send away any locals who might come along looking for work or trade, 'for I wolle [will] repeople agayne the towne with pure Englysshemen'. Ethnic cleansing, some might say, but in fact Edward was just showing what a scholar he was, because this was the Ancient Greeks' favourite model of colonization.

He imported a governing class of 300 burgesses (upper- and middle-class merchants, mainly), and gave them either a house or permission to build themselves one. And soon a large English garrison was patrolling the most impregnable fortifications that (plundered French) money could buy. The town itself was protected by high walls, with a deep moat that was in some places 50 metres wide. Within this fortified citadel of some 2,000 buildings and 12,000 people stood a castle, surrounded by a deep ditch and armed with cannons that commanded a field of fire over the surrounding country-side and down into the town itself – if your house was captured by invading Frenchmen, your china ornaments would stand little chance of surviving.

The sea entrance to the harbour was guarded by a notorious fortress called the Rysbank, which bristled with cannons and made it impossible for undesirable ships to get anywhere near the town. Only in herring season (the end of September to the end of November) were foreign boats allowed in the harbour in any numbers.

Sluice gates were built so that the outlying marshes could be completely flooded with seawater in case of attack, though this line of defence could not always be depended upon – in 1530, for example, it was discovered that the English mayor of Calais had drained a vast area of marsh for his personal use as farmland, and he had to be forced by a Royal Commission to flood it again.

But why all the fuss and expense? Surely it wasn't just to infuriate France by hanging on to one last small chunk of their territory?

Well, yes it was, but there were also much more pragmatic reasons for doing so.

The first was financial. Calais was set up as a trading post, a self-financing marketplace for English wool. From 1359 to 1558, the town had a monopoly on exports of English wool, which was by far Europe's most important raw material for clothing (cotton being rather exotic and Lycra a few centuries away from being invented). It was almost as if Italy had seized Saint-Tropez, peopled it with Neapolitans and declared that this was the only place Europe could buy spaghetti.*

Calais's merchants – known as 'staplers', because they belonged to the so-called Company of the Staple at Calais – had not only the continental buyers but also the English sellers by the throat, to put it politely, and took full advantage of the opportunity to put the squeeze on them. For example, according to a ruling of 1473, bundles of wool packed in England did not have to be unpacked in Calais before being sold on. Consequently, unsuspecting foreign buyers often found themselves to be the proud owners of large rocks and sandbags that had

* Actually, Saint-Tropez might be a lot more attractive if it was used for this purpose rather than as an exhibition space for oversized boats and failed facelifts.

been sneaked in with the wool to make up weight. The victims of fraud had three months to make a compensation claim, after which any complaint was invalid. And who was in charge of the claims court at Calais? A stapler, of course.

The merchants were required to give a cut of their profits to the central government in London, and at the height of the town's success in the fifteenth century it was providing a third of government revenue. The occupation was all the more profitable for England as a nation because, in return for their monopoly, the merchants were expected to pay for the garrison and the upkeep of the fortifications. In peacetime there was a permanent force of around 500 men, in wartime 1,000.

The staplers also had to make sure that a set of very specific rules for guarding the town were obeyed. There were four main gates, all of which were closed at noon, when the whole town seems to have taken a break for lunch. They reopened around one, and then closed for the night at 4 p.m., with a changing-of-the-guard-type ceremony that included a Mass to celebrate God's kindness in continuing to let England annoy the French in this way.

At night, one set of soldiers, the 'scout watch', patrolled outside the ramparts, while a second, the 'stand watch', guarded the town walls, and a third group, the 'search watch', guarded the guards. Any man found sleeping* at his post three times was suspended in a basket over the moat and given bread, water and a knife. When he got hungry and thirsty, his only choice was to cut the rope holding the basket, and hope that the other guards would fish him out of the moat before he drowned. If he

---

* A guard was judged to have been sleeping if a member of the search watch could sneak up and grab him by the nose.

survived, he was banished from the town for a year and a day. Any soldier who revealed the password to a civilian, or who started a fight while on guard duty, was executed. Yes, protecting Calais from surprise attack was taken very seriously indeed.

The bling-bling king

Royal visits to Calais were a great highlight, and they were frequent, because they made it clear to friends and enemies alike that this was English soil.

In June 1500, Henry VII threw an immense party in Calais for an anti-French friend, Duke Philip IV 'the Handsome' of Burgundy. It was held in a church that was requisitioned for some highly unreligious goings-on. The holy building was divided into seven areas, including a bedroom for the Duke, which was strewn (according to a contemporary chronicler called Richard Turpyn) with 'roses, lavender and other sweet herbs', and a 'secret chamber' for the Queen. The belfry was used as a pantry, and Turpyn gives a mouth-watering account of the refreshments: wine, beer, venison pie, 'the greatest number of lambs I ever saw', an English ox, strawberries, cream and 'seven horseloads of cherries'.

Turpyn notes that the King's guests were resplendent in 'clothe of golde', with a special mention for the Duke of Buckingham, whose gown was decorated with little golden bells. And halfway down the guest list was a certain 'tresorier of France', no doubt invited so that word of the fantastic opulence, and the relaxed way it was enjoyed, could be taken back to Paris.

Twenty years later, Henry VII's son Henry VIII went one better, and actually invited a French king, François I, to Calais to see for himself how cosy it was. The so-called Field of the Cloth of Gold was ostensibly a friendly meeting in the summer of 1520 between the two monarchs to seal a non-aggression pact that they had signed two years earlier. Everything was carefully arranged so that they would be seen as equals – they were to bring a similar number of soldiers and courtiers, and the valley where they met was even resculpted so that their two camps would be on the same level. Neutral ground was chosen for the gathering, just outside English-held territory. However, one glaring inequality could not be ignored: all this was happening on the French side of the Channel, which meant that the French King was a guest in his own home.

François I seems to have decided that there was no point making a scene about this, and joined whole-heartedly in the fun. And fun there certainly was, because both sides went to unbelievable extremes to impress the other. We think we live in an age of bling-bling today, but our chrome-rimmed car wheels, chunky watches and glittery mobile phones would not even have registered on the blingometer in that summer of 1520.

We know all the details of Henry's preparations from Richard Turpyn's chronicle; he tells us that the King imported 300 masons, 500 carpenters and 100 joiners, as well as painters, glaziers, blacksmiths and tailors to make a gigantic, 10-metre-tall marquee that was painted to look like a palace. A jousting stadium was built, with a gallery to seat all the noble spectators. Some 2,800 smaller tents were set up around the main palace, most of them made of silk interwoven with gold thread – a shimmering sight that gave the gathering its name.

Henry brought his queen (it was still wife number one, Catherine of Aragon) and several dozen of her aristocratic girlfriends, as well as Cardinal Wolsey (the King's right-hand man), two archbishops, a hundred or so knights with wonderful Harry Potter-style names like Sir Griffen Aprise and Sir Edward Bellknappe, 'minstrels of all manner', twenty-four trumpeters, and a few thousand ordinary soldiers – all of them, in the French King's eyes, trespassers on his land.

Henry was clearly worried about fitting everyone in, because strict rules were laid out governing the number of servants and horses that could be brought along: an archbishop could have 50 servants and 20 horses, a duke the same, whereas an earl could only bring 30 and 10 respectively. The total number of English guests (not including the soldiers) was 4,334 people and 1,637 horses.

François I set up a similar camp on his side of the valley, and even managed to impress the over-the-top English. As Shakespeare notes in his play *Henry VIII*, the French were 'all clinquant, all in gold, like heathen gods'.

The two kings arranged a solemn meeting, at which it was agreed that each would ride down alone through his host of courtiers, who had been ordered on pain of death to remain totally silent. At the bottom of the valley, at a carefully calculated central point, the two monarchs embraced – still on horseback – and then dismounted and embraced again, with a great show of friendship and mutual respect.

They were both young, active men – Henry was not yet thirty, a tall, fit redhead, François a well-built Latin lover – and had come to prove their manhood. There was jousting, with both kings breaking plenty of lances (the yardstick by which a knight's prowess was judged). During one bout, François suffered a broken nose at the hands of the Earl of Devonshire.

The rivalry between the two men was amicable but intense. To prevent diplomatic mishaps, neither king jousted against the other, and a story that Henry was disgruntled because he lost a wrestling match against

François is usually discredited as a French fabrication. But they competed in other ways. Henry had had staggeringly expensive suits of armour prepared for the occasion – on one day he turned up for the jousting in a suit encrusted with 2,000 ounces of gold and over 1,000 pearls. François, meanwhile, played at the alpha male. At the first ball, he impressed everyone by going around the whole dance tent kissing all the ladies present, 'except,' one commentator noted, 'four or five who were too old and ugly'. He proved himself a keen and elegant dancer, despite the fact that he apparently had bandy legs and flat feet.

The games, dancing and feasting went on for two whole weeks, with each side inviting the other to increasingly lavish receptions. Henry's camp consumed some 2,200 sheep, it is recorded, plus an equivalent amount of 'other viands', while a fountain kept up a permanent stream of red wine. These days, the newspapers are up in arms if a prince gets a free ticket to a nightclub party, but in 1520 no one dared criticize royal extravagance, especially when it was designed to dazzle the French.

And it did more than just dazzle. Henry had to reach deep into his coffers to pay for the party, but François was forced to borrow to pay for his half of the bill. In short, by inviting François to the Field of the Cloth of Gold, Henry was daring the French King to live way beyond his means. And every penny spent on partying was one less penny available to pay an army to retake Calais. It was bling with a sting.

Camping proves expensive for the French

Not that the chance to party French kings into bankruptcy was the most important reason for keeping Calais. As well as a trading post, it was a vital stopping-off point for invading troops. The Hundred Years War was over, but this did not prevent English armies nipping over to do a bit of unofficial peacetime raiding. And possessing Calais made it ridiculously easy. Invading English forces did not have to worry about making a risky beach landing. They sailed into the protected harbour of Calais, and as soon as enough troops had been amassed there, they simply marched out of the town gates into France.

Richard Turpyn describes some almost casual raiding by Henry VII in 1492. The King landed at Calais on 2 October, waited seventeen days while his fleet shipped over men and supplies, and then calmly went to besiege the nearby French town of Boulogne, completely unopposed.

Hearing about the siege, the French sent an ambassador to sue for peace, 'whiche', Turypn says, 'the kynge of England graunted upon a condition that the Frenche kynge shud paye every yere lii thowsand [52,000] crownes to the kynge of England during bothe theyr lyves'. The French agreed, Henry VII marched back to Calais and 'toke his shipe and sayled to Dovar'. Never has a month's camping holiday in France been so profitable.

Henry VIII did pretty much exactly the same in 1513, personally leading an army of 30,000 men to grab the important French textile town of Tournai,* which he then sold back to France for a small fortune.

It was a bubble that couldn't last, however. As raw wool became less important than woven cloth, Calais's merchants began to make less money. They couldn't skimp on paying the garrison for fear that the soldiers would mutiny, but they became markedly less scrupulous

---

* Tournai is now in Belgium, making it the only Belgian town ever occupied by the British. Until the hen parties started invading Bruges in the early twenty-first century, that is.

about the upkeep of the town's battlements, which started to look the worse for wear.

When Henry VIII's daughter Mary came to the throne in 1553, she provoked religious conflict which divided the citizens of Calais. The new French King, the swash-buckling Henri II, saw his opportunity and began to mount regular attacks . . .

Comic failure to send relief

When the inevitable fall came, it was completely farcical.

In the dying days of 1557, Queen Mary's government in London received word that the area around Calais was swarming with French troops, and Mary decided to raise an army to send across the Channel. Word was sent out for the 'levies' (reserve troops) to report for duty. However, no one told them to bring their own weapons, and most of them arrived unarmed. They were sent home to get their ironmongery, and when they returned, it was found that the fleet was too unseaworthy to transport them.

On 2 January 1558 the French attacked Calais. The logical thing to do was open the sluice gates and flood the marshes. However, the town's deputy (the head stapler acting as governor) hesitated – as he later explained in a letter of apology to Queen Mary – because this would have meant 'infesting the water wherewith we brew' with salt water. Better to lose control of the town than spoil the beer.

In the end, parts of the marshland were flooded, but the water was shallow and froze over, allowing the French to march across and attack the town walls. The prophecy carved over the town gate was coming true: iron guns and lead cannonballs were 'swimming' – on ice. The French began to fire on the town with seventy cannons, a bombardment that lasted for two days and nights.

Meanwhile, Mary had finally gathered enough decent ships to transport her (now armed) troops across the Channel to Calais, but a storm blew up, scattering and partially destroying this new fleet, and the soldiers were sent home again.

In any case, by now it was too late. On 7 January, Calais fell, and the evacuating English garrison failed to blow up the castle before they left because the fuse on their gunpowder was damp. All that remained in English hands was an outpost just inland, at Guînes, where a courageous knight called Lord Grey was holding out and refusing to surrender. In the end, though, fearing they would be killed if they resisted, his soldiers surrendered for him. They let the French in, and were rewarded by being sent home to England alive.

With this debacle, English rule in the Calais area was simply snuffed out, and the nation slipped into mass depression at the loss of what some had called 'the jewel of the realm' (for its value, of course, not its beauty). Queen Mary proved she could empathize with the national mood of mourning by making her famously gruesome declaration that 'When I am dead and opened, you shall find "Philip" [her husband] and "Calais" engraved on my heart.' Perhaps it was this very early attempt at keyhole heart tattooing that killed her at the age of forty-two, only eleven months later.

So there it was – the French could finally start spelling Calais correctly again, and France was completely free of English occupiers. The dashing King Henri II had finally achieved what every French monarch had been trying to do for more than two centuries. He must have been very pleased with himself for the slap in the face he had given the *Anglais*.

Although, as we'll see in the next chapter, a Brit was about to slap him back . . .

6

Mary Queen of Scots: A French Head on Scottish Shoulders

There is no disputing that Mary Queen of Scots was born in Scotland and that she was therefore, strictly speaking, Scottish. But even the most patriotic Highlander could not deny that Mary spent her formative years, between the ages of five and nineteen, in France. Her mother was French, and throughout her life Mary wrote most of her letters in French, even those to her English cousin Queen Elizabeth I. What's more, she always signed her name 'Marie', no doubt preferring it to the English spelling because at the time *mary* was how the French spelt their word for husband (these days it's *mari*). For a few years Mary was even Queen of France. To put it simply, the woman we know today as Mary Queen of Scots was a French creation. She was as Scottish as foie-gras-flavoured haggis.

If, in her final years as a captive in England, you had asked Mary what she thought of Scotland, she would probably have given a perfectly diplomatic reply (in French) about her undying love for her native land. But behind the political façade, she would almost certainly have been thinking, *Merde*, don't talk to me about bloody *Écosse*.

And Mary's bitterness would have been well founded, because during her few short adult years as a reigning monarch in Scotland, she was betrayed by pretty well all the Scottish nobles, nearly murdered by a gang of them, and kidnapped and raped by one. And when she was killed, a large faction of Scots didn't really care at all, because she had long ceased to be of any use to them. In fact, by lopping her head off, the English weren't trying to provoke Scotland at all – they were striking a blow against the French.

Let's have a closer look at the tragic life of Mary (or Marie), *French* Queen of Scots.

For sale: one royal baby

More recent British royals have complained about being thrust too early, or too often, into the limelight. But Mary knew nothing else, almost from birth.

She was born on 8 December 1542, in the lakeside palace of Linlithgow, 30 kilometres from Edinburgh. The date was promising: it was the Feast of the Immaculate Conception of the Virgin Mary. The place was less so: people born in Linlithgow are often nicknamed 'black bitches' after the dog on the town's coat of arms.

Mary's mother, Marie de Guise, was the second wife of King James V of Scotland. His first wife, who died of tuberculosis, had also been French, and his marriage to Marie was arranged to re-cement the Franco-Scottish Auld Alliance. It was a union that annoyed the English intensely – Henry VIII, apparently feeling lonely after executing Anne Boleyn and losing Jane Seymour in child-birth, had also put in a bid for Marie de Guise's hand.

Marie was relieved when her family turned down Henry's offer. Horrified by the beheading of Anne Boleyn, she is said to have quipped, 'I may be a tall woman, but I have a small neck.' It was a joke that would turn tragically sour when, fifty years later, Marie's daughter Mary Queen of Scots had her own slender neck severed by an English axe on the orders of Anne Boleyn's daughter, Elizabeth I.

So Marie de Guise married a Scot and moved to Edinburgh, taking a collection of French knick-knacks with her to ease the transition: things like pear trees, wild boars, tailors and, *naturellement*, doctors.

In quick succession, she and King James had two sons who died in infancy, and then Princess Mary came along. But the King, in a state of nervous exhaustion over a war with England, was already on his deathbed, and gave up the fight for life six days later, aged only thirty. At less than a week old, the newborn Mary was Queen of Scotland, with her French mother as regent. The baby was also, as a great-granddaughter of Henry VII, next in line to the English throne after Princess Elizabeth. Quite a responsibility for one so young.

As a result, before Mary's eyes had even learned to focus, the gaze of every European head of state was fixed upon her. Aged eleven days, she received her first proposal, when Henry VIII tried to make up for losing Marie de Guise by betrothing baby Mary to his son Edward, who was then aged five (years, that is). The offer was refused, probably because of the age difference – Edward was, after all, about 150 times older than Mary.

But as we all know, marriage was a touchy subject with Henry VIII, and he was so angry at being turned down a second time that he unleashed a series of punitive raids on Scotland, rather humorously dubbed the 'Rough Wooing' (which shows how tough courtship must have been in those days), and he finally bullied the Scots into signing a betrothal contract between Mary and Edward.

Marie de Guise must have been relieved when Henry

VIII died in 1547, before he could bring his plans to fruition, but this didn't mean that the pressure was off, because practically every nobleman in Scotland was suggesting sons and cousins as potential bridegrooms. Marie knew enough about the Scots lairds to realize that these offers might well be accompanied by attempts to lock little Mary away in the family's castle while the laird assumed the regency, so she turned to her homeland for help.

As luck would have it, King Henri II of France was a childhood friend of the Guise family, as well as being virulently anti-English. He stepped in and betrothed the infant Scottish Queen to his own son, François, who was a year younger than Mary. To make sure that neither the English nor the Scots would keep the two royal children apart, Henri sent his own ship to fetch Mary – but not her mother, who stayed in Scotland with a French army to protect France's hold on the Scottish Crown.

It was July 1548, Mary was five, and she was already being treated like a tiny, but vital, piece in a big political jigsaw.

The 'wild' Scots arrive in France

The little Queen was apparently a good sailor, and amused herself during the long, storm-battered voyage to France by making fun of her seasick travelling companions – two or three of her half-brothers, a guardian, a governess and four young ladies-in-waiting (all called Mary) and their various servants. The ship suffered a broken rudder in the mountainous seas, but eventually Mary landed safely in the country that was to be her home for the rest of her childhood.

At first, the Scottish party probably had a dizzy sense of *déjà vu*, because they went ashore in western Brittany, the rainy, granite-clad southern cousin of Scotland, where the locals spoke a language not unlike Scots Gaelic. Mary herself didn't know any Gaelic – in Edinburgh, people spoke Lowland Scots, a dialect of English – but Brittany must have felt comfortingly familiar.

Things became progressively more French, though, during a two-month trek eastwards to the royal chateau at Saint-Germain-en-Laye, just outside Paris, where the courtiers were in a veritable frenzy of anticipation about their new princess-to-be, and poets were composing odes to Mary's beauty before they'd even seen her.

When she finally arrived there, the Parisians apparently got quite a shock. Little Mary herself they found exquisite, but they thought her Scottish servants and courtiers were *farouches* – meaning wild, in the animal rather than partying sense.

Mary's future in-laws and her grandparents decided that she was in dire need of a French upbringing so that she would be suitable for her role as Queen of France, which was considered much more important than that of Queen of Scots. She was treated a bit like a youngster who arrives at Manchester United after being spotted scoring goals for Linlithgow Rovers. Yes, she'd been a star in the minor league, but now it was time for some serious training.

Freed from the threat of war and kidnap, Mary began an idyllic French childhood as one of a gaggle of youngsters in King Henri II's household. Amongst her new playmates was her future husband, the sickly, stuttering François, who seems to have suffered birth defects after his mother, Catherine de' Medici, had taken fertility potions – in the sixteenth century, there were no health warnings on packaging (mainly because there wasn't any packaging).

The merry royal party moved from one luxurious chateau to the next – Saint-Germain-en-Laye, Fontainebleau, Blois – with Mary, a charming, lively girl, delighting everyone. As well as being a favourite of Henri, she was taken under the wing of his glamorous mistress, Diane de Poitiers, who is remembered in France today as a sort of sixteenth-century sex goddess. Diane was twenty years Henri's senior but so alluring that Henri's wife, Catherine de' Medici, had holes bored in the ceiling of the King's bedchamber so that she could watch her husband and Diane in full frolic and presumably pick up some tips.

It has never been suggested that young Mary Queen of Scots received *that* kind of education from Diane, who was also a highly literate woman and a great conversationalist. But Mary spent some time at Diane's love nest, the romantic chateau of Anet in Normandy, which is unjustly ignored by foreign tourists, probably because it is so far from the Loire. Its only recent claim to fame is that it features at the beginning of the James Bond film *Thunderball*, as the location for the first meeting of the evil SPECTRE agents. It is amusing to watch Bond's enemies planning to destroy the world with atomic bombs and think that Mary Queen of Scots once played children's games there for real.

As she toured the royal households, Mary quickly acquired a French fashion sense, wearing brightly coloured dresses, stockings and shoes, and showing an apparent fondness for dogskin gloves. She was also schooled in more intellectual matters, of course. On her arrival in France, Mary spoke mainly Scots, which sounded horribly barbarous to French ears,* but her

* This shouldn't be taken as an insult, because every language except French does.

French was soon fluent, and she also learned Italian, Spanish, Latin and Greek.

A future queen had to master the courtly arts, and Mary practised French dances and sang French songs, and – one of her passions in later life – began to write French poems every time emotions welled up in her increasingly Gallic chest.

Despite all this, Mary didn't forget her origins, although her memories of Scotland seem to have become blurred, because when she amused the court by dressing up as a Scot one day, she donned a costume consisting mainly of loosely draped animal skins. She had apparently come to view her Scottish compatriots as Neanderthals.

Mary was fifteen when she received the news in 1558 that the port of Calais had been captured from the English by one of her Guise uncles – a family success that made her an even more prestigious member of the French royal household. And as a consequence of the victory, her marriage to young Prince François became all the more urgent. It was to be the final Franco-Scottish nail in the English coffin.

By now, Mary was every inch the ravishing French princess. And there were a lot of inches. She was very nearly six feet tall, with the slender neck that she had inherited from her mother, and fashionably pale skin despite her love of outdoor pursuits like hunting. Her hair was gradually turning from childhood blond to the rich auburn that it would become in adulthood, and her eyes were light, almost golden brown. She was charming and witty, and possessed a melodious voice (now that she had stopped speaking that raucous Scots).

She was also self-confident enough to insist that her beauty would be best enhanced if she wore a white wedding dress. Not an unusual decision for a virgin bride, one might think, but at the time it was a daring, almost offensive, choice, because white was the colour that French queens traditionally wore in mourning. Given the subsequent fates of her three husbands, she might have agreed in hindsight that it was tempting fate just a little too much.

Her request was granted, but only because she was losing out in so many other ways. The marriage contract between the French and Scottish royal houses was breathtakingly one-sided. For a start, Mary was to sign over her claim to the English throne to her French husband François. In addition, Scotland would have to pay for all aid it had received over the centuries – a fiendish French accounting trick to empty Scotland's coffers into Henri II's pockets. And to cap it all, France and Scotland would be united, with François as king. Yes, Scotland was to become a French colony. If all this had subsequently gone to plan, today Scotland might well be a spa resort for Parisians, and France would be claiming to have invented whisky. Worse still, the French would be annoyingly good at golf as well as all the other individual sports they win trophies for.

Mary was only a teenager, but surely she knew the consequences when she scratched 'Marie' at the bottom of her marriage contract. It was, quite simply, a complete betrayal of her native land's sovereignty.

Cousin, cousine

It was to be a very eventful period for Mary. After the capture of Calais and her wedding, Mary learned that her English first cousin once removed, also called Mary, had died. In those medically primitive times, it was not at all uncommon to lose a relative, but this other Mary was significant – she was Queen of England.

Elizabeth I was immediately given the throne, but in Catholic eyes, including those of the French royal family, the true successor was Mary Queen of Scots. Elizabeth was the offspring of Henry VIII's post-divorce second wife Anne Boleyn, and was therefore considered illegitimate, whereas Mary was the indisputably legitimate grand-daughter of Henry VIII's sister Margaret Tudor.

Henri II of France seized the opportunity to press Mary's claim on her – and his son's – behalf, and even had a provocative royal standard made, featuring the English and Scottish arms. (Attentive readers will recall that Edward III and Henry V of England had used exactly the same strategy for annoying France more than a century earlier – proof that the French never forget an insult.)

Mary Queen of Scots was now a living symbol of Catholic opposition to the new, and highly sensitive, Queen Elizabeth of England. By extension, Mary was also a weapon in the religious conflicts that were erupting all over Europe. And, unfortunately for her, no sooner was she propelled into the front line than her protector was killed – ironically, by a Scotsman.

Henri II, who had removed Mary from danger in Scotland when she was an infant and made sure that she spent a cotton-wool childhood in his chateaux, was just as much of an alpha male as his father, François I, had been (see Chapter 5 for François's antics at the Field of the Cloth of Gold). Henri loved to joust, showing off his prowess as a knight by breaking lances on the shields of the best horsemen in Europe.

On 30 June 1559, Henri was at a tournament in Paris, in the Château de Tournelles, on the site of what is now the picturesque place des Vosges. The games had been arranged to celebrate the marriage of Henri's daughter Elisabeth to King Philip II of Spain, the recently widowed husband of Queen Mary of England. The wedding was another major anti-English coup, the perfect excuse for a party.

Despite the fact that it was a family occasion, the King was jousting in the black-and-white colours of his mistress, Diane, under the nose of his wife Catherine. It was late in the day, and he had already broken several lances, but Henri fancied one last joust, and issued a challenge to a Norman-Scottish knight, the Count of Montgomery (an ancestor of the general of the same name who would lead the Normandy landings in 1944). The Count refused politely, but the King ordered him to mount up and charge.

Apparently Catherine begged Henri to call it a day, because she had dreamt that he would be killed by a lance piercing his eye. (Though this doesn't seem to have bothered her during his previous jousts, and may well have been a backdated prophecy, a sort of extreme 'I told you so' with which to irritate him on his deathbed.) To make matters worse, the King was planning to ride a horse with the unfortunate name of Le Malheureux – Unlucky or Unhappy.

Laughing off the superstitious warnings, Henri II charged at Montgomery. There was the usual clash of lance on shield, but this time Montgomery's lance splintered and a shard of wood shot through the slit of Henri's helmet and into his eye socket.

He was carried into the chateau and took ten days of suffering and raving to die of an infection. His furious widow Catherine had the chateau demolished and, even though the fatal injury was sustained by accident during a joust instigated by the King, had Montgomery thrown in prison. She also banished Diane de Poitiers from court, and forced her to live in obscurity in Normandy. The fun was over, by royal decree.

Two months later, still mourning for her lost protector, Mary, aged only sixteen, was crowned Queen of France in Reims cathedral, alongside her fifteen-year-old husband,

King François II, a shy adolescent whom a contemporary chronicler described as having 'constipated genitals'. It was not seen as a promising sign that that the new King was too frail to keep the crown on his head without the nobles holding it in place for him.

Teenage kicks, and teenagers getting kicked

Mary's immediate reaction to becoming queen of a second country was to infuriate her French hosts. She demanded an inventory of the crown jewels, and ordered that anything belonging to a reigning queen should be sent to her by her mother-in-law, the ex-Queen, Catherine de' Medici. But if this was meant to be a show of strength, it was a catastrophically self-destructive one. With a single request, Mary made a lifelong enemy of the most powerful – and vindictive – woman in France.

Meanwhile, the news that the French had a new, weak king had spread quickly. In Scotland, Protestant lords rose against Mary's mother, Marie de Guise, and invaded Edinburgh, calling for the French interlopers to be thrown out. The English naturally waded in to the fight and laid siege to the port of Leith, just outside Edinburgh, where Marie had taken refuge with her troops. To avoid total disaster, she had to give in to the pressure and send her French troops home. Suddenly, the Auld Alliance was in tatters and so, soon afterwards, was Mary's life – on 11 June 1560, her mother Marie died of dropsy, or oedema, a painful swelling caused by fluid retention. Cruel proof that it can be fatal for a French woman to get fat.

Mary was still grieving when her French ladder was kicked out from under her once and for all. In December, her husband King François died, just three days before Mary's eighteenth birthday, apparently of an aggravated ear infection. In a few short months, Mary had gone from almost total stability at the heart of Henri II's court to the state that the French fear most of all: *précarité*, precariousness, the threat of an uncertain future.

Mary had one attractive option – she had been given the title of Duchess of Touraine, the posh part of the Loire Valley, and might have been able to put her feet up in a nice Renaissance chateau like Amboise or Chenonceau and wait for a good Catholic husband to come along, no doubt a member of an important French or Spanish family.

But Catherine de' Medici made it pretty clear that Mary wasn't welcome in France any more. Just twenty-four hours after François's death, Catherine took revenge on her bereaved daughter-in-law by demanding the return of all the crown jewels that Mary had received on becoming Queen of France. With mums-in-law like that, who needs evil stepmothers?

Mary's family, the Guises, weren't exactly supportive, either. When she went to seek solace from her uncles and cousins in their homeland of Lorraine, in the east of France (Joan of Arc country), they advised her to go back to Scotland. Harsh advice to give a lone, eighteen-year-old girl, but they obviously wanted to use her to hold on to their remaining royal ties. Mary was, after all, still regarded by a large proportion of the Scots as their queen. Once back in Edinburgh, the Guises told her, she could try to buddy up to Elizabeth to prevent future inter-ference north of the border by the Medici clan. In a typically medieval confusion between family and patriotic allegiances, these Catholic Frenchmen were encouraging Mary to unite with a Protestant* English queen.

* I will be using the term 'Protestant' as shorthand to describe Anglicans and other groups, simply to distinguish them from Catholics. For the purposes of this book, the most important distinction is between people who felt they owed allegiance to the Pope, and those who didn't.

The Guises' ultimate aim was no doubt to put one of their own on the throne of England. If Mary became Elizabeth's ally, the English Queen might accept her as a successor. And with Catherine de' Medici hovering over the French throne for the foreseeable future (her son Charles IX was now King, and she had five more children potentially in line for the crown), the Guise family stood a much better chance of gaining power and influence in England than in France.

The problem that the Guises must have known about, and chosen to ignore, was that the English were violently opposed to Mary. As a French Catholic, and the niece of the man who'd snatched Calais, she could barely have been less attractive to the people of England if she'd had leprosy.

In short, teenaged Mary was being thrown to the lions by her own French family because of her potential usefulness in their political games.

Unwelcome home

In the summer of 1561, the obedient Mary set off for Scotland from newly French Calais, sobbing 'Adieu, France!' as the coast disappeared from sight (one can only assume that Calais was much more picturesque than it is nowadays). She had already guessed that life wasn't going to be as easy as the Guises implied, because Queen Elizabeth had refused to guarantee her a safe land passage through England. As a result, Mary was obliged to take a risky North Sea route infested with English pirates. And as if rough seas, pirates and the prospect of a hostile reception weren't enough to worry about, there was something else to make the trip unpleasant – at that time, French galleys were rowed by slaves (mostly convicts), and Mary constantly had to beg the captain not to have the rowers whipped.

She arrived in Scotland on 19 August, still aged only eighteen, and when her boat landed at Leith, she was greeted by the locals just like any beautiful princess on a royal visit – they were in awe of her chic dress and delighted when she made a speech in Scots (no doubt with a cute French accent).

But in her heart, Mary felt totally foreign – contemporary French commentators were probably mirroring Mary's own impressions of mid-sixteenth-century Scotland when they said that it was a barren, hostile land inhabited by uncouth, treacherous people who were constantly engaged in inter-family vendettas. Welcome home.

She took up residence at Holyroodhouse, the royal palace in the centre of Edinburgh, which her mother's French masons and interior designers had decorated with ornamental ceilings and magnificent wall hangings. Mary took an instant like to her refuge – it was in the city but had gardens where she could practise archery, and it was right next to a park full of animals for her to hunt. Mary also liked to go out on to the heath and play golf, a game she had loved since her Scottish childhood. She is credited with inventing the term 'caddy' – her clubs were carried by the young sons of French noblemen, known as *cadets*, which is pronounced 'cadday'.

Indoors, Mary preferred French amusements. She imported French musicians and jesters, and began to organize musical dinner parties and dances – none of which went down well with the local Puritans.

In her innocence, or perhaps under the influence of her French relatives, Mary had not realized how serious the religious issue was to be. Scotland was a newly Protestant state, and although the Catholic Mary declared her intention not to interfere in the country's official religion, she was horrified when her first attempt to celebrate Mass almost caused a riot. Her priests were threatened with violence, and music during services was deemed out of the question. Poor Mary must have felt all the more foreign – and all the more French.

However, one thing her French education had taught her was how to exert her charms. Buoyed up by a Parisienne's confidence that everyone will fall under her spell, she toured Scotland, meeting and greeting her people. And they quickly succumbed, despite what seems to have been a dodgy French sense of humour inherited from her mother. When visiting the priory of Beaulieu (a common name in Britain at the time, given by un-imaginative medievals wanting to christen any 'beautiful place'), Mary quipped, 'Oui c'est un beau lieu.' Which is a bit like someone arriving at Portsmouth harbour and saying, 'Ah-ha, this must be the mouth of the port.'

If the Scots were beginning to warm to their monarch, the feeling wasn't completely mutual. As Antonia Fraser puts it in her biography of Mary, the Queen thought of the Highlanders as noble savages and the Lowland lairds as savage nobles – she knew that rival factions of Catholic and Protestant Scottish lords were hatching wild plots with her at the centre, often involving kidnap schemes which would have ended in a forced marriage to the eldest son of the family.

But Mary and her own family had bigger ambitions. The Guises were actively looking for a husband who would be acceptable not only to the Scots but – most of all – to Mary's nosey neighbour, Elizabeth I.

In fact, both queens seem to have agreed that it was a pity one of them wasn't a man, because they would have made an ideal political match. If only same-sex marriage had been legal, history would have been very different, and a whole lot of suffering (especially on Mary's part) would have been avoided. The two women would have had to adopt children, of course, but that would have been easier than it is for modern celebrities, because in those days queens made laws.*

But it wasn't to be, and Mary's name was linked with various continental Catholics before she settled on an Englishman, a hotheaded teenager called Henry Darnley. He was a Catholic cousin of Mary's (they shared the same English grandmother), a swaggering, good-looking lord of nineteen. In 1565, he came north to visit Mary and cunningly 'fell ill', so that he was forced to stay at Stirling Castle while she nursed him. The 22-year-old Mary, who was almost certainly still a virgin, fell in lust with Henry and, despite the avowed opposition of both Elizabeth and all the Scottish Protestant lords, they married. The ceremony at which Henry was crowned King of Scotland was marked by total silence from the lords.

If Mary's life had been precarious for the past few years, with this marriage she was done for. From here on, she would know almost nothing but imprisonment and bloodshed.

Domestic violence is common in the upper classes, too

The first casualty was Mary's French-Italian secretary, David Riccio, an ugly little man who kept the Queen – who was now pregnant – amused with card games and music while her young husband was out catching syphilis. Scottish intriguers convinced the frankly dim-witted Henry Darnley that Riccio was Mary's lover, and

* It also seems a shame that none of Mary's letters to Elizabeth contains a pun on her French name – something along the lines of 'would that this *Marie* could become your *mary*'.

one evening in March 1566 a gang of them burst into her chamber, dragged the squealing secretary out into the hallway and stabbed him over fifty times, while Henry looked on and one of the lords held a pistol to Mary's stomach.

Although intrigue and murder were a part of everyday royal life in the sixteenth century, and France had been racked by religious massacres even while she was living there, only now did Mary seem to realize what a violent world she was living in. She suspected that scheming lords had promised Henry the Scottish throne in his own name, and she was probably right to believe that the attack on Riccio had been intended to end with her own murder, and that she had only been spared because the killers had lost their nerve.

So she fought down her feelings of disgust towards her husband and managed to convince him that she had forgiven him for the Riccio misunderstanding. And the stratagem worked; as soon as the scheming lords saw that Henry had defected back to his wife's side, the plot fell to pieces. For the time being, at least.

In June 1566 Mary gave birth to a son, James, in Edinburgh, and took the daring step of having him baptized in the Catholic tradition (although she refused to adhere to the prevalent custom of having a priest spit in the baby's mouth). The celebrations included a sort of pantomime organized by Mary's French valet, a man called Bastian Pages, during which French clowns made lewd gestures at some English guests, a bad joke that almost got Bastian stabbed.

There was one notable absence from the baptism – the baby's father, Henry, who was becoming increasingly estranged from the wife he had almost had murdered, and who now began plotting the kidnap of his own son.

But Mary didn't have to put up with him much longer

– in February 1567, while convalescing from a bout of syphilis in a house near the walls of Edinburgh, her errant English husband was murdered by gang of scheming Scotsmen, led by the charismatic Earl of Bothwell.

Their plot very nearly failed. They were stuffing the basement of the house with gunpowder when Henry awoke, guessed that something suspicious was going on and jumped out of a window in his nightshirt. But he was caught and strangled by the plotters, who blew the house up anyway.

Incidentally, the first man on the scene after the explosion was a certain William Blackadder, a soldier in Bothwell's pay. Blackadder was initially cleared of any involvement in the murder, but was later offered up as a scapegoat by the conspirators and convicted at a show trial, after which he was hanged, drawn and quartered, and his severed limbs were nailed up at the gates of four different Scottish towns. Not exactly the stuff of sitcom.

Although a single mother with increasingly severe nervous-health problems, Mary Queen of Scots was suddenly a very eligible widow again. She also knew full well how precarious life had become, and went to visit her son James, who was safely locked away in the loyal castle of Stirling. However, on the way back to Edinburgh, Mary's party was intercepted by the Earl of Bothwell, who convinced her that she was in immediate danger and needed to hide – why not back at his place? She accepted the invitation, and Bothwell took her to Dunbar Castle, just outside Edinburgh, and raped her.

This was a brutal but politically astute move – it meant that any child born to Mary within at least nine months could justifiably be claimed as his. And Bothwell also knew that in Catholic Mary's mind, unlike that of modern French-educated women, sex and marriage were inextricably linked. In essence, the rape forced Mary to marry him.

Objectively, Bothwell was actually a good match – a Scottish lord who had shown himself ruthless enough to rape the Queen was the kind of man the country needed to give it a bit of stability (in the sixteenth century, that is). The couple were married three weeks later – the delay caused by the fact that Bothwell was already married and had to rush through a divorce. The wedding itself was a dull, functional affair, and afterwards Mary gave her new husband a single, hurriedly selected, gift: a piece of fur taken from her mother's old cloak.

If there was any stability, though, it was cruelly short-lived. Just a month later some scheming Scots lords, who were all related to each other and seemed to change sides approximately every week, raised an army against Bothwell and his supporters. As the two forces were assembling on a battlefield just outside Edinburgh, the French ambassador came to plead with Mary to leave Bothwell and go with the rebels, who, he said, were loyal to her personally and were promising to restore her to her position as sole Queen of Scotland (which would, incidentally, therefore make her a potential French puppet again).

Mary refused, pointing out that many of these rebels had only recently been conspiring on Bothwell's side. By this time, she had come to the sad conclusion that she could trust absolutely no one in Scotland except her closest entourage of French servants. And she certainly couldn't trust the French ambassador, because his boss was her old enemy Catherine de' Medici, who wanted to preserve the Franco-Scottish alliance but would probably prefer to see the easily manipulated infant King James on the throne rather than an adult Queen Mary.

In the end, the great battle simply fizzled out, because

when Bothwell went forward to accept a challenge to man-to-man combat, most of his army sneaked off. Mary, left alone on a hilltop overlooking the scene, was escorted away by her new 'allies', whose soldiers welcomed her by shouting 'burn the whore' and 'drown her'.

Locked away by the loch

Suddenly more vulnerable than ever, Mary – who was still Queen of Scotland – was taken to Lochleven Castle, a remote fortress in the middle of a loch. Here, she was imprisoned in a tower and denied any communication with the outside world. Meanwhile, false rumours about her complicity in Henry Darnley's death were circulated in an attempt to destroy any remaining support she might have amongst the people. The most damning evidence against her was that she had played golf just after the murder – being a sportswoman was a sure sign of guilt, apparently.

And in case the propaganda campaign didn't work, Mary was also threatened that if she didn't sign abdication papers in favour of her one-year-old son James, she would have her throat cut. It was an offer she couldn't refuse.

An even bigger shock was to come when James's regent was chosen: it was James Stewart, the Earl of Moray. He was Mary's half-brother, one of her father's illegitimate children, and had previously acted as one of Mary's closest advisers. In a spectacular piece of back-stabbing, he now took power and seized all of Mary's jewels. After losing her French jewellery, Mary was now to be deprived of all her family heirlooms. This was the final Scottish straw. Mary had had enough of northerners – she wanted to go back to France.

Although she was only twenty-four, she offered to bow out of politics for ever and shut herself away in a French nunnery or live quietly with the Guises. She even managed to smuggle out a letter to Catherine de' Medici, begging for some French troops to come and free her. Perhaps unsurprisingly, the answer was a crushing *non*. Far from offering help, Catherine immediately sent an official request to the Earl of Moray for some of the confiscated jewels.

In desperation, Mary also wrote (in French) to Queen Elizabeth of England, pleading for assistance. But on the very day she penned her cry for help, cousin Liz was admiring some of Mary's jewels that had been sold to her by Moray.

So Mary had to fall back on her own guile to escape from the castle. After ten months of imprisonment, in May 1568 she used her charm (but apparently nothing more than that) to win over a young cousin of her captors at Lochleven, who spirited her out lying flat in the bottom of a boat. Hearing that she was free, yet another army of so-called loyal Scottish nobles offered to fight for her cause, only to defect in mid-battle before her very eyes, exactly as they had done before.

Mary must have felt desperately alone, having been betrayed or abandoned by absolutely everyone who had promised her help. She was faced with a life-or-death choice.

Should she go 'home' to France? No, this was impossible, because Catherine de' Medici was too vindictive an enemy. What's more, France was in the midst of vicious religious wars in which her own family seemed to be playing a decidedly bloody role.

Or should she stay in Scotland, claim that her abdication had been obtained under duress, and try to wrest power away from the regent? But no, that wasn't possible, either, because of the lack of reliable supporters and the risk that her son and herself would be killed.

So Mary turned south, to England, throwing herself on the mercy of her cousin Queen Elizabeth. And we all know what a bad move that was going to be . . .

Mary gets a guided tour of the castles of England

Here begins the story that everyone knows so well, of Mary's incarceration from 1568 until her execution in 1587. She was held first in Carlisle, then Bolton Castle in North Yorkshire and most lengthily, for fifteen years, at Tutbury Castle in Staffordshire.*

Mary's first and last trip to England got off to an inauspicious start – she crossed into Cumbria by water and stumbled while coming ashore, falling to her knees just as William the Conqueror and Henry V had done. Mary's entourage seem to have been well aware that royals are genetically incapable of getting out of boats, because they knew that it was customary to comment on the omen, and declared it a good sign, indicating that Mary was coming to get her hands on England.

However, this was not the right kind of thing to be saying on English soil, even if it was spoken in Scots or French, because Elizabeth I was very nervous of Mary's claim to her throne. So instead of being taken to see her cousin, Mary was immediately incarcerated while a law was passed making it treasonable not only to plot against Elizabeth but also to be the unknowing beneficiary of such a plot.

Mary acknowledged this law, and promised to

* Tutbury was originally built by one Henri de Ferrières, who fought in William the Conqueror's army at Hastings, and whose descendants include that other tragic royal, Diana, Princess of Wales.

relinquish her claims on the English Crown. She even swore never to seek a new Franco-Scottish alliance, and to make the saying of Catholic Mass illegal in Scotland. But none of these concessions secured her freedom.

Worse still, Elizabeth seemed to believe the lies being spread about Mary in Scotland by the Earl of Moray, especially since new 'evidence' had been conveniently found in Edinburgh implicating Mary in the murder of Henry Darnley. This was in the form of the so-called Casket Letters, which had supposedly been written by Mary to Bothwell (the man who abducted and raped her), and, if real, suggested that Mary had known about the plot to kill her husband, and had already been having an adulterous fling with Bothwell. The fact that some of the letters were signed 'Mary', a spelling she never used, and that one letter in French was full of grammatical mistakes which fluent Mary would not have made, did not seem to worry anyone.

Mary sent out a stream of letters to Elizabeth pleading for just one meeting – cousin to cousin, woman to woman – where they could cut through all the lies and the politics. One of these pleas was a poem in which Mary likened herself to a poor ship cast adrift on the stormy seas of fate. (It was, of course, written in French.)

Mary also wrote to King Charles IX of France, a younger brother of her first husband, King François, asking him for help for old times' sake. No luck. *Au contraire*, under the influence of Catherine de' Medici, Charles withheld the pension due to Mary as an ex-Queen of France, and even confiscated her lands in Touraine.

So Mary was forced to accept her imprisonment, and made the best of things by setting up her own mini-France again, with thirty servants, including a French secretary to write her letters and, of course, a

French doctor and apothecary (pharmacist). She managed to obtain permission to go on French-style spa treatments at the thermal baths in Buxton, near Tutbury, and – like any French girl staying with an English family – she also took English lessons, or at least managed to perfect her English, which until now had apparently been decidedly wonky.

But Mary wasn't just any old French expat. While she was having thermal bubble baths and practising English conversation, the Pope was urging Spain to invade England, rescue Mary and marry her off to Philip of Spain's brother, who would then take over the English throne and convert everyone back to Catholicism. Meanwhile, France was actually considering an alliance with England by marrying another brother of King Charles IX, Duke Hercule-François of Anjou, to Elizabeth. In terms of English politics, Mary was becoming at best expendable, and at worst a threat.

It was therefore logical that her final downfall would be engineered by the English secret services, with the French Embassy in London taking an apparently un-witting part in the plot. Secret letters intended for Mary had been accumulating atthe embassy, awaiting the day when she might be able to receive them. Some of these were treasonable, but Mary could only be convicted if she actually read them and, better still, replied. So a potential postman, an English Catholic called Gilbert Gifford,* went to the embassy and offered to smuggle the letters into Tutbury, and the French handed them over to him.

And so it was that a correspondence began between

---

* Gifford was granted an English pension for his part in the plot against Mary. After her conviction, he went to France, became a priest, was arrested having a bisexual threesome in a brothel and died in the Bastille.

Mary and her French sympathizers, all of them blissfully unaware that every letter was being read by the spymaster Sir Francis Walsingham, head of Queen Elizabeth's secret service. Walsingham was waiting for one word that could be used as evidence of high treason, and he couldn't believe his luck when a new penpal stepped in, an English gentleman called Anthony Babington who saw Mary as a kind of Catholic saint and had decided to mount a swashbuckling bid to rescue her.

In July 1586, Babington sent a letter announcing his intention to assassinate Elizabeth and put Mary on the throne. Fatefully, Mary replied saying that if she were to become Queen of England, French aid would be necessary. In her biography, Antonia Fraser seems to hint that Mary might not have approved of killing Elizabeth, and that this reply was merely a theoretical 'what if . . .' supposition, a sort of French inability to stay out of a philosophical discussion. But it was enough for Walsingham. Mary had countenanced Elizabeth's death, and was therefore guilty of high treason.

Mary tried in vain to claim that, as a foreign head of state, she could not be tried by an English court. And this would normally have been true, but Elizabeth's law making anyone liable to prosecution for plotting her downfall extended even to foreign queens.

Realizing that she was in mortal danger, Mary played her I've-got-important-friends card, and made one of her most famous pronouncements, a veiled threat of French and Spanish intervention if she were harmed: 'Remember,' she warned the commissioners at an initial hearing, 'that the theatre of the world is wider than the realm of England.' This sounds as if it was translated from the French, and was probably enough in itself to ensure that Mary would be having a tête-à-tête with the axeman. What? Suggest that there was something bigger out there than Elizabethan England? Off with her head!

Catherine de' Medici wasn't exactly fond of Mary, but she couldn't let an ex-Queen of France be executed like a common criminal, especially not by the *Anglais*. So the French King, now Henri III, another of Mary's ex-brothers-in-law, made a promise that he would not support any future plots against Elizabeth, if only Mary were spared. Unfortunately, though, the English didn't need, or trust, French promises, and Henri was quite simply ignored.

Scotland, meanwhile, was silent – which was not surprising, given that Mary's son, King James, who was now an independent-minded twenty-year-old, had signed an alliance with Elizabeth. And when English ambassadors asked James whether he would break the alliance if his mother was beheaded, he said no.

Poor Mary was doomed.

Two strikes and out

Mary seems to have been very sanguine about her imminent demise, and accepted that the game was up. She declared that she was happy to become a martyr to her religion – 'with God's help I shall die in the Catholic faith' – and even went as far as to say that Philip of Spain should take the English throne and put an end to Protestantism.

Despite this last defiant piece of politicking on Mary's part, Elizabeth I was still reluctant to sign the death warrant. She seems to have been unwilling to create a martyr, and fearful of reprisals from Catholic nations. She even tried to persuade Mary's jailers to kill her on the quiet – as we have seen before, there have been many examples of royals meeting with unfortunate accidents while in custody, inadvertently impaling themselves on red-hot pokers, for example. When the jailers refused (Mary's charms were still effective), Elizabeth deliberately engineered things so that she could sign the warrant 'innocently'. She got her secretary to hide it in a pile of other papers, and claimed that she 'didn't notice' what she was signing. Once the deed was done, she made a great show of not wanting to part with the document, but did little to stop her aides having it delivered to Mary's final place of incarceration, Fotheringhay Castle in Northamptonshire.

On the evening of 7 February 1587, the 44-year-old Mary was visited at Fotheringhay and told by the Earls of Kent and Shrewsbury that she was to be executed next morning. Mary had been prepared for this, but swore on a bible that she was innocent of any plot to kill Elizabeth. The Earl of Kent objected that her vow meant nothing, because it was a Catholic bible. Mary replied with piercing French logic: 'If I swear on the book which I believe to be the true version, will your lordship not believe my oath more than if I were to swear on a translation in which I do not believe?' The poor earl was probably still trying to work that one out when she was executed.

Mary spent her last night making her will and writing letters. She asked for Masses to be said in France, and made a bequest to the monks of Reims. She also put in a formal plea to be buried in France, in one of the royal cathedrals of Saint-Denis or Reims.*

Next morning, she walked to the block courageously, and instructed her servants to 'tell my friends that I died

* This was refused, and her coffin was left unburied for a year in Fotheringhay and then buried in Peterborough. It was eventually moved to Westminster Abbey by her son when he became King James I of England, and is still there – on the opposite side of the abbey's Lady chapel to Elizabeth I.

When Mary Queen of Scots' head was removed in 1587, so were France's hopes of grabbing the crown of England from Queen Elizabeth I.

a true woman to my religion and like a true Scottish woman and a true French woman'. When her servants started wailing, she asked them, in French of course, to be quiet.

After the deed was done (with, it is said, two blows of a bloody butcher's axe), the executioner lifted Mary's head by her famous auburn hair, and a wig came away in his hand. The head fell to the ground, its real hair turned prematurely grey by the stress of the long imprisonment.

France mourned, in the best tradition of political hypocrisy, with a Requiem Mass at Notre-Dame attended by Henri III and his mother, Catherine de' Medici, who, it is hoped, refrained from wearing any of the jewels she had confiscated from Mary. An archbishop gave a sermon, spitting with fury that 'the axe of a vulgar executioner disfigured that body which had graced the bed of a King of France'. In French eyes, it was of course doubly wrong to execute a beautiful woman.

Up in Scotland, Mary's son, King James, reacted to the news of her death with a stoicism that some might call indifference. He was unmoved, except to say, 'now I am sole King.' Later, he declared that her execution was 'a preposterous and strange procedure'. Not what you could call filial or patriotic outrage.

All of which begs the question: Mary Queen of *Scots*?

Well, strictly speaking, yes, although, given that she was betrayed by almost every Scotsman who had enough power to do so, it is not surprising that, at her death, she clearly saw herself as French. It was in France that she wanted to be buried, and the very last thing Mary wrote was a letter to King Henri III, saying that she was being killed because she posed a French threat to the English throne. She seems to have forgotten that her maternal relations, the Guises, had risked her life by implicating her in their religious power games, and that Catherine de'

Medici, who was Queen or Queen Mother for Mary's whole life, had been – excuse my French – such a bitch to her.

And in political terms, it was the French, not the Scots, who lost out when Mary lost her head. With her death, France was deprived of the only person in Europe who could realistically have sat on the English throne without being nasty to the French ambassador. Mary's son, King James of Scotland, was much too chummy with Elizabeth for France's liking, but even at forty-four years old, Mary could in theory have been married off to a Frenchman, inherited the English crown on Elizabeth's death (from either natural or unnatural causes) and brought her errant son, King James of Scotland, to heel. It could have been a fantasy outcome for France: with Mary on the throne of England, and James in power in Scotland, the whole of Britain could have been ruled from the French side of the Channel again, just as it had been in William the Conqueror's day.

But with one or, more exactly, two blows of an English axe, this French dream had been shattered. France had lost a potential colony, and all because of its dismal failure to throw its full weight behind the person who best represented its interests. It was a trend that was about to be repeated right across the globe . . .

7

French Canada, or How to
Lose a Colony

The French think that their cousins in Canada are quaint historical throwbacks. The Québécois speak with an accent that most French people find primitive, comical even, a sort of seventeenth-century peasant patois. They use amusing words like *char* (cart) for car, and *blonde* for girlfriend, and their swearwords are old religious terms like *sacrament!* and *tabernacle!* When a Quebecker is interviewed for French TV, he or she is often subtitled in 'normal' French, as if the language they speak in francophone Canada is so barbarous that Parisians won't be able to understand it. In a word, the French think of Quebeckers rather like New Yorkers see Alabamians. There's just a little knuckle-on-floor-scraping involved.

But at the same time, any mention of the history of Quebec rouses burning anti-British and anti-American outrage in a French person's heart, as if someone was talking about a favourite café of theirs that had been turned into a Starbucks. Canada was stolen from France, they will allege, and if the word 'Acadie' comes into the conversation, the outrage can turn to a blazing condemnation of British genocide. (As long, that is, as the person has heard of Acadie. Many French people have no idea what it is – a pop singer, maybe, or a pet name for the Académie Française?)

Acadie (in English, Acadia) was the French name for what is now Nova Scotia, a peninsula in northeastern Canada that in 1713, after more than a century of brinkmanship, was finally ceded to Britain by treaty and, rather unkindly one has to admit, ethnically cleansed in the 1750s when the French colonists refused to swear allegiance to the British Crown. Some 12,600 Acadiens (Acadians) were forcibly sailed out of Canada, most of them ending up as refugees in New England, Britain, France and Louisiana (the word 'Cajun' is a corruption of 'Acadien').

If you go to the island of Belle-Île-en-Mer, just off the coast of Brittany, you can see a permanent exhibition in the capital, Le Palais, dedicated to the Acadiens who settled there. The island's official website has a heart-rending page on these refugees, which talks about the 'diaspora of this humble, peace-loving people whose whole civilization was based on faith in God, respect for their ancestors and the honour of work'. In short, Acadie is one of those names, like Joan of Arc, that conjure up images of dastardly British treachery and heartless Francophobia.

However, just as they did with Joan of Arc, the French seem to be forgetting their own none-too-glorious role in the affair . . .

No room for France in the New World

As soon as Columbus returned from his first transatlantic outing, the Kings of Spain and Portugal got the Pope to grant them ownership of the newly discovered territories.

This the Holy Father did, allowing them to draw a line down the known map of the western world, stretching from pole to pole and slicing the Atlantic in two. Everything to the east of the line – the coast of Africa, the vast tracts of ocean and the jutting-out bit of Brazil – went to Portugal. Anything discovered lying to the west was to belong to Spain. Roughly speaking, on 7 June 1494, almost the whole of North and South America became, by divine command, Spanish.

France was mightily peeved, although it was probably not surprised, because the Pope in question, Alexander VI, aka Rodrigo Borgia (yes, one of *those* Borgias*), had recently been appointed after an election campaign that had involved political lobbying, vested interests, lofty promises and – it is alleged – a certain amount of back-handers. And France had backed Borgia's rival, giving him 200,000 gold ducats (in modern money, a helluva lot). Not surprising, then, that France was left off the papally approved map of the New World.

The French thought that this was all the more unfair because they claimed that they had, in fact, discovered the New World long before Columbus. (No one accepted that the Native Americans might have discovered the place rather than sprouting up there like plants, and no one knew about the Viking expeditions in the eleventh century. They were mentioned in the Icelandic Sagas, but the *Groenlendinga Saga* wasn't in many French public libraries. Probably because in the fifteenth century France didn't have any public libraries.)

A 1940 history of French colonization by Henri Blet

---

* This Pope was more than just a *Holy* Father. The *Catholic Encyclopedia* concedes that he had 'relations with a Roman lady' who bore him four children, including the notorious Lucrezia. It doesn't mention his three children by other mistresses.

alleges that a church in Dieppe was decorated as early as 1440 with mosaics depicting Native Americans, and that the town's archives contained reports written by sailors who had been to South America at least fifty years before Columbus. Tragically, Monsieur Blet writes, this evidence was all destroyed during a 1694 bombardment of Dieppe by the *Anglais*. Our fault, as usual.

The same author mentions that 'fishermen from Bayonne' (in the southwest of France) had long been going to Newfoundland on the Canadian coast on whaling trips, but shoots himself in the foot by mentioning that they called the island Baccalaos, a transcription of the Spanish term for cod. These fishermen were in fact Basques, not Frenchmen, who had been drying and salting fish there for centuries, and keeping the rich fish stocks secret for obvious reasons.

Monsieur Blet adds that fishermen from Normandy, Brittany and La Rochelle had also been going to Canada for decades before Columbus crossed the Atlantic, and concludes that 'the French were not absent from these great discoveries. But their voyages were discreet . . .' Surely the first (and last) time in history that the French have ever been discreet about their achievements.

Anyway, as Signor Borgia, alias Pope Alexander VI, probably said, 'Quid. Semper.' (Latin for 'What. Ever.') The New World was to be Portuguese and Spanish, by divine decree. Which is slightly ironic because one of the discoveries that Columbus brought back was syphilis, a disease that the unchaste Pope would later catch.

Henry VII of England braved papal disapproval and sent out the explorer Giovanni Caboto (an Italian, like Columbus), changing his name to John Cabot so that his discoveries would sound more convincingly British. Cabot duly 'discovered' North America (Columbus had been no further north than the Caribbean) in 1497, although he probably waved to the Basques when he arrived in Newfoundland – if he did at all. His charts were not accurate enough for anyone to be sure. Which probably explains why he disappeared completely on his second mission in 1498.

The French, meanwhile, contented themselves with whinging about the Pope's ruling. According to Henri Blet, King François I did little more than protest to the Spanish that 'the sun shines for me just as it does for other people, and I would like to see the article in Adam's will that excludes me from the share-out.' Which was witty but not very productive, because the Spanish simply ignored him.

Sorry, wrong address

It wasn't until 1524 that a Dieppe ship-owner called Jean Ango convinced King François to put his money where his mouth was and support an expedition designed, quite literally, to put France on the map of America.

Ango was not only interested in mapmaking, of course. Like everyone who had ventured west of the Azores, he was in it for the money. They all wanted to find a quick sea route to Asia and its spices, which usually had to travel through pirate-infested seas around the Cape of Good Hope and up the west coast of Africa, or overland, where a chain of merchants would add their commission to the prices.

Ango therefore hired yet another adventurous Italian, Giovanni da Verrazzano, to do the actual transatlantic sailing for him, and told Verrazzano to explore the coast of this new continent and find a way through it to Asia. Verrazzano set off in 1524, and discovered a lush, uncharted peninsula that he called Arcadia because it reminded him of the region of the same name in Greece.

It was, we now know, the part of North America to the north of Chesapeake Bay.

Continuing north past the mouth of the Hudson River, which he thought was a lake, Verrazzano finally reached Newfoundland and Nova Scotia before returning to France. There, he proudly announced to Ango and King François that France now possessed the vast new continent of Gallia Nova, which encompassed the whole of North America, known and unknown, above the Spanish territories of Florida and Mexico. Ango probably answered, 'Très bien, but what about my spices?'

Verrazzano made two other trips looking for the route to the east, and is said to have met an untimely end in 1528 at the hands of cannibals, who might or might not have eaten him as revenge for his telling them that they were now French.

Still, at last France had an official foothold in the Nouveau Monde, and set about mapping it. The only problem was that when later French travellers found the tree-lined peninsula that is now Nova Scotia, they thought they'd arrived in Verrazzano's Arcadia, and the name began to appear on maps in the wrong place. It was also misspelt, appearing as Lacardie, Accadie and Cadie before settling down as Acadie.

It was hardly a good start for the colony – both its geographical location and spelling were wrong. Verrazzano must have been turning in his grave. (Except that he didn't have one because he'd been eaten.)

Cartier takes over the watch

Verrazzano's successor on the French exploration scene was a Breton sailor called Jacques Cartier, who had prob-ably accompanied the Italian on at least one of his missions, and who, it is said, had already been on fishing expeditions to Newfoundland. He was commissioned by King François I to go and find a passage to Asia, deposits of gold or at the very least a nice piece of fresh cod.

In April 1534 Cartier crossed the Atlantic with two ships and sixty-one men, located Newfoundland with no trouble at all, and began to map the gulf of the St Lawrence River. There, he encountered some Native Americans, the Micmacs, with whom he traded knives and cloth for animal skins. The Micmacs, incidentally, remained on friendly terms with the French settlers throughout the troubled history of Acadie, and even helped to protect the Acadiens against British invaders. In return, *un micmac* has entered the French language as a slang term for dirty dealings. Talk about gratitude.

Before leaving the area in July 1534, Cartier erected a 10-metre crucifix with the inscription 'God Save the King of France', and formally claimed the territory for his country. But, like Verrazzano, who had flattered the King with his 'Nova Gallia' ploy, Cartier essentially returned empty-handed apart from a few bits of beaver skin, and was promptly sent back again.

In 1535, he took a small force of armed men up the St Lawrence River in canoes as far as an Iroquois village called Hochelaga ('beaver dam'). It was set on a hilltop that Cartier renamed (presumably without informing the Iroquois) Mont Royal, or 'royal mountain' – later to become Montreal. Perhaps out of guilt for appropriating their hill, Cartier decided to give the whole region an Iroquois name, and asked them what they called it. 'Canada,' they replied, and this was duly written on the French map, with Cartier presumably not realizing that his question had been misunderstood – it was a word meaning village.

The chief of the Hochelaga Iroquois gave Cartier good news. It was, he said, possible to continue a long way upriver, and if the strangers travelled for three moons, they would eventually arrive in a land rich in gold. In view of what happened next, however, this might well have been a mistranslation of the Iroquois for 'bugger off and leave us alone.' When Cartier was given gold nuggets and diamonds, he rushed home to the King with this proof that his missions were worthwhile, only to be told that the stones were iron pyrites and quartz. Poor, intrepid Cartier was branded a loser and lost his job. Though he did leave his mark on contemporary France – his experiences inspired a new expression that became very popular at the time, 'as fake as a Canadian diamond'.

Colonization is cut off in its prime

France now embarked on a round of bloody religious conflicts between the Catholics and the Huguenots (Protestants), which would have diverted attention and money away from transatlantic exploration except that the persecuted Huguenots, who formed a large and very influential section of French society, began looking for places to hide. Like the Pilgrim Fathers, who would set sail from England in 1620, the Huguenots thought that the Americas might be a good bunkhole.

One of the most ambitious and powerful of them was called Gaspard de Coligny, and in 1562 he organized an expedition to set up a colony in what is now South Carolina. He sent over a Dieppe sailor called Jean Ribault, who built a settlement near present-day Charleston and left twenty-eight men to guard it while he returned to France to tell the Huguenots that he had found their promised land.

Unfortunately, back at home, religious conflict had turned into outright war, and Ribault was forced to take refuge in England. But the Brits had heard what he was up to, and arrested him on suspicion that he would steal English ships and use them to supply his new French colony in America.

After a year, the twenty-eight men stranded in South Carolina eventually realized that no one was coming to relieve them, so they built some boats and set off back across the Atlantic. Unbelievably, they reached the coast of England, and were rescued just in time, because the survivors had resorted to eating their shipmates.

Ribault was eventually released, and returned to Carolina with 600 French soldiers and settlers. There, he was pleasantly surprised to find his fort intact, and to see that he'd arrived just in time because some Spanish ships were nosing around. Leaving a few men to guard the settlement, Ribault sailed off to scare away the Spaniards.

What he didn't know, however, was that the Spanish had also sent up an army by land, and the soldiers captured the fort and massacred the male inhabitants.

At the same time, a hurricane smashed Ribault's fleet, killing many of his men. A few hundred shipwrecked survivors surrendered to Spanish soldiers, only to be tied up and interrogated about their religion. Anyone who said he wasn't Catholic had his throat slit, and all but a handful of the Huguenots told the truth and died on the continent that was meant to be their refuge. Ribault was among the truthful dead. His backer, Gaspard de Coligny, was soon to follow him along the path of religious martyrdom.

Back in France, Coligny was making himself highly unpopular with the Catholic establishment. In 1568, he recruited an army of English privateers and launched a fleet of fifty ships to rampage up and down the Channel attacking Catholic shipping, including French vessels. These Protestant privateers weren't out to slash Catholic throats, however. They stole the ships' cargoes, which they took to Plymouth or Coligny's home port of La Rochelle, and set the captured vessels and their crews free so they would come back to be robbed again. It was, it seemed, an early example of recycling.

Given this level of high-profile anti-Catholic activism, it was only a matter of time before the religious question caught up with Coligny, and in 1572, it did so in the most spectacular way possible.

On 22 August of that year, he was the victim of an assassination attempt in Paris. A shot was fired from a house belonging to the Guises, Mary Queen of Scots' family, who were prominent Catholics. Coligny was not seriously wounded, suffering only a severed finger and a broken elbow, and went to recover at his house nearby. Here, he was visited by the King, Charles IX (a Catholic), who promised to punish the attacker and even brought his physician along to treat Coligny's wounds. A later visitor wasn't quite so caring, though – one of the Guise family's servants, a Bohemian called Charles Danowitz, came to the house and stabbed Coligny in the chest. Half dead, he was thrown into the street, where he was beheaded, castrated and disembowelled, all of which amply made up for the earlier marksman's failure.

With rumours of a Huguenot uprising being spread by King Charles IX's mother (and Mary Queen of Scots' ex-mother-in-law), Catherine de' Medici, a massacre began, and up to 15,000 Huguenots were killed by mobs throughout France, most of them on 24–5 August 1572 – an event which is remembered in France as St Bartholomew's Massacre, as if Jesus' apostle were himself responsible for the killings.

In any case, Coligny, the man behind France's drive to explore and colonize the Americas, was left lying, minus a few vital body parts, in the street near the Louvre. The

French weren't going anywhere for the time being, except into a deep pit of bankruptcy caused by their religious wars.

The French get cold feet

In the race to divide up the riches of the New World, the English were taking full advantage of the power vacuum north of the Spanish territories. Queen Elizabeth I granted Sir Walter Raleigh the right to colonize and exploit any American lands he could grab – in exchange for 20 per cent of the profits – and in 1584 Raleigh sent out two explorers, Philip Amadas and Arthur Barlowe, to do the grabbing for him. They 'discovered' what is now the Carolina coast and claimed the whole unexplored region for England as Virginia, conveniently ignoring the fact that much of it was already in Spanish hands and that France had claimed it as Nova Gallia.

At the same time, English ships were trading with Huguenot refugees who had fled to Newfoundland and were eking out a living there despite an astonishing lack of support from France. Colonization was just not fashionable amongst French politicians. Even when relative stability was restored in France in the 1590s, the country's chief financial minister, a man with the glorious name of Maximilien de Béthune, baron de Rosny et duc de Sully, was fiercely opposed to gallivant-ing about overseas in search of potential income. 'Ploughing and grazing are the nipples of France,' he famously said, referring of course not to nipples' sexiness but their ability to feed the country.

Unlike Sully, though, the new French King, Henri IV, saw the way the New World was being divided up, and had no doubt heard about this new trend called 'smoking' that was being popularized in France by a monk called Frère André Thévet, who declared that it cured 'humours of the brain' (he didn't know about the tumours of the lungs).* King Henri duly began to grant licences to set up companies to trade with the Americas.

Canada, Henri decided, looked like a good proposition – for a start there were plenty of Norman, Breton and French Basque sailors who knew how to find their way there and back. And the French Huguenot refugees were already over there, trading in furs and fish. Admittedly, so far they had been trading mainly with the English, but surely they would welcome overtures from their king?

There were just two minor problems with the contract that Henri began to offer his trading companies. First, it demanded that his land in the New World be turned into Nouvelle-France – literally, a new France, with the same agriculture and society as there were back home. This meant that the colonists would be peasants who were to clear the land and then hope that it was suitable for growing wheat, vines and animal foodstuffs. Which brings us to the second point: Henri had decreed that French settlements were to be started above the line of 40° latitude, safely north of interference from the Spanish. In doing so, he was assuming that the climate at 40° latitude in North America is the same as that in Europe. To say that some of the future French colonists were going to get cold feet is a cruel understatement. They were in danger of losing all their extremities . . .

* Nicotine is named after a Frenchman, Jean Nicot de Villemain, France's ambassador to Portugal in the mid-1500s. He sent some tobacco snuff to Catherine de' Medici, who sniffed it and was so delighted with the effects that she tried to have tobacco renamed Herba Regina.

A French colony is pillaged . . . by the French

Thus it was that in mid-1604 Pierre Dugua, sieur de Monts, a Protestant from the Vendée coast of western France, was named viceroy of a chunk of Nouvelle-France, and set off with a hundred peasants and craftsmen to colonize a section of the Canadian coast. They settled in an inlet that they dubbed French Bay (now the Bay of Fundy), where half of them died during the first winter, their faint cries of 'hang on, aren't we on the same latitude as Venice?' being swallowed up in the arctic gales.

As soon as it was possible to travel, the survivors moved across the bay to the slightly more temperate climes of a place they patriotically named Port Royal, which became the first settlement on Acadie. Finding that life was actually possible here, de Monts returned to France to fetch more colonists.

However, when he got home, he hit an iceberg. Not a real one, which would have been bad enough, but a political one with a much greater capacity to inflict damage. The problem was that de Monts's royal licence to colonize had included a monopoly on the trade of furs and cod from his new territories, which had enraged merchants back in France so much that they persuaded Henri IV to revoke the monopoly. De Monts was told that he could keep his colony as long as he agreed to carry on sending out settlers to cultivate the land and convert the Native Americans to Catholicism. Understandably, the Protestant de Monts told France where it could stick its farm implements – which he had already realized were going to be of little use in the permafrost anyway – and abandoned his plans to colonize. The Acadiens were on their own.

Miraculously, they hung on, largely thanks to some

Native Americans who took pity on the stranded Europeans and taught them to fish and trap efficiently. And they might actually have made a go of it if the French mainlanders hadn't sabotaged things for them.

Yet again, it all came down to religion. The Acadiens surviving on cod liver oil and beaver meat were, as we've seen, Protestants, but the regime back home was Catholic and was convinced that the New World had to be saved by saying Catholic Mass. In 1610 it was therefore decided that supply ships taking provisions out to Acadie should also carry Catholic priests to help with the conversion of the Native Americans. This didn't go down too well with the Protestant shipowners, however, who refused to let the priests on board. No problem: a Catholic royal attendant, Antoinette, marquise de Guercheville,* bought out the shipowners, thereby obtaining the licence to supply Acadie as well as a large batch of shares in the colony itself.

Inevitably, tensions arose between the colonists and the priests because of their incompatible priorities, and soon settlers began to abandon Port Royal to set up small independent communities on their own. The formerly thriving colony of Port Royal fell into a steep decline, and was effectively killed off by Antoinette just three years later.

In 1613, she sent over a ship called, interestingly, the *Fleur de Mai* (*Mayflower*), with ten Jesuit priests and 120 workmen on board. They docked in Port Royal, where

* Antoinette is famous for becoming the first known example of a woman refusing the advances of a French king. She told Henri IV: 'my rank is not noble enough for me to become your wife, but my heart is too noble for me to become your mistress', a line that, in a more modern form, is still used today by countless French secretaries resisting their bosses.

the remaining colonists were waiting anxiously for supplies. But when the *Fleur de Mai*'s passengers came ashore, they declined all offers to exchange moose heads for bottles of wine, and set about stripping Port Royal of everything useful. The ship simply loaded up with Antoinette's legal share of all the timber, crops, furs and fish in stock, and sailed away again to found a new colony.

The site the pillagers chose was a place that had been baptized Saint-Sauveur (St Saviour) on an island off what is now Maine. Here, the *Fleur de Mai*'s crew immediately split into two factions: those who wanted to build a fort first, and those who thought it wiser to clear land for planting. The French love a good intellectual debate, and were still theorizing about how to colonize North America when the deciding argument sailed over the horizon in the form of an Englishman called Samuel Argall.

Argall had discovered a new, fast transatlantic route. Instead of heading south towards the Canaries and then west with the trade winds, he sailed due west from the Azores to Bermuda and thence to the new English colony of Virginia. There, Argall had been instrumental in the kidnap of Pocahontas, who would of course go on to become a Disney film star. This was clearly a man at the heart of American history, and it was a very unlucky day for the colonists at Saint-Sauveur when he was ordered to explore the coast north of Virginia and eradicate any French settlements he found.

In July 1613, he interrupted the French debate on *La Méthode de colonisation idéale*, burned the *Fleur de Mai*, set one group of settlers adrift in a boat, and made prisoners of the rest, half of whom were presumably saying, 'See, I *told* you we should have built a fort first.'

Amongst Argall's captives was a priest called Father

Biard, and it is alleged that Biard now betrayed his own countrymen by telling the Brits that they might like to stop off and destroy the settlement at Port Royal. Luckily for the colonists there, almost everyone was away working in the fields or hunting when Argall sailed up. So the English contented themselves with burning the houses and stealing anything of value or use, and were just about to sail out of the bay when the horrified settlers returned and recognized Biard on deck.

The rivalry between French Protestants and Catholics had dealt an almost fatal blow to Acadie, and it was going to take the intervention of a famous Frenchman to resuscitate it . . .

Beaverskin handbags at ten paces

Cardinal Richelieu is remembered today as one of the most ruthless and ambitious politicians France has ever had (which is really saying something). Before he became the fictional anti-hero in Alexandre Dumas's novel *The Three Musketeers*, he was the all too non-fictional prime minister of King Louis XIII, and an avowed enemy of the English.

Born into a poor but noble family in 1585, Richelieu (full name: Armand-Jean du Plessis cardinal-duc de Richelieu et duc de Fronsac) had become a bishop aged only twenty-one and a cardinal at thirty-seven. He quickly made a reputation for himself as a clear-thinking administrator who took the most logical and efficient action as soon as it was needed, even if this meant having an innocent person executed to dissuade others from opposing him. He also had a superstitious streak, and used to consult soothsayers. And one of the things he was most anxious to know was when he would defeat the English.

So when Richelieu received a letter from Acadie begging for assistance against the English, he thought it was a divine message. The letter came from a settler called Charles de Latour, who was theoretically Governor of Acadie but in reality little more than the leader of a gang of stranded fur trappers. Latour was married to a Native American, but apparently even this close co-operation with the locals was no guarantee that his ailing colony was going to survive the onslaught of the elements and the English.

It was 1627, and the British and French were enjoying one of their frequent minor wars. The Protestant port of La Rochelle on the west coast of France was under siege by Richelieu and Louis XIII's Catholic army, and England was meddling in France's religious strife by sending ships to the Protestants' aid. For once, fate seemed to be on France's side, because the man leading the British mission was the Duke of Buckingham, who, it was alleged, had been selected not because of his military prowess but because he was a close friend of the royal family – it was widely accepted that he had been the lover of the previous King of England, James I.* Under orders of a new king, Charles I, Buckingham tried to capture the Île de Ré, the long island that lies like a sea wall guarding the access to La Rochelle harbour, but failed miserably, losing several thousand men in the process, mainly from starvation and sickness because of his bad preparations. When La Rochelle capitulated, Richelieu saw Buckingham's

* The rumours were fired by King James's pet name for Buckingham – his 'sweet child and wife' – and the Duke's appointment as a Gentleman of the Bedchamber. Buckingham reciprocated the royal affection, writing to James that 'I naturally so love your person, and adore all your other parts, which are more than one man ever had.' In modern English, this would probably translate as something like: 'Let's do it again, big boy.'

absurd defeat as proof that heaven had decided it was time to stick it to the English once and for all.

Richelieu and Louis XIII therefore decided to answer Charles de Latour's cry for help with four ships, all laden with men and supplies destined to relaunch France's colonization of Acadie. But in a tragi-comic anti-climax, the miniature rescue fleet was intercepted by British ships, and the short-lived excitement was over. If it was a sign from heaven, it was two fingers to France.

To make matters worse, these British ships had been on their way to Nova Scotia with seventy Scottish colonists. They arrived safely, no doubt pleased to have the extra French provisions on board, and set up camp at Port Royal, the place that the French had so kindly prepared for settlement. The houses had been burnt, but overall it was, they found, an excellent site for a colony, near a good fresh-water supply, and the land around it had been cleared for planting. There was even a well-built French mill nearby. The Scots decided (unanimously) to start off by building a fort, and when that was done they set about consolidating their settlement.

Worse was to follow for Charles de Latour. His begging letter to Louis XIII and Richelieu had been delivered by his father, Claude, who had been returning to Acadie on one of the ships that were captured by the Scots. Perhaps they had plied him with whisky, because Latour Senior seems to have become convinced during the Atlantic crossing that in the long run France was totally incapable of maintaining its foothold in Canada.

He therefore offered to go and persuade his son to give up his French governorship of Acadie and accept a more concrete land grant from the Brits. And when Charles refused to bow to British rule, Claude even led an Anglo-Scottish force to attack his son's fort.

Charles, though, had learned from his countrymen's

past mistakes, and had built himself a decent stronghold. The French held on, and an abashed Claude de Latour had to march his men back to Port Royal, where he was promptly thrown out by his disgruntled hosts, leaving him with no option but to return and beg forgiveness from his son. Today, at Fort St Louis in Nova Scotia, there is a small stone pyramid with a plaque immortalizing the family argument in both English and French. It says that 'In 1630 Claude de Latour arrived here with an Anglo-Scottish expedition and strove in vain to induce his son Charles to surrender the last foothold of France in Acadia. From the consequent displeasure of the Scots at Port Royal, Charles later offered him refuge near this fort.' Which sounds as though the father was forgiven but had to stay out in the woodshed.

Soon afterwards, political events in Europe interceded to save the de Latour family from further embarrassment: the short war with England had ended with the Duke of Buckingham's La Rochelle debacle, and Richelieu demanded reparations. These he received in 1632, when Nova Scotia was restored to France as Acadie. The Scottish colonists at Port Royal were ordered to destroy their settlement and ship everything moveable back to Britain. Incredibly, the Acadien dream had risen from the ashes.

But it didn't take the French long to flatten it again.

France's main problem: nuns don't have many babies

Richelieu was now convinced more than ever that Acadie was part of a divine mission, and hatched a plan to make Canada one enormous evangelical playground. New settlements were to be basically missionary outposts with enough peasant helpers to feed the priests and nuns. A less devout man might have suspected that communities in which lay people were merely expected to produce food for missionaries were not going to be as dynamic as settlements where everyone concentrated on massacring the local wildlife and selling the meat, fish and fur for maximum profit, but that doesn't seem to have occurred to Richelieu.

Nevertheless, one man took up Richelieu's challenge: Samuel de Champlain, a veteran campaigner who had founded a short-lived colony on the site of Quebec in 1609. In 1633, Champlain was given the title of 'the King's lieutenant for the St Lawrence River' and sent to Canada with 200 French peasants, carefully chosen for their 'good morals' – that is, they were all devout Catholics. Champlain took them up the St Lawrence to Quebec, where he built a new stronghold (diplomatically named Fort Richelieu), a Jesuit college, a convent, a home for newly converted Native Americans and a large brothel. No, that last one was a joke.

As we all know, Catholic priests and nuns (even French ones) do not usually produce many offspring. Which explains why, by the end of the 1600s, the population of the whole of Nouvelle-France (French Canada), including a new settlement in Montreal, was only around 20,000. By contrast, the English colonies stretching from Virginia up to Maine were already home to some 200,000 people, and it was this basic mathematics that was going to put an end to French rule in Acadie.

Throughout the late 1600s and early 1700s, the French army kept launching raids into British-held territory, but instead of driving the foreigners away, this merely seems to have persuaded London that life in its northeast American colonies would be much more relaxing in the long run if they kicked the French out of Canada once and for all.

Call Mr Darcy!

In 1713, France ceded possession of coastal Canada to Britain by signing the Treaty of Utrecht, in which, amongst other things, King Louis XIV revoked his claims on Newfoundland and Acadie in return for a reduction in taxes on French imports into Britain, as well as possession of Alsace. In short, coastal Canada was bargained away for more valuable interests closer to home. It's the kind of thing that makes the Quebeckers hate France even today.

Ever since 1713, waves of English-speaking colonists had been arriving in Acadie, as well as large numbers of soldiers. In 1749, the Brits founded the new town of Halifax, to give themselves a separate, non-French-speaking capital. Nervous Acadiens were not reassured when in 1754 a man called Charles Lawrence was appointed Governor of Nova Scotia. Here was a type familiar to anyone who has read Jane Austen or seen one of the adaptations: an arrogant English bigot who was convinced that the law was on his side and that he was therefore free to act as odiously as possible. Jane Austen would have sent in Mr Darcy to take him down a peg, but all this was taking place a long way from the rustic tranquillity of the English countryside, on a wild peninsula perched on the edge of the known world, where death was a storm away and whole communities had been wiped out or displaced countless times within living memory.

Lawrence, a military man, was a sadist with almost unlimited powers. Added to this, he was highly suspicious of the Acadiens, and one of his first acts was to demand that they take the oath of allegiance to Britain and agree to do active military service against any invading force – France, for example. The Acadiens naturally refused, not only because they were loath to shoot their former countrymen, but also because they didn't want to be called away from their fields and traps every time some snooty Parisian commander decided to come and cause trouble.

Lawrence responded by imposing absurdly harsh penalties for any signs of disloyalty. For instance, if an Acadien was told to supply a British settlement with firewood and did not obey quickly enough, his house was to be demolished for fuel. Lawrence also had Acadiens' guns and canoes confiscated – both essential tools in hunting and fishing communities – and made plans to convert all the French settlers to the Church of England. Not surprisingly, the Acadiens began to seek refuge away from the English madman, which wasn't hard, Nova Scotia being a vast and mostly undeveloped peninsula with plenty of rivers and streams where a resourceful trapper could make a living.

No doubt furious that the wily Frenchmen kept defying his authority, on 28 July 1755 Governor Lawrence gave the order to begin deportation.

He sent an order down to New England for a fleet of two dozen cargo ships, which were to be refitted to turn their holds into prison cells without windows or sanitary arrangements (the New Englanders were pretty familiar with this kind of transport, because they were avid slave traders). Meanwhile, soldiers – also New Englanders – were encamped near the village of Grand-Pré, Nova Scotia, but instructed not to act yet, as it was harvest time and the Governor wanted the Acadiens to leave behind a good supply of fresh food.

Wondering what the soldiers were up to, the peaceful settlers got on with their lives, but began to suspect that something not too pleasant was going on when five empty cargo ships arrived offshore, and Charles Lawrence issued a summons, commanding all males over the age of ten to attend a meeting at 3 p.m. on 5 September at the village of Grand-Pré, in St Charles Church. (It's not clear whether the choice of venue was a joke. Probably not. Charles Lawrence does not seem to have had much levity about him.) It was announced that attendance at the meeting was obligatory 'on pain of forfeiting goods and chattels'.

On that afternoon, over 400 men and boys assembled, to be told by one Colonel Winslow that they were to hear 'His Majesty's final resolution to the French inhabitants of this, his province of Nova Scotia, who for almost half a century have had more indulgence granted them then any of his subjects in any part of his Dominions'. Colonel Winslow said that what he was about to do was 'very dis-agreeable' to him, 'as I know it must be grievous to you who are of the same species'. (So at least he conceded that the Acadiens were human.) He went on to announce that 'your land and tenements, cattle of all kinds and live-stocks of all sorts are forfeited to the Crown with all your other effects, savings, your money and household goods, and you yourselves to be removed from this Province'.

This was a shocking announcement to say the least, but Winslow showed that the Brits believe in fair play by adding: 'I am through His Majesty's goodness directed to allow you liberty to carry of your money and household goods as many as you can without discommoding the vessels you go in', which, given that the cargo ships had been given strict targets of numbers of people to be packed on board, was a cleverly phrased lie.

He also promised that 'whole families shall go in the same vessel' – another lie, as is proved by an order that Lawrence sent to one of the other soldiers organizing the expulsion, a certain Colonel Robert Monckton: 'I would have you not wait for the wives and the children coming in, but ship off the men without them.'

Initially, the announcement in the church must have been greeted by bewilderment, because almost the only English words the Acadiens knew were 'cod' and 'beaver'. Apparently, the sole linguist in the room was an Acadien called Pierre Landry, who translated the British declaration as soon as he'd got over his shock.

Immediately, the pleas for more lenient treatment began. Some Acadiens offered to pay for their release and move to French-settled territories inland, but this was refused. Others begged to be allowed to go and tell the women what was happening, so that they could make arrangements to leave. Eventually, a small delegation was freed to go and inform the waiting families, while Winslow held the others as hostages, sending 250 young men to be imprisoned on the waiting ships.

It wasn't until 8 October that the rest of the cargo fleet arrived and the mass deportation could begin in earnest. In the interim, twenty-four men had jumped ship, and two had been shot while trying to escape. Women and children arrived to join the men, bringing as many belongings as they could carry, but despite British promises these were left behind on the shore, and stayed there until they were found by English settlers arriving in the area five years later.

On 27 October, fourteen vessels set sail with almost 3,000 people on board, packed in as tightly as slaves and with barely enough food to survive. If the Acadiens had had portholes, they would have seen the smoke and flames rising from their settlements as the soldiers burned houses and barns to ensure that the departure was final.

At other places in Nova Scotia, the deportations were equally brutal but less efficient. Men escaped from captivity and many families hid out in the woods, evading search parties as best they could but suffering the hardships of the climate and lack of food. In some cases, whole villages upped sticks and migrated inland to set up new settlements where the Brits couldn't find them.

To make sure that the Acadiens would receive no help from the friendly Native Americans, Lawrence put a bounty on Micmac heads, offering £30 (a small fortune) for every male and £25 for a woman or child captured alive, and, chillingly, £25 for every male scalp – though how you tell between an adult male scalp and that of a woman or child is not very clear.

This was ethnic cleansing on a scale that hadn't been practised by the Brits since the Hundred Years War, the only difference being that the victims were killed by over-crowding and starvation or while 'trying to escape' and 'helping the enemy', rather than being randomly put to the sword.

In all, an estimated 12,600 Acadiens, of a total of around 18,000, were deported between 1755 and 1763. It is thought that 8,000 died, including many of those who fled or hid.

Not that France was very sympathetic to the plight of its colonists. It is generally accepted that the acid-tongued writer Voltaire was only saying what pretty much everyone in Paris felt about Canada when he wrote a letter after the disastrous 1755 earthquake in Lisbon saying: 'I wish that the earthquake had swallowed up that miserable Acadie instead.' He is also famous (in Quebec at least) for having complained in 1757 that Britain and France were at war for 'a few acres* of snow near Canada'.

* The unit of measure Voltaire actually mentioned was the *arpent*, which in France was an area 220 'King's feet' (71.48 metres) square. In Nouvelle-France, i.e. French Canada, it was only 200 'King's feet', or 64.97 metres, square. Even the units of measurement snubbed the French Canadians.

And French Canadians, who have a whole list of similar quotes, are equally pleased with Voltaire's declaration in 1762 that 'I'd rather have peace than Canada.'

Even so, the deportation of the Acadiens was not exactly Britain's, or New England's, finest hour, which is probably why these events appear in Anglo history books a little less often than the heroic goings-on inland . . .

A wolf in Wolfe's clothing

In 1756, a year after the deportation of Acadiens began, the Seven Years War broke out, and rather than engaging in skirmishes, France and Britain were now officially embroiled in a full-scale battle for military possession of their colonies in North America and elsewhere.

Acadie had been more or less abandoned to its fate, but an experienced soldier was chosen to defend France's interests in the rest of Canada: Louis-Joseph de Montcalm-Gozon, marquis de Saint-Veran (usually referred to in these less wordy times as Montcalm), who had fought in several European conflicts and received both sword and musket wounds for his pains. In spring 1756, he crossed the Atlantic with 1,200 soldiers to bolster a force of some 4,000 troops already based in Nouvelle-France. He also had 2,000 or so local militia-men at his disposal, although he knew that the latter were notoriously fickle fighters, much more interested in the whole animal-gutting scene than international wars.

At first, Montcalm carried out successful raids against the Brits, capturing forts and their much-needed cannons and ammunition. But the aid promised by Paris did not arrive because a large proportion of French convoys were being captured by the British, and in September 1759 Montcalm took refuge in the well-defended town of Quebec.

It was here that the English General James Wolfe came looking for the final showdown. On 13 September 1759, Wolfe arrived in Quebec, having brought a huge army of 9,000 soldiers and 18,000 sailors some 450 kilometres up the St Lawrence River in 170 boats – thanks in part to a thirty-year-old captain called James Cook who had a gift for surveying and mapmaking that was to stand him in good stead in later years.

With the French feeling very cosy in their fortified town on top of an impregnable cliff, it looked as if Wolfe's long river journey had been for nothing. But the General refused to accept defeat, and sent a section of his troops to attack the base of the river cliffs. This would not have bothered Montcalm except that the Brits had landed cannons, and he was afraid that the town would be bombarded, so he personally led 5,000 men out to chase the invaders back into the river.

Wolfe was also leading his troops, and had developed a daring, cool-headed way of dealing with frontal attacks. He let the charging Frenchmen come on until they were just 40 metres away, and then ordered his soldiers to unleash a single, murderous volley of musket fire, breaking the charge with one blow and sending the survivors – many of whom were the only half-convinced militiamen – into instant retreat. The battle was over in a quarter of an hour, and Quebec was taken.

Outside the city, both leaders were lying mortally wounded by musket fire. When Wolfe was told that the enemy were retreating, he said, 'God be praised, I will die in peace,' before doing exactly that. Montcalm, meanwhile, was informed that he wasn't going to survive his wounds, and moaned 'tant mieux' – 'so much the better'. He seemed to know the fight for Canada was lost.

Go home (if you know where that is)

France's other main town in inland Canada, Montreal, was surrendered the following year. The Brits left most of the non-military residents in peace, and they stayed there, cut off from France, preserving their archaic accent and having Catholic-sized families to try and boost their numbers – until just a generation ago, most Quebeckers had ten brothers and sisters.

The Acadiens were allowed no such luxury. For those who survived the initial imprisonment and expulsion, the suffering wasn't over yet.

The British colonies hadn't been warned of the refugees' imminent arrival, even though Governor William Shirley of New England had been involved in the whole business. Around 1,500 Acadiens disembarked in Virginia and North Carolina, but were refused entry and forced to live on the beach or on their ships until passage could be arranged to take them across to England. When they left again, two boats sank in the Atlantic, drowning about 300 people, and the survivors fared little better. For years, there were Acadiens living in huts by Southampton harbour, in disused potteries in Liverpool and in ruined buildings in Bristol, all of them considered prisoners of war.

Some 2,000 refugees arrived in Massachusetts, only to die of smallpox or be forced to take jobs as servants. And just down the coast in New York, 250 were imprisoned or forced into servitude.

In Maryland, the Acadiens were treated little better than slaves, and put in prison if they did not find a job, however menial, immediately. If they tried to leave the colony, they were shot. In Pennsylvania, meanwhile, they were packed into a shanty town outside Philadelphia (the 'city of brotherly love') and denied the right to work.

Many of them were encouraged to emigrate to Haiti, where they were used as slave labour by the island's French governor to build a naval base. *Bienvenus en France*.

In 1763, the French and British signed the Treaty of Paris, by which all of Canada except for a couple of tiny islands off the Atlantic coast – Saint-Pierre and Miquelon – was ceded to Britain. One effect of this peace was to improve relations enough for France to get back their prisoners of war, the Acadiens. Or, to put it another way, now that the war was over, the Brits and American colonists had a good excuse to get rid of the troublesome French-Canadian refugees.

Accordingly, almost all the Acadiens who had managed to survive their years of imprisonment, slavery, deprivation and bad English lessons were 'allowed' to emigrate from the American colonies and England. Several hundred went to Haiti, but soon regretted it – as before, the French treated them as badly as the English had done, and half of them died of malnutrition or disease. A few dozen were taken to the Falklands, but were quickly shipped out again when France gave the islands to Spain. Around 1,500 Acadiens made their way to French-held Louisiana, to have their name misspelt and become Cajuns.

And almost 4,000 went to France, amongst them seventy-eight families who were resettled on Belle-Île. These new Bellilois were the people who now have their own museum in the fortress at Le Palais. In the permanent exhibition, they are represented in heart-rending scenes of exile and separation in Canada, or gazing gratefully on the little cottages in their new homeland.

On the island, they were given land and livestock (which was a lot more than most French peasants had at the time) and, according to Belle-Île's tourist-office website, they 'didn't take long to integrate with the island's families, and mixed marriages were performed in the first year'.

Apart from the fact that the phrase 'mixed marriage' seems strange when applied to people of the same linguistic and ethnic origin (it seems strange whenever it is used, but even more so here), this can't have been the whole truth, because an Acadien-Cajun website says that 'due to livestock epidemics, crop failure, drought, *and local resistance** the colony failed in seven years.'

So it seems that the Acadiens weren't made to feel at home in France, either. They were, after all, taking land, food and work away from struggling French peasants. What was more, they kept trying to get off with the local *blondes*, and probably set up beaver traps that caught the islanders' cats and dogs. And to cap it all they spoke with funny accents.

Within a couple of years, over 1,500 of the Acadiens who had been 'repatriated' to France left again, most of them heading to join their former neighbours who were now getting established in Louisiana. This new refuge was to be temporary as well, though, because France was just about to sell it to those same welcoming American colonists.

Sacrament and *tabernacle*!

---

* *Mes italiques.*

8

Charles II: The Man Who Taught Everyone to Distrust French Motives for Doing Absolutely Anything

If France had decided to cast the French Canadians adrift on a leaky political raft, it was mainly because Canada was very low on their list of priorities. In the sixteenth, seventeenth and eighteenth centuries, France was much too busy harassing the countries huddled around it on the map of Europe to bother worrying about what was going on in the frozen north.

It was also during this time that the hostility between France and Britain took on its modern form. That is to say, there would be plenty more wars – right up to the defeat of Napoleon in 1815 – but even in peacetime, the two nations would be in a state of permanent suspicion. It was in the late seventeenth century that the childhood and adolescence of Anglo-French rivalry came to an end, and a fully mature relationship of fundamental distrust began. Which is why, today, British politicians constantly appear to be thinking: what are the French up to, how will it affect us, and should we sabotage it?

It's a feeling that has spread way beyond Anglo-French relations, and now causes practically every country on the planet to wonder what France really wants whenever its attention strays outside the haven of its modern borders.

And the person who brought this distrust of the French to fruition was a rather genial, frivolous man who was much more interested in hunting, playing cards and chasing women than politics – a fairly typical English king, in fact. He was Charles II.

What is most ironic is that, like so many English kings before him, he was half French. His mother was Henrietta Maria (or Henriette-Marie de France as she is more correctly called), daughter of France's King Henri IV, sister of King Louis XIII and aunt of the Sun King himself, Louis XIV.

In 1625, Henriette-Marie played her first, albeit passive, part in creating Anglo-French tensions during the preparations for her marriage to England's Prince of Wales, the future King Charles I. Negotiations over the dowry and the political implications of the union were highly complicated, and the diplomatic mission was entrusted to the hopeless Duke of Buckingham – the same man who ballsed up a British campaign to help the French Protestants hold on to La Rochelle.

While over in Paris to discuss pre-nuptials, the bisexual Buckingham had taken advantage of his visit to the French court to try and seduce one of the local aristocratic ladies. For a man of his position and good looks, this would have been nothing out of the ordinary. It could even have been seen as a gesture of international friendship – the Parisian beauty winning the approval of an English duke.

But the nice-but-dim Buckingham had set his sights on Anne, the wife of King Louis XIII. Imagine President Sarkozy coming to London for trade negotiations and trying it on with the Queen. Anglo-French relations would not exactly benefit (and neither, probably, would

President Sarkozy). This flamboyant frontal assault on the French Queen's honour did not go unnoticed at court, and it was fortunate for Buckingham that political necessity overrode King Louis's desire to have him castrated and thrown in the Seine. Despite the close diplomatic shave, the match between Charles II's parents went ahead, and history was allowed to take its course.

Gatecrashing the Louvre

The marriage was reasonably stable (particularly once the omnipresent Buckingham died and left the couple in peace), although the devoutly Catholic Henriette-Marie is often blamed for causing Charles I to stand up so unbendingly to the Protestant English Parliamentarians and thereby provoking the Civil War. In 1644, when the fighting got too hot for comfort, she went into exile in Paris, where she was joined in 1646 by her son, Prince Charles.

At this point, Henriette-Marie was even more at the heart of the French court than ever, because her brother, Louis XIII, had died and France was being ruled by the boy King Louis XIV and his mother Anne, who was Henriette-Marie's sister-in-law. Henriette-Marie was therefore one of the senior royals living in the Louvre, all of whom were bonding together to preserve their family's fragile hold on power via the *enfant* Louis.

The brain behind the throne, though, was an Italian-born cardinal called Mazarin. He was the regent Anne's guiding hand – and some say his hands did much more than just guide her. Mazarin was wholly in favour of welcoming the royal refugees from England. A Catholic, he didn't want a strong Protestant republic across the Channel giving the militant French Protestants, the Huguenots, ideas. Mazarin was therefore keen to have

Prince Charles in France as a potential weapon to be unleashed against England if the monarchy fell.

However, despite his distaste for Protestants, he didn't want to exclude altogether the chance of allying with a future Protestant-ruled England to fight his arch enemy, Spain. He was even considering marrying a French princess to Oliver Cromwell's son in order to defuse any future Anglo-French tensions. It was therefore important to him not to make it obvious that he was supporting Charles I in the Civil War.

Poor sixteen-year-old Prince Charles had no idea what a Parisian hornets' nest he was stepping into. He just thought he was going to live with his mum while his dad got a few domestic policy issues sorted out. So when he arrived at the French court in June 1646, Charles was dismayed to feel as though he was gate-crashing a garden party – instead of being welcomed into his mother's family, he was completely ignored by Mazarin, King Louis XIV and the Queen Mother Anne for two whole months, and forced to hang around the corridors and anterooms of the Louvre hoping for an invitation to something more exciting than a wig-weaving display by the second cousin of the third wife of a duke's hunting horse.

Not surprisingly, Henriette-Marie was shocked by this implied insult to her own royal status, and repeatedly asked for an explanation as to why her son, a prince, was not granted so much as a five-minute audience with anyone of his own rank.

The excuses given by Mazarin were a miracle of political evasiveness. The protocol of this unplanned visit was, he said, so complicated that lengthy discussions were needed before an audience could take place. The problems were endless. Should Charles see the King in one of his salons? If so, who would sit and who would stand? And where exactly would the sitting, if it happened at all, happen? The chairs at such get-togethers were arranged in a strictly pre-defined order, and who sat (or did not sit) where was a matter of endless gossip and rivalry. Since Charles was heir to a throne, it might be necessary for him to take precedence over Louis XIV's younger brother, Philippe, who could construe this as a snub. And Louis himself, who was only seven at the time, was in a delicate position vis-à-vis his English cousin Charles, who was a teenage giant at nearly six feet; it must not look as if Louis was being belittled.

In short, Charles and Henriette-Marie would just have to wait on the sidelines of court life until all the practical details had been hammered out.

Charles uses the French art of mime

In truth, of course, Mazarin was simply trying to make it look to the outside world as though Charles was an unwelcome guest, and it wasn't until August 1646 that Charles and his mother were invited by Louis and Anne the regent for a three-day stay at Fontainebleau castle, a royal country residence south of Paris.

The visit did not get off to a good start. When they arrived at the chateau, Charles disappointed his hosts because he couldn't speak or understand a single word of French. Parisians are never pleased when Anglophones are unable to speak their language, but in Charles's case it was even less excusable – not only had he been living in France for two whole months but his mother was French. Was he stupid, they wondered, or was this a deliberate insult?

Luckily for Charles, his immense height and royal bearing argued in his favour. 'His mouth was large and ugly but he had a very fine figure,' observed one generous French courtier.

Next day Charles at last had an official audience with Louis XIV, who, it was noted, let his English cousin sit in an armchair. This was judged to be a great compliment, not because it was Louis's favourite chair, but because very few people on the planet were allowed to park their backsides so close to a French monarch – and not just on some low, stumpy-legged stool, either, but a comfy chair. It was the ultimate accolade, and clearly worth waiting two months for.

Observers were even more impressed when, at the end of the audience, Louis was seen to accompany his guest as far as the staircase. This was an almost unheard-of honour – most visitors were obliged to reverse out of the room, bowing and scraping, hoping that they didn't make fools of themselves by backing into a duchess or falling down the stairs.

The only blot on the diplomatic copybook was that, aside from the niceties of protocol, the audience was a complete farce. Both boys spent the whole half-hour or so in silence, smiling at each other but not saying a word for fear of making grammatical mistakes in a foreign language or not being understood in their own. Even if they had learned '*bonjour*' and 'hi', they weren't going to risk having their accent laughed at.

However, life at court must have seemed fairly absurd at the best of times, and no one appears to have taken offence. The two boys did some male bonding by hunting together, and at the end of three days the visit was declared a success. From the English point of view, it hadn't been perfect – Charles didn't receive any gifts or money, for example – but as one English courtier observed, 'these civilities are better than neglects'.

That winter, the French court returned to Paris and this time Charles was allowed to join in the fun. He ignored his tutors' entreaties to study, and devoted himself to enjoying balls, masques (costume parties) and plays, the only irritation being that his mother Henriette-Marie had taken it into her head to try and improve their family finances by marrying him off to one of his immensely wealthy, and hugely patronizing, French cousins.

The lucky girl was Anne-Marie-Louise d'Orléans, known at court as Mademoiselle – the title traditionally given to the most senior female heir to the throne. She was the daughter of a brother of Louis XIII, a blood princess three years older than Charles and, by her own account at least, a good catch. In her memoirs, she wrote of 'my fine figure, my good looks, my pale complexion, the splendour of my fair hair'. Not exactly a shrinking violet.

Charles's mother had no problem convincing Mademoiselle that the English Prince was crazy about her – how could he be anything else? But Charles was having none of his mother's schemes, and began a single-minded sabotage campaign. Not only did he refuse to woo Anne-Marie, he said that he couldn't speak to her because he didn't know any French. He was forced to squire her to functions and escort her home afterwards, but didn't open his mouth except to eat and drink. It was almost as though he had bets going on how long he could hold out.

His mother alternated between bouts of fury at her stubborn son and desperate face-saving sessions with Anne-Marie. Charles was just shy, she said, and his silence was nothing more than a symptom of his infatuation – though this lie became slightly less credible when courtiers observed that Charles had learned enough French to chat up the lovely duchesse de Châtillon, who was notorious for her string of noble lovers. He was also seen dancing and joking with maids of honour at the same soirées where he maintained a stony silence with Anne-Marie. The Princess's bafflement soon turned to indignation, and the marriage was officially called off.

In purely financial terms, this was annoying, and politically it was a total disaster, because the new Republican rulers of England were demanding that Louis XIV should hand over his royal refugee for imprisonment. Unmarried and tied to France only by his mother's nationality, Charles was in danger of becoming Cardinal Mazarin's latest bargaining tool.

But then in the spring of 1648, Charles was spirited out of Paris to join his father's cause, leaving behind him at least one furious princess, a few fondly smiling French ladies and a general impression that he was a bit too fun-loving and disrespectful to be a political threat if ever he came to power in England – which goes to show that you shouldn't underestimate a man just because he wears a big floppy wig.*

No way to win a wife

When Charles returned to Paris shortly after his father's execution in 1649, he was a king without a country and – worse – without any money. And it seems to have been sheer poverty that drove him to give in to his mother's pleas and have a more serious go at courting Mademoiselle Anne-Marie-Louise.

Henry Jermyn, Henriette-Marie's secretary, was duly sent to Mademoiselle with letters professing Charles's boundless admiration for her. This time, even Mazarin was in favour of the match and informed Mademoiselle that Charles was 'passionately in love' with her, despite all the evidence to the contrary.

* Apologies to historical hair experts for this anachronism. In fact, according to the diarist Samuel Pepys, Charles did not start wearing a wig until his hair went grey in 1663.

With the tradition of marrying princesses off at the age of twelve to wrinkly old kings in exchange for a promise not to declare war in the near future, it seems strange that everyone should have gone to such lengths to convince Anne-Marie that this was going to be a love match. But she was acutely conscious of her wealth and status, and had an annoying habit of trying to organize her own marriage. The only option was to appeal to her vanity and convince her that she was irresistible.

Charles (or, more likely, his mother) sent word that although he was now a poor, landless king – with the word 'king' no doubt written slightly larger than 'poor' and 'landless' – if Anne-Marie consented to the match, he would marry her, and then go away to 'seek his fortune'.

The ploy failed. The surprisingly modern Mademoiselle said that she was not some object to be wed and then abandoned, and refused. Even so, it seems that she was tempted by the offer, because she later confessed in her memoirs that all she wanted was for Charles to woo her by whispering sweet nothings – *douceurs* – to her: 'Without being a coquette, I might listen to a king who says he wants to marry me.' If Charles had only played the French lover and told her that she was as scrumptious as foie gras and sweeter than *crème brûlée*, he could have become a ridiculously wealthy chateau-owner, living it up in the Loire Valley until the English decided to invite him back.

Despite her initial refusal, Anne-Marie was persuaded to give the young Englishman yet another chance and meet him at the royal chateau of Compiègne, north of Paris. On the day of the visit, Anne-Marie even got up early to have her hair curled, a piece of coquetry for which she was teased by her ladies in waiting. It seemed that Charles was just one 'oh, you've changed your hair-do' away from a massive dowry.

The French royal party, including the young King Louis XIV, accompanied Anne-Marie out into the forest, where it had been agreed that Charles would meet them. And when the English King arrived, the reunion was an affectionate one. Protocol demanded that Charles talk to Louis first, and this he did, chatting amiably in French about hunting while the expectant Anne-Marie waited for him to turn his attention to less gory matters. But when his man-to-man with Louis came to an end and the ladies tried to engage him in more flirtatious conversation, to everyone's astonishment he said he couldn't speak French and, once again, didn't utter a word to poor Anne-Marie.

After dinner at the chateau, things got even worse. Someone was unrealistic enough to suggest that the happy couple-to-be might want to be left alone, and poor Mademoiselle had to suffer the indignity of watching Charles repeat the mime act he had perfected on so many previous occasions. This time, he sat completely mute by her side for a full quarter of an hour. Finally, in desperation, Anne-Marie summoned a gentleman to join them, at which point Charles came out of his trance and began merrily chatting to the newcomer in French.

Charles knew, of course, that this was no way to win a woman, French or otherwise. By now he was quite an expert on the subject. So why did he go to such elaborate lengths to insult Anne-Marie? Was her new curly hairdo too ridiculous for him? Did he still have the bet on with his courtiers? Or perhaps he really did want to marry Anne-Marie for financial and political reasons but was just too sincere to go through with it. He was, after all, still a teenager, and not (yet) a cynical man of the world.

In fact, it seems that he had two main motives for annoying Mademoiselle and having a bit of a joke at Mazarin's expense. First, he was probably just paying lip service to his mother's urgings. She was behind the marriage idea, and was much keener than Charles on an Anglo-French union. Secondly, and perhaps more importantly, Charles could not forgive the French for failing to send their condolences when his father was executed – to avoid appearing overtly Royalist in Cromwell's eyes, Mazarin had not even sent a message of sympathy. Charles didn't blame the affable young Louis, but he wanted nothing to do with the French political establishment.

When he left France this time, Charles told his mother that he was going to 'obey his own reason and judgement' from now on, and 'did as good as desire her not to trouble herself in his affairs'.

The seeds of the great Anglo-French falling-out had been sown.

Say it with chairs

In 1651, after an aborted attempt to regain the English throne, Charles returned briefly to France and regaled the court with the story of his dramatic escape disguised as a woodcutter, and his risky trek across England during which he had actually had to cook some of his own meals. He had been hidden and helped by a whole succession of loyal supporters, he told everyone, but refused to reveal a single name for fear of treachery. He no longer trusted the French.

He was now even more penniless than before, and seemed unlikely ever to reign – which may explain why he resorted to torturing poor Mademoiselle Anne-Marie yet again. This time, though, he deigned to speak to her, and even turned on the charm, saying how good it was to be back in Paris and that he hoped they would get the chance to dance together soon. Against all odds,

Anne-Marie actually gave him the time of day, and they began to meet up, with Charles breaking protocol and leaving his allotted armchair to go and squat with the girls. An English Cromwellian spy noted that the King had taken to 'wit and jesting' with Anne-Marie. At last, it seems, Charles had learned to fake it the French way.

But so had Anne-Marie. It turned out that she was simply playing her old English tormentor along, and had set her mind on marrying Louis XIV – an absurd plan, because Louis was eleven years younger and planning to marry a foreign bride. In any case, Charles was definitely off her wish list. And as soon as he discovered this, Charles gave up all pretence. At soirées, he began to stay in his designated armchair rather than sitting with Anne-Marie. Royal seats said it all once again – the on-off courtship was finished.

The inevitable result of this was that Charles and his mother began to feel the pinch. Begging from Louis XIV produced plenty of promises but little cash, and Charles would often lose that at cards.

Several of Charles's courtiers complained that they had no carriage and had to travel around Paris on foot, and King Charles himself was, as one of his followers said, 'reduced to so low a condition that he is forced to eat his meals in taverns, having not the commodity of dining at home'. French restaurants clearly weren't Michelin-star standard in those days.

In the end, it was Mazarin who gave Charles the cash he needed. In 1654, the cardinal decided that he wanted the troublesome Englishman out of France so that he could sign a formal treaty with Oliver Cromwell. So Mazarin gave Charles a lump sum, and the young English exile left Paris on horseback, with his clothes and bedding travelling alongside in a simple cart. He went to seek refuge with his sister Mary, who was nominally

Queen of Holland and had some reasonable accommodation to offer him, even if the Dutch court was a tad more Puritan than Paris.

Charles was in danger of becoming just another bitter ex-royal stranded far from his throne, like some Romanian princeling photographed in a Swiss casino alongside a gaggle of face-lifted nouveau-riche widows. As one of Charles's courtiers reported (rather exaggeratedly), 'the King is now as low as to human understanding he can be.'

Charles signs a pact with the *diable*

Of course, as we now know, Charles was not destined to sponge off his sister for ever, because Oliver Cromwell died in 1658, and in 1660 the Royalists took control of England and told the King he was back in a job.

He wasn't a great success as a monarch, and as his friend, the satirist John Wilmot, Earl of Rochester, wrote, he 'never said a foolish thing, nor ever did a wise one.' His biggest weakness was his calamitous financial management, and it was this that drew him dangerously close to France.

In 1661, Charles married his youngest sister, Henrietta Anne, to Louis XIV's brother Philippe, and although the marriage was an unhappy one – mainly because Philippe was a violently jealous husband despite being openly gay – at least Charles had a reliable ally in Paris. And it was Henrietta Anne who began the negotiations with Louis for what would later become known as the Secret Treaty of Dover. (Obviously, it was not called that at the time because it might have made it obvious that Charles was trying to hide something.)

There was a good reason for keeping the discussions secret, because if they had been public, some influential Englishmen might well have decided to send the King straight back into exile, or worse. In essence, Charles was willing to guarantee that, in return for a sizeable annual backhander from Louis XIV, he would support France's territorial claims in Holland – with which Charles had family connections, don't forget – and convert England and Scotland back to Catholicism. He would even allow a French army to come to England and 'assist with the conversion'. Charles was selling not only his soul but his family and his country.

The Secret Treaty was signed in 1670, and led to Charles's Royal Declaration of Indulgence in 1672, in which he surprised everyone by offering his countrymen complete religious freedom. This was purportedly aimed at ending the persecution of non-conformist Protestants (like the Puritans who sailed to America on the *Mayflower*), but Parliament rightly suspected Charles of trying to open the way for a national conversion to Catholicism, and blocked the move.

Charles had therefore failed to deliver on the religious clause of the treaty, but he kept his word on the military front, and entered into what is now known as the Third Dutch War. And it was during this relatively minor conflict that Anglo-French relations took their irreversible turn for the worse.

The war began in April 1672, when a French army invaded Holland by land while a Franco-British fleet tried and failed to impose a blockade on Dutch shipping. Baulking at the cost of the campaign, Charles quickly offered the Dutch a peace agreement whereby he would recognize their independence and even cede the British herring quota, in exchange for (you guessed it) a large cash payment. But these negotiations failed and the war lumbered on, characterized mainly by some bizarre naval encounters.

In June 1672, for example, Dutch ships crossed the

Channel, hoping to attack the Anglo-French fleet as it lay at anchor off the Suffolk coast. The French spotted the Dutch on the horizon and quickly raised anchor, but instead of engaging them, the French ships 'accidentally' took the wrong course, sailing away from the enemy and contenting themselves with shooting from a distance. This left the English to fight alone and in the ensuing Battle of Solebay, the English commander, Charles's brother James, had to change ships twice when his flag-ships were destroyed under him, and the Earl of Sandwich (an ancestor of the inventor of the snack of the same name) was killed, his charred body recognizable only from remnants of his clothing.

A year later, in June 1673, the first Battle of Schooneveld went much the same way. In this engagement off the Dutch coast, a massively superior Anglo-French fleet commanded by Charles II's German cousin, Prince Rupert of the Rhine, was unexpectedly beaten off by the Dutch – a defeat that was mainly caused by a large gap that suddenly appeared in the French line, enabling the Dutch to launch a piercing counter-attack. This rapid manoeuvre was acknowledged by the French as a piece of brilliant sailing, and they practically applauded as the Dutch floated by and started to fire broadsides at the English.

In the second battle of the same name a week later, a similar debacle occurred when French ships failed to follow the English into an attack, claiming that they did not understand Prince Rupert's signals. Worse, when the French came under fire, they disengaged immediately rather than replying, and left the English fleet to take all the punishment.

In English minds, these French failures to hold their own at sea suddenly took on a sinister aspect. Was it all down to misunderstandings between the Brits and the French in the heat of battle? Or could it be that France's plan all along was to let England and Holland destroy one another's shipping and bankrupt themselves with excessive military spending, so that France could step into the void and conquer them both?

Charles II was no genius, but he began to see that he had been royally had by Louis XIV. The French had even managed to destabilize England's internal politics – by agreeing to attack Protestant Holland, Charles had fuelled fears at home that he was a closet Catholic. Parliament had tried to clarify the situation by passing a law requiring all government officials to denounce Catholicism as 'idolatry and superstition', only for Charles's brother James to resign from the military rather than take the vow. Suddenly, the two sides of Britain's religious schism were shaking crucifixes at each other again, and Charles II was forced to make peace with the Dutch to avoid a repeat of the civil strife that had cost his father his head and his throne.

As with Charles's treatment of Anne-Marie, a very basic question about his motives has to be asked: what the hell was he up to? This was far more serious than snubbing a French princess – it was treason. And his only possible excuse for trying to sell his realm's independence was that his former poverty and insecurity made him do foolish things for money. Or that he had matured into a frivolous, cash-loving cynic. If the truth had been known at the time, he might well have ended up on the same chopping block as his dad.

But in the final analysis Charles can probably be forgiven, because his crude attempt at subterfuge actually strengthened his country in one vitally important way.

From now on, no one in Britain – Catholic or Protestant, king or queen, soldier or civilian – would ever trust French political motives again.

9

Champagne: Dom Pérignon Gets It Wrong

> 'Women are like champagne – when they come in French wrapping, they're more expensive.'
>
> M. Ageyev, *Novel with Cocaine*

France is a very protectionist country, especially where its culture is concerned. And the part of its culture that it is most protective of, and cares most about, is not cinema, painting or the great French novel, but food and drink. It is no coincidence that the French words for culture and agriculture are the same – both are *la culture*.

And the part of its (agri)culture of which it is proudest, and which brings it the best combination of cash and prestige from abroad, is champagne. Or Champagne with a capital C, because it is of course a proper name.

In fact, France cares so much about Champagne that it had a clause protecting the name inserted into the Treaty of Versailles, the peace agreement that marked the official end of the First World War. Yes, a whole generation of young Frenchmen lay mangled in the mud, several hundred thousand civilians had been killed, a barely

236

credible 10 per cent of the French population had been wounded in the fighting, and France still found time to worry about wine labels.

Their concern arose from the fact that during the war the area around Reims had suffered terribly from bombardments and trench-digging, and Champagne production had understandably fallen. It is, after all, quite difficult to harvest grapes while you are being mortar-bombed. France was therefore afraid that other sparkling wines, from America, Italy, Spain or even Germany, might step into the gap in the market. Consequently, Article 275 (out of 440) of the Treaty of Versailles states that 'Germany undertakes . . . to respect any law . . . in force in any Allied or Associated State . . . defining or regulating the right to any regional appellation in respect of wine or spirits produced in the State' and that 'the importation, exportation, manufacture, distribution, sale or offering for sale of products or articles bearing regional appellations inconsistent with such law or order shall be prohibited by the German Government and repressed.'

In essence, this meant that, yes, world peace was important, but only as important as the exclusive right to call France's sparkling wine Champagne.

As a result, it is against international law to prefix the brand name with a national adjective like 'English' or 'Spanish'. And it is practically a human-rights abuse to use the words 'Champagne' and 'elderflower' in the same sentence. Only America has stood up to Champagne's official regulatory board, Le Comité Interprofessionnel du Vin de Champagne (CIVC). The US government insists that wine made in California using the same types of grape and the same methods may be marketed as 'Californian Champagne' – a stand that is possible because although America signed the Treaty of

Versailles, it never ratified it. (No fools, those Americans.)

Still, one might say, the French winemakers are entirely justified in protecting their unique product. After all, it was invented by a French monk called Dom Pérignon in 1668, right?

Wrong.

Sorry, France, but Champagne is English in all but name.

A man of some Merret

The French version of the Champagne story has a partially sighted Benedictine monk, Pierre (aka Dom – an honorary title derived from the Latin *dominus* or master) Pérignon, a native of the Champagne district, becoming the accountant and cellar master at the abbey of Hautvillers near Épernay in 1668, and developing the Champagne we know today by perfecting the fermentation process and turning still wine into fizz.

In reality, though, he spent much of his career at the monastery doing everything he could to make Champagne *less* bubbly, because the bottles at his winery kept exploding. Wines bottled in the autumn would go to sleep, as it were, during the winter, only for their yeasts to come out of hibernation in spring and turn the wine cellars into an early version of French underground weapons testing.

Dom Pérignon therefore set about trying to make the wine purer, to prevent excess fermentation. He had his grapes picked early in the morning, when it was cool, decreed that damaged grapes should be thrown away, and developed a gentler way of pressing the fruit so that the juice from the flesh of the grape would not interact too much with the skin. In this way, he was able to make a white wine from red grapes, which gave the abbey's

Dom Pérignon, the French monk who supposedly 'invented' Champagne, suffers an attack of premature excorkulation. In fact, he wanted to *reduce* the sparkliness of his region's wines.

finances a real boost – red grapes were much less susceptible to bad weather, while white wines sold for better prices.

The abbey was now producing purer wines and making higher profits, but still had to cure the explosion problem, which was actually getting worse – when Dom P. (if one may be so familiar with the legendary monk) began sealing his bottles efficiently with corks instead of wooden pegs, it only caused the wine to burst out of the bottom of the bottle.

It is often said that when Dom Pérignon first took a gulp of fizzy Champagne, he exclaimed, 'I am tasting the stars!' But that was just an advertising slogan invented in the nineteenth century, and in fact he is more likely to have groaned something about the 'bubbles de merde'.

A short distance to the north, however, there were some people who were perfectly happy with exploding Champagne, and who had been happy even before Dom Pérignon started to purify it. Well, they weren't so keen on the actual explosions, which they tried to remedy, but they loved the joyful bubbliness of the wine.

They were the English.

It was just after the Plague of 1665 and the Great Fire of London. Britain had recently got rid of Cromwell and his Puritans, who had forbidden dancing, music, theatre and anything in life that might make people giggle, and had inherited Charles II, the King who had recently emerged from something as close as a monarch can get to poverty. All in all, the Brits were game for a bit of fun. They had taken French bubbly to their hearts and were so relieved that it was legal to enjoy themselves again that they had probably invented games like Stick a Champagne Bottle up Each Nostril and Jump.

Wine from the Champagne region had first been made popular in England in the early 1660s by a French soldier, writer and bon vivant called Charles de Saint-Évremond, who had been forced to seek exile in London after getting into trouble in Paris for criticizing the all-powerful Cardinal Mazarin. The wine that Saint-Évremond imported from France in barrels was meant to be still, but frothed a lot in the large containers, and had a tendency to explode when bottled. This, however, ceased to be a problem for English wine merchants when glass production was industrialized thanks to the development of coal-fired furnaces in Newcastle. Suddenly, it was possible to make much thicker and more resistant bottles than any being turned out in France, and Londoners could have fun with the controlled pop of a Champagne cork instead of diving for cover under the table.

In case French readers feel tempted to contest all this, there is documentary proof in an article presented to the Royal Society in 1662 by a scientist called Christopher Merret.* He was born in Gloucestershire in either 1614 or 1615 (the Champagne seems to have clouded his memory), studied at Oxford (a notorious training ground for heavy drinkers), and in 1661 translated and expanded an Italian treatise on bottle manufacture. It seems to be this that drew his attention to the question of exploding Champagne, because the following year he published a paper entitled 'Some Observations Concerning the Ordering of Wines'. In this, he tried to explain why wine became bubbly, and identified the second fermentation in the bottle as the main cause. He also described adding sugar or molasses to wine to bring on this second fermentation *deliberately*. Sparkliness was a positive thing, Merret said, and could be produced in

* Merret, whose name is sometimes spelled Merrett, was a friend of Samuel Pepys and got drunk with the diarist on 22 January 1666. Whether it was on Champagne, Pepys doesn't say.

any wine, particularly now that England was making bottles that were capable of holding in the bubbles. Thus, while Dom Pérignon was trying to do away with the fizz, the Brits wanted more.

And these days, they're not the only ones; modern Champagne-makers use Merret's method, and add doses of sugar to give their wine its characteristic sparkle, a technique they call *méthode champenoise*, although strictly speaking, if one respects the concept of a discovery belonging to the person who first publishes a scientific paper on a subject, it should surely be called the Merret Method, or *méthode merretoise*. After all, if you don't respect that concept, what is to stop me claiming credit for the theory of relativity? (Apart from the fact that I don't understand it, of course.)

Sparkling English wit

Champagne (or 'Champaigne' as contemporary Brits spelled it, continuing the art of misspelling French place names they had begun so honourably with Agincourt and Calais) was celebrated in seventeenth-century British literature. The Irish dramatist George Farquhar, for example, an exile in London after he almost killed an actor while using a real sword in a stage fight, sings its praises in his 1698 play *Love and a Bottle*.

'Champaigne,' one character says, 'a fine liquor which all your great Beaux drink to make 'em witty.' Another describes the 'witty wine' in words that capture all its sparkle: 'How it puns and quibbles in the glass!'

It was this popularity amongst British socialites that made the French wonder what all the fuss was about, and convinced King Louis XIV to adopt Champagne as his wine of choice, making it de rigueur amongst the French some time after London's witty beaux had started the fashion – and, of course, only once it had become safe for the Sun King to drink thanks to the sturdy English bottles being imported into France.

Meanwhile, Dom Pérignon was perfecting his wine-making techniques, and invented the method of stocking Champagne bottles with their necks pointing diagonally downwards so that sediment collects near the cork and can be removed more easily. But this again was to stop his bottles exploding rather than to generate more fizz.

And so there we have it. Champagne is a wine that owes its sparkle to a technique identified by an English scientist, its marketability to English bottle-making technology, and its popularity to the fun-loving dandies of seventeenth-century London.

Naturally, the French can lay claim to the regional name, because Champagne is undeniably in France, but in all fairness one could argue (if one really wanted to annoy the French) that the drink should be called Champagne à l'anglaise, 'English-style Champagne', to distinguish it from the flat, bubble-free wine that Dom Pérignon wanted to produce. One could even write to Moët & Chandon and suggest that they change the name of their Dom Pérignon brand to Merret. Less fancy-sounding, perhaps, but more accurate.

Of course, given that they're protected by the Treaty of Versailles, EU regulations and (probably) a little-known clause in the Declaration of Human Rights, the French can shrug off such suggestions. But for historical reasons, there really is no reason why they should object to labels marked 'American Champagne' or 'English Champagne'. If it's quality they're worried about, then they can stop worrying right away – sparkling wines produced in the USA have been highly respected for a long time, and now English-made bubbly is on the rise, too.

This improvement in the English product is apparently

due to the onset of global warming, which is causing ideal Champagne-producing conditions to shift north from France towards vineyards with similar soil on the other side of the Channel. It's a delicious historical irony – all the big industrial nations that signed the Treaty of Versailles (including France) are polluting the atmosphere with carbon dioxide and returning Champagne to its true spiritual home, England.

Santé!

10

Eclipsing the Sun King

Louis XIV called himself le Roi Soleil, 'the Sun King', to make it blindingly clear to his people that he was the source of life itself in France. A democrat he was not.

Louis also referred to himself as Jupiter, the king of Roman deities, god of the sky and guardian of law and order on Earth, though this was mainly to convince his male courtiers that it was OK for him to sleep with their wives. 'There is no shame in sharing with Jupiter,' he would say as he escorted away a duke's young bride for a royal rogering.

Louis XIV still holds the record for the longest-reigning European monarch ever – seventy-two years – surpassing Queen Elizabeth II and even Queen Victoria. And although the modern French may not admit to being monarchists, they revere him almost as much as Joan of Arc, Napoleon and Johnny Hallyday.

However, as we saw in Chapter 8, the Sun King's supposed omnipotence did not make him infallible. And it was precisely Louis's belief in his God-given powers that would lead him to underestimate two great leaders who, before the end of his reign in 1715, were able to

King Louis XIV (1638–1715) thought of himself as a god, but his taste in clothes was not exactly divine.

secure Britain's place at the heart of world power – that is, in direct opposition to France.

And it was all to do with his intestines . . .

The daily life of a god

For Louis XIV, sleeping with his courtiers' wives was just one way of flaunting his divine power. In fact, his whole lifestyle was geared to proving his magnificence. Every day at court followed a rigid pattern determined by the King – like the sun, it was said, one always knew where he was. More importantly, the courtiers therefore knew where they had to be.

In 1682 Louis moved the court to his father's old chateau at Versailles, 16 kilometres southwest of the Louvre, even though a massive renovation scheme was only half finished. There were still around 20,000 workmen laying out the gardens, building new wings on the palace and decorating the interior.

Louis had his reasons for forcing the French aristocratic establishment to uproot itself from Paris. There, rival factions had their strongholds, and intrigue and rebellion were possible. In this isolated chateau in the middle of a forest, the nobles were either at court or they were not – there was no half-measure. And, given that Louis was the dispenser of all power within France, they had better be there if they wanted money or influence.

Soon, a whole new town grew up around the palace as the courtiers built houses, either for themselves, if they were not important enough to be invited to reside *chez* Louis, or for their servants, who were forbidden to live at the palace.

At eight thirty every morning, the Sun King would rise, awoken with a mug of tea or broth to perform the *levée*, or getting-up ceremony. And quite a performance it was, conducted in the presence of the *petites entrées*, the small group of people who were permitted to see the King in his nightshirt. These were usually his doctors, his valets and the *porte-chaise d'affaires* – the 'carrier of the business chair'. No, he wasn't an office furniture remover; he was the man who brought in the commode. This officer of the court, who had paid a small fortune to acquire the hereditary job for his family, arrived carrying a highly decorated Portaloo, on which Louis would sit while his barber straightened his morning wig (less high-rise than the afternoon and evening one) and then, on alternate days, shaved him. Meanwhile, Louis would do his *affaires* – his business – and the doctors would examine the results for signs of ill health.

Once the ceremony was over and the royal backside had been wiped with a cotton swab, the King was ready to receive the select group of courtiers – males only – who were allowed to watch him being dressed. This honour was granted to about a hundred of them, and the crowds in the bedchamber were so dense that pick-pocketing of watches and purses was not uncommon. It was very expensive to live at Versailles, and impoverished aristocrats were not above supplementing their incomes with a dip of their manicured fingers.

At ten o'clock, Louis attended a thirty-minute Mass, which often included new choral music written for him by France's most gifted composers. On his way to and from the chapel, the King would touch sick people who had been allowed to enter the palace to take advantage of the divine monarch's self-declared healing powers.

Later, after two hours or so conferring with his ministers and hearing petitions from people who had managed to talk, bribe or sleep their way into an audience, Louis had lunch. Starting at one o'clock sharp, he would eat alone, usually facing a window with a view of his gardens. That is to say, he was *eating* alone, but he was watched by a huge crowd of people as he consumed an immense meal that might consist of a whole pheasant, a whole duck, a joint of mutton and slices of ham, accompanied by salads, pastries and fruit. As with his *levée*, the Sun King's chewing and guzzling was deemed a fascinating ceremony that the courtiers were privileged to attend.

At 2 p.m., the King's afternoon entertainment would begin. This varied slightly, and might include a walk in the park with a group of ladies, shooting in the grounds of Versailles, or hunting on horseback in the forest. With Louis at large, courtiers had a great opportunity to attract his attention and obtain a royal favour – an invitation to the *levée*, for example, a post in one of the King's ministries, promotion in the army, or a grant to improve their chateau.

People were noticed because of their fine clothes (courtiers would change outfits several times a day), by making some witty remark as the King passed (a juicy titbit of gossip about one of his enemies, for example), or simply by being a beautiful woman.

One thing that no courtier could do, though, was break the strict rules attached to these activities. When the monarch rode, for example, no one could stop or dismount unless he did. And Louis was possessed with that dangerous combination: a cruel sense of humour and a large bladder. He could ride for hours after lunch without peeing, unlike most of his courtiers. It was the ultimate in control freakery – Louis's lackeys were forced to wet themselves rather than breach royal protocol.

Starting at 6 p.m., a *soirée d'appartement* began, and Louis would stroll 'casually' through his apartments, stopping to chat to courtiers as they gambled at cards, played billiards, danced, or just conversed. Everyone was, of course, obliged to be having a wonderful time, and it is easy to imagine the bets rising extravagantly, the trick shots getting more daring and the jokes growing louder and more rehearsed as His Sunniness approached.

At 10 p.m. dinner, or *souper*, was served. It was a less lonely affair than lunch, attended by several hundred courtiers and servants, all of them standing except the royal family, who were seated at table to eat, and the duchesses, who were allowed to watch while squatting on stools. Again, there were strict rules – Louis hated to be distracted while eating, so everyone was required to be silent as he and the family members in attendance took their pick of the forty-odd dishes on offer. The food was brought to table by a procession of servants who would march through the palace from the kitchens, and anyone seeing the caravan on its way to the King had to bow or curtsey to the lucky dishes that were about to disappear into the divine entrails.

Finally, at eleven o'clock came the official sundown, the *couchée*, which was the *levée* in reverse, ending with the King doing his *affaires* again, removing his wig, getting into his nightshirt and going to bed. Though he didn't always stay there, and often preferred to pad along one of the passages that led to nearby bedrooms where his favourites would be waiting for Jupiter to appear on their horizon, no doubt with the occasional husband hiding under the bed whispering, 'Don't forget to ask him about that shipbuilding contract.'

All in all, during his typical day, Louis would be observed and admired by up to 10,000 people, most of them obliged – if they wanted to retain their status in the country – to spend the vast sums of money necessary for court life. They had to buy new clothes, wigs, jewels and carriages, take part in the obligatory gambling and bribe palace officials for the smallest favours. It was a life of tyranny by politeness, a dictatorship of boredom and butt-licking, a never-ending pantomime designed to keep the potentially troublesome French aristocracy firmly in its place.

Meanwhile, the lower strata of the population were informed of the King's continuing godliness with a constant supply of etchings, pamphlets, paintings, tapestries and medals celebrating his every act. The monarchy was so self-assured that opposition was unthinkable.

Or was it . . . ?

William of Orange gets his juices flowing

William of Orange, who would later usurp the throne of James II and become King William III of England, was originally little more than the feudal lord of a tiny independent state in southern France. Orange, consisting of a few square kilometres around the ancient town of the same name, was a sort of mini-Liechtenstein that had been inherited by a Dutch family, the Nassaus, in the mid-sixteenth century.

Although it was such a tiny fiefdom, its rulers claimed the right to be called Princes of Orange, probably to compensate for the fact that in their native country, Holland, they had the much less glamorous title of *stadhouder*, or 'lieutenant', the prosaic name given to the hereditary rulers of a large part of Holland.

William had not even been born when he had this responsibility thrust upon him – his father died of smallpox a week before his birth in 1650 – and at first his Dutch territories were ruled by a regency that included William's mother, Mary, the sister of King Charles II of England.

William's family was stripped of the title of *stadhouder* in 1650, a reaction to their dictatorial ways, and it looked as though William would grow up, like the young Charles II, as a jobless prince. His prospects looked even gloomier when his mother died – also of smallpox – in 1660 during a trip to England to visit her brother, thus weakening the family's royal connections. And things could have hit rock bottom in 1672 when Uncle Charles attacked Holland, having made a secret Anglo-French pact with Louis XIV.*

That year is still known in Holland as the *rampjaar*, the *annus horribilis*, but it was a blessing in disguise to William, who rose spectacularly to the occasion. He had his family's rivals bumped off, took charge of the army, and even came up with Dutch history's most famous quotation. When threatened by the Anglo-French that his country would be trampled out of existence if he didn't surrender, William replied, 'There is one certain means by which I can be sure never to see my country's ruin. I will die in the last ditch.' This bit of repartee became so famous that 'last-ditch' was adopted into the English language.

William then ordered his citizens to pull their fingers out of the dykes (Holland's second most famous quotation), and flooded vast tracts of land, which was not very beneficial to the tulip harvest but stopped the French army's advance at a stroke.

Louis XIV was understandably frustrated by his failure to crush a few clog-wearing herring fishermen, and took his revenge by annexing William's tiny fiefdom of Orange, which was much easier to invade – it was in France, and had no ditches to flood. He gave the territory and title to a noble French namesake, Louis, marquis de Nesle et de Mailly.†

However, far from being trampled out of existence, by

* For the full details of the Secret Treaty of 1672, see Chapter 8.
† Incidentally, this new Prince Louis of Orange had five daughters, four of whom would go on to be squeezes of King Louis XV.

the time peace was restored in early 1674, the 23-year-old formerly unemployed Prince William had regained the *stadhouder*ship of his ancestral lands in Holland, and even been given power over some other small independent Dutch states.

And more than all of this, he had resolved to devote his life to annoying the main instigator of the war: the arrogant Louis XIV.

Louis squeezes the orange

William decided to strengthen his hand in the European poker game by asking to marry his cousin Mary, the niece of King Charles II of England. The rather glamorous Mary is said to have wept bitterly at this idea, not because she was going to have to eat Edam for the rest of her life and be known as a *stadhoudersvrouw*, but because William was an ugly man with a reputation for preferring male soldiers.

Mary's father, the future King James II, would have liked to marry his daughter into the French royal family, but her Uncle Charles II saw the chance to appease the Protestants in England and gain an ally against Louis XIV, and threw his weight behind the Anglo-Dutch union. It went ahead, and Mary was in a flood of tears throughout the wedding ceremony.

Piqued by this new anti-French entente, Louis made two fatal mistakes. First, in 1685, he revoked the Edict of Nantes, the law that had protected Protestants in France against persecution, thus causing a flood of refugees – including military men – into Holland. Then, under-estimating the belligerent *stadhouder*, Louis signed a naval pact with James II as soon as he became King of England, and issued an order impounding any Dutch trading ships anchored in French ports. Two French gauntlets had been thrown at the Dutchman's feet.

To Louis's, and especially James's, astonishment, William didn't only rise to the challenge, he grabbed it by the balls and made a breathtaking tactical riposte. Instead of sending a few ships out into the Channel to harass the English and French fleets, which was what most Dutch aggression had amounted to in the past, he simply sailed to England and snatched the throne.

In doing so, he rightly claimed that he had been invited over by some Protestant MPs and the Bishop of London. The pretext for their invitation was that James II's second wife, an Italian Catholic princess called Mary (at the time, there was an edict whereby all female royals were to be called Mary to confuse future readers of history books), had just given birth to a son. Until then, although James had converted to Catholicism, the next in line for the throne of England had been his Protestant daughters from a first marriage, the eldest of whom was another Mary – William of Orange's wife.

At the time, the religious question alone might have been enough to topple an English king – everyone had had enough of the waves of persecution that had swept across the country in recent decades – but James was also a despotic ruler who modelled himself on Louis XIV, and had apparently forgotten what happened when his father, Charles I, had shown similar disdain for his people and their Parliament.

With a stroke of almost incredible daring (and, one could argue, dictatorial ruthlessness), in November 1688 William gathered an army of Dutchmen, French Protestant refugees and mercenaries from all over Europe, and sailed them along the south coast of England, aiming to land in Torbay in the extreme southwest. Thanks to a piloting error, the fleet of some 250 ships almost missed England and got blown out into the

Atlantic, but a so-called 'Protestant wind' guided the ships back northeast, and they eventually managed to land.

Meanwhile, King James's fleet was trapped by onshore gales in the Thames Estuary, then got becalmed off the coast of Sussex, and finally retreated, with some of its captains already going over to the Protestant cause. Similarly, on land, James led an army out to resist William, but with desertions growing, he had a nervous breakdown and fled to France.

William's mixed bag of foreign soldiers marched towards London, surprised to find themselves being welcomed as liberators, and suddenly, without a shot being fired, England had a Dutch king. True, he had an English queen, but no one believed that she wore the political trousers. The Bloodless or Glorious Revolution of 1688 was complete.

Louis XIV sponsored an attempt to regain James's crown via an invasion of Ireland, but it failed when William personally brought an army to defeat him at the Battle of the Boyne near Dublin in July 1690. This was a calamity not only for James but also for Irish Catholics, who had to strap themselves in for about three centuries of Anglo-Protestant domination.

Louis XIV was still determined to restore James as a puppet ruler in England, however, and planned another campaign on his behalf. On the menu this time was a naval attack to destroy the English fleet, to be followed by a Franco-Irish invasion of England that would sweep James back into power.

But things went very wrong. Ignoring the fact that a combination of bad weather and worse planning had reduced the French fleet to half strength, Louis gave express orders to its unfortunate commander (who was male, despite being called Anne-Hilarion de Tourville) to attack a massive Anglo-Dutch force that had sailed across to Normandy in a pre-emptive strike.

Over several days of fierce fighting and pursuit in thick fog, the Anglo-Dutch put de Tourville to flight, fired on beached French warships to make sure they were completely destroyed, and sent men ashore to burn vessels that had retreated into port. Between 29 May and 4 June 1692, the threat of a French invasion of England was blown out of the water, largely thanks to Louis XIV's recklessness in ordering his depleted fleet into attack.

Among the French losses were ships called *Saint-Louis* and, most painful no doubt, the magnificent *Soleil Royal*, which was set alight by a fireship and exploded – a supernova that left only one survivor.

Louis offered to give James the Polish throne as a consolation prize, but James turned the job down and settled into his French retirement home at the palace of Saint-Germain-en-Laye – not at Versailles, where the political action was. And on 20 September 1697, Louis formalized James's status as a loser by agreeing to the Treaty of Ryswick, in which he recognized William and Mary as rulers of England and promised to give no future aid to supporters of James II.

As he sat on his commode on that September morning, Louis may have realized that if he had lost all influence over his neighbour across the Channel, scuppered his chances of reigning as a Sun King over the whole of Europe, and vastly increased the power base of his Protestant enemies, it was all his own fault. And if all these reflections did trouble the King's *levée*, his doctors no doubt noted some signs of stress in the results of that morning's *affaires*.

But worse indigestion was to come . . .

Winston Churchill's son

Flashback to 1650: John Churchill, 1st Duke of Marlborough, the general who is about smash Louis XIV's land armies and have the Sun King begging for peace, is born. His father's name: Sir Winston Churchill.

No, this is not a feat of time travel. Sir Winston was not a twentienth-century prime minister who had been teleported back to oppose Louis XIV, like a historical Terminator. This Winston was a member of the landed gentry in southwest England who had fought as a Royalist cavalier in the Civil War and was almost bankrupted by the huge fine he was made to pay when the fighting ended. His wife, Elizabeth Drake, was the greatniece of that reckless fop the Duke of Buckingham* – fortunately, though, the idiot gene seems to have mutated into a more calculated bravado as it seeped down the family line.

After the Civil War, in recognition for the Churchills' loyalty, Winston and Elizabeth's eldest son John was given a position as a page boy to Charles II's brother James (the future James II). The teenager often accompanied his master to military parades, and it is said that one day, when James asked the impressionable John what he was planning to do when he grew up, the lad fell to his knees and begged for a commission in the army.

John's wish was granted when he was seventeen, because, as a nineteenth-century biographer called Charles Bucke puts it, James's wife Anne 'had indicated more kindness and favour to the young aspirant than her husband thought prudent'. In twenty-first-century terms, James suspected they were shagging. John was therefore

* See Chapters 7 and 8 for full details of his recklessness and foppery.

sent to serve as an ensign with the Guards in Morocco, where he saw action in skirmishes with the Arabs, who were none too pleased that the English had taken up residence at their seaside.

John didn't get castrated with a scimitar, which might have been what James secretly hoped, and on his return the dashing young officer leapt straight back into action – this time with one of King Charles II's mistresses, Barbara Villiers. She not only granted John her sexual favours but also showered him with cash, a welcome supplement to his meagre army pay. In an amusing parallel, the cash gifts given to John by the royal mistress amounted to almost exactly the sum paid by his father as a fine after the Civil War. A neat and pleasurable way to rebalance the family accounts.

John and Barbara began a scandalous affair, no doubt made all the more outrageous by the fact that Barbara was also related to the Duke of Buckingham. It must have been this combination of family good looks and reckless-ness that made the two of them indiscreet, and they were eventually caught in the act by King Charles himself. When young John hid in the wardrobe, Charles pulled him out and laughed, saying that he forgave the youngster 'because you do it to get your bread'.

Despite his laughter, Charles seems to have thought it wise to follow his brother James's example and send the randy young soldier on another dangerous mission abroad – and this is where Louis XIV comes into the picture.

Fighting for the French

John Churchill was one of the 6,000 men sent by Charles II to join the French army that invaded Holland in 1672, under the command of the Duke of Monmouth, one of

Charles's illegitimate sons, who was just a year older than John Churchill. Together, the two young men cut a dash across Holland, earning a name for themselves at numerous battles and sieges. John's courage so impressed his French comrades-in-arms that at the siege of a small town called Nimeguen, the Marshal of France, vicomte de Turenne, made a wager that John would win the battle for him. French soldiers had just lost control of a vital command post, and Turenne said, 'I will bet a supper and a dozen bottles of claret that my handsome Englishman will capture the post with half as many men as the officer who lost it.'

Of course it is possible that young Churchill had been sleeping with Turenne's mistress and the Frenchman wanted to get rid of him, but the bet was taken and won, with the result that Churchill became a folk hero amongst the troops.

At the siege of Maastricht, John went one better, offering to be part of the so-called 'forlorn hope', the nickname for the suicidal first wave of soldiers sent to attack a fortress. In this battle, he not only saved the Duke of Monmouth's life but was also the first man to break through the defences, and personally planted the victors' flag on the ramparts. (The French flag, that is.)

Louis XIV was so grateful that he congratulated Churchill for his gallantry and made him lieutenant general of the Anglo-French army in Holland. After the war ended, Churchill stayed on to serve with the French alongside Turenne, adding tactical know-how to his bravado, and quickly mutated into that most valuable and inspirational of soldiers: a leader who was idolized by his troops.

Rather unwise of Louis, then, to unleash the same man *against* France a few years later.

Marlborough makes a packet

Fast-forward to 1701: during the Glorious Revolution, John Churchill had wisely chosen to support William of Orange instead of his old protectors, Charles and James. This was not just because he was a man with a keen nose for winners. He had also become disillusioned during the intervening years – he had served as a diplomat for Charles, and had been led to believe that he was negotiating for England when the King was in fact double-dealing with France. In return for his support, William and Mary made Churchill the Earl of Marlborough.

It was now that Louis XIV stirred up the hornets' nest of his own making.

On James II's death in Paris in 1701, Louis XIV recognized the exiled King's young son as James III of England, a flagrant breach of the peace treaty he had signed with William of Orange four years earlier. Naturally, this enraged the English, who began to prepare for war – preparations that were only briefly postponed after William fell off his horse while hunting at Hampton Court.

Before dying of his injuries, William told his successor, Queen Anne (one of James II's Protestant daughters), to adopt Marlborough as her principal adviser in the forthcoming struggle against Louis. This she did, and as Marlborough's nineteenth-century biographer so excitedly puts it:

> ... happy was it for Europe, as well as for England, that Marlborough possessed so great an influence over the new sovereign; for the exigencies of the times fully demanded the public exercise of the best and most fortunate genius. The power of France exceeded all

precedent in modern history, and it would have been easy, with such a combination of resources as its king possessed, to have effected the subjugation of Europe, had not this country [England] stood in the breach and won the palm of victory.

You can almost hear 'Rule Britannia' playing in the background.

And most commentators agree that it was Marlborough's tactical genius that won this 'palm of victory'. As an experienced diplomat, he was sent to negotiate with England's allies – Austria, Holland (part of which had been annexed by Spain), Portugal and most of the independent states in Germany. All of these countries were already at war with France because Louis XIV's grandson Philip had just inherited the crown of Spain, thereby creating the potential for a frighteningly powerful alliance of the two countries. These days, we are just mildly amused to know that King Juan Carlos of Spain is a descendant of Louis XIV and the Archdukes of Austria, but 300 years ago this royal intermingling caused a whole encyclopedia of wars.

Initial fighting saw gains for both sides in Holland and Germany, and made Queen Anne of England happy enough to give John Churchill, Earl of Marlborough, a dukedom. Meanwhile, the French had identified their most dangerous opponent, and decided that the only way to win was to contain Marlborough's army in the north while they went to grab Austria with their allies the Bavarians. Marlborough saw the danger and began a forced march south down the Rhine valley into Germany, keeping his tactics so secret that he didn't even tell his allies where he was going.

Five days later, he popped up by the Danube. He had covered 250 kilometres, which sounds to us like a none-too-strenuous mountain-biking holiday but gets military historians very excited indeed. Back in the early eighteenth century, such a rapid advance on foot and horseback would usually have decimated an army, with large numbers of soldiers dropping from exhaustion or disease caused by drinking bad water. Marlborough, though, made sure that his troops were constantly fed and watered along the way, so that, according to one of the officers present, 'the soldiers had nothing to do but pitch their tents, boil their kettles and lie down to rest.'

The French, on the other hand, had been hampered in their attempts to follow Marlborough because every change in tactics and direction had to be approved by the power-mad King Louis XIV, and Versailles was several days away. Worse, dispatches from abroad could only be read to Louis at certain times of the day, taking second place to the straightening of the royal wig and other more intimate ceremonies.

On the banks of the Danube, Marlborough met up with Prince Eugene of Savoy, the head of the Austrian army, yet another enemy created by Louis XIV. Eugene was born in Paris to one of Louis's lovers, and would have served in the French army had the Sun King not rejected him. He subsequently went to Austria and became head of the Habsburg army instead – the very troops who were about to join up with Marlborough and inflict one of France's greatest military defeats.

Blenheim: another Agincourt

The Battle of Blenheim in 1704 was, like that other famous victory over the French, Agincourt, a misnomer. It was actually fought around a village called Blindheim in Bavaria, and in misnaming it, the English annoyed both the French and the Bavarians.

To non-military eyes, the battle looks very much like just another of those days in history when men were ordered to charge straight at cannons and muskets, with victory coming to the side who showed the most suicidal courage. In this case, some 52,000 Anglo-Austrians were sent against 56,000 Franco-Bavarians who had taken up what they thought were impregnable positions in and around the village of Blindheim, which was set behind marshland and surrounded by protective woodland. And a French general had just sent off a message to King Louis saying that the enemy would never dare attack when Marlborough and Eugene came marching over the horizon at dawn on 13 August 1704.

The suicidal charges carried on all day, and the battle was finally lost by the French rather than won by the Anglo-Austrians. More exactly, victory was made possible by Marlborough's ability to spot what the French were doing wrong and exploit the situation instantly. When they packed too many of their troops into the village, he held back his charges and poured withering fire into the buildings, setting many of them alight and scaring the defenders out into the open. When the French commanders disagreed over strategy and left a lightly defended gap in their lines, Marlborough immediately struck at their weak point. In the end, 30,000 French troops were killed – including about 3,000 cavalrymen who drowned when they tried to escape across the fast-flowing Danube – and over 10,000 of Louis XIV's best infantry were forced to surrender when they were left isolated by their uncoordinated generals.

This not only removed France's ally Bavaria from the war also made Marlborough even more famous in France, and he became the hero of a popular song, 'Marlbrouck s'en va-t-en guerre' (or 'Mispronounced Marlborough goes to war'). More importantly, the ditty served as a cruel blow to Louis XIV's ego. No one dared tell him of the defeat until his mistress, Madame de Maintenon, plucked up the courage to break the terrible news that 'you are no longer invincible.'

From here on, the long-drawn-out war progressed with Louis alternately suing for peace and then launching offensives, while Marlborough marched around the continent inflicting one brilliant defeat after another on the French army. He even got to the stage where he could have attacked Paris itself if the political will had been there to let him do so.

But by now the backlash had set in. Marlborough was like a pop star who has had one too many hit singles, and the British military establishment turned on him, accusing him of corruption and self-aggrandizement. He was dismissed from his command.

Even so, France had lost the war, and Louis signed the 1713 Treaty of Utrecht, in which he recognized the new line of British succession, ceded control of large chunks of French Canada and – far more humiliating – agreed that the Crowns of France and Spain would never be united, even if they were held by the same royal family. Basically what Louis was signing away was his dream of world power.

The sun goes down on France

The Sun King died on 1 September 1715, of gangrene due to bad circulation, which his doctors initially diagnosed as sciatica and then tried to treat with smallpox medicine. And although he is remembered today as the glorious Roi Soleil – mainly by people in awe at the size of the Château de Versailles and envious of all his mistresses – at the time it was more a case of 'bon voyage and don't come back'. His funeral procession was jeered by a mob as it travelled to the royal necropolis at Saint-Denis Cathedral, just north of Paris. (Though this might just be a local tradition, because a French president going through this northern suburb today, alive or dead, would get the same treatment.)

On his deathbed, Louis seems to have recognized the error of his ways, telling his five-year-old successor, the future Louis XV, 'j'ai trop aimé la guerre' ('I loved war too much'). Perhaps he was trying to simplify things for the youngster, because even he must have seen that there was a little more to it than that.

Louis XIV had squandered away all of his country's wealth on lost wars and a palace as big as a town, encouraged the aristocracy to become foppish layabouts, and over-taxed the commoners who would finally lose their patience and start chopping off privileged heads seventy-four years later. What was more, by mobilizing two of Europe's most ambitious and daring soldiers – William of Orange and the Duke of Marlborough – Louis had blown France's chances of spreading its influence right across the continent.

To add insult to injury, 'Marlbrouck' took the wealth he had accrued during his spectacular career and built his own Versailles, a glorious chateau in the English country-side (mis)named after a French defeat: Blenheim Palace. The building is literally a monument to French humiliation, and its entrance features a sculpture of the Duke's coronet on a cannonball that is crushing a fleur-de-lis, the device on the French monarchy's coat of arms. And the insults don't stop there. The palace was built on land donated by the grateful nation, and to this day the Marlboroughs still present the British monarch with an annual symbolic payment in the form of a fleur-de-lis banner.

In short, the Churchill–Marlborough family home is

an eternal reminder of Louis XIV's historic cock-ups, a three-century-old anti-French joke that is enjoyed by half a million visitors – and the British royals – every year.

11

God Save the National Anthem

Although almost every Anglo-French conflict throughout history seems to have been the result of British provocation, occasionally the French have a go at stirring up trouble. Sadly for them, their attempts often end up going awry. One such case is their assertion that French monarchs were being serenaded by the song we now know as 'God Save the Queen' some fifty years before Londoners first started singing it in around 1745.

National anthems are a touchy subject, and Britain has done its own share of mischief-making in this domain. Depending on one's point of view, it is either a symptom of British jingoism or a healthy reflection of our famous sense of humour that we have shamelessly hijacked other countries' national anthems.

For decades, the BBC radio comedy show *I'm Sorry I Haven't a Clue* has opened with a short excerpt from 'Deutschland Über Alles', apparently played by a brass band that has been at the schnapps. Similarly, whenever a Brit or American hears the opening notes of 'La Marseillaise', there is a fair chance they'll think that a bunch of hippies from Liverpool are about to sing 'All You Need Is Love'. We have no respect.

But for once the Brits can retort that it was France who started it, because in the nineteenth century the French claimed that 'God Save the Queen/King' had been written by a Frenchman and later stolen by *les Anglais*. It's a claim that is still frequently repeated as fact today, and which could be taken as a compliment. After all, Britain's national anthem has a fairly memorable tune and a very easy-to-remember title. What's more, we usually simplify it by singing only the first verse, limiting it to just seven lines that consist almost entirely of the words 'God', 'save' and 'Queen'. It's short and catchy, a sort of royal pop song.

Perhaps the only problem with the anthem is the inherent complication in its title – the need to change the name of the song whenever the monarch switches gender (or rather, whenever the crown passes to a person of a different gender – a transsexual royal is probably a long way off).

Most countries go in for a more radical update of their anthem after a regime change. It is usually not the done thing to keep the old tune and just cross out 'king' or 'queen' on the official lyric sheet, replacing it with 'democratically elected president' or 'your friendly new dictator'. When Germany's Kaiser fell at the end of World War One, his family's anthem 'Heil Dir im Siegerkranz' ('Hail to thee in the victor's crown' – a title that by 1918 had become cruelly inaccurate) was swapped for 'Deutschland Über Alles' ('Germany above all'), which Hitler would later try to make more accurate. France, of course, did the same at the Revolution, ditching Louis XVI's religious hymn 'Domine Salvum Fac Regem' in favour of the bloodthirsty but atheistic 'La Marseillaise'.

Britain, true to its tradition of moderation in

everything except football, tattoos, bare cleavage and alcohol consumption, merely tweaks the title of its anthem once or twice per century. Perhaps it is this adaptability that has ensured the song's longevity – and inspired France to try and steal it.

The French insist that 'God Save the Queen/King' dates back to the seventeenth century, when Louis XIV was having a few problems staying on his throne . . .

The Sun King gets burnt

As we saw in Chapter 10, King Louis XIV of France believed in the divine right of kings, and called himself '*le Roi Soleil*', subconsciously implying that *le soleil* shone out of his posterior. And it might well have been extreme solar heat that, in January 1685, caused the onset of severe regal discomfort in the anal region.

Readers of a sensitive nature should probably skip the next seven paragraphs, because the medical details of the King's condition and its treatment, especially in an age of surgery without anaesthetic or disinfectant, are almost too horrendous to record. Suffice it to say that at the beginning of 1685, Louis could no longer ride or sit comfortably. A swelling between his buttocks turned into an inflamed abscess, and on 2 May a fistula was diagnosed – that is, an opening between the anal tube and the skin, effectively a second, unnatural anus that became infected because of the contact between faeces and the open wound. (Readers of a slightly less sensitive nature who have made it this far will be excused for abandoning the narrative now and skipping the next six paragraphs, because we are about to go into surgery.)

Fistulas were not uncommon amongst aristocrats and royals who spent much of their time in the saddle, giving their posteriors a serious pounding. The royal doctors therefore tried the conventional treatments, which mostly involved poultices, creams, enemas and blind faith. None worked, and the quacks began to panic.

There were other fistula sufferers at the royal court in Versailles, and the doctors sent some of them to test the healing waters at Barèges in the Pyrenees. But they returned with their fistulas in place, and in some cases worsened after bumping hundreds of kilometres over unmade roads.

Louis's condition was not improved by the fact that he hardly ever washed, because bathing had been banned by the Church on the grounds that nakedness provoked excessive sexuality (not that Louis needed baths to encourage him in that direction). Even under normal conditions, staying in the same room as Louis XIV was an ordeal despite all his perfumes. With a long-term anal infection, the royal air must have become unbreathable.

All of which makes a man called Charles-François Félix a true hero. He was a fifty-year-old barber-surgeon from Avignon, accustomed to shaving people and performing operations that often ended in death by infection or pain-induced shock. Louis XIV's doctors invited him to operate, presumably on the grounds that it would be good to have someone else to blame for the King's demise. The idea was to cut away the infected flesh and seal the wound – without anaesthetic, of course. Félix agreed to try, but he had never treated an anal fistula before, and wisely asked for time to prepare. Poor Louis was going to have to wait six months for his operation – proof that France's health service was not always as efficient as it is today, even if you went private.

Félix requisitioned seventy-five fistula sufferers as guinea pigs, mostly expendable prisoners and peasants, and practised on them. Their fate is not recorded, but those who were incised to death or eaten away by infection during the trials may have gained some consolation from the fact that they helped Félix to develop two new surgical tools – a long, curved scalpel and a silver 'anus widener', a sort of three-pronged bottle opener.*

On 18 November 1686, after a night of enemas, Louis was finally laid out on a table in his palace, his naked backside propped in the air like a twin royal sunrise. He was accompanied by Madame de Maintenon (his mistress), his Minister of State, four of his doctors and his confessor, Père Lachaise (who would later give his name to Paris's most famous cemetery). For the next three hours, the King showed almost superhuman courage, uttering barely a sigh as the curved blade cut away at his inflamed rectal passages, before Félix was able to pronounce the wound clean and seal it with a cloth soaked in liniment and egg yolk. That same morning, Louis was sitting up in bed and receiving well-wishers. Less than two months later, he was walking normally again.

The surgeon – who had probably risked his own life as much as that of his patient – was ennobled and rewarded with a fortune in cash – 50,000 *écus*, the equivalent of several million pounds today – and a similar amount in land. However, because of what we would now diagnose as post-traumatic stress, he was forced to retire soon afterwards because he could no longer hold a scalpel without trembling. A cynic might assume that with all his new-found riches, he was probably happy that he never had to slit open another anus or hear a patient screaming in agony again.

Meanwhile fistulas became highly fashionable, and many of the King's fawning courtiers demanded the operation, even if they didn't need it. A doctor practising in

* Both are now on display at the Musée de l'Histoire de la Médecine in Paris.

Versailles, Pierre Dionis, noted that 'those who had minor oozing or simple haemorrhoids did not hesitate to present their posteriors to a surgeon and ask for an incision; I saw more than thirty who wanted the operation, and whose folly was so great that they were angry when informed that there was no need to perform it.' Other surgeons were less scrupulous, and the sight of bandaged backsides became very common around Versailles. Anything to resemble *le Roi Soleil*.

The King's miraculously swift recovery was celebrated throughout the nation with prayers, poems and music. And this is where the story of Britain's 'stolen' national anthem rears its head.

God save *le roi*

France's claim to both the tune and the words of 'God Save the King' (as it was first called in English) is often affirmed as a straightforward fact. It can be found, for example, on a website dedicated to anal fistulas, presumably to console sufferers for their pain and humiliation. The French assertion is that a certain Madame de Brinon, the mother superior of La Maison Royale de Saint-Louis, a school for poor young aristocratic ladies in Saint-Cyr, near Paris, was inspired by the King's survival to write a poem. She took as her source a line from the Latin version of Psalm 19, 'Domine salvum fac regem' (attentive readers may remember it from the beginning of this chapter), and adapted it to give the following verses in French:

> Grand Dieu, sauvez le Roi!
> Grand Dieu, vengez le Roi!
> Vive le Roi!
> Qu'à jamais glorieux,

Louis victorieux
Voye ses ennemis
Toujours soumis!
Grand Dieu, sauvez le Roi!
Grand Dieu, vengez le Roi!
Vive le Roi!

In other words:

Great God, save the King
Great God, avenge the King
Long live the King!
Forever glorious,
Louis victorious,
May he see his enemies
Always defeated
Great God, save the King
Great God, avenge the King
Long live the King!

This may not read very much like a poem of thanks for a successful operation – why the need for revenge? A punishment for the saddle-maker, perhaps, who caused the medical problem in the first place? But in the eyes of French royalists, that's just nit-picking.

At the same time, Louis XIV's court composer, Jean-Baptiste Lully (or Giovanni Battista Lulli to give the Florentine his original name), was commissioned to write a celebratory *Te Deum* to be performed at Versailles. He, so the French story goes, decided to use Madame de Brinon's poem, and wrote a melody to accompany it – the tune that we now know as 'God Save the King (or Queen)'.

Tragically, though, while rehearsing for the concert, Lully injured himself. Because he was working with a large orchestra, he was marking time by tapping a long stick on the floor rather than using a short baton. At one point during rehearsals, infuriated by the orchestra's incompetence, Lully slammed the baton down so hard that he impaled one of his toes. The wound became infected, and doctors recommended that the toe should be amputated. A keen dancer, Lully refused, and died of gangrene on 22 March 1687.

Not that Louis XIV would have attended the concert if Lully had been conducting, because the King had fallen out with his court composer over the latter's 'Italian morals'. The bisexual Lully had had an affair with one of the page boys from the royal chapel, and the subsequent scandal had dampened Louis's enthusiasm for his music.

But the celebratory concert went ahead at Easter 1687, and according to French legend, this was the first public performance of the song that the British would later falsely claim as their own. The French-language Wikipedia page on 'God Save the Queen' states categorically – with no use of subjunctives or conditionals to imply doubt – that 'the ancestor of "God Save the Queen" is the song "Grand Dieu sauve le Roi"'. It goes on to say that Handel arranged the song 'perhaps after a visit to Versailles'.

We can almost see the provocative glint in the eye of the French person who wrote the entry. So, *Anglais*, you think you're clever borrowing our 'Marseillaise' for a pop song? What do you think of *that*?

Merci for the memoirs

Well, what this particular *Anglais* thinks is that the story is a hoax. And a French one at that. France's claim to authorship of the song is usually based on a book called *Souvenirs de la Marquise de Créquy*, first published in

1842. This hefty eight-volume autobiography purports to be the lost memoirs of one of Louis XIV's courtiers who died in 1803, and covers the golden age of the monarchy, the Revolution, and even the beginning of Napoleon's empire. The Marquise knew everyone who was everyone, and the book brings them all to life, wittily, suggestively, and – in the case of the kings – reverently.

The Marquise tells us that one of her 'most unforgettable impressions' was hearing 'a sort of motet, or rather a glorious national anthem, with words by Madame de Brinon and music by the famous Lully'. She remembers seeing it performed for Louis XV (the successor to Louis XIV, of course) in the middle of the eighteenth century, and reprints the French verses quoted above. She tells her grandson, to whom the book is addressed, that 'you will have no trouble procuring the music, given that a German called Handel acquired it during his trip to Paris, and dedicated it to King George of Hanover in return for a financial reward, and that *Messieurs les Anglais* have now adopted it, and perform it openly as one of their national anthems.' *Quel scandale!*

In a 'new, corrected, expanded' edition of the *Souvenirs* published in 1873, the editor strengthens the Brinon/Lully authorship claim further by citing 'a statement signed by three nuns from Saint-Cyr who wholeheartedly confirm the author's revelation'. And who could doubt the word of three French nuns?

The only problem is that the patriotic Marquise de Créquy – who really existed – almost certainly didn't write all of her own memoirs. The Bibliothèque Nationale de France's catalogue confirms this, ascribing the authorship of the so-called 'autobiography' to one Maurice Cousin de Courchamps, a shady character who is also known to have plagiarized a book about Protestantism.

It's impossible to know how many of the Marquise's anecdotes were her own, and how many were ghost-written later by Monsieur de Courchamps, but they make amusing reading, especially when aiming barbed remarks at *les Anglais*.

For example, we are told the story of an heroic French innkeeper called Mam'selle Lhopital, who, in the early years of the eighteenth century, saved the life of England's King-in-exile, James III, the Catholic claimant to William and Mary's throne. James was living in France, and one night, while he was travelling through the countryside somewhere near Paris, Mam'selle Lhopital apparently stopped his carriage and warned him of an English Protestant ambush at her inn on the road ahead. She told him that she had recognized a group of rowdy customers as criminals because 'these good-for-nothings are all Englishmen, and one of them spoke out against our Holy Father the Pope'.

Similarly, the Marquise (or Monsieur de Courchamps) expresses some wonderfully French disdain for the English language. As a young woman, we learn, she had a Scottish language tutor, but he was only allowed to teach her Spanish 'because no one would have thought of studying English at the time, or any language from the north. The people of the north learned French, but the French only ever learned Italian or Spanish. We naturally turned towards the south, towards good wine, sunshine and beneficial climates.' The Marquise (or Monsieur de Courchamps) informs us that civilization came from the south, and that a list of venerable French women like Madame de Maintenon and the writers Mesdames de Lafayette and de Sévigné – 'models of perfect education . . . surely knew not a word of English or German'.

The implication is clear: the Anglo-Saxons are all barbarians, and everyone looks to the south to find civilization, so it is quite obvious that the English must have stolen their national anthem from France, *n'est-ce pas?*

A *réalité* check

The question about 'Grand Dieu, sauve le Roi' is: where does truth begin and elaborate hoax end?

Well, all the characters mentioned in Courchamps's version of the song's origin were real. Madame de Brinon was the head of the school at Saint-Cyr, and died in 1701. Lully really was rehearsing music for the celebration of Louis XIV's recovery when he pulped his toe. And it is true that by the end of the eighteenth century Louis XVI of France was using this same tune, either with its Latin text or the French words 'Grand Dieu sauve le Roi' etc. as his anthem before the Revolution came along and it was replaced by 'La Marseillaise'. But that is where truth seems to end.

For a start, the text of Lully's *Te Deum* is in Latin, not French, and does not contain the lines 'Domine salvum fac regem'. What's more, Lully wrote it in 1677 – not for Louis XIV but for the baptism of his own son. Lully presumably thought the piece would be appropriate to mark the King's re-birth after his brush with death. And if that weren't enough, the *Te Deum*'s many baroque twists and turns do not stray anywhere near the tune of 'God Save the King'.

It could be argued that this doesn't matter. After all, the Marquise never mentions a direct connection with the fistula and the *Te Deum*. She (or Courchamps) only says that the song was penned by that little-known song-writing duo Lully and Brinon, and performed for French kings before English kings. This is what is important to the French: the dates of the songwriters' deaths mean that the anthem must have been composed decades before the Brits began using 'God Save the King'.

However, what French sources fail to provide is documentary proof – a score, a handwritten poem, an early published version of the song. All we are left with, in fact, are unsubstantiated claims, alongside some juicy anti-English anecdotes. And, of course, the 'three-nun' statement in a later edition of Courchamps's book – not that we are given a glimpse of the statement itself.

The conclusion seems to be that when Courchamps wrote – or more probably expanded upon – the memoirs of the real Marquise de Créquy, he almost certainly threw in the patriotic story of the national anthem as French royalist propaganda. He might well have been trying to revive the song to rouse support for the French King reigning at the time, Louis-Philippe. If so, it would have been politic to make the anthem as French as possible, and not just a loan from the English. To achieve this French purity, a new creation myth was needed.

Moreover, Courchamps wasn't the only Frenchman up to this kind of mischief at the time. In November 1852, a man calling himself 'un vieux Versaillais' (which literally means an old man from Versailles, but which could also be interpreted as a veteran royalist from the court at Versailles) wrote to a French music magazine called Le Ménéstrel complaining that its editors had wrongly attributed 'God Save the King' to an English composer called John Bull, who was Queen Elizabeth I's music teacher in the early seventeenth century. The 'vieux Versaillais' says that the name John Bull sounds much too English to be genuine, and disingenuously asks how he could have written 'God Save the King' when a queen was on the throne.*

* There really was an English composer called John Bull, who lived from 1562 or 1563 to 1628, and who seems to have borne no relation to the stereotypical Englishman of the same name invented as a satirical figure in the early eighteenth century.

The 'vieux Versaillais' repeats the Créquy/Lully/Brinon story, and says that if readers want confirmation, they should look at the 1834 edition of a periodical called *La Revue de Paris*, where the true origin of the song is explained by the composer and musicologist Castil-Blaze (the pen-name of a man called François-Henri-Joseph Blaze).

It is true that in volume 8 of *La Revue de Paris*, published in August 1834, Castil-Blaze asserts that Lully composed the tune, although he doesn't mention the fistula and says that the music was written for Louis XIV's mistress, Madame de Maintenon, and sung by the girls of Saint-Cyr every time the King came to their chapel. It is a very similar story to the one published by Courchamps in 1842.

Castil-Blaze ends his article by saying that it is ironic that 'God Save the King' – 'composed at Versailles by a French-Italian and taken to London by a German' – should be 'the musical work that inspires the most vanity in the English'. And this seems to be the key to the whole French claim – Maurice Cousin de Courchamps, the 'vieux Versaillais' and Castil-Blaze were all using the song as a pretext for anti-English jibes that were an essential part of a campaign to arouse patriotism and restore the French monarchy. French kings had always fought *les Anglais*, and the battle for the national anthem was just another patriotic war.

Not that claiming ownership of 'God Save the King' was of much use to the French, because Louis-Philippe, the last king of France, was ousted in 1848, and although royalists continued to campaign in favour of restoration for several more decades, all their attempts failed.

Louis-Philippe, the fourth French king in a row to be either guillotined or forced into exile, fled to England, and, as we shall see in Chapter 22, he died there in mysterious circumstances. God, it seems, was never very keen on saving French kings.

The dark side of the tune

It was not difficult for the French to claim that they wrote Britain's national anthem because, in fact, no one seems to know exactly where it came from. The *Encyclopaedia Britannica* says that the origin of both the words and the music is 'obscure', and cites the English composers Thomas Ravencroft and John Bull as possible sources of the melody. *The Oxford Companion to Music* says that a version of the tune was first published by John Bull in 1619, but that it was 'traditional' in origin. This might well be another explanation for its popularity – it is a kind of folk song.

The first undisputed sighting of the melody as we now know it was in a publication variously called *Harmonia Anglicana* or *Thesaurus Musicus*, 'a collection of songs, several of them never before printed', published in 1744.

As for the words, they are sometimes attributed to an eighteenth-century writer called Henry Carey, though he never claimed authorship. They were clearly inspired by the King James Bible of 1611, which contains several uses of the phrase 'God save the King', or something very similar – 1 Samuel 10:24, for instance, reads: 'And Samuel said to all the people, See ye him whom the Lord hath chosen, that there is none like him among all the people? And all the people shouted, and said, God save the king.'

The first known printing of the words and music together, with the topical first line 'God save great George our King', is in an edition of *Gentleman's Magazine* dated 15 October 1745, where it is listed as 'a new song'.

According to the official website of the British

Monarchy (which can surely be trusted when talking about its own anthem, *n'est-ce pas?*), in September of that year 'God Save the King' had been arranged and performed by the leader of the orchestra at London's Theatre Royal as a patriotic reaction to the uprising in Scotland led by the Young Pretender Charles Edward Stuart (alias Bonnie Prince Charlie). The website says that 'it was a tremendous success and was repeated nightly' – by popular demand, it seems; no question of it being used as anti-Pretender propaganda.

The song apparently became especially popular in England after the Battle of Culloden in April 1746, when Bonnie Prince Charlie's Highland Army was defeated by George II's government forces. This was a blow not only to the Young Pretender but also to the French, who were supplying him with money, ships, muskets and men. Bonnie Prince Charlie's army included French soldiers as well as Irish and Scots troops who had previously been serving in the French army. Even the Royal Scots regiment was sponsored by France, and officially branded the *Royal Écossais*. All of which means that when 'God Save the King' was being sung victoriously in England in the 1740s, it was at least partly directed at the French.

And to cap the whole story, proponents of the old cliché that French troops surrender too easily will be delighted to note that after the Battle of Culloden, out of 376 'Scots' prisoners, 222 were from French units – a statistic made even more telling by the fact that the Scottish army consisted of about 7,000 men, of whom 652 were from French units. In other words, at Culloden over 30 per cent of the French army's troops surrendered, compared with less than 3 per cent of the native Scots.

All in all, then, not only is the French claim to the British national anthem unproven, but the song first became popular as a victory chant after the defeat of a

French-sponsored attempt to grab the British throne. It is a musical double-whammy.

As so often throughout history, when a Frenchman like Maurice Cousin de Courchamps tries to provoke *les Anglais*, all he does is invite the Brits to retort with a vicious knockout blow.

12

Voltaire: A Frenchman Who Loved to Get France in the *Merde*

When it comes to annoying the French with the written word, one man takes the *gâteau*. Not Shakespeare, although he did get in some incisive digs at France in his history plays. Not Winston Churchill, even if his remarks about de Gaulle during the Second World War were often pretty incendiary. And certainly not the horde of American writers who gave the French a verbal gang-banging in the wake of the Iraq War.

No, the writer who annoyed the French – or more exactly the French establishment – most efficiently was a Parisian who has been credited with striking the first real blow of the French Revolution.

He was Voltaire. No first name, just a single nom de plume at a time when the French upper classes had titles as long as their family trees. Anyone who was anyone was called something like Philippe-Maximilien de Thingy de Wotsit, comte de Gubbins et marquis de Howsyourfather, and yet here was a man adopting a two-syllable name that sounded like a newly invented unit of measurement to calculate the amount of electricity in the atmosphere. And during his long life (1694–1778), Voltaire aimed some real bolts of lightning at his country and its snobbish establishment.

Choose your weapon

Voltaire's real name was François-Marie Arouet, but almost no one in France knows that. Mention his pseudonym though, and even someone who has never read him (which is unlikely if they went to a French school, because he's required reading in class) will know that you're talking about a man who proved that the pen really can be as mighty as the sword.

Incidentally, the saying 'the pen is mightier than the sword' has a French connection – it comes from a play about France called *Richelieu, or The Conspiracy*, written by one Edward Bulwer-Lytton* and first performed in 1839. The full quotation adds some essential subtlety to the expression – 'Beneath the rule of men entirely great/The pen is mightier than the sword.' It's true – less noble rulers will simply unsheath their sword and decapitate any writer who criticizes them. Which is exactly what worried Voltaire for most of his life.

He was born into a well-to-do, but non-aristocratic, Parisian family. His father was a government officer in charge of the revenues generated by the spice trade, and sent the young François-Marie to the best schools in the hope that he would follow in Papa's safe and predictable footsteps. However, the tactic backfired when the future Voltaire became obsessed by the classical literature he was studying, and at the age of seventeen he dropped out and announced that he was going to be an *homme de lettres*

---

* Bulwer-Lytton is also credited with coining the phrase 'the great unwashed'. In fact, though, he used 'the unwashed' to describe the Parisian poor.

– a writer. At the time, this was roughly the equivalent of saying he was hoping for a career in graffiti painting – hardly anyone made money from literature, and writing anything controversial would get you arrested. Louis XIV had recently died, but it was still an age of an absolute monarchy that thought of itself as divine.

Papa, of course, blew a fuse, so François-Marie agreed to sign on at law school, and spent his time drinking and wenching with the Paris in-crowd. Being French, this also involved lots of talking, and Voltaire found that he had a real talent for witty remarks and acerbic put-downs. These days, to rise in French society you have to go to a good school and have friends in the right places (or if not friends, at least people interested in your sexual favours). But in the early eighteenth century a sharp tongue could get you a long way, even if you only used it for talking. A well-placed jibe or witty speech would quickly do the rounds of polite society. On the other hand, if you didn't have a comeback for an insult, you would be a laughing stock, and watching reputations rise and fall was a favourite spectator sport. The young François-Marie Arouet was a skinny, hook-nosed commoner, but he was a skilful exponent of this parlour game, and by the time he was twenty-one he was something of a celebrity in fashionable Paris, with everyone waiting to see what pithy piss-take he was going to come out with next.

The danger was, however, that you could let your wit run away with you, and in 1716 Voltaire did just that, and was banished from Paris to deepest Corrèze (the provinces, the ultimate punishment) for writing rude poems about the regent, Philippe d'Orléans, uncle of the boy King Louis XV. He was forgiven after a few months, and returned to the capital, only to repeat his offence and get himself thrown into the Bastille for almost a year.

This seems to have brought him to his senses, and on

his release he changed his name to Voltaire and put his witty pen to more profitable use, writing plays and epic poems that immediately brought him fame if not fortune.

His fame, though, caused his downfall. The son of a civil servant mixing with the high and mighty? The man who had insulted the regent lording it over polite Paris society? It was too much for the snobs to bear.

With French friends like these . . .

Accounts vary as to exactly how Voltaire's demise came about. The most convincing version sets the story at a dinner with Voltaire's friend, the duc de Sully. (This duke was a descendant of King Henri IV's famous right-hand man of the same name.)

Amongst the dinner guests that night was a dandy from one of France's oldest aristocratic families, Guy-Auguste de Rohan-Chabot, chevalier de Rohan, comte de Chabot (yes, that is just one person), who was hated by practically everyone, even his friends. He was arrogant, dull (one commentator neatly describes him as 'a lord among wits, but never a wit amongst lords') and known to be a crooked moneylender. He only seems to have been invited to the party because he was a cousin of the Duke.

The conversation over dinner was cut and thrust, with Voltaire at his rapier-like best. But when he dared to contradict the chevalier, the affronted aristocrat turned to the Duke and asked pointedly, 'Who is this young man that speaks to me so loudly?'

Quick as a flash, Voltaire replied for himself, 'He is a man who does not drag a great name about with him, but who honours the name he bears.' The other guests must have held their breath in anticipation of a fight.

Behind the elegant phrasing, this was a vicious putdown. A modern equivalent might be something like: 'Hey, loan shark, you think you're better than me just because all your ancestors married their brothers and sisters?'

As soon as he'd worked out the insult, the chevalier stormed off. Instead of being affronted by the anti-aristocratic remark, though, the duc de Sully thanked Voltaire for getting rid of the boring snob. The incident seemed to be over.

However, a week later, at another dinner *chez* the Duke, the meal was interrupted by a messenger saying that someone wanted to talk to Voltaire outside 'about doing a good deed'. Voltaire went down to find a carriage waiting in the street. A voice called him over, and as soon as he put his foot on the step, three men sprang from nowhere and grabbed him. Two of them held his arms while the other started hitting him with a cane. A few thwacks later, the voice, now clearly recognizable as the chevalier de Rohan, called out, 'Enough!' and the carriage drove off.

Voltaire was shocked more than hurt, but decided that he was not going to take the affront lying down – or even standing up. He went back indoors and told everyone what had happened, and asked for volunteers to come and make a formal complaint.

But it was now that Voltaire found out where he really stood in Parisian society. He had been friends (or so he thought) with the duc de Sully for six years, he had been entertained as an honoured guest in all the best houses in Paris, and now he couldn't find anyone willing to bear witness against the chevalier. It was OK for a commoner to make jokes about the establishment, but he wasn't allowed to question its ultimate authority.

Voltaire decided to go it alone. He found himself a fencing teacher, and as soon as he was good enough to take on a toff, he challenged the chevalier to a duel. The aristocrat accepted, but ran straight home to his family to report Voltaire for breaking the law that forbade commoners challenging noblemen. The Rohans immediately went to see the Prime Minister, who signed a *lettre de cachet*, an order that could be obtained by aristocrats to imprison anyone who was bothering them. So when Voltaire turned up to the duel, the police were waiting for him, and he was dragged off to the Bastille again. Although he stayed there for just a month this time, he was only released on condition that he promise to leave France and not return without the King's permission.

The haven he chose was England.

Revolutionary French letters

After his novel *Candide*, Voltaire's most famous work is a hymn in praise of the traditional enemy across the Channel, a book so controversial that its title was changed to lessen the scandal. It is usually known as *Lettres philosophiques*, but when Voltaire published it in 1734 he wanted to call it *Lettres écrites de Londres sur les Anglois* et autres sujets (Letters Written from London on the English and Other Subjects)*.

Voltaire wrote most of the *Lettres* between 1726 and 1729 during his English exile, which seems to have been the most eye-opening experience of his life (except, presumably, his initiation into the debauched ways of his high-society friends when he was a student).

---

* Yes, that does say *Anglois* and not *Anglais*. At the time, 'ais' was often written 'ois'. This is why the French have the first name François, which simply means Frenchman, and why in English we speak of being a connoisseur, a word adopted from French before they changed the spelling to 'ais'. In French, a connoisseur is *un connaisseur*.

288

Voltaire was not your average political refugee. He didn't have to queue for days in government offices begging for a visa and a work permit. He was strapped for cash, but he was a well-known writer and had letters of recommendation from a few loyal friends in Paris that ensured him a soft landing in London. His only major problem seems to have been getting used to the local sense of humour. Instead of being subtly witty, Londoners talked surreal nonsense. He was horrified, for example, to discover that they had been joking when they told him that you should never ask an Englishman a favour if the wind is blowing from the east.

Voltaire experienced a bit of anti-French hostility, which was only natural given that the two countries had just emerged from a long series of wars, but he was cushioned from this by being accepted into a literary crowd that respected him for his work. He was good friends with writers who, like him, enjoyed taking a swipe at the establishment: Alexander Pope, the poet famous for his satirical work *The Rape of the Lock*, a mock epic about a lord who steals a lock of a society girl's hair, and Jonathan Swift, whose *Gulliver's Travels* is of course not a children's story about miniature people tying up a giant but a vicious satire on human self-importance.

Voltaire's closest friend, though, was a merchant called Everard Falkener, a common-born businessman who was afforded a million times more respect in London than he would ever have received in Paris. Falkener, who would later become Britain's ambassador to Turkey, was the living proof to Voltaire that French society was stuck in the past, and that it was possible to end its dictatorship of snobbery and hereditary privilege.

The businessman also inspired the writer to indulge in a little private enterprise, and Voltaire got his influential friends to find subscribers for a special edition of one of his plays, the *Henriade*, about King Henri IV. To Swift he wrote 'the subscription is only one guinea, payable in advance' – his English was coming on fast – and the scheme was a huge success, making Voltaire a highly respectable profit of £2,000.

Like many more recent immigrants to London (at least before the 2008 credit crunch), he decided that this was the land of opportunity, and started to write a book about the place. The result, *Lettres écrites de Londres, etc.*, is a kind of love letter, a gush of almost unquestioning admiration for Britain's political and religious freedoms, and for its attitude to the arts, business and science. He even liked its aristocrats, who were much less snobbish than their French counterparts. Yes, an eighteenth-century English lord as a model of democracy – it gives you an idea how bad things must have been in Paris.

As the book's title suggests, it is in the form of letters from London to a French friend, but it goes way beyond the scope of 'wish you were *ici*'.

Voltaire starts out with a subject close to his heart – religious freedom – and writes: 'An Englishman is free, and takes whichever path he chooses to heaven.' This was at a time when it was practically illegal in France to be anything but Catholic. He also aims barbed remarks at the supposedly chaste French clergy, many of whom preached strict morality while living a life of Parisian debauchery: 'The priests here [in England] are almost all married. And the awkward manners they acquired at university, coupled with their limited contact with women, means that most bishops make do with their own wife.'

He goes on to whinge about France's treatment of its writers and thinkers. We call ourselves an intellectual country, he says, but look at the difference between the French philosopher Descartes and the Englishman Isaac

Newton (whose magnificent state funeral Voltaire attended in 1727):

> He [Descartes] had to leave France because he was looking for the truth . . . and died prematurely in Stockholm, of a bad diet, surrounded by his scientific enemies and treated by a doctor who hated him . . . Newton lived for eighty-five years, peacefully, happily, honoured in his homeland. His luck was to be born in a free country, so that the world could be his student and not his enemy.

This is provocative enough, but Voltaire goes still further and strikes at the root of France's problems – the monarchy:

> England is the only nation on Earth that has managed to limit the power of kings by resisting them, and has finally established a wise system of government in which the ruler is all-powerful when it comes to doing good, and has his hands tied if he attempts to do evil.

So far, Voltaire had written rude poems about the regent and challenged a chevalier to a duel; this, though, was revolution.

The book came out after Voltaire's return to Paris, and struck France like a thunderclap. Voltaire knew it would, so he published it anonymously and was able to deny any knowledge of its authorship when his apartment was ransacked by the authorities. Copies of the book were burnt, and Voltaire himself would not have fared much better if there had been any hard proof against him.

The scandal ensured that the book was a bestseller. Then, as now, the French loved books that undermine authority, and this one scythed at all the pillars of their establishment. Copies were sold as fast as they could be imported (editions came in from England and Switzerland), and it is said that even people who could barely read wanted to own the book just for the thrill of it.

There was no conclusive evidence against him, but everyone knew who had really written the *Lettres*, and Voltaire had to rely on influential friends to make sure that the sword of authority did not come down and cut off his pen in its prime. He moved to the northeastern corner of France to live with his mistress (and her very understanding husband), then to the court of Frederick the Great of Prussia in Potsdam, and finally to Geneva and a chateau on the Swiss border. An attempt to return to Paris was met with an order of banishment by Louis XV himself.

At last, in 1778, after Louis XVI had come to the throne, the 83-year-old Voltaire was allowed home. Social change was in the air, and at a performance of one of his plays, he was hailed by an admiring crowd as a returning hero. He died soon afterwards, apparently telling the priest who was urging him to renounce his free-thinking ways and make his peace with God, 'Now is not the time to be making new enemies.'

Merde in England

The *Lettres écrites de Londres* . . . caused trouble in more than one way. As well as igniting a revolutionary flame in French minds, Voltaire also made everything English – clothes, literature, art, card games, even swearing – incredibly fashionable. In the middle of the eighteenth century, a Parisian nobleman called Count Lauraguais wrote a letter to an Englishman saying:

> We are all metamorphosed into English. Our dandies, who formerly were dressed, painted and perfumed like

dolls at ten in the morning, now ride in the environs of Paris in a plain shirt and frock [coat] like English jockeys. Our delicate ladies, who never ventured to stir out in the morning, run all over Paris in the genteel and loose dress of milkmaids. We hunt, swear and determine all disputes with bets, like your nobility.

This fashion also encouraged the French to cross the Channel and see the *Anglois* for themselves, even though war-free years were few and far between. From 1756 to 1763, for example, the two nations were embroiled in the Seven Years War, which involved vicious land and sea battles right across the globe. Voltaire famously depicted English brutality in *Candide*. The hero arrives in Portsmouth to see an admiral, blindfolded and on his knees, being shot by a firing squad that puts twelve bullets into his skull 'as calmly as you like'. He asks what is going on, and is told that the English admiral is being executed for 'not killing enough people' during a battle against the French, and that in England, it is considered wise to kill an admiral occasionally 'to encourage the others'. Candide refuses to land in such a violent country. Voltaire was clearly shocked by this episode, but seems to be criticizing the war itself (which was a shared Anglo-French responsibility), and warmongering in general, more than the English as a whole. And this doesn't seem to have discouraged French travellers from popping over to London.

When they arrived, however, they often got a shock. Voltaire may have been able to bury the hatchet and learn to love his enemies (one of his harshest criticisms was that Oxford professors spoke Latin with a terrible English accent), but the Brits were not so forgiving. And even though some French people dressed *à l'anglaise*, many of them still paraded about in London in their foppish

293

Parisian fashions, which made them stand out like ballerinas in a rugby team.

A poet called Anne-Marie du Bocage, who made a name for herself with her French adaptation of Milton's *Paradise Lost*, went over to London in the 1760s and was horrified by how unrefined it all was. 'Their so-called palaces would be no more than large houses in Paris,' she wrote, and 'their bedrooms have almost no armchairs.'

She was even more upset when she went to the theatre. 'One of their favourite stage characters is a ridiculous Frenchman. With his face powder, his snuffbox, his watch, his box of beauty spots always at the ready and his endless bowing, he seems terribly caricatured. But then gradually we realize it is all too lifelike.'

Londoners could smell a scented Parisian coming half a mile away, and had plenty of time to plan a hearty welcome. One French traveller called Pierre-Jean Grosley reports in his book *Londres*, published in 1770, that even though he tried to avoid dressing like a Parisian dandy, 'at every street corner, my French appearance called forth a shower of insults through which I slipped, thanking God that I didn't understand English.'

During a stroll by the Thames, 'twenty boatmen stopped work, lined up and assailed me with every horror in the English language' (Grosley knew this because an English friend was kind enough to translate). He also describes a Frenchman who is flattered that a small crowd seems to follow him everywhere he goes, only to be told by his interpreter, 'They're making fun of you.'

And it was not just the over-perfumed upper classes who fell victim to anti-French prejudices. Grosley's manservant was walking down Oxford Street after watching a public hanging when he was picked on by a mob, and was lucky to be rescued by three deserters from the

French army who had been drinking in a nearby pub and came to see what the bilingual shouting was about.

Grosley is perturbed by all this verbal and physical abuse, and devotes a whole section of his book to possible reasons for it; at least if you understand *why* you're being insulted, he tells his French readers, it might make the experience less painful. He gives a long list of wars and religious disagreements, and says that Londoners probably get tired of loud Parisian aristocrats throwing their money about. By contrast, London is 'currently the refuge for every bankrupt man in France' and these spongers get on people's nerves by begging for money.

But Grosley concludes his section on 'why they hate us' by advising his readers not to judge Londoners too hastily. They aren't always being *deliberately* impolite, he says. It's not just because you're French that 'they elbow you off the pavement and push you into the mud – it is because the English are very punctual, and are therefore in a hurry to get to their appointments on time'.

Either this was a masterful piece of Voltairesque irony or one of Grosley's London friends had been *teking ze pisse*. In any case, it shows that the wars against France had spread far beyond the battlefield.

In the eighteenth century, French tourists might have been able to forget the constant wars and fall in love with Britain (or Voltaire's idea of it, anyway), but the average Londoner liked nothing better than to take a pot-shot at every perfumed Frenchman who strayed within smelling distance. If it was a love–hate relationship, the hate was all being aimed France's way.

13

Why Isn't America Called L'Amérique?

There is a small part of every French brain that never stops throbbing.

This is not the section given over to sex, which the French actually find quite easy to forget – when they are discussing food, illness or workers' rights, for example. Neither is it a colony of bacteria that entered their skull hidden in a particularly lively cheese.

No, these are the brain cells devoted to the idea that Barack Obama ought to be French. That when Neil Armstrong stepped on the moon, he should have talked about 'un bond de géant pour l'humanité' rather than a 'giant leap for mankind'. And that instead of getting hooked on a global brand of hamburger, the world really should be tucking into takeaway *boeuf bourgignon*. OK, the sauce would dribble everywhere, but a French engineer would invent an ingenious device to collect it.

In short, what the throbbing neurons keep repeating is that America really ought to be a French *département* like the Caribbean islands of Martinique and Guadeloupe.

The response to this suggestion is quite obvious, and involves asking why English words like debacle, disaster,

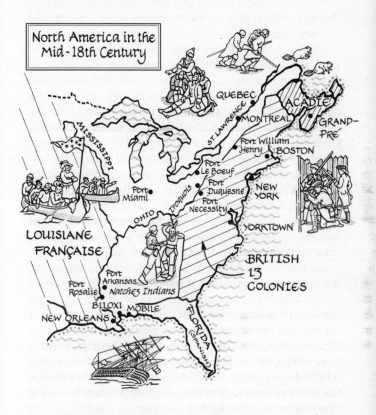

North America in the Mid-18th Century

QUEBEC

MONTREAL

ACADIE

GRAND-PRÉ

ST LAWRENCE

Fort William Henry

BOSTON

Fort Le Boeuf

Fort Duquesne

Fort Necessity

NEW YORK

YORKTOWN

MISSISSIPPI

Fort Miami

OHIO

IROQUOIS

LOUISIANE FRANÇAISE

BRITISH 13 COLONIES

Fort Arkansas

Natchez Indians

Fort Rosalie

BILOXI

MOBILE

NEW ORLEANS

FLORIDA (SPANISH)

France's policy in North America was to hem in British colonists on the coast and then push them into the Atlantic. And it could have worked, if the French themselves hadn't made such a dog's *petit déjeuner* of it.

297

calamity and defeat were all originally borrowed from French.* The sad fact is that France had its chance in America and blew it. Not just once, but at every step of the way, over at least a century of screw-ups. (Or should one say *faux pas?*)

This is because, at one point, the French had a master plan for colonizing not just Canada but the whole of North America and, as we'll see, they really could have pulled it off. But they lost or sold it all, except for a couple of islands and some street names in New Orleans.

The French would counter this insolence by saying, *Oui, mais* you Brits lost even more than that, because North America was your colony until you were unceremoniously ejected from it by revolutionaries who, to add insult to injury, threw a cargo of your precious English tea into Boston Harbour. *Touché!*

Oui, mais in terms of square kilometres alone, this is inaccurate, because Britain only ever possessed colonies on a relatively thin band of the eastern seaboard.

And more importantly, in most British brains the throbbing neurons just aren't there. (Well, not because of America anyway – there are plenty of other gripes that get our brains aching.) We Brits feel no resentment about 'losing' our American colonies. We're quite fond of independent Americans, and see them as distant cousins who can't spell our language properly. We've co-operated with America pretty amicably on projects like liberating Europe and inventing pop music. And we have no desire whatsoever to try and govern Texans.

To this day, though, the French still fret about the USA as the one that got away – the dead cert who said he or she was nipping to the loo and slipped out of the back

---

* Admittedly, victory, triumph, success and glory are also French words, but that would weaken my argument.

door of the restaurant; the unknown actor who left France and then became world famous. It drives their subconscious mad, and is the main reason why they constantly moan about French not being the universal language.

And the tragi-comic thing is that their downfall was caused by some French soldiers who threatened violence on an unarmed Anglo-American cow . . .

France takes a walk on the wild side

Today, the average French man or woman doesn't know how much they lost. They are vaguely aware that they held on to Louisiana for a while after American independence, and one of their few criticisms of Napoleon Bonaparte is that he sold that last little corner of the Southern USA to the English-speakers.

But what they don't generally realize is that Louisiana was originally much, much more than a little corner. At its outset, the French territory of Louisiane, named to flatter Louis XIV, was immense, and covered practically a third of the present USA, an area as big as the whole of Europe, an expanse of unexplored land stretching from the Great Lakes down to the Gulf of Mexico, from Illinois halfway to the Pacific.

Louisiane was conceived as a barrier against the Brits or the Spanish exploring the west, and was also an attempt to encircle the non-French colonies on the Atlantic coast, from New England down to Spanish Florida, and – *pourquoi pas?* – shove them into the ocean and claim the whole North American continent for France. It was a daring plan – and it could have worked.

It all started much like a Molière play, with a defrocked priest in a curly wig. René-Robert Cavelier de La Salle was a Norman merchant's son who had studied to become a

Jesuit priest but dropped out because of what he described as his 'moral infirmities'. Seeking his more worldly fortune, he left France for Canada in the mid-1660s and was soon to be found wandering the rivers and lakes, looking for a quick route to China. He was so obsessed with this idea that when he obtained some land near Montreal, the other settlers jokingly started calling it 'la Chine'.

La Salle didn't let jokes discourage him, though, and joined forces with an Italian banker's son called Tonti, a formidable man who had had a hand blown off by a grenade, and had replaced it with an iron fist that he would often use as a club.

On New Year's Day 1682, La Salle and Tonti wrapped up warm and set off from the Fort des Miamis, on the southwest coast of Lake Michigan near present-day Chicago, to find China.

These frontier 'forts' were often little more than a large log cabin surrounded by a wooden palisade, the idea being to convince unfriendly Native Americans that it would be dangerous to attack them. The Native Americans were courageous fighters, but saw no sense in suicide – as one Jesuit priest remarked, 'They fight to kill, not to be killed.' Even so, when La Salle walked out of that tiny fort, he knew that he was leaving behind his last protection on this part of the planet, and entering an untamed wilderness – which was one of the reasons why, as well as twenty-two armed Frenchmen and eighteen Native Americans, he took along a priest. He thought he might need a little help from a friend higher up.

The party began to trudge slowly south through thick snow and, on 6 February, they found the Mississippi. Its waters were freezing cold because their source was 400 kilometres further north, but the river was wide and fast-flowing, and looked navigable.

La Salle's party therefore built some rafts, climbed on board, and didn't stop floating until they hit the Gulf of Mexico, a good thousand or so kilometres south. To be fair, La Salle probably realized right then that, given the lack of Buddhist temples, the river didn't lead to China, but the trip took them through fertile-looking country that wasn't neck-deep in snow – a very novel thing for French explorers used to travelling in Canada.

La Salle was so pleased that he decided to claim the whole vast region for France – the entire length of the Mississippi (even though he didn't know where its source was) and its tributary, the 1,500-kilometre-long Ohio River, which led northeast to the very edge of the English colonies. So he put on a red coat with gold embroidery that he had brought along in case he met the Chinese Emperor, and held a naming ceremony. In a picture of the occasion (admittedly drawn after the event) he even seems to be wearing a curly wig.

In the presence of a lawyer, a plaque made out of a melted cooking pot was nailed to a giant crucifix to inform the world (or its French-speaking inhabitants, anyway) that this was now officially the southern border of the new territory of Louisiane.

La Salle returned north and bullishly decreed that one of the areas he had travelled through – Illinois, west of the English colonies – should become the new centre of French colonization. He rightly judged that its climate was far more clement than Canada and that the land would therefore be much more productive. It was also teeming with beaver.

The region was used by the Iroquois as hunting grounds, but they were generally on good terms with the French, so La Salle saw no reason why an immediate colonization programme should not begin. His initial plan was to implant 15,000 people, who, he predicted, would have far fewer problems getting established than the poor freezing fishermen and trappers up north. The numbers he suggested were plausible, too – France had the biggest population in Europe, nineteen million compared to Britain's eight million, with plenty of peasants to spare.

The ambitious plan never got off the ground, though, and for the Frenchest of reasons.

The priest who always accompanied La Salle on his travels, and who blessed all his discoveries, was not a Jesuit (the most powerful Catholic group in France) but a Récollet; the Récollets were a branch of the Franciscan order. The Jesuits were very active in the colonization of Canada (as we read in Chapter 7), and saw the Native Americans' souls in much the same way as the secular settlers saw beaver skins – they wanted a monopoly in the trade. To make things worse for La Salle, the Jesuits had influence over the Governor of Nouvelle-France, a sixty-year-old called La Barre who knew he would soon be meeting his maker, and they all wrote to Louis XIV demanding that this excitable La Salle should be discouraged from any more colonization. Sadly for La Salle, Louis agreed, and wrote back to the Governor that this exploration outside Canada was 'completely pointless, and similar expeditions should be prevented'.

Even more negative waves were being generated by the French-Canadian merchants who didn't want competition from new southern territories. Some bizarrely un-American gene seems to have stopped the French merchants thinking, *Formidable*, we can open up new trading centres in Illinois!

All in all, the French reaction to La Salle's idea was like saying, 'No, I don't want your lottery prize money. For a start, you ticked the numbers with the wrong brand of pen. And secondly, I'd have to walk at least a kilometre to pick up the winnings.'

All washed up

Amazingly, La Salle didn't abandon hope. He returned to France to pitch a scheme for attacking the Spanish colonies in the Gulf of Mexico and Texas so that they wouldn't pose a threat to French colonization in the region. All he needed, he said, was 200 soldiers. The rest of his manpower would be recruited amongst the friendly Iroquois, who were probably even more friendly now that their Illinois hunting grounds were not going to be invaded.

This was a message Louis XIV was willing to listen to – one thing he liked was sending French armies to attack people. So the King gave the plan his backing, and in July 1684 La Salle left France with 5 ships, 200 soldiers and 100 civilian colonists. Typically, though, instead of giving command of the expedition to the man who knew the region (La Salle), the navy appointed its own leader, an aristocratic sailor called Tanguy le Gallois de Beaujeu, the son of a royal valet. At the time, a Frenchman without at least one 'de' in his name was considered incapable of leading anything more complicated than a visit to the rubbish tip.

Rivalry between La Salle and Beaujeu festered throughout the transatlantic voyage, and became even more toxic when one of their ships was lost to pirates in the Caribbean. And as soon as the surviving vessels arrived at their destination, any resemblance to *Love Boat* came to an end. According to which version of the story you believe, either La Salle couldn't find the mouth of the Mississippi or Beaujeu refused to follow his directions. In any case, they sailed on westwards looking for a suitable place to land, until disaster struck and one of the ships got caught up in treacherous currents and sank, taking its cargo of provisions with it.

When La Salle finally set foot on dry land he was so furious that he apparently told Beaujeu to 'sail off back to France', or words to that effect. If this was the case – and other accounts of the expedition accuse Beaujeu of simply dumping the colonists onshore and hightailing it – it was a temper tantrum that La Salle would not live long to regret.

He built a fort and unloaded some of the supplies from his one remaining boat, *La Belle*, which was generously stocked with dried meat (2,000 kilos), wine and brandy (10 barrels), gunpowder (4,500 kilos) and guns, as well as plenty of salt, vinegar and oil (they were obviously planning to find some potatoes and start producing crisps). A secure outpost was soon established and things seemed to be looking up – even if they had mislaid the Mississippi.

Leaving a party of soldiers and settlers at the fort, La Salle set off east to locate the river. Some of his men paddled through the shallows in canoes while *La Belle* followed in deeper water. And their misfortunes started almost immediately: first, *La Belle*'s captain choked to death on the spines of a prickly pear, and soon afterwards a group of men, including the ship's replacement captain, were killed by Native Americans while sleeping onshore.

La Salle decided that their only option was to leave the ship at anchor with a crew of twenty-seven men, women and children while he and some of the soldiers went on alone in the canoes. He would return, he said, as soon as he had found the mouth of the Mississippi. But La Salle was gone for weeks, and the drinking water on board *La Belle* started to run dangerously low. Five men were sent out on the ship's longboat to fetch fresh supplies, but they never returned, so the skeleton crew began to drink the wine and brandy they had on board. Sadly though, even French livers can't last long on an alcohol-only diet, and when people began to die of dehydration, the survivors decided to sail back to the fort. They didn't have an experienced captain or pilot, however, and soon lost control of the ship, which ran aground on a mudbank and sank into the goo. Only six of the twenty-seven survived and made it to the fort.

As soon as La Salle returned to the fort and found out what had happened, he made the only logical decision, which was to start walking to Canada in search of help – a 1,500-kilometre trek through the wilderness that makes modern-day TV survival programmes look like armchair chat shows.

He took thirty-six men with him, promising the people he left at the fort that he would hike back to rescue them as soon as possible.

Unsurprisingly, though, by this time confidence in his leadership was not running high, and he became one of the first men ever to be gunned down in Texas, receiving a single bullet in the head from one of his own men, apparently in an argument about the share-out of meat. The French have never been good at vegetarianism, and it seems that American blueberries just weren't enough for them.

In a cruel irony, the career of one of France's most ambitious and far-sighted explorers was ended with a musket ball that he had brought all the way from France. If La Salle had time for one final thought before his brain stopped working, he probably wished he had listened to Louis XIV and ended his 'pointless discoveries'.

Meanwhile back in the wilds of Texas, the survivors

struggled on northwards, their numbers continually depleted by the elements and hostile Native Americans. In the end, five men reached a French settlement in Canada, all of them claiming that it was someone else who shot La Salle, of course. None of those who stayed down on the Gulf of Mexico were ever seen again.

Sugar is not so sweet

La Salle's death didn't end French attempts to colonize North America. They still sent out raiding parties from Canada to annoy the New Englanders, and in 1689 they even launched an attack on the large and prosperous colony of New York, which the Brits had recently swapped with the Dutch for Suriname. Luckily for the New Yorkers, though, the French fleet got lost in the fog and sailed back to Canada.

The French were also still interested in settling the Gulf Coast, mainly because they had realized thanks to La Salle that the Mississippi would be a great trading route between Canada and their Caribbean island colonies, which were becoming very rich indeed thanks to sugar plantations.

Ever since Europeans had stumbled across America, they had thought of it as a possible El Dorado, and with sugar they had found liquid gold. Even better, they didn't have to mine it or pay for it – it grew on trees. Well, in plants, anyway.

The Brits were especially fond of this exotic natural sweetener that had suddenly become plentiful and relatively cheap. As well as putting it in desserts and pastries, they used sugar for making alcohol and to sweeten their new national drink, tea. The French didn't use sugar quite as much in alcohol – they had wine – or in their cooking,* but they loved to sell it, which is why sugar was the product of the New World that, much more than tobacco, financed the wars in America and made the Brits determined to hang on to their American colonies.

The sugar that the Brits bought or produced wasn't all shipped back across the Atlantic – it was a vital part of a hugely profitable trade network between the colonies and England. Often referred to as the triangular trade, it was much more complex than that. English-manufactured goods like cloth were shipped down to Africa, where they were sold and the money used to buy slaves. This human cargo was hauled across the Atlantic and the survivors were sold to the sugar planters. The profits went on sugar that was either shipped back to Europe or sent up the Atlantic coast to the rum-thirsty colonists. The colonists in turn would often fill the same ships with their salted cod, which Africa was willing to trade for slaves that the northern colonies could either use on their own tobacco plantations or sell to the French.

All this had a very high cost in human misery, but generated enough profit to make everyone ignore it – it even made the Brits and the French forget when they were at war. There was a fair bit of mutual piracy going on, and some attempts to grab each other's Caribbean islands, but at the end of the seventeenth century, business was generally allowed to carry on as usual so as not to cut off the flow of easy money. The Brits were the biggest slave merchants, and the French their biggest customers because of the need

* These days, the French make fun of English food because, for example, 'les Anglais eat jam with meat' (they mean mint jelly). But almost everything British that the French grudgingly admit to liking is sugar-based. They love our fruit cakes so much that they make a rather pale version of it that they call generically *le cake*. The name has even entered French slang, and a common term for someone with pimples is '*tronche de cake*', or 'cake face', because of all the fruity bits.

for labour on their sugar islands – Saint-Domingue (Haiti), Martinique and Guadeloupe.

Thus it was that between 1687 and 1701 the number of slaves bought by the French planters rose from 28,000 to 40,000, with sugar production and the consequent profits rising accordingly.

Despite France's failure (as yet) to push the Brits into the Atlantic, and despite the painfully slow development of Louisiane, it looked as though America was going to be a source of considerable wealth for the cash-strapped French.

Which was when a Scotsman stepped in and sank their hopes in a quagmire of debt.

Beware of letting a banker run your economy

John Law of Lauriston is remembered by French historians as the man who was responsible for the Mississippi Bubble. This sounds like a painful tropical disease, but was in fact like Britain's South Sea Bubble – the same sort of crazed investment scheme that contributed to global economic meltdown in 2008.

Law was born in Edinburgh in 1671, the son of a gold-smith who, like many goldsmiths of the time, also acted as a banker. When John was only seventeen, he inherited his father's money, and immediately decided to devote his life to spending it. He cultivated an image as a young dandy, chased after society ladies, and frequented Edinburgh's fashionable gambling dens. And he soon found that instead of spending money, he was actually accumulating it, because he had a brilliant mathematical brain and an eye for a good scam.

According to William Harrison Ainsworth, author of a nineteenth-century novelized biography with an almost superhero title – *John Law: The Projector* – Law became adept at a high-betting card game called faro, which was a favourite amongst punters because they stood a much better chance of winning than at other games. However, it was also very popular with seasoned gamblers because it was easy for the banker/dealer to cheat invisibly, which is why it later became notorious in the Wild West as a quick way of relieving gold prospectors and cattle men of their earnings.

Ainsworth defends Law against charges of dishonesty and quotes a French aristocrat who says that Law was 'so skilful at play that without the slightest trickery, he could do that which appears incredible – win enormously'. But as Law toured Europe hosting faro games, he was politely asked to leave several cities, including Paris, where King Louis XIV personally signed the expulsion order. Strange, then, that when Law returned to France in 1715, almost as soon as Louis had been put in his tomb, he was hired by the regent, the duc d'Orléans, as his chief economic adviser.

The Duke was not planning to fill the nation's coffers by organizing faro tournaments (although more modern governments have realized they can do the same thing with lotteries). Law, a friend of the Duke from gambling *soirées* in the old Louis XIV days, had come back to Paris with the news that he had conceived a foolproof way of making money, not just for himself but for whole countries. It didn't bother the duc d'Orléans that several other European monarchs had already said no thanks, *nein danke, no grazie* and similarly negative things to Law's ideas. France was desperate – Louis XIV had got the country into massive debt with his warmongering and the new regent needed a miracle.

Law's system was simple, new and very convincing. His theory was that money generates wealth by changing hands. Especially by entering his own grasp, of course, but more generally by passing through several sets of fingers, thereby enabling each person to sell their wares or services. For example, rich Parisian A has 1,000 *livres* (the French currency of the time) and spends it on a high-class prostitute. The prostitute spends her money on a diamond ring, the jeweller buys Champagne, the wine-seller gets himself a wig and a suit, the tailor treats himself to a new treatment for syphilis, and so on, until the money no doubt ends up back in the pocket of rich Parisian A. Everyone has benefited.

It was the opposite of what often happened to French money at the time. The rich aristocrats would usually sit on their cash, living off the interest. They had to spend large amounts to maintain a show of wealth, but left even larger amounts dormant. Law's plan would wake up the dormant cash and get it out into circulation. It would, he told the regent, make France rich again.

The Duke agreed wholeheartedly with the idea that had got the Scotsman thrown out of less gullible countries, and in 1716 Law was allowed to launch the Banque Générale, which began to issue banknotes, the value of which was backed up with a supply of royal gold and silver. The bank was such a raging success that in 1718 its name was changed to the Banque Royale, the ultimate seal of approval. By this time, though, it was issuing far more notes than it could honour with gold or silver, and confidence in its reputation was only kept high by the Duke's very public support for the scheme.

Meanwhile, Law created a company, the Compagnie d'Occident (Company of the West), and had friends in such high places that he was given exclusive trading rights between France and Louisiane. At the same time, he began to buy land near the Mississippi, which was ridiculously cheap – bits of the untamed swamp were trading at around a zillion square metres for one beaver skin. He had no intention of doing anything with the land – it was pure speculation – but the news that Law himself was buying boosted confidence in his company's shares, which began to sell to the enthusiastic get-rich-quick French at rapidly rising prices. And Law took a personal 4 per cent commission on every deal.

On the strength of this success, Law was given control of all the other colonial *compagnies* dealing with Africa, China and India, and in 1719 he merged them into the optimistically named Compagnie perpetuelle des Indes orientales. Cleverly, he fixed a new share price, obliging investors to give four old shares to acquire one new one, and justified this massive inflation by exaggerating the imminent riches to be had in these undeveloped continents: gold, diamonds, timber, furs and spices, not forgetting cod.

He also deluged France with tales of huge mineral finds around the Mississippi,* trying to tempt new settlers. When none came forward, he (or his representatives) tried less subtle recruitment tactics, rounding up tramps, prostitutes, convicts and lunatics and kidnapping children. All told, some 4,000 potential French-Americans were shipped out and dumped in 'forts' that had been set up along the Gulf Coast, notably in Biloxi, which was devastated by Hurricane Katrina in 2005, and wasn't much more hospitable back in 1719 because the French had built their settlement practically on top of a Native American village.

Soon, the purely speculative nature of the colonization began to tell, and the forty-odd settlements in Louisiane – along the Mississippi and Ohio valleys, in Texas and the prairies – were all close to extinction, mainly because the

* For once, Law was actually telling the truth, but sadly oil wouldn't be found there until after the French had sold Louisiane.

Compagnie had a nasty habit of not paying for the furs and other goods that it bought. As a result, almost all the new immigrants died or drifted away to set up their own independent communities.

Back in France, though, Law's guile and self-confidence were still keeping things afloat. He merged the Compagnie and the Banque, got himself appointed France's Contrôleur général des finances in January 1720, and even arranged to lend the state over a billion *livres* – all of it in his own paper money. In just three months, the shares in his new company rose from 500 *livres* to a staggering 20,000 *livres* – a 4,000 per cent increase, which was a pretty competitive rate of earnings by any standards.

At this point, some canny shareholders said that they would like to cash in their investment, *s'il vous plaît*, and began to sell. Others asked to exchange their pretty Banque Royale banknotes for lumps of more solid precious metal – as was their right – only to discover that the Banque had a billion *livres'* worth of notes in circulation and a mere 330 million in gold and silver.

The whole system sank as quickly as a supply ship stuck in the Mississippi mud, and took everyone down with it. Well, nearly everyone – Law, the captain, fled to Venice in December 1720, abandoning France to its fate. He had persuaded an estimated one million French families to buy shares in his various companies, and all of them were left with worthless bits of paper. The same went for anyone with his banknotes in their safes or mattresses. 'Last January I had 60,000 *livres* in paper money,' a French lawyer wrote in 1721. 'Now I haven't even got enough to give my servants their Christmas box.' Which shows how hard it was hitting.

Britain catches the French disease

The comic thing was that, while John Law's Mississippi Bubble was bursting, the Brits decided to inflate their own South Sea Bubble. It was almost as if they wanted to outdo France's insanity.

The South Sea Company had been making money for a decade or so out of slave trading with South America (the name 'South Seas' referred to the Spanish-controlled part of the Atlantic), and had been promising exaggerated profits but bankrupting no one until early 1720. Then, just as Law's system was heading for the toilet, an investment frenzy took off, with corrupt English politicians accepting shares in return for speeches about how the South Sea Company was on the verge of making a fortune from Peruvian gold, and similar Lawesque nonsense. The share price rose from £120 to about £1,000 – an absurd increase, although a modest one compared to France's 4,000 per cent.

At the same time, a whole multitude of copycat schemes sprang up, with British companies promising to do things like develop perpetual motion and insure people against damage caused by their servants. There were companies to 'improve the art of making soap', to 'trade in hair', and, most notoriously, for 'carrying on an undertaking of great advantage, but nobody to know what it is'. The director of that particular start-up offered 5,000 shares at £100 each, with a guaranteed dividend of £100 per annum per share. All he was asking at the outset was a £2 deposit per share. He opened his office door in London one morning at 9 a.m. to find a crowd waiting. By 3 p.m., he had taken 1,000 deposits, and at 3.01 p.m. precisely he disappeared, never to be heard of again, having made £2,000 profit (minus a day's office rental and some printing) in six hours – this at a time when a skilled tradesman might make £200 a year.

The scenario was repeated, with only slightly less dishonesty, a hundred times in London. Shares were issued in the morning, a stock-crazy public would meet their brokers in coffee houses to buy them, the company directors would sell immediately to grab their profit, and the company would fold overnight. It was total madness, and one asks oneself why people were gullible enough to keep offering themselves up like pigs knocking on the wolf's front door. (Though the answer to that question is, of course, quite simple: as the recent collapse of the Madoff 'investment' scheme has shown, we human beings have an almost limitless talent for gullibility as soon as someone promises us unrealistic returns on our investments.)

When the British bubble inevitably burst, many investors were ruined and a gaggle of top politicians lost their jobs. A certain Lord Molesworth asked Parliament to vote on a motion that the 'contrivers and executors of the villainous South Sea scheme', who had started all the trouble, should be 'tied in sacks and thrown into the Thames'. The newly appointed First Lord of the Treasury, Robert Walpole, wryly replied that they should make good the losses first, and the South Sea Company's directors had their assets confiscated. The damage was severe, and confidence in the government was virtually destroyed, but – vitally – the crisis hadn't dented Britain's faith in empire-building. Amazingly, the Company itself was restructured and survived until the 1850s.

John Law wasn't so lucky. He didn't get thrown in the river, but he suffered a similar fate, dying in Venice in 1729 after contracting pneumonia while out on a gondola. He was not mourned much on either side of the Atlantic, because the damage he inflicted had bitten deep. He had not only lured France into bankruptcy but had also done irreparable damage to the Louisiane brand.

Ironically, the only people who didn't realize this were a few poor French colonists trying to live there.

Way down in New Orleans

In 1721, a year after John Law's corrupt scheme had collapsed, construction work began on a new settlement on the banks of the Mississippi. It was going to be called Nouvelle-Orléans in honour of the regent, the duc d'Orléans, and the settlers had decided that they wanted something a little grander than the usual palisade-around-a-hut arrangement. Accordingly, an engineer called Adrien de Pauger had been commissioned to build a real town on a strict grid system, with six blocks by eleven of building plots.

Right from the start, though, de Pauger hit problems. Not because of the financial hurricane that was sweeping France, but because the settlers seemed incapable of sticking to his neat grid plan – they kept trying to build houses at the wrong angles and in the middle of his projected streets. This drove the short-tempered de Pauger to distraction, and he began to get into fights with the French colonists, some of whom were whinging that he was building the town in completely the wrong place and ought to move it further downstream.

Amazingly, though, the town gradually grew according to de Pauger's grid system, and a new style of architecture developed with it: French colonial, with its elegant wooden façades and classical columns. De Pauger also built the first levee to protect the town against the unpredictable waters of the Mississippi. He didn't do it all himself, of course – it took 4,231 man days of slave labour to finish.

When Nouvelle-Orléans was officially named the capital of Louisiane in 1723, it looked as though the colony might actually pull itself out of the political and financial mire. Until, that is, the French shot themselves in the foot yet again. With, it should be said, a little help from the Brits.

At this time, French colonists in America enjoyed good relations with some of the biggest and most powerful Native American peoples like the Iroquois and the Hurons, whom they had persuaded to fight against the English. The small French settlements of Fort Rosalie and Fort Arkansas on the eastern bank of the Mississippi depended for their survival on the goodwill of the Natchez people. The Natchez had developed a highly complex agricultural society, and lived not in one big tepee village as Europeans might imagine, but spread out in family farms, with a territorial capital built on a large ceremonial mound. They made excellent cloth and pottery, had a well-defined class system, and enjoyed inter-tribal lacrosse tournaments. All in all, they were a lot more civilized than most of the European settlers in the area, and had even helped to build Fort Rosalie by supplying much of the timber.

British agents provocateurs (ironic that the name should be French) were constantly trying to spoil this cosy relationship, and some of them had been getting at the Natchez, warning them what would happen if France got too strong a foothold on their land – yes, those grassy lacrosse pitches would get covered in gravel and used for *pétanque*. And one day in 1729, the commander of the French garrison at Rosalie confirmed the Brits' propaganda by building his house on the site of a Natchez farm.

The Natchez duly attacked Fort Rosalie, massacring 60 slaves and 183 French (mainly male) settlers and taking the women prisoner. The French army was quick to react, and came marching into Natchez territory to exact revenge. A first expedition recovered 50 French women and 100 slaves. A second incursion was pure genocide: all but 1,500 or so of the 6,000 Natchez were slaughtered. Of the survivors, 500 were sent to the sugar plantations of Saint-Domingue as slaves, and the rest managed to escape and were taken in as refugees by other peoples such as the Creeks, Cherokees and Chickasaws.

As stories of the genocide spread, previously neutral Native Americans turned against France. In 1736, the Chickasaws began preparing for war, urged on by the surviving Natchez. The French got wind of this, and sent two small armies into Chickasaw territory. The first, consisting of 400-odd men, was attacked and burnt alive. The second was beaten back and retreated to the coast.

And the fighting had far-reaching consequences beyond the immediate ethnic cleansing of the Natchez territory. King Louis XV declared the whole of Louisiane a free-trade zone, undermining Nouvelle-Orléans's status as an obligatory stop-off for goods coming in and out of the region. And the newly created town's situation was made even more precarious because its customers – the French settlers – took fright and began moving away en masse.

Thanks to an ill-advised French housebuilding project and some British troublemaking, France had lost its hold on a huge swathe of eastern Louisiane.

And a cow was about to evict them from the rest.

A tale of two Georges

In 1752, a certain twenty-year-old man took an oath of allegiance to his monarch, England's King George II, and was made an army officer. The young soldier served the British Governor of Virginia reliably, and soon his reputation was so good that he was chosen to lead a vital mission against the French.

This stalwart English patriot's name was George Washington. Yes, *the* George Washington, the first President of the USA. Americans tend to blur everything in his biography between the chopping down of his father's cherry tree and his part in the anti-British revolution, but a snapshot of him in the early 1750s would probably have shown him singing 'God Save the King' (which was a recent hit, having first been published in 1744) while saluting the Union Jack (which had been officially adopted as the Great British flag in 1707).

Washington, the son of a planter and slave-owner, had begun his working life at sixteen, surveying land for a distant relative of his, Lord Fairfax, the only English hereditary peer living in North America and a fierce Loyalist who would remain pro-British even after the Revolutionary War. Now young George was going to be given a much more political job.

Throughout 1752 and 1753, the Governor of Virginia, Robert Dinwiddie, was becoming increasingly concerned about French fort-building along the Ohio River, to the west of his colony. This was an area claimed by France as part of Louisiane, but it was also in the territory that the newly formed Ohio Company had appropriated for itself with a view to fur-trading. Governor Dinwiddie happened to be a shareholder in the company, so he gave the young Washington, who was a major in the Virginia militia (Britain's local civilian army), a mission – to go and tell the French to get out of Ohio, or else.

Washington took an ultimatum to Fort Le Boeuf in Pennsylvania, which he found to be a well-built outpost equipped with several cannons and manned by an experienced French-Canadian officer and a hundred men. The French, Washington reported, looked as though they intended to stick around.

The news worried Dinwiddie, who wasn't surprised when his ultimatum was ignored and the fort-building went on. But when he heard that the French were establishing a settlement on the site of a former British fort and calling it Fort Duquesne in honour of the Governor of Nouvelle-France, he decided the provocation had gone far enough. He promoted Washington to lieutenant colonel and sent him out to deliver another eviction notice to the French trespassers. Washington did as he was told; being a polite planter's son, he asked them to leave. Being French soldiers, they refused.

What happened next is rather controversial, and is often glossed over when the future First President's life is discussed.*

According to the French, when Washington saw that Fort Duquesne wasn't going to be dismantled, he decided to build a base for himself, which he diplomatically opted to call Fort Necessity (as in 'don't blame us, Messieurs les Français, you're making us do this'). Fort Duquesne's commander wasn't going to let this happen without a fight, so he sent forty or fifty of his men to warn the British off.

The raiding party was led by an officer called Jumonville (his name was much, much longer, but we won't interrupt the suspense by going into that here), who began roaming around threatening violence to any English-speakers he could find. One of his victims was a farmer called Christopher Gist, who arrived in Washington's camp during the night of 23 May 1754, complaining that some French soldiers had burst into his cabin and told him that if he didn't leave the area, they would kill his cow.

* By American writers, that is. The French love to talk about it.

Yes, an Englishman's milker was in danger of being turned into French *steak-frites*. Clearly, the British had no option but to declare war. Guided by a Native American called Tanacharison (who could relate to the cow because he claimed that the French had boiled and eaten his father), Washington immediately went out and found Jumonville's raiding party encamped amongst the trees in a rather attractive rocky glade. About forty Virginians and twelve of Tanacharison's men encircled the camp, and at dawn on 24 May 1754, Washington gave the order to fire. A few minutes later, a dozen Frenchmen lay dead and twenty-three were captured, including their wounded leader, Jumonville.

The battle was won and fighting had officially stopped, but Tanacharison, perhaps deciding that Jumonville looked like the man who had cooked his father, stepped up and bludgeoned the poor Frenchman with his tomahawk, before washing his hands in his victim's brains.

As an officer and a gentleman, Washington probably disapproved of this kind of behaviour, but these were violent times – after all, his men had just ambushed a dozen sleeping Frenchmen to stop them committing some serious animal abuse. So, not letting his conscience get in the way of his mission, Washington went ahead and built Fort Necessity.

It was a grand name for a spindly construction consisting of one hut surrounded by a ring of two-metre high logs, and therefore stood no chance of resisting the 700 Frenchmen who came looking for vengeance.

They were led by Jumonville's brother, Louis de Villiers (his full handle was much longer, but he did have one name in common with his sibling), who began to riddle Fort Necessity with French musket balls. It seemed likely that Washington would soon have to capitulate or be turned into Emmental, but de Villiers was impatient to see justice done, and sent over a message threatening that if the Brits didn't surrender, the pro-French Native Americans would scalp any survivors.

While George was mulling this over, a group of Virginians took advantage of the lull to break out the garrison's rum ration and get roaring drunk. This, plus the pouring rain that was dampening the British gun-powder, convinced Washington to accept the French proposal. He and his men would abandon their fort and march back to Virginia.

First, however, de Villiers gave Washington a document to sign. George, being a typical Brit of the time, couldn't read French, but signed it anyway. What did a piece of enemy paper matter? They were out in the apparently infinite forests of Ohio, where de Villiers was (according to the Brits, anyway) an illegal alien, so his supposedly legal document was worthless.

Unfortunately, what the document said was that he, George Washington, admitted full responsibility for the murder of Jumonville. Yes, according to the French legal profession, the kindly-looking white-haired Father of the Nation was a confessed murderer.

On 4 July, a date that would later be associated with the signature of a less incriminating document, Washington marched his men out of the fort, trying his best to ignore the taunts of the triumphant Frenchmen and Native Americans who grabbed guns and supplies from the retreating soldiers. It was, American historians are keen to point out, Washington's only military defeat.

His confession, meanwhile, was published and used as proof that the British were a brutal race of cold-blooded killers, although as we saw with the slaughter of the Natchez, this was one monopoly that British colonists couldn't claim. And there were, after all, mitigating circumstances in Washington's case, because everything

he did was for a noble cause: the defence of an innocent
cow.

Scalps should be rinsed before use

By 1756, France and Britain were formally at war rather
than just fighting each other. Then, as now, there was a
technical difference between the two. In fact, rather like
a playground football match, the Seven Years War (it
wasn't yet called that, of course) was only declared once
a respectable array of players had been assembled. After
some jostling, the two sides were Britain and Prussia
against Austria, Spain and France. At stake, as usual, was
who would be the most powerful nation in Europe.

At first, things went rather well for the French,
especially outside America. In April 1756, a huge invasion force of ships and soldiers invaded the
British-held island of Menorca. An inadequate British
rescue force was sent down to relieve Mahon, the island's
capital, but failed to do so – it hardly even engaged the
enemy. France celebrated by inventing a new sauce, *la
mahonnaise*, designed specifically to be too complicated
for English chefs to make properly.

Britain sulked so much that the admiral sent to save
the Mahon garrison, Sir John Byng, was court-martialled
for 'not doing his utmost' and shot. His was the
execution that so shocked Voltaire that he described
the incident in his novel *Candide*.

Even more British outrage was caused in August 1757
when 6,000 Frenchmen and 2,000 Native Americans
attacked Britain's Fort William Henry in upstate New
York, which was defended by about 2,200 British regular
soldiers and colonial militiamen. As they had done
with Washington at Fort Necessity, the French got
some shooting and bombarding out of their system

and then offered the Brits the chance to surrender.

The French leader, Montcalm (who would die in 1759 defending Quebec), promised that the defeated troops and all their civilian camp followers could leave unmolested. So it came as some surprise when the departing Brits were leapt upon by the pro-French Native Americans. Men, women and children were slaughtered, while guns and scalps were snatched as trophies. Apparently the warriors had been under the impression that they would be able to do some killing and looting, and didn't agree with the generous surrender terms.

Estimates vary, but it is likely that almost 200 people died before Montcalm was able to live up to his name and calm his bloodthirsty allies. No one ever asked him to sign a confession admitting to mass murder, but history has been much less kind to him than to Washington, because in 1826 the events at Fort William Henry were immortalized in James Fenimore Cooper's novel *The Last of the Mohicans*, which tells the story of an attempt by two Native Americans to save the British commander's daughters.

History took more immediate revenge, too – after the massacre, some Native Americans returned to the scene of their crime and dug up the bodies, hoping to get more scalps. What they actually got was smallpox, which they passed on, starting a raging epidemic that caused countless deaths amongst the French and their allies. And one of the victims may well have been Washington's accuser, Louis de Villiers, who died in Quebec of smallpox in 1757.

Gifting America to the Brits

Officially, the Seven Years War lived up to its name, and lasted until 1763, but in practice it was pretty well over after only three years. By this time, France had lost Quebec and a largely unsung English naval hero called Sir Edward Hawke had done so much damage to French shipping that France had almost no way of transporting soldiers and supplies across the Atlantic. Paris therefore began to put out feelers for a negotiated end to the war in late 1759.

Naturally, the French didn't admit this to everyone, which was why one poor Breton was still wasting his energy trying to make a go of Louisiane.

As governor of the territory, Louis Billouart, chevalier de Kerlerec, was doing his best to bring order to total chaos. Everyone in Nouvelle-Orléans seemed to be arguing with everyone else – the military with the merchants, the clergy with the lay people, the Jesuits with rival religious groups – and when the penniless Acadien refugees started to pour in after having been expelled from Canada, they became a whole new source of expense and argument.

Kerlerec feared that the Brits could just stroll in and take Nouvelle-Orléans whenever they wanted, so he had a wooden palisade built around the town and moored an old ship in the Mississippi so that it could be sunk to block a British invasion fleet. He also asked Paris and Canada for more troops, but these requests were ignored. He was on his own.

Kerlerec's only choice was to try and convince the Native Americans that the French weren't all like the troops who had massacred the Natchez. And at first he was successful, persuading the Cherokees to help him defend Nouvelle-Orléans if the Brits came calling.

In the event, though, he didn't need to call on the Native Americans, because, as the French historian Henri Blet puts it, Nouvelle-Orléans 'wasn't attacked. It had to defend itself against itself.' In other words, France was perfectly capable of losing colonies without help from the *Anglais*.

Kerlerec's problem was that he was a rather stuffy naval officer in charge of a vast area populated by trappers, fur merchants and slave-owners – people who were perpetually living on the verge of bankruptcy and violent death, and therefore given to bouts of dishonesty and corruption. The only bribes that Kerlerec willingly paid were sweeteners for the Native Americans. The chiefs had to stay pro-French, and to ensure this, regular gift presentation ceremonies were held. The Governor would invite tribal representatives to a great banquet, during which he would formally hand over large quantities of gunpowder, bullets, billhooks, axes and red paint (the Native Americans loved to decorate themselves and their villages in red) which the chiefs would then distribute amongst their warriors.

The budget for this exercise was managed not by the Governor but by his *ordonnateur*, or financial controller, in this case another naval man called Vincent de Rochemore. But budgets were a sore point with Rochemore. Even before he arrived in Nouvelle-Orléans, he had been complaining that his salary wouldn't be enough to keep himself and his family, and that he would have to spend his own money to maintain a decent lifestyle. A financial controller with money issues was not a happy combination, and soon there were rumours that Rochemore was stealing the Native Americans' gifts and selling them for his own profit. And as Kerlerec was keenly aware, a Cherokee deprived of his French axe or paint pot might go looking for more generous allies.

The Governor had no choice but to send Rochemore back to France, where the disgraced *ordonnateur* immediately set about destroying Kerlerec's reputation. It was alleged, for example, that the Governor wanted to have the gift ceremonies in Nouvelle-Orléans, whereas it would have been safer to have them at Mobile, where there was a large French fort as well as a town. Why would Kerlerec want the ceremonies close to home if it wasn't to steal some of the red paint for himself?

The upshot was that Kerlerec was recalled and thrown into the Bastille, then exiled from Paris and ordered to stay 30 leagues away from any royal palace (presumably the authorities were afraid he would paint red graffiti on the walls).

In essence, Louisiane's last chance of staying French was lost because of an argument over presents. It was like a family's Christmas Day squabble that ends when the house burns down.

Meanwhile, France's Fort Duquesne, which had got George Washington into such hot water, had been lost, and a new British outpost built in its place – this was Fort Pitt, which would later become Pittsburgh, in honour of Britain's prime minister.

The 1763 Treaty of Paris, which marked the official end of the fighting, was a total humiliation for France. King Louis XV signed over Nouvelle-France (Canada), preferring to hang on to the sugar islands of Guadeloupe and Martinique. The fighting had involved Spain, too, and in an exchange of territories, Britain obtained Florida, while France gave Spain its lands on the west bank of the Mississippi, which included Nouvelle-Orléans. (Although no one dared tell the town the bad news until September 1764.) Meanwhile, Britain received the east bank of the Mississippi, meaning that Louisiane was split down the middle and lost. The French humiliation even stretched all the way back home – France agreed to dismantle the forti-fications in its own port of Dunkirk so that England would feel less threatened by an invasion.

You can feel the lasting pain in a French government website. 'The Treaty of Paris', it says, 'annihilated two centuries of effort by colonists, explorers and royal officials. It was the end of the dreams of a French America.' And it was all their own fault. As Napoleon himself once said, 'Our ridiculous national fault is that the greatest enemy of our success and glory is ourselves.'

In other words, the French really should not have provoked George Washington by threatening to kill that cow. Never has a piece of steak cost a Frenchman so dear.

14

American Independence – from France

There's one thing you can't accuse the French of, and that is giving up on trying to outwit the Brits. Even after the humiliation of the Treaty of Paris, which robbed France of practically every square centimetre of land it had owned in America, the French didn't abandon hope of spoiling things for the *Anglais* on the other side of the Atlantic. First they helped the Americans gain independence (though they received scant gratitude for that), and then they went one better and tried to turn America into Britain's arch enemy in world politics – and we all know how well that turned out.

And the final move in their American power play was so disastrous that even today, almost no one in France knows the whole truth . . .

Merci but *non merci*

American independence really started not with the Boston Tea Party but with a huge, and uncharacteristic, British mistake: having fought a vicious seven-year guerrilla war to hang on to America, the Brits went soft.

And the Americans were all too quick to show them that softness was for wimps.

The first sign of flabbiness was King George III's Proclamation of 1763, which forbade European settlement west of the Appalachians, the mountain chain that runs parallel to the Atlantic coast from Canada down to Alabama. It was a surprisingly modern proposal – the Brits were effectively saying that the vast majority of the American continent would be better off in the hands of its rightful owners, the Native Americans.

This provoked immediate fury in the American colonies, because it hemmed them in even more efficiently than the French had ever done. Worse still, eviction orders were issued to settlers living west of the Appalachians, including those in Ohio, where the Seven Years War had originally broken out. Leading Americans like George Washington were horrified – they'd fought and died for this land, expelled the French army, and now they were meant to give the territory away?

Britain then showed its total flaccidity by passing a second compassionate law, the Quebec Act, in favour of those other enemies of the American colonists – the French-Canadians, who had provided so much help to France. The Act finalized the separation of Canada from the American colonies, and gave the French Catholics living there religious freedom and even some independence within the new British territory of Quebec. The British-Americans, many of them hard-line Puritans, didn't take kindly to this at all.

So the American patriotism that had united the disparate colonies against the French now turned against the Brits, especially when London began to try and recoup some of the costs of the war by imposing higher colonial taxes. It was one of these taxes that provoked the Boston Tea Party in 1773, the famous protest by a gang of

Bostonians who dressed up as Native Americans, as if they hoped to prove that the Iroquois and Cherokees were too badly behaved to own a whole continent.

France couldn't resist the temptation. It saw the breach in Britain's empire, and decided to fill it with French gunpowder.

Famous names join the war

Louis XVI's Minister for Foreign Affairs, Charles Gravier de Vergennes, was virulently anti-British, and wanted revenge for the Seven Years War and the Treaty of Paris. When divisions began to appear between the Brits and the Americans, he saw his chance. 'Providence,' he said, 'has chosen this as the time for the humiliation of England.'

At the same time, Benjamin Franklin was over in Europe, ostensibly as the Colonies' representative in London, but also making *amis* with France. The French apparently fell in love with the easy-going, unpretentious American immediately, even though he was a vegetarian. He was a self-made man, a successful writer and inventor turned politician, and seems to have cut through Parisian snobbishness like a tomahawk.

The French may also have felt an affinity with him because he, like them, had a talent for eccentric and ultimately useless inventions – he conceived the glass harmonica, a musical instrument that enabled the player to make the sound of running his or her moistened fingers around the rim of a glass, only using a much more complicated method. Franklin did useful research too, notably into electricity, and even though he was a rather stout, plainly dressed man, his eccentricity seems to have endeared him to the Parisiennes. It might well have been this success that led him to develop his theory that the best protection against sexually transmitted disease was a hearty post-coital pee. Not one of his better ideas.

Anyway, when Franklin arrived in Paris in late 1776 to ask the French to help defend America's newly declared independence, he was welcomed with open arms by the Minister for Foreign Affairs. The only condition that the anti-British Vergennes wanted to impose was that no one should know that France was supporting America, so the minister looked around for someone to be their unofficial go-between.

The man Vergennes chose was Pierre-Augustin Caron de Beaumarchais. He is famous today for his plays *The Barber of Seville* and *The Marriage of Figaro*, but before achieving literary fame, this former watchmaker and harp tutor to the royal family was engaged in less public, and often much shadier, activities. His first two wives both died in mysterious circumstances, leaving him to inherit their fortunes, and on one occasion he was sent to London to shore up the reputation of one of Louis XV's mistresses. Now, Vergennes asked Beaumarchais to become an arms dealer. Comedy writer as gun-runner for revolutionaries? It was as if Ricky Gervais had been shipping missiles to the Tamil Tigers.

Beaumarchais set up a fictitious company called Roderigue Hortalez et Compagnie (the Spanish name was chosen to disguise its true origins) and began trading French arms with America in exchange for tobacco. In all, he shipped around 30,000 muskets and 2,000 barrels of gunpowder across the Atlantic, as well as cannons, uniforms and tents.

One man in France was advising caution, however. This was the Contrôleur général des finances, a rather dull and un-Beaumarchaisesque economist with a woman's first name – Anne-Robert-Jacques Turgot. He suggested that the French should stay well out of the

American Revolutionary War – otherwise, he said, the Brits would turn against France and embroil the country in a war it couldn't afford.

Ironically, Turgot was probably the most pro-American politician in France. He supported the revolutionaries' egalitarian ideals, and was lobbying for economic reforms to reduce social inequality amongst his own countrymen. And it was for precisely this reason that his warning was ignored. He had made too many enemies amongst the French aristocracy, and they were fed up with him trying to tell them what to do with the country's money.

In the event, of course, Turgot was right. Vergennes's and Beaumarchais's 'these aren't French weapons, honest, even if they're being shipped from France and have "Made in France" stamped on the boxes' ploy was fooling no one. The Brits had long seen through the pretence, mainly because some very prominent Frenchmen were giving the game away.

The most famous of these was Lafayette, America's favourite Frenchman. This nineteen-year-old nobleman, whose real name no American would have been able to pronounce – Marie-Joseph Paul Yves Roch Gilbert du Motier, marquis de La Fayette – came from an almost genetically anti-British family. One of his ancestors had fought alongside Joan of Arc, and his father had been killed by an Anglo-German cannonball during the Seven Years War. So in April 1777 Lafayette sailed to America to join the cause célèbre, despite the pleas of Louis XVI to be a bit more discreet.

Soon, there was no point pretending, anyway. In February 1778, the French signed an alliance with the Americans, causing the Brits, who had been preparing for just such an eventuality, to declare war. France now had to start pumping real money into the conflict.

At this stage, things weren't looking good for American

independence. There were more pro-British Loyalists in the Colonies than there were Patriots fighting for Washington. Meanwhile, most Native Americans were siding with George III, who wanted to grant them land rights, and around 100,000 slaves had run away from their owners after they were offered freedom if they fought for the Brits – George Washington was one of the men who lost valuable unpaid workers in this way. His own soldiers were deserting and mutinying, too. He was in desperate need of French support.

And he got it. The USA may have forgotten it during the Iraq War, but France really did go all out to win independence for America. It even sent one of its best old soldiers, a man called Rochambeau, to Newport, Rhode Island, with an army of over 6,000 troops.

At first, relations between these French troops and their American hosts were tense. The French were gamblers, and seemed to be able to ogle right through the chaste Puritan women's clothing. To avoid a diplomatic incident, only officers were allowed out of camp, and their elegant manners soon charmed the locals, who were touched that such noblemen would come to help their fight for democracy. And when Washington visited his new allies, he was received warmly. The French seemed to have forgotten that he had fought against them in the Seven Years War and signed a confession admitting to the cold-blooded murder of one of their officers.

Such a cosy atmosphere couldn't last for ever, though, and the French didn't take long to start squabbling amongst themselves. Rochambeau got into an argument with Lafayette, who had been made Washington's aide-de-camp*

* Incidentally, Rochambeau's own aide-de-camp was the dashing Swede Count Hans Axel von Fersen, who is seen swashbuckling Marie-Antoinette in Sophia Coppola's film. The royal adultery has never really been proven, though.

and thought he knew a thing or two about war. The young marquis had already been shot in the leg while helping the Americans to lose a battle in Pennsylvania, and he now tried to tell Rochambeau how to deploy his troops. This elicited a superb putdown – the older man wrote 'as a father to a dear son', accusing Lafayette of personal ambition:

> It is all very well to consider the French invincible, but I am going to tell you a great secret that I have learned in 40 years of experience – no one is easier to beat [than French soldiers] when they have lost confidence in their leaders, and they lose it immediately if they feel that they have been endangered for the sake of personal gain.

In summer 1779, to take the pressure off Washington's hard-pressed men, France mounted a farcical attempt to invade Britain. An army of some 30,000 troops was amassed on the Channel coast and loaded on to French and Spanish ships. However, many of the ships had been supplied with dirty drinking water, and when they tried to provoke the Brits into a naval battle in the Channel, the English fleet kept sailing out of range, drawing the French away from their potential landing points. In the end, with French soldiers and sailors dropping like flies from scurvy and water poisoning, the invasion force simply sailed back to France. It is said that so many French corpses were floating round the Channel by this time that the Cornish stopped eating fish.

The French win American independence

Luckily, over in America, Rochambeau was making a better job of helping Washington, and in October 1781 a combined army of some 8,000 French and 9,000

Americans won the victory that, in American folk memory at least, finally clinched independence. They besieged the last big British army – 6,000 men – that was holed up in Yorktown, Virginia. Half of these men were wounded or suffering from smallpox and other diseases, and the British commander, Charles Cornwallis, was only holding out because he had been promised reinforcements from the north. But when a French fleet cut the reinforcements off, Cornwallis was forced to surrender Yorktown, and British resistance to American independence ended with it.

The surrender ceremony was a touching moment of Franco-American togetherness. Cornwallis, claiming to be too ill to attend, sent his second-in-command, an Irishman called Brigadier General Charles O'Hara, who tried to give his sword to Rochambeau. The Frenchman politely refused, implicitly forcing the British officer to recognize the legitimacy of the American cause. O'Hara turned to Washington, who also refused to accept the surrender from an inferior officer, and O'Hara was finally obliged to present his sword to the American second-in-command, Major General Benjamin Lincoln (no relation to Abraham).

As well as giving this diplomatic support at the end of British rule, the French had also suffered more casualties than the Americans during the siege of Yorktown – around 200 to the Americans' 80. And it was their fleet, after all, that had sunk Cornwallis's last hopes of rescue. It might therefore seem ungrateful on the Americans' part that they started negotiating a formal end to the war with the British, excluding the French from the discussions.

In the subsequent agreement, the Americans and the Brits essentially got together to screw France. Britain had to recognize the independence of the American Colonies, but held on to Canada. The Brits and Americans guaranteed each other unmolested access to the Mississippi River. And as soon as the war was over, the Americans turned their back on the French traders who had been shipping over weapons and supplies, and started doing business with the Brits. Very quickly, the two former enemies were the best of business buddies.

The Native Americans, of course, received zilch, and having lost the protection of their old friend George III were not going to enjoy the nineteenth century very much.

All that France got out of the deal was the excitement of helping downtrodden Americans rebel against their monarchy – an idea that Frenchmen would soon apply at home. Poor Louis XVI thought he was giving his English neighbours a sly stab in the back. In the event, though, he had slotted his own head into the guillotine.

I've got a Bonaparte to pick with you

Incredibly (some might say masochistically), France managed to revive its dream of a French America one more time. And the man who rekindled the flame (and subsequently peed all over it, as most French leaders tended to do) was Napoleon Bonaparte.

When America gained its independence from Britain, it only possessed the eastern half of the country. Spain owned much more of North America than America did – in the 1763 Treaty of Paris, it had received French Louisiane, the vast, mostly unexplored, expanse of land west of the Mississippi that included Nouvelle-Orléans.

But the Spanish were having problems getting the most out of their possessions. There had been a revolt by the French population of New Orleans that had been violently put down by an Irish mercenary working for Spain called Alexander O'Reilly, and the Spanish had tried and failed to stop the Americans getting free access to the vital trade route up the Mississippi. America also had 'right of deposit' in New Orleans, which meant that they could use the city as a storage centre for merchandise going to and from their settlements on the east bank. Spanish colonization, meanwhile, was stagnating.

The year was 1800. France had come through the upheaval of the Revolution, and its new leader, Napoleon, was turning his attention to matters outside the country's borders. He looked at the Spanish dossier and saw a way of furthering King Charles IV of Spain's and his own interests with one neat swap – France would take back the troublesome former Louisiane in exchange for extending the territory governed by Charles IV's son-in-law, the Duke of Parma, in Italy. Even today, there are many who would agree that a few square kilometres of Tuscany are worth all of Missouri, Kansas, Oklahoma and a whole bunch of other American states, and back then Charles seems to have been very satisfied with the deal. However, Napoleon insisted that Spain should not brag about its new Italian acquisition, because he wanted to keep the agreement a secret from the Americans. As a result, no one told the French Louisianans themselves, who thought that they were still living in a Spanish colony.

It was a difficult secret to keep, though, and before the handover had even been made, the Americans sent envoys to France to make sure that their old access agreements to the Mississippi would be respected.

Thus it was that in 1801 President Jefferson sent a New York lawyer, Robert R. Livingston (Americans had already started celebrating their independence from Britain by inserting initials in their names), to Paris to try and buy New Orleans. It was a mission impossible, though, mainly because Livingston had to deal with a notoriously slippery character: Napoleon's Foreign Minister, Charles-Maurice de Talleyrand-Périgord.

Talleyrand was a womanizing nobleman with a limp, a non-believer who had become a bishop in order to get rich, only to abandon the clergy when religion became taboo during the Revolution. By 1801, he was renowned as a politician who had no real principles except self-advancement – he once said: 'Treason is a matter of dates.' Talleyrand's boss, Napoleon, was no fan of his Foreign Minister, and apparently called him 'a piece of shit in a silk stocking'. A difficult man to do business with, then, especially because he was rumoured to want a personal cut of any financial deal he did for the French government.

Talleyrand was the right man to negotiate with the Americans,* though, because he understood their aspirations. He had spent a couple of years in exile in America after the French Revolution, selling land in Massachusetts and books and condoms in Philadelphia.

The 1801 negotiations to sell New Orleans fell through, but by 1803 Napoleon was in urgent need of cash – he was at war with Britain and there was a revolt in his sugar colony of Saint-Domingue (Haiti), which threatened to lower his income even more. Worse, he owed the Americans 18 million francs ($3.75 million) in reparations for French acts of piracy committed on American shipping since their independence.

So when Robert R. Livingston (bizarrely, the 'R' stood for Robert – it was also his father's name) came back to Paris in April 1803, hoping to buy unlimited access to the Mississippi for $2 million, he was astonished to be

---

* Incidentally, Talleyrand's former home on the place de la Concorde is now the American Embassy in Paris.

offered the whole of Louisiane west of the river for $15 million, minus the above-mentioned reparations. Livingston's co-negotiator, James Monroe, arrived a few days later, and the two of them concluded that it had to be a trick – they weren't empowered to discuss such a massive deal, and thought the French were trying to buy time by forcing the two men to wait for consent from Jefferson.

America was not built on prevarication, though, and Livingston and Monroe quickly decided that it was an opportunity not to be missed. The price, they worked out, was less than three cents an acre. Even 200 years ago, this was ridiculously cheap. What's more, Jefferson had told them that they could, at a pinch, spend $9 million on river rights and the ownership of New Orleans. For $6 million more, they were being offered half a continent. The only real worry seemed to be that the French refused to say exactly where they considered Louisiane's frontiers to be. The Mississippi formed a natural border on one side, but America would just have to work out the rest for itself.*

Nevertheless, it was an unbelievable opportunity. Terrified that Napoleon would change his mind, the two Americans scribbled out a contract, the so-called 'letter that bought a continent', by which France would receive 80 million francs ($15 million), minus the 18 million francs that it owed America, in exchange for all remaining French possessions in America. The agreement was signed on 30 April 1803, and announced to the Americans on 4 July (that date again). The Louisiana Purchase (or Louisiana Sale – Vente de la Louisiane – as the French logically called it) was complete. Napoleon

* One map drawn up by the French Treasury even seems to suggest – falsely – that Louisiane stretched west as far as Washington state.

had kicked himself and his country out of North America once and for all.

At the time, he claimed to have won a great coup against the Brits by elevating America to the rank of a world power: 'I have given England a maritime rival who sooner or later will humble her.' But this was proved wrong almost immediately. Just two years later, an Englishman called Nelson would humble (or rather, blast to smithereens) Napoleon's own maritime force at Trafalgar. And Britain and the USA became firm friends in the early nineteenth century and have stayed so ever since.

It's cruel, really. Rather like *Monty Python*'s blue parrot, the French have never stopped pining for Louisiane. And it's lucky they don't know how many square kilometres they actually lost, because they have grown so distressed at letting America slip through their fingers that they even had to invent Johnny Hallyday, their own imitation American, to try and ease the pain.

And the cruellest thing of all is that Britain had the last laugh.

The Americans paid $3 million of the Louisiana Purchase price in gold and the rest in government bonds, redeemable for cash. However, French banks were too nervous to accept bonds, and two foreign banks had to step in to provide the cash. The first was Hope and Company, a bank based in Amsterdam but set up by Scotsmen. The second was a London bank, Barings (which was then a healthy institution, two whole centuries away from being bankrupted by rogue trader Nick Leeson). Napoleon was in such dire straits that he agreed to sell the bonds to these two banks at a 12.5 per cent discount. Basically, Boney gifted the Brits, his worst enemies, a million-plus dollars in commission for doing the deal.

It's no wonder that French accounts of the whole Louisiane debacle tend to gloss over the details. There's only so much American-inspired pain that a French person can take.

15

India and Tahiti: France Gets Lost in Paradise

As we have seen earlier, there were several problems with French explorers and colonizers. First, even as early as the sixteenth, seventeenth and eighteenth centuries, the Brits travelled the globe as they do now, thinking, 'Hey, I could buy a house here and do it up' (or, in areas without houses, build a new one). They would then start up an import–export business and run it until someone kicked them out.

The French, on the other hand, were more prone to deciding, 'Oh, this place isn't as nice as France – as soon as I've earned enough money, I'm going home to settle in the village where my parents and grandparents grew up.' If they were forced to stay in an unpleasant colony, they usually ended up hating it and causing total anarchy there in order to show everyone just how awful it was. This is probably why French settlers prospered in North Africa, which was a sunnier extension of the Côte d'Azur, in West Africa and Vietnam, where the colonies mainly needed engineers and short-term managers to ship out the natural resources, and on various sunny islands that could be turned into Club Meds. In general though, the concept of *la colonisation* quickly acquired a decidedly bitter taste in France.

There remained, however, two places that seemed to be perfect candidates for gallicization. They were blessed with a warm climate, valuable resources and (in one case) exceedingly willing women . . .

The Pondicherry on the cake

France's most cynical writer, Voltaire, who famously made insulting remarks about Canada, seems to have been genuinely sad that France lost India. In an essay called *Fragments historiques sur l'Inde*, he says of the Brits in India that 'happiness followed them everywhere, and this happiness was the fruit of their worthiness, their prudence and their solidarity in the face of danger. It was discord that doomed the French.'*

Voltaire was all the more depressed because he knew that France could have done spectacularly well in India. Unlike wild and untamed North America, India was already civilized. It had well-organized rulers who needed only a little persuasion – backed up by military threats if necessary – to let Europeans build trading posts and start making serious money exporting spices, timber, cotton and saltpetre (an ingredient of gunpowder).

And in the early eighteenth century, both France and Britain were rupeeing it up in India, because they had a gentlemen's agreement not to let purely European conflicts interrupt the flow of Asian money into their pockets. Britain's East India Company was trading profitably out of major cities like Madras, Calcutta and

* What Voltaire doesn't mention is that he had invested some of his personal savings in French India, and was unhappy to lose *them*, and not so much the colony.

343

Bombay.* The French, meanwhile, had built their very own luxury business park in Pondicherry, some 150 kilometres south of the British-dominated port of Madras on the southeast tip of the sub-continent.

Ever since the 1680s, Pondicherry had been flourishing like a French orchid on the trunk of India. By the 1740s, it had grown from a fishing village into a colonial capital of around 80,000 inhabitants, with wide avenues, grandiose Indo-French administration buildings, flamboyant churches, classical gardens, fortified walls and even a shopping district – in short, it was a decent-sized French new town. Pondicherry's several hundred European residents were doing so well that when France and Britain returned to their usual state of war in 1756, the French felt cocky enough to want to end the gentlemen's agreement and kick the Brits out. So they chose one of their most fanatical Anglophobes as the new governor for their Indian affairs, and set him loose . . .

A Frenchman goes doolally

Thomas Arthur, comte de Lally, baron de Tollendal (Lally for short), was born in 1702, the son of a French noblewoman and an Irish baronet. Lally had fought against the *Anglais* at the Battle of Fontenoy in 1745, at the head of Louis XV's Irish brigade, and had been promoted on the battlefield by the King himself. You might therefore conclude that he was the perfect man for the India job – a leader with battle experience who had volunteered for the Indian mission because he was dying for a chance to have another go at the Brits. But in fact he was exactly

---

* Today these are called respectively Chennai, Kolkata and Mumbai, and Pondicherry is now officially Puducherry, but I shall stick to old colonial names in this chapter on colonialization.

the wrong man, for several typically French reasons.

Lally is described by the nineteenth-century historian G. B. Malleson as 'a daring soldier' and 'a man of hasty temper, yet possessing a ready mind'. On the other hand, Malleson says that the Franco-Irishman had 'a supreme contempt' for anyone who had been living the spicy life out in the colonies and filling their pockets while people like him had been fighting to defend France. Just like his contemporary in New Orleans, the chevalier de Kerlerec (see Chapter 13), Lally was possessed by the noble but misguided conviction that he owed it to France to rap a few corrupt knuckles amongst his own colonists. It was time, he naively declared, for a bit of honesty. And as if to prove the depth of his naivety, he sent 100,000 francs to Pondicherry with a note instructing the city's councillors to spend it on supplies, labourers and pack animals to support his arriving troops.

'Cash?' said the councillors. 'That will do nicely,' and the money disappeared without trace.

The corrupt Pondicherrians had plenty of time to secrete their ill-gotten gains because Lally's journey from France to India took almost twice as long as necessary. He could probably have canoed there faster. This was because the admiral chosen to transport Lally and his 2,000 soldiers was, to quote G. B. Malleson again, 'the feeblest, the weakest, the most nerveless of men' and 'the most unfit man in the world to be the colleague of Lally'.

Anne-Antoine, comte d'Aché (yet another Frenchman with a girl's first name) was an ageing Norman noble-man who would probably have been hanged from the yardarm if he'd been in the British navy.

Shortly after leaving France, d'Aché had chanced upon a lightly defended British cargo ship and captured it. Piracy like this was an integral part of sea warfare at the time, but d'Aché decided to take the ship to a safe harbour, Rio de Janeiro, and sell the cargo there, and it took six valuable weeks to complete the deal. Lally obviously had no jurisdiction over his naval escort, because not only did he put up with this delay, but when they finally made it to the Indian Ocean, he also had to endure long periods when d'Aché refused to sail because the wind was too strong. It was rather like Admiral Nelson chickening out of Trafalgar on account of mild seasickness.

Lally's relief at finally reaching Pondicherry in April 1758 was tempered by the welcome he got from the French community when his ship entered the harbour. Somehow, the cannons fired to salute him had been loaded with live ammunition, and five cannonballs smashed through the hull of Lally's own ship. *Un accident, bien sûr*.

Lally's bad day got worse when he was told that a British fleet that had set out from Europe three months *after* d'Aché had arrived in Madras five weeks earlier. It is easy to imagine the corrupt councillors' suppressed amusement as they broke this news, and even easier to picture them pointing out to sea and adding, 'Oh, and by the way, *voici les Anglais* now.'

Before Lally's troops had even disembarked, the British ships attacked, their gunners wreaking havoc on the densely crowded French decks. In reply, the French fire was so wild that most of it flew way over the attacking ships, and a complete defeat was only avoided because high shots damaged the Brits' rigging.

If the British navy had taken the offensive so quickly, it was because they knew that Madras was incapable of defending itself from a land assault. The British governor of the region, the legendary Clive of India, was away taking revenge on the Bengalis for having locked British prisoners in the Black Hole of Calcutta (and, incidentally, robbing the East India company of £2 million in revenue), and in his absence Madras was being guarded by a skeleton force of soldiers who had been deemed unfit to go and fight in Bengal.

As soon as Lally heard this, he gave the order to load up the supplies he'd ordered and march north. It was his very first day in India, he still hadn't got the salt air and sea biscuits out of his system, and he was leaping into action.

Again, it is not difficult to imagine the local councillors feigning bafflement – 'Er, what supplies are these? You say you sent money? Well, we never got it. Anyone seen *Monsieur*'s hundred thousand francs? No, sorry.'

Although by now Lally must have been close to either a nervous breakdown or a murderous rage, he shrugged off this new setback and issued a decree conscripting all Indians within Pondicherry into service as bearers for his army. It was a strategy that might well have worked in a slave economy, or even in a conquered European country, but in India it broke just about every taboo possible, enraging both the high castes who could never envisage doing such lowly work and the lower castes whose only consolation for their poverty and inferior social position was that it was all part of the rigid caste system.

The French colonials must have realized that it was going to be even easier to sabotage this righteous hot-head Lally than they thought.

The Rajah's tennis match

The question is, of course, what were these Frenchmen up to? Lally had come out to India to defend their interests and they were doing everything to stop him bar poison his chapattis. The answer is that the merchants didn't care who was ruling India, because they knew that international politics weren't going to affect the insatiable European market for spices and cotton. Whatever happened, for them it would be business as usual.

Lally seems to have been too tunnel-visioned to realize this, because he just kept on charging ahead with his military plans. Only partially deterred by his failure to recruit bearers, he decided to besiege a closer target: Fort St David, a 30-kilometre trot south of Pondicherry – that is, in the opposite direction to Madras. Fort St David was Clive's main base in the region, but like Madras it had also been left lightly defended. If Lally could capture the town, he would put a successful stamp on the start of his campaign and show everyone that he meant business.

So he marched his men south and began a siege, and everything seemed to go well for ten days. Lally wasn't too disheartened when he received news that British ships had left Madras and been sighted off Pondicherry, heading south on their way to defend Fort St David. This was no great problem, he replied, d'Aché's ships could intercept them. Well yes, he was told, in theory that was true, but the Admiral's sailors were refusing to set sail until they been paid the arrears they were owed. They were on strike.

Pondicherry's rich French councillors naturally didn't see why they should advance the money, so Lally had to ride back to town, pay off the sailors out of his own cash and convince d'Aché to put to sea immediately. And, miracle of miracles, it worked – harried by the French fleet, the small force of British ships couldn't get close enough to help Fort St David, and the garrison capitulated. To prevent any future mishaps, Lally simply razed the fort to the ground.

Giddy with success, he then tried to persuade d'Aché to sail north with him and attack Madras. Total victory in southern India was in their grasp.

But once again, colonial success just wasn't to be. D'Aché initially said that most of his sailors were too sick to fight, and when Lally insisted, he abruptly changed tack and said that he was going off to see whether he could find some British merchant ships to plunder – his crew were clearly not too sick to do that. So, ignoring Lally's argument that the defeat of the whole British presence in South India outweighed the off-chance of capturing a few spices and rolls of cloth, off d'Aché sailed, taking 600 badly needed troops with him. Lally probably didn't go down to the harbour to say *bon voyage*.

The old soldier was now in deep *merde*. He had no money and no Frenchman willing to lend him any, no naval back-up and no way of transporting his much-reduced army's food and equipment overland.

His only hope, he decided, was to do a bit of debt-collecting. The Rajah of Tanjur, the ruler of a region about 150 kilometres inland from Pondicherry, owed a large amount of money to France, enough to equip an army. All Lally had to do was march there and scare the Rajah into paying – the only problem being that his men would have little or nothing to eat until they got to Tanjur. He set off anyway, feeding his disgruntled troops on rice (the same diet as most of the local peasants) and promises of some pre-emptive plundering on arrival.

The journey across country was tough but relatively uneventful, and the pillaging went well, with both private houses and temples yielding enough booty to keep the troops happy and convince the Rajah that Lally was not intending to leave empty-handed. In fact, the Rajah was so convinced of this that, while playing for time over delivering the money, he sent word to the Brits that if they were in the mood for some fun, a tired and underfed French army was camped outside his town.

Lally smelled a rat and issued an ultimatum: if he

didn't get his money, he would send the Indian and his whole family off to France as slaves. This had exactly the opposite effect to the one he intended. The Rajah was so offended by Lally's threat that he decided not to wait for British help, and immediately began firing at the French.

Lally was taken completely by surprise at this sudden turnaround. He had more soldiers than the Rajah, but had brought so little ammunition that his artillerymen were soon reduced to picking up Indian cannonballs and shooting them back. And in the middle of this absurd tennis match, a messenger arrived to tell Lally that the second-in-command he had left in charge at Pondicherry, an officer called the chevalier de Soupire (*soupir* aptly meaning sigh), was threatening to abandon the town because 800 British soldiers were on their way, and he only had 600 to defend it. Lally was forced to retreat yet again, and even had to abandon three of his heavy cannons because he no longer had enough oxen to pull them.

Back in Pondicherry, he found d'Aché, who had returned from his pirate cruise to a fiery welcome from the British navy. The Admiral was wounded, and refusing to fight any more. Sportingly leaving behind 500 men to strengthen the garrison, he sailed away to safety in Mauritius.

Lally had now been in India for about three months, and it must have begun to dawn on him that the whole sub-continent was up in arms against him. The Brits were determined to kill him, but they were only slightly more dangerous than his own compatriots in Pondicherry. His naval back-up had backed out, and his number two had no backbone. And to cap it all, he had managed to turn all the Indians against him.

Given this disastrous state of affairs, you have to admire the man for calling an emergency meeting of Pondicherry's French officials and haranguing – or maybe blackmailing – them into contributing enough money from their own pockets to finance an attack on Madras using every man they had: 2,000 French foot soldiers, 300 cavalrymen and 5,000 sepoys (Indian troops).

Lally must have known as he set off north with his newly subsidized army that the forthcoming siege was going to be all or nothing. And deep down, he probably suspected that it would be nothing.

Once more unto the breach? *Non merci*

No sooner had the French troops arrived in Madras than everything started to go wrong. A faction of them ransacked Black Town – the racist name for the area where the Indian dockers lived – and looted everything they could carry. It seemed the attack on the British garrison could wait.

When serious fighting did begin, one of Lally's generals, Charles-Henri d'Estaing,* accidentally offered himself up as a prisoner when he mistook a group of British redcoats for some of his own volunteers and tried to lead them in a charge against themselves.

There can be little doubt that this really was an accident, because d'Estaing was known to be a brave officer, and when the Brits subsequently released him, he broke his promise to them and returned to the fighting, an offence against the military code of honour that almost got him hanged when he was captured a second time. And in fact he did end up on a scaffold, but a French one – he was guillotined as a traitor during the

* This is not an ancestor of the former French President Valéry Giscard d'Estaing, whose family pulled all kinds of strings to add the d'Estaing tag to their name in the 1920s.

Revolution. During his trial, he refused to defend himself against trumped-up charges, and told the court: 'When you have cut off my head, sell it to the English; they will pay you well for it.'

Meanwhile, back in Madras, Lally was settling in for a long siege. The Brits had received reinforcements, and the only hope was to starve them out. However, instead of concentrating on making life miserable for the enemy, many of Lally's troops began roaming the area for booty and drinking away their profits.

The French merchants had also got in on the act and had turned the siege into a fully fledged business opportunity: looting warehouses and using the bearers who had been hired by Lally to keep his army supplied with food and ammunition to haul sugar and pepper to Pondicherry. Some even forged Lally's signature on orders procuring boats to sail their treasure down the coast.

The resolve of the soldiers who were taking an active part in the siege was sinking by the day. The money Lally had raised had been spent and, unlike the looters, the troops weren't getting paid. Food was running out – officers were complaining because they were on ordinary soldiers' rations, and the hired sepoys were leaving. Morale was weakened still further by French deserters inside the British fortifications who would climb up on to the ramparts, a bottle of wine in one hand, money in the other, and call out to the French troops to come and join them. In an exchange of prisoners, the Brits cunningly handed over 500 of these Frenchmen who had been well fed and looked after, and as soon as they were returned to their own underfed army, they led a mutiny.

Lally's only option was to focus his troops' attention by starting a bombardment, which he somehow managed to keep up for forty-two days. (Perhaps his men went and asked the Brits for their cannonballs back.) And the tactic did more than concentrate French minds – it actually made a breach in the fortifications, opening the way for an attack on the battered garrison inside.

Yet again, victory was in Lally's grasp, and yet again, his own men let him down. His officers had clearly never heard Shakespeare's 'once more unto the breach' speech. To charge the fortifications would mean certain death, they said, and refused point blank to lead the assault. Instead of having them all shot for cowardice (or sending them out to buy a copy of *Henry V*), Lally decided to go it alone with his best troops, and was just putting together a plan of attack when a British fleet sailed over the horizon.

As luck would have it, Admiral d'Aché was back in India on one of his frequent guest-star appearances, and actually agreed to get into the action. He sailed up to Madras and engaged in a brutal stand-off with the British ships. But when no clear victory was won for either side, the Admiral declared once and for all that fighting these people was pointless. Lally begged him to stay, explaining that this time Pondicherry really would be lost if he left, and even threatening to report d'Aché to the King. But the aged mariner simply sailed away again, ignoring British ships as they cruised past him to close in on Madras.

Like a madman sinking in quicksand, Lally flailed pointlessly on. He gave up the siege of Madras and retreated to home base, but as G. B. Malleson puts it, he 'found the enemies he met with inside the walls of Pondicherry worse than those he had to combat without'.

Inevitably, the Brits came marching along the coast to take back all their pillaged cloths and spices and – *pourquoi pas?* – do some plundering of their own. And when they arrived at the French colony to besiege it, Pondicherry's civilian residents refused to put on army uniforms to fool the attackers into thinking the city was well defended.

Eventually, after four months, Pondicherry simply ran out of food, and Lally was forced to surrender on 16 January 1761. As he was escorted away by the British troops, the civilians who had conspired against him came out to yell insults at him, and he only escaped with his life thanks to his captors' protection. A seventy-year-old, nearly blind general called Dubois wasn't so lucky. When the French civilians realized that he was attempting to leave Pondicherry with documents proving the corruption that had been largely responsible for Lally's failure, the old man was impaled on a sword, and the incriminating documents were spirited away.

Poor Lally's sufferings were far from over. He was taken back to London as a prisoner of war, and while there, heard that his old adversaries had returned from India and were blaming the loss of Pondicherry – and, effectively, the whole of South India – on him. Even Admiral d'Aché was heaping accusations on Lally, and the old fool had wangled himself a medal for his supposed valour during the campaign: the Grand Cross of the Royal Military Order of St Louis, no less. Lally's temper and sense of honour got the better of him and, released on parole, he went back to Paris to defend himself.

It was a literally fatal mistake. He was thrown in prison for two years, then subjected to a show trial and condemned to death. The sentence caused a public outcry, and many expected King Louis XV to spare him, but the anti-Lally lobby was too vehement and the sentence was carried out only three days later.

And still the humiliation wasn't over. Lally was taken to the scaffold bound and gagged so that he wouldn't be able to proclaim his innocence. There, still denied the chance to make a final speech, he was laid on the block and the executioner's sword came down on his allegedly treacherous neck. It was probably lucky that he was gagged, too, because the blow failed to kill him, and the swordsman's father (a retired executioner himself) had to jump up and finish the job.

The cruellest irony was that by the time Lally was executed, France had in fact regained control of Pondicherry thanks to one of the few favourable clauses in the Treaty of Paris that marked the end of the Seven Years War – Lally's supposed failure to hold on to the colony was already old news. And the territory had a new French governor, a certain Jean Law de Lauriston, the nephew of John Law, who fifty years earlier had caused the financial ruin of France with the connivance of the great-uncle of the same Louis XV who let Lally go to his botched execution.

In the long run, France triumphed in Pondicherry, which, despite two more British occupations at the end of the eighteenth century and the beginning of the nineteenth, stayed in French hands until 1954, seven years after the rest of India had gained independence. There would be over fifty more French governors, and Lally's ghost was no doubt present at every single investiture, howling its frustration through its gag.

Bougainville, the flower of France's explorers

We are constantly reminded that at least one Frenchman successfully travelled the tropics – tourist brochures for practically every sunny city in the world feature gardens dripping with pink bougainvillea. The South American plant is named after Louis-Antoine de Bougainville, France's most famous explorer, who became a celebrity in March 1769, when he completed a 28-month circumnavigation of the globe. His idyllic descriptions of free love amongst the coconut palms also made Tahiti famous, and sent Parisian philosophers into a frenzy of idealization about the 'Noble Savage' islanders and their pre-biblical innocence.

Only one man put a damper on all the hero worship – and he was, of course, a Brit. When James Cook arrived home after his first Pacific voyage in 1771, it quickly became clear that, compared to him, Bougainville hadn't actually achieved very much. For a start, the Frenchman hadn't really discovered anywhere new, and had somehow failed to notice Australia. And – worst of all – Bougainville was accused by Cook of infecting the Noble Savages with sexually transmitted diseases.

Once again, an *Anglais* was gatecrashing France's colonial party . . .

Louis XV tries to stir up the Pacific

Shortly after Cook's return to Europe, Bougainville published an account of his trip, catchily and simply called *Voyage autour du monde* (*Voyage around the World*). He did so mainly as a record for future mariners who might want to sail that way themselves – his book is full of depth measurements and latitude co-ordinates. But he also seems to have been determined to refute Cook's allegations in public.

To be fair, Bougainville is full of praise for Cook, and charmingly honest about his own modest achievements. Far from presenting himself as a conquering hero, as his nation would have liked him to be, Bougainville deliberately or inadvertently dispels several myths about his voyage.

The most important of these is that he is usually said to be the first Frenchman to circumnavigate the globe. This is only natural because it was the official reason for his trip. Louis XV wanted a morale-booster for the country after the traumas of the Seven Years War, and in 1766 he commissioned Bougainville to sail around the world, 'taking the time in different places to erect poles and attach to them orders of possession in the name of His Majesty' – a fancy way of saying 'get us some colonies out in the unexplored Pacific before the other European nations grab them all.'

In his preface to *Voyage autour du monde*, Bougainville is slightly coy about this claim to be the first French circumnavigator, saying only that he is the first of his countrymen to 'carry out a voyage *of this sort* in Your Majesty's ships' (my italics). A little further into the book, the reason for his strangely precise wording becomes clear when Bougainville mentions that a French explorer called Le Gentil de la Barbinais might actually have sailed around the world before him. Not that this changes anything, Bougainville adds, because Barbinais had set off in a privately owned vessel, so it wasn't an official mission. What's more, he had also stopped off in China for over a year, and then sailed home in a different ship. 'In truth, he [Barbinais] did personally go around the world,' Bougainville concedes, 'but one couldn't call it a circumnavigation carried out by the French nation.' Like so many things in France, exploration was all about who you knew.

How to lose the Falklands without a battle

Bougainville's book makes no comment on the name of his purpose-built flagship, even though it was called *La Boudeuse*, or *Sulky Lady*. It was a strangely pessimistic name for a vessel that was meant to carry a crew of superstitious sailors on such a long and dangerous journey, but it was appropriate, because Bougainville knew that the first major event of his trip was going to be a sad one.

He had been ordered to stop in the southern Atlantic and take part in a ceremony to hand the Falkland Islands, then a French territory called Les Malouines (or 'Islands of Saint-Malo'), over to the Spanish. Three years earlier, Bougainville had gone out there to establish a French colony, a task he had achieved by stranding seventy-five Acadien refugees from Canada at the end of a relatively sheltered bay and naming the settlement Port Saint-Louis in honour of the Kings of France past and present. This had caused much annoyance in Spain, which claimed the whole of South America, and now Louis XV had agreed to give the islands back, and was making the man who had settled them in the first place make the presentation.

Poor Bougainville describes the historic ceremony in one laconic sentence: 'I handed over our settlement to the Spaniards, who took possession of it by raising the Spanish flag.' He then read out a letter from King Louis to the Acadiens, informing them that after being ousted from Canada, they were now being kicked out of the Malouines too. France had let them down again, and it probably came as no surprise that several of the families decided to take their chances and become Spanish, even though their windblown outpost had now been rather too frankly renamed Puerto Soledad – Port Solitude.

Bougainville had hoped to put this indignity behind him by setting off immediately for the Pacific, but he was now forced to hang around in the newly Spanish 'Malvinas'* waiting for his supply ship, L'Étoile (The Star), which was meant to rendezvous with him at Port Saint-Louis, sorry, Puerto Soledad. Bobbing impatiently at anchor in the recently lost French colony, La Boudeuse probably lived up to its name more than ever.

* The islands wouldn't become the Falklands until the Brits grabbed them in 1833, though the French still call them Les Malouines today.

It wasn't until two months later that Bougainville finally met up with the *Étoile* in Rio, where two key characters joined the French mission. The first was a botanist called Philibert Commerson, the man who later discovered the flower that bears Bougainville's name. The second was his assistant, Jean Baré, who would turn out to be a very unusual man indeed.

Not such a virgin island

When Bougainville's two ships finally sailed out of the stormy South Atlantic and into the shimmering Pacific, he must have felt a huge weight lifting off his shoulders. At last, a year after he had left France, he was getting down to the fun part of his job. Reading his book, you get a palpable sense of his glee as uncharted islands begin to appear on the horizon. But he seems to have forgotten the wording of Louis XV's commission, because instead of 'erecting poles and attaching orders of possession to them', often he simply logged their position, gave them French names, and didn't take the risk of getting snagged on a reef or attacked by fierce-looking natives.

When, in April 1768, the *Boudeuse* and *Étoile* came in sight of a larger-than-usual mountainous island at a latitude of 17 degrees 35 minutes and 3 seconds South (Bougainville's measurements, not mine), he was delighted with his discovery and named it Nouvelle-Cythère, after the Aegean island of Kythira.

The natives seemed friendly, too. The men who canoed out to meet the French ships were brandishing coconuts, bananas and other 'fruits délicieux' rather than spears and battle clubs. Everything, Bougainville notes, 'augured well for their good character'.

As soon as he landed, however, he got two major shocks.

First, if he understood the islanders correctly, another ship full of pale, overdressed men had been there before. He would find out later that this was the Cornishman Samuel Wallis, who had visited Tahiti in June of the previous year, while Bougainville had been waiting around for his supply ship. So the French hadn't discovered the island, after all – those blasted Brits had.

Never mind, though – Bougainville did his best to tell the islanders the advantages of being a subject of Louis XV (long holidays, unlimited access to the Malouines – oh no, forget that one, but there were lots more), and consoled himself that no one seemed to be waving Union Jacks.

The second surprise was even greater. When the botanist Commerson and his assistant Jean Baré went ashore, they provoked a minor riot. Not because the islanders' religion forbade botany, but because the men were crowding around Baré and making lewd gestures that implied they wanted to have sex with him. The Frenchmen tried to explain that sexual intercourse between males was taboo (despite anything the Brits might have told them about French sailors), but the islanders made it clear that this wasn't a problem because they were sure the young assistant was not a male. And when Bougainville's men managed to extract Baré from his admirers and get him back on board, Jean tearfully confessed to being Jeanne. She had disguised herself, Bougainville writes, because she knew that a woman would never have been allowed to join the expedition. (In fact she was obviously the married Commerson's mistress, but Bougainville is too discreet to reveal this.)

It might seem unbelievable to us that a woman could have been on board ship for ten months without being discovered. Bougainville admits that there had been rumours amongst the crew that she was female because of her lack of beard and her 'meticulous care not to perform her necessities' in front of the other men, but, with all the sexual prejudices of his age, he explains that you would never have guessed she was a girl.

'How could you see a woman in the indefatigable Baré,' he asks, 'an experienced botanist, whom we had seen following his master on all his gathering trips, through the snow and up the icy mountains of the Straits of Magellan, carrying food, weapons and plant books with such courage and strength?' In short, she was a hard-working scientist, so she obviously couldn't be a woman.

Now that her true nature had been revealed, though, Bougainville had a chance to get his mission into the record books for an indisputable reason: Jeanne would be the first woman ever to sail around the world. But he didn't let her steal his glory, and later put both Commerson and Baré ashore in Mauritius, where they stayed until Commerson died in 1773. Jeanne sub-sequently returned to France, completing her circuit of the globe and probably becoming the first woman to do so – although, by Bougainville's rules, her stopover had no doubt disqualified her from making the claim.

In fact, Bougainville didn't get rid of her in case she grabbed the limelight – it had become, he says, 'difficult to prevent the sailors from alarming her modesty', because the stay in Tahiti had really got their hormones raging . . .

Nailing the Tahitians

The first canoes to greet the French had been crewed entirely by men. But after this friendly encounter, things rapidly got more co-ed. When the *Étoile* and the *Boudeuse* came closer to shore, a whole flotilla of canoes paddled out, and the sailors were astonished to see naked women in them, 'making tempting movements'. Even more incredible, the men were signalling that the Europeans were welcome to choose a woman, and 'were gesturing to show us exactly how we should make her acquaintance'. It was every mariners' dream come true, and Bougainville was as dumbfounded as the rest of his crew: 'I ask you: how, before such a spectacle, is one supposed to restrain 400 Frenchmen, young sailors, who haven't seen a woman for six months?' (Presumably if they had been British, they would have been much easier to control.)

At first Bougainville forbade all shore leave, and only one man disobeyed – a cook, who came back 'more dead than alive'. He told his captain that he had gone ashore, been instantly stripped naked by the islanders, and had every part of his body gazed and prodded at, before being given a girl and told to perform with her in front of everyone. When he didn't rise to the task, the disappointed Tahitians brought him back to the ship.

Once the French did go ashore en masse, they found a society where sex was as exchanged as freely as bananas. It was perfectly natural for the sailors to be invited into a house where a young girl would be offered as a sign of hospitality, and a crowd would gather to watch the ceremony. 'Each coupling is a cause of national celebration,' Bougainville says, and he admits that the Tahitians were mystified at the foreigners' preference for privacy. 'Our morals forbade such a public show,' he assures his readers, 'though I cannot guarantee that all of my crew remained reluctant to adopt this local custom.'

His book was dedicated to Louis XV, who was quite a ladies' man himself, and must have been delighted with the description of a way of life that was probably his fantasy of how Parisian court life should be. And the followers of philosopher Jean-Jacques Rousseau were even more excited – they believed in the Noble Savage, the innocent primeval man unspoilt by the hypocrisies of modern civilized life, and the Tahitians' ability to walk around naked and engage in public humping clearly proved that they were free of Adam and Eve's original sin.*

Other aspects of island life confirmed this idealistic view. There was no concept of locking anything away, and Bougainville states that 'everyone picks fruit from the first tree they see, or takes it from any house. It would seem that the necessities of life can be no individual's property, and belong to all.'

The Noble Savage fans didn't read Bougainville closely enough, though, because he also stated that Tahiti was constantly at war with other islands, and that their methods of warfare were far from noble – when the Tahitians won a battle, they kidnapped the women to be their sex slaves and killed all the men and boys, scalping the chin of anyone with a beard.

Bougainville also pulled no punches about the true relations amongst Tahitians: 'The kings and nobles have the power of life and death over their slaves and servants, and have the same rights over the people they call *Tata-einou*, or low men. It is from this class that they choose the victims for their human sacrifices.' Not quite such a paradise after all, even if it did make for a pleasant fortnight's stopover on the Frenchmen's round-the-world trip.

But there was one aspect of life on the island that robbed it of its Garden of Eden status even for the sex-hungry sailors – and this is where those annoying Brits came in.

When James Cook returned from his own circumnavigation on 13 July 1771, he was able to list all the

---

* The same can presumably be said of the people who do similar things every summer at France's biggest naturist resort, Cap d'Agde.

discoveries that the French explorer had missed: Australia, the Great Barrier Reef and the fact that New Zealand was made up of islands rather than being the fabled southern continent, for example. And the Englishman also began to spread malicious rumours about Bougainville and his crew.

In his journal, Cook talks about the *Tahitiennes*' easy morals. He says that he had to punish his men for stealing nails to exchange for sex, and he accuses the French of making the situation even more complicated. In his log for 6 June 1769, he describes the islanders telling him that two ships (clearly the *Boudeuse* and the *Étoile*) had stopped at Tahiti ten or fifteen months earlier. He adds that 'they [the Tahitians] likewise say that these ships brought the venereal Distemper to this island where it is now as common as in any part of the world.'

An open-minded man, Cook considers the possibility that either he or Wallis, the man who had beaten Bougainville to Tahiti, might have caused the epidemic. But he dismisses both charges: 'No such thing happened to any of the Dolphin's [Wallis's ship] people while they were here,' he states. And Cook's own men get a clean bill of health, too: 'I have the satisfaction to find that the Natives all agree that we did not bring it here.' The conclusion is obvious – it was the Frenchmen's fault.

Cook rubs salt into Bougainville's moral wound by predicting that, given the islanders' sexual habits, the disease would spread throughout the South Seas 'to the eternal reproach of those who first brought it among them'. And he closes the long entry for 6 June 1769, which is entirely given over to sexually transmitted diseases, with a killer piece of circumstantial evidence – he has seen several islanders with iron tools that 'we suspected came not from the Dolphin, and they now say they had from these two ships'.

French ironwork in the hands of Tahitians could mean only one thing: Frenchmen having sex with the local girls and giving them an STD as a farewell gift. QED.

In fact, we know from Wallis's account of his voyage that his men had also exchanged nails for sexual favours, and he eventually had to forbid any contact with the islanders for fear that the *Dolphin* would fall apart for lack of iron. But Cook didn't know (or didn't care to acknowledge) this, and the accusation was there in his travel diary for all in Europe to see: Bougainville had visited Adam and Eve and given them the clap.

Bougainville couldn't let Cook get away with this. 'Their [the Brits'] accusations that we gave the unfortunate Tahitians the disease are groundless,' Bougainville pleads in his book, 'and we would perhaps be more correct in suspecting that it was passed to them by the crew of Monsieur Wallis.' It is amazing, more than two centuries later, to read two of the world's most famous explorers locking horns over sexual hygiene.

Bougainville goes even further, and widens the issue to health in general. Here, he is on more solid ground, and ends his book with a mean jibe at Cook. The British captain had lost thirty-eight crew members during his voyage, mainly to an outbreak of dysentery caught in Indonesia. Bougainville, on the other hand, could boast that the *Boudeuse* entered Saint-Malo 'having lost only seven men in the two years and four months since leaving Nantes'. And, as if to convince any floating voters, he appends a footnote to the effect that the death toll on the *Étoile* was an even more healthy two. The subtext is clear: who had the disease-bearing crews, *les Français ou les Anglais?* Do the maths, dear readers, the final score was 38–9 in France's favour.

Case closed.

Final impressions of Tahiti

Sadly for Bougainville, his initial claim to French sovereignty over Tahiti was ignored. He died thirty-one years before France finally got its hands on the island. In 1842, a rogue French admiral sneaked in and annexed the place while the British Consul was away. Even then, it was something of a joyless acquisition – by this time, the previously innocent islanders had been got at by British missionaries, and the girls were hiding their natural charms inside tent-like Victorian dresses.

When the French painter Paul Gauguin arrived there at the end of the century (bringing his own case of European syphilis), he was horrified to find that Bougainville's description of a nation of promiscuous love goddesses was cruelly out of date. And if you look at the Tahitian paintings that don't feature his lover or models, Gauguin's *Tahitiennes* are decidedly covered up. It really was a case of paradise lost.

16

The Guillotine, a British Invention

'There is only one cure for grey hair. It was invented by a Frenchman. It is called the guillotine.'

P. G. Wodehouse

Before France plunges itself into the self-flagellation that they called a revolution, one key historical mistake has to be cleared up: the guillotine, which will play a surprisingly limited role in the ensuing action, was not French. The earliest references to a decapitation machine with a falling blade are British.

To put it bluntly, Docteur Guillotin never invented such a machine, and in fact he was most upset that his name had been misappropriated to describe a way of cutting off people's heads. In any case, the first French guillotine was built by a Prussian.

So, the guillotine – a French invention? Apologies to France (and P. G. Wodehouse), but it's another misconception that has to be knocked on the head.

Killing with (and without) kindness

As the executioners responsible for the deaths of Mary Queen of Scots and King Charles I would probably agree, the main problem with cutting an important person's head off is accuracy. The axe is heavy, your hands are sweaty, you're wearing a mask, and you're being watched by some very powerful people. To make things worse, you know that if you mess things up, the story will be repeated in history books for ever more. What could be more natural than to let the blade stray right or left, to cut into a shoulder or take off a scalp? This was why it was a privilege in England to be executed with a sword. There was much less chance of a messy, multi-swing botch job.

If you *wanted* to get messy, there were of course some spectacular ways of killing people. The French used to enjoy watching criminals broken on the wheel, for example. The victim would have their arms and legs smashed with a metal bar and their chest caved in, and then they would be tied to a wheel with their broken limbs folded under them and left hanging there until they died. This method was commonly used in France as a way of executing robbers right up to the Revolution.

French traitors, meanwhile, would usually be torn limb from limb by horses pulling in four different directions. François Ravaillac, who stabbed King Henri IV to death in 1610, was executed like this, but only after having the hand that held the knife burned off with sulphur, and then having molten lead and boiling oil and resin poured over his flesh. (Henri IV was a popular monarch, and France was pretty angry at Ravaillac.)

It seems surprisingly humane, then, that elsewhere people were experimenting with quicker, cleaner ways of taking off a head. And the earliest type of what we mistakenly call the guillotine was probably invented in

The guillotine was introduced into France in the eighteenth century as a quick, humane method of execution. But decapitation machines were already in use hundreds of years earlier in Yorkshire – and were occasionally operated by animals.

Halifax, northern England, a town whose only other claim to innovation is that it was home to confectioner Violet Mackintosh, the woman who invented Rolos and Quality Street toffees.

The Halifax Gibbet looked a lot like the French version, though it was a much sturdier, stockier beast. A large wooden block, about five feet long and one foot thick, held an axe blade like a single tooth. This block was raised approximately fifteen feet in the air between two wooden posts, before being allowed to drop on to the victim below. And from the look of the modern replica standing in Gibbet Street, Halifax, today, if that thing came down on your neck, your head would fly halfway across Yorkshire.

The earliest reference to its use is the execution of a criminal called John Dalton in 1286, though town records of executions before Elizabeth I have been lost. We do know, however, that the gibbet claimed twenty-five heads during her reign, and that it was last used in anger on 30 April 1650.

Not that Halifax was a hotbed of treachery and murder, or a centre of excellence for execution where other towns would send their most fiendish criminals to be beheaded. In *The Every-Day Book* by William Hone, an almanac for 1825–6 with a text for every day of the year, the anniversary of the execution of Louis XVI – 21 January – has a few paragraphs about the Halifax Gibbet. Hone says that it was used for crimes committed in the forest of Hardwick, which belonged at the time to the lord of the manor of Wakefield. If a thief was caught there with goods valued at more than 'thirteen pence halfpenny', then he or she was taken for trial to the lord's bailiff in Halifax and if found guilty, beheaded on a market day (a Tuesday, Thursday or Saturday).

A much earlier text, written in 1577 by a man called

William Harrison, gives a highly detailed description of the method, and suggests that the people of Halifax took a sort of collective responsibility for the executions (though the lord of the manor probably kept his hands clean).

Harrison wrote that the Halifax Gibbet's axe was held in place by a wooden pin:

> ... unto the midst of which pin there is a long rope fastened that cometh down among the people, so that, when the offender hath made his confession and hath laid his neck over the nethermost block, every man there present doth either take hold of the rope (or putteth forth his arm so near to the same as he can get, in token that he is willing to see true justice executed), and, pulling out the pin in this manner, the head-block wherein the axe is fastened doth fall down with such a violence that, if the neck of the transgressor were as big as that of a bull, it should be cut in sunder at a stroke and roll from the body by a huge distance.

This is gruesome enough, but he adds a final, frankly bizarre, detail:

> If it be so that the offender be apprehended for an ox, oxen, sheep, horse, or any such cattle, the self beast or other of the same kind shall have the end of the rope tied somewhere unto them, so that they, being driven, do draw out the pin, whereby the offender is executed.

Cows executing cattle rustlers ... market days must have been very lively in medieval Halifax. No risk of people driving out of town to do their shopping at the mall.

There are also records of guillotine-type machines in

use in Ireland in 1307 and in Scotland in 1564. Two centuries later, in 1747, a Scot, Lord Lovat, a convicted traitor who was due to be executed in London, begged the government to introduce the technology down south. 'My neck is very short,' he said, 'and the executioner will be puzzled to find it out with his axe.' Apparently he also hoped that the new London machine would be named after him. In the event, though, he got the axe, and was lucky – his head came off with one blow. If, of course, you can call that luck.

The cutting edge of technology

So where did Guillotin come in?

As we will see in the next chapter, the French Revolution was marked by wholesale massacres, and in fact, Royalists were more likely to be hacked to death by a mob than have their necks neatly sliced. Docteur Guillotin was therefore doing a humanitarian good deed when he suggested that a swift decapitation, not preceded by torture, should be the standard form of capital punishment in France. He was also proposing a democratization of the death sentence, because until then only aristocrats had been decapitated – lower-class citizens had suffered the hideous punishments mentioned above.

Joseph-Ignace Guillotin, a physician from Saintes in the southwest of France, was a politician as well as a doctor. He was elected a *député* (Member of Parliament) for Paris in the first post-revolutionary parliament, the Assemblée nationale constituante, and it was at a session of the Assemblée on 10 October 1789 that he outlined his ideas for a new code of punishment. As well as suggesting that everyone should get the same punishment for the same crime, and that all executions should be by decapitation machine, he also proposed that the body of an execution victim should be returned to the family and given a decent burial. All in all, a thoughtful man.

His only fault seems to have been a tactless sense of humour. At the October session of the Assemblée, his ideas had not been listened to very attentively, so he brought them forward again in December, when he compared a swift decapitation machine to the long and cruel process of hanging: 'With my machine,' he boasted, 'I can cut off your head in the wink of an eye and you won't feel a thing.' His pun got a laugh, but the other *députés* were so shocked by his levity that they called a halt to the debate.

Guillotin's quip was reported outside Parliament, and inspired a comic song that mocked 'Hippocrates' representative' for wanting to massacre people as quickly as possible. And it was this song that first gave a name to the as yet non-existent killing machine – the 'Guillotine'.

Eventually, in 1791, all the doctor's proposals were voted through, and the Ministry of Justice began looking into exactly what kind of machine they wanted. Antoine Louison, the secretary of the Academy of Surgeons, remembered Guillotin's proposal and recommended this kind of machine. Guillotin was summoned by the Procureur général (State Prosecutor) to enlarge upon his suggestions, but it is not sure that the doctor attended the meeting, because by this time he had learned that, as a homage to his dedication (and possibly to the song he inspired), the new machine really was going to bear his name. He was apparently horrified.

Various people began to tender for the job of making the decapitation machine. The man who usually did the ministry's scaffold-building, a carpenter called Guidon, put in a prohibitively high bid because his workers didn't want to be associated with the project. Even when the government offered to make all contracts totally anonymous, the workers still refused to have anything to do with the guillotine. In Strasbourg, though, an officer of the court called Laquiante agreed to design a machine, and got a Paris-based Prussian harpsichord-maker called Tobias Schmidt to make it.

Completed in early 1792, Schmidt's prototype included a platform twenty-four steps off the ground to give the public a good view of the killing, and a leather pouch to hold the severed head. At first, the blade was rounded or straight, but Schmidt soon exchanged it for the 45-degree-angled edge that we know so well. This was one harpsichord-maker who had missed his vocation.

The prototype was set up in the rue Saint-André-des-Arts in the Latin Quarter, where Schmidt had his workshop, and tested out on sheep and calves. It was then moved to the Paris suburbs and tried out on corpses from a hospital, a prison and an old people's home. The results were considered satisfactory and, on 25 April 1792, an armed robber called Nicolas-Jacques Pelletier gained the dubious honour of being the first man to be guillotined in the place de Grève (the square in front of the modern Hôtel de Ville – Town Hall – where criminals were traditionally executed).

The new machine worked so well that it actually became something of a fashion icon – children's toys were all the rage, and guillotine earrings were a must-have accessory (or should that be the *neck plus ultra*?) for Parisian women. For a short while, anyway – the novelty palled after the execution of Louis XVI on 21 January 1793, when it suddenly became fashionable to accuse perfectly innocent people of counter-revolutionary activities and slice off their unfortunate head.

It is not known exactly how many people died during the Terror of July 1793–July 1794, but it may have been as many as 17,000. Guillotin himself barely escaped with his neck intact – he was imprisoned on suspicion of Royalist sympathies after a condemned aristocrat asked him to care for his wife and children. On his release from prison, Guillotin withdrew from public life and was so discreet that he was thought to be dead. He actually survived until 1814, however, and no doubt spent his final years wishing that one of the other popular names for the decapitation machine would replace his own – by now, the machine had been nicknamed 'le rasoir national' (national razor), 'la raccourcisseuse patriotique' (patriotic shortener), and, more seriously, 'le Louison' after Antoine Louison, the secretary of the Academy of Surgeons who had commissioned it. But the name guillotine stuck and was even turned into a verb, *guillotiner*.

In the end, though, Dr Guillotin had only himself to blame. If he hadn't made his memorable joke in Parliament about 'ma machine', he might have been remembered for his democratic intentions rather than a gruesome method of execution. And the guillotine might even have been given a more historically accurate name – 'le Halifax', for example. Which would actually have been quite fun, because 200-odd years later, the Académie française would probably still be debating whether to allow the verb *halifaxer*.

17

The French Revolution: Let Them Eat Cake. Or Failing That, Each Other

The chorus of the French national anthem says it all: 'Marchons, marchons, qu'un sang impur abreuve nos sillons', which could be loosely translated as 'Let's march, let's march, and may our fields be irrigated with impure blood.'

Not only is it a shade more violent than 'God Save the Queen'* (which harks on about defeating Britain's enemies but wishes for nothing more violent than that God will 'frustrate their knavish tricks'), it is also a touch misleading. In fact, most of the blood shed in the cause of the French Revolution was not what the author of 'La Marseillaise' would have thought of as 'impure'. It was French as opposed to foreign, and only a small proportion of it was aristocratic.

The words and music to 'La Marseillaise' were written in 1792 by a soldier called Claude-Joseph Rouget de Lisle. He composed his stirring song for French troops

---

* 'The Star-Spangled Banner' rules itself out as a comparison, because it has a gruesome line about kicking anti-revolutionary forces out of America: 'Their blood has washed out their vile footsteps' pollution.'

marching into battle against the Germans, and it was adopted as the national anthem after some volunteers from Marseille sang it in the streets of Paris. Ironically, however, Rouget himself (his name means 'red mullet', by the way) was later imprisoned as a traitor for protesting against the internment of the royal family, and narrowly avoided shedding his own blood. He spent the rest of his life in poverty, earning a crust translating English texts into French, while desperately trying to emulate his first hit. 'La Marseillaise' didn't fare much better than its composer – it was banned by Napoleon, and only restored as the national anthem in 1879.

All in all, the circumstances surrounding the song are a perfect illustration of the bloody chaos that reigned during the Revolution.

Today, most French people think that events went something like this:

Day 1, fair-minded but hungry liberators storm Bastille and release political prisoners.

Day 2, a people's tribunal votes to cut off heads of evil King and his wife who made a tactless remark about cakes.

Day 3, the same tribunal votes to cut off heads of everyone else who is posh and against liberty, equality and fraternity.

Day 4, freely elected Republican idealists introduce glorious era of democracy that still reigns in France today.

But the annual Bastille Day celebrations hint at what really went on. If you go to Paris on 14 July, who will you see, parading down the Champs-Élysées? Is it the people who make France the successful nation it is today: the *pâtissiers*, winemakers, fashion designers, mineral-water salesmen and nuclear engineers?

No. Tanks rattle along the avenue; camouflaged helicopters roar overhead; students from the country's top engineering school, the École polytechnique, march past in military uniform, their swords chinking. The streets of the City of Lights are ablaze with weaponry, just as they were 200-odd years ago. The only difference is there aren't quite as many heads being paraded about on pikes or people getting hacked to death by the mob. Which is lucky, because it might scare away the tourists.

And the Brits, as usual, were to blame for all the mess. Or so said a Frenchman who was there at the time – Maximilien Robespierre, the so-called 'bloodthirsty dictator' who sent so many real or imaginary traitors to the guillotine before ending up there himself. In 1793 he made a speech saying that the Revolution was started by London 'to lead France, exhausted and dismembered, to a change of dynasty, and put the Duke of York [Prince Frederick, George III's son] on the throne of Louis XVI. The execution of this plan would have given England the three objects of its ambitions and jealousy – Toulon, Dunkirk and our colonies.'

Robespierre was on the paranoid side, and he was trying to rewrite history in order to stir up hatred for a new anti-British war, but he might have had a point. Some historians say that without the Brits the French would never have had the will to revolt. The Seven Years War of 1756–63 and participation in the American War of Independence had effectively bankrupted France, and the arguments about how to get out of the financial quagmire had caused the first real cracks to appear in its political establishment. Commoners demanded that Louis XVI and his landowning courtiers take radical action to ease the hardship, and the King was too out of touch, ill advised and weak to deal with the situation. The calls for reform turned to outright revolt, and today the country is a republic.

So actually, the French should be grateful to the Brits –

except those French people who had their heads cut off during the Revolution, or who were torn limb from limb, drowned, shot or roasted alive, of course. They probably wished that things had stayed a little more peaceful in 1789.

Pourquoi la Bastille?

The storming of the Bastille on 14 July 1789 was by no means the first event of the Revolution, or its most meaningful.

In the same area of eastern Paris, on 28 April, there was, for example, a dramatic attack on a paper factory. It belonged to Jean-Baptiste Réveillon, the man who made the decorated paper skin of the first Montgolfier balloon. Réveillon was no aristocrat – he was a commoner who had built up a business manufacturing and selling wallpaper, and had made his mark on French history by hosting the first ever balloon flight in the grounds of his factory. So why attack him? Well, a rumour sprang up that Réveillon was planning to cut wages at his factory in line with the recently lowered price of bread, and the news provoked a riot. A mob of several thousand people attacked the building where he lived and worked, burning his merchandise and designs, smashing or stealing his furniture, and looking for the boss himself with a view to using his blood to paint a wallpaper motif. Troops fired on the rioters, killing thirty of them and provoking the rest into terrorizing the whole neighbourhood.

In fact, though, the rioters had got it all wrong. Réveillon had made a speech saying that the price of bread ought to be cut so that badly paid workers could afford it. But he didn't hang around to point out that he'd been misquoted – he and his family climbed over a wall, only just escaping with their lives.

Even so, one could argue that the mob had had revolutionary intentions, and that the riot had provided thirty martyrs, so this outbreak of public violence might justifiably have replaced the Bastille in the national calendar. There was, however, a major linguistic problem: Réveillon Day wouldn't have worked, because 'le réveillon' is Christmas Eve, and it would have created confusion to have two Christmas Eves, one of which was at the end of April. So the hunt for a national holiday was still on.

On 13 July, a mob attacked the convent at Saint-Lazare, where it was rumoured that a vast supply of wheat was being hoarded. This time, the story was accurate, and the attackers came away with fifty-odd wagonloads of grain. The problem was, however, that the convent was a charitable institution, and the wheat might well have been intended for distribution to the poor. And anyway, Convent Pillaging Day wouldn't have sounded good. Something more politically correct was needed.

Next day at 10 a.m., Parisians attacked the army barracks at Les Invalides and, unopposed by a sympathetic garrison, seized some 30,000 muskets. An army mutiny in favour of the people – a great cause for celebration and, *pourquoi pas*, a national holiday?

Well, *non*, for two reasons. First, Invalids Day wouldn't have been at all sexy. And secondly, they had the guns but no powder to fire them with, or bullets to fire. It was a damp squib of a day.

Enter the Bastille, an old fortified prison in the east of Paris. It was due for closure, and held only seven forgotten prisoners, none of them revolutionaries. There were four forgers, who had been jailed for a banking scam, two lunatics and one count who was accused of helping his sister run away from her husband. The

Marquis de Sade (who had been shut away by his wife's family because of accusations of sexual violence) should also have been there on 14 July, but he had been transferred a few days earlier after yelling out of his cell window at passers-by that the inmates were all being murdered.

In Charles Dickens's novel set during the Revolution, *A Tale of Two Cities*,* the released prisoners are borne aloft like liberated heroes, but in fact the Parisians weren't interested in freeing this motley crew of prisoners (indeed, all of them apart from the count were locked up again after the prison had been stormed). The mob targeted the Bastille because it was rumoured to contain a veritable gunpowder mountain, guarded by a squadron of only eighty-two semi-invalid soldiers. The pickings were too easy to resist. It was around 10.30 a.m. on 14 July 1789, and history was about to be made.

A delegation was sent into the prison to demand that the governor, a marquis called Bernard-René Jordan de Launay, hand over the gunpowder. The petitioners were invited in for lunch (yes, even in mid-Revolution, the French took time out for a civilized meal) but then sent away empty-handed. And when a second delegation was no more successful, the mob gathering outside the prison walls began to get impatient.

De Launay should perhaps have seen the way the political wind was blowing and opened the gates, just as the soldiers at Les Invalides had done. But just after lunchtime, at which he might have had a glass of wine

---

* The novel, published in 1859, paints a balanced picture of the climate of exhilaration, idealism and pure savagery during the Revolution, as the book's famous opening words suggest: 'It was the best of times, it was the worst of times, it was the age of wisdom, it was the age of foolishness . . .'

too many, he made the mistake that would cost him his head.

Around 1.30 p.m., a crowd broke into the prison's outer courtyard, and were fired on from the ramparts. This enraged the attackers, who could do little about it other than wave their empty muskets in protest. Unfortunately for de Launay, however, they were soon reinforced by mutinous soldiers, who brought along a couple of cannons and began pounding the gates. At about five in the afternoon, de Launay accepted that his meagre garrison was not going to hold out, even if they did have several tons of gunpowder and musket balls. He wrote a polite note asking the mob for the usual terms in such situations – surrender in exchange for humane treatment – and really ought not to have been too surprised when his request was refused. Almost a hundred attackers had been shot dead, and one had been crushed when the chains holding up the drawbridge had been cut. The stormers of the Bastille were in no mood for polite negotiations.

De Launay finally opened the gates, and the mob surged in to take possession of the prison. Half a dozen of the defenders were picked out and killed for having been too enthusiastic in their defending, and de Launay himself was marched off to the Hôtel de Ville, which had been occupied by the rebellious townspeople. On the way there, he was badly beaten by his captors, and no doubt guessed what kind of violence lay in store for him. So, deciding that he'd had enough, he kicked one of his tormentors in the groin, a final crime for which he was stabbed and shot, before having his head carved off with a kitchen knife.

This attack on a barely inhabited prison was not the glorious start to the Revolution that it is usually held up to be, but it was very symptomatic of what was to come

– the mixture of trial by mob and decapitation was a theme that would be repeated all over France for at least the next five years.

France wanted an English king

At this stage of the Revolution, no one was talking about killing Louis XVI, or even deposing him. What most politicians wanted was a constitutional monarchy, like the one across the Channel. These days, we might think of George III of England as a drooling idiot who thought the King of Prussia was a tree, but in the late eighteenth century he was pretty popular in Britain. He had chosen a brilliant Prime Minister in William Pitt, and, seen from Paris, seemed to be the embodiment of what Voltaire had described in his *Lettres écrites de Londres*, when he praised Britain's 'wise system of government in which the ruler is all-powerful when it comes to doing good, and has his hands tied if he attempts to do evil'.

In May 1789, Louis XVI had reacted to the growing discontent amongst his citizens by giving up a day's hunting and summoning Parliament to Versailles so that he could hear the *doléances*, or grievances, brought by the members from all over the country. This was not the list of petty complaints one might imagine – Parliament was not being asked to vote on the maximum height of a hedge in South Brittany, for example. Instead, the members came with lists of truly idealistic demands: there should be a universal system of taxation regardless of rank; key state jobs should go to the best qualified rather than most aristocratic candidate; a national education system should be set up to help the poor, etc., etc. Hopes were running high and even the King, who had got dressed up in his finest jewel-encrusted finery for the occasion, was optimistic that the air could be cleared so that he could get back to hunting in peace.

Typically, however, the members became embroiled in a row about voting before they could debate any social reforms. The Parliament, or États généraux, was divided into three États (Estates). The First Estate was the clergy, and its 291 representatives spoke for 10,000 or so people. It paid no tax on its vast landholdings. The Second Estate was the nobility, which consisted of about 400,000 people, and had 270 representatives. They were not taxed either, and had feudal rights over many members of the Third Estate, the 25 million commoners, who had 585 representatives at Parliament. Theoretically, the commoners had a slim majority, but they now demanded that all MPs should represent equal numbers of constituents. By this system, the commoners would have had 50 times more members than the other two Estates put together.

King Louis, who was no doubt beginning to sweat behind his diamond façade, tried to get everyone to discuss taxation, which was the issue that would rebalance the nation's accounts, bring down food prices and put a stop to the smouldering popular discontent. Critically, though, he didn't have the necessary power or charisma to keep his Parliament in check, and the Third Estate went off to debate in private – deciding it could do without the others, it declared itself an Assemblée nationale. And instead of trying to placate the commoners and bring them back into the fold, Louis simply locked them out of the proceedings.

With one turn of the key, he had sealed his own fate. Almost 150 members of the clergy and two aristocrats joined the Assemblée nationale, and suddenly the absolute monarchy was finished. An alternative government was in place, and a precedent had been set. You could say *merde* to the King and get away with it.

Even so, the breakaway Parliament, which also called itself les Communes as an apparent homage to its British role model, did not want the King's head on a plate, or even in prison headgear. The leader of the Assemblée was a count – Honoré-Gabriel Riqueti, comte de Mirabeau – who had been elected to represent the Third Estate for Aix-en-Provence and Marseille. Mirabeau was a Marquis de Sade-like eroticist who had once been imprisoned because of his salacious writings, but he now turned his energies to campaigning for a British-style constitutional monarchy. He tried to persuade the King that absolutism and feudalism had had their day, and that he could hold on to the throne if he would only agree to govern beside ministers, as George III of Britain was doing.

Louis XVI wouldn't listen, though, and neither would Marie-Antoinette, who – it was rumoured – tried to bribe Mirabeau into dropping all this foolish democracy nonsense. And when the exhausted Mirabeau died of heart disease (one of the few politicians to die a natural death over the next few years), the monarchy's last chance died with him.

Nobbling the nobility

From now on, the Revolution proceeded with a mixture of idealistic political debate and violent destruction. In August 1789, while the Assemblée was hammering out the details of France's Declaration of Human Rights, the *Déclaration des droits de l'homme et du citoyen*, article two of which is about the inalienable right to property, peasants were burning chateaux and landowners' houses all over the country. Like the Storming of the Bastille, this round of demolition was given an official name – 'la Grande Peur' or Great Fear, not because the landowners were frightened of getting burned along with their furniture, but to explain the peasants' actions. Apparently the Fear was caused by scaremongers spreading rumours that the *aristos* had – *horreur!* – invited the *Anglais* to invade.

Understandably, the landowners took the hint and started to leave the country, along with many high-ranking army officers. Grabbing whatever they could of their remaining possessions, the refugees streamed over the borders into Italy, Holland, Germany, Austria (Marie-Antoinette's homeland) and Britain.

The impoverished aristocrats who chose to take refuge in England must have been nervous about the kind of reception they would receive. After all, they were running for help to the traditional enemy, and many Brits were known to be in favour of the Revolution. The idealistic egalitarian demands of the Assemblée excited libertarians – the poet Samuel Taylor Coleridge, then a teenage student, burned the words 'Liberty' and 'Equality' into the lawns at Cambridge (presumably he was stopped before he could get to 'Fraternity'). Even Royalist Brits were pro-Revolution because they thought that the internal strife would exhaust France and rule it out once and for all as a rival for world power.

Generally, however, the fleeing French *aristos* were kindly received, especially because they presented such a pitiful spectacle. Escaping from France was difficult and expensive – the price of a one-way boat trip from Dover to Calais had risen spectacularly. Many of them arrived with little more than the clothes they stood up in, and even the flounciest silks and most perfumed handker-chiefs began to get jaded after a few months of poverty.

There is an episode of the *Blackadder* sitcom about French exiles in London, in which Rowan Atkinson meets a snooty *aristo* who is reduced to eating 'horse's willy' in a cheap café. For once, though, the *Blackadder* episode was even tamer than the truth. A wonderful book called *Histoire générale des émigrés pendant la Révolution française*, written by Henri Forneron in 1884, is full of sumptuous anecdotes about French goings-on in London in the 1790s. Forneron tells the story of the writer René de Chateaubriand, a nobleman, who was having to live in a shared hovel, and was so cold at night that he slept under a chair to try and stay warm. In the morning, he and his French roommate would often wake up thinking: where's the servant with breakfast? before remembering that they had no servant, or money to buy breakfast. They would boil water and pretend it was English tea.

The English writer Frances Burney met a French family who were so penniless that they were sleeping in their carriage outside an inn in Winchester. Well, they weren't exactly a family – the carriage was home to a countess, her brother, a noble lady and the countess's lover, whom she apparently treated alternately 'with scornful impatience and a seductive sweetness'. Frances Burney wrote that they told her tearful stories of burnt chateaux and murdered friends, but reserved their strongest emotion for an English lady who confessed that she had never been to France.

'What, you've never seen Paris?' the countess gasped. 'How terrible!'

Frances Burney did her bit for Anglo-French solidarity by marrying an impoverished French general, whom she fed with her royalties, but other Brits found slightly less generous ways of helping out.

London newspapers were full of adverts offering instant cash for French jewels, silks and silverware. The Marquess of Buckingham set up a shop selling handicrafts made by the émigrés, with *marquises* and *comtesses* working ten hours a day as salesgirls. The enterprising Buckingham also created a tapestry workshop employing 200 priests – some 8,000

French clergymen fled to England during the Revolution, and, not being qualified (or willing) to work for the Anglican Church, had to find other employment. Many of them got work as teachers (Latin and French were much in demand) or doing manual work such as making wooden crates or paper flowers.

One clergyman found a less conventional position. An abbot moved in with a German singer, who pretended he was her uncle. She was fooling no one, though, and the émigré community loved to gossip about the way she would bully him to into composing French poetry that she sold to a publisher. Not only that but she would hit him, prompting a fellow émigré to remark that 'if you're going to have a niece, you should choose her more carefully.'

Scandal also dogged a certain chevalier de Saint-Louis (something like a Knight of the Garter), who is named in Henri Forneron's book only as Aimé M**** de la V***. Aimé claimed to have a job as a servant in Carnaby Street, but it was common knowledge that he was living with a prostitute he had picked up in Jersey on the way over from France. This outraged the exiles so much that a group of chevaliers held an emergency meeting and officially kicked him out of the Ordre, even going as far as publishing their decision in a London newspaper.

Adapting to life in Britain was tough for many of the émigrés. One is quoted as saying that she 'hates this country without sunlight, where French fruit is unavailable'. The worst thing was that after being cloistered at court, the *aristos* were suddenly out in the big wide world. One exile complained that she had had 'no news of the royals for long periods, which is troublesome because one really should not marry without their permission'.

These British-based refugees clung on to hopes that the excitement in France would die down and they would be able to return, but the more adventurous ones crossed the Atlantic to start completely new lives in America.

One hard-up émigré called Brillat-Savarin went to Connecticut, where he was taken in by an American family with four daughters – a dream scenario for a roving Frenchman, you might think, but his amorous instincts seem to have been dulled by pure hunger. He had to go out hunting for the family's food, and would often shoot turkeys and squirrels. On one occasion, the girls put on their best dresses and sang what he refers to as 'Yankee Doddee' for him. But instead of wondering which daughter he would most like to undress, he confesses that all the time they were singing, 'I was thinking of how I was going to cook my turkey.' Providing even further proof that the French are more interested in food than sex, he goes on to report that 'the turkey wings were served *en papillote* and the squirrels boiled in a Madeira wine *jus*.'

Brillat-Savarin did seem to be pleased with his country of refuge, though. One evening, he had dinner with some Englishmen and was disturbed to watch the two Brits drinking like fish while he ate and supped in moderation. After dinner, the Englishmen sang 'Rule Britannia' and then passed out under the table. It seems that English tourists haven't changed much in 200 years, and they convinced Brillat-Savarin that he was better off on the other side of the Atlantic.

Wise words from a Burke

Life might have been hard for the émigrés living amongst the less than sympathetic Brits, but in November 1790 they gained a very respectable ally.

Edmund Burke was a renowned lawyer and politician, a 61-year-old former MP who was born in Dublin but had served in the London Houses of Parliament, and had given a famous speech in 1774 pleading for an easing of the dictatorial rule over the American colonies. His advice was ignored* and two years later the Americans rebelled.

Given his democratic sympathies, Burke might have been expected to come out in favour of the upheavals in France, but in fact his book *Reflections on the Revolution in France* did exactly the opposite. In it, he considered the attempts to cure France's economic and political ills, coupled with the outbreaks of murderous violence, and decided that something was fundamentally wrong with the Revolution.

'In viewing this monstrous tragi-comic scene,' he writes, 'the most opposite passions necessarily succeed and sometimes mix with each other in the mind: alternate contempt and indignation, alternate laughter and tears, alternate scorn and horror.'

He talks about the violence in Paris and the Grande Peur and concludes:

Were they the inevitable results of the desperate struggle of determined patriots, compelled to wade through blood and tumult to the quiet shore of a tranquil and prosperous liberty? No! Nothing like it. Their cruelty has not even been the base result of fear. It has been the effect of their sense of perfect safety, in authorizing treasons, robberies, rapes, assassinations, slaughters, and burnings throughout their harassed land.

This was not a fashionable opinion, and Burke pro-voked outrage amongst the chattering classes. The most

* Although MPs might have been asleep – Burke's speeches were known to last eight hours.

famous of these was Thomas Paine, the English revolutionary who had been one of the Founding Fathers of the United States. Paine reacted in March 1791 by publishing his *Rights of Man*, in which he accuses Burke of being 'afraid that England and France would cease to be enemies' and of pouring forth nothing but 'rancour, prejudice, ignorance' and 'copious fury'.

Paine also defends the French against Burke's charge that they have rebelled against a 'mild and lawful monarch', stressing that 'the Monarch and the Monarchy were distinct and separate things; and it was against the established despotism of the latter, and not against the person or principles of the former, that the revolt commenced, and the Revolution has been carried.'

Paine takes a hearty swipe at monarchy in general, and Britain's system of government in particular. He outlines the ideals of the French Revolution, and predicts 'political happiness and national prosperity' there.

He also put his money where his mouth was and went to France to support the Revolution, despite being unable to speak a word of French . . . although his departure might also have been due to the fact that the British authorities were after him for sedition.

Paine's is the best-known response to Burke's book, but in fact the first to react had been feminist writer Mary Wollstonecraft, who published *A Vindication of the Rights of Men* only three weeks after Burke. Because it was written so quickly, the book has been criticized for being disorganized. And because it was written by a woman, it was also slammed by her male contemporaries for being too emotional (as soon as they found out who had written it, that is – the first edition was anonymous).

Wollstonecraft rips into Burke for supporting hereditary privilege and government by an elite. She also mocks the old man for his apparent infatuation with

Marie-Antoinette. On 6 October 1789, a mainly female mob had marched to Versailles, decapitated several members of the palace guard and brought the royal family back to Paris in a procession led by protesters carrying heads on spikes. Burke had described the 'horrid yells, frantic dances and unutterable abominations of the furies of hell, in the abused shape of the vilest of women'. In a very modern-sounding critique of his language, Wollstonecraft takes him to task for criticizing these women just because they were poor and uneducated compared to the refined Queen. The women's yells would have seemed less abominable, she says, if they hadn't had to earn their living selling fish.

This public row about France was highly entertaining and very profitable. All three books were major publishing successes* on both sides of the Channel, with Paine and Wollstonecraft easily outselling Burke because their publisher undercut his cover price. Cruelly, however, only one writer's prophecies came true.

For all his elitism and misplaced gallantry, Burke had seen the way things were going. The politicians soon got tired of intellectual debate and began purging moderate elements. The name of the Assemblée nationale kept changing – Assemblée constituante, Assemblée législative, Convention and Directoire were some of its new identities over the next five years – and each change brought not just sackings but wholesale executions as different factions – the Girondins, Montagnards and Jacobins – took power. It was Voltaire who said that 'in a

* Though none of them came anywhere near the huge success of Dickens's *Tale of Two Cities*, published more than fifty years later, which has since become the best-selling English-language novel of all time, with 200 million copies sold. The sales figures seem to imply that no literary subject fascinates Anglos as much as the French Revolution. The French would be proud to know it.

government, you need both shepherds and butchers.' The problem in France was that the butchers kept killing the shepherds, while the sheep turned cannibal.

Earth-shaking laws were being implemented – the abolition of slavery, the legalization of divorce, the adoption of the metric system – but it was in a climate as devoid of political principles as a drunk footballer in a brothel.

After Louis XVI and Marie-Antoinette made a pathetic attempt to escape from France in June 1791, organized by the Queen's alleged Swedish lover Count Fersen, a climate of paranoid fear had set in. Anyone suspected of being a Royalist was liable to be 'tried' by a tribunal and either guillotined or, more often, handed over to the crowds outside for lynching.

In September 1792, a rumour went around that a counter-revolution was being planned in Paris's jails, and that prisoners had been heard chanting 'Vivent les Autrichiens' (long live the Austrians, a reference to Marie-Antoinette's family). In each section of the city, the prisons were opened up, the inmates hauled out and tried for treason. Thousands were killed and, in an apparent confusion about buildings with high walls, the massacres were even extended to monasteries.

The most famous of the victims was Marie-Antoinette's First Lady of the Bedchamber, Marie-Louise, princesse de Lamballe, who was suspected of having a lesbian affair with the Queen. She was taken out of La Force prison (in the picturesque Marais district of Paris) and told to swear an oath of disobedience to the royal family. When she refused, she was hacked to death, and her head was paraded under Marie-Antoinette's window at the nearby Temple prison by a crowd calling to her to come out and kiss her lover.

It was all exactly as horrific as Burke had predicted.

A Frenchman ate my hamster

Again, this violence was given an official title – 'la Terreur' – and as news of the atrocities filtered out, the last vestiges of British sympathy for the Revolution dissipated completely. London's newspapers had a field day describing the bloodshed.

Reporting the princesse de Lamballe's killing, *The Times* said that 'her thighs were cut across, and her bowels and heart torn from her, and for two days her mangled body was dragged through the streets.' The newspaper also enjoyed itself immensely over the September 1792 massacres, raging that 'the most savage four-footed tyrants that range the unexplored deserts of Africa, in point of tenderness, rise superior to these two-legged Parisian animals.'

On 10 September, *The Times* gave an eye-witness account of the killing of 220 Carmelite monks:

> They were handed out of the prison door two by two into the Rue Vaugirard, where their throats were cut. Their bodies were fixed on pikes and exhibited to the wretched victims who were next to suffer. The mangled bodies of others are piled against the houses in the streets; and in the quarters of Paris near to which the prisons are, the carcases lie scattered in hundreds, diffusing pestilence all around.

On 12 September, the paper did its best to drum up sympathy for the imprisoned royals, though it seemed to be scraping the barrel just a little: 'The victuals given to the King and Queen is worse than that of any of their guards, and the jailors oblige them to eat such dishes as they know they dislike most. They drink the same wine as their guards.'

Then as now, journalists had much more fun when

they were allowed to concentrate on pure atrocities:

The mob ordered one of the Swiss soldiers to dress the hair of a young Swiss officer, a very handsome young man; and when it was done, they ordered him with a hand-saw to take off his head, and to be cautious not to spoil his headdress, saying it was too fine a head to put upon a pike, but to the best advantage. The soldier refused to obey, and was immediately cut to pieces; and two women sawed the officer's head from his body. He was not heard to make the least complaint, and it was near an hour before the head was quite off.

Another story, if true, was just as gory:

At the Place Dauphin, the mob had made a fire, and before it several men, women and children were roasted alive. The countess Perignan with her two daughters, the daughters first, and the mother after, were stripped of their clothes, washed with oil, and roasted alive, while the mob were singing and dancing round the fire, and amusing themselves with their cries and sufferings. After the repeated prayers of the eldest girl, not more than 15 years old, that someone would with a sword or a pistol put an end to her horrid existence, a young man shot her through the heart, which so irritated the mob, that they immediately threw him into the fire.

You can almost feel the British glee that the political chattering was over and the violence had really got under way.

Un petit Soupir à la Parisienne. — A Family of Sans Culotts refreshing after the fatigues of the day

Epigram extempore on seeing the above Print.

Here as you sit, well as his beyora. On Maigre Days each had his Dish But now his human Flesh they grow
Frenchmen were Cannibals we groan. Of Soup, or Salad, Eggs, or Fish. And every Days a Mardi Gras.

Frighteningly, British illustrator James Gillray's grotesque view of the French Revolution contains elements of truth. Cannibalism was almost certainly not on the menu, but massacres, mutilations and even roastings were common during the Terreur.

When is a cake not a cake?

Soon afterwards, Thomas Paine's theory that the King was not under personal threat was proved bloodily wrong. On 21 January 1793, Louis XVI was driven through the streets of Paris in a carriage and guillotined on the place de la Révolution (today the place de la Concorde), his final words drowned out by a drum roll and the yells of the crowd to get on with it. On 16 October, Marie-Antoinette followed him, after being tried for treason and (bizarrely) incest. She did not get the carriage treatment and had to ride to her execution on the back of an open cart, taunted by the crowd.

These days, many French people think of Marie-Antoinette as a victim of the Revolution rather than one of its causes. They pity the Austrian girl who had been married off for political reasons at the age of fourteen to an impotent French prince, and was then kept in a gilded cage while her hapless husband let France sink into the mire. But back then, she was regarded as a haughty harlot, the foreign princess who dressed up as a shepherdess in her custom-built model farm in the grounds of Versailles while real peasants were starving to death nearby.

All of which probably explains the 'let them eat cake' rumour – the story being that the Queen uttered these callous words when she heard that Parisians were rioting because they couldn't afford bread. Opinions vary on whether she actually made the remark, although one thing is certain: whatever she said, it wasn't 'let them eat cake', which has to go down as one of the worst translations in history. It's as if 'vive la différence' were translated as 'let the difference live'. It doesn't mean anything.

The actual quotation attributed to her was 'qu'ils mangent de la brioche', which means something like 'then why don't they eat brioche?', and would need a little footnote explaining that brioche is a posh version of bread made with eggs, butter, sugar and milk.

If she did say this, some might say she deserved to have her head cut off, or at the very least bashed with a brioche. But in fact it's almost certain that she didn't say anything of the sort – the phrase is actually taken from the autobiography of philosopher Jean-Jacques Rousseau.

In *Les Confessions*, Rousseau tells a story about working as a live-in tutor to the children of a certain Monsieur de Mably and falling in love with the local white wine – so much so that he often sneaked away a bottle to have a quiet drink in his room. But, he says, he could never drink without eating. 'How was I to get bread?' he agonizes. He couldn't be seen taking baguettes up to his room, and if he asked the servants to buy bread, his host would be insulted. Finally, to quote the original, 'Je me rappelai le pis-aller d'une grande princesse à qui l'on disait que les paysans n'avaient pas de pain, et qui répondit: Qu'ils mangent de la brioche.' In other words: 'I remembered the solution suggested by a great princess, who was told that the peasants had no bread, and answered: Then why don't they eat brioche?' Rousseau is not bothered at all by the political incorrectness of the story, and goes out to the patisserie to buy brioche for himself, which was apparently an acceptable thing for a well-bred young man to do, being a luxury rather than a staple food.

He was writing about the year 1736, nineteen years before Marie-Antoinette's birth, and was probably suggesting that the brioche remark had been made by the wife of the Sun King, Princess Marie-Thérèse, daughter of

Philip IV of Spain. This is a perfectly credible idea – Louis XIV's court was totally cut off from reality and lived by its witticisms. Anything was good for a joke.*

Whatever the truth about the whole cake/brioche story, Rousseau's autobiography came out in 1782, seven years before the Revolution, and was the perfect source of a misappropriated quotation when people were looking for nasty things to say about Marie-Antoinette. As we've seen, it was a time when rumours caused riots and massacres. No one was going to disbelieve such an easily quotable quip, and it was destined to stay with Marie-Antoinette for much longer than her head.

A day for parsnips

It would be a shame to think of the French Revolution as one long round of bloodletting and demolition, however. Among the power-seekers, there were real innovators who leapt at the chance to rethink a whole society from scratch.

Apart from the metric system, the most radical of these new ideas was the Revolutionary Calendar, a superbly crackpot scheme to begin again at Day One and reshape the year to fit French life. It was doomed to fail, for a reason we will see in a moment, but in a way the opponents of the old calendar were right. After all, several of the months were named in incorrect Latin – September was the ninth month and October the tenth. What kind of lesson was that for schoolkids learning dead languages? And what was all this business of having different-length months, and the Catholic

* Although Marie-Thérèse has her defenders, too, who argue that the remark could actually have been a pertinent suggestion. At the time, if there was not enough bread, bakers would lower the price of brioche.

nonsense of decreeing that a week should have seven days?

It was time, the Revolutionaries thought, to do away with it all and start afresh.*

The new calendar was developed by a wonderfully French combination of people – two mathematicians and two poets. The mathematicians did the groundwork, deciding that the year should have twelve months of thirty days. Fortunately, being mathematicians, they quickly realized that this wasn't enough, and added five extra holidays – six in leap years – so that France would stay in alignment with the natural calendar.

The poets chose the names of the days and months, using French plants, animals and tools for the days, and making the months rhyme in groups of three. Winter, for example, was divided into *nivôse*, *pluviôse* and *ventôse* (names derived from the French words for snow, rain and wind). For the days, the poets didn't want to be tied down to simply replacing *lundi*, *mardi*, *mercredi*, etc., so they gave each individual day of the year a name. In autumn, for example, there was parsnip (30 September), pumpkin (8 October), aubergine (17 October) and spade (20 December). In spring, 8 April was beehive, 4 May silkworm. All very picturesque, but the drawback is obvious . . .

'What's the date today?'

'Parsnip.'

'*Merci.*'

'Or hang on – is it carrot? Or horseradish?'

This wasn't the fatal flaw in the idea, however. The

---

* Or nearly afresh. The scheme was voted in on 5 October 1793, eleven days before Marie-Antoinette was executed, but was deemed to have begun a year earlier in 1792, which was posthumously named Year One, thus depriving the people of a New New Year's party.

Revolutionary weeks were to be ten days long, and you don't have to be an expert mathematician to work out that this automatically reduced the number of weekends, which is one thing you cannot do to a French person. To rub it in, the government declared that 'Sunday is abolished in the name of reason'. As well as this, the new calendar's five or six holidays were peanuts compared to all the old Catholic saints' days. The people were more than happy to hack a few priests to death, but they didn't want to lose their saints' days.

So it came as some relief to the French when the Revolutionary Calendar was abolished in 1805 by Napoleon, who restored the illogical old system with the added bonus of a new holiday – 14 July, which would otherwise have been rather limply called sage.

The French are aliens

Whatever the Brits might have thought about the pros and cons of the Revolution, eventually France forced their hand.

First, in November 1792, the Convention nationale, as the French ruling body was called that week, issued an Edict of Fraternity calling on the downtrodden subjects of all Europe's monarchs to rise up and overthrow their rulers. The Convention declared that it would provide aid to the citizens of any country who decided 'to recover their liberty'. Understandably, monarchies like Britain, Prussia and Spain did not take kindly to this public invitation to rebel, and on 1 February 1793 (known in the French Revolutionary Calendar as broccoli, the 12th day of pluviôse, Year 1) France made things even clearer by declaring war on Britain.

A new law was passed, obliging every able-bodied, unmarried man to join the Revolutionary Army.

Predictably, this caused a rush for marriage licences as single men proposed to any woman who would have them. It is said that French widows have never been merrier. Even so, about half a million men joined up and although many of them soon deserted or mutinied, France still represented a daunting opponent.

Britain was suddenly faced by a triple French threat – war with Revolutionary France; trouble stirred up at home by the 70,000 or so Royalist exiles; and a British revolution fomented by Paris.

Britain couldn't trust its French exiles, partly just because they were French, but also because the highest-ranking of them – the comte d'Artois (a grandson of Louis XV) and his son the duc de Berry – were fully fledged members of the Bourbon family of Louis XIV, who had virtually bankrupted Britain with his wars. So Pitt and his government voted through an Aliens Act, forcing French émigrés to register with a Justice of the Peace, and thereby putting them on a kind of open-ended probation.

This was reinforced by the Traitorous Correspondence Act, which called for letters written to France to be opened and censored, and forbade all trade with France or active support for the Revolution.

Fear of a British revolution made Pitt and co. become dictatorial themselves. Public meetings were banned and troublemakers were shipped off to the handy new penal colony of Australia. Pitt also decided that it would be much easier if he paid France's other enemies – especially Austria and Prussia – to fight the French, which might explain why Britain's direct interventions against France became slightly half-hearted.

In the summer of 1793, for example, the Brits sent a fleet to capture the southern French port of Toulon. Local officials actually welcomed the invasion, but the invaders announced that they hadn't come to enforce a regime change, and were soon evicted by a daring 24-year-old Corsican artillery captain called Bonaparte, who recaptured strategic forts and was able to bombard the Brits into retreat. When Toulon was retaken, Royalists were brutally executed, some of them being blown apart by cannons. As usual, being a counter-revolutionary was proving to be a messy business.

At the same time, Napoleon's home, Corsica, rather insultingly asked to become part of the British Empire with George III as its king. The island was briefly occupied, but was deemed too difficult to defend because of its many ports and its hilly terrain, and the Brits soon left the Corsicans to the mercy of their vengeful French overlords. Ten thousand Corsicans fled the subsequent persecution, and relations with the French mainland have never been friendly since.

In July 1794, a French Royalist army, with British backing, landed in Quiberon Bay in Brittany. But the aristocratic French leaders could hardly understand the Breton peasants they had come to liberate, and the British fleet had to set sail again because of bad weather, leaving the invasion force unprotected. In the end, the Revolutionary Army cut them off, executed 700 of the returned exiles and captured 20,000 British muskets. If this wasn't bad enough, the Quiberon cock-up also provoked France into launching a retaliatory attack.

In February 1797, 1,400 French troops, including 800 convicts, were dressed up in British uniforms captured at Quiberon and sent to attack Bristol under the command of an Irish-American soldier called William Tate (who couldn't speak French). The ships got lost, however, and landed in Wales, where the hungry ex-cons went on a scavenging spree and then gave themselves up to a group of red-cloaked Welsh women whom they mistook for soldiers. Twelve drunk Frenchmen were captured by a lone woman wielding a pitchfork. The French regular soldiers occupied a farm but were then tricked into accepting an unconditional surrender by a local militia leader called John Campbell who told them (falsely) that they were outnumbered. The Frenchmen and their American leader simply marched down on to the beach and piled up their weapons. It was a thirty-six-hour fiasco that France can proudly claim as the last foreign invasion of British soil.

Revolution – what is it good for?

If this Anglo-French war seems to have been a tepid affair (it wouldn't heat up until Nelson and Wellington got involved), it was partly because France was having greater success attacking more accessible neighbours like Holland, Prussia and Italy, and was also very busy killing its own people.

Anti-Royalist massacres plunged Brittany and the Vendée (southwest of the Loire) into genocide that hadn't been seen since the English *chevauchées* during the Hundred Years War. In Nantes, thousands were executed by drowning. In the Vendée, Revolutionary troops were told to 'burn windmills and demolish ovens' (the two vital tools for making bread and feeding the population) and ordered: 'If you find women and children, shoot them – they all support our enemies.' Today, if the north-west of France is a hotbed of support for the right-wing National Front and extreme Catholic Royalists, it might well be a reaction to the atrocities committed there during the Revolution.

Generally, though, after Robespierre was guillotined by a rival faction in 1794, the violence subsided and the Revolution began to peter out. It was as if the French had

had enough of politics. After all, apart from a flowery calendar and some bloodletting therapy, the Revolution hadn't brought much benefit to the poor it was meant to help. True, the top layer of privileged aristocrats had been stripped away, but they had been replaced by bureaucrats wielding just as much power and violence as the *aristos*. At the end of 1795, six years into the Revolution, the economy was still in a state of collapse, and the poor were dying in droves of famine and cold. Meanwhile, the *nouveau riche* bourgeoisie was amassing fortunes in black-market trading, and making sure it would hang on to its wealth by dishing out backhanders to corrupt officials. In 1797, free speech was ended when press censorship was introduced. In 1802, slavery was legalized again and an amnesty was granted to all the *aristos* who had run away to Britain and other countries and survived the hardship, humiliation and horse's willies. Within a few years, France would have a military dictator who would call himself emperor, create a new 'imperial aristocracy' and marry a great-niece of Marie-Antoinette. To crown it all (if that's not a bad pun), in 1814 King Louis XVIII, a grandson of Louis XV, would arrive in Paris to cheers of 'Vive le roi!' Twenty-five years after the Storming of the Bastille, France would be more or less back where it started. Not what you would call lasting change.

Democracy had come to certain aspects of French life, though, notably the military. If it hadn't been for the Revolution, a Corsican with an incomprehensible regional accent and bad grammar would never have risen through the ranks of the French army by merit alone. An aristocratic general would have made sure that the young upstart Bonaparte was kept in his place – ordering horse-feed, perhaps, or going on suicidal charges.

Yes, Napoleon, the so-called 'little Corporal', was

probably the most important product of the French Revolution, an enemy as dangerous to Britain as anyone since William the Conqueror – and with similar ambitions.

And strictly speaking, as we shall see, Boney was a British product . . .*

---

* So much so that I have opted throughout the book to use the English spelling for Napoleon, without the accented é. In a spirit of equality I have done the same for Josephine.

18

Napoleon: If *Je* Ruled the World

The illustration opposite is a cartoon of Napoleon's planned invasion of Britain. It was drawn in around 1804, at a time when the attack was a real possibility and lookouts along the south coast of England were on constant alert for the first sighting of a Corsican in a sailboat.

The drawing shows hot-air balloons wafting troops over Britain's Channel defences, invasion barges being rowed across a surprisingly narrow Straits of Dover, and a tunnel crowded with French footsoldiers, cavalry, cannons and even what looks like a small collection of prostitutes. In F. E. Halliday's *Concise History of England*, the cartoon is laconically captioned 'Napoleon's projected invasion of England by tunnel, sea and air. A French fantasy'.

It may seem like a fantasy to us now, but for a few years in the early nineteenth century it was the keystone to Napoleon's plans for global domination. He thought that if he could just annex England, he would rule the world.

Designing a new uniform for the Emperor of Earth (Napoleon adored inventing uniforms, flags and coins

Napoleon dreamt of invading England using all the latest technology at his disposal, and some that didn't exist – the Channel Tunnel, for example. In the end, he abandoned his plans because even the supposedly reliable technology didn't work: his invasion barges sank.

for his new possessions) was a dream that was largely inspired by the British – and destroyed by them, too. Which is why Napoleon, like Joan of Arc and the Six Nations rugby tournament, provokes outbursts of acute Anglophobia in French patriots. When the Empereur died, there were Frenchmen who claimed that he had been murdered in a cunning British poisoned-wallpaper plot, even though all the medical evidence pointed to a hereditary disease.

And the fervour lives on today. In March 2008, when former French Prime Minister Dominique de Villepin sold his collection of Bonapartist books and documents (modestly catalogued as 'The Imperial Library'), the Parisian auction room was crowded with bidders and spectators. Books that had belonged to 'His Majesty the Emperor', as the supposedly Republican auctioneers referred to Napoleon, sold like hot croissants, and an autograph went for 28,000 euros.

But one of the most emotive moments came when a British anti-Bonaparte pamphlet was snapped up by the Musée Napoléon Premier in Fontainebleau, just south of Paris. No doubt celebrating that it hadn't fallen into the hands of the enemy, spectators cheered and shouted, 'Vive l'Empereur!'

This continuing hero worship is understandable. In his few short years as military dictator and then self-appointed Emperor of France, Napoleon won more battles than France had done for centuries, and has done since. At one point, he had annexed more of Europe than Hitler ever managed with his aeroplanes and Panzer tanks. And Bonaparte wasn't just a warmonger – he balanced France's disastrous finances and almost personally wrote the law books still used in modern French courts. He even created one of the nation's proudest cultural traditions – the *maison de tolérance*, or legal, state-regulated brothel.

His only real mistake was to scare the Brits into taking him prisoner and exiling him on the most godforsaken island in their empire – alone and vulnerable to attack by fiendish wallpaper poisoners . . .

The not-so-little corporal

There are two myths about Napoleon that get in the way of people's judgements of who he was and what he achieved.

Numéro un, he was a poor prole from Corsica who made it good. Actually, no: he was born into the island's aristocracy. Of course, as far as a Parisian *marquis* was concerned, the noblest Corsican was about as aristocratic as a chamber pot, but Napoleon came from a privileged background, and would never have made it to military academy otherwise.

Numéro deux, he was a midget. Wrong again: Napoleon was just over five feet six inches or 168 centimetres tall, a respectable height for the times. Stories of his extreme shortness seem to come from Englishmen wanting to throw doubts on his masculinity, and from a mistake by the doctor who performed his autopsy – an incompetent French quack who got the metric-to-inch conversion wrong.

So let's look at the facts about the man who was to be both France's most successful ruler since Charlemagne, and then its most spectacular failure.

Napoleon's family, the Buonapartes, came to Corsica from Italy in the twelfth century. An ancestor of his called Ugo is listed in the army of Frederick the One-Eyed, Duke of Swabia, who invaded Tuscany in 1122. Ugo's nephew later became one of the ruling councillors of Florence. The Corsican branch of the family had very little money, however, and rather than any flashiness of lifestyle, their rank was reflected in the size of their houses and their prominent position in society. Napoleon's grandfather, for instance, served the island as Inspector General of Roads and Bridges, an enviable post because Corsica had almost none of either.

When King Louis XV of France bought Corsica from the Italians in 1768, Napoleon's father Carlo was one of the leaders of the short-lived resistance campaign, and fought the French invaders in the *maquis*, accompanied by his pregnant wife Letizia. When she gave birth on 15 August 1769, they decided to name their son Napoleone after an uncle who had died in the struggle for independence. Yes, France's future national hero was born an anti-French guerrilla.

Louis XV's men soon gained full possession of Corsica, and instead of punishing the resistance fighters, the King set about winning over the most influential locals by offering them membership of France's aristocracy. Families only had to prove that they had lived on the island for 200 years, and had noble ancestry – which was easy for Carlo Buonaparte, who got his Tuscan cousins to vouch for him. As soon as his application was accepted, Carlo began to sport a powdered wig and silk stockings, and bought a library of 1,000 books as if to prove his poshness, trappings which he could now afford because, like all French aristocrats, he was exempt from taxation.

Another privilege, of even greater consequence to the young Napoleone, was that the children of French aristocrats could go free of charge to France's most prestigious schools. And in May 1779, the nine-year-old took up a scholarship to the military academy in Brienne, in the Champagne countryside.

His fighting instincts were tested as soon as he arrived, because as a weedy, dark-skinned, non-paying student with a coarse provincial accent, he instantly became something of a social outcast. He adapted well, though – he lost the telltale accent and even began to develop his talents as an invader by annexing other boys' spaces in the college's garden. Every student was allocated an area to cultivate, but not all of them could be bothered, so Napoleone took over their land, erected a defensive palisade and declared it his territory. When some students on an adjoining plot accidentally damaged Napoleone's trellis, he attacked the perpetrators with a hoe and sent them running for cover. The pattern for his future military behaviour was set in a vegetable patch.

When, at the age of twelve, Napoleone decided that he wanted to join the navy, he began sleeping in a hammock. A school inspector approved of his choice: 'He is very bad at dancing and drawing. He will make an excellent sailor.' And when, in 1783, Britain and France lapsed into a temporary peace, he applied to transfer to an English naval college, giving rise to a fascinating historical possibility – the Corsican serving under Nelson at Trafalgar ('Kiss me, Napoleon'), or even becoming the country's military dictator and forcing Queen Victoria to win the throne as a counter-revolutionary warrior.

But it was not to be. Napoleone Buonaparte was offered a place at the crack École militaire, and left Brienne for Paris, a self-confident teenager with a French name, Napoléon Bonaparte (he'd conveniently lost the Italian spellings), excellent skills in mathematics and gardening, and atrocious grammar. It was just five years before the Revolution, and he was off to join the King's army.

At the École militaire, the new Corsican student showed even more of the belligerence that had won him respect in the Brienne vegetable garden. During a drill exercise one day, he made a mistake and was rapped on the knuckles. Hitting students was against regulations, and Napoleon launched his rifle at the instructor's head, swearing that he would never attend a lesson with him again. Judging that an attitude like this might be useful in battle, the school simply found him a new instructor.

And Napoleon was punished, but not expelled, for his most serious breach of discipline. During a balloon display by the pioneer aviator Blanchard (of whom more later), Napoleon got impatient because take-off was delayed by unfavourable winds,* and eventually took matters into his own hands, cutting through the ropes with a knife and sending poor Blanchard floating away out of control. Blanchard survived, only to die falling from another balloon a few years later.

In 1785, Napoleon graduated from the École (in only one year instead of the standard two), and because there were no places in the navy, accepted a post as an artillery officer, a job that would enable him to use his mathematics and get aggression out of his system by firing large lumps of metal at people. Napoleon was sixteen and his military career was beginning in earnest. He received his commission from Louis XVI in person, the man he would soon (albeit briefly) replace on the throne of France.

Napoleon got himself posted in Valence in southern France and as well as attending lectures on cannonball trajectories, started reading history books. One of his favourites was a history of England from the Roman invasion to the present day, which stopped early so that French readers wouldn't be traumatized by all of Marlborough's famous victories against the army of Louis XIV. (This was nothing unusual – the textbooks

* This impatience and misjudgement of the wind was to scupper Napoleon's British invasion plans some twenty years later.

413

Napoleon had studied at Brienne omitted to mention any English victories during the Hundred Years War, claiming that Agincourt and Crécy were won by Gascons – that is, other Frenchmen.)

The conclusion Napoleon drew from his favourite history book was a typical one for the time – like many Frenchmen just before the Revolution, he came to admire Britain's constitutional monarchy and made notes to this effect, writing that if the British King abuses 'his great power to commit injustice, the cries of the nation grow to a thunder, and the King backs down'. He decided that this might be a good thing for Louis XVI's regime to think about.

In the event, of course, Louis did no such thing, and the Revolution began, with the new National Assembly's laws hitting straight at Napoleon's privileges. Under royal rule, his family hadn't paid tax, and his siblings were getting a free education at the poshest schools.

Napoleon could have been forgiven for becoming a Royalist, but he embraced the Revolution in its initial, moderate form and pledged allegiance to the new state. He even congratulated people who bought up houses that had been confiscated from aristocrats and the clergy – safe in the knowledge, of course, that no one in Corsica would dare try the same thing with his own family's property for fear of provoking a vendetta.

He did feel the need to be closer to home, however, and in 1791 he went to Corsica and put himself forward to be elected leader of the local Garde nationale, the voters being the guards themselves. In order to guarantee that the electorate got it right, he billeted 200 guardsmen in his mother's house, where they were fed on Mama's best home cooking. He also had one of the election officials kidnapped, and got a gang of 500-odd guards-men to intimidate his main opponent during a campaign speech. He was only twenty-two, but he had already learned to combine his Corsican heritage with his military training, a terrifyingly efficient mix that he would soon be trying out on the rest of Europe.

A chance to bash the Brits

It was only during the Terreur that Napoleon became disenchanted with the direction the Revolution was taking, and he was highly relieved when France went to war with Britain in 1793. At last, he was going to get the chance to put everything he had learned in artillery class to practical use against some uppity foreigners.

On 27 August, the port of Toulon rebelled against the Revolutionary government, tore down its tricolour and beckoned in some British and Spanish ships that happened to be sailing nearby. Napoleon begged to be allowed to go and evict the invaders, even if they had been invited in. Luckily for him, the local artillery commander had recently been wounded, and Napoleon was given the job of bombarding the ships in the harbour.

The officer in charge of the army was a typical product of the French Revolution – a painter who had decided that he would make a good general. When he ordered Napoleon to fire at the nearest ships, the young officer pointed out that it would be pointless, given that they were at least two miles out of cannon range. Impressed by the young man's expertise, and ignoring grumbles from fellow officers that this newcomer was a treacherous *aristo*, the general decided to give Napoleon carte blanche, an opportunity that was too good for the ambitious Corsican to miss. He had cannons towed to Toulon from as far away as Monaco, and brought in 100,000 sacks of soil to build a massive gun emplacement on the seashore. Within a few weeks, the artillery aimed at the British fleet was not only within firing range but had also grown from just five to almost 200 cannons. When Napoleon let fly, the ships began to take serious punishment, and the shots they fired in reply just embedded themselves in Napoleon's soft earthworks. The ships were forced to back off, weakening their hold on the port.

Emboldened by this success, Napoleon put forward a daring plan to retake the town from its Royalist occupiers using his cannons. He had spotted that a single section of Toulon's ramparts, a fort known as Little Gibraltar, held the key to the British defences. If it fell, the French would be able to use it as a base to bombard the other enemy outposts and end the siege. Brilliant, the new general (a former sugar planter) said, much better than our old plan of randomly firing at the city walls now and again and hoping that the Brits would go away.

So Napoleon built another of his gun emplacements outside Little Gibraltar, and began a forty-eight-hour slogging match with the enemy artillery, grabbing short bouts of sleep lying on the ground, wrapped up in his overcoat. He then mounted up and led a cavalry charge at the weakened fortress, during which his horse was shot from under him and he was stabbed in the thigh by a British blade.

As Little Gibraltar fell, closely followed by the whole of Toulon, a star was born.

Napoleon himself expressed it nicely: 'In revolutions, there are two types of people – those who make them, and those who take advantage of them.' The newly promoted Brigadier General Bonaparte was the living embodiment of this. As a reward for his actions in Toulon, he was appointed Inspector General of Coastal Defences for the whole Côte d'Azur, and given a luxurious villa outside Antibes. Things were looking decidedly rosy.

Not now, Horatio

Unfortunately for Napoleon, just out of telescope range of the new Bonaparte residence, a British sailor was finding out that what he enjoyed most in life was firing cannons at Frenchmen.

This was Horatio Nelson, the humble son of a rector in Norfolk, who had joined the navy at the age of twelve and was now gaining his first experience as a captain in wartime.

Nelson possessed a contemporary Englishman's instinctive loathing for the French. When, in 1783, he visited France, he concluded simply, 'I hate their country and their manners.' And after spotting British officers adopting the dandyish French fashion for wearing epaulettes, he declared, 'I hold them a little cheap for putting on any part of a Frenchman's uniform.' When he took up his command in 1793, he went even further, telling a new midshipman: 'You must hate a Frenchman as you hate the devil.'

And so it was that, in 1794, Nelson flung himself into action, blockading Corsican ports in support of a British army invasion of the island. The Brits eventually abandoned their plans to use Corsica as a Mediterranean base and withdrew, but Nelson had got a taste for the kind of in-your-face cannon battles that Napoleon himself enjoyed, and left the area with his reputation for bravery established. As he wrote to a friend, 'even the French respect me'.

Soon they would do much more than that.

Napoleon would have loved to come and defend his island, of course, but he was marooned on the mainland. As the French Revolutionary politician Pierre-Victurnien Vergniaud said, 'It is to be feared that the Revolution, like Saturn, will devour all of its children one by one.'* This was a reference to the Greco-Roman myth about a god who, fearing that his children would overthrow him, ate each one at birth. Napoleon himself, so recently the hero, now almost became one of those devoured children.

While Nelson was bombarding Corsica, Napoleon was under investigation for being Italian and therefore a potential traitor. Accused of being too close to the brother of the guillotined leader Robespierre, he was only saved from a similar fate when the appetite for political bloodletting suddenly subsided, and France regained a semblance of sanity.

But Napoleon's reputation was in tatters because of the allegations against him, and he considered suicide, and then (more seriously) emigration to Turkey, where artillery officers were much in demand. He was in Paris getting together the necessary papers when fate again presented him with an unmissable opportunity.

In September 1795, Paris was in turmoil as moderate Republicans wrestled for power with Royalists, many of whom had adopted English accents, calling themselves the 'Incoyables' – the word *incroyable* pronounced *à l'anglaise*, without the letter R. When the British landed (or rather dumped) a Royalist army in western France, things came to a head and counter-revolutionaries marched on the Tuileries Palace, the seat of government.

Always wanting to be at the heart of the action, Napoleon went to the public gallery of a parliamentary debate, where he was spotted and offered the chance to defend the Republic. His reply was one characteristic sentence: 'Where are the cannons?'

The answer was that there were forty guns out in

---

* As if to prove Vergniaud right, he was guillotined at the height of the Terreur.

Neuilly (the suburb where President Sarkozy began his political career), so Napoleon sent troops to fetch them, and positioned his artillery at strategic points around the Tuileries. And when the massive rebel army of 30,000 men stormed into central Paris, it was Napoleon's deadly cannon fire that enabled 8,000 Republican troops to rout them.

In just one day of action, he had repaired all the political damage of the previous year. In October 1795, aged only twenty-six, he was appointed commander-in-chief of the Armée de l'intérieur. He wasn't allowed to design his own uniform, but the gold-braided coat was pretty fancy, and he wouldn't have long to wait before he would be his own stylist.

Rose by any other name

Soon afterwards, Napoleon won an even greater prize: Josephine, she of 'not tonight' fame. The French will tell you that he never uttered those words and that they were just another piece of anti-Bonaparte propaganda invented by the Brits, but, as we'll see, the story probably wasn't far off the mark.

Josephine, real name Rose Beauharnais, was six years older than Napoleon and a mother of two. She was the widow of a guillotined aristocrat, and had narrowly escaped the chop herself. This seems to be why she decided to enjoy life to the full, entertaining a series of lovers including the national hero General Hoche and one of France's political leaders, Paul Barras. Probably the last thing she expected was the slavish devotion of a youthful Corsican soldier who decided he didn't like her name and began calling her Josephine. She slept with him, of course – he was a novelty in Parisian society – but was disconcerted when the serious young man wrote her a long love letter at seven the next morning and then began interrogating her about whether she'd also slept with Barras.

It was only when he offered to marry her that he got her full attention. She was a widow with no income except her friends' generosity. He was a newly promoted general with excellent prospects and, if the worst came to the worst, a decent pension. So she accepted, and Barras sportingly gave Napoleon a wedding present – command of the Army of the Alps.

This was not just so that the newly-weds could go on a skiing honeymoon, however. The Armée des Alpes was due to invade Italy, and Napoleon was being sent into action. Josephine must have been as delighted as English King Henry V's bride, who was taken on a besieging honeymoon.

Napoleon made things even worse – for the trip, he loaded up with books on military history and alpine topography. And when Josephine suggested doing something more amorous than revising geography, he told her: 'Patience, my darling. We will have time to make love when the war is won.'

Which is just a less catchy version of 'not tonight, Josephine'.

Denying the Nile

Napoleon found his new army literally in tatters. The 40,000-odd men stationed in Nice were in ragged trousers and patched tunics, some of them still sporting the white jackets worn under Louis XVI. Their hats ranged from hairless bearskins to dented helmets, and their footwear from clogs to simple lengths of cloth wrapped around their feet. They were underfed and demoralized, hardly able to march in time across a parade ground, let alone 'liberate' Italy from Austrian occupation.

Napoleon's first act was to spend all his available funds on food and brandy, and to borrow enough money to buy a three-month supply of flour and 18,000 pairs of boots. This won him the instant adoration of his troops, and boosted morale so much that just a few weeks later, on 10 May 1796, he won his first great victory and gained a new nickname.

At Lodi, near Milan, he managed to persuade his foot-soldiers, who had so recently been on the verge of starvation and enforced nakedness, to carry out a suicidal charge across a narrow bridge. At the same time, using the sense of strategy that was to make him such a dangerous opponent, he sent some cavalry to cross the river upstream and surprise the Austrians by galloping down on them when they had all eyes and guns fixed on the river. The plan worked like a dream, the bridge was taken and the victorious Frenchmen, many of them long-serving veterans, dubbed their young leader 'le petit Caporal', little realizing that the Brits would later use the nickname to make jokes about his height.

Over the following year, the 'little man' was to win more battles in Italy than any French army for the previous three centuries, in the process capturing over 1,000 highly valuable Austrian cannons and vast amounts of loot. One of the principles of the Revolution was that works of art that had been in the possession of royalty, aristocrats or the Church became the property of the people. Napoleon applied this principle to the Italians, and it was now that Paris's collection* of great Italian paintings and documents was founded, with works by Raphael, da Vinci, Correggio and Mantegna

---

* The Louvre had been transformed into a national museum in 1793.

being shipped north for the greater glory of the Revolution. Even the Pope was made to contribute, and Napoleon personally chose some of the hundred works of art pillaged from the Vatican. It was hardly surprising that he was later excommunicated – no one robs the Vatican without incurring divine discontent.

Napoleon's next move was the one that would bring down Nelson's wrath upon him.

It was the end of 1797, and Napoleon had been made commander-in-chief of the Armée de l'Angleterre. No, the Brits had not yet begun buying up French talent, and this was not a football-style transfer. The French had formed a whole army dedicated to invading Britain, but after inspecting the troops available to him up on the Channel coast, Napoleon decided that an invasion was (for the moment at least) too risky, and turned his sights to Egypt. This, he claimed, was to capture the land routes to the East and threaten Britain's presence in India, although cynics might say that he'd caught the art bug and just wanted to add a few sarcophagi to his rapidly growing collection.

In a move that baffled his superiors, Napoleon declared that he didn't just want to take soldiers with him. He also assembled a small army of scientists to study what he confidently expected to be a new French territory, as well as artists and poets to record his victory for posterity. Was a touch of megalomania creeping in, perhaps? His officers certainly disapproved, and christened the civilian hangers-on 'the Pekinese', because they followed Napoleon around like lapdogs.

The French invasion fleet sailed out of Toulon on 18 May 1798, stopped off to capture Malta, and then won Egypt in a single battle, proving the first of Napoleon's theories about Egyptian culture – namely that scimitars are not effective against cannonballs.

Napoleon proceeded to grab the money and jewels belonging to the country's rulers, the Mamelukes, but showed that his sense of equality, liberty and fraternity was limited by giving the spoils to the officers rather than letting all his troops benefit from the pillaging.

All in all, though, it had been a highly effective expedition. Not only had Napoleon won a new colony for the Republic, but he had also come up with one of his most famous quotations. To motivate his troops, he had told them: 'Soldiers, from the crest of these pyramids, forty centuries are watching you.' Slightly inaccurate – the pyramid of Gaza was forty-three centuries old at the time – but eminently quotable.

What Napoleon didn't know was that the sailor from Norfolk was about to spoil the party.

The Brits had been wondering for a few months what Napoleon was up to. The wily Frenchman had initially thrown his enemies off the scent by spreading false rumours about a planned invasion of Ireland, and when this didn't materialize, the alarm bells sounded. Nelson (who had now been promoted to Rear Admiral) had been sailing around the Med looking for signs of French activity, using all the search facilities available before the invention of satellite reconnaissance – spies, rumours overheard in harbourside taverns, spottings of masts on the horizon, and his own instincts about what the sneaky Corsican might be plotting. And in August 1798 Nelson struck floating gold. He stumbled across the French fleet riding peacefully at anchor in Aboukir Bay, near Alexandria.

The fleet's Vice-Admiral, François-Paul Brueys d'Aigalliers, was an aristocratic survivor of the Terreur. He had prepared for a potential British attack by chaining his thirteen battleships together in a defensive prow-to-stern line close to the shore, with his main force of guns pointing out to sea. He saw Nelson's fourteen warships approaching at sunset on 1 August, and thought that he had plenty of time to prepare for a fight or escape. Surely no one would attack such an impregnable line of ships in darkness, especially with the risk of running aground?

Grande erreur. The Frenchman didn't know that he was up against a man who was just as daring and unconventional as Napoleon, and he couldn't believe his telescope when the Brits, with the wind behind them, not only sailed straight into attack, but also began sweeping around to the landward, undefended flank.

Nelson's fleet took the French on from both sides, battering away with a double blast of broadsides while the unattacked ships further down the line looked on helpless, chained up and unable to sail into action against the wind. Vice Admiral Brueys's flagship, the *Orient*, caught fire and was destroyed in an immense explosion that so shocked both fleets that they actually stopped fighting to watch the fireworks.

The boy stood on the burning – ouch

It was an explosion that would echo down the years.

Giocante de Casabianca sounds like an Italian wine, but he was a boy sailor aboard the *Orient*, who stayed at his post while the ship blazed and was killed in the subsequent explosion. He was immortalized by the English poet Felicia Hemans in 1826 in her poem 'Casabianca', which opens with the famous line: 'The boy stood on the burning deck'. Hemans tells the tragic story of Giocante's heroism, although she rather spoils the poignancy by saying that he was waiting for an order from his father (an officer on the *Orient*) to abandon ship while other sailors were jumping overboard. Only around 100 of the 1,000-strong crew survived, all of them by swimming for it before the unstoppable fire reached the ship's powder magazine. It is heroic but perhaps a little silly to stand there while your more experienced shipmates tell you to jump for your life. As the comedy writer Spike Milligan once said:

> The boy stood on the burning deck
> Whence all but he had fled –
> The twit!

Nelson meets his Josephine

Nelson was another sailor who very nearly ended his career at Aboukir. He was hit on the forehead by a piece of shrapnel and so badly cut that a flap of flesh was left hanging down over half his face. 'I am killed,' he told his crew, but for once he was wrong. He was stitched up and able to enjoy the sweet taste of victory. Of thirteen enemy ships, only two escaped destruction or capture. The French Mediterranean fleet was non-existent.

As a reward, the victor was ennobled as Baron Nelson of the Nile (a clear message to Napoleon that Egypt didn't belong to him), and became an even bigger hero, attracting the attention of a famous groupie, Lady Hamilton.

She was very much Nelson's Josephine – a woman with a colourful past and a changed name. She was born into poverty in Cheshire as Amy Lyon, and went to London as a teenager to become a maid. After getting the sack for her immoral night-time activities, she became a stripper and prostitute, and finally struck lucky at the age of sixteen – while on long-term hire to a drunken aristocrat, she met a dull-but-nice earl's son called Charles Greville who set her up as his mistress. He renamed her Emma Hart in a vain bid to limit a scandal, but when he decided that the time was right to marry an heiress, he couldn't take any risks, so he sent Emma to stay with his uncle, Sir William Hamilton, the British ambassador to Naples.

Greville fully intended to reclaim his mistress once he'd got his wedding out of the way, and didn't think it necessary to explain his plan to Emma, who believed she was being sent on a long Italian holiday. When she realized what was happening, opportunistic Emma turned on her charms and got gullible old Sir William to marry her, much to Greville's annoyance.

Lady Hamilton was the shining light of Naples society when Nelson first met her in 1793, and on his return trip after the Battle of the Nile, she fainted into his arms at the sight of his wounds and whisked him away to her villa to nurse him back to health.

Their affair became highly public, but old Sir William was just as star-struck as Emma with their famous guest, and didn't seem to mind that his wife was receiving broadsides under his own roof.

Nelson's good luck was all the more galling for poor Napoleon back in Egypt, because his defeat at Aboukir had had a highly embarrassing side effect. The French fleet had been Napoleon's only means of communication with France, and alongside his official despatches he had sent personal letters, including some very private ones to Josephine.

While Napoleon was away, she had been getting friendly with a dashing cavalry officer who, instead of lecturing her on the art of warfare and reading her passages from books on alpine geography, preferred to tell jokes and show off his riding skills, as it were.

Nelson was now able to intercept French communications easily, and one of the treasures he captured in late 1798 was a lovelorn letter from Napoleon about the pain of Josephine's affair (although it no doubt also contained a few lines on the topography of the Nile Delta). Forgetting for once the tradition of honour amongst officers, Nelson sent the letter home to be published in the London newspapers. The story was soon picked up in Paris and Napoleon suddenly found himself living every Frenchman's nightmare – he was the *cocu*, the guy whose wife was getting it elsewhere.

Predictably, Napoleon immediately began riding around Cairo in the company of the pretty blonde wife of one of his infantry officers. He had to show Paris that if his marriage had hit a rocky patch, it wasn't because of his lack of virility.*

The Brits didn't restrict themselves to making fun of Napoleon's love troubles, though, and launched a propaganda offensive about the wimpish campaign that Napoleon was carrying out in Egypt. Instead of surging straight across the desert to overrun the surrounding countries and dig a canal through to the Red Sea (an idea that had been doing the rounds for quite a while), the Frenchman was getting scientists to crawl inside pyramids and dig up old heaps of stone like that ridiculous Sphinx thingy. He even had artists copying out hieroglyphs, as if a few sideways-walking pharaohs and gods with cats' heads might be of any military use. Artyfarty French nonsense, what?

The British government also persuaded Turkey to declare war on France, and suddenly Napoleon had a serious opponent in the desert. His planned stroll across

* There is a remarkable historic parallel with President Sarkozy, who is often compared to Napoleon because of his height and need to be in constant control. When Sarko's second wife, Cécilia, was reported to be having an affair, news was immediately leaked that he was seeing rather a lot of a beautiful French journalist.

the Middle East had turned into a hellish, flies-in-the-wine, sand-in-the-sandwiches slog across the desert, pursued by Turks who combined the fury of the medieval Crusades with the might of modern (British-subsidized) military technology. Eventually giving up, Napoleon sneaked home on a little frigate in August 1799, leaving his army to fend for itself.

Napoleon gets stoned

This ignominious exit must have hurt, but worse was to come.

The Brits realized that Napoleon had really cared about Egypt. He had had windmills built there and founded a large hospital. He had started a programme to combat the bubonic plague, which was still at epidemic levels in the country. And of course he had launched a campaign to record and understand ancient Egyptian culture. One of the key finds his scientists made was the Rosetta Stone. This was a vital lump of (as its name suggests) stone, inscribed in around 200 BC with a text in three scripts: Greek, Demotic (an Arab-like alphabet for writing ancient Egyptian) and hieroglyphs.

The 760-kilo slab of granite-like rock was found by French soldiers while they were building a fort to defend themselves against the British in the Nile Basin. Its importance as a tool for translating hieroglyphs was immediately recognized by Napoleon's scientists, which was why, when the Brits invaded Egypt and kicked out the remaining French troops, they demanded that the stone be sent back to its rightful home, the British Museum (at that time, it never occurred to anyone that the rightful home of an ancient artefact was where it was originally found). The French were so incensed that they threatened to burn all the priceless ancient manuscripts in the Alexandria Library if they weren't allowed to leave with their treasures, casting something of a shadow on their devotion to ancient culture. But according to a British scholar called Edward Clarke, the French were trying to smuggle the stone out of Egypt when he and some colleagues caught up with them in a Cairo back street* and appropriated it. The huge trophy was escorted back to London, where someone at the museum duly defaced it by painting on two inscriptions – 'Captured in Egypt by the British Army in 1801' and 'Presented by King George III'. Now no one could doubt its Britishness.

A foggy day in Paris town

Napoleon's excursion to Egypt may have ended in failure, but back in Paris things were looking promising. In his absence, France had gone down the *toilette*, and it was now at war not only with Britain and Turkey but also with Russia, Austria and Nelson's friend the King of Naples. France had lost all the territory Napoleon had gained in Italy, as well as its possessions in Holland and Switzerland. And the Royalists were feeling cocky enough to announce the imminent arrival in Paris of London's most prominent French exile, King Louis XVIII.

The returning General Bonaparte saw only one solution to the nation's troubles: himself. Along with two political nobodies called Emmanuel-Joseph Sieyès and Pierre-Roger Ducros, whom he quickly discarded afterwards, Napoleon organized a coup, the so-called Coup d'état du 18 brumaire, this being the Revolutionary Calendar date for 9 November 1799. It was an apt name – *brumaire* comes from the French word for mist,

* Though you should never believe what someone called Clarke tells you about what he's been up to in a back street.

brume, and that Saturday was apparently very foggy.

First, Napoleon went to the Orangerie of the Château de Saint-Cloud to try and persuade Parliament into accepting him as their leader (or First Consul), but the statesmen howled the uncouth young soldier down. He was, after all, still a fresh-faced thirty-year-old. So, no doubt recalling his more modest campaign to become head of the Corsican branch of the Garde nationale, he pulled out his trump card – a troop of soldiers with fixed bayonets – and was delighted to see the politicians jump out of the windows of the Orangerie and flee through the Château gardens. He had effectively taken power.

Napoleon promptly designed himself a new uniform (a long red velvet jacket with gold buttons and braid, over very fetching tight white trousers with swirling gold embroidery down the thighs) and an outfit for his servants (pale blue with silver lace) and on 17 February 1800 he moved into Louis XVI's old apartments in the Tuileries Palace.

One of his first acts was to erect a gallery of sculptures which included Alexander the Great, Caesar, Hannibal, George Washington and – ominously, perhaps – Britain's great general, the Duke of Marlborough.

Like all efficient military dictators, Napoleon then got himself voted leader for life and began to complain about his wife's reputation for extravagance. Josephine, who had dumped the cavalry officer in the light of her husband's increased social status, was a real fashion victim and soon became notorious for her dressmakers' bills. She did, however, make a concession. Given that hubby was now in public office, she gave up wearing the low-cut, almost transparent, dresses that she and her circle had been fond of wearing, in favour of more prim, opaque styles. She also exchanged partying for gardening, and it is a little-known fact that she is responsible for a revolution of her own, in horticulture. At the time, the rose (Josephine's real name, of course) was a small, short-lived and unfashionable bloom. Wanting to improve its image, she began to create hybrid varieties, and eventually crossed the Provence and China roses to produce the Tea rose, a repeat-flowering variety. This was developed further by the Victorians to produce the Hybrid Perpetual, the basis for most garden roses today. In short, the much-maligned Josephine's work in the garden was to prove just as long-lasting as her husband's future achievements with law books.

Napoleon got busy reforming his new country. He was a total control freak, and would spend his days (when he was not off battling the Austrians, Italians, Dutch, Poles, Brits, Germans and Russians) making laws on every aspect of French life. Between 1800 and 1810, he oversaw the drafting and implementation of, amongst others, his *code civil*, *code pénal* and *code du commerce*, many elements of which are still applied in modern French courtrooms. He set up a state education system, including a university, law schools and the École normale supérieure, the teacher-training college that produces France's most elitist academics today. And he introduced an efficient, and fair, system of taxation that soon balanced the country's accounts. In this he was helped by the cash he got from selling off what he considered the least important item in his real-estate portfolio, Louisiana.*

Napoleon's sense of democracy was a product of the Revolution, but he also helped the upper classes to prosper, allowing the bourgeoisie to get rich by buying up land and pretending to be *aristos*. He actually created a new aristocracy of 1,000 barons, 400 counts, 32 dukes

---

* Though to see how big a mistake that was in the long run, see Chapter 13.

and 3 princes, and even granted the émigrés an amnesty, permitting them to return to Paris society after their hard years of exile in England and elsewhere as dancing teachers, gigolos and eaters of horses' willies. Some 40,000 families returned.

All of which was a prelude to the obvious next step – if the country was now overflowing with new and old aristocracy, and Napoleon was its leader for life, shouldn't he have the poshest title of all? Which was why in 1804, at the ripe old age of thirty-five, he appointed himself Emperor of France. The new uniform? White silk with a short purple cape embroidered with the emblem he chose for himself – the bee, a motif dating back to the Franks, a royal dynasty before Louis XVI's family, the Capets, had taken power.

No one except the snootiest returned *aristos* seemed to mind this self-elevation. By now, everybody in France loved Napoleon, especially the men, the biggest beneficiaries of his *code civil*, which was more egalitarian than the old regime's laws, but a disaster for women. They couldn't sign contracts or vote, and all education beyond primary school was for boys only – Napoleon thought that 'young women are best educated by their mothers.' The *code civil* also decreed that a wife couldn't work without her husband's permission, and even then he would receive her salary. As another of Napoleon's sexist maxims expressed it: 'If there is one thing that isn't French, it's that a woman should be able to do as she pleases.'

Men, on the other hand, needed to be free, which was why the Emperor cooked up some highly unfair laws on adultery. He decreed that a wife could only sue for divorce if her husband kept a mistress in an apartment that he rented for her – just having sex with another woman was fine. The wife, of course, had to reserve her favours for hubby, or risk being thrown out of the house (even if it was hers when they got married). And if a man had sex with a prostitute, that wasn't adultery at all – it was human nature. Napoleon thought that 'prostitutes are a necessity. Without them, men would attack respectable women in the street,' which was why he legalized prostitution. Prostitutes had to be registered and undergo regular health inspections, and if they obeyed these rules they could work legally in a quaint-sounding *maison de tolérance* or brothel. These institutions could be set up in any town or city, their only concession to public modesty being that the windows should be shuttered so that passers-by and neighbours wouldn't be shocked by what went on inside – hence the brothel's other name, *maison close*.

Napoleon's ambition was to have them installed all over his empire, which, he hoped, would soon include Britain. Not that he was a regular client of prostitutes, though he had lost his virginity to one, whom he 'got talking to while out walking one evening'. No, his reasoning was that venereal disease was a real headache (if that's not a mixed metaphor) for his generals – syphilis and other STDs could ravage a campaigning army, especially if, like Napoleon's, it was usually trailed by a horde of female 'camp followers' providing services for any soldier who had money, loot or a bed for the night. Getting prostitutes registered and health-checked was therefore part of Napoleon's military strategy. Marching wasn't the only thing an army did on its stomach.

Angleterre, here I come

It was of course the Brits who would put an end to Napoleon's imperial idyll of law-making and institutionalized sexism, but like so much in French history, the debacle to come was all France's own fault.

In 1802, Napoleon had persuaded the British that he sincerely wanted peace. He wrote a personal letter to King George III saying so. Far from believing that it had been written by a tree, the temporarily sane King called the Empereur a Corsican tyrant and refused to reply. But after the Prime Minister, William Pitt, resigned from office, Britain's anti-war campaigners got the upper hand, and in the same year France and Britain signed a treaty, the Peace of Amiens, which included an exchange of captured territories and even – a huge political concession – an agreement whereby George III crossed 'King of France' off the long list of the British monarch's historic titles. Napoleon was so pleased that he put a bust of his old English tormentor Nelson on his dressing table.

Opinions differ as to whether Napoleon was sincere about peace or, like Hitler in 1938, just wanted a breathing space to get himself ready for war. In fact, it seems that neither side was playing things entirely straight. The Brits failed to honour parts of the peace treaty, including the promised evacuation of Alexandria, and the British press waged a campaign of vicious anti-Napoleon propaganda. Cartoons appeared showing him as a rotund dwarf; racist allegations were made about the dark hue of his skin; and French-language émigré newspapers in London regaled their readers with rumours about Napoleon's impotency and, illogically, his habit of sleeping with Josephine's daughter from her first marriage.

It was now that Napoleon became completely obsessed with crushing Britain, and conceived an ambitious two-pronged campaign – both parts of which were to fail spectacularly.

Prong one: he would mount a serious invasion attempt, and predicted that he would be received like a new William of Orange – perhaps forgetting that William had invaded England to do away with a pro-French King, James II.

He also boasted that England would become just another French island like Corsica or Oléron. For those who don't know it, Oléron is a 25-kilometre-long sand-bank off the west coast of France, and never possessed a fleet of several hundred warships crewed by rabidly anti-French sailors like Admiral Nelson.

The Empereur's blood was up, and his first concrete move was to establish an immense base for his invasion force in Boulogne, just opposite the White Cliffs of Dover. Here, in full view of the English (on a sunny day, of course) he began to amass troops, and eventually had 200,000 men languishing by the seaside, mugging up on English irregular verbs and demanding to know when they were going to be let loose in the pubs just a few kilometres north. To placate them, Napoleon made frequent morale-boosting visits to the camp, handing out campaign medals before any actual campaigning had been done, and even getting the men to erect a rather presumptuous triumphal column.

Meanwhile, Napoleon was making the plans that inspired the cartoon included at the beginning of this chapter. An engineer called Albert Mathieu really did suggest a secret road tunnel running under the Channel, and a contemporary drawing shows horse carriages travelling through it, breathing air supplied by chimneys sticking up out of the water – which would have been a bit of a giveaway, and might have attracted the un-welcome attention of British warships. One bomb down the chimney and Napoleon's carriage would have got rather wet, which was probably why he rejected

Mathieu's project as unrealistic. Apart from anything else, in the drawing the sea looks about 4 metres deep, and Napoleon knew they would have to dig a bit deeper than that.

He wasn't against new methods of warfare, though, and appointed a woman called Sophie Blanchard his Chief Air Minister of Ballooning. She was the wife of the man whose balloon Napoleon had cut adrift in his École militaire days, and had since made a name for herself as a kind of artiste of the sky, putting on shows that included dropping fireworks from the air and throwing dogs out of her balloon (equipped with parachutes, of course). Napoleon consulted Madame Blanchard on the feasibility of sending troops across the Channel in balloons, but she told him that the winds would be too unreliable to take them across. She knew all about the dangers of primitive air travel, and, like her husband, was to die in a flying accident, after fireworks set light to her balloon.

A piece of new technology that Napoleon was probably also wise to turn down was the submarine. An American called Robert Fulton, who was living in Paris, had offered to build the French a submarine for use against the all-powerful British fleet, 'a machine which flatters me with much hope of being able to annihilate their navy', Fulton said. There was a precedent for such an attack. In 1776, an American pedal-powered sumarine called the *Turtle* had attempted to drill a hole in a British warship in New York harbour, and had come close to succeeding. Fulton carried out tests with his own prototype, which was capable of reaching depths of 7 metres and an underwater speed of 4 knots, but every time he went near a British ship, it saw him and sailed away. The French naval minister is reported to have told Fulton, 'Go away, monsieur. Your invention is perfect for the Algerians or pirates, but we have not yet abandoned the sea.'

Instead, Napoleon decided to develop his own war machines, and asked for public sponsorship to help him build a fleet of invasion barges capable of carrying 110 men each, precursors to the ones that would cross the Channel in the other direction in 1944. And the 'your name here for only 20,000 francs' campaign was very effective, unlike the barges themselves. When, against the advice of his navy, Napoleon ordered a test run in choppy seas, several of the vessels sank, causing many deaths and denting morale so much that the story had to be hushed up.

On the other side of the Channel, the Brits were taking the threat of an invasion very seriously. Fortifications were built and public panic was taking hold. One English drawing of the time depicts a totally unrealistic French floating castle, supposedly able to carry 60,000 men and 600 cannons. Even the poet Wordsworth, who initially supported the Revolution, now turned against France, writing in his *Prelude*:

> Frenchmen had changed a war of self-defence
> For one of conquest, losing sight of all
> Which they had struggled for . . .

Harsh and realistic words from a Romantic poet better known for his poems about clouds and daffodils.

Everyone knew, though, that no floating castles or invasion barges were coming anywhere near Dover as long as the British fleet reigned supreme on the seas – which was where Napoleon needed one of his cunning tactical schemes. So he decided to send his two fleets, based in Brest and Toulon (the latter being bolstered by Spanish ships), across the Atlantic to make the Brits think he was planning something in the West Indies – a massive rum festival, perhaps. Then, as soon as all his ships had met up, they would speed back to Europe to support the Channel invasion force and destroy any British ships that hadn't been lured away on the wild-goose chase to the Caribbean.

It couldn't fail, *n'est-ce pas*?

Meet you in Trafalgar

In January 1805, the scheme was set in motion, and the southern French fleet slipped out to sea from Toulon. It was commanded by one Admiral Pierre-Charles-Silvestre de Villeneuve, an aristocrat turned pro-revolutionary with a decidedly un-Napoleonic trait – caution.

Nelson, who had been ordered to keep a watch on Villeneuve, set off in pursuit but then, in an error of judgement that would haunt him for the ten remaining months of his life, lost the French fleet entirely. He hunted Villeneuve from Sardinia to Egypt, from Naples to Cadiz, going mad with frustration that his instincts had failed him and that no one had seen any sign of a French sail.

The letters and despatches he wrote during the chase paint a vivid picture of the national hero floundering across the globe, unable to find anyone to fight. 'I am very, very miserable,' he wrote, and: 'O French fleet, if I can but once get up with you, I'll make you pay dearly for all that you have made me suffer.' He didn't even take time to stock up with fresh supplies: 'Salt beef and the French fleet is far preferable to roast beef and Champagne without them.' He finally returned to Portsmouth in defeat, furious that his cannons had remained unfired.

In fact, though, he had nearly caught up with

Villeneuve. As well as scouring practically the whole Med, Nelson had also made a search of the Caribbean, and spooked the over-cautious French admiral into returning to Cadiz instead of making for the Channel as Napoleon had ordered him to do.

In September, Nelson heard the news that the Franco-Spanish fleet was back in Cadiz, and sailed off at once in the optimistically named *Victory*. He was a veritable torpedo launched at Napoleon's navy.

With a massive, all-important battle at last a certainty, Nelson seems to have attained a fatalistic serenity. On hearing that Villeneuve had finally left Cadiz to head for the Channel and was now vulnerable to attack, the Admiral made preparations for the heroic death of every-one in his fleet, encouraging his men to write last letters home, and doing the same himself. 'My mind is calm,' Nelson wrote, 'and I have only to think of destroying our inveterate foe.' As the communications ship was sailing away from *Victory* carrying the letters, a coxswain appeared on deck looking agitated. Nelson asked why. When he was told that the man had not got his letter into the mail sack on time, the Admiral gave the order to recall the ship: 'Who knows that he may not fall in action tomorrow. His letter shall go with the rest.' Like Napoleon, he was a leader who understood that men fight better if they know they are respected.

Nelson formulated his battle plan: he would sail at the Franco-Spanish fleet at right angles and smash its line in two, from the centre. It was as unconventional as his tactics at the Nile, and involved considerable personal risk to Nelson himself – his would be one of the first ships into action, and would come into French cannon range long before the *Victory* could bring its guns to bear.

But as he sailed into battle on 21 October 1805 just off the Cape of Trafalgar, about 40 kilometres along the coast from Cadiz, he retained his deadly cool.

'I will now amuse the fleet with a signal,' he announced, and dictated: 'Nelson confides that every man will do his duty' – 'confides' here meaning 'is confident that' – a message of trust from the Admiral to his men.

When an officer suggested making it more official-sounding by putting 'England', Nelson accepted, but then got a little irritated when the signaller asked whether he could send 'expects', because 'confides' would have to be spelt out, whereas there was a single flag for 'expects'. Nelson told him to get on with it, because he had other signals to send before the cannonballs started flying, and his famous message was quickly broadcast to the fleet in its edited version.

Things now got very sticky for *Victory*. It was the fastest ship in the fleet and sailed in first, taking a full forty minutes of punishment from the French flagship, the *Bucentaure*, without replying. As was the custom, Nelson and his officers simply stood on deck watching the cannons puff and the lumps of hot metal fly towards them. It would have been dishonourable to do anything else. The Admiral's secretary was killed, as was his replacement, but the ship held its course despite ripped sails, shattered woodwork and tumbling sailors.

Soon, though, it was the crew of *Bucentaure* that was panicking, as *Victory* headed steadfastly for its stern. The French knew that unlike their ships, which had most of their guns aiming high to topple masts and disable an enemy at a distance, Nelson liked to set his cannons low, to get up close and fire short-range broadsides right into the body of ship.

Sure enough, as *Victory* swung astern of the *Bucentaure* – so near that its yardarms grazed the French ship – Nelson gave the order to light the fuses. At last, *Victory* unleashed its firepower. The cannons had been loaded with regular cannonballs as well as chainshot – two or more balls linked by chains – and musket rounds. From a range of just a few metres, this varied collection of British projectiles smashed through the length of the *Bucentaure*'s gun deck, doing horrific damage. Each chainshot decapitated dozens of French gunners as it flew by, and many others were killed just by the shock-wave of passing cannonballs. It is estimated that some 400 men were killed in that first salvo, almost a quarter of all Franco-Spanish deaths in the battle. Villeneuve could be in no doubt about what his fleet was in for.

Nelson didn't stop there. Pulling alongside a second French ship, the *Redoutable*, he fired point-blank into that one, too. A hellish close-range battle between the two interlocked ships began, as they exchanged cannon fire into each other's hulls and masts, while Nelson and his right-hand man, Captain Sir Thomas Hardy, stayed on deck discussing strategy, despite the fact that French musketeers were posted in the rigging almost directly above them. Their one concession to the need for self-defence was to walk back and forth on the far side of the ship, even though this took them only fifteen or twenty metres from the *Redoutable*'s side.

Sure enough, a musket shot from above hit Nelson in the shoulder. Captain Hardy noticed that he was talking to himself, and turned back to see Nelson fall to his knees, then collapse flat out.

'Doctor, I am gone,' the Admiral told the surgeon, and this time he was right. The bullet had passed through his lung and smashed his spine.

Above decks, the battle raged on for four hours, with all the British ships adopting similarly destructive tactics, and Nelson died just before the Franco-Spanish fleet surrendered. As everyone knows, shortly before expiring, he asked the bald, portly Sir Thomas to kiss him – which he did, on Nelson's battle-scarred forehead. The Admiral's very last words were not 'kiss me, Hardy' though. They were probably 'drink drink, fan fan, rub rub' – gasped requests for water, more air, and for the doctor to massage his chest to relieve the pain. But for obvious historical reasons, what sound like a pop star's demands for a groupie to do obscene things to him have been replaced by the phrase Nelson kept repeating on that surgeon's table, 'Thank God I have done my duty.'

That he certainly had. Eighteen French and Spanish ships had been captured and one destroyed, and yet again Napoleon's great invasion plans had been sunk. There was no way those French barges were going to risk setting out across the Channel now.

Buy French? *Non merci!*

The second prong of Napoleon's anti-British toasting fork was a trade embargo that he called his *Blocus continental*. After the failure of his invasion, as of 1806, he set about trying to force all the countries where he had troops or influence to stop doing business with the Brits. In this he would be helped by his brothers – Louis, whom he had made King of Holland, Joseph, King of Spain, and Jérôme of Westphalia – as well as allies or occupying armies in Russia, Poland, Italy and Denmark.

Forbidding all British imports, and even confiscating any ship that had docked in Britain before arriving in the French Empire, Napoleon wanted to put a clamp on the artery of Britain's wealth – foreign trade – and bankrupt his enemy into submission.

It was a bold plan, and quickly started to have an effect. Between 1806 and 1808, Britain's exports dropped by 12 per cent, and imports of raw cotton, vital for the new mills clattering away in the North of England, fell by a terrifying 80 per cent, causing widespread unemployment. But there was a fatal flaw in Napoleon's scheme. The Bostonians might have started a revolution because of high-priced English tea, but most people actually wanted to do business with the Brits. Their cotton and steel were amongst the best and cheapest in the world. Their scissors and razors were highly sought after – Napoleon himself shaved with a British blade. Chocolate, spices, sugar, rum and tobacco all had their European addicts, and Britain was their dealer of choice.

The result was that soon everyone was ignoring Napoleon's orders. Smugglers set up huge warehouses in Gibraltar, Malta, Sicily, Greece and Heligoland (a group of islands just off the northwest coast of Germany), and with the British fleet usually willing to lend a hand as bodyguards, the traffickers were able to open up supply lines as regular and reliable as before the blockade, even into France itself, where soldiers often took bribes to escort smuggled goods past the customs men. The racket was so organized that a German company even started selling the bigger smugglers insurance against loss of their cargoes.

As the Anglo-Saxons say, the customer is always right, and even Napoleon had to admit defeat in the face of overwhelming market forces.

But he seems to have given a French shrug of the shoulders at this setback, because he began to plan another scheme to beat the treacherous *Anglais*.

And this one was *sure* to work . . .

19

Wellington Puts the Boot in on Boney

As Londoners and Parisians know, Anglo-French history is all about railway stations. In 1805, rail passenger travel was still a couple of decades away, but the score for future station names was 1–0 to France. The French already had Austerlitz (Paris's only mainline station named after a battle), a victory won by Napoleon six weeks after the defeat of the French fleet at Trafalgar, whereas the Brits were a long way from Waterloo.

Napoleon was feeling fairly confident. Nelson might have destroyed or stolen most of his ships, but his armies ruled dry land. And Britain didn't have a land-based Nelson, did it?

No, but (unfortunately for Napoleon) it soon would have – a certain Arthur Wellesley, former Irish MP and ex-Governor of Mysore in India. Wellesley was, of course, the future Duke of Wellington. He had returned home to England in 1805, coincidentally stopping off at the rocky island of St Helena and staying in a house that would soon have a very famous French guest, and had taken part in the Anglo-Austro-Russian campaign that foundered at Austerlitz.

At the end of 1805, Wellesley's career was at a low, but he was about to pick himself up and give London the railway station name that the French would never forget.

From Russia without love

It wasn't until 1808 that Wellesley started to give Napoleon headaches.

The Empereur had recently installed his elder brother Joseph as King of Spain, and Wellesley was sent there to stir up revolt. Napoleon was busy occupying Berlin and Warsaw, but was obliged to come all the way down to Spain to chase the irksome Brits out of his brother's kingdom. The French army forced the invaders to re-embark for the UK, but the troublemaker Wellesley would soon be back.

Meanwhile, Napoleon gave in to two distractions from his ultimate aim of ending British interference in his affairs. First, he decided that, as an emperor, he needed a royal wife. He therefore walled up the doorway connecting his room to Josephine's and, as if this wasn't enough of a hint, explained to her that he was granting himself a divorce on the grounds of irreconcilable differences in social status. There was nothing poor Josephine could do except go out to her country house (which she got in the divorce settlement) and prune her roses.

In a beautiful piece of historical irony, Napoleon set his sights on Marie-Louise, daughter of the Austrian Emperor Franz II and a grandniece of Marie-Antoinette. Yes, just fifteen years after France had guillotined its Austrian queen, it was getting a new one. Napoleon was in such a hurry to marry Marie-Louise that he had the ceremony performed by proxy and then, when she arrived in France by carriage, rode out to meet her and insisted on having sex immediately. The eighteen-year-old apparently liked the rough touch, because afterwards she told him, 'You can do it again if you want.' Although a cynic might say that this was Napoleon's version of events, and how do we know she didn't say, 'Is that it, then?' And an even crueller cynic might go further and say that even if she did say, 'You can do it again if you want', it would imply that the first time was rather brief. But those are just typical Anglo remarks, and perhaps it is kinder to conclude that the new Empress of France was not unhappy to be married to the dashing forty-year-old general. After all, she could have ended up with an ancient madman like George III. And just a year later, she gave birth to a son, whom Napoleon named Napoleon (of course – hadn't France just had a series of Louis?). As a christening present the baby was given Rome. Not a model or a picture, but the city itself, of which Napoleon Junior was immediately crowned king.

Napoleon's other, and far more destructive, distraction was Russia. As we now know, this was a big mistake, but at the time it seemed like a very good idea indeed. Russia was, after all, a vast empire in itself, and ruled by a tsar who had an army about the same size as Napoleon's – great odds to a gambler like the Empereur. And the French didn't go in alone – all told, the invading army consisted of over half a million soldiers from all the countries of Napoleon's empire, supported by a 10-kilometre-long wagon train of supplies that included 28 million bottles of wine and 2 million bottles of brandy. It was going to be the biggest party ever.

In the event, of course, the party was well and truly pooped. Everywhere Napoleon went, the Russians left a trail of destruction, and there's just no fun in conquering a wasteland – no vodka for the troops to steal, no icons to send back to the Louvre. And when he occupied Moscow, the Russians simply set fire to it. Napoleon then made the tactical error of trying to dash back to France ahead of the winter, and his Grande Armée was soon transformed into a shivering mass of frostbitten extremities, its once glorious soldiers reduced to dis-embowelling horses so that they could curl up inside the rib cage and keep warm. Of his half a million men, only about 25,000 made it back to France. Not all the others were dead – some 100,000 had been taken prisoner, and German and Austrian troops simply stopped off on the way back west. But it was a catastrophic defeat.

Strangely, Napoleon blamed it on England. 'If the *Anglais* had left me alone,' he said as he rode in a sleigh towards Warsaw, 'I would have lived in peace.' Whether this was true or not, peace was something he would rarely enjoy again. Well, not in France, anyway. The Brits were planning to give him lots of peace elsewhere.

Wellington hits the jackpot

While things were going so horrifically for Napoleon in the east, Britain had never let up on his western weak point. By 1813 Spain and Portugal were as full of pasty-faced men as they would ever be in the tourist boom 150 years later. At their head, instead of a travel rep, was the Marquess of Wellington, who had been ennobled for winning a battle near Madrid.

He was now back in Spain and, like Nelson, fired up for vengeance on the French. Even more fiery were the Spanish guerrillas, who had had enough of their French King Joseph and were doing all kinds of unpleasant things to any French soldiers and officials they could lay their hands on.

Together, the Anglo-Spanish forces were driving Joseph's army steadily back towards France, and on 21 June 1813 Wellington forced a showdown in the Basque country on the north coast of Spain, at a place called Vitoria.

While Joseph was otherwise engaged with a mistress, Wellington's men pounced on the unprepared French troops, who simply turned tail and ran. Joseph himself only just escaped – a British cavalryman fired a shot into his carriage but was then distracted by the vast amounts of booty to be had. While a few focused soldiers made sure that the French kept running, the rest fell upon Joseph's supply train, snatching all his artillery (151 cannons) and millions of bullets, as well as more glittering prizes – the whole royal bankroll, all of Joseph's jewellery and hundreds of women, the French officers' 'travelling companions'.

The greatest find of all, though, was a chamber pot. This had nothing to do with a lack of British toilet facilities. There were plenty of Spanish trees to pee against, and the more refined members of Wellington's army had no doubt packed their trunks with all the necessities for a long stay abroad. No, this was a very special chamber pot, a gleaming silver receptacle belonging to King Joseph himself, and when the 14th Light Dragoons found it, they instantly adopted it as their regimental mascot. They christened it 'The Emperor', and no doubt had a soldierly laugh performing symbolic acts in it and imagining that they were doing those things to Napoleon himself. This chamber pot is still used to drink Champagne in the regiment's mess today, and is placed on the drinker's head after each toast. Like the Marlborough family's banner (see Chapter 10 on Louis XIV), it's an anti-French joke that has remained alive across the generations.

Wellington was less pleased with the trophy, however, and was furious with his men for not finishing off the French while they were down. He even wrote a letter to

England complaining that 'we have the scum of the Earth as common soldiers.' But he got a consolation prize – promotion to Field Marshal – and he needn't have worried because, despite being loaded down with booty, his men kept pressing forward and swept Napoleon's army right back across the border. They didn't stop there, either, capturing Toulouse and Bordeaux, where Wellington was hailed as a liberator. It was like the days of Eleanor of Aquitaine and Henry II all over again. Southwest France was in British hands, and Napoleon, the keen historian, must have been heartbroken.

Camping it up on the Champs-Élysées

Meanwhile, further north, things weren't going any better for the Emperor – Napoleon, that is, not the chamber pot. The Prussians were marching into France, led by the wonderfully named Gebhard Leberecht von Blücher. This was doubly hurtful for Napoleon. Apart from the basic fact that a vast army was coming to attack him, half the troops belonged to his father-in-law, Franz II of Austria. People tell mother-in-law jokes, but the male version can be a lot less funny.

To make matters worse for Napoleon, one of his old sidekicks, Talleyrand, the French diplomat who negoti-ated the sale of Louisiana, had turned traitor and was going around Paris telling everyone that the so-called Emperor would 'crawl under his bed and hide'.

But Napoleon wasn't that kind of man. He took an army out to meet Blücher and, in yet another historical coincidence, fought him at Brienne, where he had been to school. Inspired perhaps by the symbolism of it, the French troops forced the Austro-Prussians to retreat, and, despite incurring heavy losses that they couldn't afford, kept up the fight for a full month, with Napoleon always in the thick of things, exposing himself to death as if he preferred to go out in a blaze of glory rather than ending it all with a meek surrender. At a place called Arcis-sur-Aube in the Champagne district (the birthplace of the Revolutionary leader Georges Danton), Napoleon was particularly suicidal. He galloped his horse past a time-delay shell, killing the poor animal and sending himself, singed and bruised, crashing to the ground. But he took another horse and continued his charge, as musket and cannon fire whistled around him and slashed holes in his uniform (a plain grey overcoat – the time for gold braid was past).

Determination and suicidal bravery weren't enough, though, because Napoleon simply didn't have enough troops to keep up his resistance, and soon Paris was under attack from Prussians, Austrians and Russians, all of whom were in the mood for a bit of payback for all the damage that the French had done while marching through their own countries. It is something that the Parisians forget, but in March 1814 there were Cossacks camping on the Champs-Élysées, near the building site where Napoleon's Arc de Triomphe was slowly, and not very surely, being erected.

To his credit, Napoleon did not flee into exile. Instead, he tried to talk his way out of trouble. He even attempted to soften his father-in-law's hard imperial heart by sending him an engraving of his grandson, Napoleon Junior.

His Eastern European enemies weren't all set on deposing him, either. When Tsar Alexander of Russia, King Friedrich Wilhelm of Prussia and the Austrian Emperor's representative Prince Schwarzenberg arrived in Paris at the end of March 1814 (the Brits were still in the southwest of France), they were open to suggestions. All they really wanted was a guarantee that Napoleon would never come back to visit them with his Grande Armée.

The worm in France's apple, though, was – as so often – a Frenchman. Talleyrand was acting as the nation's self-appointed negotiator and kept the anti-Napoleon poison flowing. He was already in the pay of the Prussians, and now he sucked up to the Tsar, telling him that lasting peace would only be assured if Napoleon abdicated and the royal family returned. The Tsar wasn't at all convinced – crossing France, he had never heard anyone say a good word for the old royal regime, and he had seen French soldiers shouting 'Vive l'Empereur!' with their dying breath. But Talleyrand was an experienced and unprincipled smooth talker (hence Napoleon's quip that he was 'a shit in silk stockings'), and had the clincher in his pocket – a document demanding that Bonaparte abdicate in favour of Louis XVIII. All the Tsar had to do was sign, and peace would come. The Russian was an affable, easy-going man, and in the end he took the proffered pen. Napoleon's fate was sealed.

Unless, of course, he refused to go. He still had 60,000 loyal men at his disposal, all of them more than willing to bayonet Boches and Russkies. But the one moderating influence on Napoleon's megalomania had always been the voice of his generals, and now his closest and oldest associates argued that it was a lost cause. They had seen what had happened to occupied Moscow, and didn't want the same thing to happen to their own favourite city. It was one thing to see a few Russian Orthodox churches go up in flames, but Notre-Dame? The Louvre? The *maisons de tolérance*?

Finally, after one of his marshals went even further and defected to the Austrians with 16,000 soldiers, Napoleon agreed. And to be fair, more than losing his throne and his set of uniforms, what seems to have pained him most of all was that the royals might undo his reforms. He dearly hoped that they would do nothing more than 'change the sheets on my bed'. (In fact, he wasn't far off the truth – one of the first changes the returning King made was to have fleurs-de-lis sewn over the bees on the Tuileries' carpets.)

On 6 April 1814, Napoleon abdicated. It was his all-time low – worse than his arrest as a traitor in Nice, worse than Moscow, worse even than when the British newspapers published the stories about Josephine having it off with a hussar. It was that moment in a Hollywood film when the hero wanders off alone and gets mugged after selling his last possession, the gold watch he bought himself when he made his first million.

In Hollywood, of course, things turn around, and twenty minutes later he is taking off an even bigger watch before getting into bed with the female lead, but Napoleon's low point was to last much longer. He rather unrealistically asked to be sent with his family into exile in England, where he saw himself retiring as a country gentleman (plenty of scope for tweed uniforms). But he obviously hadn't seen all the propaganda directed against him. His request was refused, and Marie-Louise and Napoleon Junior were spirited away to rejoin *Vater*-in-law. Napoleon was never to see them again.

He tried to commit suicide, but took poison that was past its sell-by date and vomited it up. In the end, he accepted a lesser fate – exile to the Italian island of Elba, just east of Corsica. It wasn't going to be that unpleasant. He was to be made king of the island (this might have been a British joke, but he took it very seriously), granted a very generous French pension and escorted into exile by 600 of his most loyal soldiers. This last condition would later seem, in retrospect, a little unwise.

After a heartfelt speech to the troops he was to leave behind, which had everyone in tears, including the Prussians, Austrians and Brits overseeing his departure,

Napoleon grabbed hold of the Old Guard's standard, inscribed with the long list of its victories, and told his men, 'Adieu, and don't forget me.' It was a great 'hasta la vista' moment, and his troops would have less than a year to wait before the Napoleonator made his triumphant comeback.

Napoleon gets the Elba

In May 1814, the blobbish Louis XVIII, trussed up in a British naval coat and ridden with gout, flopped on to the throne vacated by his brother Louis XVI, and set about making his family unpopular in France all over again. He had Napoleon's Constitution ceremonially burnt (in the Royalist town of Bordeaux, just to be safe), ignored the Senate's demands for him to adopt the post-revolutionary tricolour flag, gave confiscated properties back to returning *aristos*, and quickly reneged on his promises to cut taxes on the people's pleasures (cigarettes and alcohol).

There were celebratory parties, of course, but relations with the King's benefactors were strained. Wellington was appointed British ambassador to France – a provocative choice. At one dinner, when he was given the cold shoulder by French courtiers, the Field Marshal retorted, 'Tis of no matter, I have seen their backs before.' *Touché*.

Napoleon, meanwhile, was enjoying himself in his new kingdom. Just like France in 1800, there was plenty of room for improvement in Elba. It didn't have a flag, for one thing, so he designed a new one, adding three gold bees to the old Medici family standard, a red diagonal stripe on a silver background. The island had virtually no agriculture and depended on imports (a concept Napoleon hated because of Britain's strangle-hold on the seas), so he had vegetables, olive trees and chestnut trees (Corsica's favourite) planted. He found a spring that produced sparkling water and got the islanders to market it. He learned to plough with oxen and to spear tuna, and even invaded the nearby islet of Pianosa and claimed sovereignty over it. He slept on his old camp bed in a town house, and seemed to see the whole exercise as yet another foreign campaign.

Clouds did pass over his island idyll, however. In May, Josephine died of pneumonia and what one French historian described as a 'gangrenous throat infection',* and although Napoleon hadn't exactly treated her gently during their divorce, he was so devastated by the news that he mourned in isolation for two solid days.

The more permanent annoyance was an Englishman by the name of Sir Neil Campbell, the British Commissioner to Elba – in other words, Napoleon's jailer. He observed and reported the ex-Emperor's every move, and Napoleon knew that he had to be careful because Talleyrand was still out there lobbying European leaders to have him moved even further away, to the Azores.

Talleyrand was nervous because there was an underground campaign to bring Napoleon back to France, where it was clear to all but the most privileged *aristos* that the restoration had been a huge, foreign-influenced mistake. Paris had been given back to the powdered fops, the most powdered and foppish of the lot being the King. A popular song mocking Louis XVIII blamed it all on the Brits, ending with the line 'I owe my crown to the English'.

But if Louis and co. hoped to keep Napoleon on his island, they shouldn't have made a fatal error. They

* Josephine's illness was the result of a chill caught while giving Tsar Alexander (one of Napoleon's enemies) a tour of her rose garden at Malmaison. This was probably not a euphemism, but does suggest that she was underdressed for the occasion.

neglected to pay the pension he had been promised, and few things annoy a Frenchman more than someone meddling with his pension rights. Napoleon duly started to plot his escape.

In February 1815, he got his chance. Sir Neil Campbell announced that he had to go to Florence to see a doctor about his hearing problems (unofficially, it is said that he wanted to spend some time with his mistress) and would be away for ten days.

No sooner had the Englishman left the harbour than Napoleon sprang into action. He had a ship painted in British colours, fitted out with cannons and loaded up with all his gold. Knowing that the island was crawling with Talleyrand's spies, he sent his silverware and carriages to Naples and, to create a semblance of normal continuity, had his soldiers start to dig flowerbeds.

His plan was almost revealed when a spy learned that he was really intending to sail to France, but the only way of getting a message out would have been to pass it on to a British ship that came to see how things were going in Campbell's absence, and the French spy didn't want to share information with the *ennemi*.

Napoleon's secret was safe, and on 26 February he set sail for France with 600 members of his Old Guard, 300 Elban and Corsican volunteers and 108 cavalrymen who had saddles but no horses. And on the afternoon of 1 March, this determined but undersized army of liberation landed on the French mainland near the town of Antibes.

The Emperor was back.

The Emperor's old clothes

For once, Napoleon didn't design a new uniform, choosing to play the nostalgia card and stick to his old grey coat, white waistcoat and black hat. He did need a new battle standard, though, and got his men to make a wooden eagle out of some pieces of a bed. He then set off for Paris, minus twenty-five of his soldiers who had gone to liberate Antibes and got locked inside the town walls.

News of the Emperor's return spread quickly, and he was well received, with some of his old subjects giving him bunches of violets (his signature flower because it was imperial purple), and others contributing horses and donkeys – at a price – for his mountless cavalrymen. He made startlingly fast progress, and on 4 March, his small army popped up near Grenoble in the Alps, to be faced by their first real test – a force of 700 men sent out to oppose him. Napoleon had numerical superiority for the moment, but didn't want to provoke hostilities. After all, France had a good deal more than 700 soldiers waiting for him further north.

So he rode slowly towards the opposing lines and, a few dozen metres from their muskets, dismounted and continued on foot. With a dramatic gesture, he swept open his grey coat to give the troops a clear shot at his white waistcoat, and asked if they wanted to kill their emperor. A young captain told his men to fire, but they ignored the order, calling out: 'Vive l'Empereur!'

Similar incidents were repeated in almost every garrison in the country. In Lyon, the King's brother, Charles, comte d'Artois, personally went to organize the resistance, but when a general ordered the city's troops to shout 'Vive le roi!' his lone voice echoed across the parade ground. The comte politely asked one of the soldiers to show the others how it was done, but the man courageously kept mute. The comte saw the way things were going and fled straight back to Paris. On 19 March, in the middle of the night, his brother the King followed his lead and sneaked off to Belgium.

Back in 1803, when Napoleon was planning to invade Britain, he had said that he wanted to be a new William of Orange. Now he had become just that in France, leading a bloodless revolution to oust an unwanted monarch. It was a happy ending, surely? Cue credits and soaring music over a shot of Napoleon standing on the Arc de Triomphe as his exiled son comes up behind him and shyly takes his hand. The Emperor turns and sees his wife smiling from the top of the stairway. The camera pulls away and, as the reunited family embraces, we pan out over the streets of Paris, where can-can dancers, accordion players and similar anachronisms capture the mood of French celebration. The End, *Fin*, gather up your half-empty popcorn bucket and leave the cinema.

Well, not quite.

Nap nips to the 'Loo

It was in Napoleon's interest to keep the peace. Sure, his troops were prepared to shout 'Vive l'Empereur!' to anyone who would listen, but there weren't enough of them to take on the whole of Europe. And Napoleon had to undo Louis XVIII's damage, and reintroduce a more democratic form of government. To make things more complicated, the restoration had dented the Emperor's aura of omnipotence, so there were demands for greater liberties – trial by jury, for example, and freedom of expression. Parliament wanted a whole new constitution. There was a lot of work to be done.

But that old scoundrel Talleyrand had seen this coming and had his speech ready. By coincidence (probably) he was at a ball in Vienna with Wellington, Tsar Alexander and the Austrian Emperor's Minister of State, the Prince von Metternich (full unpronounceable name Klemens Wenzel Nepomuk Lothar, Fürst von Metternich-

Winneburg zu Beilstein) when a messenger burst in with news that Napoleon had landed in France. Immediately, Talleyrand set about whipping up an armed response, and extracted promises from the British, Austrians, Prussians and Russians to provide 150,000 troops each. It was a massive force against France's 200,000 men, but Napoleon had no choice but to prepare for war.

In mid-June, Wellington and Blücher marched into Belgium, planning to meet up and invade France. Unfazed, Napoleon rode out from Paris in his carriage, and said that he was looking forward to this new challenge. For some reason, he had never personally led an army into a pitched battle against the Brits. First, though, he was going to attack the Prussians – he knew how they operated, and it would give him a chance to see whether he'd still got that old Boney magic up the sleeve of his famous overcoat.

He joined his troops near Charleroi in Belgium on 15 June, and over the next couple of days he beat up the Prussians pretty successfully. He even came close to capturing Blücher when the Prussian fell off his horse. Meanwhile, Napoleon asked his old friend Marshal Ney to keep the Brits occupied until he was ready to knock the two enemy's heads together and drive them out of Belgium. He confidently predicted that they would grab Brussels that night, and the war would be over within a day or two.

Ney, though, committed a mistake that was to cost Napoleon his throne and rob the French of the chance to score the killer goal in the battle to name railway stations. Ney hesitated, and instead of attacking, waited long enough for Wellington to draw up his troops on high ground near an unknown village called Waterloo.

To be fair to Ney, though, Napoleon must share some

of the blame. On the morning of 18 June 1815, he heard a rumour that the British and Prussians were planning to join forces in a combined attack. Unlike Nelson, who always took intelligence into account, Napoleon ignored the rumour. He was convinced that he had given the Prussians too much of a beating already, and that they would continue to retreat. He was wrong.

He also committed a much graver mistake in underestimating Wellington. Napoleon is reported to have said that 'Wellington is a bad general, the English are bad troops and it will be a walkover.' Overconfidence is never a good weapon, especially against Wellington, the kind of Englishman who used to say things like 'we always have been, we are, and I hope that we always shall be, detested in France'.

The problem was that Napoleon had been out of the battle game for a while, and was not *au fait* with the latest tactical developments. Wellington knew that the best defence against the conventional opening gambit of a Napoleonic army – an artillery bombardment – was to withdraw slightly behind a ridge of high ground. This simple strategy meant that many of Napoleon's cannonballs splatted harmlessly into the rain-sodden Belgian earth.* This English-style rain, the French allege, was the key to Wellington's victory, because even if Napoleon's artillery fire fell short, he always counted on causing havoc amongst his opponents with murderous ricochets. But nothing ricochets off wet mud.

The French give several more unconvincing explanations for their subsequent defeat. According to one

---

* Strange, perhaps, that so many British World War One commanders would put the same blind faith in cannons in the same Belgian mud before sending their troops to get mown down by machine guns.

story, before every battle, Napoleon drank Champagne. One of his mottos was: 'In victory you deserve it, in defeat you need it.' He had developed a taste for bubbly while studying in the Champagne region and thereafter, the story goes, he never failed to stop off on his way to foreign parts to stock up. It is a credible theory because the road from Paris to Prussia, Russia, Poland and Belgium leads through Champagne (although the theory doesn't work quite so well for Austria, Italy or Spain). Anyway, before Waterloo, Napoleon apparently didn't drink Champagne, and paid the price for his abstinence. All in all, it sounds like a neat bit of drinks marketing rather than a credible explanation for losing a battle.

An even more outlandish story is that Napoleon's fighting abilities were impaired because of haemorrhoids. These were usually treated with leeches, but apparently on 16 June, between battles against the Prussians, the leeches were lost or escaped. It was therefore painful for Napoleon to stay in the saddle and be mobile during Waterloo, and the laudanum he took to alleviate the pain dulled his mental faculties. This, though, would seem to be an absurd myth – apart from the fact that Napoleon was seen galloping ferociously across the battlefield of Waterloo to order his cavalry into the attack, once Wellington and Blücher's troops finally joined up as planned, there was no way the most alert French commander could have won.

As so many battles before it, Waterloo consisted of men and horses charging, or in many cases walking, straight into hails of gunfire. No camouflage uniforms, body armour, tanks, air support or laser-guided missiles. You just headed for the enemy and hoped they would either die or run away before they killed you. At that time, generals joined in, too, rather than sitting in comfy command posts and radioing in their orders while sipping tea. As we've seen, Napoleon and Nelson were not averse to getting shot at, and at Waterloo Marshal Ney personally led several cavalry charges at the Thin Red Line, having several horses shot from under him.*

On 18 June, it is estimated that about 25,000 Frenchmen were killed or wounded, along with around 15,000 of Wellington's army and 7,000 of Blücher's. In a ten-hour battle, that amounts to 4,700 casualties an hour, or more than one man falling, dead or injured, every second. And given the medical technology of the day, the chances of surviving a musket-ball impact, lead poisoning, or an operation to have a smashed limb sawn off without anaesthetic were slim.

The French poet Victor Hugo wrote a poem about the demise of Napoleon, and described the gore of Waterloo very effectively: 'The plain,' he wrote, 'where torn flags shuddered, was transformed, in the death rattles of dying men having their throats cut, into a flaming abyss, red as a forge.' Not the stuff of army recruitment brochures.

If the battle had been a boxing match, at the end of it, the two battered, broken-nosed, puffy-eyed, blood-blinded fighters would have been slumped in their corners, with the victory given on points to the heavier man simply because he had landed more blows. But for history's sake, let's call it a victory. Not a *British* victory, of course – without Blücher, Wellington wouldn't have won. Indeed, the Duke was heard uttering a prayer in the afternoon of 18 June: 'Give me night or give me Blücher.' And Wellington's own army was not entirely British, either. In fact less than half of them were – the rest were

* Not that it did him much good. Six months later Ney was found guilty of treason by the royalists for going over to Napoleon's side and executed by firing squad in Paris. Courageous to the last, he refused a blindfold and gave the order to fire.

soldiers from Holland and small German states like Hanover, Brunswick and Nassau.

But, as at Agincourt, it was the Brits who got to name the battle. It could have been called Mont Saint-Jean, after the high ground where Wellington started the fighting, but he wanted a more English-sounding name and chose the handy village nearby.

In French minds, the Battle of Waterloo has gone down as a Franco-British horror story. It can be no coincidence that in 1940, General de Gaulle chose to make his famous appeal from London for the French to resist Hitler on 18 June, thereby wiping the national shame off the calendar. And in the popular French imagination, it is still the defeat to end all defeats, and has entered the language, as I found out for myself soon after arriving in France. I knew that a colleague had been having trouble with his boss, and asked what the mood was like in the office.

'Oh, c'est Waterloo!' he exclaimed.

'Très bien.' I smiled, assuming that things were obviously on the up. He had to explain to me that, no, he meant that it was all-out war, and he was coming off worst.

Yes, almost 200 years later, Waterloo still has the ability to make the French suffer.

Reunion with Nelson

The pain wasn't over for Napoleon yet. He fled back to Paris to be told that the Assemblée (the Parliament) wanted him to abdicate. He did so, in favour of his son, who was (as he put it) a prisoner in Vienna. At least this way, he might get to see the boy again, and even play at regent. But Wellington came and sabotaged his plans, warning the Assemblée that there was no way that Britain or its Prussian friends, who would be here soon,* were going to let a Bonaparte stay in charge of France.

Napoleon decided that the only thing for it was to take exile in America. Unlike in the early twenty-first century, the French were highly respected there, and with the ploughing and fishing skills he had learned on Elba, as well as the gardening tips he had picked up at school, he hoped to make a new life for himself.

He made a run for it to the Atlantic port of Rochefort on the west coast of France, but found it blockaded by the British ship *Bellerophon*, popularly known as 'Billy Ruffian', a warship that had seen action both at the Battle of the Nile and Trafalgar. Nelson had come back to haunt Napoleon.

After much hesitation, the French fugitive decided to surrender to the British, remembering perhaps his old fantasy of living out his days in the English countryside, and thinking that he would be allowed to reminisce with old soldiers about the scraps they'd enjoyed in their youths. He was received gracefully, and even given the captain's cabin as the ship set sail for England. But the British government had already decided that it would send its most important political prisoner since Mary Queen of Scots somewhere a bit further away than an English village.

Saint where?

If you ask Google Maps how to get from Paris to St Helena, you will get the response: 'We could not calculate

---

* When the Prussians did arrive, Wellington prevented them from expressing their high spirits by dynamiting key parts of Paris, including the pont d'Iena, named after Napoleon's victory against the Prussians in 1806. The French might not like the English Duke, but he protected their capital for them.

directions between Paris France and Saint Helena Island.'

Actually, you'll get the same response about the island and practically any destination in the world, and that is in the twenty-first century. In 1815, getting exiled to the volcanic hump situated some 2,000 kilometres from the nearest continent was like being sent to the Moon. It was a real statement of intent, as were the conditions of Napoleon's detention – he was isolated from the other islanders, guarded by 125 sentries, and if a ship came in sight, all St Helena's cannons were pointed in its direction and a warning shot was fired. Napoleon was not meant to return to Europe unless the British went to fetch him. He certainly wasn't going to nip home to France and dispossess the newly reinstalled Louis XVIII.

There was to be no playing at king on St Helena either, no turning the island into a miniature Napoleonic empire. The climate was about as far from the Mediterranean balminess of Elba as you could get – it was characterized by Atlantic rainstorms and lashing winds, especially at his new residence of Longwood, a rat-infested farmhouse some 500 metres up on a damp plateau.

Napoleon did manage to add a courtly touch to some elements of his life there. He designed a posh uniform for his maître d'hôtel – a silver-embroidered green coat, black silk trousers and white silk stockings – and after dinner the former Empereur would read scenes from Molière, Racine or one of the other great French dramatists to the group of friends who had been allowed to accompany him.

He spent most of his days dictating his memoirs, but reserved his greatest energy for battles with his British captors. A constant war of petty sniping went on. Napoleon would deliberately hide so that the officer charged with personally setting his eyes on the prisoner twice a day would get into trouble. In return, the Brits would seize gifts sent to St Helena, and on one occasion even refused to allow Napoleon to order a new pair of shoes unless he personally presented an old pair to the British governor, a slightly sadistic soldier called Sir Hudson Lowe.

The ex-Emperor also objected to Lowe's insistence on calling him General Bonaparte, and in a fit of pique declared that he wanted to change his name altogether, to Baron Duroc (the Baron of the Rock). The Governor forbade this too.

More than ever, the odds were against Napoleon, though, and the war of attrition gradually wore him down. He stopped going for rides because he objected to being followed by British officers, and at one point stayed indoors for two months so that he would not be seen by his guards. His physical condition declined, and serious stomach aches began.

Napoleon put in a request for a personal physician, and his letter was sent to France. The French duly added their own dose of cruelty to the British mistreatment, and a full eighteen months later, a certain François Carlo Antommarchi arrived. He had a medical degree, but had until recently been employed as a prosector, or dissector's assistant, preparing corpses for anatomy classes at the University of Florence. Not exactly the top Paris physician that the ailing Napoleon had hoped for.

His stomach pain grew steadily worse, a condition initially diagnosed as hepatitis, and treated by Antommarchi with laxatives, which only made the pain worse. Governor Lowe thought Napoleon was faking, or at the very least imagining things, and suggested that someone should rush into his bedroom and scare him into getting up.

By April 1821 Napoleon was bedridden and declining

rapidly, unable to keep food or painkilling medicines down. He dictated his last wishes, asking for his body to be buried 'on the banks of the Seine' (in Paris, of course, rather than Le Havre). His second wife, Marie-Louise, was also in his mind, though spookily it was in a request to have his heart preserved and sent to her as a farewell gift.

He also had enough fight in him for one last stab at the Brits: 'I die prematurely,' he said, 'assassinated by the English oligarchy' (an oligarchy being a system of government by an elite, like Napoleonic France, for example).

The former Emperor of most of Europe died at 5.49 p.m. local time on 5 May 1821, and his death at last gave Antommarchi a chance to perform the job he had been trained for. At Napoleon's request, he did an autopsy, and found a large stomach cancer. As Napoleon had feared, it was the same disease that had killed his father, and he wanted to be sure so that his son could be forewarned. A British doctor present at the post-mortem added a detail to Antommarchi's report, noting that Napoleon's penis and testicles were 'very small'. Even at the end, the Brits couldn't resist kicking the Emperor when he was down.

Though if we are to believe certain allegations, an even crueller blow was struck after the autopsy. It has been suggested that, once the witnesses had dispersed, Antommarchi secretly removed Napoleon's penis and gave it to Ange-Paul Vignali, the priest who had administered the last rites and conducted the funeral service. Napoleon's valet even alleged in a magazine article that Vignali cut the Emperor's 'baguette' off himself as a souvenir – and this was in 1852, long before it became fashionable to accuse Catholic priests of sexual perversion.

Either way, when Vignali's family sold off his collection of Napoleonic souvenirs in 1916, they included a lock of the Emperor's hair, a death mask and an item described as 'a mummified tendon taken from

Napoleon's body during the post-mortem', which was listed in the auction catalogue as 'rare' (though, if it was the penis, 'unique' would surely have been more accurate). The curios were bought by an American collector called A. S. W Rosenbach who put the gruesome piece of flesh on show at New York's Museum of French Art in 1927, where it was confidently identified as the imperial organ. Amused onlookers described the exhibit as a shrivelled eel, a shoelace, a sea-horse and a raisin. Not very flattering.

The Petit Caporal's *petit caporal* came up for sale again in London in 1969, but didn't sell, and when it came under the hammer (apologies to male readers for that image) in Paris in 1977, the French state did not try to acquire it. It was bought by John Kingsley Lattimer, a New Jersey urologist (a man with a specialist knowledge of the nether regions) to add to his collection of macabre historical objects that included Abraham Lincoln's bloodstained collar, Hermann Goering's empty cyanide capsule and pieces of the upholstery from JFK's Dallas limousine. Lattimer refused to exhibit Napoleon's specimen, although according to one person who saw it after the collector's death in 2007, it looked like 'a baby's finger'. If so, it had clearly grown, since it was a mere shoelace in 1927.

All in all, the story whiffs strongly of Anglo-Saxon mischief, and when I asked a member of Napoleon's family to comment, she told me, 'I've never heard of this story, and I can't help you.' It is not a subject that worries modern Bonapartes, or the French in general, which must cast doubt on the object's authenticity.

But the Emperor's 'baguette' is not the only part of his body that has caused controversy. His hair, too, has had tongues wagging ever since he died. There are those, and they are mostly French, who accuse the Brits of poisoning, and point to traces of arsenic found in locks of Napoleon's hair. A piece of wallpaper from Longwood House was examined and found to contain the poison.

Exactement! the accusers cried – before Napoleon moved in, his captors fiendishly poisoned the décor, certain that over the years bits of it were bound to flake off and fall into the imperial coffee cup or wine glass. And wasn't it a well-known fact that Frenchmen like to lick walls?

The actual explanation for the presence of poison in the house is far more prosaic. In those days, green dye commonly contained arsenic, and the same colours, and levels of toxicity, would have been found in practically every house on the island. Which is not to say that it is safe, of course. No one wants toxic wall coverings. But it wasn't a British plot. Furthermore, in the early nineteenth century, arsenic was thought to cure baldness (although it has since been proved that it has the opposite effect), and Napoleon is known to have bathed his head in the poison. Arsenic stays in the body, so it is not surprising if it was found in locks of the vain Emperor's hair. The banal truth is that poor old Boney died of hereditary cancer, probably aggravated by gastric ulcers, at the premature age of fifty-one.

His body wasn't sent back to be enshrined by the Seine, of course, or put on the mantelpiece by his widow. Governor Howe was under orders not to let it leave the island, and it was not until December 1840 that it returned to France, and was driven on a carriage under his Arc de Triomphe, which had only been finished four years earlier. It was finally laid to rest in the Invalides, although the shrine-like tomb that France commissioned wasn't completed until 1861.

Not that France can let the matter rest. Ever since the Emperor's coffin was repatriated, there have been rumours that it was either empty or contained the body of a valet called Cipriani. Even today, there are French historians who maintain that Napoleon's remains were smuggled off St Helena by the *Anglais* and secretly buried in Westminster Abbey. It seems rather bizarre that they haven't spotted the weakness in their own theory – it would mean that in the early nineteenth century the Brits accorded their former enemy *numéro un* the honour of a resting place alongside their greatest monarchs and poets. Incredible to say the least, but the allegation is still made at regular intervals, the most recent outbreak of paranoia being a book published in 2000 called *The Enigma of the Exhumed Body of 1840*.

There is, however, one intriguing thing about Napoleon's tomb at the Invalides that is rarely discussed. Interestingly, a space was left for Napoleon's son, Napoleon Junior, who died in 1832, but his remains weren't transferred there until 1940, by an avid Austrian fan of the Empereur – Adolf Hitler.

Napoleon wins the Eurovision song contest

So what was Napoleon's lasting legacy? There's 'not tonight, Josephine', of course, and the tendency to compare any autocratic Frenchman (and there are lots of them) to him. There is the deep-seated British glee at winning Waterloo and Trafalgar, and the two national heroes Napoleon helped to create, Nelson and Wellington. There are his laws, of course, which still shape France's entire way of thinking. Not forgetting Abba's Eurovision-winning first hit, which name-checks Napoleon in the first line and gives no mention of either Wellington or Blücher.

But to my mind, his true legacy has nothing to do with wars or politics.

When Napoleon went to invade Egypt, he didn't have to fill his ship with scientists. He could have done it the conventional military way and taken extra troops, cannons and gunpowder – that was what his own soldiers wanted him to do. But he defied them, and it was his archaeologists who found the Rosetta Stone, which in 1822, just months after Napoleon's death, enabled Jean-François Champollion to make one of the biggest breakthroughs in the study of ancient history – the deciphering of hieroglyphics. Surely that is a much greater gift to humanity than legal reforms, a few elitist schools and a couple of railway stations named after battles?

However, even this is not a totally French success story. The fact is that Champollion wouldn't have got anywhere without a Brit called Thomas Young, who translated the demotic script on the Rosetta Stone, revealing a text celebrating the first anniversary of the coronation of Pharaoh Ptolemy V. Young then made a start on the hieroglyphics, but got bogged down because he didn't realize that the hieroglyphs paraphrased the other texts rather than giving a word-for-word translation. In reality, Champollion expanded on Young's work rather than doing it all himself, and actually had to correct one of his articles about the transcriptions when Young pointed out key errors.

So Napoleon's legacy only became possible thanks to an *Anglais*. Sorry, Monsieur l'ex-Empereur, but did you really expect to enjoy even a posthumous moment of triumph without British interference?

Addendum: The Brits pour scorn (and more) on Napoleon

New evidence of Britain's never-ending taste for Napoleon abuse has recently come to light.

In July 2013, Bonaparte's last desk was put up for auction in London. This was the writing table on which he must have braved the pain of his stomach cancer to scratch out some final notes, and maybe even sign his will. An impressive six and a half feet long, made out of ebony and mahogany, one would think that it was an escritoire fit for an emperor, albeit a deposed one. But one would be wrong, mainly because the desk was English.

It was commissioned in 1815 by the then Prince of Wales, the future George IV, to be sent to Napoleon in his new home on the distant island of Saint Helena (hence, no doubt, the use of two woods that are resistant to extreme damp). However, this apparently kind gesture on the Prince's part was tempered by a healthy dose of royal *schadenfreude*. George specified that the desk should bear no symbols signifying Napoleon's former rank – none of his family bees, no violets, certainly no capital N, not even a cannon or two.

What was more, although Prince George commissioned the desk from George Bullock, one of England's foremost furniture makers (no doubt as a prince, he only knew the foremost people in any field), he ordered a design that was the opposite of French tastes at the time: the desk was stark and rectangular, its only decoration a few inlays of funereal ebony, whereas Napoleon preferred rounded forms with plenty of gilt ornamentation.

Despite its simple design, the desk wasn't cheap – it cost just over £68, the equivalent of about £5,000 in modern money. But then the Prince of Wales didn't really mind the expense, because he charged Napoleon the full price. It was not so much a gift as a punishment that the victim had to pay for.

The desk, which was in Napoleon's residence at Longwood House when he died, is still in perfect condition, proving that *l'Empereur* did not vent his frustration by kicking in the plain English side panels or by scratching anti-Wellington insults to decorate its bare surface. After Napoleon's death, it was bought by his jailer, Sir Hudson Lowe, and later sold to Cecilia, Countess of Strathmore, whose daughter Elizabeth was to become the Queen Mother. Quite a provenance for a piece of furniture coming to auction, but it was Napoleon's name in the catalogue that attracted buyers' attention.

At the sale on 14 November 2013, the desk fetched £110,500, a 1,600-fold increase in value since it was first shipped out to Saint Helena to depress the fallen French Emperor. Napoleon would no doubt have been flattered to know that a piece of furniture that he owned for five years would soar in value by association with his name, but any satisfaction he felt would have been diminished by the thought that it was those capitalistic Brits who had pocketed the profit.

A low blow at Napoleon

Napoleon's furniture-related humiliation didn't end there. When commissioning the desk, the Prince of Wales had also instructed George Bullock to make some smaller objects to decorate the Frenchman's luxury prison – including a chamber pot that came up for auction in London in 2005.

A very elegant, double-handled, cream earthenware piece, with an orange-leaf motif around the rim, it looks more like a slightly squashed vase than a traditional chamber pot. A bouquet of dahlias would look perfectly at home in it. Because of its Napoleonic connection, it was listed by Bonham's of London as 'an important chamber pot' and sold for £2,880 – not a bad price for a second-hand portable toilet.

The sad thing, both for Napoleon and the sellers, was that the imperial posterior never came anywhere near the 'important' pot. If it had, the price would no doubt have been much higher. The chamber pot, and other items in a china bathroom set designed by George Bullock in 1815, were never sent to Saint Helena because the Prince of Wales thought that the leaf motif looked like a crown of victor's laurels. There was no way the British royal family was going to let Napoleon feel triumphant, even on the toilet. Bullock therefore had to find another buyer for his chamber pot, and in 1817 he provided it as part of an order for the Great Tew estate in Oxfordshire, where it stayed until the owner of the estate gave it away in the 1960s as a jokey engagement present.

Not that lavatory humour at Boney's expense is anything new. An exhibition called *Rude Britannia*, held at Tate Britain in London in 2010, included a charming Napoleonic exhibit made in 1805: a flowery chamber pot containing a head-and-shoulders bust of a resigned-looking French Emperor, hatless and open to bombardment from above.

Where Napoleon is concerned, no British blow has ever been too low.

20

Food, Victorious Food

The worst thing about wars is that they don't stop for lunch.

No, obviously that's not true at all – the worst thing is that people can legally kill each other. But wars do disrupt dining habits. The combatants have to eat the rations doled out to them in open-air canteens, with neither a tablecloth nor a clean glass in sight (except for the officers, of course). And civilians have to make do with whatever doesn't get requisitioned by the government or stolen by marauding troops.

Peace, on the other hand, can liberate the palate. As soon as the fighting stops and lingering food shortages have been overcome, borders open up and people move around, bringing their culinary ingredients and ideas with them.

This is exactly what happened after the Napoleonic Wars. The victorious nations, especially the Brits, Prussians and Austrians, poured into France as both tourists and occupiers, and began to lap up the world-famous French cuisine.

Or so the French would have us believe. In fact, the

visitors found certain things lacking and had to import their own foods – and some of these proved so popular with the French that they adopted them and are convinced that they invented them. But as we saw with Champagne in Chapter 9, these claims really must be taken with a pinch of salt (plus a little pepper and maybe even a *soupçon* of English sugar), and three staples of French everyday cuisine are in fact foreign imports.

It's a steak-out

In the early nineteenth century, the richer Brits used Paris as a kind of second home, and introduced many elements of upper-class British life into France.

Horse-racing started in earnest, and large meetings were held on the Champs de Mars, outside Napoleon's old school, the École militaire. Famous British horse trainers moved to France, and a stud farm and racecourse were set up near the chateau of Chantilly just outside Paris to take advantage of the high-quality turf there. Soon Epsom-style race meetings were all the rage with the Parisian upper classes and their new British friends.

At the same time, the first mounted fox hunt in France started harassing animals in the forests around Pau, near the Pyrenees, which had been adopted by the Anglo-Scots as a spa resort. The practical French had always hunted for food, and (like Oscar Wilde later in the century) must have thought the Brits slightly stupid for trying to catch something so inedible, but what they failed to understand was that that was exactly why foxes were hunted – to show that you were too posh to have to run after your dinner.

It was also in Pau that the Scots baffled locals with their habit of digging holes in the ground and hitting little white balls at them.

All of these activities were eventually taken up by the French and are still the preserve of the country's upper classes today. Cricket didn't have so much luck, probably because it involves throwing a hard ball at the batsman's testicles, and that is one risk that a Frenchman won't take.

At the same time, food fashions also crossed the Channel. British cakes and puddings started to appear in bakeries and cafés, while British soldiers introduced Paris to a slightly barbarous but tasty way of cooking beef.

Beef, of course, is inescapably associated with the Brits in the French mind. A slightly old-fashioned nickname for the *Anglais* is '*les rosbifs*', a phonetic transcription of 'roast beef', and the original French name for what they now call *le steak* was *le bifteck*, or beefsteak.

The French have been grilling meat ever since the Neolithics found out what they could do with fire, of course, but until post-Napoleonic times, the fashionable way to cook beef in France was to boil it or stew it in a sauce.

Apparently, this all changed when redcoats came to camp in the Tuileries gardens. It seems that the Parisians were distracted from their promenades by smells of soldiers grilling beef, and were tempted to try the simple but effective recipe for themselves.

The writer Alexandre Dumas, famous not only for *The Three Musketeers* but also for a *Dictionnaire de la cuisine*, got his first job in Paris just after the *Anglais* arrived, and in his dictionary's entry for *Beef-steak ou bifteck à l'anglaise*, he reminisces: 'I remember seeing *le bifteck* arrive in France just after the campaign of 1815, when the English stayed for two or three years in Paris. Until then, our cuisines had been as different as our politics.' He says that at first the French were suspicious of this British import, but soon, 'being a nation without prejudices, we gave the *bifteck* a certificate of citizenship'. He gives a drooling description of how best to grill the meat, and concludes: 'Every time I go to England, I eat it with renewed relish,' regretting only that the Brits don't know how to make gherkins to go with their steak.

The origin of the *frites*, or French fries (as the French don't call them), that accompany *le steak* is lost in the fatty mist of culinary history. Everyone claims to have invented them, though it is pretty safe to say that the method of cutting potatoes into long sticks when deep-frying them probably didn't exist in France at the time they adopted the steak. Dumas's dictionary, like other cookbooks of the time, suggests cutting the potatoes into slices, not sticks.

Anyway, at the very least, one half of France's national dish of *steak-frites* is British in inspiration – a nice historical irony on a linguistic level because the word 'beef' originally came from the French *boeuf*.

The French stick baguettes down their trousers

All cultures have their creation myths, and the French are no different. Their theory about the creation of the baguette ranks amongst one of the funniest.

They tell a story about the long stick loaf first being baked for Napoleon's soldiers. Before then, it is alleged, bread had always been round – after all, the word *boulanger* comes from *boule* or ball. But Napoleon, who oversaw every part of his soldiers' lives, wanted a loaf that was easier to transport when his armies were on the march, as they often were. He therefore asked his bakers to make a long bread stick that the troops could carry in a pocket in their trousers. Why this method of transport is more efficient than putting a round loaf in their backpack is not explained. Anyway, it is almost certainly a complete myth, and as the French-language

Wikipedia page on the baguette very rationally puts it, 'the baguette would have inconvenienced the soldier during the day and probably arrived in bad condition.'

The French do insist that baguettes date from about this time, however. The flour company Retrodor has a website which suggests that the baguette was invented after post-revolutionary bakers were no longer forced to make coarse 'bread of the people' and were allowed to bake white bread. At the same time, so the company's website says, beer yeast was introduced into the baking process, making it possible to create a lighter dough, perfect for the slender stick loaf. What they seem to be saying is that the baguette is entirely French.

However, less patriotic food historians agree that the baguette isn't really French at all, or at the very least avoid the subject.

In her book *A History of Food*, the French author Maguelonne Toussaint-Samat doesn't mention the development of the baguette. She describes the evolution of bread in the ancient Greek, Jewish and Roman civilizations, talks about Joan of Arc dunking 'sops' of bread in wine, and pinpoints the location of the baker's oven in medieval French towns (not too close to the neighbour's wall). But she steers clear of the origin of the baguette.

In fact, the archetypal French bread seems to have originated *chez* one of the allies who occupied Paris after 1815 – and the light, fluffy texture referred to by English bakers as 'Vienna bread' gives us a clue to which ally this might be.

In the mid-nineteenth century, the Austrians developed a new type of gas-fired oven fitted with steam injectors. The oven could be heated to over 205°C, and the steam jets made the crust expand before it was baked, leaving the inside of the loaf light and airy. The highly efficient oven was soon being fitted in *boulangeries* all over France.

What's more, far from being a centuries-old French tradition, the baguette only became really fashionable in the 1920s, for two reasons. First, at the end of the First World War, many of France's bakers and apprentice bakers were lying buried under the mud of the Somme and other battlefields, so there was a labour shortage, making the easy-to-prepare Vienna-style bread an attractive proposition.

Secondly, a new French law made it illegal for bakers to work before four in the morning, so that the baguette became the only loaf that they could be sure of having ready for breakfast time.

It had another advantage for the *boulanger* too: it only stays really fresh for about half an hour. (OK, a bit longer, but an hour or so after cooling it will start to dry up just under the crust and give a less pleasant crunching sensation.) If customers want fresh bread, they throw their 'old' baguette away and come back for a new one. It's a great business plan.

So in the 1920s everyone was happy with the baguette, and the Austrian loaf became a symbol of France just as evocative as its giant metal cousin, the Eiffel Tower.

Since then, the French stick's reputation has drooped slightly. In recent years, its sheer whiteness has caused diet-conscious France to move over to healthier breads made with wholewheat, cereals, bran and rye. The baguette has been forced to evolve, and practically every *boulangerie* now sells a *baguette de tradition*, which has a softer crust and a darker dough with less yeast, and is usually slightly wonky, so that it looks as if it has been made by a half-blind medieval baker. But it is a misleading name, and in fact it is the fluffy, unnaturally white baguette with the golden crust that is *de tradition*. And that tradition is Viennese.

The twisted history of the croissant

The croissant, the ultimate French breakfast (and breakfast-only) food, isn't French, either. Like the baguette, it is Austrian. This is no surprise – Austria is a country founded on pastries, and a visit to a Viennese coffee shop makes you wonder how a nation that devotes so much energy to producing its dizzying variety of delicious *Kuchen* and *Torten* could ever have done something so hideously uncakelike as support Hitler in 1938. And one thing's for sure – the Austrian corporal didn't get enough of his country's cakes when he was a boy, otherwise he could never have turned into a genocidal dictator.

Crescent-shaped cakes have been made in Europe for centuries. The crescent is, after all, a strong symbol associated with the moon and the Orient. Legend has it that the Austrians first started making what we call croissants after the siege of Vienna in 1683, when the Turks began burrowing tunnels under the city walls and were heard by bakers working in their cellars at night. As a reward for alerting the authorities rather than trying to sell an early breakfast to the invaders, the bakers were granted the right to make pastries reminiscent of the crescent on the Ottoman flag.

That is one theory. Others say that the Austrian croissant, or *Kipfel*, has been made since the thirteenth century, which doesn't really contradict the siege story. It probably amused the bakers who saved Vienna to see that their traditional *Kipfel* cakes looked like the crescent on the Ottoman flag.

One thing seems certain, though – the croissant in its modern form came to France from Austria.

Romantics say that it was introduced by Marie-Antoinette, who was of course famous for her interest in bread and cakes. More pragmatic historians are sure that it was imported by an Austrian, a soldier turned business-man called August Zang, who opened a Viennese bakery in Paris in 1838 or 1839. His Boulangerie Viennoise at 92 rue Richelieu, near the city's National Library, started the fashion for croissants and inspired the development of the *pain au chocolat* and *pain aux raisins*, the other pastries that the French still call collectively *viennoiseries*.

French writers make no reference to the croissant until 1853, when the chemist Anselme Payen published his highly ungastronomic *Des substances alimentaires*, in which he talks about croissants and English muffins in a section on 'fantasy or luxury breads'.

By 1875, croissants seem to have become more standard fare, because in a book called *Consommations de Paris* (which could be roughly translated as *Paris Food and Drink*), a writer called Armand Husson refers to croissants and coffee as an 'ordinary' as opposed to a 'lux-ury' meal.

Today, of course, croissants form the centrepiece of the continental breakfast, and are as French as the peculiar breed of waiters who serve them. And they are for break-fast only – almost no café will have any left after ten o'clock in the morning. Not because they will have gone off, but because practically no French customer would ask for one so late in the day.

Which is why the French were rather confused when in the 1990s, the Anglo-Saxons started eating them for lunch, stuffed with all sorts of unsuitable fillings. I was living in Glasgow at the time, and remember the sudden invasion of trendy 'continental' foods when the city became European City of Culture. Suddenly cafés were brasseries or bistros, pubs were wine bars, and the city's food menus became decidedly un-Scottish. Out went deep-fried pizza (in the cafés I went to, anyway) and in came ciabattas, paninis and stuffed croissants. I was working for a bilingual publisher, and can remember my French colleagues frowning at the croissant I bought myself at a city-centre brasserie one lunchtime. Not only was it twice the size of a French croissant, it was pasty white and – the ultimate heresy – overflowing with spinach and Gruyère cheese.

They stared in amazement for a few seconds, and then burst out laughing at the absurdity of eating this breakfast food at lunchtime. One of them was also mystified at the perversion of his national food.

'The cheese is French,' I defended myself, but this didn't win him over.

'There are some things you can't do with another nation's cuisine,' he lectured me. 'What would you think if we started putting cheese in tea or English beer?' (Which is something that a trendy chef has no doubt done since.)

In his defence, I should add that this was a long time ago, when people thought they were living on the cultural edge by putting pineapple on pizzas, and hadn't even dreamt of mango sushi.

But what I would have loved to answer, if I'd known it back then, was 'Actually, *mon ami*, it's not your cuisine at all. Has no one ever told you where France got *le steak*, *les baguettes* and *les croissants*? They were all imported by Napoleon's enemies after we sent him to St Helena.'

Though on second thoughts, it was probably a truth that he simply wouldn't have been able to digest.

21

The Romantics: The Brits Trash French Art

In the early nineteenth century, the French thought they had the world sussed. Descartes and Voltaire had described it (albeit with a little help from Sir Isaac Newton); dramatists like Racine and Corneille had idealized it; Napoleon had encoded it in his laws; and Jacques-Louis David had painted it, turning contemporary people and situations into the stuff of Greek and Roman history. The world was classical, symmetrical, logical and governed by strict rules. In short, it was French.

All of which was highly ironic, because France itself was in total upheaval.

French artists and writers really should have got the message much earlier. David, for example, was forced to abandon his giant painting of the *Serment du Jeu de paume*, the 'tennis court oath' at which breakaway democrats had vowed to write a new constitution in 1789, because by the time he had finished sketching it out, half the oath-takers had been declared traitors.

France's artistic establishment resisted change, though, until the fall of Napoleon, when the country was suddenly flooded with British painters and writers and their new chaotic ideas. Romantics like Byron, Mary and Percy Shelley, Wordsworth and Turner came swooning and posturing across the continent, raving about passion and nature and heroism, and generally infuriating France's cosy cultural elite.

The most infuriating thing of all was that the Brits all claimed to have been influenced by the raw energy of the French Revolution, whereas the savagery of the Terreur was something that France was trying to forget. Rioting, mass hysteria and blood in the streets? Nothing to do with us logical French – you must have made an *erreur*!

Too emotional for the French

The battle between Classicism and Romanticism embodied the difference between the airs and graces of a wigged and powdered Parisian and the brash social freedom of the English. William Wordsworth and Samuel Taylor Coleridge's *Lyrical Ballads*, published in 1798, were heavily influenced by folk ballads, the kind of poems and songs recited by country folk, handed down since time immemorial. But to the French establishment, country folk were just ignorant bumpkins, great for mucking out horses and making cheese but incapable of anything artistic.

In his preface to the *Lyrical Ballads*, Wordsworth wrote that the poems 'were written chiefly with a view to ascertain how far the language of conversation in the middle and lower classes of society is adapted to the purpose of poetic pleasure'. This would have had French poets chuckling into their perfumed hankies. What kind of 'conversation' did the lower classes have? Arguments about the price of bread? Or how to get cowpats off clogs? Not the stuff of poetry, that was for sure.

One of Wordsworth's poems in the collection begins:

> Strange fits of passion have I known:
> And I will dare to tell,
> But in the Lover's ear alone,
> What once to me befell.

Short lines, everyday vocabulary, illogical 'fits of passion', and not a single reference to a Greek god? In France, it would have been binned.

But the Brits loved everything about Nature, including the people who lived in it. Not surprising, really, because the Industrial Revolution was starting to carve up the British countryside and suck the rural population into the slums, making Nature a precious thing in need of protection. This was in part why painters like Constable, Turner and the lesser-known but just as important Richard Parkes Bonington were fascinated by foggy, overgrown natural scenery that was a million miles away from French artists' statuesque Greek and Roman landscapes.

These Brits were respected artists at home, but when Eugène Delacroix adopted their Romantic style after a visit to England in 1825, all he earned in Paris was insults. His painting *La Mort de Sardanapale* depicts the murder of an Assyrian king's concubines before he commits suicide, a theme taken from a play by Lord Byron. Classical in subject matter but violently Romantic in execution, it was described by Parisian newspapers as 'a bizarre work' and 'a painter's mistake'. In short, it was much too *anglais*.

Another Romantic influence that scared the French Classicists to death was women. Napoleon's *code civil* had set their inferiority in stone and deprived them of an education. The most widely respected female French writer of the Revolutionary years, Olympe de Gouges, author of the *Déclaration des droits de la femme et de la*

485

citoyenne (*Declaration of Women and Female Citizens' Rights*) and a play condemning slavery, was guillotined in 1793 for opposing the death penalty. In other words, if you can't control your mouth, *chérie*, we'll have to chop your whole head off.

In the early nineteenth century, Parisian males thought that ladies were perfect for evenings of witty conversation and adulterous sex, or for producing the right number of heirs, but little more. And then in 1821, across the Channel came Mary Shelley's *Frankenstein*. Translated by a writer called Jules Saladin who preferred to remain anonymous, signing himself J. S***, and published with a mistake on the title page (the author was presented as 'Madame Shelly'), the French translation was the first foreign edition of the novel, which had been a big hit in the UK in both book and stage form.

Shelley was the daughter of the feminist Mary Wollstonecraft, who had been in Paris during the Revolution, so perhaps it was not surprising that some French critics seized upon this to slam the book for its lack of 'femininity'. The *Revue encyclopédique* for 1821 calls the novel 'the bizarre product of a sick imagination', and regrets that 'the work of a woman' does not 'offer likeable and gracious images instead of revolting and hideous objects and stories'. The book 'has no moral goal, does not enlighten the mind or uplift the soul', and the reviewer concludes with the ultimate French Classicist put-down: 'Let us hope that the author will apply the principles of the great masters – good sense and reason must be the primary guidelines for a writer.' It wasn't what he called *littérature*.

But this moralizing lesson meant nothing to the Brits, and Romantic novels like Emily Brontë's *Wuthering Heights* and Charlotte Brontë's *Jane Eyre* kept up the cross-Channel storm of 'irrational' female emotion and unbridled passion. Even prim Jane Austen produced something of a Romantic bodice-ripper in Mr Darcy. Fair enough, women were by no means equal in Britain (Mary Shelley got some bad reviews there, too, and Mary Ann Evans called herself George Eliot so that she would be taken seriously), but such a concentrated outpouring of respected female fiction was unheard of in France. Only one Frenchwoman, Aurore Dupin, alias George Sand, came close, and she was (and is) known more for her scandalous love affairs than her writing. And it is a sign of how slowly France changes that since the creation of the Académie française in 1635, only four of its 710 members have been women.

How do you say 'damned spot' in French?

The most frightening attack on French Classicism, though, came from a man, and a dead one at that – Shakespeare.

The Académie, whose mission has always been to protect the purity of France's culture and language, despised him – even Voltaire, who recognized Shakespeare's genius with words, had felt obliged to mount an anti-Shakespeare campaign before he died, calling the Bard a 'drunken savage'. Everything about his plays was disorderly and unclassical. Servants talked to kings like equals, words were invented willy-nilly, emotions got out of control, and quite a few of the characters said nasty things about the French, especially in the history plays. Worse still, instead of declaiming their lines like statues in a Greek temple, the actors actually moved. They acted. *Quelle horreur.*

When an English theatre troupe performed a selection of Shakespeare's plays in Paris in 1827 and 1828, the actors confirmed all the Académie's prejudices. Hamlet and Romeo were played by a 52-year-old and Othello by a drunk. They ranted and raved their way through the monologues and – even more shocking for Parisian audiences – played other scenes like real human beings. Sometimes they actually sobbed or laughed.

All of which delighted France's most famous pioneer of Romanticism, Victor Hugo (or to give him his full first name, Victor-Marie). Before finding worldwide fame in the 1980s as the author of a hit musical comedy, *Les Misérables*,* Hugo was a soldier's son turned writer, and a pioneering French fan of Shakespeare. The best-known pictures of him show an old white-bearded man resting his head on one hand, but in his youth Hugo was a rabble-rousing literary hothead whose chat-up line 'why don't you come up to my apartment so I can explain all about Romanticism?' he tried out on any society lady or housemaid who came his way.

Legend has it that Hugo fell under Shakespeare's spell in 1825, flicking through a copy of the play *King John* while attending the long, boring coronation of France's King Charles X. By 1827, the sheer freedom of Shakespeare's writing had got under the 25-year-old Hugo's skin and he poured out his newfound passion in the preface to a play about the English hero Oliver Cromwell. (The play itself, incidentally, was considered too long and boring to be performed.)

Hugo's preface idolizes pre-classical man and his primitive emotions. 'He lets himself go. His thoughts, like his life, resemble a cloud that changes shape and direction with the wind.' (The exact opposite of French Classicism.) Hugo goes on:

* In fact, *Les Misérables* was first a highly successful five-volume novel published in 1862. When it first came out, Hugo enquired about its sales by telegraphing his publisher with the message '?'. The publisher, with a bestseller on his hands, replied '!'.

Shakespeare is Drama. And Drama breathes the grotesque and the sublime, the terrible and the farcical, tragedy and comedy, in the same breath. [There were no comic scenes in Racine's tragedies.] Let us take a hammer to theories, politics and systems! Let us tear down the plaster façade masking the face of art. There are no rules or models. Or rather, there are no rules except the laws of Nature.

All in all, it was like playing 'Anarchy in the UK' at an Académie française garden party.

When Hugo put his theories into practice in his play *Hernani*, it had a predictable effect. The play itself is a rather overblown story about a bandit who falls in love with a noblewoman, but the plot was the last thing that interested the crowds on its opening night in February 1830. The verse was choppy and Shakespearean, the emotions bordered on hysteria, the hero was a common thief. Hugo was so nervous about the play's reception on its opening night that he marshalled his friends and supporters like a Napoleonic army. The teenaged poet Théophile Gautier wore a bright red waistcoat and lime-green trousers to shock the Classicists. Pro-Romantics were strategically seated beside well-known adversaries and placed near the expensive boxes to shout down hecklers.

The play's opening scene contains a piece of dialogue that got the Classicists howling with outrage. The King of Spain, a rival for the heroine's affections, wants to hide in her bedroom. The maid, though, tries to throw him out, producing the following exchange:

'Hide me here.'
'You?'
'Me.'

'Why?'

'No reason.'

'Me, hide you?'

'Here.'

'Never.'

Perhaps it reminded the men of Paris's literary establishment too much of visits to their lovers' apartments. In any case, it was not the classical verse they wanted to hear at the theatre, and a riot broke out between the pros and the antis. It was a battle between the young and the old, between adherence to rules and free expression, between Shakespeare and the French. And it spilled out of the theatre into fights and even duels all over France.

Hernani was pretty profitable for Hugo – the scandal kept the play running for several weeks. But it got him evicted from his apartment after noisy opponents exasperated his landlord, and it took a lot longer to win the battle to impose Shakespeare's disorderly literary conduct on French culture. The main problem seems to have been that the French language just couldn't cope with him. Translations weakened the Bard's poetry, because Latin-based French is too rigid and refined. For example, you just cannot translate the witch's line in *Macbeth*, 'ditch-delivered by a drab', without pulling it to pieces. Fair enough, a drab is an old word for prostitute, so modern English-speakers might not get the reference either, but an 1844 French translation by the poet Émile Deschamps renders these punchy seven syllables as 'd'un enfant de fille de joie,/Sur la borne écrasé par sa mère en naissant' or 'the child of a lady of the night, smashed at birth by its mother on a milestone'. The result isn't a hag's spell, it's a posh poet's explanation.

Deschamps was a Romantic, and did his best, but some of the translators didn't dare give a full French version of what they read. The most common translation of *Romeo and Juliet* performed in the early nineteenth century had no fight scenes and no balcony. In Shakespeare's original *Othello*, Desdemona loses a handkerchief decorated with a strawberry motif, but in nineteenth-century France, a *mouchoir* was considered too humble an object to provoke a tragedy, and strawberries were too rustic, so in early French versions she lost either a embroidered piece of Oriental cloth or a diamond-studded headband.

On a more profound level, despite all their claims to be a passionate nation, the nineteenth-century French were overwhelmed by Shakespeare's emotions. Teenagers committing suicide for love; a king's blood dripping from an imaginary knife; witches warning that a forest will walk – France was too Catholic for such pagan Anglo-Saxon goings-on.

In the end, though, the French Romantics won their battle to impose a toned-down version of the new aesthetics that the Brits had shown them, and made it all their own.

The poet Charles Baudelaire, a big fan of Romantic art and gothic novels, began writing his *Fleurs du Mal* in the early 1840s, basically by taking British-style Romanticism and adding a dash of absinthe and a dose of syphilis. He was as uncontrolled and unclassical as you could get, as were his libertine successors Verlaine (who went to live in England for a while) and Rimbaud.

The Impressionist painters, meanwhile, took Bonington's and Turner's love of quickly executed paintings and turned them into a quintessentially French movement that still sells almost as many posters as the late Michael Jackson.

Even so, it wasn't until the late 1850s that Victor Hugo's son François-Victor published a translation of

Shakespeare's plays with Desdemona losing a strawberry-spotted *mouchoir*.

A mere 250-odd years after it was written, *Othello* finally stopped being too modern for the French.

22

How Britain Killed Off the Last French Royals

During the French Revolution, Britain had offered support, exile and no doubt endless cups of tea to the surviving members of France's royal family. Ever since, the French ruling classes had felt quietly confident that, even if the two countries had been at war almost constantly since the Norman Conquest, they could always find a friend in Buckingham Palace (which first became the official royal residence in 1837 when Victoria moved in).

Thus it was that, in the mid-nineteenth century, every time France embarked on one of its frequent bouts of political self-flagellation, the deposed rulers dived across the Channel in search of refuge.

However, exile *chez l'ennemi* wasn't always a good idea, as the families of both Louis XVI and Napoleon Bonaparte were about to discover . . .

Louis-Philippe lives the dream

King Louis-Philippe was descended from the brother of Louis XIV, and belonged to a secondary branch of the

Bourbon dynasty that had always been just out of range of the French throne. When the Revolution came, Louis-Philippe's side of the family had even supported it, hoping that the upheavals might send the crown their way.

However, their wish didn't come true until 1830, when King Charles X, who had succeeded his brother Louis XVIII, was ousted from power for the usual reason – trying to control Parliament instead of doing it the British way and adopting more of a figurehead role. Charles was forced to flee to England, where he was taunted by tricolour-waving crowds and hounded by creditors from his first exile during the Revolution.

Meanwhile, instead of calling for another Republic, the Paris mob and the politicians offered the throne to the moderate Louis-Philippe. They remembered his father, who had renamed himself 'Philippe-Égalité' and served the Revolution faithfully until he was guillotined for treason in 1793. Perhaps, the people thought, King Louis-Philippe would usher in a more democratic monarchy.

And at first, Louis-Philippe didn't disappoint them – he went all out to try and change the royal image. 'I don't like gambling or hunting,' he proclaimed, 'and I don't have a single mistress.' Victor Hugo admired him for this simplicity and congratulated the King for 'sleeping with his wife and having servants in his palace whose duty it is to show the conjugal bed to the bourgeois'.

Louis-Philippe went even further – he used to sing the 'Marseillaise' and walk the streets shaking hands with passers-by (though when doing this he would always wear a specially kept old glove). There is a photo of him, one of the first daguerreotypes, looking like a bourgeois gentleman, stuffed into a tight waistcoat, a top hat on the table beside him. His characteristic piled-up hair, side parting and bushy sideburns make him look modern for the times rather than an eighteenth-century throwback. His expression is rather snooty, but this might well have been because in those days you had to pose without moving a muscle for several seconds so as not to blur the photo.

The King tried to immobilize his critics in much the same way. The caricaturist Charles Philipon was put in jail for a drawing that showed Louis-Philippe's chubby, wide-jawed head mutating into a pear – a piece of repression that backfired when Honoré Daumier produced a version of the caricature that was a hit all over Europe.

It took an assassination attempt to give the King some breathing space. In 1835, Giuseppe Fieschi, a Corsican ex-convict who had previously benefited from an amnesty of political prisoners by Louis-Philippe, fired a *machine infernale* made out of twenty-five rifle barrels at the King's carriage as it was trotting along the boulevard du Temple in Paris. The home-made gun killed seventeen people and injured Fieschi but only managed to graze the King's forehead. Although wounded, Louis-Philippe went on to review an army parade, and was hailed as a fearless hero when he made a joke during the ceremony. One of his generals had been killed, and other members of his entourage mown down, which was why, the King quipped, 'I'm the one driving the coach.' Not exactly a side-splitter, but standards were different in Paris in 1835.

In the subsequent trial, it turned out that Fieschi was a paid assassin, hired by anarchists who wanted the *machine infernale* to blow up and kill him, thus covering their traces. The State finished the job for them, guillotining Fieschi and two accomplices. Even here, Louis-Philippe showed his popular touch by ordering that the condemned men should be the first royal attackers in French history not to be tortured in public before their execution. All in all, every inch (or centimetre) the nice guy.

His popularity didn't last long, however, because soon Radicals were accusing Louis-Philippe of being too friendly with the Brits. When Queen Victoria came on a state visit to Normandy in 1843, Louis-Philippe responded to her gesture of support with a speech that used the term *entente cordiale* for the first time (albeit the wrong way round – he used the English-sounding *cordiale entente*). The young Queen got on well with the cordial King, who spoke good English, and she invited him to pay a return visit. This he did in 1844, in full knowledge of the dangers it involved – if he got too warm a welcome in Britain he would become unpopular at home; if he was coldly received by the London crowds, he would be laughed at on both sides of the Channel.

As it happened, the British crowds cheered him. 'The English are grateful because I know them well enough not to hate them,' he told Victor Hugo. But, as the King had feared, this rapprochement didn't go down well at home. Britain's industrial powerhouse was accused of causing unemployment in France, and the expansion of the British Empire by their detested and still all-powerful fleet was seen as a direct threat to French prestige.

The Anglophobes weren't the only ones complaining. Louis-Philippe might be the 'people's king', but the people he was fondest of were his rich friends, to whom he started to give lucrative contracts to build the country's new railways. The poor were getting left out again, and their survival was still index-linked to the slightest variation in bread prices, just as it had been in 1789.

Advisers begged Louis-Philippe to make concessions. He was, for example, spending fortunes on all the royal chateaux. 'But I have such a big family,' he is said to have answered. He had ten children and pleaded that he needed to make sure they had decent places to live. Which was not an entirely unfair claim – in the past, French kings had often requisitioned whole palaces for their mistresses.

Unfortunately for Louis-Philippe, his family housing plan came to an abrupt end in February 1848, when the wave of revolution that was sweeping across Europe broke over Paris. The mob put up the barricades, soldiers fired at demonstrators and the Second Republic was proclaimed. Louis-Philippe slipped out of the side door of his palace, just as every monarch since Louis XVI had done. He headed, naturally enough, for England and his chum Victoria.

The lead pipes of peace

Alexandre Dumas gives a wonderful cloak-and-dagger account of the royal dash to safety in his book *Histoire de la vie politique et privée de Louis-Philippe*. He describes the King, shorn of his trademark bushy whiskers, disguised in dark glasses (*lunettes vertes*) and a scarf, and speaking with an American accent so that people will think he's a foreigner fleeing the troubles.

Louis-Philippe, or Bill Smith as he introduced himself to all-comers (seriously – that is not a joke), first tried to escape via Trouville. There, he paid a captain 5,000 francs, but when the man's boat was prevented from sailing by a storm, he asked for his money back and the sailor betrayed him to the authorities.

Rushing along the coast in a simple cart, the King found an English steamer, the *Express*, which took him on board at Honfleur and sailed him, accompanied by only his wife and a servant, to

Newhaven, from where they took the train to London.

Freedom at last. The only trouble was that the bumbling King, who seems to have been a French version of P. G. Wodehouse's hapless Lord Emsworth,* had forgotten to bring any money. He remembered distinctly bundling up a wad of cash and putting it on his desk, but that was the last he saw of it.

Louis-Philippe's old friend Victor Hugo paints a tragic picture of the royal in exile. In an entry in his memoirs for 3 May 1848, Hugo notes that the King and his family have only three servants and 'are literally in poverty. There are 22 of them at table and they drink water' (lack of wine being, of course, a sign of extreme famine in French eyes).

The only cash they had was the Queen's income from her Italian family and the interest on some spending money that the absent-minded King had deposited in a London bank during his visit to Victoria in 1844 and forgotten about. When Sir Robert Peel and Lord Aberdeen came to see him, they felt so sorry for the refugee family that they discreetly slipped them a gift of £1,000.

Perhaps because of this poverty, Louis-Philippe was being allowed to stay free of charge at Claremont House near Esher in Surrey. Some historians suggest that this was a kind of banishment from court by Queen Victoria, who didn't want to appear too friendly to the deposed monarch so that relations with the new regime in France could stay at least workable if not cordial. But in fact, the Queen loved Claremont, and had been a frequent visitor

---

* Interestingly, Dumas compares Louis-Philippe not to Lord Emsworth (who hadn't been created yet, anyway) but to King Lear, a Shakespeare reference that would have been unthinkable in French literary circles just a few years earlier, and proof that the Bard had finally made it big in France.

there in her youth. The house belonged to her Uncle Leopold, who had moved out when he became King of Belgium. Leopold was also married to Louis-Philippe's daughter Louise-Marie, so Claremont was a family home.

It was a beautiful new house designed by Capability Brown, with landscaped gardens so picturesque that they have since been bought by the National Trust (the house itself is now a school). But one of the mod cons in this state-of-the art residence was running water, and pipes at the time were made of lead. The French royals, as Victor Hugo pointed out, were drinking water instead of wine at mealtimes and fell ill. The King began suffering from severe weight loss, and his doctors sent him to the chic new seaside resort of St Leonards near Brighton for some invigorating fresh air. It is not certain whether they forced him to go in the sea, but the English climate seems to have finished the job that the running water started, and by August 1850 Louis-Philippe was so ill that they sent him home to Claremont to die.

When the doctors told him that he would soon be joining his ancestors, the affable old man apparently said, 'So what you're telling me is that it's time to pack my bags?'

The last King of France was buried in Weybridge, Surrey, the funeral procession watched by a mix of French expats and bemused English countryfolk. Dumas describes the scene in his book about Louis-Philippe, and is so shocked by the obituaries in the English papers that he quotes them at length.

The *Morning Chronicle*'s obit writer trumpets: 'We can't say that a great and good man has just expired. He won his crown by duplicity and held it by oppression.' *The Times* talks of the King's 'absence of mental faculties'. The *Daily News* says that 'in the 18 years of his reign, not one great or generous idea emerged'. And, true to form, the *Sun* jeers: 'Old Pear Head falls out of his tree.' No, it didn't really say that – the paper wouldn't go tabloid for another 100-odd years – but it criticized the King for trying to suppress the Republic that he saw emerging, and said that he had finally got his 'just punishment'.

And poor old Louis-Philippe thought that the Brits liked him. If the lead piping hadn't killed him, the obituaries would have.

Napoleon III: any Southport in a storm

Napoleon III (original name Charles-Louis-Napoléon Bonaparte) was the son of the first Napoleon's brother Louis and the famous Josephine's daughter from her first marriage, Hortense. The Bonapartes believed in keeping it in the family.

After 1815, Hortense took little Charles-Louis-Napoléon into exile in Switzerland, leaving her husband behind in France. Hortense had followed in Josephine's footsteps and got herself a reputation as something of a *femme fatale*, and her husband wasn't sure that he was the father of any of their children.

By 1836, the Bonaparte genes (if there were any) had come to the fore, and the 28-year-old Charles-Louis, etc. returned to France and tried to stage a coup. His plan was to enter France in Strasbourg, get the garrison on his side and then do what Uncle Boney had done after his exile on Elba and march on Paris, gathering support as he went. In the event, though, no one was interested, and King Louis-Philippe had the young rebel put on a ship and sent to America.

But he wasn't giving up yet. He returned to Europe and tried exactly the same trick again in 1840, sailing from England to Boulogne, trying to convince the local troops to support him, and getting arrested yet again.

This time Louis-Philippe was less indulgent, and had

Charles-Louis, etc., who was now calling himself Prince Louis Napoleon, imprisoned in a fortress called Ham, in the Somme, which had once played host to the Marquis de Sade. Here, the prisoner enjoyed himself in a Sade-like way, fathering two children with the fortress's laundry-woman before eventually deciding to escape. In 1846, he switched clothes with a guard and fled to Southport* in Lancashire.

Southport proved to be an inspiration to the exiled wannabe emperor. At the time, it was a chic seaside resort, visited by the grandees of Lancashire industry, and the self-appointed Prince Louis Napoleon lived on a wide, tree-lined boulevard called Lord Street. It has been suggested that Lord Street inspired the future Napoleon III to redesign the centre of Paris when he became emperor, and that the capital of France should really be known as 'the Southport of the South'. There are even those who say that when Prince Louis Napoleon returned to Paris, he thought to himself: Let's build Southport here, only bigger.

But we are getting ahead of ourselves. It wasn't until 1848, after the turmoil of the Revolution had cleared up, that Louis Napoleon headed back to France to stand for election as the President of the Second Republic. To everyone's surprise, he won by a landslide. Not content with this, he staged yet another *coup d'état*, from the inside this time, and became a dictator in 1851. It was only one typically Bonapartist step from this to declaring himself Emperor Napoleon III the following year.

At this point, the French decided to enjoy a period of relative peace and spectacular growth. Instead of arguing

---

* The reader will note the complete absence of jokes about exile in Southport being worse than imprisonment in a fortress in the Somme.

amongst themselves and changing their system of government for the umpteenth time in sixty years, they kicked back and prospered. The industrial revolution finally set up shop in France, railways spread like vines across the country, new mines positively spurted out coal, share prices rocketed, and Napoleon III had Paris's slums knocked down and the Southport-style Haussmann boulevards built. (Though this was also a means of creating wide access routes for troops should another Parisian mob try to take power. And it is also much harder to barricade a boulevard than a medieval lane.)

Napoleon III believed in free trade, and sent French products all over the world. It was a French company that brought his uncle's Egyptian plans to fruition by building the Suez Canal. The new Emperor even took the air of change to its extreme and formed an alliance with the enemy, Britain, in the Crimean War – the only friction here being that the French thought the heroic Charge of the Light Brigade an absurd waste of men and horses. (Which it was.)

The Brits spoilt the new friendship, however, by trying to have Napoleon killed in 1858. It wasn't a government plot, of course, just a bit of typically English private enterprise.

Britain finishes off an Italian job

One of Napoleon III's grand plans was to take over Italy (another idea borrowed from his uncle), which didn't go down too well with a group of Italian nationalists exiled in London. They got a Birmingham engineer to make them some fragmentation grenades, which were tested by their English allies and then taken to Paris. On 14 January 1858, three Italians, led by a man called Felice Orsini, whose father had served with the first Napoleon's army in Russia, sent their English grenades into action.

As Napoleon III and his wife Eugénie were on their way to the opera in Paris, the Italians hurled the bombs. They didn't aim too well (maybe they should have got some training from English cricketers in the art of throwing), and managed only to blow up some horses and kill eight passers-by. As with Louis-Philippe's carriage attack, the intended victims were unharmed, and increased their popularity by carrying on as if nothing had happened. Napoleon and Eugénie took up their seats at the opera and watched *William Tell*, no doubt flinching during the arrow-firing scene.

During Orsini's subsequent trial,* the plot's English connection came to light and caused a major diplomatic flurry, with the British government eventually having to resign after it became impossible to appease both the French (who were, strictly speaking, allies) and the Francophobe Brits. It was Napoleon III himself who defused the crisis, inviting Victoria and Albert to a party to celebrate the opening of a naval base in Cherbourg.

So it was all *ami-ami* again, and Britain had to wait another dozen years before it got its chance to kill a French emperor – until 1870, in fact, when Napoleon III's plans for continental expansion finally got the better of him. Trying to emulate his uncle again, Napoleon III attacked the Prussians, only to lose the Battle of Sedan to Otto von Bismarck and end up as a prisoner of war. This stirred up bad memories of Waterloo, and Napoleon III was deposed. After a short bout of imprisonment, he headed for England to join Eugénie and their teenage

* Orsini and one of his fellow conspirators were guillotined, and an accomplice called Carlo di Rudio was transported to Devil's Island, the notorious French prison camp in French Guiana. He escaped and later fought alongside General Custer at Little Big Horn. True to form, he survived.

son, Napoléon-Eugène-Louis-Jean-Joseph, who had already sought refuge *chez* Victoria.

The deposed Emperor and his family took up residence at a house called Camden Place in Chislehurst, Kent, which had been given a French flavour by its English owner – he had imported French furniture, installed wooden panelling salvaged from a French chateau and bought the wrought iron gates from the entrance to the 1867 Exposition universelle in Paris. The rent was a comparatively modest £300 a year, but Napoleon didn't plan on staying for ever. He was already plotting his return to power.

It was a British doctor who put a stop to that.

Ever since the mid-1850s, Napoleon III had been plagued by stomach ailments, which ran in the Bonaparte family. He had suffered from painful prostate and bladder infections, kidney problems and bladder stones, and had once called in a London specialist called Dr Robert Ferguson to treat him in Paris. Ferguson had betrayed the Hippocratic Oath (which presumably didn't apply to foreigners back then) and gleefully reported to the British government that the Emperor was suffering from nervous exhaustion that had a 'debilitating effect upon sexual performance'.

Now, in 1873, the deposed Napoleon III was suffering from bladder stones, and was again at the mercy of English doctors. The eminent surgeon Henry Thompson, a specialist in sexual diseases and author of a fun-sounding treatise on the *Health and Morbid Anatomy of the Prostate Gland*, was summoned to Chislehurst. He had already performed a successful kidney stone operation on Leopold of Belgium, Queen Victoria's uncle, using lithotripsy, a method of disintegrating the stone with acoustic shockwaves. This is a non-invasive process, but can be very painful because the sound waves cause bones to vibrate, so Thompson decided to knock the Emperor out with chloroform and perform the operation in two stages on 2 and 6 January. At first, everything went swimmingly, but Napoleon died during the second operation, and Thompson and his anaesthetist Dr Joseph Clover (a pioneer in his field) quickly signed the death certificate giving kidney failure as the cause of death.

Whether this diagnosis was true or whether, as some allege, Thompson bungled the operation, the fact is that the last Emperor of France, the nephew of the great Napoleon Bonaparte, died at the hands of the British medical profession in 1873 and was buried in Chislehurst.

But wait – there was a successor, his son, the dashing young Louis Napoleon. Perhaps France would have another Emperor after all?

Well no, actually, because the Brits were about to nail him too, in even more farcical circumstances.

Napoleon the Third-and-a-Half

Napoléon Eugène Louis Jean Joseph (Louis to his friends) had seen military action when he was only fourteen. He had ridden with his father against the Prussians at Saarbrücken in Germany, and only fled to England when the tide of war turned against the French.

So, after a brief spell studying physics at King's College London, the young man applied for a place at the Royal Military Academy at Woolwich. He had big ambitions for the future – there were rumours of an engagement to Victoria's daughter Beatrice, and he hoped that his country would one day call on him to lead them out of their political confusion.

However, being invited to rule France as Napoleon IV didn't look like an imminent prospect. On his father's death, the French Republicans dubbed him Napoléon

Emperor Napoleon III with his son, whom the French later nicknamed Napoleon the Third-and-a-Half. Both were to suffer bizarre
deaths while in exile *chez* the Brits.

Trois et Demi (three and a half). He therefore opted for a spell in the British army, which would pass the time and might also prepare him to lead a military power struggle in France.

A Frenchman in a British military school – he must have felt like his great-uncle, the Corsican amongst the French mainland aristocrats. Young Louis was good at horseriding and fencing, but was no academic, and was even beaten in the French exam by an English cadet. He graduated, though, and was sent to join the Royal Artillery, yet another homage to his great-uncle the cannon expert.

In 1879, Britain declared war on the Zulu nation, which was impolitely demanding that the colonials give back its homeland in South Africa, and the young 'Prince Impérial', as Louis styled himself, decided that this was a playground where he would be able to prove his worth as a soldier and a man.

Britain's Prime Minister, Benjamin Disraeli, was horrified at the political ramifications of sending a French emperor-in-waiting to fight a British war, and refused permission. But Louis's mother Eugénie begged Queen Victoria to let the boy go and have some fun, and finally Disraeli agreed to have the Frenchman sent out as an observer. He would be allowed to wear an artillery-man's uniform, but must display no insignia or any sign of rank, to avoid attracting any dangerous attention.

The French were furious: the Republicans because a Frenchman was serving in the army of the traditional enemy, and the Imperialists because they suspected that a war in Africa might be a dangerous place for their Last Hope to be dashing around. Louis himself told his partisans not to worry – a quick and highly publicized military outing would have France clamouring for his return.

Louis arrived in South Africa in May 1879, and spent the next couple of weeks hassling commanders to let him see action and chasing any Zulu he saw, despite orders not to expose himself to risk.

Finally, the British commander in South Africa, Baron Chelmsford, allowed Louis to accompany him into Zululand, but assigned him to help the Royal Engineers rather than putting him into a battle unit. The orders were not to let the Prince near any fighting, and that he should not go anywhere without a strong armed escort.

Strange, then, that the man in charge of the Royal Engineers, Colonel Richard Harrison, let Louis go out on a scouting mission with a certain Lieutenant Carey, a vicar's son who had been educated in France. Carey would regret accepting the tagalong Frenchman for the rest of his short life.

Louis was delighted. At last, he was going to see action. On 1 June, impatient to leave, he badgered Carey into going out without the full escort. In a party of only nine men, they rode along the ominously named Blood River, the proud Prince sporting his great-uncle Napoleon's sword. The valley was thought to be free of Zulus, which may explain why the small group of soldiers rode several miles out into the bush, where Louis spotted a deserted kraal, a Zulu settlement, and suggested that they go and brew up coffee there.

There were signs of very recent occupation, and the grass around the kraal was so high that it was impossible to see if anyone was lurking nearby. But Louis insisted that the troops rest up and have a coffee.

Finally Carey became really anxious and ordered the party to leave. Louis pulled rank on him (although technically Carey was the superior officer) and told him to give it ten minutes more. The extra time was almost up when they were stormed by forty armed Zulus, charging out of the long grass and yelling 'uSuthu!' which meant 'kill!' rather than 'forty espressos, please'.

Spooked by gunfire, the British horses bolted. Louis managed to cling on to his saddle holster and was pulled along by his mount until the leather strap broke. Shoddy English workmanship, he no doubt thought as he hit the ground and injured his right arm.

He looked for his sword, but couldn't find it. So, firing his revolver with his left hand, he ran as best he could until he was hit in the thigh by a Zulu spear. He bravely pulled it out and turned to face his pursuers, but another assegai caught him in the shoulder, and he went down fighting.

Carey and four surviving soldiers had got on their horses, and met up about 50 metres away. However, instead of returning to try and save the Prince, Carey rode back to base camp without firing a shot.

When a search party came out, they found Louis's body with eighteen assegai wounds. It had also been disembowelled, a Zulu practice meant to guarantee not only that the injured man was actually dead, but also that his spirit would not return and avenge the death (an unwitting and ironic reminder of Napoleon Bonaparte's belief that an army marched on its stomach).

Carey made his report about Louis pulling rank and refusing to leave the kraal, but the man he was meant to protect was too important. All the fingers of blame were pointed at Carey, especially those of Eugénie and Victoria. There were even rumours that Victoria herself had planned the whole thing to prevent the Frenchman's marriage to her daughter. To make things worse, the Zulus said that if young Louis had been wearing royal regalia, they wouldn't have killed him. Inevitably, a court martial found Carey guilty of 'having misbehaved before the enemy.' A scapegoat had been found and sacrificed. However, a couple of months later, the conviction was quietly overturned, mainly on the grounds that the British army held the Frenchman largely responsible for leading the patrol out into such dangerous territory. Once the fuss was over, Carey was allowed to return to service.

Meanwhile, the Brits shipped Louis's badly embalmed remains back to England, where French officials unwisely insisted on opening the casket to formally identify the body. One of them fainted at the sight of the putrefying, mutilated corpse, which was only identifiable thanks to a childhood abcess scar on his hip.

Louis was given a state funeral, which was attended by Queen Victoria but boycotted by the French ambassador. The young Prince's mother Eugénie was there, but was so grief-stricken that she had to be informed when the service was over and it was time to get up off her knees. After the ceremony, the coffin was taken to Chislehurst, to lie alongside the body of Emperor Napoleon III.

Louis had a theoretical successor, his cousin Victor Jérôme Frédéric Napoléon Bonaparte, who declared himself Napoleon V and later returned to France to demand a plebiscite on restoring imperial rule. All he achieved, though, was to get himself arrested, proving that the dashing young soldier Louis Napoleon had been his family's last realistic chance of regaining power in France.

And so it was that the hopes and dreams of both the Bourbon and Bonaparte dynasties were buried in southeast England. France's royal and imperial families had come looking for asylum in Britain and had ended up receiving little more than a fancy funeral. It was nothing personal, of course. A bit of lead piping, a medical mishap and an encounter with over-zealous Zulus – it could happen to anyone.

And the fact that it was the Brits, so fond of their own royal family, who ensured that France would be a Republic for the foreseeable future, was an unfortunate accident, a complete coincidence. *N'est-ce pas?*

23

Why All French Wine Comes from America

In the 1860s, an epidemic came very close to killing off all the vines in France. Winemakers in the most famous grape-growing areas of the country could only stand helplessly by as their plants withered and died. A mystery disease was eating at the very root of the French wine industry, and the extinction of Chablis, Champagne and Chateau Margaux was a real possibility (along with Beaujolais, Bordeaux and Burgundy, St Émilion, Sauterne and Sauvignon, and all the other letters of the alphabet, of course). Only a miracle could save them.

And that miracle, when it came, was American. Which would subsequently prove to be rather ironic . . .

Horrifying green acne

The first ominous signs that something was up were spotted in 1863, in a village called Pujaut, on the left bank of the Rhone Valley near Nîmes. A few plants in one of its vineyards seemed to have sprouted a horrifying case of acne – the smooth green leaves were a mass of little buboes. Soon they yellowed, dried up and fell. Weirdly,

'The Phylloxera, a true gourmet, finds out the best vineyards and attaches itself to the best wines.' A not-at-all French view of the deadly phylloxera aphid that bugged, and almost bankrupted, the country's winegrowers in the second half of the nineteenth century.

the spots then cleared up and the plant produced grapes, but the following year the vine produced less fruit, and the wine was acid and had no bouquet. By the next season, the plant had shrivelled and when it was pulled up, its roots were black, as if the disease had exhausted it. Worse, it had infected the surrounding plants, which suffered exactly the same three-year death rattle.

Soon reports came in of similar shrivellings in the nearby villages of Roquemaure and Villeneuve-lès-Avignon, and in 1866 a second outbreak was diagnosed near Bordeaux. As the plague spread out in concentric rings across France, panic set in. No one knew what was causing the epidemic. Farmers thought it was a kind of vine tuberculosis, even though plants don't have lungs. It wasn't until 1868 that three French scientists at Montpellier University finally found the cause.

The team was headed by the director of the Botany department, Jules-Émile Planchon, a local man who had worked at the Royal Botanical Gardens at Kew in London, one of the world's leading centres for the study of plants. Planchon dug up dead and dying vines and found that the roots of the sick plants were infested with a tiny yellow aphid, almost invisible to the naked eye. He recognized it as a deadly new mutation of an existing pest and, a man with a sense of occasion, gave the bug a name that sounds like a baddie in the *Astérix* comics: *Phylloxera vastatrix* (meaning more or less 'devastating dry leaves').

The aphids were quite attractive, if you like that sort of thing. They were a very pleasant colour, a sort of pale saffron yellow that looks great in a Van Gogh painting, but, crawling over every root in your vineyard, was the stuff of nightmare. The bugs' life cycle, Planchon discovered, was a model of destructive efficiency. The female laid her eggs beneath the surface of the leaf in summer (hence the buboes); on hatching, the insects would make their way to the stem of the vine, where the female hatch-lings sneakily laid a second generation of eggs – up to 600 each – that gestated throughout the winter; the following spring, a mass of wingless yellow aphids were born and stampeded down to the root, which they demolished like English tourists at a drink-all-you-can beach bar. At which point, the host plant went to meet its maker, and the overfed little insects staggered off to find their next victim. And the tragic thing was that the females were capable of laying eggs through asexual reproduction – there wasn't even any pleasure involved. It really was a soulless, evil plague.

The question was, how to stop it, especially as the bugs were marching across Europe as efficiently as one of Napoleon's armies. Within twelve years, they had popped up in every major wine-producing country in Europe. They even made an appearance in Australia (having got there on imported vines rather than by burrowing through the planet from Europe). But the hardest-hit country was France – between 1875 and 1889, its wine production fell from 8.4 billion litres to only 2.3 billion and around 40 per cent of French vines were dead.

Yes, more than twenty-five years after its symptoms were first noticed, the disease was still spreading, and the only solution seemed to be to destroy practically all the surviving vineyards in the country.

The Americans liberate France

Some French growers and scientists wanted to use cure rather than prevention – either spraying with noxious insecticides or temporarily flooding the vineyards (it had been found that the bugs were not very fond of water). But curing infected plants, argued Planchon, was a waste of time. What was needed was a kind of vaccine.

And this was where the Americans came in.

As early as the 1870s, an entomologist called Charles Valentine Riley, a Londoner living in Missouri, had found that phylloxera bugs were present in USA (where they had been given a more English name, the grape louse), but did not seem to cause damage to vineyards. For some reason, the American plants were resistant to the bugs.

Riley began sending American rootstocks to Planchon, who agreed that these plants were indeed immune. Why not replant all France's vineyards with American grapes, he wondered? The answer, of course, was obvious: the French were sure that their native vines produced superior wine. But two Bordeaux winegrowers called Léo Laliman and Gaston Bazille had a solution to this quandary, too. At their suggestion, Planchon began grafting branches of the French plants on to American roots, and soon confirmed that the resulting plants were also resistant.

The discovery split the French wine industry down the middle between the sprayers and the grafters, with anti-Americans derisively calling the supporters of Planchon's method 'wood merchants'.

As the argument dragged on, French winegrowers were going out of business en masse – many emigrated to America and North Africa – and merchants were importing wines from abroad. Even if the grafting worked, it looked as though it might be too late to save the industry.

A typically French scandal held things up even further. The government had offered a prize of 320,000 francs to the first person to find a cure for phylloxera. The Bordeaux winegrower Laliman claimed it, even though he had been working alongside Planchon and Bazille. This in itself might seem dubious, but worse was to come – Laliman was turned down because of accusations that he had been the man to import the infected vines in the first place.

Almost miraculously, given the arguments that were raging, grafting and replanting slowly began to have an effect. About 2,500 hectares of new vines were planted in 1880, rising to 45,000 hectares in 1885. Soon a Franco-American army of liberation was marching across the country.

It is said (probably by Americans) that if their vines hadn't been parachuted in, the yellow aphids would have wiped out almost the whole European wine industry. Because of its isolation, Cyprus was untouched, but pretty well every other country would have lost its vineyards. The only European grape that is immune to attack by phylloxera is the Assyrtiko, which is native to the Greek island of Santorini.

In any case, the day was saved thanks to some solid botany, creative thinking, a Darwinian belief in the survival of the fittest – Charles Darwin's *On the Origin of Species* had been published in 1859 – and the hardy American plants. A big transatlantic *merci* was in order.

Or was it? Because some people were also saying that the Americans, with a little help from Darwinism, had helped to cause the phylloxera outbreak in the first place.

Ever since the end of the 1850s, French winemakers (including, it was alleged, the Bordeaux grower Léo Laliman) had been experimenting with ways of boosting production by improving upon Nature. They had been planting foreign vines in their vineyards, including root-stocks from the USA. And judging by the way Laliman came forward with the grafting theory, he was probably experimenting with grafting on his own farm.

Everyone now agrees that the pest was originally shipped over from the New World in one or more of these batches of vines ordered from an American plant catalogue. Of course it was an unfortunate accident, but infecting a country with a deadly plant disease and then selling them the cure is exactly the kind of sharp business practice that makes the French suspicious of the Anglo-Saxons to this day.

Wherever the fault lies, though, one thing is for sure – if a French winegrower holds up a glass of Bandol, Bordeaux, Burgundy or one of the enormous numbers of wines belonging to B or any other letter of the alphabet, and claims that it is superior to anything that the New World could ever produce, there is an all-too-simple response.

That French wine *is*, in part at least, a product of the New World.

24

Edward VII Has a Frolicking Good Time in Paris

Dirty Bertie and the Entente Cordiale

British and French monarchs have been visiting each other's countries ever since William the Conqueror started the fashion for regular cross-Channel tourism. Some of them, like Henry II and Edward III, travelled abroad to patrol their own possessions and pillage those of others, like Charles II and Louis XVIII, to escape political troubles back home, and a few to get killed in bizarre mishaps – Napoleon III and Richard the Lionheart spring to mind.

Modern monarchs go on diplomatic state visits, but probably the only royal who travelled purely for pleasure was Edward VII. He was a man who understood just how pleasant it was *not* to be at war with France.

Albert Edward, Prince of Wales, eldest son of Queen Victoria, 'Bertie' to his friends and lovers, made France his adventure playground in the last decades of the nineteenth century. When he wasn't playing musical bedrooms in English country houses, he was 'gadding about' (as his mother put it) in Paris and Cannes, flitting from the racecourse to the Folies Bergère and his favourite *bordels*. He was such a regular reveller that he had his very own room in one of Paris's poshest brothels equipped with custom-designed erotic furniture – but more of that in a moment.

Even when tensions between France and Britain arose, Bertie made sure that politics didn't stand in the way of pleasure. He got on equally well with French Royalists and Republicans, who were all his *amis* as long as they didn't try to tell him that Britain should have a revolution or a French-style monarchy. Republicans who resented the presence in their country of such a high-profile royal melted as soon as they came to lunch at his hotel, which in turn infuriated the Royalists, who thought that he should be helping them reinstate their deposed monarchy.

But Bertie just wanted everyone to be friends so that he could get on with having fun. It could even be argued that his sexual exploits forced France kicking and screaming into talks about the Entente Cordiale, the agreement that buried the ancient hatchet of Anglo-French warfare once and for all in 1904.

In short, never in the field of human conflict was so much owed by so many to one man's libido.

Paris, a most un-Victorian city

Bertie first fell in love with France when he was thirteen. He came to Paris on a royal visit to the court of Napoleon III and realized that palaces didn't have to be as dull as his parents' house. Queen Victoria and Prince Albert believed in making princes learn boring stuff like Latin and history rather than just letting them be princes. They wanted him to be a Victorian, with all the moral constraints which that entailed.

In Paris, though, Bertie danced while chic ladies teased him about what he was hiding under the kilt that his parents made him wear. The Empress Eugénie was a glamorous fashion icon who took Bertie under her wing and no doubt caused un-Victorian stirrings behind his sporran. Napoleon III, a bit of a lad, talked to him man to man, and the young Prince must have realized that here was a city where you made up your own morals day to day. After all, in French *avoir le moral* means to feel good, so in France good morals must mean anything that makes you happy, *n'est-ce pas*?

Bertie had to wait a few more years until he got the chance to enjoy France to the full. First, his parents wanted to finish his education. They sent him to Oxford and made him go to highbrow London plays. But he wasn't cut out for the intellectual things in life, and once shocked theatergoers by asking loudly, 'Can anyone tell me what this damned play is about?'

By the 1860s, though, he considered that his formal education was over and more informal proceedings could begin. He started coming to Paris on annual pleasure sprees, often accompanied only by an equerry. And even if wifey came along (in 1863 he had married Alexandra, the daughter of the Prince of Denmark), she liked to go to bed early, so as soon as he'd seen her back to the hotel, Bertie could go out on the town for some extra-marital R&R.

He went to the Folies Bergère (here at last was a stage show that he understood perfectly), toasted the dancers with Champagne, and even found that the freedom of being in Paris cured his speech impediment. Back home, he had trouble saying his Rs. Here, though, they rolled off his tongue as easily as the witty remarks that made all the ladies giggle.

At the theatre, any danger that the play might be too

intellectual was overridden by the pleasure of gazing at the gorgeous actress Sarah Bernhardt. And he once got even closer to her by wangling himself a bit part as a corpse, and lying on stage while 'la divine Sarah' wept over her dead prince.

After the theatre, he would go on to dinner at the Café Anglais, where the notorious English call girl Cora Pearl was once served up, naked and smothered in cream, as a dessert. (And the French say English cuisine is boring.)

Not that Bertie did all this on the sly. He usually rampaged around Paris with a gang of friends from the Paris Jockey Club, and he loved everyone to know that he was the Prince of Wales. The ladies were much more attentive as soon as they heard his name, and were sometimes willing to entertain him two at a time.

It wasn't long before rumours about these princely perversions seeped back to London, where the scandal sheets were all too happy to repeat the juicy details of his exploits. In 1868, a cartoon appeared depicting the Prince abandoning Britannia for a French harlot. And one newspaper story had him showing serious disrespect for his rank. He was just about to go out, it was said, when he got news that a distant royal relative had died. His friends asked what he thought they should do. 'Put on black studs and go to the play,' the Prince replied. Queen Victoria was probably not amused.

Bertie invites the Republic to lunch

In 1870, Bertie was seriously afraid that the fun might come to an end. The Franco-Prussian War had broken out, and Victoria's family was German. Would the French suspect Britain of being secretly pro-Prussian? And, even more importantly, would patriotic French can-can dancers refuse to flash their stockings at him?

It was time, Bertie told his mother, for a diplomatic visit to Paris to smooth things over between the two nations. Victoria wasn't fooled – she seemed to spend her whole life begging him to stay at home and improve his mind – but the politicians thought it was a good idea. So off he went again, getting up to all his usual tricks and showing the French that the Brits still loved them (preferably in threesomes).

He also did the political rounds, appeasing and annoying everyone in Paris by allowing French Royalists to toast him with Champagne but refusing to utter an anti-republican word. 'These Republicans may have hot heads,' he lectured a *duc*, 'but they have generous hearts.'

Sure enough, Anglo-French relations survived intact, and Bertie was invited by a newly elected Republican government to help organize the Paris Exposition universelle of 1878. He accepted of course, and contributed his personal collection of Indian treasures for the British pavilion. He was so determined to make the trip that he agreed to send the collection even after insurers refused to cover him. When the exhibition opened, a few Republican deputies tried to provoke the Prince by chanting 'Vive la République!' but he simply laughed. He wasn't going to let politics spoil a launch party.

Meanwhile, another diplomatic crisis had flared up. The Turks had ceded the island of Cyprus to Britain, and the French were enraged, because this gave the detested Royal Navy yet another stronghold in the Mediterranean and threatened to destabilize the fragile balance of power in the region.

No worries. Bertie simply invited France's most influential (and most Republican) politician, Léon Gambetta, to lunch.

Wanting to keep the meeting secret, the Prince sent a carriage to fetch Gambetta. At first, conversation was stilted and general. Bertie was shocked by the petit bourgeois politician's appearance. Gambetta wore vulgar patent-leather boots and an ill-fitting frock coat, and his table manners were awful. Gambetta in turn was expecting a scornful snob, a French-style *aristo* with an English accent.

The Prince's opening conversational gambit seemed to confirm his prejudices – Bertie asked why France didn't let its aristocrats take an active part in the country's life. 'They don't want employment,' Gambetta replied, 'they just want to sulk. That is their occupation.' The Prince then suggested that the French do things the British way, which was to give industrialists and scientists a peerage and liven up the aristocracy. It wouldn't work, Gambetta said, because a hereditary French baron wouldn't talk to a *duc de l'industrie*. The Prince sportingly conceded the point and said that now he understood French Republicanism.

The astonished Gambetta said later that he had had an excellent lunch, and that the Prince had even shown 'Republican bonhomie'. In short, thanks to Bertie, it was infuriatingly difficult to be angry at the British over the Mediterranean or anything else. At the end of the meeting, Gambetta grudgingly conceded that there was nothing France could do about Cyprus, anyway. Bertie had seduced the leading French Republican just as efficiently as he did the Parisian *dames*.

A throne with a difference

There was a reason why the Prince was in such a permanent good mood. Hard to believe, perhaps, but in 1878 Paris had become even more hedonistic. A new attraction had opened its doors in the city's theatre district, and made Bertie's wildest dreams come true.

King Edward VII believed that the *entente* with French ladies should be much more than *cordiale*. Here he indulges in a bit of conjugation with the girls from his favourite Parisian brothel, Le Chabanais.

Le Chabanais was a luxury brothel financed by some of France's richest businessmen and run by an Irish madam. Behind its prim street door was a hidden world of orgasmic delight. The girls were all very high-class, chosen to look like famous actresses of the day, and the clients were selected just as rigorously. Men didn't just come to get laid, they came to drink Champagne, be flattered and fawned over by semi-naked beauties, have their witticisms laughed at, and then drift upstairs with their 'conquests' to one of the plushly decorated bedrooms.

It was all legal, too, thanks to Napoleon Bonaparte, who had created the *maisons de tolérance* in the early 1800s. His law stipulated that the working girls had to undergo regular medical examinations, which made prostitution not only legal but safe. There was no danger that syphilis or another sexually transmitted disease might give the game away to wifey – or was there? Doctors were often corrupt, and infection was only diagnosed if a madam wanted to get rid of someone. And behind the luxury of the reception rooms, Le Chabanais didn't even have showers for its live-in girls.

The clients didn't see the sordid side, of course, and for Bertie it was love at first sight. He reserved a private room and chose the décor himself. He wanted a copper bathtub that he would fill with Champagne, and he designed his famous 'fellatio seat', on which two or three people – including one portly Englishman – could have simultaneous oral sex.

The two-tier velvet and gold lacquer chair was a miracle of ingenuity. Victoria might even have been proud of her son for showing such dedication to the science of sex. The top 'floor' of the seat consisted of a stool with handgrips and stirrups, so that Person One could sit there with their legs splayed. Below this were footrests that allowed Person Two to stand or squat in front of the occupant of the top floor. At ground level was a long divan where Person Three could lie down with their face just under the genital region of Person Two. It must have taken some long, Champagne-soaked evenings to design it, and even more to get the positions just right.

Interestingly, the love seat later contributed almost as much to international relations as Bertie did when he was alive. During the Second World War, when the high-class Paris *bordels* were reserved for Nazi officers, the occupying troops decided not to remove the Prince's coat of arms from the chair 'because he had a German mother'.

But back to 1878. Bertie returned to London, no doubt with a huge smile on his face, and reported his success with Gambetta. The Foreign Office was duly grateful and enquired whether the Prince would be willing to take on this diplomatic role on a more permanent basis. He was being offered his dream job.

Bertie's international career

Another threat to the Prince's life of lust and luxury came in 1889, when even Bertie realized that it was diplomatically impossible to attend that year's Exposition. It was, after all, being held to commemorate the centenary of the Revolution. Sorry, the reply came, but the Prince of Wales was obliged to refuse the invitation.

However, that didn't stop Bertie the private citizen going.

Back to Paris he came, on a purely unofficial visit you understand, accompanied by his wife and his good friends Lord and Lady Warwick – a nice, calm family trip, then. Well, not really, because Lady Warwick was in fact the Prince's lover, a hot-blooded London socialite called

Daisy Greville.* She was the woman who inspired the song 'Daisy, Daisy', the chorus of which refers to her looking sweet upon the seat of a bicycle made for two. The songwriter had clearly heard about Bertie's furniture designs.

By now, despite his obvious Francophilia, Bertie had begun to annoy a small but important section of the French population – the secret police, who had been told to keep an eye on him in case he was exchanging seditious messages with Royalist women (not that conversation was easy on his fellatio seat). Agents had to follow him about and check up on all his lovers – an arduous task, indeed. So the police were probably relieved when, as well as bringing English lovers to Paris with him, he also developed a taste for travelling American heiresses, who were, after all, citizens of a republic.

Not that the Prince ever confined his attentions to one lucky lady. Montmartre at the turn of the naughty nineties was about as naughty as it would ever get. The coquettish Parisiennes dressed up in swathes of skirts and petticoats, but unlike their Victorian counterparts, the layers of clothing weren't a moral shield. As one of the Prince's biographers put it: 'Dress was a fortification. Each rampart had to be stormed in turn, and the final surrender was all the more valued for the siege that had preceded it.'

Bertie went to war with a vengeance. He had an affair with La Belle Otero, the Spanish star of the Folies Bergère, whose stupendous breasts inspired the twin domes of the Hotel Carlton in Cannes (although it is hard to believe

* When the Prince broke up with Daisy after finding out that he wasn't her only lover, he began a relationship with Alice Keppel, the great-grandmother of Camilla Parker Bowles.

that they were quite that big, grey or pointed). Bertie was also seen around town with Hortense Schneider, a French singer so famous for her aristocratic lovers that she was nicknamed 'le passage des princes'.

He went to the Moulin Rouge to watch the can-can dancer La Goulue ('the Glutton' – because she used to drain men's glasses while she danced). She would hold one leg high in the air, her petticoats practically slapping the audience's faces, revealing the heart sewn on her knickers. Her party trick was to kick the front row's hats off their heads, which shows just how close the men would get to her titillating thighs. She noticed the Prince one night and shouted out, 'Evening, Wales! Are you going to buy me Champagne?' Needless to say he did, even though he was slightly shocked that she called him 'tu'.

As the century wound down, with the Prince getting older and expecting his mother to die or abdicate at any moment, he seemed keener than ever to cross the Channel and enjoy himself.

The exception was 1900. The French were mad at Britain again, this time because of the Boer War. France might be hanging on to its colonies in West Africa, but it didn't want the Union Jack flying over South Africa. For once, Bertie accepted the advice of the Foreign Office, and called off a planned visit to Cannes. It was a precaution that nearly cost him his life.

He and his wife Alexandra had decided to go and visit the in-laws in Denmark, and were changing trains in Brussels when a fifteen-year-old boy called Jean-Baptiste Sipido fired four shots into their carriage at point-blank range. None of the bullets found their target, prompting the Prince to write and tell a friend, 'Fortunately, anarchists are bad shots.' But the incident only served to increase tensions with France, because while the court was deliberating about his age, Sipido escaped from custody and fled to France, where the police refused to arrest him. Next time, Bertie probably thought, I'll go to the Moulin Rouge – it's much safer.

The Entente Cordiale reaches its climax

In 1901, Queen Victoria died, her last word being 'Bertie'. Her dying wish had been that the Prince would keep both his first names as homage to her dear husband Albert, but Bertie decided to call himself simply King Edward. Two names, he said, would be too French.

What with the funeral arrangements and a coronation to organize, the new King didn't get the chance to return to Paris until May 1903. As head of state, it would have been pretty difficult to nip across with his equerry and hole up in Le Chabanais, so this was an official visit with a valid political excuse. France was still unhappy with the Brits over the defeat of the Boers, and suspicious about signs that Britain might be thinking of a rapprochement with Germany – the new King of England and his cousin the Kaiser had been brought closer together over the death of Victoria.

Bertie therefore offered to go to France and 'do some diplomacy'. The Foreign Office was against the idea, as were the Germans, who were very glad to have two major European powers arguing, but the call of Paris was too strong and Bertie got his way, the only concession being that instead of crossing the Channel and arriving in Paris from the north, he would enter the country via Italy (and maybe stop off at the Carlton in Cannes to admire La Belle Otero's architectural breasts).

When Bertie got to Paris, though, things looked ominous. He drove along the Champs-Élysées to shouts of 'Vive les Boers!' The only Brit who got a cheer was an army officer who was mistaken for a Boer because of his khaki uniform. One of the embassy staff remarked that 'the French don't love us'. 'Why should they?' Bertie replied, deciding that this trip required even more charm than usual.

So that night, during a speech at the British Chamber of Commerce, he uttered a sentence that was unheard of for a British monarch:

A Divine Providence has designed that France should be our near neighbour, and, I hope, always our dear friend. There may have been misunderstandings and causes of dissension in the past [a slight understatement] but all such differences are, I believe, happily removed and forgotten, and I trust that the friendship and admiration which we all feel for the French nation and their glorious traditions [here he was probably thinking of the Folies Bergère and Le Chabanais rather than the Revolution and Napoleon] may in the near future develop into a sentiment of the warmest affection and attachment between the peoples of the two countries.

Back in London, the ground beneath Westminster Abbey must have been shaking as Edward III, Henry V, Elizabeth I, William of Orange and a whole host of past monarchs spun in their graves.

Even this smooth talk didn't win Parisians over, however. Rather undiplomatically, Bertie was taken to see a blatantly pro-republican play at the theatre, and, for the first time in his life, had to resist the temptation to applaud the actresses. Worse, he had arranged for La Belle Otero to be there, and the theatre managers had her thrown out. He was being subjected to both political and personal snubs.

Luckily, strolling through the foyer during the interval,

he spotted a French actress he knew (and he knew many). He went up to her and told her that he remembered applauding her performances (ahem) in London, and that she had 'represented all the grace and spirit of France'. He said this in French, of course, and his diplomatic quote was soon doing the rounds of Paris high society.

He kept up the charm offensive next day at the Hôtel de Ville, telling the guests, 'I can assure you that it is with the greatest pleasure that I return to Paris each time, where I am treated exactly as if I were at home.' Which was a lie – neither his mother nor wife ever let him have a fellatio seat in his bedroom.

And finally, thanks to the sheer force of Bertie's bonhomie (and perhaps some moral support from the Parisiennes), the climate began to change. The previous day's Chamber of Commerce speech got a glowing write-up in the French press, and when Bertie left Paris, it was to shouts of 'Vive le roi!' He had single-handedly turned the diplomatic situation around. It was as if all his years of Champagne dinners and *bordel* parties had borne fruit. He had swept aside the political differences like the petticoats of a Montmartre *fille de joie*. He had sweet-talked the French into becoming his lovers, and had them crowded around him on his diplomatic fellatio seat.

On paper, the Entente Cordiale, signed just under a year later on 8 April 1904 by the British Foreign Secretary, Lord Lansdowne, and the French ambassador to Britain, Paul Cambon, was just an agreement not to interfere in each other's colonial mischief in Morocco and Egypt, with a side clause limiting French fishing rights in Canada. And it was an *entente* – an understanding rather than an alliance – that was *cordiale* – polite but by no means *amicale*. It was as if two neighbours had agreed not to throw hedge cuttings on to each other's lawn any more. It didn't mean that they would be inviting each other to barbecues.

But in the minds of the French and British people, it was much more than this – it was a vital breakthrough, a promise of friendlier times to come. And it was all thanks to Edward VII, the King formerly known as Dirty Bertie.

Because, in a nutshell, the Entente Cordiale, the agreement that would shape Anglo-French relations for the next century (at least), was born in a private room in a chic Parisian *bordel*. Surely it's not going too far to say that the Entente was just a political metaphor for the convoluted couplings that used to go on in Bertie's copper bathtub and on his custom-made erotic furniture.

Vive le roi indeed.

25

Marie Curie's Debt to a Jealous Brit

Pierre and Marie Curie are rightly regarded as France's greatest scientists. Admittedly Marie was born in Poland, but she made her discoveries in France and co-wrote most of them with her Parisian husband, in French. Their combined nationality is not in doubt.

The Curies are highly respected in France, as well as being remembered with real affection because of the way they mixed research with romance. The French like to picture the scientific couple sharing radium-lit dinners after a hard day studying radioactivity, and fondly comparing each other's symptoms of radiation poisoning. And like so many great love affairs, theirs ended tragically, when Pierre was run over by a horse-drawn carriage on the Pont Neuf in Paris. For years afterwards, Marie would write tender love letters to her departed husband. They were the Romeo and Juliet of nuclear science.

In 1995, a century after their wedding, the couple received France's greatest honour when their remains (sealed in lead-lined, radiation-proof coffins) were moved into the Panthéon, the national mausoleum in the centre of Paris. Even so, Marie was probably spinning

like a split atom at the inscription above the entrance –
'*Aux grands hommes, la patrie reconnaissante*' ('to great
men, the nation is grateful'). She was the first woman to
be entombed there on her own account – the only other
female occupant was the wife of a scientist who refused
to be separated from his spouse in the afterlife.

In the Curies' case, it could be said that Pierre was the
one accompanying his wife – Marie, after all, won two
Nobel Prizes to his one.

And what is not very well known about this French
success story is that some of the credit for the second
Nobel Prize, won by Marie Curie alone in 1911, should
go to a Brit. Though not for very honourable reasons . . .

A doubting Thomson

The Curies first met in 1894 when Marie applied for a job
as Pierre's lab assistant, but she quickly convinced him
that she had some revolutionary ideas, and they soon
became equals, working together on the study of radioactivity (a new word coined by Marie). By the turn of the
twentieth century, they had identified two new radioactive elements: polonium (which they named after
Marie's homeland) and radium.

Meanwhile they, or more particularly Pierre, had been
receiving support in the form of friendly letters from a
prominent British scientist, Lord Kelvin (original name
William Thomson), best known for his work on identify-
ing absolute zero as a temperature. Irish by birth (at a
time when the whole of Ireland was a British territory),
Kelvin had been ennobled in 1892, largely in recognition
of his public opposition to Irish independence – hence
his choice of a Scottish river as his aristocratic title.

Lord Kelvin is often depicted as a benevolent older-
generation scientist supporting the young Curies, and it

is true that he made a public show of solidarity with them in 1903, when the male scientific establishment was in uproar over the nomination of both Curies for the physics prize. (At first, Marie had been excluded, but Pierre had warned that he could not accept a nomination without her.)

In the spring of that year, the couple were invited to give a lecture in London as guests of the Royal Institution. Or rather, Pierre was invited to speak, as the RI did not allow female lecturers. Marie was relegated to a mere audience member. But while Pierre described their work, paying tribute to Marie for her major role in their discoveries, Kelvin very publicly sat beside her, and hosted a lunch for them both the following day.

However, beneath the genial surface, it seems that Lord Kelvin was bubbling with an almost radioactive fury, because the Curies were disproving one after the other of his fundamental pronouncements on science. He had, for example, said that 'there is nothing new to be discovered in physics now. All that remains is more and more precise measurements'. This was not uncommon belief at the time, although Dmitri Mendeleev, who created the periodic table of elements in 1869, had openly admitted that there were probably many more elements still to be discovered.

Kelvin was less open to progressive ideas. He scoffed, for example, at the idea of radio communications: 'Wireless is all very well, but I'd rather send a message by a boy on a pony.' Although the Curies' work proved that the atom was not the smallest particle of matter, Kelvin maintained that atoms were indestructible. He didn't believe in practical uses of radioactivity, either: 'X-rays will prove to be a hoax.' And he shot the idea of aeroplanes out of the sky: 'I can state flatly that heavier-than-air flying machines are impossible.'

Even worse for Kelvin, the Curies' discovery of radio-activity disproved at a stroke his theory that the Earth could not be more than 20–40 million years old (his estimate of the sun's age).

As the old man entered his twilight years, the glow of radioactivity emanating from the Curies' lab was driving him to distraction. He was not a happy scientist.

While Pierre was alive, Kelvin held back from direct public assaults on the Curies' ideas, but as soon as Marie's husband fell beneath the wheels of that Parisian carriage, the old lord let rip. On 9 August 1906, less than four months after Pierre's accident, he published a letter in *The Times* refuting the discovery of radium. Kelvin claimed that it was merely a mixture of lead and helium atoms, and not a new element at all. Despite the fact that many scientists accepted the Curies' theories, Kelvin's name added weight to his argument, and Marie's reputation seemed to be in real danger of withering faster than an irradiated lab assistant.

The first person to win a second prize

Marie was forced to set her grief to one side and embark on the arduous process of proving beyond any doubt the existence of radium as an element. To do this, she had to isolate it in its metallic state, one stage purer than the radium chloride compound that she and Pierre had discovered earlier. When she finally achieved this after four years of hard labour reducing ore to metal, Marie was again awarded a Nobel Prize, this time for chemistry.

Kelvin had died in 1907, but the award was a post-humous slap in the face for his reactionary ideas, and Marie's acceptance speech delivered the knockout punch. On 11 December 1911, she paid homage to her husband and then launched into a devastating attack on any remaining doubters: radium, she said, 'is a perfectly defined and already well-studied chemical element', meaning that certain people had been senselessly denying the obvious. 'It was of real importance to corroborate this point,' she added, 'as misgivings had been voiced by those to whom the atomic hypothesis of radioactivity was still not evident.' In other words, they (and especially Kelvin) had been too stupid to understand. She also underlined the sheer amount of hard labour that had been necessary to prove her theory beyond all doubt: 'Tons of material have to be treated in order to extract radium from the ore.' In other words, *merci beaucoup*, Lord Kelvin.

It could be argued that Marie Curie owed at least some gratitude to the aged Brit: after all, it was thanks to him that she had gone the extra mile and isolated radium in its purest form. Without Kelvin's goading, she might well have branched out and helped other scientists to identify the new elements that they were working on. Instead, she was forced to undertake the years of toil that earned her a second Nobel Prize and sealed her reputation as the world's most famous female scientist, an inspiration to generations.

In much the same way as the British Egyptologist Thomas Young pushed Jean-François Champollion to complete his translation of hieroglyphs (see Chapter 19), Marie Curie's proof that radium was a new element was a case of a Brit annoying a French person (or one who had adopted French nationality, anyway) for their own good.

And if that weren't enough of an annoyance for Madame Curie, her 'British-inspired' second Nobel Prize infuriated the French press. While the global scientific community was honouring her – and incidentally French science as a whole – France was indulging in a nuclear war of scandal against her.

The reason for the press's fury was that after five years of widowhood, Marie had had an affair with one of her husband's former pupils, Paul Langevin, a gifted scientist in his own right who would later discover sonar. Langevin was married, with four children, and the xenophobic, sexist French press leapt upon the opportunity to brand Marie Curie 'a Polish woman who has come here to destroy a French household'. When she became the first person ever to win two Nobel Prizes just a month after the love-triangle scandal broke, it was a decidedly unwelcome distraction from the French press's hate campaign, and French newspapers ignored the award almost completely.

The French journalists couldn't tolerate the idea of a brilliant female scientist having an affair with her husband's pupil, five years her junior: in short, Marie Curie was being too French even for the French.

26

Britain and France Fight Side by Side for Once

August 1914: it must have been a very strange sensation for the French. An invasion force of British troops was streaming across the Channel, but not (for once) to rape and pillage. And they weren't pointing their guns at Frenchmen. Well, not deliberately, anyway – the British army was actually here to defend France after ten centuries of attacking it at every opportunity.

For the Brits, too, it must have felt very new. They had fought on the same side as the French a few decades earlier in the Crimea, but that was little more than a colonial expedition. This was a mainland European campaign covering all the old battlefields of northern France and Flanders. Once again, soldiers were clashing in the Somme valley, near Crécy and Agincourt, yet this time *les Anglais* were side by side with les Français. It was highly suspect, as if the Duke of Wellington had changed sides in the middle of Waterloo and turned on the Prussians. Many were wondering how long the partnership would last . . .

An Englishman called French

The British government knew that the sight of a hundred thousand or so English-speaking soldiers sailing towards France might shock the locals, so they decided to break them in gently. In August 1914, the first British troops to disembark were Highlanders, reminders of the Auld Alliance and living ambassadors of France's all-time favourite Brit, Mary Queen of Scots. The men in kilts paraded through the streets of Boulogne playing the 'Marseillaise' on their bagpipes. Yes, the welcoming crowds must have thought, this is going to be a pretty surreal war.

The mood of subtle diplomacy was heightened by the nomination of a certain Field Marshal Sir John French to lead the incoming army, the British Expeditionary Force (or BEF). Not only did he have the perfect surname, but he was also a great fan of Napoleon and an avid collector of Napoleonic memorabilia.

The tactic worked (initially, at least) – the French were delirious to see the Brits coming to defend them. One English artillery officer recalled later that when his unit drove inland it was 'flowers all the way' from the cheering crowds. 'The cars,' he said, 'look like carnival carriages. They pelt us with fruit, cigarettes, chocolate, bread.' And when he stopped to buy some driving goggles to keep out the dust, the shopkeeper refused to let him pay. Someone even bought him lunch.

The free lunches didn't last long, though. Very soon, the Brits were no longer flavour of the month. The advancing Germans might not have received as many bouquets as the BEF, but they were making fast progress through Belgium and encroaching on France. The Kaiser's orders were to ignore the French and 'exterminate the treacherous English and walk over Sir John French's contemptible little army'.

In this, they were helped by Sir John himself. Although he no doubt owned some of Napoleon's books, he can't have read any of them, because he was a lousy tactician. His first move was to march his troops to Belgium despite warnings that he would be out on a limb and vulnerable. The Germans duly pushed him back, forcing the BEF to abandon most of the trucks that the French had so recently covered with flowers.

In retreat, the Brits resorted to their old pillaging tactics, emptying orchards, helping themselves to chickens, eggs and milk, and stealing coal or ripping down whole farm buildings for firewood. It was the Hundred Years War all over again.

Worse, the retreat meant that a mood of Anglo-French distrust set in almost immediately. The French were angry at Sir John for apparently giving up the fight, while the British Field Marshal defended himself by saying that he was forced to pull back because sudden, unannounced withdrawals by the French kept leaving his men exposed. In the end, Sir John had to be persuaded by a combined force of French leaders and Britain's Secretary of State for War, Lord Kitchener, not to pack up his army's troubles in their kit bags and march straight back to Boulogne.

And as the two Allies bickered, the Germans came stomping through France. By the beginning of September, just a few weeks into the First World War, they were within 50 kilometres of Paris, with the prospect of a siege sending a shiver down the capital's spine.

Not-so-gay Paree

Only forty-three years earlier, in the autumn and winter of 1870–1, Paris had suffered a four-month siege at the hands of the Prussians. From September to January, Otto von Bismarck's army had camped in the suburbs and bombarded the city. The starving Parisians had ended up eating dogs, cats, rats and all the animals at the zoo – a famous restaurant menu for Christmas 1870, the ninety-ninth day of the siege, featured stuffed donkey's head, antelope terrine, camel roasted *à l'anglaise* and *consommé d'éléphant*. The siege had ended in French defeat and the temporary occupation of Paris by the Prussians, with a victory ceremony in the Château de Versailles – all this within living memory of many of the city's residents in the summer of 1914.

The glittering days (and nights) of Edward VII's gay Paree were at an end. Indeed, the mere prospect of war had snuffed out the city's notorious gaiety before a single shot had been fired, and any initial gung-ho excitement about the declaration of war was suppressed as Paris went into hibernation. Martial law was declared, café terraces were cleared away, the sale of absinthe was banned (the country needed its men sober), and *cafés-concerts* were not allowed to play music. The cabaret dancers hung up their frilly skirts, and trade for Montmartre's *filles de joie* became morbidly slow – most of their younger clients disappeared when the men received their call-up papers. Suddenly the only males on the streets were boys, older men, a few stunned American tourists and the police patrols, as Paris became seized by the fear that German spies might already be inside the city planning for another siege.

When the German army arrived at the river Marne at the beginning of September, the city was on full alert, and one of the first emergency measures was a decision to commandeer all Paris's taxis for use as military transport vehicles. This was an excellent idea, in theory at least – the city had 10,000 taxis, belonging to several different private firms, with enough seats to transport 50,000 men.

In practice, though, there were some major headaches. For a start, 7,000 of the taxis were out of service because their drivers had been called up. The others were being driven by men too old for military service.

When the order was issued on 6 September for all available taxis to gather at Les Invalides, outside Napoleon's tomb, only 350 turned up. It was a disappointing turnout, but these, along with some 250 buses and private cars, were loaded with supplies and sent out of the city towards the front line about 50 kilometres to the northeast. On the way, there were rumblings of mutiny. As the taxis came within hearing of the artillery fire, a few of the drivers got scared and wanted to turn back. An officer had to threaten to disable the vehicle of any man who turned around, leaving his car to be captured by the Germans or destroyed in battle. Others complained about the lack of food, or its quality – the older men were having trouble chewing the hard army bread.

Overall, though, the supply mission was declared a success, and next day began the troop convoy that has gone down in French history as the 'Miracle of the Marne'.

Several hundred more taxis had been requisitioned by now, and they all flowed out of Paris in a long snaking line towards the battle that was raging in the Marne valley. The order was to carry five soldiers per cab – one in front with the driver and four in the back – though many soldiers travelled in luxury, only two or three per vehicle (even today, Parisian taxi drivers hate to carry more than three passengers, and are especially allergic to having someone sit up front with them).

Contrary to popular belief, the troops weren't all picked up in Paris; many of them were based out in the northeastern suburbs, much closer to the fighting. And progress was slow – in convoy, the taxis could only travel at around 25 kph (15 mph), so the drivers took forty-eight hours to ferry 6,000 or so troops out to the front line. This was in fact a tiny contribution to the Battle of the Marne, which eventually involved a million men on either side (half of whom would be wounded or killed). But in Paris, which had been holding its breath in terror, the Taxis de la Marne took on instant legend status. People began saying that these few brave civilians had saved the city, and the taxi drivers were seen as modern embodiments of St Genevieve, the fifth-century nun whose prayers supposedly kept Attila the Hun from attacking Paris in 451 (he went to ravage Orléans instead).

And it is true, as symbols of national unity and resistance, the small army of taxis had a huge impact on French morale. With a little help from 250,000 British troops, the French army and its taxi drivers had halted the German advance. Paris would not be occupied, and the fighters could stay out in the countryside and dig in for a few years of trench warfare.

The French turn beer and wine into water

And dig they certainly did, because by the end of 1914 there was a 700-kilometre line of trenches stretching from the coast of Belgium to the Swiss border, and the First World War as we know it had begun – that is, each time there was to be a major offensive, the Allies or the Germans would open up with artillery, obliterating not only trenches but also any French or Belgian towns and villages nearby. Then soldiers would march forward across what used to be fields and orchards, and litter the ground with their bullets, shrapnel and dead bodies. The survivors would dig in, and the whole pantomime would start over again. France was being defended, but it was also being destroyed.

The stagnation of trench warfare changed French attitudes towards their British guests. They had been happy to shower the Tommies with flowers, chocolate and driving goggles when they thought the Brits were not going to stay any longer than lunch. Even Christmas hadn't seemed too far away. But soon it became obvious that the Tommies were going to be there for much, much longer, along with the Aussies, Kiwis, other colonial troops and, later, the American Doughboys. By the end of the war, there were over two million Allied troops in France, almost all of them billeted *chez l'habitant*.

Even at the beginning of the war when French opinion of the Allies was at its highest, the billeting didn't always go well. The problem was that many of the British regular soldiers had served in the colonies, and treated their French hosts no better than they had the Indians and Africans, to whom they hadn't been exactly respectful. In short, there was a whole class of British soldiers who saw French villagers as little better than primitive savages.

The French reacted with predictable logic – they profiteered. Knowing that they could get bombarded at any moment or forced out of their homes by a German advance, they did whatever they could to survive. Even so, the exploitation infuriated the Tommies and their Allied comrades.

The most vociferous critic of the profiteers was probably the poet and novelist Robert Graves, who wrote a bitter account of his time in the trenches ten years after the war, when he had had plenty of time to let his outrage about the inhumanity of war come to the boil.

In *Goodbye to All That*, he is shocked to learn that the French railways are actually charging British hospital trains £200 a day to use their rails. He also savages the

French civilians around the town of Béthune where he was based: 'The peasants did not much care whether they were on the German or the British side of the line ... They just had no use for foreign soldiers and were not at all interested in the sacrifices that we might be making for their dirty little lives.'*

He fumes at the way these French civilians exploited the 100,000 men billeted around Béthune in 1916, saying that as soon as a soldier gets his pay 'he spends it immediately on eggs, coffee and beer in the local *estaminets*; the prices are ridiculous and the stuff bad. In the brewery at Béthune, I saw barrels of already thin beer being watered from the canal with a hose-pipe. The *estaminet*-keepers water it further.' He even says that after the war, French peasants made claims for damages for property they had never had.

One soldier who took the profiteering more lightly was an American called Arthur Guy Empey, who joined up in 1915 to serve in France alongside British Tommies. In his book *Over the Top*, he gives a wry glossary of vocabulary used by the troops:

> *Allumettes*: French term for what they sell to Tommy as matches, the sulphurous fumes from which have been known to gas a whole platoon ... *Estaminet*: A French public house or saloon, where muddy water is sold as beer ... *Vin Rouge*: French wine made from vinegar and red ink. Tommy pays good money for it ... *Vin Blanc*: French wine made from vinegar. They forgot the red ink.

A French writer, André Maurois, confirms these impressions in his book *Les Silences du Colonel Bramble*.

---

* Graves was up in arms about the whole war, and was equally damning about British civilians and their misplaced patriotism.

The hero, Aurelle, like Maurois himself, is a Frenchman assigned to liaise with the Brits, and in one scene his regiment arrives in a French village. All the shops have been turned into Tommy traps. The haberdasher has thrown all her buttons and cottons in the back room and 'like everyone in the village, she was now selling Quaker Oats, Woodbine cigarettes and embroidered postcards saying "from your soldier boy"'. Aurelle tells a villager to protect his savings, if he has any, by putting them into government bonds. 'I've already got 50,000 francs' worth,' the man informs him. Everyone in Maurois's book is getting rich except for the troops whose priority was much more basic – to stay alive.

And amongst the richest of all were the mesdemoiselles.

Voulez-vous coucher avec moi?

There were some forms of profiteering that the soldiers didn't mind at all.

When the first wave of British troops arrived in Boulogne, they were carrying a letter from the Secretary of State for War, Lord Kitchener, telling them to 'be brave, be kind, be courteous (but nothing more than courteous) to women'. Kitchener was of Edward VII's generation and knew all about French mesdemoiselles. He was also the soldier who had been in overall charge of the British army that fought the Boer War, and knew what discourtesies his troops were capable of when they occupied a country (mainly because he'd ordered them to do it).

But the Tommies were also getting more concrete advice on how to deal with French women. A wartime report by France's Conseil national des femmes françaises (National Council of Frenchwomen) denounces a British booklet called *Five Minutes'*

Conversation with Young Ladies, which told soldiers how to put Kitchener's courtesy to practical use. This 'disgusting production,' said the report, was helping to 'facilitate vice by foreigners', teaching the soldiers such phrases as 'Voulez-vous accepter l'apéritif?', 'Permettez-moi de vous baiser la main' and 'Où habitez-vous?' From 'Bonjour' to 'Let's go back to your place' in five minutes – quick work even by French standards.

The same report criticized American troops in Paris who 'call upon women quite rudely in the street without being concerned whom they are addressing'. Not that the Parisiennes were unwilling – the report expresses shock at 'young girls leaving their lessons to let themselves be easily approached on the pretext that they know how to speak English'.

And amongst the English phrases the girls probably knew were ways of discussing prices. Part-time prostitution was rife in France during the whole of World War One, and understandably caused extreme anguish amongst French troops, who suspected that their wives and fiancées might be showing excessive hospitality to foreign soldiers. For many widows, of course, it was more a matter of survival – a way of balancing the books now that the man of the house had been blown to bits in a trench somewhere. There were more than enough foreign men to help an enterprising homeowner or waitress supplement her income.

Robert Graves tells a gruesome but typical story of how billeting often led to horizontal fraternization. Two of his fellow officers tell him that they have been staying *chez* a mother and daughter, and tossed a coin to decide who slept with whom – or rather, to see who won the mother because the daughter was 'a yellow-looking scaly little thing like a lizard'.

Graves's colleagues chat endlessly about the hostesses

they have slept with, making fun of Frenchwomen's false coyness. In bed, they rarely agreed to get completely naked because it wasn't *convenable* – not right. It seems that the women's nightgowns were their own last line of defence against complete indignity.

Eventually, Kitchener had to concede defeat in the war of the sexes and put Napoleon's ideas into practice. Bonaparte had legalized brothels in France and the rest of his empire to protect his troops against sexually transmitted diseases, and the Brits took advantage of his law to set up their own French *maisons de tolérance*, fronted with blue lights for officers and red for other ranks. It is estimated that there was an army of over 50,000 Frenchwomen supporting the British war effort from their mattresses.

Robert Graves gives an unromantic description of one of the brothels:

A queue of a hundred and fifty men waiting outside the door, each to have his short turn with one of the three women in the house . . . the charge was ten francs a man [which was about two weeks' pay for the ordinary soldier]. Each woman served nearly a battalion of men every week for as long as she lasted. According to the assistant provost-marshal, three weeks was the usual limit: 'after which she retired on her earnings, pale but proud.'

Actually, Graves (or the assistant provost-marshal) is romanticizing a little here, because a battalion could be up to 1,000 men, which works out at about fifty customers a day per woman. No human body can stay 'proud' after taking that much bombardment – especially from men who, through no fault of their own, suffered from appalling personal hygiene.

The Allied soldiers immortalized French womanhood in the song 'Parley-vous'. No one is sure who originally wrote it (some say it was French, dating back to the 1830s) and it's a ditty that seems to have had a life of its own, because countless verses sprung up throughout the war, improvised by anonymous soldiers. Here is a small selection that shows the high esteem in which the Allied troops held their hostesses.

> Mademoiselle from Armentières, parley-vous,
> Mademoiselle from Armentières, parley-vous,
> She's the hardest working girl in town,
> But she makes her living upside down,
> Hinky-dinky, parley-vous?

> Mademoiselle from Armentières, parley-vous,
> Mademoiselle from Armentières, parley-vous,
> She'll do it for wine, she'll do it for rum,
> And sometimes for chocolate or chewing gum,
> Hinky-dinky, parley-vous?

> You might forget the gas and shells, parley-vous,
> You might forget the gas and shells, parley-vous,
> You might forget the groans and yells,
> But you'll never forget the Mademoiselles,
> Hinky-dinky, parley-vous?

Amex will do nicely, Monsieur

That 'parley-vous' in the song is just one example of the pidgin franglais that evolved in the Allied ranks. The Brits and French already had an amusing exchange of vocabulary going on before the war. To 'take French leave' was known as *filer à l'anglaise* ('to run away English-style'), syphilis was known as 'the French disease' and a

'French letter' was *une capote anglaise* or 'English great-coat', which speaks volumes about the thickness of winter clothes supplied to British troops.

Mispronounced phrases like 'toot sweet' for *tout de suite* and 'san fairy ann' for *ça ne fait rien* ('it doesn't matter') soon became an everyday part of the Tommy's language. And even though *soixante-neuf* was already used to describe mutual oral sex (France's nineteenth-century brothels and prolific pornography industry have a lot to answer for linguistically), the use of the word 'French' to describe fellatio dates from 1917, when ordinary soldiers discovered pleasures that until then seem to have been reserved for Edward VII and other cross-Channel travellers.

Like a linguistic bout of *soixante-neuf*, the pleasure was mutual, and the French adopted many English words. A 1920 dictionary of *anglicismes* gives a list of English terms that entered the French language during the war, including business, Tommy, chips, no good, no man's land, all right (apparently pronounced American-style as 'olrède'), lorry, tank and three words for American soldiers: Sammy, Yank and Amex. The last one does not prove that American troops were rich enough to have credit cards – it comes from American Expeditionary Force.

The author of the dictionary seems to feel almost guilty about listing these foreign additions to the French language. 'It is highly likely that our Allies, forced to learn a few words of French during their stay with us, have taken back to their respective homes a much richer harvest of Gallicisms than this meagre crop of Anglicisms and Americanisms,' he reassures his countrymen, displaying the paranoia about the 'purity' of French that continues to this day.

The French get a kick out of the war

The French picked up more than just vocabulary from the foreign troops, however.

In 1914, a French soldier wrote a letter home after seeing Scots soldiers ignoring incoming shellfire to brew up and have a shave. He couldn't believe his eyes – 'No danger deflects them from their allegiance to the razor and the teapot.'

In *Les Silences du Colonel Bramble*, André Maurois paints a far more ambivalent picture of British officers. He admires their stiff upper lip but clearly thinks their priorities are insane. In one conversation he has a British major describe a 'typical' Englishman's thoughts on war and revolution in a way that would have had a Frenchman howling with derision.

'In England,' the Major says, 'it would be impossible to organize a revolution. People would come and shout outside Westminster, then the policeman would tell them to go away, and they would leave.' (Political passivity being one of the worst crimes imaginable in French eyes.) The British major goes on:

> We are a funny people. To get a Frenchman interested in a boxing match, you have to tell him that national honour is at stake. To interest an Englishman in a war, the best thing is to tell him it's like a boxing match. Tell us that the Hun is a barbarian and we will agree politely, but tell us he's a bad sportsman and you will rouse the whole British Empire. Bombarding neutral cities is almost as unforgivable as fishing for trout with a worm or killing a fox with a shotgun.

A British colonel interrupts: 'Don't exaggerate, they haven't done *that* yet.'

But then, sport was an area where the Allies and the French didn't see eye to eye. The Tommies seemed to be football mad. At Mons, in some of the first fighting in the war, the French were amazed to see British soldiers going into attack with footballs hanging from their backpacks. Whenever they could find flat ground and free time, the Brits would have a kick-about. The French were right about this British obsession – one Tommy wrote a letter home in 1914 describing the war as a giant football match. He called it a 'great match for the European Cup. The Germans haven't scored a goal yet, and I wouldn't give a brass farthing for their chances of lifting the cup.'

After their initial amazement, the French troops joined in with the kick-abouts. It was a new game for the vast majority of them and, at first, they would get thrashed anytime they took on a British team. But with coaching from the Tommies, they improved and even began organizing matches of their own. Soon, football had become a French national sport.

In fact, you could say that France's victory in the 1998 World Cup was all thanks to the Brits. An apt date, too – it came eighty years after the armistice that allowed the young Frenchmen who survived to go home and perfect their ball control.

We've won the war, now we want blood

The guns stopped firing at 11 a.m. on 11 November 1918, which must have seemed horribly cruel to the men who were killed between midnight and 11 a.m. In any case, the end of the war had come too late for an estimated 8.5 million dead and 21 million wounded.

The peace was almost as much of a carve-up as the fighting. The only Allied leader who came out of it with impeccable honour was American, President Woodrow Wilson. He was apparently appalled at the slaughter, and amazed that the supposedly great European civilizations had been capable of dragging the world into such barbarism. He insisted that everyone should disarm, join a new League of Nations, and guarantee self-determination for the smaller European countries that had been swallowed by the great powers.

Britain's Prime Minister, Lloyd George, thought the Allies should be less lenient on the Germans. He wanted to punish them while keeping their country healthy enough to act as a barrier against the new Communist state of Russia in the east.

The French, though, were obsessed with bringing Germany to its knees. Remembering the Franco-Prussian War, France's Prime Minister, the 77-year-old Georges Clemenceau, was determined that the Germans should never be strong enough to invade France again – which makes it hard to understand why he insisted on a peace treaty so harsh that they would come back looking for vengeance only twenty years later.

Clemenceau declared that the pacifier Wilson and anti-Russian Lloyd George were timewasters with overblown political theories. 'I find myself between Jesus Christ on one side and Napoleon Bonaparte on the other,' he quipped. And he didn't mean this as flattery – Clemenceau was an anti-Bonapartist who had been imprisoned in his youth for opposing Napoleon III. He had also been against any form of appeasement with the Germans throughout the war, and had had a former French Prime Minister, Joseph Caillaux, arrested for suggesting surrender.

Clemenceau wanted something much more punitive than peace – reparations. Germany, he said, had to pay for every French house, barn and turnip destroyed by the war. According to the Treaty of Versailles, damages were to be paid to:

> ... injured persons and to surviving dependants, by personal injury to or death of civilians caused by acts of war, including bombardments or other attacks on land, on sea, or from the air, and all the direct consequences thereof, and of all operations of war by the two groups of belligerents wherever arising.

This last phrase implying that Germany had to compensate French people killed by *Allied* shelling.

To give people time to calculate how many relatives, buildings and turnips they had lost, Clemenceau insisted that the treaty should not fix a sum – the Germans had to sign a blank cheque promising to pay whatever the Allies demanded later. And when the invoice finally came, it was for a crippling amount: 226 billion Marks, a meaninglessly huge fine on which Germany began to default as early as 1922.

Clemenceau was also determined to cripple German trade, so the treaty stipulated that Germany had to accept all imports from Allied countries. Clemenceau was furious that penknives engraved with 'La Victoire', on sale in France, had been made in Germany. The exports, he said, had to start flowing in the other direction.*

In short, Clemenceau wanted total humiliation, and the Germans were so incensed that they seriously considered climbing back into the trenches and starting the war again. The German Chancellor resigned, and the Foreign Minister who signed the Treaty of Versailles on 28 June 1919, Herman Müller, was branded a traitor.

---

* And as mentioned in Chapter 9, the French even sneaked in a clause protecting French Champagne against foreign imitations.

Even the Americans decided not to ratify the treaty.

For the French, though, getting Germany to sign its own bankruptcy notice was a victory, and after the signing ceremony, Clemenceau emerged smiling broadly and commenting: 'It is a beautiful day.'

He didn't realize that he had set in motion a storm that would burst over France just over twenty years later and spoil much more than the weather.

Joan of Arc rises from the ashes

As soon as the Treaty of Versailles negotiations were over, the French took the opportunity to annoy one of its supposed friends – Britain – by resuscitating Joan of Arc.

Her memory had been revived by Napoleon in the early 1800s, and again in the 1870s when the Prussians had grabbed Alsace and Lorraine, Joan's native region. However, both the Napoleonic and Franco-Prussian Wars had resulted in French defeats, so her magic seemed to be temporarily ineffective.

It wasn't until the turn of the twentieth century, when an organization called Action française (a group of right-wing Catholic Royalists) was battling to bring down the Socialist government in France, that Joan's name was put forward as a serious candidate for canonization. The Pope, Pius X, wanted to support Action française, and accepted a petition to make the 'Witch of Orléans' a saint.

A hearing was held at the Vatican, during which serious objections to her sanctification were made. For a start, it was said, Joan did not actually *want* to die for her beliefs, so she wasn't a true martyr. She had also killed quite a few people in battle – how Christian was that? And the cardinals were troubled by the fact that, in several accounts of Joan's life, male witnesses commented on her breasts, which they had usually glimpsed while she was being forced to change from men's to women's clothes. Could she really be a saint if she'd let men ogle her boobs?

But Joan's canonization was too much of a political necessity for both the Pope and Action française, and these objections were brushed aside. The obligatory three miracles were found – a convenient trio of French nuns who swore they had been cured by praying to Joan, including one who had been suffering from leg ulcers – and she would have been declared a saint in 1914 if the First World War hadn't broken out and interrupted papal proceedings.

However, as soon as the guns fell silent, France, now in dire need of a heroine to symbolize its victory and to expunge the awful memories of slaughter in the trenches, put pressure on the Vatican again, and in May 1920 St Joan of Arc officially came into being.

Yes, just eighteen months after Britain had sacrificed a whole generation of its young men to defend Joan of Arc's homeland against invasion, the French adopted an anti-English patron saint. *Merci beaucoup, les amis*.

Worse, not only is she the patron saint of France, but Joan is also – according to various slightly contradictory sources – the protector of soldiers, prisoners, funeral directors . . . and Anglophobes.

And one of her most devoted worshippers, and France's most fervent Anglophobe of the twentieth century, was a tall soldier with a large nose who would soon be crossing the Channel to make life for another World War One veteran, Winston Churchill, very annoying indeed . . .

27

World War Two, Part One

Don't mention Dunkirk

The subliminal French version of World War Two goes
something like this . . .

In 1940, the Germans cheated by sneaking around the
side of the Maginot Line. They pushed the weak *Anglais*
into the sea at Dunkirk and then temporarily occupied
France (but only half of it). Meanwhile, General de
Gaulle was in London telling Churchill how a war should
be run. The fat old Brit was a waste of time, but luckily
America entered the war on the French side and agreed
that the most important thing to do was invade
Normandy and link up with the Resistance, who had previously cleared the way to Paris by blowing up all the
railway bridges. OK, bit of a contradiction there, but
never mind, because the French capital was already being
liberated by General Leclerc and his tanks, after which
the war was over, apart from some minor tidying up in
Germany (which the Russians and Americans got all
wrong – they couldn't even catch Hitler alive). Oh, and
there was some messy stuff in Hiroshima that ended the

conflict in Asia which was not very important anyway because it was so far away from France.

That is an exaggeration, of course, but only just. If you talk to French people about the Deuxième Guerre, it immediately becomes clear that we remember events very differently. And the funny thing is that the contradictions and confusions were all there between 1939 and 1945. Here are a few real, unexaggerated, quotations that show how complicated relations were between France, Britain and the USA:

Churchill on de Gaulle: 'He is like a female llama surprised in his bath.'

De Gaulle on the Brits: 'England, like Germany, is our hereditary enemy.'

President Roosevelt's nickname for de Gaulle: 'The temperamental lady.'

De Gaulle on the attempts by the Brits and Americans to liberate Nazi-occupied French colonies: 'We must warn the people of France and the whole world of Anglo-Saxon imperialist plans.'

And we thought we were Allies.

Party like it's 1939

In the interwar years, the Brits and Americans did anything *but* annoy the French. *Au contraire*.

The American heiress Peggy Guggenheim brought her dollars over and almost single-handedly bankrolled the French avant-garde art movement.

An African-American erotic dancer called Josephine Baker lifted the Folies Bergère out of the doldrums and restored Paris to its pre-1914 status as world capital of sex. Her semi-naked dance with bananas hanging from her waist would not be considered very PC today, but back in the mid-1920s this sassy chorus girl from

Missouri became a massive star in Paris and embodied France's lack of racial prejudice. A whole host of black musicians followed in her wake, instilling in France a love of jazz that has never faded.

English-speaking writers also flooded into the country. Henry Miller wrote *Tropic of Cancer*, and made Paris the capital of both sex and alcohol. James Joyce and Samuel Beckett arrived and it became the new epicentre of Irish literature. Ernest Hemingway hit town and made machismo respectable. (George Orwell also nipped over to do some washing-up in poor Parisian restaurants, but that has left less of a mark on the French artistic consciousness.)

By 1940, France was the capital of contemporary Western culture, and it was just a shame that the ham-fisted Nazi philistines came and spoilt the cultural idyll.

The last *ligne* of *défense*

The artists might have been enjoying themselves between the wars, but there hadn't been quite as much fun and frolicking in the political world, especially where Anglo-French relations were concerned.

France saw the rise of Hitler as a direct challenge to its demands in the Treaty of Versailles. Determined to stand up to him, it quickly erected* a line of fortifications that was a throwback to World War One – a kind of massive armoured trench designed to stop Germany invading through Alsace and Lorraine. They called it the Ligne Maginot, after their Minister of War, André Maginot. Yes, even in peacetime, the French had kept on a Minister of War.

* Strictly speaking, France only finished off the Ligne Maginot during the Hitler years – work had actually begun in 1928.

The Brits, meanwhile, hung back and watched the agitation on the continent with a naïve hope that things would settle down so that everyone could get together for a nice cup of tea. Initially, their only reaction to the rise of Nazism was a polite suggestion that Herr Hitler might like to consider some minor arms limitations – a proposal that enraged the French because, under the Treaty of Versailles, Germany wasn't supposed to be arming itself at all.

In March 1936, Hitler tested the troubled Anglo-French water by occupying the Rhineland, a sector of Germany on France's eastern border that was supposed to be demilitarized. He sent in a small force of 3,000 men to see what would happen, and the answer was hot air – France blustered but didn't want to invade Germany and risk starting a war. Churchill, who wasn't yet Prime Minister, added a sort of lukewarm air of his own by saying, 'I hope that the French will look after their own safety and that we shall be permitted to live our life in our island.' You can almost hear the 'More tea, vicar?'

The problem for Britain and France as they decided whether or not to stand up to Hitler was that both countries' top politicians and military men had served in World War One. It was less than twenty years since the trench slaughter had ended. The leaders' schoolfriends had been killed, mutilated men were still begging on street corners, and war widows were marrying off children who had never known their fathers.

But their reactions to the situation were very different. Britain was disturbed by France's eternal anti-German belligerence and felt rather guilty about the vengefulness of the Treaty of Versailles, while France was aghast at Britain's apparently short memory. Meanwhile, America wisely decided to stay out of all this old-fashioned European posturing – it was just recovering from the

Depression and didn't need a war to bankrupt it again.

All of which explains why the Munich Conference in September 1938, between France, Britain, Italy and Germany, was such a farce.

The motive for the summit was that Hitler wanted international permission to 'repossess' the Sudetenland, a mainly German-speaking region that had become part of Czechoslovakia after World War One. The French Premier, Edouard Daladier, was all for saying *non*, and warned Britain's PM, Neville Chamberlain, that 'if the Western powers capitulate, they will only hasten the war they wish to avoid'. Daladier even predicted that Hitler was aiming for a 'domination of the continent in comparison with which the ambitions of Napoleon were feeble'. Quite something, coming from a Frenchman.

Chamberlain, though, dearly wanted to believe Hitler's assurances that once Germany had taken the Sudetenland, everything would become peaceful again. The 69-year-old old-school Englishman had already been to visit Hitler at his alpine hangout in Berchtesgaden (taking an aeroplane for the first time in his life) and returned to London announcing that they had had a 'friendly' talk. He told Daladier that Hitler was sincere, and actually persuaded the Frenchman not to oppose the Führer's 'one last invasion' request.

The conference itself, which took place in Munich on 29 September 1938, was therefore a mere rubber-stamping session. The British and French delegations hadn't even met to discuss their strategy. The photos taken just before the agreement was signed show Chamberlain resembling a cross between a tailor's dummy and a startled chicken, Daladier looking as if someone is about to shoot him (which, politically, they were), Mussolini unsure whether to burp or pout, and Hitler a picture of pure serenity. It was a shotgun wedding at which France and Britain were the brides, and Hitler the groom with a prior agreement to use the honeymoon tickets to take his best man, Mussolini, to Las Vegas. (In separate bedrooms, of course.)

Worse still, from the French point of view, next morning Chamberlain had a private meeting with Hitler at which they co-signed a non-aggression pact that didn't even mention France.

Chamberlain then flew home to Heston aerodrome near London (later used as a base for Hurricanes, Spitfires and B17 bombers), which was where he famously waved his 'peace for our time'* letter, the scrap of paper signed by Hitler that morning. Pointedly excluding his supposed French allies, Chamberlain spoke to the assembled crowd: 'We regard the agreement signed last night . . . as symbolic of the desire of our two peoples never to go to war with one another again.' The Brits and Germans, he promised, were going to work together 'to ensure the peace of Europe'. Later that day, he made another speech telling everyone to go and sleep soundly in their beds. Less than a year later, the same people would be sleeping much less soundly in bomb shelters.

It is very easy to glower back with perfect hindsight, of course. In archive film footage, Chamberlain looks like a nice old man who wants everyone to be friends. But as he is making his optimistic speech at Heston, there is a younger man in the background, a reporter or plain-clothes policeman perhaps, looking sceptical, not joining in any of the cheers or applause. He was one of the men who would soon be doing the fighting.

On the other side of the Channel, Daladier, like

---

* Chamberlain is often misquoted as saying 'peace *in* our time', probably because of the line in the *Book of Common Prayer*, 'Give us peace in our time, O Lord.'

Chamberlain, returned home from Munich to a hero's welcome. His reaction, though, was less rosy-eyed. Looking out at the cheering crowds, he apparently told an aide, 'Ah, les cons.' The twats.

And when Hitler invaded Poland less than a year later and Chamberlain announced that Britain and Germany weren't going to have any more friendly talks for a while, there was a resounding cry from French politicians of 'we told you so'. Not that Daladier got much of a chance to scoff. In 1940 he was arrested by the pro-Nazi French regime, and later sent to Buchenwald concentration camp. He was one of the few prisoners who survived.

A quick outing to France

Dunkirk was never a peaceful place. Like its sister town of Calais just along the coast, it has been fought over for centuries, and changed hands countless times. Dunkerque, to give it its real French name, actually had three owners in one day on 25 June 1658. In the morning, it was under Spanish control, and then it surrendered to a besieging army of Frenchmen, before Louis XIV gave the town to Oliver Cromwell as a goodnight present. France finally bought the title deeds back from King Charles II of England in 1662 for around £320,000 (the current price of a small farmhouse in the region). In World War One, the Germans tried to take the town, sending Zeppelins to bomb the Dunkerquois into submission, but it held out and became a vital supply port for the Allies.

So it probably felt like business as usual when the Second World War swept over the town and made its name for ever synonymous with British pluckiness – or, in French eyes, British cowardice and desertion.

Britain and France didn't go into war the best of allies,

and started out just as they had done in 1914, with a joint catastrophe.

The army that was shipped across to prevent Hitler from invading France was called the British Expeditionary Force (the same name as the small bunch of soldiers sent to get a beating in the autumn of 1914). The karma could hardly have been worse if they had been called The King's Own Royal Losers.

This force of just under 400,000 men, most of them carrying World War One weapons and less ammunition than the average hunter takes on a rabbiting trip, arrived in late 1939 to play their part in the French army's master plan for defending its borders against attack from the east, helping to plug the gap between the Maginot Line and the Channel coast.

And France's ploy worked after a fashion – when the Germans began Blitzkrieging westwards on 10 May 1940, the Maginot Line wasn't breached, because the Nazis simply ignored it and entered France by the side door. The Panzer tanks swept through the Ardennes hills (which the French had claimed to be impregnable) and encircled the British and French troops who had been waiting for an attack further north.

This Blitzkrieg army wasn't the all-new, 100 per cent stainless-steel cutting force that popular myth has remembered. The front edge was made up of new tanks and dive bombers, but behind them came the same plodding First World War-type infantry that the French and Brits possessed. The trouble was that the Blitzkrieg machines scattered everyone before them, sending their confused opponents reeling backwards before the more vulnerable German troops came within range.

The French, needless to say, wanted to dig in and defend Paris, but the Brits quickly saw the way things were going. Winston Churchill – who had taken over as leader of the wartime government the day the Nazi attack began – decided that having practically the whole of Britain's regular army stuck in a POW camp would not be of use to anyone. Now was the time for the French to 'look after their own safety', as he'd put it.

So, on 26 May 1940, barely two weeks into the campaign, Churchill told his men to come home. However, he neglected to inform his hosts that their visitors were leaving, and the French fought on, thinking that they were covering a strategic British retreat with a view to making a stand on the Channel coast. When the French found out what was really going on, they were understandably angry, especially because the Brits had blocked roads so that no one, friend or foe, could follow them.

The evacuation from Dunkirk began on 27 May, with only 7,000-odd Brits being loaded on to waiting naval ships that day. The Ministry of War saw that this wasn't going to be enough, and sent out a plea to private boat owners to join the flotilla. The next day, civilian vessels came teeming across the Channel. Over the course of nine hellish days, soldiers trooped down to the beaches and jetties, often having to queue for hours in shoulder-deep water as shells and bombs churned up the sand and sea around them. The shallow-bottomed civilian boats had to manoeuvre inshore under intense fire and haul the exhausted troops on board, filling every square inch of deck, cabin and hold before they set off, either to shuttle men out to larger ships offshore or to head straight back to England with their priceless cargo. As well as some 200 military vessels, over 700 small craft, including private yachts, trawlers and river Thames pleasure boats, made the Channel crossing once or more. In all, some 200 boats were sunk during the rescue operation.

The Brits think of the Dunkirk evacuation the same way that France remembers the Taxis de la Marne, the fleet of cabs that ferried French reinforcements out to repel the German army that was advancing towards Paris in 1914. But, as we saw in Chapter 26, the French are always keen to remind the Brits that their taxis were taking men in to attack, whereas the Dunkirk boats carried out a massive retreat – a desertion, even – leaving the heroically battling French army to its fate.

This is not entirely fair. As soon as the main force of Brits were on their way back home, the boats started loading up with Frenchmen, and eventually got almost 140,000 of them out safely. In addition, thousands of Brits stayed on in France to fight a hopeless rearguard action, defending both the French and British escape, and only surrendering when they ran out of ammunition or their French commanders waved the white flag. These Brits spent the rest of the war as POWs, and their self-sacrifice wasn't even mentioned in Allied news reports of the time because it would have been bad for morale.

Instead, on 4 June Churchill made his battling Dunkirk speech to the House of Commons, proving despite his lisp that he, rather than the old softie Chamberlain, was the man for the job. And although the speech annoyed the French for a reason that will become clearer in a moment, this must be one of the greatest pieces of political rhetoric ever. You can listen to it on the internet, and the unwavering voice from seventy years ago still stirs up the emotions.

First, Churchill gives a breathtakingly lucid analysis of the reasons for the Nazis' success. 'The great French army was very largely cast back and disturbed by the onrush of a few thousands of armoured vehicles,' he says. A few days into the fighting, and already the Blitzkrieg held no more secrets.

Churchill concedes that Dunkirk 'is a colossal military disaster . . . We must be very careful not to assign to this deliverance the attributes of a victory. Wars are not won by evacuations.' But, he adds, 'there was a victory inside this deliverance' – the RAF had won the battle in the skies, protecting the beaches and the escape fleet from potentially disastrous air attack. Churchill predicts that the success of Britain's defence against invasion will hang on this completely new tactical weapon: the aeroplane. The first real fighting of the war has just begun and he has got it all worked out.

The speech climaxes with the oft-quoted catalogue of places where the Nazis could expect to meet British resistance:

> . . . we shall fight on the seas and oceans, we shall fight with growing confidence and growing strength in the air, we shall defend our island, whatever the cost may be, we shall fight on the beaches, we shall fight on the landing grounds, we shall fight in the fields and in the streets, we shall fight in the hills, we shall never surrender.

He has come a very, very long way since the 'More tea, vicar?' days, and the brilliant thing about the speech, apart from its pure morale-boosting toughness, was that it confirmed everything that both the Germans and the French thought about Britain.

The Nazis really were afraid of setting foot in Britain and unleashing the kind of ferocious, house-by-house opposition that was the complete opposite of their dash through France. Dunkirk had shown what individual, civilian Brits were capable of, and Churchill had put their spirit into words.

The French, meanwhile, were thinking: Those *Anglais* are only concerned about their own little island – as usual. If a Frenchman had been listening carefully, he would have heard the words 'we shall fight in France' slipped in just before the mention of seas and oceans, but he probably wouldn't have believed them. No one expected a British army to come rushing back across the Channel just yet – it's probably the only false note in the whole speech.

And if they hadn't had more pressing things to worry about, some French military historians would also have been calling copyright lawyers, because they would have recognized the theme of the speech. Churchill, a highly aware military historian himself, had clearly borrowed it from France's former leader, Georges Clemenceau, who had motivated his troops in World War One by promising them: 'We will fight in front of Paris, we will fight in Paris, we will fight behind Paris.' Yet even the most patriotic French soldier would have had to admit that Churchill had taken what sounds like someone reading from a grammar book and turned it into a rabble-rousing tear-jerker.

Meanwhile, somewhere in France, in between attempts to evacuate himself and his family to Britain, a very tall Frenchman was gasping with outrage and telling everyone: 'But that was my idea!'

Back in the 1920s and 1930s, General Charles de Gaulle had been one of the earliest proponents of mechanized warfare. He had opposed the construction of the Maginot Line as an outdated concept, and been ignored. He had long been calling for France to spend its money on tanks and aeroplanes, and the Nazis had stolen his proposal and thrown it back in his face. He had been proved horribly right, and now Churchill was claiming the credit for his analysis of the way war was evolving. Not only that, the Englishman was suggesting that deserting France was a victory. It was almost like a conspiracy between the French-hating Germans and the sneaky, self-obsessed *Anglais*.

De Gaulle was an angry, bitter man – and he was on his way to London.

The Frenchest of Frenchmen

Charles André Joseph Marie de Gaulle was born on 22 November 1890, the son of a minor aristocrat – hence the 'de'. It was a name that was to stand the Général in very good stead because it was so perfectly French. 'Charles of Gaul' sounds like an ancient king from the days of resistance against the Roman invaders (which was a failed resistance but is remembered as a heroic one nevertheless, like so many French military campaigns). If the name hadn't existed, it could have been invented for a character in the *Astérix* comics.[*]

The boy Charles was brought up a strict Catholic (he had been christened one, too – note the inclusion of both Joseph and Mary in his list of first names), and destined for a military career. He studied at Saint-Cyr, the military school founded by Napoleon.

De Gaulle served in World War One as an officer under Marshal Pétain (the future pro-Nazi collaborator), and was wounded five times before being made a POW at Verdun in 1916. After the war, under Pétain's guidance, he wrote a military history, *La France et son armée*, with no mention of Waterloo.

In short, it would have been hard to find a Frencher Frenchman.

Not that de Gaulle realized this yet. When he arrived in London as a refugee on 16 June 1940, he must have been taken aback to find that he was suddenly the

---

[*] In a way, you could say the same thing about Churchill. A church on a hill does seem to conjure up something profound and unchanging about the peaceful English countryside.

number-one Français in town. He popped up like the sole repatriated passenger of a bankrupt airline who realizes that it's up to him to rally public opinion and get the stranded tourists out of Corfu airport – and who also sees the chance to get free air travel for life.

He was in the right place at the right time. Ten days or so previously he had been made a member of the crisis government as France realized that his modern warfare theories might be useful after all. But all the other senior men in the government had stayed at home to capitulate. Most French politicians were as good as saying that the fight was over, and Paris had been offered up as an 'open city', meaning that it was surrendering to the Nazis without a struggle so as to preserve its historic monuments. Meanwhile, the French navy was refusing to sail to British-held ports to ensure that its ships wouldn't be press-ganged into the Nazi battle fleet.

And then on 17 June Pétain made a radio announcement that was the diametric opposite of Churchill's rousing speech. 'It is with a heavy heart that I say to you today that you must stop fighting,' he told his troops. 'I contacted our opponent last night to ask if he would be willing, amongst soldiers, after an honourable struggle, to seek a way of ending hostilities.'

No armistice had been agreed by the Nazis, no conditions set, but Pétain was giving up.

The French troops immediately began laying down their arms, and around one million offered themselves to the Nazis as prisoners of war. About 100,000 of these had been evacuated from Dunkirk, and had returned to France after a short stay in England.

The surrender was a key moment in Anglo-French relations, as important as Agincourt, Waterloo or even Dunkirk (yes, two key moments in a single month – it was an intense time). Churchill had announced that the

Brits were for fighting on (albeit from the safety of their own island, having left the French in the *merde*) and now the arch Anglophobe Pétain was saying *non merci*.

In a way, France was also showing that Paris was the centre of their universe. There had been plans to regroup Allied forces in the west and use ports like Brest and Bordeaux as bases for a British-aided fightback. De Gaulle himself had suggested evacuating French troops to the territories in Africa and the Middle East, and then launching an invasion of France. There were already hundreds of thousands of unconquered French and colonial troops out there, ready to fight.

But no, unlike in 1914, when they had mobilized old men and taxis to sweep the Germans off their doorstep, the Parisians had decided that it was all over. Hitler was going to take Notre-Dame, the Champs-Élysées and the all-important cafés on the boulevard Saint-Germain, so there was nothing left worth fighting for.

France won't 'sleep with a corpse'

Fortunately, de Gaulle wasn't a Parisian (he was from Lille in the north), and didn't agree with his defeatist colleagues. He even put his genetic Anglophobia to one side for a while to embrace an idea that would make modern-day French and British people shudder with horror.

The French ambassador in London, André Corbin, and Britain's top diplomat, Sir Robert Vansittart,* had dreamt up a crackpot plan to unite France and Britain as one nation.

True, similar things had been tried by a whole host of British monarchs, but their plans had usually involved conquering France and simply taking it over. Napoleon

* He was Lawrence of Arabia's second cousin.

had envisaged a similar scheme, but he had wanted to make Britain a wholly French territory, adopting his laws and introducing *maisons de tolérance*.

In the past, each country had essentially wanted to rape and possess its neighbour. This 1940 plan was to be a consensual union, a merger. Everyone would have joint citizenship, and the governments would share power over their two countries and empires just like a political alliance between two parties. The two nations would be one.

It was, of course, little more than a propaganda exercise, a way of enabling Hitler's enemies to say that France hadn't been conquered because its London-based territories were still free. Even so, de Gaulle immediately embraced the scheme and got on a plane to pitch it to his defeatist colleagues back in France.

Their answer was predictable. Pétain said that Britain was finished. It was like suggesting union with a corpse. Besides, he was already making plans to sleep with the (all too alive) enemy.

De Gaulle wisely returned straight to London, where Churchill – against the advice of his own Foreign Office – secured some BBC airtime and encouraged the Frenchman to give his own 'the fight will go on' speech.

De Gaulle speaks and the world says, 'Pardon?'

It was on 18 June, the 125th anniversary of Waterloo, that the Général went on the radio and made his Appel du 18 juin. Despite its name, this was not a charity appeal. It was a call (*appel*) for France to resist Nazi occupation, a French version of Churchill's speech, full of rhetorical questions, repetitions and exclamations.

'Must all hope disappear?' de Gaulle asked. 'Is defeat final? No! Because France is not alone! She is not alone!

She is not alone! She has a vast empire to back her up. She can unite with the British Empire that rules the seas.' Which had to be the first time in history that a Frenchman had ever been pleased to announce British naval superiority.

He went on to recognize rather sportingly that this was a world war, not limited to France, and then got in a little plug for his ideas: 'Although we have been blitzed by mechanical force, we will win using even greater mechanical force. This is the world's destiny.'

Soaring to a dramatic finale, he promised that 'whatever happens, the flame of French resistance must not, and will not, be extinguished'. It was a good ending, though he spoilt it by announcing that he'd speak again next day, which he didn't.

Nevertheless, de Gaulle had just given the most famous speech in French history – the name if not the text of l'Appel du 18 juin is known by every French schoolkid. The only problem was that almost no French listeners heard it. It was on English radio, practically unannounced, and given by a man whom no one in France had heard of. And unfortunately, the BBC thought the talk so unimportant that they didn't record it.

All of which might explain the muted response to the speech. De Gaulle had invited all the Frenchmen in the UK, both soldiers and civilians, to join him, but very few did. Of 10,000 French immigrants in Britain, only 300 volunteered, and of the 100,000-odd soldiers temporarily on British soil, only 7,000 stayed on to join de Gaulle. The others went back and were quickly made POWs.

Worse, despite a flattering reference to America in the speech, President Roosevelt refused to recognize de Gaulle as a leader of France. Almost right up until 1940, the Americans held out hopes of working with Pétain and the defeatists and turning them against Hitler.

Only Churchill stood by the Général, and made an official announcement to the effect that 'His Majesty's government recognizes General de Gaulle as leader of all free Frenchmen, wherever they may be.'

It was an act of solidarity that de Gaulle would often forget in the years to come.

Pineapple or banana?

The insults and backstabbing that went on between de Gaulle, Roosevelt and Churchill were as bad as anything in a boy band's dressing room.

Although America didn't enter the war until 1941, Churchill was constantly trying to show Roosevelt that the Allies were a cause worth supporting. Right from the start, he had one eye on the Nazis and another on America's huge supplies of men and war machines.

De Gaulle, though, was so obsessed with French interests and his own position as a future leader of the country that he often lost sight of the bigger picture. He saw only France and the need to discredit and destabilize Pétain's government. This shortsightedness and mis-placed patriotism caused almost every Brit or American who had any dealings with him to unleash a torrent of abuse about his arrogance, ingratitude, unreliability and – quite cruelly – about his appearance. Here are a few more famous quotes about le Général.

Hugh Dalton, Churchill's Minister of the Board of Trade, said that de Gaulle had 'a head like a banana and hips like a woman'. Alexander Cadogan of the Foreign Office said the same thing except that he replaced the banana with a (more credible) pineapple.

The novelist Sylvia Townsend Warner called the French leader 'an embattled codfish. I wish he could be filleted and put quietly away in a refrigerator.'

And to H. G. Wells he came across as 'an artlessly sincere megalomaniac'.

Even Churchill, a romantic Francophile who had fought in the trenches and loved France in much the same way as Edward VII had done, soon realized that de Gaulle couldn't be trusted. Though in fact de Gaulle occasionally had good reason to act up, because Britain did some highly unpleasant things to the French . . .

Britain sinks French hopes

Mers-el-Kebir is a name that means nothing to most English-speakers, but just mentioning it to de Gaulle after 3 July 1940 would have been like saying 'Joan of Arc' while barbecuing a kebab.

On that day, Churchill decided that the French navy could not be relied upon to keep its ships out of Nazi hands, and ordered that all French vessels docked in British-held ports anywhere in the world should be seized. Two hundred of them were boarded and effectively stolen from France.

The main French war fleet was in Algeria, at the Mers-el-Kebir naval base near Oran. Some British ships went to invite its commander, Admiral Marcel Gensoul, to join the Brits (and de Gaulle, of course) in resisting the Nazis. An officer called Captain Holland delivered the invitation in person, and asked the Admiral in French to sail to Britain, America or the Caribbean, with a reduced crew so that his ships would not be at battle stations. Either that, or he might prefer to scuttle his fleet. It was a thinly veiled ultimatum, with a deadline of 6 p.m. for a reply.

But the Admiral simply huffed that a mere captain had been sent to deliver the ultimatum, and decided to call the Brits' bluff.

This was a big mistake. Churchill was determined to

show that war was war, and at 6 p.m. precisely, having got no reaction, the British guns opened up for nine minutes, disabling two French battleships, blowing up another, and killing over 1,250 French sailors.

De Gaulle was predictably horrified. His Appel had been widely quoted in the (as yet) free French press, and recruits were trickling in. Now his supposed Allies had apparently declared war on France.

Worse, when a deeply troubled Churchill announced events at Mers-el-Kebir to the House of Commons, MPs of all parties gave him a rousing cheer of support. Roosevelt, too, was quick to send a message of approval. In British and American eyes, it was clearly OK to bombard Frenchmen.

It took de Gaulle almost a week to accept that victory against the Nazis was more important than French pride, and he made a speech acknowledging that, had the ships not been sunk, Pétain would almost certainly have allowed Hitler to get his hands on them.

By now, Pétain was the Général's mortal enemy – literally. The Paris-based government handed France over to the Nazis on 10 July with an official armistice that divided the country in two. Hitler was to get the northern half, including all the Channel ports and most of the industrial resources, and Pétain was to take his puppet government to the spa town of Vichy, just the other side of the demarcation line between Occupied and Unoccupied France. One of Pétain's first acts was to pronounce a death sentence *in absentia* on de Gaulle. The Général rose to the provocation by promising to set France free (although at the time he had an army of just 2,200 men and an even smaller navy), and by adopting as his flag of resistance the Croix de Lorraine, Joan of Arc's anti-British battle standard. Churchill must have been delighted at the symbolism, and to show it, he was soon ordering another attack on a French colony.

In September 1940, the Brits decided to grab Dakar in Senegal. It was in pro-Vichy hands, and was a potential Nazi submarine base that worried the Americans because it was just a short underwater cruise from their Caribbean back door.

This time, de Gaulle decided to go along for the ride and try to prevent the British from bombarding French ships and troops. He was sure that his presence alone would persuade the Pétainist garrison to come over to his side. He also knew that the gold reserves of the Banque de France had been sent to Dakar, and would buy him enough weapons to free him from his slavish dependence on the Brits. An added prize would be that success here would put him on the map with America.

The Général duly went to get fitted for a tropical outfit at a London clothes shop and, chatting merrily, told the shop assistant where he was going. His French troops based in Liverpool did exactly the same. Soon the security of the mission was totally blown, and a surviving fleet of Vichy ships broke out of the Med and set sail to defend Senegal.

A despairing Churchill wanted to call it all off, but de Gaulle threatened to take his men and march overland to Senegal. So, deciding that it would be fun but not good for the war effort to let the loose-tongued Frenchmen die of thirst in the Sahara, the Brits eventually agreed to go ahead with the mission.

True to form, it turned into a complete farce as soon as the British fleet moored off Dakar.

Two Free French aeroplanes took off from the aircraft carrier *Ark Royal* and flew in with a message from de Gaulle to the Vichy governor. But instead of heeding his new leader's call to arms, the Governor simply had the messengers thrown in jail.

Meanwhile, a small boat sailed into harbour with three emissaries who were fired upon, and only just escaped with their lives. Just along the coast, Free French troops landed, expecting to be hailed as liberators. They too were beaten off by the pro-Vichy garrison.

A deflated de Gaulle decided that the time had come to pull out, but the very next day, the British ships were ordered by Churchill himself to begin bombarding the port. They damaged a submarine and a destroyer before sustaining hits themselves and opting to leave. In retaliation, Vichy French aeroplanes bombed the British base at Gibraltar. It was an out-and-out Anglo-French war, with each of the two countries hammering away at each other's colonies, exactly the kind of spat Napoleon and Nelson used to enjoy.

Getting into the spirit of things, the Vichy government began producing anti-British propaganda posters, one of which recalled the whole long history of conflict between the two nations. It proclaimed:

> Yesterday England shed French blood, Joan of Arc was burnt alive in Rouen, Napoleon was in his death throes in St Helena. Today, at Dunkirk, the sacrifice of our boats and soldiers allows the English troops to escape, England sheds French blood at Mers-el-Kébir. Tomorrow, what will they take from us?

It was 1805 all over again – it was almost a shame that the Nazis were there to complicate things.

The Dakar mission had been a disaster for Churchill, but de Gaulle was the biggest loser of all. Roosevelt decided that he was a nobody and opened an American consulate in Dakar to negotiate with the Vichy government about the potential U-boat threat. In effect, America was recognizing the legitimacy of the Pétain regime – de Gaulle's biggest nightmare. It didn't mean that Roosevelt was pro-Hitler. On the contrary, he was totally anti-Nazi, and came out in favour of Britain, announcing that he would supply them with weapons and be 'the arsenal of democracy'. But it did show all too clearly what Roosevelt thought of the French: they could only be relied upon to squabble amongst themselves and distract attention from the real aims of the war.

These prejudices were confirmed in Occupied France, where the Communists, whom one would have thought would be anti-Nazi, declared their support for Hitler because of the non-aggression pact he had signed with Stalin. Later on in the war, the Communists played a major role in the armed Resistance, but in July 1940, their newspaper *L'Humanité*, which is still published today, ran an article congratulating Parisian workers for 'showing friendliness to German soldiers'. With comrades like that, who needed enemies?

France's first great victory over Nazi tyranny

In December 1941, de Gaulle hatched a plot that proved beyond all doubt to Churchill and Roosevelt (who had recently entered the war after the attack on Pearl Harbor) that he was too much of a nuisance to be consulted on anything.

Admiral Émile Muselier was one of de Gaulle's faithful, and had been the first to use the Croix de Lorraine to distinguish his ships from those loyal to Vichy. On 23 December 1941, Muselier was moored off the Canadian coast in Halifax, Nova Scotia, with a French submarine and three ships. De Gaulle ordered him to sail to the nearby islands of Saint-Pierre and Miquelon, 242 square kilometres of windblown but French-owned rock, and liberate them from the pro-Vichy governor 'without telling the foreigners' (that is, the Brits and Americans).

At dawn on Christmas Eve, the four-vessel French fleet sailed into Saint-Pierre harbour, and Muselier's men seized control of the island. This was a relatively simple matter, and involved little more than taking over the lone radio transmitter and the Western Union telegraph office and arresting the Vichy governor. Once these objectives had been achieved, the Admiral cabled Churchill, who was at the White House conferring with Roosevelt, to inform him of this momentous development in world events – a tiny group of Canadian islands had been liberated from the Nazis. At last the tide of war was turning!

Roosevelt was furious. This was effectively a *coup d'état*, and no one changed regime in the Americas without asking him first. He therefore declared that the islands would be run under joint British, Canadian and American rule for the duration of the war, after which they would be returned to whichever regime was then governing France.

De Gaulle, though, wasn't going to let anyone spoil his first successful invasion, and announced that his men would open fire if the Allies tried to send in their troops. He must have been hugely satisfied when, to everyone's amazement, Roosevelt backed down. France had stood up to the giant America and won.

In fact, of course, the President had only done so because at such a critical time, with the whole course of both the Asian and European wars in the balance, he couldn't be bothered to argue with a few Frenchmen in a Western Union office somewhere up the Canadian coast. Besides, Admiral Muselier was now in a huff because de Gaulle had ruined his good relations with the Americans, and was threatening to rebel against the Général and take the navy with him. The French were fighting amongst themselves again, and didn't need any outside interference to screw things up.

The affair tipped Roosevelt and Churchill over the edge. If de Gaulle wanted to behave like a rebellious teenager, they decided, then he was grounded. He was in London, entirely dependent on British transport to go anywhere further than the local French restaurant, and there he was going to stay.

Meanwhile, Churchill was hatching a plan of his own that was going to have the Frenchman spitting with fury . . .

Mad about Madagascar

In May 1942, a British force invaded the island of Madagascar, off the east coast of Africa. The Allies were afraid that it could be used as a base by Japan to torpedo shipping in the Indian Ocean and off the Cape of Good Hope, and Vichy's recent surrender of its colony in Vietnam had convinced Churchill that the same thing could happen in Madagascar. The Brits duly sent out an invasion force from South Africa and attacked the French garrison at Diego Suárez, the island's largest harbour.

De Gaulle only learned about the invasion when a journalist called him and asked him for a quote. He was trebly furious. For a start, the *Anglais* were trying to steal a French island. Secondly, they were doing it behind his back.* And worst of all, just like the whole mechanized warfare business, they had stolen his idea – he was the one who had suggested the Madagascar scheme to Churchill in the first place.

---

* Though surely Churchill's main motive for secrecy must have been that if de Gaulle had been informed, he would have gone out and asked the local chemist what anti-malarial drugs you needed for a trip to Madagascar.

The Frenchman lapsed into an even deeper paranoia than usual and sent a cable to his men in Africa and the Middle East, saying, 'We must warn the people of France and the whole world . . . about Anglo-Saxon imperialist plans.' He added that 'under no circumstances must we have any relations with the Anglo-Saxons', and complained that he was being held captive by the British in London.

The cable was encrypted in a French code, but was easily deciphered by the Brits and, no doubt, by some delighted Nazis.

The Bogeyman comes to Casablanca

The Allies knew that if they were to control the Mediterranean and keep valuable oil resources out of Nazi hands, then it was necessary to liberate all the French colonies* in North Africa. As well as the Nazi occupiers, in 1942 there were over 100,000 potentially dangerous Vichy troops stationed there.

Churchill and Roosevelt kept de Gaulle out of the loop yet again – wisely, as it happened, because when the Frenchman got wind of a combined British and American landing near Algiers, he told one of his men, 'I hope that the people of Vichy throw them into the sea.' As if they were following his orders, French troops fired on the Americans who came to liberate Casablanca before being overrun.

Unsurprisingly, in January 1943, when the Allied leaders held their conference at Casablanca on the future of

---

* I use the word colony loosely. Morocco and Tunisia were protectorates, while Algeria was actually considered part of France, and all Algerians were (legally speaking) French citizens. However, to the locals of all three countries, the French were *les colons*.

Europe and Africa, they were cagey about inviting the volatile de Gaulle, or 'Joan of Arc' as they had jokingly taken to calling him.

Churchill sent a telegram to de Gaulle inviting him to join them for the discussions, but without saying exactly where. Theoretically the Général was still under a travel ban, and subject to an even tighter information blackout. The reply was blunt. De Gaulle refused to discuss the fate of France and French colonies with foreign nations. OK, Churchill and Roosevelt said, in that case we will deal with a more malleable World War One veteran called Henri Giraud, one of de Gaulle's adversaries in the pre-war arguments about modernizing the French army.

The threat had the desired effect, and the Général quickly changed his mind.

When he arrived in Casablanca, he was his usual tetchy self. He pointedly snubbed Giraud – official photos are often cropped to show de Gaulle apparently sitting alone between Churchill and Roosevelt – and said how indignant he was to find American troops everywhere. (Yes, he was reminded, they're here to stop the Nazis overrunning the place and to keep the Vichy men from shooting you.)

The conference was carried out in the same spirit as the preliminaries. The Général issued a declaration that 'I am the Joan of Arc of today' and must have wondered why he could hear laughter in some quarters. He went on to refuse any talk of power-sharing in Africa and demanded to be flown back to Europe. With a stunning lack of diplomatic tact, he refused to leave in an American plane on the grounds that a US pilot, being a late arrival in the war, would probably land him in Nazi-occupied France by mistake.

This singular lack of co-operation simply earned de Gaulle yet another bout of naughty-boy punishment.

Not only was the travel ban upheld, but his offices were now bugged by the British secret services, which had come to the conclusion that the Général was not interested in the wider war effort, but only in his own political power over France and its empire. Churchill went so far as to describe de Gaulle as 'Fascist-minded, opportunist, unscrupulous, ambitious to the last degree ... his coming to power in the new France would lead to a considerable estrangement between France and the Western democracies'.

He didn't know that his prediction would come true well before the war was over.

28

World War Two, Part Two

The Brits protect the Resistance from the French

Ever since the debacle at Dakar, the Brits had warned de Gaulle about security breaches, but his men in London refused to accept that their codes could be broken. Which was why, almost from the start, the Allied security services resolved to share no sensitive information with the Free French, even if it involved France. The Français were being kept in the dark about Allied goings-on in their own country – it was a situation that would annoy anyone.

In 1941, the British Special Operations Executive (SOE) had begun setting up Resistance cells within France, using French agents, but had refused to tell de Gaulle where they were or who was running them. De Gaulle came up with the typically French wheeze of centralizing the management of Resistance groups under an umbrella group called the Conseil national de la Résistance, which would have brought them all under his control, but would also have meant that catching one key member of the network would expose absolutely everyone else to mortal danger. As a result, the SOE decided to ignore de Gaulle's suggestion and run small, independent cells that wouldn't even know the existence of any other group.

In the early years of the war, the Resistance was less about blowing up railways and killing Germans – the type of actions that could get innocent hostages killed in reprisals – than smuggling out Allied airmen. Churchill's prediction about the importance of superiority in the skies had quickly come true, and it was vital that Allied bomber and fighter crews who came down on the wrong side of the Channel should return home safely.

Active resistance therefore began with a few brave French people risking their lives to hide the men until they could be brought out. They weren't so much underground fighters as people-smugglers and owners of safe houses, whose addresses would be given to pilots verbally before they left on a mission. Hiding Allied servicemen in their attics, cellars or barns, these ordinary civilians got almost 6,000 airmen, escaped POWs and other stranded troops safely out of France during the war.

And sad to say, the biggest danger to the escapees and their rescuers was not cracked codes, it was other ordinary French civilians. Because Pétain and his political cronies weren't the only collaborators.

There is one foolproof way of exasperating a Frenchman, and that is to mention collaboration. Either he will tut – 'Oui, oui, it's all been said before' – or he will say that it's lucky Britain and America weren't put to the test like France was. But there is no getting away from the scale of everyday cooperation between French civilians and their German occupiers.

A recent article in Britain's *Daily Telegraph* pointed out that informing on your neighbours is such a common habit in France that French has two distinct terms for informing on someone. *Dénonciation* is doing the right thing by giving the authorities information, whereas *délation* is telling them something you shouldn't. During the war, the issue became so painful that nowadays both types of informing are taboo in France, which is why there are fewer security cameras in the streets and almost no public appeals to help the police to track down killers and rapists.

It has been hard for France to come to terms with the fact that, under Nazi occupation, ordinary French men and women informed on their fellow citizens for hiding Allied servicemen, belonging to the Resistance, being Jewish, listening to the BBC or simply saying something unflattering about Pétain. And the first on the scene to investigate these 'crimes' were either the French police or the more overtly pro-Nazi paramilitary *milice*.

Of course, some ordinary *gendarmes* did refuse to work under the Nazis – during the war, 338 were executed and 800 deported to Nazi prison camps. But many of them guarded transit camps for prisoners on their way to extermination, and turned Resistance fighters and fugitive servicemen over to the Nazis for inevitable torture and execution.

Up *merde* creek without a paddle

One story illustrates the complex relationship between all these factions. It was a British raid known as Operation Frankton, which was made famous in a 1955 film called *The Cockleshell Heroes*.

On 7 December 1942, six two-men canoes were launched from a British submarine called HMS *Tuna* (a joke, surely – a tin can called 'Tuna'?) about 15 kilometres off the west coast of France. The team of twelve men was led by a 28-year-old major called Herbie Hasler, who had previously been awarded the French Croix de

Guerre for his bravery in support of the Foreign Legion during a mission in Norway. Hasler had planned the almost suicidal Operation Frankton himself. The idea was to canoe up the river Gironde (difficult in summer, almost impossible against the winter tides, especially in canoes that were so small they were nicknamed cockleshells) and sabotage Nazi ships that were lying at anchor in Bordeaux, waiting to take on a cargo of radar equipment to Japan and return with raw materials. Destroying them would also block the harbour and render the port unusable.

Meanwhile, the submarine was not going to wait around for the twelve men to return. They had more than 100 kilometres to paddle and no one expected them to make it back, their only potential escape route being across country to Spain. The men had been told to go to a village called Ruffec, 160 kilometres northeast of Bordeaux, where, it was said, they could get help. For security reasons, no names or addresses were given, meaning that the survivors would just have to take their chances. And to make things even more perilous, Hitler had recently issued an edict ordering all captured British commandos to be executed as soon as they had been interrogated. They were too dangerous to be left alive.

In a nut(or cockle)shell, the twelve men had volunteered to give their lives to knock out a vital strategic harbour.

The operation got off to a catastrophic start. One canoe was damaged as soon as it was launched, and its crew was unable to take part in the mission. Two more of the little boats capsized in the surf at the mouth of the Gironde and two men (George Sheard and David Moffat) drowned; the other two (Samuel Wallace and Robert Ewart) were captured by Nazis as they struggled ashore. The team was already down to half strength and they hadn't even covered 10 per cent of the journey.

Paddling upriver by night, without the aid of lights, it was almost inevitable that the remaining three canoes would become separated. One boat got left behind and hit an underwater obstacle on the night of 10–11 December. Its crew, John McKinnon and James Conway, made it ashore and decided to head straight for Spain rather than turning north to Ruffec. They hiked 40 kilometres to a village called Cessac, where a French couple called Jaubert hid them for three days. The Jauberts said that the best way to get to Spain was by train from the town of La Réole, 20 or so kilometres further on. The two men made it to La Réole, but were arrested by French *gendarmes* and handed over to the Gestapo. It's easy to imagine the conversation between the commandos and the policemen: 'But we're your Allies, you can't just give us to the Nazis to be shot.' 'Sorry, *monsieur*, but your identity papers are clearly fake, and your French accents are atrocious.' McKinnon and Conway must have wished they'd learned a few more French swear words before leaving the UK.

Meanwhile, two canoes were still paddling upriver, their presence unsuspected because the four captured Marines revealed nothing about their mission under interrogation. And in the night of 11–12 December, the two remaining crews clamped their limpet mines to five ships, set the timers and paddled the hell out of there.

The men now had to hide their canoes and get 160 kilometres across occupied territory to Ruffec. Things got a bit more urgent when, just before dawn, the mines exploded and the Nazis realized that the men they had captured hadn't been alone. Marines Wallace and Ewart were summarily executed.

Two of the successful saboteurs, Bert Laver and Bill Mills, managed to get about 60 kilometres to a place called Montlieu-la-Garde before some locals betrayed them to the *gendarmes*, who also did their duty and delivered the commandos to the Nazis. They too were interrogated, sent to Paris along with McKinnon and Conway, and executed in March 1943.

Not knowing that they were the only men still at large, Herbie Hasler and his co-paddler Bill Sparks trekked on. They had to beg for food, and were occasionally refused help but never betrayed. On 18 December, they finally got to Ruffec where, not knowing whom to contact, they took a chance and went into a restaurant called La Toque Blanche (the White Chef's Hat). They struck lucky – the owner, a man called René Mandinaud, was sympathetic and put them in touch with the Resistance 'pipeline'.

At this point, a French government website about the Resistance, which tells the story of the mission, suddenly launches into a hail of details. Every person who helped Hasler and Sparks is – quite rightly – named. We learn each one's profession, how long the fugitives stayed with them, and whom they passed the men on to. We know, for example, the name of the teacher (Monsieur Paille) who interviewed them and confirmed that they were real Brits rather than spies, and that of the woman (Marthe Rullier) who went to alert the Resistance, as well as René Flaud (who drove the men to the Unoccupied Zone in his baker's van) and the Dubreuille family (who hid them for forty-one days on their farm).

The final link in the Cockleshell Heroes' escape chain was an English expat called Mary Lindell, who had married a French count and settled in the southwest of France. When the Nazis arrived, she went back to Britain, but returned to France in 1942 as a Resistance leader with the codename Marie-Claire. It was her eighteen-year-old son Maurice who smuggled Hasler and Sparks to Lyon, where Marie-Claire herself took the two men in hand.

Her first instruction was that Hasler should shave off his moustache – the blonde Marine looked as French as a Christmas pudding. She also warned him to stay away from the mademoiselles. In her experience, the biggest danger to escaping servicemen was their eye for the ladies, which would make them forget even rudimentary security. And she was right to be careful – just a few months later, she was wounded during a mission and sent to Ravensbrück concentration camp. She survived captivity, but one of her sons did not.

Following Mary Lindell's 'pipeline' of safe houses, Hasler and Sparks went to Marseille, Perpignan and finally over the border into Spain. Posing as tramps, they made their way to the British consulate in Barcelona, and both of them eventually got back to Britain safely via Gibraltar.

Of the ten paddlers who died, two drowned, two were captured directly by the Nazis and four were betrayed. In short, for men on a mission to save France from Nazi Occupation, just being seen by a French civilian – especially a *gendarme* – was twice as dangerous as canoeing through icy waves in the middle of a winter's night. It's probably a statistic that the French would prefer to forget.

What did you do in the war, Jean-Paul?

The moral conflicts in occupied France were great material for French writers, and those with a political conscience immediately took up their pen against the Nazis. A group of them created the publishing house Les Éditions de Minuit (Midnight Editions), which began distributing its books hand to hand to avoid censorship. Big literary guns like Louis Aragon, Paul Éluard and François Mauriac went underground and relinquished fame and royalties in favour of being read by a few people who could be trusted to pass the books on to friends instead of handing them over to the *gendarmes*.

Les Éditions du Minuit published books with titles like *Chroniques interdites* (*Forbidden Chronicles*) – a selection of banned texts – and *L'Honneur des poètes*, which speaks for itself. Print runs were small for obvious reasons, and although the company survived after the war, it spent many years on the verge of bankruptcy because of its refusal to accept Nazi or Vichy money.

On the other side of the coin were French writers who came out as overtly pro-Nazi – Louis-Ferdinand Céline, the author of the classic novel *Voyage au bout de la nuit* (*Journey to the End of the Night*), revealed himself as an anti-Semitic maniac, making statements in favour of deporting and killing anyone with one Jewish grandparent. Only slightly less dubious was Jean Cocteau, who claimed to be apolitical, but had influential friends in the Nazi regime to make sure he was never troubled.

Others simply sat on the fence, not overtly collaborating, but remaining ambiguously silent. The two most famous of these were Jean-Paul Sartre and Simone de Beauvoir.

This revered pair of intellectuals are regarded in modern-day France as untouchables – Sartre because he was arrested on the barricades during the uprising of May 1968,* and de Beauvoir for her seminal feminist book, *Le Deuxième Sexe*.

Many French people won't hear a word against them, but this is an extreme case of denial, because for most of the Occupation the pair kept their heads down and actually prospered under Nazi rule. Both were practically unknown before 1940, and rose to prominence in the

---

* Sartre was released on the orders of President de Gaulle, who said, 'You don't arrest Voltaire.'

talent vacuum of Nazi Paris – with a large proportion of the literary establishment in exile or underground, it was far easier to get published, and far more likely that their books would be read.

Sartre and de Beauvoir were anything but naïve or stupid, and must have known that French publishers had signed a collective self-censorship agreement with the Nazis, guaranteeing that no seditious literature would threaten the status quo of the Occupation. Any 'dangerous' writers simply wouldn't be published through traditional channels, and to circulate unofficial anti-Nazi reading matter was a severely punished crime.

Sartre had begun the war in the French army, but was captured by the advancing Nazis in 1940 and sent to a POW camp in the west of Germany. There he became the head of the escape committee and risked his life several times helping his fellow prisoners to tunnel out and join de Gaulle's army in Britain . . . No, actually he didn't do that at all. What he did was write a play and then get himself released and sent home back to France, claiming that his bad eyesight affected his balance. This could, of course, be interpreted as a clever escape ruse, but members of the Resistance would later find his easy release highly suspect.

A free man again, Sartre accepted a teaching job at a Paris *lycée* that had become vacant because a Jewish teacher had been forced to quit – an embarrassing fact that was kept quiet until a French magazine revealed it in 1997.

His best-known plays, *Les Mouches* (*The Flies*) and *Huis Clos* (*No Exit*) were first published and performed during the Nazi Occupation. The premiere of *Les Mouches* was held in 1943 in a theatre owned by a Frenchman whom the Germans considered *deutschfreundlich*, a venue that had been called Le Théâtre Sarah Bernhardt until the

Nazis renamed it because she was Jewish. The play received a glowing review in the Nazi newspaper *Pariser Zeitung*, which shows just how politically unthreatening it was.

Sartre redeemed himself by claiming that his works were allegories of resistance, and by joining the Comité national d'écrivains (the National Writers' Committee), which busied itself naming other writers as collaborators. His fellow existentialist Albert Camus, who had at first been amongst the politically dubious stay-at-homes, preferred to climb off the fence and take up arms in the Resistance.

Sartre's partner, Simone de Beauvoir, was equally ambiguous during the war. She was sacked from her job as a *lycée* teacher, but not for anti-Nazi activities – it was because the mother of one of her female students, a girl called Nathalie, had complained that de Beauvoir had slept with her daughter.

After this, de Beauvoir worked for Vichy's national radio, a station that was vital to the Nazis because it gave French people an alternative to tuning in to the BBC. It used to broadcast non-sensitive programmes alongside propaganda to give it a veneer of respectability,* and de Beauvoir presented a historical show that wasn't in itself pro-Nazi, but was effectively helping to boost the audience figures for propaganda. To get this job, she had to sign a form attesting that she was not a Jew, thereby openly accepting the regime's racist stance, even more so than Sartre with his teaching job.

Meanwhile, de Beauvoir was writing, and her first novel, *L'Invitée* (*She Came to Stay*), was published in

---

* Film star Catherine Deneuve's father, Maurice Dorléac, acted in radio plays on the same station. After the war, he was banned from performing for six months.

1943. She was touched when it was praised by the leading pro-Vichy writer Ramon Fernandez, and she expressed hopes of winning France's most prestigious literary prize, the Prix Goncourt, even though it was common knowledge in literary circles that the committee were overt collaborators.

In short, it is hardly surprising that much of Sartre's and de Beauvoir's post-war writing was about reinventing moral codes.

Some French painters were no more laudable. André Derain and Maurice de Vlaminck went to Germany as part of an artists' group visit, to much trumpeting by the Nazi propaganda machine. The sculptor André Maillol came up to Paris from the south of France to visit an exhibition of Nazi-approved art, and was entertained by the Germans after the show – all this while Expressionist paintings were being stolen from murdered Jewish collectors and either destroyed as 'degenerate art' or sold off to fund Hitler's war effort.

Other hugely famous names in French culture came out of the war just as tarnished. The crooner Maurice Chevalier, who had been something of a Hollywood star in the 1930s, stayed in Paris for the duration and enjoyed a successful career – though he refused to sing on Vichy radio. Édith Piaf also stayed on, singing for Nazi officers and even inviting them over to her place for drinks.

Of course it could be said that singers provided a valuable morale boost to the downtrodden French public, but it sounds as though occupying Wehrmacht troops got just as much of a kick out of their songs, and no doubt returned to the front whistling 'Je ne regrette nichts'.

Amongst the worst offenders, though, was the fashion designer Coco Chanel. Today, the Chanel brand is as impeccably clean as the lines of Coco's classic dresses, and her name conjures up everything quintessentially

French: effortless elegance, classy simplicity, the smell of luxury.

When war broke out in 1939, however, Chanel closed her fashion house, sacking her 4,000 seamstresses in the kind of mass redundancy that French unions make almost impossible these days. Perhaps she sensed that a European war would make it difficult to stage international fashion shows. She was also old enough (fifty-six) to remember that there had been a serious fabric shortage during World War One. Either way, she declared that she was going to devote all her energies to marketing her successful Chanel No. 5 perfume.

Although, to be exact, it wasn't *her* perfume. She had created it in 1921, but sold most of the rights to a pair of businessmen called Pierre and Paul Wertheimer. They were Jewish, and took refuge in the USA as soon as France was occupied, although not before setting up an Aryan-run umbrella company – wittily called Bourjois ('bourgeois' with a J in the middle) – to prevent the Nazis seizing their business interests.

Chanel knew about this manoeuvre and informed the Nazis about Bourjois's fake Aryan credentials, hoping that she would be able to regain control of her perfumes. She was well placed to do the informing, because it was common knowledge that her lover was a prominent SS intelligence officer called Hans Günther von Dincklage. Not only that, but she was living at the Ritz Hotel, one of the Nazis' headquarters in Paris. She wasn't only sleeping with the enemy, she was spending her days *chez* him, too.

In 1943, Coco became involved in a bizarre attempt to bring peace between Britain and Germany. It was apparently the brainwave of another SS man, called Walter Schellenberg, a close aide of Himmler's and the officer responsible for drawing up a list of dangerous Britons to be arrested as soon as the Nazis won the war – not the kind of man most people would credit with a plan to secure world peace.

The scheme involved Coco taking a message to Winston Churchill, a vague acquaintance whom she had met once or twice during her love affair with an English duke in the 1920s. To arrange this, she contacted an old high-society friend called Vera Bate Lombardi, a cousin of the Duke of Windsor (the abdicated King Edward VIII). Vera had introduced Coco's designs to the British upper classes before the war, and the Nazis were sure she had access to Churchill.

On Schellenberg's orders, Coco tried to lure Vera to Paris, supposedly to join her newer, bigger Chanel operation, but Vera, who was living in Rome, refused to have anything to do with her. The Nazis promptly had Vera arrested as an English spy.

Churchill did eventually help Chanel, though, because when she was arrested after the Liberation on charges of collaborating with the Nazis, it is said that Winston himself intervened in her favour. She was allowed to sneak away to a comfortable exile in Switzerland with her Nazi lover, Hans Günther.

The Wertheimers returned to France and, to avoid a messy legal battle, agreed to pay Coco off with $400,000 in cash, plus 2 per cent royalties on all Chanel products, as well as a monthly payment. No danger that Coco was going to suffer from post-war food rationing.

Sex 'crimes'

Famous collaborators may have been able to escape unscathed, but women guilty of so-called *collaboration horizontale* weren't so lucky. As soon as a town was liberated, the reprisals would begin, and any woman who had been openly giving a Nazi sex in exchange for food and luxuries had her head shaven and was often subjected to a public beating.

Well, *almost* any woman, because yet again, the French establishment closed ranks to suppress embarrassing details.

Napoleon's brothels played host to the enemy with little or no threat of interference. In Paris, thirty-one *bordels* were reserved for the Wehrmacht, as well as 5,000 women working the streets who were told to cater for Nazis only. Others were free to choose their clients without asking for details of their nationality or political views. In 1941, a new Vichy law was passed, assimilating brothels with 'third category entertainment', with the same status as horse and cycle racing. In 1942, the system went even further by making brothels just another part of the hotel industry, presumably so the girls wouldn't have to time their clients' performances quite so accurately.

After the war, while everyday *collaboratrices horizontales* were humiliated for the newsreel cameras, the prostitutes simply switched over to French and Allied clients. A French policeman noted in 1945 that some local authorities had 'refused to condemn prostitutes because their conduct was professional and not political'. Reading between the lines, the reason for the leniency is obvious. The Nazis weren't the only ones frequenting brothels – the local dignitaries were regulars, too, and didn't want the secrets of their wartime *amours* coming to light, especially when said *amour* had been obtained in establishments protected or used by the Nazis.

Retribution came only later, in 1946, when the political wing of the Resistance movement pushed through a law outlawing brothels. The irony was that the law bore the name of an ex-prostitute called Marthe Richard, who had been giving parties for Paris's high-ranking Nazis throughout the war, and who tried to clear her name by coming over all moralistic once the game was up.

Interestingly, it was a combination of this law and the struggle for power in post-war France that inspired Ian Fleming to write his first James Bond novel, *Casino Royale*. Not that anyone is suggesting that Fleming might have felt any personal nostalgia for the *bordels*, of course.

Pourquoi pas forgive *et* forget?

It may seem malicious to rake up all these memories of collaboration. It is, after all, an easy target, like reminding a football fan of a humiliating cup final defeat. And there were, of course, some Resistance heroes – Jean Moulin, for example, who was arrested in Lyon (sadly, during a meeting to organize de Gaulle's Conseil national de la Résistance) and died under Nazi torture; or Pierre Brossolette, an SOE agent who, although handcuffed, threw himself out of a top-floor window to his death rather than risk revealing anything to the Gestapo; or Guy Môquet, who was shot by the Germans when aged only seventeen, and whose farewell letter to his family is studied in French schools.

But there were skeletons in the cupboard – Guy Môquet, for example, was arrested by *French* policemen for illegally distributing leaflets – and after the war, France tried to keep many of them locked in there. There were plenty of show trials and head-shavings, but these mainly involved people who were either too obviously Nazi to get away with it, or who just lacked the power and friends to avoid trouble.

After 1945, the rot in the French establishment was too deep to be cut out without undermining the whole fabric of the country. François Mitterrand, who was elected President of France in 1981, was a perfect example of this. After a spell in a German POW camp, he returned to

France in 1941 and worked for the Vichy government. He was undoubtedly active in the Resistance, especially later in the war, but was also a good enough servant of the Pétain regime to be awarded the Ordre de la francisque, a Vichy order of merit. Some of his contemporaries suspected him of playing two hands simultaneously, waiting to see which side would come out on top. And in 1992 it was revealed that he had secretly arranged for wreaths to be laid on Pétain's tomb ever since the old collaborator-in-chief's death in 1951.

One common French retort to all this talk of collaboration is that the Anglo-Saxons 'l'ont échappé belle' – had a narrow, or in French 'beautiful', escape. The Brits and the Americans were never faced with the moral dilemmas of Occupation. Would a London policeman have handed General de Gaulle over to the Gestapo? We will never know.

Although that might not be exactly true, because of course a small part of Britain was occupied by the Nazis . . .

Living with the Nazi 'visitors'

As France was spiralling towards surrender in 1940, the Brits decided that the Channel Islands weren't worth defending. They announced that they would evacuate anyone who wanted to escape, and then leave the islands to the Germans. This begged the question: in that case, why had Britain hung on to them for so many centuries? The answer, of course, was obvious: just to annoy the French.

The announcement also gave the islanders very little time to make their decision. Should they leave their homes to the Nazis for the foreseeable future, or stay on and hope for the best?

Most men of military age who weren't already in uniform went to England to join up, and in all, around 30,000 people, a third of the islands' population, opted to leave. The rest decided to wait for the inevitable, and not a shot was fired when the islands surrendered one by one in early July 1940.

So how did the islanders behave during their five years of occupation? In his book *The British Channel Islands under German Occupation, 1940–1945*, Paul Sanders gives an incredibly detailed account of life under the Nazis in Jersey, Guernsey, Alderney and Sark. He paints a morally complex, often sordid, but occasionally uplifting picture.

There were collaborators (horizontal and upright), paid informers, black marketeers and fraternizers, and the wartime Bailiff of Jersey, Alexander Coutanche, was accused by some of being a Pétain-like traitor for agreeing to serve under the Nazis.

But there were subtle differences to what happened on the French mainland. The most important was that, in fact, no equivalent of the Nazi-pandering Vichy government was set up. The island was administered, yes, but not by people who secretly welcomed the Nazis' presence or wanted to implement any of their ideas.

It is true that Hitler's anti-Jewish laws were introduced on the islands. Jews had to register, and were eventually prevented from owning businesses. But the laws were not zealously applied as they were in France, and Bailiff Coutanche refused to force anyone to wear a yellow star.

Tragically, three Jews were deported from Guernsey to Auschwitz. It seems they were singled out by the Nazis because they were refugees from Austria. Auguste Spitz, Marianne Grunfield and Therese Steiner never came back. The Guernsey police did take part in their deportation, but only to inform them of the Germans' order that they had to pack a suitcase and report to the Nazis the next day. This doesn't alter the women's ultimate fate, of course, and no one stepped in to save them, but neither were they grabbed by the local police and handed over, as might have happened in France.

Most of the islands' other Jews were sent to internment camps (as opposed to concentration camps) in 1942 and 1943, as part of a group of some 1,300 deportees that included anyone not born in the Channel Islands and all men who had served as officers in World War One. They were all deemed by the Nazis to be 'undesirable influences' and shipped off to Germany in reprisal for a British commando raid on Sark. Most of them survived the war.

There was little or no Resistance movement, although the islands' first wartime administrator, Sir Ambrose James Sherwill, was imprisoned and then interned for aiding a commando raid, and a few escaped prisoners were hidden and helped to freedom. Most islanders remained passive, and contented themselves with daubing Churchill's 'V for Victory' sign on walls and listening to the BBC, a common crime for which all radio sets on the islands were confiscated in 1942. Not very disruptive, one might argue, but it would have been hard to organize an underground army when there was pretty well one Nazi soldier to every two residents, almost all of the occupiers billeted in the locals' homes.

This cohabitation predictably led to fraternization, usually to obtain food – once the shops had sold their stock, severe rationing kicked in. Fishing boats were forbidden to go out, and most people had little more than oats, potatoes and milk to eat, whereas the Germans had ample supplies that they were willing to sell or trade. The trading was, inevitably, often for things other than carved seashells and local handicrafts – many women went in for horizontal collaboration, and were dubbed 'Jerry-bags' by the disapproving islanders. As in France, the worst offenders were young girls who liked the smart, well-fed men in their uniforms, and upper-class ladies who fell for the officers' old-school Prussian charm. And there were also real love affairs. But the phenomenon was apparently much less prevalent than on the French mainland, partly because the community was so small that it was impossible to be discreet and partly because the islands were effectively in the front line and the garrison had little time for partying, but also because there was a well-run, health-inspected brothel available, entirely reserved for the troops. It was managed by a French madam and employed French prostitutes. Yes, the Nazis imported *collaboratrices horizontales*.

Artists lick the Nazis

Like their colleagues in Paris, the Germans occupying the Channel Islands were not deprived of entertainment. There were theatre performances, concerts (some mixing local and German musicians) and art exhibitions. But cultural life on the islands seems to have been characterized by some quirky acts of artistic resistance.

Claude Cahun and Marcel Moore were two French women artists who had settled in Jersey before the war. When the Nazis arrived, the pair accepted invitations to parties with the occupiers. However, they didn't do so just to drink Champagne and snaffle canapés, and given their sexuality, it is unlikely that they were interested in sleeping with the enemy. In fact, they would get themselves invited to social occasions and then slip anti-Nazi leaflets into German soldiers' pockets. These weren't simple propaganda sheets – they were works of art, such as anti-Fascist poems or cut-and-paste texts listing Nazi atrocities.

Unsurprisingly, Cahun and Moore were caught in 1944 and sentenced to death, although their executions were never carried out and they ended the war in prison. Had they been doing the same thing in France, it could have been much worse for them, as they were both Jews.

A Jersey artist who was much more mainstream was Edmund Blampied. When the war broke out he was fifty-three, an internationally renowned illustrator and one of the island's leading cultural lights. He chose not to leave the island in 1940, even though his wife was Jewish. Neither he nor his wife were mistreated by the occupiers, and he could even be accused of collaborating in that he accepted the commission to design wartime currency and stamps. A Nazi sympathizer, perhaps?

Not really. Blampied took the considerable risk of incorporating the letters 'GR', for King George VI, in his stamp designs, so that, during the whole occupation, every time an islander licked a stamp, they were poking their tongue out at the Nazis.

A British cover-up?

After the war, allegations of collaboration in the Channel Islands were investigated by the British police and even MI5. Doubts about the Bailiff of Jersey, Alexander Coutanche, were dismissed, so one could accuse the British establishment of being as self-protective as the French. But it seems that, like other politicians on the islands, he maintained working relations with the Nazis in order to ensure that the residents did not suffer too much. And not just the native islanders – he went to the Nazi commander to complain about the ill treatment of Russian slave labourers being used to build fortifications. The islanders would often give food to these men, which infuriated the Nazis so much that they put up posters saying that it was not necessary to feed the prisoners because the living skeletons actually received enough to eat.

In fact, Coutanche waged a constant niggling campaign of resistance against the occupiers, often refusing to sign orders or implement new rules, and photos of him in 1945 show a markedly thinner man than in 1940. Unless self-starvation was a cunning ploy to avoid detection, he was on the same enforced diet as the other islanders.

After the war, known black marketeers had their profits confiscated, and there were a few attacks on 'Jerry-bags'. Forty islanders were banished, and twelve were put forward for prosecution, including some paid informers, although all charges were eventually dropped. It seems that the Channel Islands, like France, preferred to put the recent past behind them.

So things weren't pearly-white, and the Brits did collaborate. But there was one big difference between Paris and Jersey or Guernsey – almost all the active male Channel Islanders had gone off to fight rather than sitting around in cafés arguing about the true meaning of moral freedom.

The French 'liberate themselves'

The tears of joy and relief that greeted the Allied troops as they advanced through Normandy in June 1944 told the real story of the Liberation. But one man was not there to see them – Charles de Gaulle.

For security reasons, he was not told about the preparations for D-Day until two days before the invasion. After everything that had gone before, Churchill was afraid that if the French had known earlier, the Nazis would have found out what was going to happen. Not through deliberate treachery, of course – there was just a risk that one of de Gaulle's aides would go to a London bookshop and order 500 maps of Normandy.

If you ask a Frenchman today whose troops were on the Normandy beaches on 6 June 1944, you will probably get the answer 'mainly Americans'. The Brits were there, he will admit, but not very many of them. And he will almost certainly forget the Canadians completely.

In fact, though, of the 156,000 or so troops who landed in Normandy on D-Day, 73,000 were American and 83,000 belonged to the British army, although admittedly only 61,700 of them were actually Brits. The rest were mainly Canadian.

There were also Frenchmen present – marine commandos who had been given diagrams of their targets a few days before the invasion. The maps had no place names, but some of the men were Normans, and recognized the targets. Their British commanders were so worried about a security breach that they had the Frenchmen locked into their camp until D-Day.

These French troops were led by a man called Philippe Kieffer, who had rallied to the Allied cause right from the start of the war, and they fought bravely, suffering proportionately high losses during the battle for Normandy – a fifth of their unit was killed. This sounds a lot, and statistically it was, but the almost unbelievable fact is that, on D-Day, the French invasion force amounted to only 177. Not 177 brigades or battalions – 177 men, making up just over 0.1 per cent of the total invasion army.

Why so few? Well, apart from the fact that most of the French army was in German prison camps or French civvie street (*la rue civile?*), the Allies had major problems getting de Gaulle to support an operation to invade France. The Général was stung by his late inclusion in the plans, and scornful of Churchill's insistence that, before the landings went ahead, it was vital to discuss how a liberated France would be governed. De Gaulle maintained that he didn't need to 'apply to the Americans' to run his own country. He even refused to let 200 French liaison officers cross the Channel with Allied units because he didn't want them politically compromised. He was concerned that the Allies might install a temporary regime in liberated zones that he wouldn't be able to control. The American General George C. Marshall was so furious at this refusal to send in Free French helpers that he made a blasting statement that 'no sons of Iowa would fight to put up statues of de Gaulle in France', which rather cleverly symbolized what de Gaulle was actually hoping would happen.

The Général held off till the last minute before he made a speech to the French supporting the D-Day landings, provoking Churchill into accusing him of being 'consumed by ambition, like a ballerina'. (Churchill obviously knew things about ballerinas that most of us don't.)

In the end, de Gaulle came round – as usual, he was just pushing things to the limit, testing Allied resilience and marking his territory – and gave a brilliant speech on the BBC's French-language service.

'The supreme battle has begun,' he began. 'After so much fighting, fury and pain, the decisive blow has been struck. Of course, it is the Battle for France and it is the Battle of France!' (That repetition is not a misprint. When I say he gave a brilliant speech, I mean by French rhetorical standards.) He went on:

Immense attacking forces – for us, rescue forces – have begun to burst out from the coast of Old England, the last bastion of Western Europe to stand firm against the tide of German oppression. It is from there that the freedom offensive has been launched. France, down-trodden for four years, but not diminished or beaten, France is on its feet and playing its part. France will battle with all its might. It will fight methodically. That is how, for the past 1,500 years, we have won all our battles.

In going so far back in history, de Gaulle seems to be referring to the invasion of Attila the Hun, whom France did indeed repel, although according to French legend, this had more to do with the prayers of St Genevieve than fighting ability.

De Gaulle called on the French to resist the oppressor 'by means of weapons, destruction or information', and concluded poetically: 'The Battle of France has begun. The nation, the empire, the army are united in a single desire, a single hope. From behind the heavy cloud of our blood and tears, at last we can see the sun of our greatness!'

You would have thought that there were 177,000 Frenchmen crossing the Channel rather than just 177. De Gaulle himself didn't boost their numbers until 14 June, eight days into the offensive, but as soon as he appeared on his home soil, it was clear that he had won his personal battle. Everywhere he went, the liberated French hailed him as the returning hero and accepted him as their new leader. His determination not to share power and not to let the other Allies interfere in France's post-war regime had paid off. According to Simon Berthon, author of the book *Allies at War*, which details the tumul-tuous relationship between de Gaulle, Churchill and Roosevelt, the Général's arrival was also very convenient for the French because he was a living embodiment of the myth that France had never been defeated. He made it look as if Liberation was simply a result of his presence in London, and that, contrary to appearances, France had never stopped resisting the enemy.

Be nice to the French – but not too nice

Armed with a booklet on how to behave *chez les Français*, the British contingent of the invasion force arrived in France. Much more respectful than the chat-up phrasebook available to the World War One troops, it was called *Instructions for British Servicemen in France*, and contained a very astute rundown of the historical hiccups in Anglo-French relations, with laconic phrases like: 'The long wars with England and the recurrent invasions from our side of the Channel have left the modern Frenchman with no grudge against us, except perhaps for the burning of Joan of Arc.'

It also recalled more recent history, pointing out that the French were not too happy about Dunkirk, Mers-el-Kebir, Dakar, Madagascar or the bombing of harbours and factories in France, and made the glorious understatement that 'it is only natural that these should have caused some resentment'.

The language section was much less suggestive than its World War One predecessor too. It stuck mainly to hellos, goodbyes and obtaining food and information – the phrase 'Are the trees in that wood thick?' was almost certainly not a chat-up line. The soldiers needed to know where Nazi tanks and troops might be hidden.

In any case, the book was very clear on the need to *respecter les femmes*. The girls at the Folies Bergère were not typical Frenchwomen, it stressed, and soldiers should not 'imagine that the first pretty French girl who smiles at you intends to dance the can-can or take you to bed'.

Not that the troops had much time for dancing and fornicating as they battled their way across the French countryside. Nor were they going to be allowed anywhere near the Folies Bergère. De Gaulle saw to that.

Who liberated Paris? *Moi!*

The French think that Paris was liberated at the end of August 1944 by the legendary Général Leclerc, who linked up with the Resistance to batter the Nazis into surrender. Leclerc, they believe, was accompanied by a few Americans who came along for the ride, but there were no Brits present.

Actually, this is pretty close to the truth, but not for the reasons that are usually given.

Churchill had arranged for a larger French force under Leclerc (full name Philippe Leclerc de Hautecloque – the last name is usually omitted, probably because it could be translated as 'tall blister') to come to Normandy at the beginning of August. Leclerc's Second Armoured Division consisted of just over 14,000 men, including 3,600 North Africans and 3,200 Spanish Republicans, and was nominally under the command of the American General Patton – though it would soon be clear that its real commander was de Gaulle.

The Allied push towards Germany was, for obvious geographical reasons, centred quite a way north of Paris.* If the Allies could make a thrust across the Seine and up to the Belgian border, the theory went, they might cut off Hitler's army of occupation and win the race to Berlin against Stalin and the Communists (the Cold War had already started in all but name).

---

* The Allies didn't let themselves be distracted by the Channel Islands, which weren't liberated until May 1945, by which time the islanders were starving and even the Nazi garrison was reduced to sneaking over to France to steal food.

This, though, did not suit de Gaulle at all. He knew that he had to get to Paris as soon as possible after D-Day if he wanted to run the whole of France. Things were hotting up in the city – a general strike began on 15 August, followed by an uprising four days later by the FFI – the Forces françaises de l'intérieur, a raggle-taggle civilian army led by a Communist called Henri Rol-Tanguy, alias Colonel Rol.

The last thing de Gaulle wanted was to let Rol take the credit, and the capital – the gratitude of a few flag-waving Normans meant nothing if Paris was liberated by the Communists. So once again, the overall strategy of the Allies was shoved into second place behind de Gaulle's and (he claimed) France's interests.

General Eisenhower, meanwhile, had his hands rather full dealing with the ferocious Nazi resistance that his men were meeting across northern France, so de Gaulle threatened to send Leclerc's small army into Paris alone unless the Allies agreed to sidetrack their advance and liberate the city. De Gaulle's daring but ill-advised scheme might well have meant destruction for Leclerc's valuable tanks (which were actually American machines), so Eisenhower agreed to support the French with a large force of American infantry, and, sportingly, to let Leclerc enter the city first.

The race was on. De Gaulle ordered his men to advance as quickly as possible into Paris to steal the Communists' thunder. Accordingly, Leclerc struck prematurely in the south of the city, inadvertently choosing to do so precisely where the Germans had set up their strongest defence. This not only got Leclerc bogged down but also alerted the Germans that a bigger attack was about to happen.

The French pulled back and tried a more westerly route, but got held up again when the inhabitants of the western suburbs came out and began to bombard the tanks with flowers, wine and hugs. Losing their patience with Leclerc, the American troops announced that they were going to hit the Germans in the south with everything they had got and march straight on into the city, and tough luck if a Frenchman wasn't at the head of the liberators. This ultimatum came on the evening of 24 August.

Afraid to let de Gaulle down, Leclerc told a captain called Raymond Dronne to take a small detachment of three armoured cars and three tanks and use their local knowledge to zig-zag through the back streets of the southwestern suburbs. They had, they were told, to get to the centre of Paris that very night.

This they did, although local knowledge didn't play much of a part in their progress – Dronne wasn't a Parisian and most of his men were Spanish. But they arrived safely at the Hôtel de Ville (Town Hall) just before midnight, and the bells of Notre-Dame Cathedral set off a welcoming chorus across the whole of Paris. All the inhabitants knew what this meant, including the Germans who had been defending the outskirts of the city – they retreated during the night, allowing Leclerc's main force of tanks to make their triumphant arrival.

The Nazi governor of Paris, Dietrich von Choltitz,* surrendered to Colonel Rol and General Leclerc on 25 August at Montparnasse Station and told his 17,000 men to stop fighting.

The victorious de Gaulle arrived on the twenty-fifth

---

* Von Choltitz is said by some to have saved Paris by refusing to obey Hitler's orders to blow up the city. However, he planted explosives under many key buildings, and in the days just prior to his capitulation he burned down the Grand Palais, destroyed Paris's cereal stocks and had Resistance fighters executed en masse. He was no Saint Choltitz.

and declared himself the head of the Gouvernement provisoire de la République française. He also objected to Colonel Rol's name appearing on the official German surrender document. The Général took possession of his old office at the War Ministry and then walked to the Hôtel de Ville, where he formally assumed military control of the city. He was invited to go on to the balcony to proclaim the return of the Republic, but refused, saying he had been leader of the French for four years and didn't need to proclaim anything.

It was at the Hôtel de Ville that he made another of his famous speeches, the 'Paris libéré' declaration, in which, ignoring the fact that Churchill, Roosevelt and all their men were still battling their way to liberate less strategic parts of France, he announced that Paris had been liberated 'by its people with the help of the armies of France, with the support and help of all France, of fighting France, the only France, the real France, of France alone'.

The Général then went even further – when he came across members of Britain's Special Operations Executive, the men who had been co-ordinating so many of the Resistance's activities, he told them to leave Paris: 'This is no place for you.' In other words, goodbye and thanks for all the cups of tea.

Next day, de Gaulle led a procession down the Champs-Élysées and across the place de la Concorde (now the route of the annual Bastille Day parades), followed by Leclerc and a host of Resistance fighters. Leclerc's tanks were kept out of the way – de Gaulle didn't want a full-scale military parade – and were parked near the Arc de Triomphe. In fact, they shouldn't have been anywhere near the procession at all, because Eisenhower had ordered them to rejoin the main Allied army now that their job in Paris was done. De Gaulle told Leclerc to ignore the order, and also decreed that the Americans could not join his victory parade.

This was de Gaulle's big day, and he engraved it indelibly on the public memory when sniper shots rang out as he crossed Concorde and, later, when he was walking towards Notre-Dame Cathedral. On both occasions, practically everyone, soldiers and civilians alike, dived for cover except de Gaulle. Cynics have suggested that the shots were pre-arranged, but it is far more likely that de Gaulle simply felt totally invulnerable. This was what he had lived for since the day in June 1940 when Winston Churchill had pushed him in front of a BBC microphone, and no cowardly sniper was going to spoil it.

All over bar the slapping

As soon as Paris was liberated, de Gaulle went into action to tighten his hold on the reins of power. He reformed the disbanded Première Armée and sent it to join the Allies who were liberating the rest of France. Supported as usual by the Americans, it then made a punitive thrust across the Rhine and the Danube into the heart of Germany.

De Gaulle also sent out troops to re-establish French control over its colonies in Asia and Africa, inadvertently committing France to a series of hideous colonial wars in the 1950s and 60s, but for the time being ensuring that the Anglo-Saxons didn't dip their sticky fingers into France's empire.

And that was about it, really – the war was over and France had won.

There were two final slaps in the face coming de Gaulle's way, however. And, surprisingly, neither came from the Brits or the Americans.

The photos of the Yalta Conference in February 1945 are singularly lacking in Frenchmen. The meeting of the

Churchill, Roosevelt and Stalin have been keeping a chair free for France's wartime leader-in-exile, Charles de Gaulle. If the Frenchman is looking suspicious, it's probably because he suspects that his 'Allies' have sawn through the chair legs.

'big three' (not the *'grand quatre'*) to discuss the post-war rule of Germany involved only Stalin, Churchill and Roosevelt. Roosevelt had vetoed de Gaulle's presence, saying that it would be an 'undesirable factor', and Stalin was even blunter, declaring that he didn't see what the French had done to warrant a place at the conference table. It was therefore largely thanks to Churchill that France was invited to join in the carve-up of post-war Germany into Allied sectors.

Even so, this wasn't too painful a slap, because apart from being absent from history's photo album, it was an acceptable result for de Gaulle: after May 1945, France got its old 1918 borders back, and was even allowed to drive its tanks around large bits of Germany. Honour had been restored.

The second put-down was much more hurtful because it came from France itself. Just like Churchill, who was voted out of office by the war-tired Brits in 1945, de Gaulle couldn't hold on to power. His newly liberated nation decided that it didn't want the Général as its supreme leader, and, fed up of trying to govern alongside the Communists and Socialists, de Gaulle withdrew from the coalition, casting a Macbeth-like spell on the country as he left: 'You will regret the path you have chosen.'

In retrospect it still seems hard to believe that, after such an obsessive wartime campaign to seal personal glory for France and himself, de Gaulle just walked away from office. But this is to misunderstand the man. He wasn't just any old wartime leader. In his head, de Gaulle was the new Napoleon.

It all adds up – the fury whenever *les Anglais* went anywhere near a part of the French Empire; the horror at the idea that les Anglo-Saxons were invading France (albeit as liberators); the victorious homecoming to the Arc de

Triomphe; the 'I am France'-style declarations; even the way in which he'd risen to prominence as the techno-savvy man of the moment. He *was* the new Bonaparte. And like Bonaparte (at least until his final exile), de Gaulle knew that his nation might reject him now, but they would soon regret it and clamour for him to come back.

And when he did return, it was the Brits and Americans who were going to suffer.

29

Le Temps du Payback

Britain, the USA and France emerged from the Second World War scarred but fundamentally happy. Despite the heavy human and economic cost, they had all, in their own ways, won great moral as well as military victories. The dictators had been toppled, the invaders repelled, their perverted ideals frustrated. Well, almost, because Stalin was proving to be something of a headache and, thanks to Churchill and Roosevelt, he controlled quite a large part of Europe. But now the Allies could sit down and plan the way forward for the brave new free Western world, *n'est-ce pas*?

Er, *non merci*, came the answer from France, a response that was repeated even more loudly and frequently after Charles de Gaulle returned to power. As the Général had shown throughout the war, France had its own priorities. It even created a new philosophy based on this – *l'exception française*, the basic thrust of which was 'we've had enough of these Anglo-Saxon *conneries.*'

But why all the French negativity? Well, like the drowning man who is pulled out of the canal by his old worst enemy, post-war France was carrying a painful burden of resentment relating to the Liberation. From 1940 to 1944, not only had the old worst enemy pulled the French out of the canal, but it had also given them a roof over their head, warm clothes and a hot meal, and then escorted them home in a chauffer-driven limousine. The implied debt of moral gratitude was too much, and after 1945 France was determined to show that it didn't need all this patronizing help. It also wanted revenge.

At last, a good French joke

While de Gaulle was in the wilderness (well, at home in the east of France writing his war memoirs), the Brits upheld their ancient tradition of annoying their Gallic neighbours.

In 1947, during one of the bitterest winters in living memory, Britain stopped exporting coal. This was a purely defensive measure, to ensure that its own home fires kept burning, but it was also a perfectly well-aimed kick in the crotch of France's slowly recovering industries, which ground to a temporary halt. Not content with this, Britain struck another cruel economic blow in 1949 when it devalued the pound, suddenly making French goods prohibitively expensive on the world market compared to their competitors across the Channel. Whatever happened to *la solidarité*?

The Americans added their own fuel to the diplomatic fire during the creation of NATO in 1948 and 1949. The French had originally seen this an international organization to protect Europe against renewed aggression from Germany, but when the Cold War started in earnest, the USA got together with Britain and made sure that the new NATO was primarily an anti-Soviet initiative. To make it even clearer that they were ignoring France's wishes, the Anglo-Saxons actually made provisions for

Germany to join the military alliance. The prospect of one day being hauled out of the canal by yet another old enemy was hard for France to swallow, even more so when British and French defence specialists discussed their exit strategy in case of an overwhelming Soviet attack, and the Brits proposed a massive evacuation via Dunkirk. They were serious, too.

France had the final laugh, though, by generously offering to host NATO's military headquarters, SHAPE (Supreme Headquarters Allied Powers in Europe). This was an obviously English name that probably irritated the French a little, but they got their own back by building the HQ at Rocquencourt, a little town 20 kilometres outside Paris that was almost impossible for an *Anglo-Saxon* to spell or pronounce correctly.

The Brits and Americans might well have wondered why the French were so keen on this Parisian suburb. Did they think the old quarry there would make a good nuclear bunker? Was it because nearby Versailles would be a nice place for the NATO soldiers to visit on their days off? Or could it possibly have been because Rocquencourt was the site of Napoleon's last battle?

You see, the Brits might be under the impression that the defeat at Waterloo on 18 June 1815 was the Empereur's swan song, but in fact, two weeks later, his army fought one last time, and actually won a great victory.

On 1 July 1815, the invading Prussians were about to enter Paris when a French army lured them into an ambush at Rocquencourt, where they gave them a good sabre-bashing and took 400 prisoners. The Prussians subsequently sent in reinforcements, chased the remnants of Napoleon's army away and captured Paris, but in French minds that is irrelevant. What really matters is that France won this last battle and that Napoleon was therefore, in the final analysis, a victor and not, as the *Anglais* always try to imply, a loser.

Almost no one has ever heard of the Battle of Rocquencourt, which probably made the French chuckle as they put the site forward to be NATO's military HQ. It had to be one of the best military in-jokes ever.

L'Empire strikes back

Meanwhile, Britain was prancing about on the moral high ground with regard to its empire. India was independent (although bloodily so) and the Brits had extricated themselves from Palestine. An uprising in Kenya was being kept under control thanks to native African troops, and Malaya had been promised independence and was therefore working with Britain to oust Communist insurgents. By contrast, the Algerians began rebelling against French rule in 1945, and the Communist leader Ho Chi Minh was leading a revolt in Indochina. France's empire was on the verge of exploding.

Unlike the Brits, who mainly steered clear of long colonial wars and advised France to do the same, the French dug in, pitching their greatest generals (apart from le Général, that is) against the Vietnamese rebels. But even men like General Leclerc could do nothing to stop Ho Chi Minh, who had honed his battle skills against the Japanese, and it all ended very messily in 1954, when the French decided to make a stand in a valley called Dien Bien Phu.

Assuming that mere Asian guerrillas would never be able to win a pitched battle, the French dug World War One-style trenches, and were horrified when the highly organized Viet Minh began bombarding them with deadly accuracy from the surrounding hills. It was almost as though the rebels had been sneakily reading Napoleon's war manuals. The French artillery commander was so heartbroken at being out-thought and outgunned that he went into a bunker and blew himself up with a hand grenade.

After almost two months of savage fighting, the Viet Minh finally overran the French, taking more than 11,000 prisoners. Independence talks began in Geneva on 8 May 1954, exactly nine years since France's victory in Europe, and took place to an infuriating background chorus from Britain and America of 'told you so'.

The French extracted the dregs of a victory by obtaining an agreement whereby, instead of letting Ho Chi Minh hold nationwide elections that he would almost certainly have won, the country was divided into two, with the southern part ruled by a puppet pro-French ruler – which planted the seeds of the Vietnam War that would so annoy the Americans a decade later.

Unfortunately for France, though, Ho Chi Minh had given other people ideas, and revolts either broke out or intensified in the French territories of Cameroon, Tunisia, Morocco and – bloodiest of all – Algeria. The Brits provoked French wrath by refusing to sell them helicopters for use in Algeria, yet again showing the *typiquement anglais* capacity for posing on the moral high ground. It was almost as if the two countries had never been allies at all. In fact, the only highpoint in Anglo-French relations during the whole period was a farcical low point in both nations' histories . . .

Britain pulls the plug on the Suez Canal

In 1956, Colonel Nasser, the President of Egypt, declared that the Suez Canal, the vital lifeline between east and west and the main artery of European presence in the

Middle East, was being nationalized. The French had built the canal, and a French company, the Compagnie universelle du canal maritime de Suez, had run it since its completion in 1869. But on 26 July 1956, Nasser passed a Nationalization Law and announced that all shares would be bought by Egypt at the day's closing price on the stock market. This was a perfectly legal move, but was obviously made to undermine British and French prestige in the region.

The French were already looking for an excuse to bash Nasser. He was supplying the Algerian rebels with military advisers and weapons – some of which had been sold to Egypt by the Brits. So France suggested a Franco-British invasion to take control of the canal. The French even offered to let the Brits command the invading army (thereby ensuring that the squeaky-clean *Anglais* would get their fingers dirty in a colonial war), and said that they could guarantee success by involving their new friends the Israelis, who were also chomping at the bit to cut the belligerent Nasser down to size.

The British PM, Anthony Eden, a Francophile who had worked as an intermediary between de Gaulle and Churchill during World War Two, was hesitant, but gave the go-ahead for hush-hush talks between French, Israeli and British negotiators. They were to meet at a top-secret location – a house in the chic Paris suburb of Sèvres – and fine-tune their joint strategy. Basically, Israel would invade and topple Nasser, and the Brits and French would then intervene, supposedly as peacemakers but in fact to regain a foothold in Egypt. A cunning plan.

As a veteran of 1940–44 London, Eden ought to have known that the concept 'top secret' was relative where Anglo-French relations were concerned, and he really shouldn't have been surprised when his men came back to London with the invasion plan written out in black and white, whereas their instructions had been to make sure that nothing whatsoever was committed to paper. It was as if the French were setting him up.

They were certainly pitching Eden against his ally President Eisenhower, who was opposed to military intervention. And when the Anglo-Franco-Israeli attack began in October 1956, the Brits showed once again where their true loyalties lay. The invasion, and the consequent doubts about Britain's role in the Middle East, hit sterling so hard on the money markets that Eden was forced to prop the currency up with borrowed American dollars, a loan he received on condition that he surrender to Eisenhower's pressure and pull out of Egypt. The French urged him to stand up to the Americans, at least until Nasser had been fatally weakened, but Eden sheepishly confessed that he had already made his promise to Eisenhower. Suez was history.

For France, this was the final straw. It was Dunkirk all over again. The Brits were as untrustworthy as ever, but were now even more despicable because they were at the beck and call of their new American masters.

The French decided that they would win their colonial wars on their own, but got themselves so deep in the mire in Algeria that their army mutinied. A crack unit of French paratroopers even invaded Corsica (wanting, perhaps, to gain inspiration from a visit to Napoleon's birthplace?) and was said to be planning an invasion of the mainland to seize political power.

De Gaulle, meanwhile, was sitting in the watchtower-cum-office he had built for himself at his house in the village of Colombey-les-Deux-Églises, gazing down on France as it made a fool of itself. He was like the wizened old player in an American baseball movie – he wrings his hands at the mess these uppity newcomers are making of his team, but deep down he knows that one day they'll call him and beg him to come and win the crunch match of the season for them.

The call came on 28 May 1958. As Paris sat at its dinner table wondering when the rebel paratroopers were going to start floating out of the sky, the French President, René Coty, invited de Gaulle to step up to the plate and take over the country. When the Général's political opponents raised objections, he countered, 'Who really believes that, at the age of sixty-seven, I would begin a career as a dictator?'

De Gaulle was back in power and mightily pleased with himself. Even Napoleon hadn't managed a come-back after twelve whole years away. Now people were going to see what a Frenchman could *really* achieve on the world stage.

The French want to kill their Général

It took almost four years for de Gaulle to sort things out at home, because a powerful section of the French estab-lishment really did not want to let go of Algeria. An army-led group called the Organisation armée secrète carried out terrorist attacks in mainland France; the police massacred around 200 Algerian immigrants after a protest march in Paris; and de Gaulle himself survived over thirty assassination attempts – not by Algerian in-dependence fighters but by Frenchmen. The worst of these was a machine-gun attack on his car, during which bullets whistled past the head of both the Général and his wife. But de Gaulle had been sniped at before, and emerged unfazed. He negotiated Algerian independence and then turned his full attention to the Anglo-Saxons.

In 1957, France had set up a Common Market with Belgium, Luxembourg, Holland, Italy and West Germany. Faced with the danger of being excluded from doing business with the above countries, in 1958 the Brits decided that they might like to join in the fun.

However, there was one part of the Common Market agreement, the Treaty of Rome, that Britain didn't want to sign up to – the agricultural policy, which even fifty years ago already looked to sceptics as though it was purely geared to keeping French farmers in business. Consequently, Britain offered to join the Common Market for all goods except agricultural produce.

The French puffed with despair at this eternal British desire to bend the rules in their favour (perhaps France thought that it ought to have a monopoly on that?) and de Gaulle broke off the discussions. He made the rejection even clearer by lobbying for the creation of a full-blown Common Agricultural Policy, which was implemented in 1962 and set French farmers up on the unassailable pedestal they still occupy so proudly today.

The British Prime Minister, Harold Macmillan, was sure that de Gaulle was excluding the Brits because he saw them both as puppets for the Americans and as rivals for European domination. The Frenchman could never, Macmillan said, forgive the Anglo-Saxons for the Liberation. And he was exactly right. De Gaulle knew that he was top dog in the new Europe, and he wasn't going to share power.

Even so, Macmillan was determined to persuade the Général to soften his stance, and invited him to come shooting on his country estate at Birch Grove in Sussex. The PM was a real old country gent, and loved nothing better than pottering about in tweeds blasting at wildlife. De Gaulle accepted the invitation, but it didn't turn out to be the cosy sporting weekend Macmillan had hoped for. Alarmed by the attempts on his life, the Frenchman always travelled with a stock of blood in case he needed a transfusion, but Mrs Macmillan, who was a bit of an eccentric (she used to garden at night in a miner's helmet), refused point blank to have the gruesome stuff in the house. The French had to bring a special fridge with them and set it up in an outbuilding. Worse, de Gaulle's security guards ruined the shooting by crashing about in the woods and disturbing the pheasants. They clearly weren't sporting men.

A return visit to the French presidential palace in the forest of Rambouillet near Paris at the end of 1962 didn't go any better. Here, de Gaulle was on a reassuringly firm historic footing. It was at Rambouillet in 1944 that he had written his 'Paris libéré' speech. The Général felt so at ease that when he took Macmillan shooting, he simply stood by and made loud comments whenever the PM missed a shot.

De Gaulle also made it clear that he saw little point in talks about Britain joining the Common Market. He told Macmillan straight that as things stood, France could veto anything it wanted in Europe and lord it over Germany, whereas if Britain came in, things would be much less comfortable. He also insisted on speaking without an interpreter, and although Macmillan spoke very good French, conversation was inevitably one-sided. De Gaulle later described Macmillan as 'this poor man, to whom I had nothing to offer', who looked so beaten that 'I wanted to put my hand on his shoulder and tell him, don't cry, Milord' – a joking reference to an Édith Piaf song, 'Ne pleurez pas, Milord'.

De Gaulle didn't stop there. He went on to make some astonishing statements that gave the *coup de grâce* to Britain's application to join the EC. Britain had been trying to exist alongside Europe without really joining in for 800 years, he said (although he could have added another couple of centuries to that). He also slammed the Brits for accepting American Polaris missiles, more evidence that Britain was in the pocket of the USA and therefore not a reliable European ally. And when one of de Gaulle's own ministers criticized him for forgetting the Entente Cordiale, he simply reminded the man of Agincourt and Waterloo. To de Gaulle, scuppering the Common Market negotiations was pure historical revenge.

Discord over Concorde

It seems hardly credible that while de Gaulle was trying to shoot Britain down in flames, the Brits and the French were co-operating – or at least trying to – on the development of Concorde.

They had been working individually on supersonic aircraft ever since the war. France was developing a small fast plane for routes to its African colonies. The British Aircraft Corporation, meanwhile, was drawing blueprints for a wedge-shaped transatlantic jet – basically, the future Concorde. Soon, though, the British project was soaring over budget rather than over the clouds, and the government demanded that outside funding be found. Hoping that a bit of technology-sharing might lubricate their entry into the Common Market, Britain turned to France.

The French were unwilling at first, but realized that they needed help building a supersonic engine, and agreed. Even so, mutual suspicion was so great that the contract became a political treaty rather than a purely commercial deal, with Britain demanding prohibitive cancellation penalties from the French state to stop it pulling out later.

In 1962, work was started on two projects – the British transatlantic plane and France's smaller version. It soon became clear, however, that no one would want to buy the French plane, and it was dropped.

Arguments also raged about the name of the aeroplane. The French wanted Concorde, but Harold Macmillan held out for the British spelling, Concord, and finally got his way. It was his one minor victory over de Gaulle, and it was to be short-lived – in 1967, when the first prototype was unveiled in Toulouse, Britain's Minister for Technology, Tony Benn, announced that the plane would be called Concorde. The final E, he said, stood for Excellence, Europe, Entente and England. (When a Scot wrote to him pointing out that the nose cone was made north of the border, Benn added that the E also stood for Écosse, the French for Scotland.)

Two prototypes were made – one in France, one in the UK – and the French beat the Brits into the air by a month, sending their version supersonic on 2 March 1969. The planes even got royal approval when the Queen flew to Toulouse in the British Concorde. Unfortunately, though, the new Anglo-French invention was a commercial flop. This was partly because of the 1973 oil crisis – Concorde used two tons of fuel just taxiing to the runway – but mainly because the Americans banned the planes from causing supersonic booms in their airspace, a move often interpreted as envy that the Europeans had achieved something they hadn't. Consequently, only sixteen Concordes were ever built, and the Brits cursed themselves for insisting on those pull-out penalties.

Technically, the planes were a huge success. Pilots all agreed that they were great fun to fly, and they delivered on all their promises. The flight time from London to New York was more than halved, to only 210 minutes, barely time for lunch and a film. And while the Concordes were in the air, they were elegant symbols of what the Brits and French, despite all their differences and constant squabbling, could achieve if they co-operated. It just seems a shame that the story came plummeting to its tragic end in July 2000, when a Concorde crashed on take-off – from (ironically) Charles de Gaulle airport in Paris.

Au revoir to the Americans

When de Gaulle agreed to work with the Brits on Concord(e) in 1962, it was no doubt because he saw it as an anti-American project. Throughout his post-war career, he kept up a steady campaign of Yank-bashing, saying most famously that Vietnam was a 'detestable war, since it leads a large nation to ravage a small one', thereby conveniently forgetting France's exploits in the same country.

In 1966, he saw the perfect opportunity to poke his political tongue out at America and Britain at the same time.

He had started to cause trouble in NATO almost immediately he returned to power in 1958, grumbling that Britain and the US were plotting together to control the organization's policy, and provoking them by asking NATO to back his colonial war in Algeria. In 1959, he had ejected all foreign nuclear weapons from French soil, forcing the Americans to move theirs to Britain and Germany, and then in 1962 he removed his navy from NATO command. His posturing for independence came to its logical climax when in 1966 he ordered all foreign troops out of France, arguing that in the event of war, he would not let French soldiers bow to American command as they had been forced to do in World War Two.

The way de Gaulle announced his new policy has gone down in history.

Apparently the Général phoned the American

President, Lyndon Johnson, to tell him that France was opting out of NATO, and that consequently all American military personnel had to be removed from French soil.

Taking part in the conference call was Dean Rusk, the US Secretary of State, and Johnson told Rusk to reply: 'Does that include those buried in it?'

1968: Parisian students discover sex

Two years later, history caught up with de Gaulle.

In May 1968, Paris students took to the barricades. Today, this revolt is remembered in France as a modern version of 1789, an uprising by idealistic youth against the tyrannical establishment. In fact, though, it all started as a bit of posturing about sex.

In March, the students at a new campus in Nanterre, a suburb just west of Paris, went on strike because of poor living conditions. The campus was a barely finished building site, and combined all the impersonality of a French *ville nouvelle* with the mud of the Somme trenches and a ridiculously undersized canteen. What was worse, male and female students were not allowed to mix in the halls of residence – in other words, sleepovers were forbidden. In protest, the frustrated students occupied the administration buildings.

Hearing about the reasons for the sit-in, de Gaulle's Minister of Education stirred things up by telling the students to cool their ardour in their new swimming pool (which sounds as though it wasn't heated). He also ordered the Nanterre campus temporarily shut down, at which point the students took their grievances to the Sorbonne in central Paris and managed to turn disgruntlement about the single-sex dorms into a call for national revolution.

The rector of the Sorbonne panicked and called in the

riot police, who cracked a few heads as they cleared the building. A protest march against this over-reaction provoked an even greater over-reaction, especially since the police violence was filmed and photographed as no French demonstration ever had been before. Soon events had spiralled out of control in typical French style, with first the students and then the workers taking to the streets all over the country.

By mid-May ten million workers were on strike, and the students' cause had been sidetracked by the unions. The call for revolution had turned into a call for a pay rise.

De Gaulle was seriously scared, though. During the protests, he took refuge on a French army base in Germany, where he discussed military intervention, and only re-emerged once things had calmed down. Ironically, the calming was done by the unions, who needed to prove that they, and not the middle-class students, were the ones who would call for revolution if and when it was required.

What French people forget is that despite all these tumultuous events, when the country went to the polls in June 1968 (to elect Members of Parliament, not a new president), the Gaullists won a spectacular victory, taking more than two-thirds of the seats. The supposed revolution had only made the people want to strengthen the status quo.

De Gaulle's veneer of invulnerability had been dented, however, and he was forced to resign the following year after a failed referendum to reform local government and the Senate, the upper house of Parliament. Rather unwisely, he had promised to quit if the result of the poll was a 'no' – always a mistake for a leader who has been in power for ten years (except if they are controlling the ballot count, of course).

The Général – Britain and the Anglo-Saxons' greatest French rival since Napoleon, and an even more successful one politically – died soon afterwards, on 9 November 1970, when an artery burst while he was sitting down to watch the TV news. He was seventy-nine.

It is almost certainly a total coincidence that just a few days before his death Britain had announced the discovery of the North Sea oilfield, which would soon be pumping huge amounts of cash into the UK economy. Surely de Gaulle's blood pressure can't have been raised to a fatal level by this bit of divine intervention on the side of the *Anglais*? No, that is a conjecture too far. But one thing is certain – if there is an afterlife, and if de Gaulle ended up in the same place as Churchill, the old British bulldog must have been chuckling contentedly when the disgruntled Général arrived to take up his cloud. Even more so when de Gaulle started to argue with Napoleon about whose cloud ought to be highest in the *section française* of the hereafter.

Hitchcock psychs up French directors

Away from the political scene, the Anglo-Saxons were being generally annoying by polluting French culture with their barbaric films and music.

At the end of the 1950s, French films were enjoying a surprising international success, thanks to New Wave directors like François Truffaut, Jean-Luc Godard and Claude Chabrol and their arty, low-budget movies. The style and philosophical themes of the films are often held up as examples of how France can inject a little intelligence into popular culture, generally raising the tone. It's true – New Wave's nervy camera techniques, abstract story-telling and improvisational feel did raise the intellectual stakes in film-making without (usually) boring the pants off the cinemagoer.

The films didn't make much money, and were largely reliant on a new French government subsidy, the *avance sur recettes* – an advance on profits that was meant to be a loan but which was only repaid if a film made enough at the box office. Few of the New Wave films repaid the loan, but the directors wore this poverty like a badge of honour. As Jean-Luc Godard once said, 'I pity French cinema because it has no money. I pity American cinema because it has no ideas.'

What is less often said, though, is that these French directors were the first to admit that they had been inspired by Anglo-American *auteurs* like Alfred Hitchcock, Charlie Chaplin and Orson Welles. In fact, French New Wave wouldn't have existed without Hollywood.

However, even though American blockbusters did better business at the French box office, thanks to the *avance sur recettes* and the new generation of directors willing to spend it, on the whole the news was good for *le cinéma français*.

Music was where the rot really set in.

At first, France had cleverly reined in the rock'n'roll revolution by simply translating hits into French and getting homegrown singers to perform them. It was a stroke of genius – you take a catchy song that's already made a fortune in the USA or Britain and get a local kid to sing your new version, thereby grabbing all the lyric royalties for yourself and creating a new homegrown pop star. It was as good as insider dealing.

Johnny Hallyday, France's musical megastar, first appeared on TV in 1960, billed as a singer *d'origine américaine*. His real name was Jean-Philippe Smet, and he had Americanized himself by adopting the stage name of his cousin's husband, a singer called Lee Halliday, and then being misspelt by a record company. Johnny became famous doing Elvis's dance moves while singing a bizarre mix of rock'n'roll and French crooning. His early hits included 'Souvenirs, souvenirs', a French remake of an American hit, and 'Be bop a lula', a partial translation of the Gene Vincent song, and his first album, *Hello Johnny*, was packed with French-language covers, including one called 'Itsy bitsy petit bikini'.*

Johnny and all those who followed in his footsteps were the acceptable face of *la musique anglo-saxonne*. They gave the French public all the excitement of American rock'n'roll without any of the linguistic pollution. They were a bit like croissants or baguettes – foreign imports mutated into something quintessentially French.

Much less acceptable were the groups and singers who came into France later on in the 1960s and showed people how it was really done – the Beatles and the Rolling Stones, for example, with their Anglo-Saxon arrogance and annoyingly singable English lyrics ('She lurv you, yé yé yé', 'Can get no satees-fax-yon', etc.).

To be fair, French singers welcomed and even promoted the Anglo musicians. Johnny Hallyday famously invited the unknown Jimi Hendrix to Paris to support him in 1966, and a singer called Hugues Aufray did a lot to popularize Bob Dylan with his translations of Dylan's songs.

But France's cultural establishment was deeply troubled. Take the Beatles, for example – the French had

---

* There was some traffic in the other direction, the most famous example being 'My Way', which is an English-language adaptation of the French song 'Comme d'habitude' ('As Usual') by Claude François. If you listen carefully to the English version you can hear that it's a French song – the melody is basically a variation on a single theme and the rhythm is totally undanceable.

thought that the *Anglais* were all bowler-hat-wearing upper-class gentlemen, and yet these working-class boys were being hailed as trend-setters, and making even a provincial city like Liverpool look cooler than Paris. (To Parisians, there are few life forms lower on the evolutionary ladder than provincials.)

And the English didn't seem to mind. They were treating these so-called musicians with more respect than they did their royal family. It was a true revolution, more profound than anything France had ever undergone. The pinnacle of cultural society was occupied by uneducated, lower-class, out-of-town youngsters, as far removed from Paris's middle-class intellectual elite as fish and chips from *foie gras*.

It was true that French stars like Édith Piaf and Johnny Hallyday were lower-class, but to the artistic establishment they were nothing more than *artistes populaires*. By contrast, people all over the world were discussing the Beatles' music and lyrics as seriously as if they were by Sartre or Camus, and none of the Fab Four had even been to university.

This, as much as the linguistic 'pollution', is what annoys French cultural conservatives even today. They just cannot accept that popular culture is as valid an art form as classical culture. In France, even pop musicians need to have studied music to be taken really seriously, which is why the French are generally so hopeless at pop music. While a Brit or American is strumming along to records and writing songs with his or her friends, a French kid is stuck at the music stand, bashing through a *How to Read Music* course with a teacher who won't let him or her near an instrument until they've mastered the theory. It's yet more proof that the student riots in 1968 didn't really change things at all. They inspired a few people to drop out of the system, but the cultural system wasn't even rocked on its foundations, and it still doesn't rock today.

French argie-bargie in the Falklands

For better or for worse, with de Gaulle finally out of the way, Britain finally joined the EU on New Year's Day 1973, and unwittingly unleashed a tide of knee-jerk anti-French bigotry.

The shock of these close political ties with the continent and fears of losing British sovereignty meant that France was always just below the surface of the public consciousness throughout the seventies, and it was this underlying Francophobia that burst out during the Falklands War in 1982. Relations between French President Mitterrand and Margaret Thatcher were relatively good at the time, mainly because Mitterrand was less haughty than his predecessors. The previous president, Valéry Giscard d'Estaing, had dismissed Mrs T. as 'une petite bourgeoise provinciale', which was absolutely accurate but rather cruel. Mitterrand, on the other hand, didn't see eye to eye politically with Thatcher, but admired her – he once said that she had 'the eyes of Caligula and the lips of Marilyn Monroe', which showed what kind of kinky stuff he was probably into.

Consequently, when Argentina invaded the islands 600 kilometres off its coast, Mitterrand went out of his way to declare his support for Britain. In doing so, he was partially covering his own back, because he didn't want anyone challenging French sovereignty over any of *his* islands. He also made a speech saying that 'France must preserve the friendships and interests that tie it to Latin America'. But he was categorical in his support for Britain, saying, 'We are the allies of the *Anglais*.'

Even so, when the Argentinians sank the Royal Navy

ship HMS *Sheffield* with a French Exocet missile fired from a French Super-Étendard fighter jet on 4 May 1982, in the British popular imagination it was the old enemy France stabbing them in the back.

Even more provocatively, the papers reported that Prince Andrew, who was then second in line to the throne, was being trained as an 'Exocet decoy'. He was flying his helicopter above ships in order to lure the radar-guided missiles away from their main targets, and it was presented as if France was plotting to shoot the (almost) heir to the throne out of the sky.

This was completely unfair, because Argentina had bought its weapons long before the conflict broke out, and France was actually providing information to the British secret services on how to disable Exocets. Whether it is a coincidence or not, the Exocet that sank the *Sheffield* didn't explode – it knocked a hole in the ship's hull and severed its water pipes, preventing the crew from putting out the resulting fire. The French even lent Britain a Super-Étendard and a Mirage – jets that it had sold to the Argentinians – so that the RAF could hold realistic training sessions.

All in all, France didn't deserve any of the accusations that it used the Falklands War to publicize its missiles. It wasn't their fault that British defence systems were unable to cope with Exocets. And the ill feeling probably wouldn't have been half as strong if the missiles had been built in, say, America. But this was France, and the British media were ready to leap in and exacerbate the traditional distrust.

Here comes the *Sun*

In January 1984, a new war broke out, this time directly between France and Britain, and almost entirely in the minds of the tabloids.

The French farming lobby caused the problem when imported British lamb began to undercut its prices. British lorries were attacked, and some lorry drivers were even kidnapped (or strongly advised to get out of their lorries and not to try and deliver their loads to French meat wholesalers). The *Sun* declared this a 'Lamb War', and decided to invade France. The paper sent an army to Calais, mainly consisting of Page Three girls skimpily dressed in Union Jack shirts and tin helmets. Watched by a few confused locals (and a *Sun* photographer, of course), they sang 'It's a Long Way to Tipperary' before planting a Union Jack on the town's place d'Angleterre.

The anti-French onslaught became even more frenzied when, in mid-Lamb War, the paper's editor, Kelvin MacKenzie, read a report saying that France consumed less soap than any other country in Europe. Instead of applying his journalistic instincts to find out why – the French were already using shower gel, and in fact thought the Brits were unhygienic for spending so much time soaking in their own discarded skin flakes while the soap melted slowly at the bottom of the bathtub – Mackenzie used his tabloid reflexes to renew the attack on France. His paper sneered, 'The French are the filthiest people in Europe', and alleged that 'many French people smell like kangaroos which have been kept in cages'. A Page Three girl was sent to the French Embassy to deliver toiletries and clean underwear as British aid to the 'needy nation'.

All of this shamed France into lifting the ban on English lamb, of course. Or rather it didn't at all. The French subsequently reduced the number of points of import for British meat, claiming that their vets were too thinly spread to carry out inspections at all the Channel ports. Thanks to the *Sun*'s provocation, the Lamb War was one anti-French conflict that the Brits didn't win.

France gets a sinking feeling

In July 1985, the most recent French act of war against the Anglo-Saxons was carried out, about as far from Waterloo as you can get without leaving the planet. The scene of the ten-minute long (and rather one-sided) naval battle was Auckland Harbour, New Zealand.

An American environmental activist called Peter Willcox was threatening to sail the Greenpeace ship, the *Rainbow Warrior* – a converted British trawler – to the Polynesian atoll of Mururoa to disrupt French nuclear testing there. There was nothing particularly Francophobic about Greenpeace; the *Rainbow Warrior* had just completed a mission to evacuate some islanders who had been irradiated by American testing on Bikini Atoll, and it had recently carried out a campaign against Russian whaling. But this time the ship was intending to lead a flotilla of boats to Mururoa, and France was not going to put up with that.

It wasn't the first time the French had tried to sabotage anti-nuclear protests. In 1966, French agents were accused of pouring sugar into the petrol tank of a yacht called *Trident*, which was on its way from Sydney to Mururoa. *Trident* managed to set sail, but one of its crew fell sick in the Cook Islands, and France put pressure on the islanders to hold the whole crew in quarantine until the series of nuclear tests had been carried out. There were many rumours of similar French sabotage attempts on protest boats, especially mysterious attacks of food poisoning amongst crews and sudden mechanical failures. But with *Rainbow Warrior*, France decided to go for the big bang.

Well, that is not exactly true. The problem seems to have been that, not wanting any written traces of their involvement, President Mitterrand and his Defence

Minister, Charles Hernu, gave such vague instructions to their foreign intelligence service, the DGSE (Direction générale de la sécurité extérieure), that the planning was left up to the head of the DGSE's 'Action Service', a paratroop officer called Jean-Claude Lesquer.

Subtlety is not one of the characteristics required of French paratroopers, and Lesquer's plan, code-named Opération satanique, therefore had about as much finesse as a demolition ball in a game of *pétanque*. Two limpet mines would be clamped to *Rainbow Warrior* while it was at anchor, a small charge to scare the crew off the ship, followed ten minutes later by a second crippling explosion to sink it.

The preparations were equally clumsy. First, Greenpeace's New Zealand branch was infiltrated by a new French recruit, a certain Frédérique Bonlieu (who was actually a French soldier called Christine Cabon), while, under the command of an agent called Louis-Pierre Dillais, two undercover operatives posing as Swiss tourists, Alain Mafart and a woman called Dominique Prieur, began to snoop rather obtrusively around Auckland Harbour.

Once the *Rainbow Warrior* had been located, a four-man team brought the bombs from the French colony of New Caledonia to New Zealand on a tourist yacht called *Ouvéa*. The transporters were three secret-service agents called Roland Verge,* Gérard Andries and Jean-Michel Bartelo, accompanied by a navy doctor, Xavier Christian Jean Maniguet.

After docking just up the coast from Auckland, the yachtsmen delivered the explosives to two divers whose identities have never been reliably confirmed, and on the

* It was apparently his real name, although *verge* is a slightly medical word for penis.

642

evening of 10 July 1985, while the *Rainbow Warrior* echoed to the sounds of a birthday party for one of its crew, the mystery pair of divers were able to sneak up and attach their limpet mines. At ten to midnight, the first bomb went off, causing the evacuation of the ship (and, incidentally, enough damage to cripple it).

Tragically, however, the crew didn't react as the French had predicted. Instead of dashing for the dockside and calling the police, they returned on board to make sure no one had been trapped there, and to inspect the damage. And a few minutes later, when the second explosion ripped a hole the size of a garage door in the hull, there were still several people on deck and one man below – Fernando Pereira, a 35-year-old Portuguese photographer who had gone to retrieve his expensive cameras. It is thought that he was stunned by the second blast, and drowned when the water flooded in. His body was found early next morning by a police diver, with his camera straps wrapped around his ankles.

The Auckland police began investigating, and quickly discovered a French theme to events in the previous days. A French-speaking 'Swiss' couple had hired a camper van and been seen lurking near the *Rainbow Warrior*. A yacht crew of four Frenchmen had shown brand-new passports to customs officers, and although one of them claimed to be a photographer, no cameras were seen on board.

Alerts were issued, and on 12 July the 'Swiss' couple returned their camper van to the rental agency earlier than expected, claiming a refund for their unused days. While they waited for their money, the police were called, and the pair were arrested. A rapid check revealed that 'Monsieur et Madame Turenge' were French DGSE agents Mafart and Prieur.

A few days later, the suspicious yacht *Ouvéa* was picked up by the Australians, but they had no jurisdiction to hold the crew, who were rescued by a French submarine that scuttled the *Ouvéa*, sending any forensic evidence that explosives had been on board to the bottom of the sea.

Despite the mounting evidence to the contrary, the French government went into a frenzy of denial, and even spread a rumour that it was the British foreign secret service, MI6, that had carried out the bombing. But after two months of *non*, the French Prime Minister, Laurent Fabius, was finally forced to confess that *oui*, France was guilty, and heads began to roll – the Defence Minister, Charles Hernu, resigned and the head of the DGSE, Pierre Lacoste, was fired.

Back in New Zealand, Mafart and Prieur pleaded guilty to manslaughter and were sentenced to ten years in prison, but the French quickly bailed them out. Threatening to get New Zealand's imports into the EU banned, France was able to repatriate the two convicts to a French atoll, where Prieur was joined by her husband. Mafart 'fell ill' and was sent back to France, and Prieur became pregnant and followed him soon afterwards. By May 1988, less than three years after the bombing, both agents had returned to a life of freedom.

Ironically, though, the sinking of the *Rainbow Warrior* had achieved exactly what France didn't want. Greenpeace had been hoping to focus world attention on French nuclear testing, and now the issue was on every front page. France was even forced to 'contribute' over $8 million to Greenpeace in damages. Meanwhile, New Zealand was transformed from a quietly sceptical nation to an out-and-out opponent of nuclear testing, and became a close ally of the small Pacific nations, effectively helping a gaggle of small, inaudible protest movements to form a single, united force. And nuclear testing in Mururoa was stopped – apart from a series of explosions in 1995, the atoll has been silent ever since.

The French did manage to save some face. Neither the mission commander Dillais or the so-called Greenpeace volunteer Christine Cabon were ever charged, and the men who planted the explosives have never been officially named.

Affair over, the French hoped.

Mais non, because the fired head of the DGSE, Pierre Lacoste, had left a time bomb. In 2005, the newspaper *Le Monde* revealed that, just after the bombing, he had written an account of the story describing how he had received a personal go-ahead for the mission from President Mitterrand, who was apparently horrified when he heard about the bungled bombing and the absurd attempts at secrecy. At last, the finger of ultimate responsibility was being pointed.

And then in 2006, while the Socialist politician Ségolène Royal was preparing her presidential election campaign against Nicolas Sarkozy, rumours emerged that Royal's elder brother Gérard had been one of the two men who planted the limpet mines, an allegation he refuted. And the French national embarrassment was made worse by the fact that the rumours were started by the presidential candidate's other brother, Antoine.

In short, although it is more than twenty years after the events, the two explosions that sank the *Rainbow Warrior* are still echoing very loudly around the corridors of French power.

Maggie goes tabloid

Margaret Thatcher was infuriated by French allegations that the Brits had framed France for the *Rainbow Warrior* bombing, but seems to have regarded the episode as a minor skirmish in the much longer-lasting and

Anti-French bigotry in the tabloid press? Or an accurate representation of British policy towards France and the EU in the 1980s and early 1990s? Well, in fact it was both.

more fundamental struggle for domination of Europe.

On 31 October 1990, she made a speech lambasting the French head of the European Commission, Jacques Delors, for wanting to force Britain to adopt a European currency and to relinquish its sovereignty in favour of a single European state. In her speech, Mrs T. defended 'the great history behind sterling' and accused Delors of 'striving to extinguish democracy'.

The next day's headline in the *Sun* was the immortal 'Up Yours Delors'. The paper didn't confine its reporting to discussion of the pros and cons of European federalism, of course – it reminded its readers of France's crimes, past and present: 'They tried to conquer Europe until we put down Napoleon at Waterloo in 1815' and 'They gave in to the Nazis during the Second World War when we stood firm.' More recently, it said, France had 'banned British beef after falsely claiming it had mad-cow disease' (of which more in a moment).

Inspired by its own headline, the *Sun* sent out a call to its readers: 'They insult us, burn our lambs, flood our country with dodgy food and plot to abolish the dear old pound. Now it is your turn to kick them in the Gauls.' At the stroke of noon, all 'frog-haters' were to face France, yell 'up yours, Delors' and 'tell the feelthy French to frog off'. For people living on the south coast of England, this was going to be easy. They just had to face the sea and they would 'smell the garlic'.

There were British voices of dissent. Julian Critchley, the Conservative MP for Aldershot, who was no slouch at insults himself, and once called Mrs Thatcher 'the great she-elephant', branded the *Sun*'s campaign 'an appalling exercise in prejudice and bigotry'.

However, Mrs Thatcher's PR man, Bernard Ingham, disagreed. He said that the *Sun* was 'expressing the prejudices and feelings of the average Brit'. The *Financial*

Times went even further. It dubbed the tabloid's campaign 'sickening chauvinism', but recognized that the *Sun* was giving 'an obvious, if wildly vulgarised, echo of what the Prime Minister was herself saying a few days earlier'.

Mrs Thatcher had set the tone the previous year with some outrageous diplomatic howlers during France's celebrations of the 200th anniversary of the Revolution. Even if the truth about the events of 1789 isn't exactly palatable to the French, it was hardly tactful of the British PM to give an interview to *Le Monde* in July 1989 pouring scorn on the whole business. The French are convinced that their 1789 declaration of human rights was the first of its kind, but Mrs T. pooh-poohed this as Gallic arrogance. 'Human rights did not originate in France,' she lectured France's most serious newspaper, 'we had our Magna Carta in 1215, our Bill of Rights in the seventeenth century, and our Bloodless Revolution in 1688 when Parliament imposed its will on the monarchy – we celebrated that last year, more discreetly than you.' She added that the French Revolution itself was 'a period of terror', another accurate but tactless jibe that infuriated the French. It was as though a French president had been invited to the Queen's Golden Jubilee garden party and then told the other guests that the monarchy was a load of outdated, elitist *merde*.

In short, the frightening thing was that the *Sun*'s storm of nonsense about the French smelling of garlic and kangaroos was not merely a yobbish outburst that went against all serious thinking in Britain – it was actually a translation into tabloid language of the British government's hostility towards France and the EU throughout the Thatcher years. It was quite credible to imagine Mrs T. smiling as she read one of the *Sun*'s headlines, just as Charles de Gaulle might well have nodded his approval of a low journalistic punch aimed by a French newspaper at Britain or America.

It is such a shame that the two leaders weren't in power at the same time. Thatcher and de Gaulle were so alike that their verbal cannonades would have been more explosive than Waterloo.

The disease the French couldn't catch

Very occasionally, it suits Britain to remember that it's in the EU, especially when its membership can be used as a weapon against the French. This was never truer than during the mad-cow crisis, which arose during Margaret Thatcher's time in office (giving the French a chance to brand her a *vache folle*), and exploded in the 1990s, shortly after she had been deposed.

It all started in December 1984, when cow number 133 at Pitsham Farm in Sussex began to act strangely. A reliable sanity test for cattle has never been developed, mainly because they can't lie down on couches and are useless at word association tests ('What does the word "mother" evoke for you?' 'Moo!' 'And "father"?' 'Moo!'), but cow 133 definitely wasn't herself. She was staggering about, drooling, arching her back and generally not spending her life chewing and mooing like all her brothers and sisters. The vets weren't sure what was wrong with the poor beast, but when she died six weeks later, the illness was ascribed to poisoning.

However, more and more cows, both dairy and beef cattle, began to show the same symptoms, and the Ministry of Agriculture realized it had a major problem on its hands. Even so, acutely conscious that the country earned millions from meat exports (Britain was, for example, the biggest exporter of beef into France), the government decided that it was not necessary to panic.

Tests were done, and more tests, sometimes by labs that didn't communicate with each other, and it wasn't until two years later, in November 1986, that the cows' staggering about was given a name. It was a new condition called Bovine Spongiform Encephalopathy, or BSE for short.

The problem, as we now know, was that modern farming methods had turned cattle from herbivores into carnivores and even cannibals. Their feed and protein supplements often contained mulched-up meat and bone that was unfit for human consumption, including the brains of sheep suffering from their own, well-documented, form of BSE called scrapie. This appetizing stuff was called meat and bone meal (or MBM – the mad-cow crisis would also cause an epidemic of abbreviations) and it had apparently caused a new sickness to develop in bovines' already somewhat floppy brains.

Not since a British cow provoked George Washington into evicting the French from America* had cattle played such a key role in *les relations anglo-françaises*. Just as in 1754, the stage was set for a major cross-Channel confrontation, and, true to form, it played out in a supremely Anglo-French bout of tit-for-tat point scoring.

Now that the cat (or cow) was out of the bag about BSE, the Brits acted quickly, banning the use of MBM in cattle feed, slaughtering all beef animals before the age of thirty months, and obliging abattoirs to remove and destroy the disease-carrying parts of the carcasses – the spinal column, intestines, brain and bone marrow. Nevertheless, they continued (it is alleged) exporting their stocks of potentially infected animal feed to France.

The EU was fairly lenient on Britain, and in 1989 it banned only the export of MBM, animals under one year

* See Chapter 13.

old, and any cattle suspected of having BSE. So, although the reputation of British meat had taken a bad beating, in theory it was business almost as usual.

The French, though, were having none of this leniency. They had always suspected that most British food was *infecte* (disgusting); now it was *infecté* (infected). Furthermore, they regard brains and bone marrow as delicacies. A Frenchman is rarely happier than when he is scraping the jelly out of a sawn-off chunk of cow's leg – an *os à moëlle*. There was no way the French would eat British beef if some of the tastiest bits of the animal were diseased, so they took the logical step and banned it.

For once, the Brits couldn't really complain about France's behaviour, and anyway they were engrossed in their own mad-cow panic, as the media bombarded Britain with pictures of vets in sterile bodysuits marching about the countryside massacring any four-legged animal that had a slightly paranoid glint in its eye (and given the scale of the cull, no British cows were looking particularly relaxed).

But when in 1990 the European Union decided that British beef was OK to eat again, it seemed that the country's surviving cattle had beaten the crisis, like a herd of mooing Winston Churchills. Probably for the first time ever, the Brits were willing to point to an EU law and say how wonderful it was.

France wasn't going to let Europe force-feed it with British food, however, so it not only upheld its ban but also redoubled its 'healthier than thou' stance. The French government refused to acknowledge that its cattle might be vulnerable to BSE – it was a *'poison anglais'*, as one magazine described it. And a new label was created: VBF or *'viande bovine française'* (French cattle meat), the implication being that French beef was sanest and safest, which it probably wasn't. The danger sign seemed to be in the VBF logo itself, which was missing the central B – was the designer suffering from BSE or its newly identified human form, Creutzfeldt–Jakob Disease?

The discovery of new variant CJD in 1995 caused a renewed EU ban on British beef that the French adopted with triumphant gusto as confirmation that only cows with Union-Jack-coloured blood could possibly be infected. And when this ban was lifted by the EU, the French refused to comply.

The Brits were so sure of themselves that they adopted French-style tactics. In 1999 farmers blockaded the ports of Plymouth and Poole to stop French lorries landing. Supermarkets announced that they would no longer stock French apples, pears and Brie, and one even cancelled an order for French mistletoe. Meanwhile, Conservative MEPs showed that their party still had a lot in common with *Sun* newspaper reporters by parading down the Champs-Élysées with a banner saying 'Let them eat British beef'. It was 'Up Yours Delors' all over again.

French politicians continued to insist that they could only trust their own cattle, but by now the policy of denial was starting to fall apart.

In 1999, it was revealed that some French wine producers were using filtering agents that contained dried ox blood. Fourteen wineries in the Avignon region were raided and 100,000 bottles were seized. It was stressed that only low-quality wine was affected, and that there was no problem with the *Appellations contrôlées* and *Vins de table* that were usually exported, but the evidence was there; the '*poison anglais*' had seeped into France's lifeblood. As one American wine lover expressed it: 'Is there a tiny chance I could go mad from drinking my 1991 Château Mouton Rothschild?'

Then, in 2000, Britain's *Nature* magazine really put the hoof in on French beef. It was very likely, the scientific journal said, that over 7,000 diseased animals had entered the French food chain, and that *le boeuf français* was far from pure. The subsequent media fallout caused a huge scare in France, and a supermarket was forced to recall massive stocks of French beef after a diseased animal was found at a large abattoir. From now on, French journalists gleefully reported every case of a homegrown cow that couldn't walk straight.

Thus it was that the British newspapers began to taste sweet revenge. In 2001, the continuing French ban on UK beef was declared illegal by Europe, and the *Sun* demanded that British cows should go back 'on the moove' into France. In 2002, the *Daily Mail* jeered, 'French Beef Unfit to Eat' amid discussions in Britain to ban imports of French beef because it had been found to contain traces of spinal cord.

In short, the Brits had successfully exported their *vache folle* crisis across the Channel and were now doing their old trick of looking down on the French from the recently attained moral high ground. And when France finally agreed to let its shops stock British beef again in October 2002, the turnaround was complete.

Not that France was going to let the *ennemi* enjoy its victory, of course. It imposed a ban on blood donors who spent six months or more in the UK between 1980 and 1996, even though for the final few years of that period, French beef was probably more dangerous.

And today, thanks to a combination of the innate trust in the noble French peasant (who, despite evidence to the contrary, is still believed to produce only hand-reared, grass-fed animals), a sense of invulnerability (for example, the French government successfully convinced many of its people that the Chernobyl radiation cloud stopped at the Italian border), and traditional distrust of British food, BSE is still seen as an inherently *anglais* thing. This was confirmed at the highest level in 2005 when President Jacques Chirac quipped that 'the only thing they [the *Anglais*] have done for agriculture is invent the mad cow'.

Little did Chirac know, however, that jokes about British (and other nations') food would soon cost his country very dear indeed . . .

30

Napoleon's Dream Comes True

From the end of the Second World War right up to the 1990s, Britain and France were like a bickering old couple, making snide remarks about one another while getting on with everyday life. And like that bickering couple, for as long as they could remember, they'd been in separate beds – in this case, on opposite sides of the Channel.

The opening of the Channel Tunnel in 1994 was therefore a seismic shock, like suddenly throwing the old couple into a double bed after years of being free to stretch out in all directions on their own single mattress. The question was, would they lunge in with knees and elbows, or choose to snuggle up? And who, if anyone, would manage to hog the duvet?

Return to Waterloo

The first realistic attempt to dig a passage under the Channel was made in 1875, when Britain and France passed simultaneous laws giving permission to a firm called the Channel Tunnel Company Limited to begin boring holes in the cliffs of Dover and in Sangatte, near Calais.

The machines to be used were British. A man from Dartford in Kent (now the site of one of London's best-known Thames tunnels) with the impossibly patriotic name of Captain Thomas English invented a boring machine that was actually very interesting, because it could dig through a half a mile of rock a month, and allowed the Brits to predict confidently that they would arrive at mid-point by 1886. They applied for public money to fund the project, but the British government was having second thoughts about doing away with the nation's greatest defence against those unreliable continentals, so it quoted a sensible-sounding law banning railway tunnels below sea level and put a stop to the project.

By this time, there was already a mile and a half of tunnel on the Dover side, its opening marked by one of the miners who had begun the digging, a Welshman who had clearly left school before mastering English spelling (his carved inscription reads 'This tunnel was begubnugn in 1880 William Sharp'). Not wanting to give up, the stubborn tunnellers carried on digging once the government inspectors had left, presumably hoping that people would believe they were just looking for fossils.

However, the inspectors came back to enforce their ban, and the boring machines fell silent. Even so, the Channel Tunnel Company was never actually wound down, and it resurfaced in 1964 when the British and French made a joint announcement saying that they both wanted to start digging again. The head of the Channel Tunnel Company, an ageing British aristocrat called Leo d'Erlanger, declared that work would take five years. The only problem was that no one on either side could say when tunnelling would actually begin – though this silence shouldn't have been too surprising given that the French president of the time was still de Gaulle, not the greatest fan of cross-Channel co-operation.

In 1967 serious planning finally began, and in 1971 a dual state-funded proposal headed by the Channel Tunnel Company and the Société française du tunnel sous la Manche was given the green light, with the two governments' commitment to getting value for money being made obvious in the way they refused to waste millions getting PR firms to think up clever names for their companies.

Digging resumed in 1973, and was going well until the Brits pulled the plug on the tunnel in 1975, saying that the project was already 200 per cent over budget and they couldn't afford it. Napoleon's dream was once again dead in (or rather, under) the water.

It was refloated by an unexpected ally, Margaret Thatcher, who in 1981 gracefully conceded that she wouldn't oppose a Channel Tunnel as long as it needed absolutely no state funding. In other words, go ahead but you're on your own.

This call for private enterprise had a predictable effect. One of the designs put forward was a crackpot scheme to suspend a tube across the Channel on 340-metre-tall pylons – the bidders clearly hadn't understood the meaning of a key word in the specifications: 'tunnel'.

A very low-costing idea was proposed by a conglomerate of ferry companies, though of course no one suspected, or suspects, them of trying to sabotage competition to their cross-Channel transport monopoly by obtaining the contract to build a tunnel and then failing to deliver.

Finally, an equally low-costing bid from Eurotunnel was accepted, and no one suspected, or suspects, them of putting in a low offer to obtain the contract and then ask for state aid once the budget ballooned to more realistic proportions. In any case, Thatcher and Mitterrand felt confident enough to sign the contract giving Eurotunnel the go-ahead in January 1986.

Digging began near Folkestone in 1987 and at Sangatte in 1988, and by a miracle of Anglo-French co-operation, the two teams actually met in the same place in the middle of the Channel on 1 December 1990, when a Brit called Graham Fagg drilled through the last half-metre of the rock that had separated England from France for an estimated 8,000 years. Fagg (sorry, but surely they could have found someone with a better name for this Neil Armstrong moment of undersea engineering?) reached through the hole and shook hands with his French counterpart, Philippe Cozette (whose name rather appropriately sounds like the French word for a cosy chat, *causette*). In fact, though, this 'break-through' was a ceremony staged for the media, and the two teams had made sure they were both in the same place a few weeks earlier, when an almost invisible hole five centimetres wide was cut between the French and British sections of tunnel.

After this moment of euphoria, digging work dragged on for a year beyond target, and it was announced that the budget had doubled to £12 billion. Britain's eternal cynicism about France's intentions turned out to be justified when it was realized that, contrary to the rules, the French state had been underpinning its side of the project because its banks were partly nationalized (one wonders why the first two words of the name Banque Nationale de Paris didn't give the game away?).

On 6 May 1994, after almost 200 years of talking and planning, the tunnel was finally completed. The Queen was allowed to invade France first, and travelled under the Channel to an opening ceremony in Calais. President

Mitterrand then returned with her to Folkestone to open the other end of the tunnel. And around 200 million similar passenger journeys have been made since that day.

There have been many financial problems in the interim, of course, as well as the occasional strike and accident to hold things up, but the tunnel has been welcomed almost universally as a miraculous innovation. The days of stumbling half-asleep across the wind-blown docks of one of the Channel ports in the middle of the night and trying to grab a seat on a clanky train that would spend several hours grinding to London or Paris are over. The ferries have also upped their game and are cruise liners compared to the tubs of the monopoly days.

Nevertheless, the weight of Anglo-French history pressing down on the tunnel roof has guaranteed that the griping and sniping won't stop just because a few engineers managed to get things right.

First, there came the French amusement that the Brits couldn't get permission for their high-speed rail link. Instead of ignoring or paying off protesters and ploughing a track through the empty fields of northern France, British planners had to ask permission of practically every suburban garden-owner in Kent, and they all said no. Consequently, as Mitterrand quipped during his first visit, French tourists would have plenty of time to admire the famous English countryside as they pottered along the old railway from Folkestone to London at 20 m.p.h.

This, though, was nothing compared to the historical snub of having the London-bound trains arrive at Waterloo, the station named after the French defeat that marked the downfall of Napoleon, the man who had actually dreamed up the tunnel project. If de Gaulle had been alive, he would probably have sent Exocets through the tunnel rather than allow the humiliation to go ahead.

The only semi-official objection to the Waterloo terminal took a long time coming. In 1998, a right-wing city councillor in Paris's 1st arrondissement called Florent Longuépée ('long sword', the name of William the Conqueror's great-great-grandfather) wrote to Tony Blair demanding that the station undergo a name change. Otherwise, Longuépée threatened, he would campaign to change the name of the Gare du Nord to Fontenoy. This meant absolutely nothing to the Brits and not much more to the Parisians, but was in fact the name of a 1745 battle in Belgium at which French troops routed an Anglo-Austro-Dutch-German army. The battle is only remembered (if at all) because the Gardes françaises chivalrously offered the English Foot Guards the chance to take the first shot. It is a gesture that is always put forward as an example of French courage, which is false for two reasons. First, it was a devious strategy – a line of musket-bearing soldiers who have just fired would take some minutes to reload, during which time their adversaries could dash towards them and take a shot from much closer range. And secondly, the French writer Voltaire tells a version of the story in which the English made the offer first, and the French cunningly saw through the ruse and threw it back in their faces.

Be that as it may, it is just another example of the way the French and Brits can never really agree on anything. As we know, neither Waterloo nor the Gare du Nord had its name changed, and in any case, the Brits have now moved the Eurostar terminal to St Pancras station, which is politically far less inflammatory. (Or is it? More on that later.)

And today, the tunnel is a symbol of Anglo-French synergy, while the Eurostar train (built by a French company, of course) is a place where you can use euros or pounds, speak English or French (and occasionally

Flemish) and even take it in turns to smile at the cute accents of the train managers who make the service announcements. Napoleon and Josephine would have been on it every weekend.

A law against English

Just a few months after the Channel Tunnel was opened, the French erected a sea wall. Not to protect itself against the effects of global warming, but to hold back the rising tide of English that (so they thought) was sweeping French off the linguistic map.

As we saw in the last chapter, France has long been suspicious of rock'n'roll and Hollywood, and in August 1994 the country's Minister of Culture and the French Language published a law designed to stop the Anglo-American invasion once and for all.

The minister, Jacques Toubon, was not first and foremost a cultural man – he was a career politician, a graduate of France's elite École nationale d'administration (ENA), a right-hand man of Jacques Chirac during the latter's career in various ministries. Toubon was as qualified to head the Ministry of Culture as he was to run the railways, a tax department or Chirac's election campaigns.

When he took over the job in 1993, he gave a speech saying that he wanted to promote 'culture that makes each man a responsible citizen'. To most of us, this sounds like total gobbledygook, but to French politicians who knew the ENA, it was a comfortingly vague piece of admin-speak – other ministers were simultaneously making speeches that were exactly the same except that the word 'culture' was replaced by words like 'army', 'nuclear power' and 'cheese'.

Toubon's first move was, typically, to reorganize large

cultural institutions like the Louvre, the Opéra national and the Bibliothèque nationale (France's national library), giving top jobs to 'associates'. Again, it was so far, so ENA.

But Toubon surprised almost everybody when he imposed his 'Law 94-665 Relating to the Use of the French Language', which sought quite simply to impose French on France. Its first article decreed that 'in the designation, offer, presentation, instructions for use and utilization,* description of size, and conditions of guarantee of goods, products, or services, as well as in invoices and receipts, the use of the French language is obligatory'.

In addition, all advertising – written, spoken or audio-visual – had to be in French; the creation of a brand name in a foreign language was forbidden if a French equivalent existed; French-based companies couldn't insist that its employees had to speak or understand English; and teaching had to be in French if a school wanted public funding (the Bretons had to fight for the right to use their language in state schools).

Toubon reserved the most severe measures for music and TV. 'Before 1 January 1996,' the law stipulated, 'the proportion of musical works written or performed by French or French-speaking artistes broadcast in popular music programmes during prime time by all radio stations must reach a minimum of 40 per cent.' Toubon added that it was compulsory for TV channels to broadcast 'at least twice a week, during prime time, programmes created in French', a move to limit the

---

* French has two words for the noun 'use' – *emploi* and *utilisation* – and in an apparent attempt to show the richness of the language, the law gives them both, even though the average French person wouldn't be able to explain the difference.

number of (highly popular) American TV series being watched.

Apart from the fact that the French hate obeying new laws, this felt a bit like the Dutch boy sticking his finger in the dyke. The English language was already an integral part of French popular culture, and stars like Serge Gainsbourg and even Johnny Hallyday had performed songs with English titles. So the fightback began almost immediately – the French love playing with words, and translated Toubon himself into English, as Jack Allgood (for the French *tout bon*). And most French people treated the law as a joke.

For others, though, it opened the way to making some serious money. With radio stations obliged to pro- gramme prime-time French music, producers were able to create a whole new generation of French-language imitators of Anglo-American styles. These days, some of them even go so far as recording most of the song in cod English, to make it sound authentic, and then adding a few words in French so that it fits the quota.

Some compliance seems to be purely symbolic. Advertising slogans have to be translated into French even when it is totally unnecessary. If, for example, a French food company wants to advertise a new American-style cookie and comes up with the slogan 'It's all good', every single French person who sees the advertising billboard will understand what they are reading, but there will always be an asterisk after the slogan and a tiny translation at the foot of the poster – 'C'est tout bon'. Coincidentally (or not), on posters for the Paris Métro, the translation will often be blocked out by the seats in front of the billboards.

It can get even more absurd. Because French is a less graphic language than English, and decency laws apply only to French words, if a French rapper brings out an album entitled *Fuck You, Motherfuckers!* (which is a real possibility), the advertising posters will almost certainly feature a line explaining rather confusingly that this means 'I have sex with you, all you people who have sex with your mothers!'

The law is being ignored more and more, especially as more and more international chains of shops arrive in France. No one, for example, has forced Gap to provide a translation of its brand and add the (slightly obscene) word *trou* on their shopfronts.

Occasionally, however, French-language campaigners call everyone to order.

As recently as 2006, an American-owned company called GE Healthcare was taken to court for not translating certain in-house documents into French, and thereby discriminating against non-English-speaking workers. The company insisted that the documents were generally intended for its Anglophone employees, but a group of unions and other workers' organizations sued GE Healthcare, and the court subsequently ordered the firm to translate its in-house software, training manuals and all health and safety instructions into French, and pay the plaintiffs 580,000 euros, plus 20,000 euros per day for non-compliance.

The moral is obvious. If you want to make some easy euros, simply go to France and complain to a lawyer that you are suffering from panic attacks because you don't understand the name of any international high-street brand. *Qu'est-ce que c'est, un Starbuck?*

You can freedom kiss my ass

The *exception française* – France's right to see the world differently – is mainly applied to culture and language at home, and rarely troubles the English-speaking world.

But when it was applied to Iraq in 2003, it caused a veritable lava flow of Francophobia.

By refusing to send troops to knock out Saddam Hussein's fabled weapons of mass destruction, France opened itself up to attacks worse than anything the *Sun* had managed in the 1980s and 1990s. This time, American conservatives were the biggest culprits, and turned the patriotism that the Bush administration had successfully whipped up to support its invasion into a loathing so strong that France was actually seen as an enemy as fiendish as Saddam. There were even bumper stickers saying, 'Iraq First, France Next!'

Telling anti-French jokes became a favourite American pastime – 'Raise your right hand if you like the French . . . Raise both hands if you are French' – and the level of ill feeling in some sections of the media was truly visceral. I went to the States to promote my novel *A Year in the Merde* in 2005, and even as late as that, a radio presenter told me that my book wasn't anti-French enough* and that 'those uncivilized Froggies are just like stone-age men, aren't they?' When I didn't agree, the interview was ended.

And it wasn't only the loony fringe of the media that indulged in the language of hatred. Farcical Francophobia was bubbling away just below the surface in serious American political circles, just as it had been in Britain during the *Sun*'s campaigns. General Norman Schwartzkopf, hero of the first Gulf War, said that 'going to war without France is like going deer hunting without your accordion'. And the cafeterias in three office buildings used by the House of Representatives famously changed the 'French fries' on their menus to 'Freedom fries', prompting a rash of copycat name-changes like

* He was wrong – it's not anti-French *at all* if you read it carefully.

Freedom toast, Freedom pancakes and even Freedom kissing.

Whatever France's reasons for staying out of Iraq – oil contracts with Saddam that they didn't want to lose, or a fear that the invasion would turn Arab countries against the West – they seem to have been proved wise in the long run. And France also won a couple of key victories.

When the French Embassy in Washington was informed of the 'Freedom fries' menu change, a spokeswoman called Nathalie Loisau replied, 'We are at a very serious moment, dealing with very serious issues and we are not focusing on the name you give to potatoes.' A putdown worthy of Larry David.

And American servicemen may not have known it, but many of them were eating real French French fries. The catering company Sodexo, which has been faithfully serving meals to the US Navy for years, is French-owned.

French industry rules the world

The Sodexo canteens are typical of the discreet way in which France, despite its claims that the Anglo-Saxons are taking over the world, is, well, taking over the world. Wherever you live, there is a high likelihood that the nearest oil refinery, nuclear power station, bus stop, advertising billboard and high-speed train will be French, whereas we usually assume that it is only the hypermarket – and most of the mineral water and cheese inside it – that came from France.

French-owned companies run bus and regional train services in many of America's biggest cities, and supply water, electricity and gas to huge swathes of Britain. To give just two examples: France's EDF entered the UK energy market in only 2002 and is already the country's biggest electricity generator and distributor. Its full name is, of course, Electricité de France, but see how many clicks it takes you on the company's British website, www.edfenergy.com, to find that out. And Veolia, which used to have the rather less discreet name of la Compagnie générale des eaux, has diversified from water supply and, after entering the US transport market in 2001, now controls transport networks in Atlanta, Las Vegas, LA, Miami, New Orleans and San Diego, amongst others.

In fact, the French are the best globalizers in the world, even if they refuse to say so because they think the word is too English. They call globalization *mondialisation*, and if you ask the average French person what this means, he or she will cite McDonald's, Coca-Cola, Gap and Starbucks, and accuse the Anglo-Saxons of trying to control the world economy. They will be surprised when you begin matching them name for name, with Carrefour, Perrier, Chanel, Danone, l'Oréal, Louis Vuitton, Occitane and Renault, for example, as well as all their big Champagne, fashion and perfume brands. Many French people just don't realize how spectacularly successful their country is.

And this *mondialisation* is important for more than just global economic reasons – it is also vital for the French business community's psyche.

Without naming any names, for obvious legal reasons, what a French company can do when it buys its way into a non-French market is go as wild as a salesman on a conference in Las Vegas. It can cheerfully get up to all the mischief that a liberalized country will permit but France forbids – it can, for example, impose price increases that would be illegal in France's protected economy and working practices that would cause a national strike.

And this globalization *à la française* has benefits on a more personal level, too. French managers are usually trained in very academic business schools and then sent to work in companies where any creativity is stifled by a rigid hierarchy and the need to respect workers' rights. To avoid staleness, the ideal solution is for a French company to send its execs to an overseas subsidiary. There, they can get all the pent-up frustration out of their system by firing inefficient workers and closing down unprofitable factories (both of which are as good as impossible in France), and then return home like crusaders after a rampage amongst the heathens. They will have sated their bloodlust and can now settle down to the more restrained style of management imposed on them by the French unions. In short, foreign workers take the punishment that French managers would dearly love to dish out to their compatriots. *Vive la mondialisation.*

How do you say *faux pas* in English?

In 2004, France and Britain continued their eternal tap dance through the minefield of history when they celebrated the centenary of the Entente Cordiale.

In March, the Queen went over to Paris, where President Jacques Chirac provoked a scandal by putting his arm around the royal waist. This perfectly anodyne French gesture was of course interpreted in the British press as a huge Gallic gaffe – the Latin lover trying it on with the monarch – and there was general outrage that France didn't understand the untouchability of royalty. It wasn't 1904 that was being remembered, it was 1789.

In June 2004, it was the sixtieth anniversary of D-Day. The Queen was invited to Normandy, along with George W. Bush, who made a speech saying that France was America's 'eternal ally', this just a year after his administration had stood by while the US media called the French every name under the sun.

In July, the British were given a great honour when their soldiers were invited to lead off the Bastille Day military parade. Amongst the regiments that were sent to march through Paris were the Grenadier Guards, who have been wearing bearskin hats ever since they nabbed them from the defeated Gardes impériales at Waterloo. (But then finding an old regiment that had never been in battle against the French would have been nearly impossible.)

And in August, Paris celebrated its liberation with a series of festivities under the banner 'Paris se libère' – Paris liberates itself, a line from Charles de Gaulle's famous 'Paris libéré' speech. France's most serious newspaper, *Le Monde*, published a forty-eight-page sixtieth-anniversary supplement, which didn't mention that non-French troops might have taken part in liberating the city until page eighteen. *Merci, les amis.*

In short, the year 2004 was meant to be special but in fact it was same old, same old.

In July 2005 there was another head-to-head, when Paris and London competed to host the 2012 Olympics. (As we now know, London won and is bracing itself for the financial consequences.)

The two cities' campaigns symbolized the deep differences between Britain and France. Paris's 2012 Committee was chaired by the city's mayor, Bertrand Delanoë, seconded by the then Minister of Sport, Jean-François Lamour, both of whom looked about as athletic as a *crème brûlée*. Meanwhile, London's bid was headed by an Olympic Champion, Sebastian Coe.

The Brits made a film that showed youngsters being inspired by the Games to become athletes themselves – a truly Olympic dream. The French, on the other hand, commissioned an arty video that was basically an advert for Paris's tourist attractions, as if the

Eiffel Tower would be competing in the high jump.

On the night before the committee's vote, Tony and Cherie Blair stayed up schmoozing with delegates in their hotel in Singapore. Jacques Chirac put in an appearance and then went to bed, declining to demean himself by begging committee members for their votes. He also (it is said) cost France the vital support of two Finnish delegates when he was quoted in the press criticizing the Brits by saying, 'You cannot trust people who have such bad cuisine. It is the country with the worst food after Finland.'

In essence, Paris was so sure of itself that it threw away the bid. Instead of playing the Anglo-Saxon game of really showing how much you want something and going all out for it, the French played hard to get. Even so, they were incensed when they lost. I was invited on to French TV news to watch the announcement live, and sat between a former Ministre du Sport and a newspaper journalist, both of whom exploded with righteous anger when the 'wrong' city was chosen. They were such bad losers that I said they were forgetting the Olympic spirit – 'Paris didn't lose,' I suggested, 'it just got the silver medal.' The politician turned to me and, live on air, replied, 'You *Anglais* think you're funny, but you're not.' Not a very sporting minister.

The Brits show Sarko their London *derrière*

France and Britain's non-stop snubbing carried on during the visit to London in March 2008 by President Nicolas Sarkozy and his glamorous wife, the model and *chanteuse* Carla Bruni. The speech-writers hit exactly the right note, with both Monsieur Sarkozy and Gordon Brown calling for an upgrade of the Entente Cordiale – Sarko suggested an 'Entente Amicale', while Brown went one further and proposed an 'Entente Formidable'.

It was only almost every other detail of the trip that turned into a diplomatic *faux pas*.

When Sarko gave his speech at the Houses of Parliament, he was taken to the Royal Gallery and shown two of its prize exhibits – immense paintings depicting the French defeats at Trafalgar and Waterloo.

Similarly, when the French first couple arrived in Windsor to visit the Queen, they were greeted by a pair of royal carriages – the Queen and Monsieur Sarkozy were to travel in the first, Prince Philip and Carla in the second. Along the way, the procession was escorted by the Household Cavalry, whose breastplates are copies of those taken from dead French cavalrymen at Waterloo. Also present were men from the Blues and Royals, whose uniform features a golden eagle, in celebration of the capture of French colours at the same battle. And to cap it all, the first horse in the parade was called Agincourt. The French visit to Windsor Castle was being met with a bombardment of historical cannonballs.

The royal banquet at the castle was just as gaffe-strewn. To reach the banqueting hall, the guests had to pass through an antechamber called (what else?) the Waterloo Room, on the walls of which hung two magnificent portraits of (*naturellement*) the battle's two victors, Wellington and Blücher. By this time, Sarko must have been relieved that they weren't going to watch a video about tourism on St Helena.

He was smiling politely as he walked to the great table in St George's Hall, laid for 160 guests. On the table sat a Sèvres porcelain dinner service that, according to a French protocol expert with whom I did a TV talk show on the day after the banquet, was acquired by the British royal family during the French Revolution, when the contents of the Château de Versailles were plundered and sold off on the cheap. The implication was that, in French eyes, the President had been invited to Windsor to eat off his own plates.

Sarko came up with a snub of his own, though. Despite saying in his speech at the banquet that 'it's like a dream to stay at Windsor Castle', he apparently declined the offer of a second night's B&B and headed back home. One day of historical humiliation was apparently enough.

And is it too far-fetched to speculate that the failure to invite the Queen to the sixty-fifth anniversary of D-Day in June 2009 was France's reaction to the historical put-downs during the previous year's state visit? Fair enough, the French were focusing all their attention on Barack Obama, the new political superstar, but how could they have forgotten the daughter of the king who allowed Charles de Gaulle to base his Free French regime in London for four years? The *faux pas* was explained away afterwards – France had expected the Brits themselves to decide who was on their guest list – but the excuse was about as convincing as one of de Gaulle's wartime declarations of friendship.

In fact, Obama could probably consider himself lucky to be flavour of the month, because in June 2009 France was still smarting from two American low punches. First, as a parting shot when George W. Bush left office, his administration seems to have taken revenge for the French stand on Iraq by singling out Roquefort cheese for an inexplicable 300 per cent import duty, effectively pricing it out of the American market. As this was almost literally the last trade measure implemented by the administration, it surely can't have been a random move.

Another American gaffe came from the newly elected Obama himself when he sent a letter to former President Chirac saying, 'I am certain that we will be able to work together in the coming four years, in a spirit of peace and friendship to build a safer world.' Hadn't Obama's advisers noticed the régime change in France back in May 2007? Shocking, perhaps, but it was almost certainly not meant as a personal insult. One could even say that the Sarkozy–Chirac confusion was a symptom of the way America sees the world – one, maybe two, superpowers on top, with Britain at America's feet, a few key enemies leaping up to attract attention to themselves, and an anonymous gaggle of less important countries bustling about below. Like it or not, to at least one adviser in the new American president's team, France was on the same level of importance as Taiwan, Mozambique and Lithuania, and who knows the names of *their* leaders?

Plus ça change, plus c'est la même chose

There are some who say that we should bury the hatchet and simply forget all our supposed differences. We are all grown-ups now and should get along as partners in the modern world. History, these people seem to be saying, is in the past. But, as William Faulkner once said: 'The past is never dead. In fact, it's not even past.'

In other words, history is in the making every day, and to ignore the past would be to deny the theory of evolution. Britain and France, and more recently North America, are the way they are today because of our constant fighting over the centuries. Our spheres of influence in the political world date back centuries. As we have seen in earlier chapters, many of Britain and France's political institutions grew up in direct opposition to what *l'ennemi* was doing. France's modern-day politicians, soldiers and administrators almost all come out of schools set up by Napoleon, and have Bonaparte's inherent mistrust, mingled with envy, of l'Anglo-Saxon.

It is because of this that every minor political alter-cation gets blown out of proportion. The reaction is never just: 'Oh, why are they doing that?' It's always: 'Bloody typical, those scheming so-and-sos, they did exactly the same thing back in 1415/1688/ 1789/1815/ 1914/1940/ 2003' etc., etc. However much we try to re-invent our relationship, it stays fundamentally the same. It's in our genes.

This doesn't mean that the French and the Anglos can't get on with each other, of course. We share such a long common history that we are like family. We're side by side or face to face in all history's photo albums, and when things are going smoothly, we can laugh nostalgically at the way we used to fight all the time. Our scrapbook really is a book about scrapping.

And we do manage to resolve some conflicts once and for all. Take the Eurostar–Waterloo problem, for example. In November 2007, the Queen officially ended any suspicion of an anti-French insult when she opened the new Eurostar terminal at St Pancras station. Diplomatic incident over, *n'est-ce pas*?

Well, no, actually. Because St Pancras, a Roman Christian who was executed in AD 303 for refusing to perform a sacrifice to Roman gods, is the patron saint both of children and of the island where his relics are supposedly to be found – Corsica. Yes, Corsica, which is not only the birth-place of Napoleon but is also the island whose masked independence fighters regularly take potshots at French administrators and blow up the holiday homes of French mainlanders. So the new London Eurostar terminal is named after the patron saint of anti-French terrorists.

But then, after 1000 years of annoying the French, what did you expect?

31

Why French-Bashing Will Never End

Since 2010, despite many distractions, like the virtual collapse of the Greek, Italian and Spanish economies, a return to cold-war relations over the Ukraine, and new or ongoing wars in (to name but a few) Syria, Iraq, Afghanistan and Libya, the British (and, to a lesser extent, the Americans) have continued to focus a sizeable amount of their attention on France. Throughout all the upheavals that the modern world throws at Western nations, there seems to be a real requirement for continuity, a therapeutic need to keep on flying the flag of French-baiting, as the following episodes illustrate.

The dangers of naval-gazing

One of the deepest and most painful scars in Anglo-French history, the sinking of the French fleet by the Royal Navy at Mers-el-Kébir in July 1940, was finally healed seventy years later in 2010. Or rather, it was given a bit of cosmetic surgery.

In November 2010, Britain and France signed a treaty

to link their two navies. Predictably, it went belly up almost immediately.

Admiral Nelson would not have been pleased about such a rapprochement between the two nations – this was the man who famously briefed a new recruit aboard one of his ships with the immortal words: 'You must hate a Frenchman as you hate the devil.' He might have approved, though, of the name of the new Anglo-French treaty: the Defence and Security Cooperation Treaty, or DSCT (pronounced, well almost, 'deceit'); and he probably would have sniggered at the chaotic build-up to its signature. Assuming a man of Nelson's gravity ever sniggered.

It all started in June 2008, when the then Prime Minister, Gordon Brown, said: 'It is totally untrue that we are trying to merge the British and French navies – that is not something we will do.' It was exactly the kind of categorical denial from a politician that implies the story is probably true. Mr Brown added that 'there is no proposal to merge the use of aircraft carrier', thereby suggesting he was unaware that any navy could afford more than one aircraft carrier, and meanwhile getting so detailed in his denial that he convinced everyone that such a merger was definitely on the cards.

While the rumours were tossed around on waves of speculation, the British and French navies themselves did their best to show that co-operation was probably a very bad idea indeed.

In early February 2009, the French Ministry of Defence announced that one of its nuclear submarines, *Le Triomphant*, had had a minor accident while on patrol in the northern Atlantic. It had collided, so the official statement said, with a submerged object, 'probably a container' (which may have been a sneaky way of blaming the Chinese, those importers of cheap goods that so annoy the makers of French luxury brands). However, British reporters began to dig around and revealed that the collision had in fact been with a British nuclear sub, HMS *Vanguard*. Typically, Britain's Ministry of Defence had not even reported the incident.

The journalists asked the obvious question: how had two vessels equipped with the most effective detection equipment ever invented been able to bump into each other? And, more importantly for us civilians, was the Atlantic seabed now littered with nuclear missiles and lumps of radioactive submarine?

Assuring everyone that there had been no nuclear pollution at all (another one of those worryingly categorical denials), France's then Minister of Defence, Hervé Morin, came up with a wonderfully French explanation for the accident. These modern submarines, he said, 'make less noise than a shrimp'. Coming from Normandy, he is perhaps more prone than other French politicians to surreal seafood similes.*

The problem seemed to be that British and French subs were often patrolling the same waters while deploying their anti-detection devices. Some naval experts therefore suggested that it might actually be a good idea if Britain and France cooperated more on naval matters. It was almost as though the accident, costly and dangerous as it was, had been arranged to support the plans to merge the two navies.

The then-President of France, Nicolas Sarkozy, also sailed in to support the merger, taking the opportunity to show off his strategic awareness, or lack of it. He stated

* Hervé Morin's flights of fancy temporarily scuttled his political career in early 2011 when, while campaigning to become a presidential candidate, he gave a nostalgic speech saying that he remembered watching the June 1944 D-Day landings. He was born in 1961.

that 'France and Britain's clocks strike the same hour at the same time,' demonstrating a surprising ignorance of the one-hour time difference between Paris and London. He seemed to mean that, for once in their long history, the two countries were on the same wavelength, militarily speaking.

As for the two navies co-operating, it looked as though it was going to be an uphill task, even if ships never have to sail uphill. After all, would French sailors really feel comfortable aboard the 'Trafalgar' class of British nuclear submarines? How would those same Frenchmen feel about serving on the frigate HMS *Iron Duke*, especially if the British crew reminded them that Wellington was once quoted as saying that 'We have been, we are, and I trust we always will be detested by the French'? And would the French navy really let lusty young British sailors board *Joan of Arc*, a training ship? In fact, the answer to that last question was no – she was decommissioned shortly before the treaty came into force, as if to save her from the indignity.

In 2011, I met a recently retired French naval officer who told me that the differences went much deeper than ships' names. Aside from all the predictable jokes about sailing on the left- or right-hand side of the sea, he said that he'd had problems during his visits to British vessels because of the very nature of the people aboard. French naval officers, he told me, are all products of the same system: an engineering background and naval school. They have all been trained since about the age of eighteen to think the same way.*

* This is the same in almost any French profession, which is why groups of French engineers are so easy to spot in airport departure lounges. They all dress in short-sleeved shirts and tight jeans. If one of them has a tie, it's to show that he's the manager.

The retired officer told me how unsettled he was to learn that the captain of the British ship he was serving on had decided on a career in the navy after a spell as a concert pianist. *Oui, un pianiste!* How could these eccentric Brits entrust a warship to a sort of failed Beethoven? Future collisions were almost inevitable, he thought.

More serious objections to Franco-British naval co-operation were raised by some sections of the French press. France, they boasted, was much more independent than Britain. The Brits have to rely on the USA for their Trident missiles, whereas French nuclear submarines fire only home-grown projectiles. *Touché!*

Nicolas Sarkozy was forced to pour oil on the troubled waters. 'Imagine that the French government decides to send a French aircraft carrier into action during a major crisis – can you believe that the British would not feel implicated?'

Er, *oui*, was the obvious answer. Monsieur Sarkozy had not only forgotten about Greenwich Mean Time, he'd also blanked out Iraq 2003, as well as France's apparent sympathy with Argentina over the Falklands. If Britain sailed back for another South Atlantic war, would the French send its ships along? Doubtful, to say the least.

In fact, though, the first field test of this new phase in France and Britain's long military relationship went smoothly. The two countries combined seamlessly in Libya in 2011, managing to avoid any collisions as they unleashed air and naval bombardments. It looked as though Anglo-French co-operation had actually gone smoothly for once, causing no annoyance to the French.

But, of course, this was too good to be true. When France and Britain combined to force General Gaddafi out of office, they were in fact removing a potential trade partner who was worth billions to France. Back in December 2007, amid great pomp and even greater controversy, the newly elected Nicolas Sarkozy had invited the General to Paris for talks, and had even put up a centrally heated desert tent for him in the gardens of a Parisian château, much to the disgust of France's taxpayers and human-rights activists. There has since been a long investigation into allegations that the Paris trip was a reward for Gaddafi having illegally financed Sarkozy's election campaign to the tune of some $50 million.

Even so, the main beneficiary of probably the most costly Parisian holiday ever was to be France. Between Gaddafi's state visit and the Libyan uprising in February 2011, Gaddafi had signed deals to equip his country with French health and transport infrastructures, and to buy two French nuclear reactors that he intended to use 'to power a water-desalination plant'. No nuclear-weapon development in mind, of course.

This was the Franco-Libyan plan before the uprising, which meant that once conflict broke out, and the newly merged military firepower of France and Britain was turned upon Gaddafi's army or his Tripoli compound, commercially speaking the French were shooting themselves in the foot – with their own missiles. Every British naval gun that fired a shell at Gaddafi's forces was effectively performing a new Mers-el-Kébir on a raft of potentially profitable French trade agreements. For the French, Gaddafi's downfall was a disaster, but here they were helping the Brits to ensure that the Libyan dictator would never honour any of his deals.

A problem-free end to 1000 years of military rivalry? *Bien sûr que non.*

The French start to miss their monarchy

One of the most enjoyable things about discussing the French Revolution with French people is to watch their reaction when you tell them that the original revolutionaries in 1789 had no intention whatsoever of beheading their royal family. As discussed in Chapter 17, all they initially tried to do was persuade Louis XVI to become more like George III of England. No, not bonkers and German – what Louis's subjects wanted was an *anglais*-style constitutional monarchy, answerable to parliament.

In the end, of course, negotiations failed, things got out of hand and heads began to plop into baskets. But if you really wanted to sum up the events of 1789 in one (provocative) sentence, you could say that the French had a chance to become more British and they messed it up.

Of course, the execution of Louis XVI did not mark the end of France's royal line – between 1814 and 1848, Louis XVIII, Charles X and Louis-Philippe all reigned, more or less disastrously, until yet another revolution sent the last of them into exile in England. But right up until the 1870s, there were many people in France who wanted a return to monarchy, and the royal family was taking advice from the future King Edward VII on how to engineer this (for more details see *Dirty Bertie: an English King Made in France*).

Naturellement, such suggestions will make your average Français guffaw scornfully (which is something they're very good at). We don't want to be ruled over by a bunch of hereditary inbreds, they will tell you. And it's true – most French people are very happy living in a republic. The royalist contender in the 2012 presidential elections didn't even get enough signatures from France's mayors to go ahead with his candidacy.

But what many French people are coming to realize is that a British-style monarchy doesn't actually *rule* over anything. Politically, all the Windsors really do is stop the prime minister of the day behaving as if he or she owned the country. And the French are becoming increasingly aware that their presidents all behave as if France belonged to them, and that there is no one to stop them frittering the country's assets away. Meanwhile, Britain's royals attract tourists with their endless ceremonies, without ever begging anyone to vote for them or spending millions on dubious election campaigns. Maybe it's not such a bad deal, after all.

This is why, every time the Brits organize any kind of royal celebration, terrible doubts start bubbling up in French minds. Certain sections of the French media and general public might shake their heads at all that hereditary privilege, but inside, many of them are eaten up with envy and regret. The French know that they have thrown it all away.

Never was this more obvious than when the most glamorous young couple in the world were married on 29 April 2011. Yes, Kate and William were *Anglais*, and the French hated it.

This suggestion, too, will make many French people do their trademark guffaw. But *Paris Match*, France's best-selling weekly news magazine, called it 'the wedding of the century' (OK, not so difficult after only ten and a half years) and plastered photos of the happy couple and all their famous – and soon-to-be famous – relatives over French newsstands for months on end. *Match*'s wedding souvenir issue was every bit as sycophantic as anything produced on British soil. The whole of the French media joined in with the 'who's going to be making Kate's dress?' debate, and they instantly adopted Pippa Middleton as one of their sex symbols, even though there were at least a million young French women of her age who possessed exactly the same dark-haired-temptress looks and posteriors.

I was lucky enough to be invited to cover the royal wedding from London by France Info, the national

24-hour radio news station. A team of half a dozen of us crossed the Channel and stayed in a luxury hotel near the Houses of Parliament. A studio was set up in the hotel's business centre, on-the-scene reporters were posted along the Mall and outside Westminster Abbey, and the whole morning's output from about 9 a.m. was broadcast from London, with non-stop coverage along the lines of 'Alors, Christophe, can you see any-sing 'appening on ze Moll yet?' 'No, Jean-Luc, nossing yet, back to you in ze studio.'

France's national news channel was making sure that its republican, anti-monarchist citizens weren't going to miss a single moment of British royal action.

During the (very long) periods when nothing was happening, I was called on to explain certain cultural quirks. Why, for example, did the avenue leading to Buckingham Palace have the name of a shopping centre, when there were clearly no shops along it? No, I told them, it's not the 'mawl'. In this case, 'mall' rhymes with 'pal'. This they thought a bit strange, because in French *malle* is a trunk or large suitcase – a stupid name for a street.

A more disturbing pronunciation problem that I kept having to correct was the reporters' habit of referring to the Goring Hotel, where Kate spent the night before her wedding, as if it had been named after the former head of the Luftwaffe. No, no, I repeatedly told them, the Royal Family may be of German origin, but they really wouldn't book the future princess into the 'Hotel Goering'.

One of the French team was fascinated by the skimpiness of Kate's wedding dress. It was a blustery, chilly day, and the bride was travelling through London in an open carriage, dressed in an off-the-shoulder outfit. Don't worry, I told him, English girls are genetically designed for all-night pub crawls in the middle of winter with their thighs and cleavage exposed to sub-zero temperatures, so bare shoulders in April are nothing. The French reporter was reassured.

But for me, the highlight of the whole day was when the groom and his brother arrived at the Abbey for the ceremony. Everyone in the studio was in ecstasy over this double helping of English military manhood in ceremonial uniform: William in scarlet, the colour of the Irish Guards, and Harry in the deep blue of his regiment, the Blues and Royals.

I had, I must admit, been waiting for this moment with malicious glee. I had done my homework on the origins of the Blues and Royals. They were formed in 1969, the regimental website told me, when the Royal Horse Guards were merged with the Royal Dragoons. Both regiments originally dated back to the seventeenth century, and both had distinguished themselves against Napoleon. Furthermore, the Horse Guards' Colonel (its commander) in the early 1800s was that veteran French-basher, the Duke of Wellington. And at Waterloo, the Royal Dragoons had captured the eagle standard of Napoleon's 105th infantry regiment, an insignia that is still worn on the Blues and Royals' uniform today. 'Today' being the operative word, because there it was, on the wedding day, emblazoned on Harry's left shoulder. I naturally felt it my duty, as a guest invited along to enlighten the listeners as to exactly what was happening on this most British of occasions, to inform the French public that the Prince's 'uniforme superbe' was a symbol of Napoleon's defeat being paraded around by the British royal family before the whole world's media.

I did point out that this was in no way a deliberate anti-French snub, even if Harry has been known to play practical jokes involving uniforms. It was just a symptom of the inescapable fact that our two armies have been enemies for most of their existence. And after all, if Napoleon had won the wars that have rather sportingly been given his name, and if his empire had lasted, no doubt France would have organized a few imperial weddings featuring anti-British symbols. Sadly for France, though, Boney was ousted, and today Harry was there to remind everyone of the fact.

Admittedly, no one, during the entire ceremony, said anything that might be construed as a desire to restore the monarchy in France, or even a Napoleonic empire, but the sentiment was clear, even amongst the most cynical journalists: we, the French, will never see anything as grand as this royal wedding *chez nous*.

Although, by a rather embarrassing coincidence, a couple of months later, they did. The wedding of Prince Albert of Monaco and his former Olympic swimmer bride, Charlene Wittstock, took place on 2 July 2011, and the celeb-hungry French made the inevitable comparison with the London extravaganza. It wasn't exactly favourable. In place of the hunky (albeit balding) William was the already coot-like Albert, dressed for the occasion in a uniform the colour of a vanilla macaroon. Rather than a soldier on leave from helicopter lifesaving, he looked like a cruise-ship captain coming to report that his liner had sunk. His blonde South African bride was very glamorous, but the tears she cried were alleged to have been inspired by everything except joy. Just days before the ceremony, amid rumours that she wanted to call it all off, Charlene had been fetched from Nice airport by the Prince's security guards before she could board an outward flight. Maybe she'd just confused the dates of their honeymoon. Ah yes, the honeymoon, during which the happy couple spent time in separate hotels and had to be practically blackmailed into kissing for the cameras, a photo opportunity that produced little more than a few sad snaps of Charlene turning away from her husband's pout.

Even though most French people acknowledge that this corner of the French south coast isn't really France at all, and many of them view the Monaco royals as glorified casino managers, it's the closest the French have to reigning royalty. The comparison with Kate and William was therefore extremely painful. It showed that Britain has the real thing – more real, for some reason, than all the other European royal families, who either do their best to pretend they're not really monarchs by riding bicycles in public, or try to inflate their importance by calling themselves things like Prinz von Muckenburg-Huffenpuff. French magazines give coverage to these other royals whenever one of them puts on a ceremonial uniform or sells the rights to baby photos, but they are usually treated as no more than celebrities with long names and a habit of intermarrying.

A year after Kate and William's wedding, the French media started bowing and curtsying all over again during the Queen's Jubilee celebrations. For days on end, it was as if France had ditched its President and reinstated a monarchy. The river pageant was given live TV and radio coverage, which meant that the French were repeatedly informed by commentators that such-and-such a boat accompanying the Queen along the Thames had been at Dunkirk, thereby showing how proud the Brits are of abandoning France to its fate in 1940. But most of all it reminded the French that they simply don't have anything up their cultural sleeve that can compare to the Windsors. France's ambassador to London, Bernard Émié, as good as admitted this when he said of the pageant: 'It is of special interest to us French – you know how much we are fascinated by the British monarchy.'

This from the representative of a supposedly republican country.

In short, Prince William's wedding and his grandmother's Jubilee brought out a real sense in France that there is something lacking from their lives. And every time a photo of Prince George's latest exploit is published in the French celeb mags, the sentiment re-surfaces.

I always tell my French friends and colleagues that I personally am not a monarchist. I see the Queen as a sort of very distant, very rich relative who will never invite me to tea or leave me anything in her will, but who is part of the family anyway – and who is very good at putting on shows. The French know that they lost their only chance of feeling anything similar when the blade came rattling down on Louis XVI in 1793. Subconsciously, many of them still share that pain in the neck.

The tragedy for France is that, where royalty is concerned, all we Brits have to do to annoy the French is be British.

How can *les Américains* do this to us?

Until 15 May 2011, there was an unwritten rule in French life: a member of France's political elite is innocent until proven guilty, and usually after he's been proven guilty, too. In some cases this unwritten rule is actually written. The President and all members of both the upper and lower houses of parliament (the *sénateurs* and *députés*) are immune from prosecution during their term of office. Get yourself re-elected and the charges against you can be put off for five more years.

Before 15 May 2011, even if French politicians did eventually come to trial, they usually got special treatment. Their arrival at court would be just another photo opportunity. While the accused smiled for the cameras, a lawyer would pooh-pooh the charges on prime-time news, and say what a scandal it was that such a great servant of the nation should be slandered in this way. And then when the guilty verdict was announced, there would be appeals, reduced sentences, and an eventual return to public life as if nothing had ever happened.

So it is easy to understand the deep sense of shock felt by France's politicians when they woke up on 15 May 2011.

On that morning, French politicians saw one of their own being paraded stark naked through the streets of New York City on the bonnet of a police car, and then publicly whipped in the middle of Times Square. Well, no they didn't, but that's what it probably felt like to see Dominique Strauss-Kahn walking handcuffed into a New York police station.

The man known to the French as DSK, the director of the International Monetary Fund since 2007, former French Minister of Finance, hotly tipped to be the Socialist candidate in France's 2012 presidential elections, and probable winner thereof, was made to stand up in front of America's TV cameras, clearly having been denied the right to a make-up session. There he was, in court, being forced to listen to the accusation that he had raped a chambermaid in a luxury hotel room.

He looked haggard and worried, which French politicians never do on French TV. Even on a post-election show, while having the extent of their landslide defeat explained to them in front of millions of viewers, they will still maintain their contented smirk. Oh well, the smirk says, the people have got it wrong this time, but I'll be back, and anyway I am still mayor of my home town, which is a nice littler earner, and yes, I'm under investigation for fraud, but who isn't?

In New York, though, things were very different. Grim and unshaven, DSK was being treated like a mere mortal, and his French colleagues couldn't take it.

François Hollande – later, of course, to be elected President of France – appealed for restraint and informed the nation: 'I think first of all of Dominique Strauss-Kahn, of those close to him, of his Socialist friends.' No need to think of the alleged victim, apparently.

Ségolène Royal, failed Socialist candidate in the 2007 elections, went on camera outside party HQ saying: 'My thoughts are with Dominique, with his family, with France.' As if he were a political hostage and not a rape suspect.

The worst offender, though, was probably Jack Lang, former Minister of Culture, who condemned the Americans' refusal to release DSK on bail on the grounds that 'nobody died' ('*il n'y a pas mort d'homme*'). That, fortunately, is true in many rape cases, but the lack of a murder doesn't mean you have to let the suspect out to roam the streets again, especially if you're afraid he'll make a run for it.

In short, the New York authorities' refusal to treat this French political star like, well, a French political star was too much for a sizeable chunk of France's establishment, including a few famous intellectuals who leapt to DSK's defence as if he'd been arrested while demonstrating for women's rights in Afghanistan. The general consensus amongst all except DSK's avowed political enemies (who admittedly put the boot in with relish) was that such a great man was totally incapable of the crime he was accused of.

It was at this point that I personally took a hand in annoying the French. Usually, I am just an observer like everyone else, but on 16 May 2011, I was asked by the *New York Times* to write an article about the reactions in

France to DSK's arrest. And when it was published on 18 May, the hate emails started to arrive.

Here, first, is an edited version of the article itself. It might explain the reaction that followed:

> Over the past couple of days, French politicians have been loudly expressing their horror at the 'violent images' of Dominique Strauss-Kahn in handcuffs. In doing so, they are not only voicing their concern for a friend and colleague – many of them are also thinking, 'There but for the grace of God (or rather the grace of being in France and not the USA) go I.'
>
> Not that all French politicians are potential criminals, of course. But the sight of a top French establishment figure being treated as an ordinary suspect is about as rare as a photo of the Queen of England in a bikini.
>
> You just don't attack the inherent dignity of the French establishment. France may think it had a Revolution, but in fact it just got a new, and even more powerful, elite. In their minds, they are so indispensable to France that trying to topple one of them is a bit like threatening to shoot a prize racehorse for nibbling your lawn. You're meant to shut up and let them nibble.
>
> This is why, to the French establishment, Strauss-Kahn, rather than the traumatized chambermaid, is seen as the victim. The same case would never have come out in the open in Paris. The woman would have been quietly asked whether she thought it was worth running the risk of losing her job and her French residence permit. She would have been reminded that it was her word against his, and frankly, who is going to be believed: the witty, famous man with the influential friends and instant access to every TV channel, or the nobody?
>
> It sounds like an exaggeration but sadly it's not. The French establishment is a boat and you don't rock it.

This is especially true about sexual morality. French politicians are known to be serial seducers, and no one bothers them about it. In France, it is widely accepted that a male politician can combine efficiency in his job with a tendency to leap into bed with as many people as possible.

The danger is, however, that their reputation as 'hot rabbits', to use the French term, can give them a sense of impunity and irresistibility. Surely it's a thin line between thinking that because you're powerful and famous everyone will succumb to your charms, and assuming that someone who resists you is being unreasonable. By this logic, forcing yourself on an unwilling partner is just making them bow to the inevitable. It's all very Louis XIV, but then the French establishment generally acts as if it is ruling by divine right.

This sense of impunity is real. To give some key examples:

In 1998, Alain Juppé, France's current Minister of Foreign Affairs, was accused of misusing public funds to finance his political party. In 2004, he was found guilty, given an eighteen-month suspended prison sentence and forbidden from standing for public office for ten years because, in the words of the judge, he had 'betrayed the confidence of the people'. He appealed, the ten-year suspension was reduced to one, and today he is the minister representing the image of France on the public stage – some image.

Ex-President Jacques Chirac was implicated in the same funding scandal, but benefited from presidential immunity until 2007. Since then, all attempts to bring him to justice have petered out. He has refunded 500,000 euros to the City of Paris, the victim of the fraud, which would seem to imply guilt, but a first hearing in March 2011 sank under the weight of legal arguments, and if he does come to trial, it won't be until at least September.*

The most telling parallel with the Strauss-Kahn case is Roman Polanski. Whatever his talents as a filmmaker, here is a man who fled from the USA to France in 1978 to avoid being sentenced for having sex with a thirteen-year-old girl, a charge to which he had pleaded guilty. When he was arrested in Switzerland in 2009, at the request of the US authorities, the whole of the French cultural establishment rose up to defend him. And today, he is a hero in France. At the 2011 Césars ceremony (the French equivalent of the Oscars), he was a guest of honour, along with the Minister of Culture, and received an award for *The Ghost Writer* which, to quote France's most highly respected newspaper, *Le Monde*, 'marked his return to the family after his legal troubles'.

Yes, to the family of the French establishment, almost getting extradited to face sentencing for sex with a minor was a 'legal trouble'. He was a prize racehorse who had been caught nibbling a lawn, and a foreign lawn at that.

All of which leads me to my personal conclusion that if Dominique Strauss-Kahn is convicted, and doesn't go to prison for the rest of his life, he will return to France, publish his autobiography (which will, of course, be adapted for the big screen by Polanski) and eventually be made a government minister – Minister of Gender Equality, perhaps?

That last paragraph was a deliberate exaggeration – a dare, almost – and has so far proved inaccurate, but everything else in my article was fact (even if no photos of the Queen in a bikini have yet come to light). This

---

* Eventually, the court found Jacques Chirac guilty of misuse of public funds and sentenced him to two years in prison *'avec sursis'*, meaning that the sentence was suspended. A purely symbolic punishment.

didn't stop an outpouring of venom from people who found my email address and vented their spleen about the treatment of their fellow countryman by the 'Anglo-Saxons'. Most of the emails were protests about the presumption of innocence, even though I hadn't said anything about DSK being guilty. Others were straight-forward anti-English rants, usually from people who'd invented a fake email address so I couldn't identify them or reply. The addresses were often quite funny – merdeauxanglais@fuckengland.com, that sort of thing – but the messages themselves weren't as witty. Racism rarely is.

Fortunately for me, there were even more messages of support, and invitations to go on French TV and radio to repeat what I'd written. For a large section of the French population, mainly female, this toppling of one of the untouchables was very welcome news indeed. And I wasn't the only person saying this type of thing, of course; while DSK's politician friends and other members of the in-crowd tried to argue themselves out of a corner, there was a huge outpouring of relief that, at last, a woman had stood up and complained, even if it was in New York and not nearer to home.

Since then, of course, all the sordid details of the case have been revealed. The criminal charges were dropped after it was alleged that the African chambermaid Nafissatou Diallo might have lied on her US visa application, and was therefore deemed to be an unreliable witness (yes, the US justice system has its weaknesses as well as its strengths).

But those images of a powerful Frenchman being brought down to earth by the New Yorkers had already had a profound effect on France. Suddenly it was OK to speak out about sexual harassment. For almost the first time, women began to believe that they would be listened to rather than patronized or ignored. A French human resources director told me that instructions had gone out that in future, known harassers should be warned to keep their hands off young secretaries' knees, and that overt sexual remarks could no longer be explained away as 'having a laugh'. Meanwhile the French police began to receive training on how to deal sympathetically with a woman who wants to make a complaint.

Now at liberty in France, Dominique Strauss-Kahn has many reasons to feel grateful to the Americans.

With one pair of handcuffs, the New York police helped him to bring about a radical shift in French public opinion. His public shaming in an American court, his incarceration in the notorious Rikers Island prison and his subsequent disqualification from the French presidential race of 2012 have all been good for his country. One day he will probably be able to appreciate the bigger picture and say *merci*, USA.

Les Anglo-Saxons do it again (and again, and again)

The French often criticize Britain for being too close to America. Or rather, of being its slave, blindly imitating its free-market economics when, in France's opinion, Britain should be opposing American globalization and showing allegiance to its European neighbours. But the uncomfortable truth is that Britain has only ever been part of the European Union for what it can get out of it. What's more, throughout history, the Brits have usually done whatever they wanted, especially if it annoyed the French. And economic events since the credit crunch of 2008 have rubbed French noses in these truths once again.

In French eyes, the credit crunch was all the Americans' fault. By lending money to people who couldn't afford to repay it, the US banks effectively put the world's economy on a greased tray and shoved it down a mountainside. When the French are not blaming their current economic woes on the Germans ('How dare they humiliate France by proving that it is possible to reboot a eurozone economy by getting the unions and bosses to work together in the national interest!'), they are blaming the Americans and their stooges, the Brits.

France often accuses both America and Britain of handing over their economies to people who think that the world is made of numbers, and who get millions in bonuses even when they screw up. Of course in many ways France is right. However, the problem for the French, and one of the reasons why their economy has been bumping along the sea bed ever since, is that just before the credit crunch, they started giving the banks exactly the same amount of power.

Until about 2005, getting a mortgage in France was like borrowing off a nervous old lady. With her questions about a borrower's health and prospects, and her strict repayment demands (monthly instalments couldn't be more than 30 per cent of the borrower's salary), she seemed wildly over-protective. In return, though, she was just as prudent with everyone's savings. The maddest get-rich scheme she was offering was the *Livret A*, a guaranteed-return savings account with an absurdly low interest rate protected by the government, invented in 1818 as a way of persuading the French that it was safe to pull their savings out from under the mattress. As such it had always attracted vast numbers of French people who knew that their money was going to be safe until they needed it to top up their ample pension.

Until the turn of the twenty-first century, like all that is best about France, the banks were old-fashioned, protectionist, and ticked along very nicely, allowing everyone to enjoy their French lifestyle in peace.

Then the French banks decided that the time had come to live the American dream, to hitch up their skirts and climb on the bucking bronco of the world economic rodeo. They began offering instant loans of several thousand euros; customers could just go in and pick up the cash, no questions asked. They were effectively urging everyone to blow their savings. What kind of old lady does that?

They also came up with borrow-and-buy-to-rent schemes in poor suburbs of Paris. *Oui, Monsieur et Madame*, you too could own a brand-new apartment overlooking a suburban railway, a homeless persons' shanty town and a crack den – and you'll easily find tenants wanting to live there. Just sign here and leave the rest to us.

Meanwhile, on an international level, the French banks had shaken off their old lady's clothing and were playing the *femme fatale*, flirting with southern Europe, lending money in exchange for (as it turned out) empty promises, playing the Wall Street big-money game. The Americans hadn't forced them to do it – the French had just believed the get-rich-quick hype. So when it all came crashing down around their ears in 2008, dragging the euro close to the abyss, France's problems were almost entirely France's fault.

The symbol of the whole French meltdown was a man called Jérôme Kerviel, a 31-year-old French trader who in January 2008 was accused of losing 4.82 billion euros of the Société Générale's money. At first he was depicted as a crazed lone wolf (or should that be 'loan wolf'?) who had illegally side-stepped banking regulations to expose himself on the international markets. And he was convicted of doing just that, and fined the slightly implausible sum of 4.9 billion euros (presumably to be paid back at 20 euros a week, over 4.9 million years).

But after Kerviel's conviction, doubts began to be raised in France – what was this French bank doing, allowing traders to take such huge risks with only minimal management surveillance? And had there really been no alarm bells ringing at any time? (As if in answer to these questions, in 2014 Kerviel's massive fine was cancelled by the courts and his prison sentence reduced to an electronic tag, implying that the losses were not entirely his fault after all.)

To save France from humiliation, the state had to step in and shore up the Société Générale with one billion of French taxpayers' money. And this was just before the credit crunch, so it is easy to imagine the horror that France's big banks and their state protectors felt when the markets started crashing in the summer of 2008. *Merde* is putting it mildly.

All was not lost, however, because the global crisis took people's attention away from the Société Générale fiasco, and gave the then President of France, Nicolas Sarkozy, a chance to leap into action and save the day. Hitching a ride with German Chancellor Angela Merkel, at the end of 2011 he very publicly took joint command of the situation and started to rustle up a European salvage plan.

Which was when those *damnés Anglais* let him down.

The trouble was that part of Monsieur Sarkozy's plan was to impose a tax on financial transactions, which the Brits saw as a French cannon aimed straight at the City's profits. At a European leaders' summit on 9 December 2011, Britain's PM David Cameron therefore walked away from the negotiating table. It was an historic moment – the first-ever veto of a European vote by a British leader.

In doing so, Mr Cameron was doing much more than making history. In French eyes, it was a case of *merde encore* – yet again the Brits were retreating back to their safe little islands, hiding behind their pound sterling and their pints of warm beer, and refusing to toe the European line.

Apparently, at the overnight meeting in Brussels, Monsieur Sarkozy got so furious with this British selfishness that he had to be physically restrained. It was Churchill against de Gaulle, Joan of Arc against Henry V, Napoleon against Wellington all over again.

The *Daily Mail*, that most Wellingtonian of English newspapers, certainly saw it as such. It printed a detailed chronology of the night's events, noting that at 4.48 a.m. (presumably Brussels time) David Cameron finally refused to co-operate with the plan to impose taxes on financial transactions, and left the meeting. At 6.50 a.m. he went to bed at the British Embassy (his symbolic island retreat) and, triumph of triumphs, at 8.15 he ordered a full English breakfast. Oh yes, when England has its back to the wall and is being attacked by the sombre forces of continental Europe, it throws the namby-pamby Mediterranean diet out of the window and goes for good old British cholesterol. No doubt those other frustrated European leaders were nibbling at croissants or pickled herrings. You could almost hear 'Rule, Britannia!' playing in the background.

And the French were as mad as the *Daily Mail* was delighted.

An unnamed French official told the media that Mr Cameron had behaved 'like a man at a wife-swapping party who refuses to bring his own wife' – a comparison that springs all too easily to the minds of French politicians, it seems.

Monsieur Sarkozy was said to have called Cameron a

'*gamin buté*', which was translated in the British press as 'obstinate kid' but is a lot more colloquial than that. *Gamin* is the normal slang word for a child, but *buté* is more along the lines of mulish or bloody-minded. And the verb *buter* has a second meaning – it's a slang word for kill. In other words, the insult was almost a Freudian death-wish. As if to confirm this, the morning after the meeting, the news agencies were posting footage of the French President blatantly ignoring Cameron's attempt at a handshake, as if he didn't even exist.

On a more political level, the Governor of the Banque de France, Christian Noyer, called for the world's credit rating agencies to take away Britain's triple-A badge.

Why were the French getting so mean? Well, not only because Britain had frustrated their plans, but because, just as when Kate and William got married a few months earlier, they were envious.

Britain had always held on to its currency to be able to face up to exactly this kind of situation, and many people in France wished that they could do the same. Almost immediately, extreme right-wingers began calling for a return to the franc. The French left also moved in for the kill, saying that the fiscal fiasco proved that Sarko didn't know how to handle '*la crise*', and that he had let the bankers take control of France's economy. Sarko had set himself up as Europe's saviour, and he'd been cut down to size by *les Anglais*.

It was no use pointing out that Britain, unlike France, had completely sold its soul to the financiers, and that the glittering towers of Canary Wharf were like so many swords of Damocles about to fall on London's neck, meaning that far from being all-powerful, David Cameron was impotent, and unable to agree to extra taxes on financial transactions. The French didn't care about Britain's problems.

The cruellest irony was that a few months later, David Cameron actually came out in support of Monsieur Sarkozy in the last stages of France's 2012 presidential campaign. It was a bit like the Brits telling the French to reinstate their king after the fall of Napoleon in 1815. Back then, the support of the *Anglais* practically guaranteed the French monarchy's ultimate downfall. In 2012, with Britain behind him, Sarko was doomed.

The *Economist* magazine, which has a high profile in Paris, went one stage further and splashed a headline across its cover – 'What France Needs' – next to a picture of Margaret Thatcher. The implication was that not only did Britannia want to rule its own waves, it also wanted to lord it over France, just like in the good old days of the Hundred Years War, and that Mrs T was the new Henry V.

Hardly surprising, then, that in May 2012 the French voted for the anti-Thatcher, anti-Sarkozy candidate – the Socialist leader, François Hollande. Even less surprisingly, on the day after his election, the new Président Hollande announced a series of anti-British measures: he would lobby for an end to Mrs Thatcher's European rebate, get Europe to impose the financial-transaction tax that Cameron wanted to veto, and – the icing on this new French *gâteau* – fight to strengthen Britain's biggest euro bugbear, the Common Agricultural Policy, which pumps massive subsidies into the French economy.

It was almost as if Monsieur Hollande was posing in tight white trousers, a grey overcoat and black hat, with one hand stuffed inside his waistcoat. He was announcing that Britain and France were embarking on a modern, carnage-free version of the Napoleonic Wars. And, of course, the fighting hasn't stopped since. There's nothing that the Brits enjoy more than going toe-to-toe with the French.

Welcome *chez nous*

It didn't take long for David Cameron to welcome the new French president to the eternal Anglo-French battle-field. In June 2012, Mr Cameron chose the highly formal surroundings of a G20 summit in Mexico to make a surprisingly informal announcement. Reacting to the French president's plan to introduce a punishingly high new rate of income tax, Mr Cameron said: 'If the French go ahead with a 75 per cent top rate of tax, we will roll out the red carpet and welcome more French businesses to Britain and they will pay taxes in Britain and that will pay for our health service and our schools and everything else.'

This was at a summit where leaders, including Monsieur Hollande, had come together in a spirit of international co-operation to debate how to save Europe from the implosion of the Greek and Spanish economies. Furthermore, Mr Cameron's flippant remarks went against British policy, which is to oppose tax evasion. He was inviting rich French people to cross the Channel and avoid income tax? Why didn't he also tell Brits to go and live in the Cayman Islands?

Well, because his comment was not a thought-out policy at all – it was just a gratuitous piece of French-baiting.

The reactions in France were pretty satisfying from a French-baiter's point of view. Every newspaper and news outlet quoted David Cameron's red-carpet remark. France's newly appointed Minister of Work, Michel Sapin, attempted a joke in reply, and failed: 'I don't know how you stretch a red carpet across the Channel. It might sink.'

France's Minister of European Affairs, Bernard Cazeneuve, was more serious – too serious: 'In the arsenal of measures we intend to introduce in favour of businesses, there are some that favour investment, and they will encourage businesses to stay in France.' As jibes went, it wasn't exactly Voltaire-esque.

The newly elected François Hollande tried to appear more statesman-like in the face of the British insult, but came over like a headmistress: 'Everyone must act responsibly when speaking; and I do.'

Meanwhile, on the French right wing, politicians and business leaders used Mr Cameron's comment as an excuse to pour scorn on every one of President Hollande's new policies.

All in all, David Cameron's single-sentence baiting session had been a spectacular success.

The Olympic spirit, and how to forget it

A couple of months after the offending G20 summit, on 22 July the English cyclist Bradley Wiggins deepened Anglo-French tensions when he won the Tour de France, causing the Champs-Elysées to break out in an infestation of Union Jacks. It was clear that the *Anglais* were determined to make 2012 a year to remember for the French.

However, a week after the Tour de France, with the 2012 London Olympics provoking a new peak in the British patriotism that had been going on virtually non-stop since the Queen's Diamond Jubilee celebrations in May, François Hollande finally got the chance to take his revenge. Or so he thought.

When the French president arrived in London on a state visit on 30 July, he seized the opportunity to strike back. Team France had got off to a great start in the Games, unlike Britain, and at a press conference Monsieur Hollande was able to slam David Cameron's red-carpet remark back across the net, like a smooth French tennis player who had just been biding his time to finish off a long rally. France's Olympic medals, Monsieur le Président said, made him 'proud to be head of state . . . The British have put out a red carpet for French athletes to win medals, and I thank them.'

Touché! Revenge is, as they also say in France, a dish best eaten cold, and this was a veritable dish of iced oysters washed down with chilled Champagne.

Though things warmed up again almost immediately, and very soon those oysters were turning decidedly rancid. After a slow start, with no golds in the first four days of competition, Team GB finally began to perform, grabbing fourteen gold medals in the next four days. The Brits would go on to win twenty-nine golds in all, including such hugely prestigious events as the men's 5,000 and 10,000 metres, the men's tennis singles, and the men's long jump. Not that it was a sexist victory – Britain also won the first-ever gold awarded for women's boxing, three of the six golds in women's rowing, and eight golds in both the men's and women's cycling. Ah yes, the cycling . . .

In two of the team cycling events, the French lost to Great Britain in the final, and these defeats let the cat out of the saddlebag. During the Tour de France, the French press had often questioned Bradley Wiggins about doping, and now the accusations were repeated about the British Olympic team. Not only that, according to the director of France's cycling team, Isabelle Gautheron, Britain probably owed its success to its 'magic wheels' – the suggestion being that the Brits were using non-regulation equipment. Madame Guatheron complained that Britain was meant to be using wheels made by the French company Mavic, as was France's team, but they couldn't be doing so, because the Brits were going so much faster.

Worst of all, during the heats of the men's team sprint,

the nineteen-year-old British cyclist Philip Hindes (who would later go on to win gold) got off to a bad start and 'deliberately' fell off his bike, thereby ensuring that the heat had to be re-run. He all but admitted this straight after the race, before hurriedly withdrawing his confession and saying that he'd been joking. The French didn't complain officially, because they had no legal reason to do so, but the bile came spurting out like air from a punctured tyre.

Isabelle Gautheron sportingly admitted that Hindes' action had been within the rules and 'you have to make the most of the rules'. But, she added, 'Hindes . . . knew exactly what to do after his poor start. We don't share the same kind of mindset.' *Bien sûr*, no Frenchman ever bends the rules in sport. Except footballer Thierry Henry who scored a goal with his hand to ensure that France qualified for the 2010 World Cup instead of Ireland. But he is the only Frenchman to cheat, ever, *n'est-ce pas?*

The French press was not exactly sporting in its coverage of the Olympic cycling. The highly respected daily sports newspaper *L'Equipe* conducted a poll and found that 70 per cent of French sports fans were convinced Britain had cheated.

The *Journal du Dimanche* ran an article about Britain's lack of fair play during the Olympics. The *JDD* was incensed not only by Philip Hindes' 'anti-sporting act' in the cycling, but also by the rowing, where the Brits had allegedly 'cheated' France out of a medal. In the qualifying heats of the men's lightweight double sculls, the British pair had requested a restart when a 'seat came loose' after a bad start. This was accepted by the judges, and the Brits went on to win silver in the final, pushing France back into a medal-less fourth place. The *Journal du Dimanche* gleefully printed French tweets mocking the favouritism being shown towards *'les athlètes de sa majesté'* by the judges. One tweet suggested that 'Usain Bolt is going to request British nationality so that he can make false starts'; another: 'if Andy Murray doesn't win Wimbledon, the tournament will be replayed a month later' (that one was about to rebound painfully); and it was alleged that 'if a British athlete gets tired during the marathon, he can complete the race in a taxi.' There was even a French tweet – not reprinted in the *Journal du Dimanche*, but gleefully picked up by Britain's *Daily Telegraph* – complaining that 'After Napoleon lost the Battle of Waterloo, no re-match was allowed.' (Well, at least this was one French person actually admitting that Napoleon had lost.) Another Twitter user warned athletes that 'anyone daring to beat an Englishman will be burnt on an Olympic bonfire'. It was Joan of Arc all over again. Clearly, history was very much on French minds.

All this Twitter activity might have counted as a case of the French annoying the British for once, except that the Brits weren't annoyed at all, thanks to the goldrush of medals they were scooping up – not just in high-visibility sports, but also in sailing, canoeing, hockey, triathlon, even dressage, in which Britain had never before won a medal.

Nevertheless, David Cameron rose to the bait and took time away from running the country to give an interview to French TV so that he could reply to these grave accusations on behalf of his nation. He obviously took the matter of fair play during the London Olympics very seriously. Or did he?

The interview, recorded for France Television's prime-time evening news – in English, of course – was a masterclass in telling the French not to be bad losers. The Duke of Wellington probably gave exactly the same kind of interview to French journalists in June 1815, and if northern France's local press had quoted Henry V in 1415, the results would have been pretty similar.

The TV interviewer asked Mr Cameron: 'There is no cheating? How can you guarantee it?' to which the PM answered, in simplified English, ensuring that he was being simultaneously smug *and* patronising (a typical *Anglais*, in fact): 'The French know our secrets because you make the wheels of our bicycles . . . I think it's very unfair just because athletes win, to have suspicions. The first reaction should be to say "well done" . . . I know it's difficult with France being such a great cycling nation, but we've done very well. If France did well in the cycling, I'd say "well done", and I'm sure the French people will feel the same.' Clearly thinking that the interview was over, he then added a final jibe in kiddies' English so that the silly French reporter would understand the gist of what had just been said: 'The wheels are round and they go very fast because they pedal hard.' As interviews go, it was as subtle and informative as punching a paparazzi in the face.

David Cameron then went on BBC radio to comment on his own taunts. 'We've got a system that seems to be delivering,' he told DJ Chris Evans. 'It's driving the French mad. I did an interview with French television yesterday and they virtually accused us of cheating. I think they found the Union Jacks on the Champs Elysées a bit hard to take.'

Adding *insulte* to *injure*, on 6 August, the Mayor of London, Boris Johnson, wrote a trumpeting opinion piece for the *Telegraph*, indirectly praising himself for hosting such a wonderful Olympics, and rubbing France's nose in its sour grapes: 'It isn't so long ago that French leader François Hollande was over here, gloating about how France was beating us hollow. Well, *M. le*

Président, mettez-ça dans votre pipe et fumez-le! Bien je jamais, eh!'

He must have hoped that the French press would pick up on his attempt at literally translated cod French – which they all did – and that they would be confused by it – which they certainly were.

The *Journal du Dimanche* commented that Johnson had written a sentence in *'un français peu correct'* (not very correct French); the political weekly *L'Express* noted that his 'tirade' was like 'the frantic work of an inaccurate translation machine'; and *L'Echo Républicain* advised that 'the interpretation of those final words is left to the judgement of the readers'. Clearly they all thought that poor Boris's brain (or computer) was not up to the task of writing an insult in decent French – though it should be noted that even though his translation ended up as word-for-word gibberish, he got all his French spellings and tenses right (unless someone at the *Telegraph* corrected them for him – a French traitor, perhaps?). In any case, once again the joke was on poor old France. And Britain loved it.

David Cameron had one final task to perform in order to make it 100 per cent clear to the world that the whole idea of the London Olympics, ever since the right to host them had been ripped from Paris's fingers in 2005 (see Chapter 30), had been to perform better than France. As the Games closed, he gave a speech to Team GB's victorious athletes, congratulating them and their backroom staff for their fantastic achievements. The mood was upbeat and informal. There was laughing, cheering and applause. And at the end, a grinning Mr Cameron summed up the Games' success by reminding everyone that 'we won more medals than the French!'

The resulting roar of approval must have set the Eurostar lines trembling all the way to Paris.

French-bashing for dummies

The English and French languages have always operated an exchange system.

English offers up technological words like 'internet', 'wi-fi' (pronounced in France as 'wiffy') and the verb *'googliser'*, meaning to google; business words like 'start-up', 'trader' and *'pitcher'* (to pitch); or simply new trends such as *'le piercing'*, *'le selfie'*, and *'le string'* (the French adaptation of 'G-string').

Meanwhile French has mainly provided the English language with cooking terms – most Anglos are now familiar with *crème brûlée*, *foie gras* and *pain au chocolat*, even if we can't actually make them – as well as moralistic terms that try to tell us how to live. *Laissez-faire*, *carte blanche*, *faux pas* and *noblesse oblige* spring immediately to mind.

The main difference is that while the English language welcomes outsiders with open arms, France often resists, with the Académie Française either rejecting the new English words or proposing French adaptations, many of which are ignored or ridiculed by the French themselves. For example, any attempt to translate 'the web' into French literally as *'la toile'* is regarded as mildly comic, and calling an email *'un courriel'* (the offically accepted word) comes across as old-fashioned and school-ma'amish.

In recent years, a new English term has been used more and more often in French, and this one annoys France's language purists for two reasons: not only is it English, it also describes, in their eyes at least, a highly unpleasant habit. It is *'le French-bashing'*.

Now that they have given it a name, the French have become much more aware of the phenomenon, and examples are reported with increasing frequency in the French press. And it must be admitted that in the second decade of the twenty-first century, French-bashing has become a British national sport, dragging cross-Channel relations back to the stormy days of 'Up Yours Delors' in the 1980s and early 1990s (see Chapter 29).

This renewed delight in provoking France seems to be partly due to the after-effects of the credit crunch. Hard times have pushed everyone further into their own corner and highlighted differences in our ways of thinking. But, as usual, it also derives from the fact that the Brits just enjoy baiting the French.

In reality, the term the French really need to learn is not 'French-bashing', it is 'French-baiting'. The former seems one-sided and passive, whereas the latter is much more fun – it is the sport (or art) of annoying the French enough for them to react with outrage. And the fact that they have learnt the term '*le French-bashing*' proves that the tactic is working splendidly.

As we saw earlier, this bashing, or baiting, is often completely gratuitous. In these politically correct times, when stand-up comedians can no longer resort to lazy jokes based on racial or religious stereotypes, the French make a perfect target. They are more or less of the same race, religion and colour as the majority of British comedians, and therefore a joke at their expense is seen as in no way reprehensible. If you can make more than one joke out of it, all the better. In 2010, for example, a BBC radio comedy series, *Bleak Expectations*, based a whole episode in France, where the heroes saw, amongst other typically French things, 'legless frogs in tiny wheelchairs' and a man with 'an air of undeserved self-satisfaction'.

That was subtle compared to some of the anti-French 'jokes' that the *très sérieux* weekly news magazine *Le Point* claimed to have identified in January 2013. In an article headed '*Le French-bashing, un exercice quotidien*' ('French-bashing, a daily exercise'), its reporter described a

Saturday gym class 'in one of London's many green and shady parks', with the trainer putting sixty or so people through their paces: 'And now raise your hands in the air, and run as fast as you can. Just like a French soldier!'

The article concluded (rather accurately, it must be said) that 'making fun of Frenchies is a guilty pleasure on the other side of the Channel, almost a way of life'.

It also seemed to be saying that with this casual mockery being grafted on to the 'sudden outbreak of anti-Froggie fever amongst the British élite' (meaning especially David Cameron and Boris Johnson), things have got out of control – as if they were ever under control. French control, anyway.

Certainly, the ideological attacks on France's economy have been hitting home. The *Le Point* article quoted the *Economist*'s front page from November 2012 calling France 'the time bomb at the heart of Europe', which caused most of the French media to go into a frenzy of self-analysis and/or anti-British outrage. The *Economist* predicted, amongst other imminent disasters, that France risked 'being left behind by Italy and Spain'. *Quelle horreur!*

There was also huge French coverage of the vicious article in *Newsweek* in January 2014 describing 'the fall of France'. The exodus of French money and business brains so provocatively predicted by David Cameron on François Hollande's election had become a flood, and *Newsweek* compared it to the flight of the Huguenots in 1685, who 'were thought of as the worker bees of France. They left without money, but took with them their many and various skills. They left France with a noticeable brain drain.' In the very near future, *Newsweek* seemed to be saying, France will have been abandoned by everyone who can understand, or even spell, economics.

Fortunately for the French, the *Newsweek* piece was

peppered with laughable mistakes that enabled reporters and tweeters alike to ignore the essence of the argument and focus on the howlers: for example, the article seemed to repeat uncritically George W. Bush's unfortunate remark about France not having a word for 'entrepreneur' (which was the equivalent of someone saying that Americans don't have a word for 'dumbass'). *Newsweek*'s writer also seemed to think that a pint of milk cost four dollars in France, proving that she was living in the kind of neighbourhood where au pairs have assistants to push the baby buggies. Not exactly everyday France.

Even so, the article hurt the French, because with unemployment reaching record levels and highly qualified young graduates finding it almost impossible to get a sniff of a long-term job, many French people were starting to agree that they might be living on a sinking ship – albeit a nicely decorated cruise liner with a well-stocked bar and a state-of-the-art sick bay.

As early as 2013, Boris Johnson was claiming to be mayor of France's sixth-biggest city, with London's French population outstripping those of such regional capitals as Bordeaux, Strasbourg and Nantes, though with his propensity for French-baiting, that might have to be taken with a pinch of *sel*. In October 2014, the French consulate in London told the *Independent* newspaper that it had identified some 400,000 French people living in London. Though earlier that year, when giving figures to the BBC, it defined London as 'the south-eastern quadrant of the UK including Kent, Oxfordshire and maybe Sussex too', proving that its spokesperson was probably a recent immigrant with a weak grasp of British geography.

Whatever the true figure, west London has been turned into a French enclave, the chicest ethnic ghetto in the world. The cafés of South Kensington have become the hangouts of a tribe of posh French-speaking *mamans* who drop their *enfants* off at French-speaking schools then gather over a croissant to complain about France and compare the locations of their families' holiday homes on the île de Ré. Meanwhile, even non-French cafés in London are almost certain to have French staff – many of them capable of understanding nuclear fission or managing a factory, but incapable of finding work in France.

Not all of these French exiles are purely economic, of course – some simply think that London is a more stimulating place to live than the small French town where they grew up, while others feel obliged to escape from the apparently unstoppable stream of state-funded French films in which middle-aged Parisian film directors explore their sexuality by asking actresses to show their boobs or getting men to dress up as women (*très shocking!*).

But by 2014, the stream of expats, many of whom have obviously been influenced by the non-stop British French-bashing, had got the French establishment seriously worried.

Amongst the lone voices of resistance were the left-leaning news magazines *Nouvel Observateur* and *Marianne*. The *Nouvel Obs* told its readers in January 2014 that the Anglo-Saxons were forgetting one important thing about France: 'the fundamental values of human rights and solidarity that must be universal, must endure, be promoted and applied'. In other words, the British and American governments don't care about their citizens – many Brits and Americans would agree with that – whereas France's economy was sinking because it carried on paying high unemployment benefits (especially to its film directors) and early pensions (especially to its state workers).

In October 2014, *Marianne* protested that British French-bashing, especially the allegations that the French don't want to work hard, was down to plain jealousy: 'Behind these condescending criticisms, one can sense a certain envious resentment. Because I have no right to this laziness, to this easy-going way of life, there is no reason why anyone else should enjoy it.' (Again, many Brits and Americans would agree.)

This defence from the pro-Socialist press did not stop France's Prime Minister, Manuel Valls, taking action. In October 2014 he travelled to London, determined to convince both the Brits and the hordes of French expats working in the City that, contrary to appearances, his government was *not* determined to banish all wealthy French people into exile. The rich expats probably knew this already – after all, during the Revolution the new government had wanted the aristocrats to stay in France, so that they could have their heads removed along with their possessions.

Monsieur Valls (who, incidentally, was actually born in Spain) courageously agreed to give a speech at the Guildhall in London. This is the HQ of the City of London, the institution that has been trying to limit or destroy France's influence in the international business community since its foundation in the twelfth century. It must have been a tough audience, a bit like David Cameron going to talk at a Glasgow working men's club just before the referendum on Scottish independence.

And, recognizing this, Monsieur Valls departed from French political tradition – which is either to bore an audience to sleep or pummel them into submission with a show of self-importance – and tried a couple of jokes.

Speaking in French (*bien sûr* – France's politicians know all too well how the Brits love to giggle at their accents when they attempt to make a speech in English), Monsieur Valls quipped that 'a French Prime Minister in London is quite an event. A Socialist prime minister is a revolution.'* No one laughed, perhaps because it was all too obvious that this was the first time in his whole life that Monsieur Valls had told a joke, but this bit of self-mockery was hailed in the French press as a diplomatic master-stroke – using English humour on the English themselves.

French journalists also got excited about Monsieur Valls's message, delivered first in French then in English, that *'j'aime les entreprises . . .* my government is pro-business'. This bilingual declaration horrified the French left, and almost certainly failed to convince the French right, but either way it was big news in France, rather as if Margaret Thatcher had said that she loved trade unions.

However, all this was mere economics. The most heart-felt section of Monsieur Valls's speech was not really political at all. He bemoaned the fact that the Brits tend to 'caricature' France, and went on to make a rather start-ling confession: 'Every day I read your press, I listen and I watch what is being said about France. Too often in some of your newspapers I see bias, prejudices and attacks.'

The implication was that the Prime Minister of France had enough free time to read the British press, listen to the radio and watch the TV, just so that he could find out what *les Anglais* thought of France on any particular day. Even allowing for some poetic licence (and a team of interns), it's hard to imagine the Prime Minister of any other European country devoting so much attention to what people elsewhere are saying about his or her country – except perhaps one of Russia's neighbours wondering whether its borders are going to remain intact.

* In saying this, he confirmed what most British voters knew, that Tony Blair was not really a Socialist prime minister.

And instead of wondering why its government didn't direct all its efforts at improving the economy, the French press approved of their Prime Minister's obsession with British public opinion. The *Nouvel Observateur* noted that 'the head of the government launched . . . a counter-attack against the anti-French mockery of "French-bashing". His speech in London was, the magazine said, part of a campaign that he had been waging 'almost every day for the last few weeks'.

It seems bizarre that one of the world's biggest economies should pay such close attention to insults coming from one of its neighbours, but there is perhaps an explanation. Unlike the farcical stereotyping of the 1980s, when British tabloids were suggesting that the French never wash or that they all have garlic for breakfast, and unlike America's jokes about 'cheese-eating surrender monkeys' during the different Gulf wars, the more recent French-bashing has been hitting a real target.

In the past, most French voters, both left and right, were content to view 'Anglo-Saxon' capitalism as vulgar profiteering. They were all more or less content with France's old-fashioned, low-profit, protectionist way of doing things. Now, more and more of them are being influenced by the apparent prosperity in Britain, the USA and Germany, and thinking that maybe a little injection of free-market thinking (just a little, mind) might not be such a bad thing. Even the Socialists have seen that punitive taxes, especially on high earners and businesses, are earning them neither improved economic results nor electoral support.

In the past, the French could laugh off French-bashing: either it was absurd (the whole 'Up Yours Delors' period) or they were proud of France's go-it-alone stance (during the Gulf Wars). Now it is not so easy. It is as though the Brits are giggling at a hole in the seat of France's trousers.

It's hard for the French government to convince its people that holes in trousers seats are fashionable, or good for them in the long run. And it is going to take so long to mend the hole that the French government would really like the Brits to shut up about it.

The trouble is, of course, that for the past ten centuries or so the Brits have loved nothing more than the chance to annoy their neighbours. And so the taunting goes on, the only consolation being that even if French-bashing today is sometimes warlike in tone, at least it is light relief compared to the slings and arrows of the past.

France draws the short (final) straw

In the aftermath of the terrorist attacks in Paris at the beginning of 2015, Britain's politicians declared a truce in the French-bashing, and David Cameron was on the front line of the massive protest march on 11 January, alongside many other world leaders. After the march, he even gave a short speech at the British Embassy in which he quoted the slogan 'je suis Charlie' in the original French – though of course it came out in an extreme British accent, with the 'Charlie' pronounced as an English name rather than the French 'shar-lee'.

However, to be cynical for a moment (just a moment), this show of solidarity with France was also in Britain's self-interest, because Mr Cameron, like all the world leaders present, was acutely aware that every country faces the same terrorist threat. And the likelihood is that the Anglo-French truce will be short-lived, because experience has shown that, except in times of crisis, the natural relationship between Britain and France is something much closer to a toe-to-toe confrontation than an arm-in-arm march through the streets of Paris.

Nevertheless, the important thing to remember is that

this spirit of everlasting conflict is not our fault. It is, in the real sense of the word, our *natural* relationship. Proof of this was given in late 2014 by *The Times*, that symbol of British fair-play and neutral reporting (ahem) founded in London in 1785.

On 30 October 2014, several British newspapers, including the Old Lady of Fleet Street, reported on a study of unhappiness and its effects on the economies of different countries. According to researchers at Warwick University, certain nations are more naturally disposed to happiness, and therefore to social and economic success. This disparity is apparently related to a deficiency amongst some populations in the brain's production of serotonin, a hormone that controls happiness. Levels of serotonin are regulated by a gene that comes in 'long' and 'short' forms – and the longer the gene, the happier the nation.

The bad news, *The Times* informed its readers, is that the average Briton has a 'short-form' version of this gene, making Britain as a nation more prone to grumpiness than, for example, the average Dane, who has the longest form of the gene.

However, there was one ray of hope in the gloom, as the headline in *The Times* pointed out: 'Britons are born grumpy,' it announced, 'but cheer up, the French are worse.'

Yes, the supposedly serious mouthpiece of British journalism was reporting on a scientific study investigating the various reasons – social and economic, as well as genetic – for a country's levels of depression, and this was what it chose to highlight: we Brits are not perfect, but at least we're less imperfect than the French, who have the shortest form of the gene of all the thirty nations studied. As Boris Johnson might say, *mettez ça dans votre pipe génétique et fumez-le.*

It's like a scene from a Monty Python version of the Battle of Waterloo – it is late in the day, and a British red-coat and a Napoleonic Garde Impériale are sprawled side by side in the mud. Both are covered in blood, their once-proud uniforms in tatters. All around them lie corpses mangled by cannon fire, musket ball and sabre. Someone somewhere probably knows the outcome of the battle, but here in this gore-smeared corner of the Belgian field, it doesn't matter. The two men look at each other, wondering whether to fight on despite their terrible injuries. But neither has the strength to lift his sword. In fact, neither has the *arms* to lift his sword. Their bodies are smashed and bleeding; life is ebbing out of them both.

'Our battle is lost,' the Frenchman finally groans, in English because he knows the Englishman doesn't understand French. 'We are both going to die.'

'Yes,' the Englishman agrees, 'but unlike you, I've still got my trousers on.'

After 1000 years of rivalry, and millions of years of evolution, we Brits are still capable of extracting a grain of comfort from the fact that we're not *quite* as badly off as the French.

However, there is one detail of these genetic findings that is even more important to the Brits. The study of the happiness gene has revealed a key scientific fact about us as a nation – a fact that fully justified the 'cheer up' newspaper headline. The researchers have ensured that from now on, without fear of contradiction, we can proudly affirm that, right down at DNA level, we're not the same as the French.

Vive la différence!

Quotations

This is not intended to be a completist compendium of quotations. It's a collection of pithy and mischievous sayings, made about or by the French, all of which I came across while researching the book and haven't used in the main text. A sort of French traffic jam of quotations, in fact.

Joan of Arc (1412–31), French soldier and saint:

'Of the love or hatred of God for the English, I know nothing, but I do know that all of them will be booted out of France, except those who will die here.'

William Shakespeare (1564–1616), English playwright, poet and occasional propagandist, in his play *Richard III*, Act I, Scene iii:

'GLOUCESTER . . . Because I cannot flatter and speak fair,
Smile in men's faces, smooth, deceive and cog,
Duck with French nods and apish courtesy,
I must be held a rancorous enemy.'

Sir Philip Sidney (1554–86), English soldier and poet:

'That sweet enemy, France.'

Fougeret de Montbron (1706–60), French writer and Anglophile:

'We are the only nation in the universe that the English do not disdain. Instead they pay us the compliment of hating us as ferociously as possible.'

'We should be flattered – every foreigner in London is called a "French dog".'

Samuel Johnson (1709–84), English dictionary writer:

'A Frenchman must be always talking, whether he knows anything of the matter or not; an Englishman is content to say nothing when he has nothing to say.'

Louis XV (1710–74), King of France:

'The English have corrupted the mind of my kingdom. We must not expose a new generation to the risk of being perverted by their language.'

Laurence Sterne (1713–68), Irish writer, in his novel *The Life and Opinions of Tristram Shandy*:

'The French believe that talking of love is making it.'

Horace Walpole (1717–97), British writer, cousin of Admiral Nelson:

'I do not dislike the French from the vulgar antipathy between neighbouring nations, but for their insolent and unfounded airs of superiority.'

Pierre-Augustin Caron de Beaumarchais (1732–99), French writer and political intriguer, in his play *The Marriage of Figaro*:

'The English do add here and there some other words when speaking, but it is obvious that "God-damn" is the foundation of their language.'

Louis-Sébastien Mercier (1740–1814), French writer, after a visit to London:

'Londoners think that in Paris we are covered in braids but are either dying of starvation or eating nothing but frogs.'

Antoine de Rivarol (1753–1801), French writer, in his book *On the Universality of the French Language*:

'Something that is not clear is not French.'

(The modern French novel had yet to be invented.)

Horatio Nelson (1758–1805), British admiral, giving instructions to a new recruit:

'Firstly you must always implicitly obey orders, without attempting to form any opinion of your own regarding their propriety. Secondly, you must consider every man your enemy who speaks ill of your king; and thirdly you must hate a Frenchman as you hate the devil.'

Napoleon Bonaparte (1769–1821), Emperor of France:

'It is in the French character to exaggerate, to complain and to distort everything when one is not happy.'

'History is a series of lies on which we agree.'

'Good politics is making people believe they're free.'

Samuel Taylor Coleridge (1772–1834), English poet:

'Frenchmen are like gunpowder, each by itself smutty and contemptible, but mass them together and they are terrible indeed!'

Stendhal (1783–1842), French writer:

'The French are the wittiest, the most charming, and up till now at least, the least musical race on Earth.'

Victor Hugo (1802–85), French novelist and poet:

'To err is human. To laze about is Parisian.'

'Let's not be English, French or German any more. Let's be European. No, not European, let's be men. Let's be humanity. All we have to do is get rid of one last piece of egocentricity – patriotism.'

Winthrop Mackworth Praed (1802–39), British politician and poet:

'John Bull was beat at Waterloo!
They'll swear to that in France.'

Douglas William Jerrold (1803–57), British writer:

'The best thing I know between France and England is the sea.'

Flora Tristan (1803–44), French writer, on returning from a trip to England:

'Traditionally, in France, the most esteemed member of society is the woman. In England, it's the horse.'

Paul Gavarni (1804–66), French artist:

'When an Englishwoman is dressed, she is no longer a woman, she is a cathedral. You don't seduce her, you demolish her.'

Gustave Flaubert (1821–80), French writer, in his *Dictionary of Received Ideas*, a satire on French prejudices:

'*Anglais*: All rich.
Anglaises: Act surprised that they have good-looking children.
Français: Most important people in the universe.
John Bull: When you don't know an Englishman's name, call him John Bull.
Monarchie: A constitutional monarchy is the best kind of republic.
Stuart (Marie): Act sorry for her.'

Mark Twain (1835–1910), American writer:

'In Paris they simply stared when I spoke to them in French. I never did succeed in making those idiots understand their language.'

Georges Clemenceau (1841–1929), French Prime Minister:

'English is just badly pronounced French.'

Paul Claudel (1868–1955), French writer:

'American democracy made its entrance into the world on the arm of the French aristocracy.'

André Gide (1869–1951), French writer and winner of the Nobel Prize for Literature:

'It is unthinkable for a Frenchman to arrive at middle age without having syphilis and the Légion d'Honneur.'

Harry Graham (1874–1936), English writer:

'Weep not for little Léonie,
Abducted by a French marquis,
Though loss of honour was a wrench,
Just think how it's improved her French.'

P.G. Wodehouse (1881–1975), English – and later naturalized American – writer, in his novel *The Luck of the Bodkins*:

'Into the face of the young man who sat on the terrace of the Hotel Magnifique at Cannes there had crept a look of furtive shame, the shifty, hangdog look which announces that an Englishman is about to speak French.'

Franz Kafka (1883–1924), Czech writer, in his diary, about a trip to Paris in September 1911:

'We could never tell whether they [the Parisians] were happy to hear us making mistakes when speaking French, or if they just found the mistakes interesting to listen to.'

George S. Patton (1885–1945), American general:

'I would rather have a German division in front of me than a French one behind me.'

Charles de Gaulle (1890–1970), French President:

'I have tried to lift France out of the mud. But she will return to her errors and vomitings. I cannot prevent the French from being French.'

'When I want to know what France thinks, I ask myself.'

Richmal Crompton (1890–1969), British writer, creator of the children's book hero William Brown, who, in her novel *William the Conqueror*, says:

'I don' wanter talk to any French folks, an' if they wanter talk to me they can learn English. English's easy to talk. It's silly having other langwidges. I don' see why all the other countries shun't learn English 'stead of us learnin' other langwidges with no sense in 'em. English's sense.'

Evelyn Waugh (1903–66), British writer:

'We are all American at puberty. We die French.'

Josephine Baker (1906–75), American dancer:

'I like Frenchmen very much, because even when they insult you, they do it so nicely.'

Billy Wilder (1906–2002), Austrian-American film director:

'France is a place where the money falls apart in your hands but you can't tear the toilet paper.'

(This was before the euro was created and became stronger than the dollar.)

Georges Elgozy (1908–89), French economist:

'A Frenchman needs a year to understand English money, ten years to understand their temperament, fifty years for their lack of temperament, and an eternity for their women.'

Pierre-Jean Vaillard (1918–88), French actor:

'Now I know why the English prefer tea. I just tasted their coffee.'

Boris Vian (1920–58), French writer and jazz musician:

'To do business these days, you have to be American. But if you can content yourself with being intelligent, you might as well just be French.'

'Ridicule won't kill you anywhere, but in America it will make you rich.'

Claude Gagnière (1928–2003), French writer:

'A man who speaks three languages is trilingual. A man who speaks two languages is bilingual. A man who speaks one language is English.'

William Safire (b. 1929), American journalist:

'One difference between French appeasement and American appeasement is that France pays ransom in cash and gets its hostages back while the United States pays ransom in arms and gets additional hostages taken.'

Édith Cresson (b. 1934), French Prime Minister, angry that men weren't ogling her during a visit to London:

'One in four Englishmen is gay.'

'The Anglo-Saxons are not interested in women as women – it is a problem with their upbringing – I think it's a sort of disease.'

Jean-Jacques Annaud (b. 1943), French film director:

'When Americans make movies they aim at the entire planet. When the French make movies, they aim at Paris.'

Anonymous French person:

'English cooking: if it's cold, it's soup. If it's warm, it's beer.'

Select Bibliography

The bibliography in a history book is sometimes so long that you wonder how the author had time to eat, sleep and go to the loo while they were doing the research. And most of them contain only a few lines that are of any relevance to the subject in hand.

I am therefore listing only the books that I've either read in their entirety, or read big chunks of, and would be happy to recommend to other people.

I must admit, though, that I didn't always flick through their yellowing pages myself. Luckily, these days, lots of libraries are putting their old books on scanners that do the flicking for us. This could be said to encourage laziness, but it's also miraculous because it means that the sources of Anglo-French history are no longer limited to researchers with access to rare and fragile documents. It is now relatively easy for anyone with a computer and a taste for hunting through online book catalogues to read medieval chronicles, seventeenth-century autobiographies and eighteenth-century travel books and see what people were actually saying about events at the time they happened.

This is why many of the books listed below are out of

print, but can be found via websites like gutenberg.org, archive.org, Google books or (for French texts) gallica.bnf.fr. You will have to read them online, but that might be more convenient than going in person to the East Louisiana Library of pre-Napoleonic Colonial Affairs.

Getting access to a medieval chronicle doesn't always mean you can understand it, of course, but the pleasant thing about French is that it has changed very little over the centuries, and you only need a short course in medieval vocabulary and grammar to be able to understand fourteenth-century texts in the original. Shakespeare's English is incomprehensible by comparison.

And for those who don't speak French, I have translated all quotations and excerpts from French sources myself.

Bonne lecture, or, as some of us Anglo-Saxons might say, have a nice read.

General Histories

A Concise History of England, F. E. Halliday, 1964
Ces femmes qui ont fait la France, Natacha Henry, 2009
Friend or Foe, Alistair Horne, 2004
The History of England, David Hume, 1810
The Story of English, Robert McCrum, William Cran, Robert MacNeil, 2002
That Sweet Enemy, Robert and Isabelle Tombs, 2006
English Social History, G. M. Trevelyan, 1942
The English Channel, J. A. Williamson, 1959
A History of England, E. L. Woodward, 1947

Specific Subjects

William the Conqueror

The Anglo-Saxon Chronicle, author(s) uncertain, 9th–12th centuries
The Bayeux Tapestry, author(s) uncertain, c. 1080
1066: The Hidden History of the Bayeux Tapestry, Andrew Bridgeford, 2004
Guillaume le Conquérant, Paul Zumthor, 1978

The Hundred Years War

Les Chroniques de Jean Froissart, Jean Froissart, 1369
La Guerre de Cent Ans vue par ceux qui l'ont vécue, Michel Mollat du Jourdin, 1975
The Hundred Years War, Desmond Seward, 1978
The Cronicle History of Henry the Fift (aka *Henry V*), William Shakespeare, 1600
Journal d'un Bourgeois de Paris, 1405–49, ed. Alexandre Tuetey, 1881
Encyclopaedia of the Hundred Years War, John A. Wagner, 2006

Calais

The Chronicle of Calais by Richard Turpyn, ed. John Gough Nichols, 1846
Calais under English Rule, G. A. C. Sandeman, 1908

Mary Queen of Scots

England under the Tudors, Geoffrey Rudolph Elton, 1991
Mary Queen of Scots, Antonia Fraser, 1969
An Examination of the Letters Said to Be Written by Mary Queen of Scots, Walter Goodall, 1754
Memoirs of His Own Life, Sir James Melville of Halhill, 1683

Charles II and Louis XIV

The Life of John, Duke of Marlborough, Charles Bucke, 1839
Louis XIV, David Ogg, 1933
The King in Exile: The Wanderings of Charles II from June 1646 to July 1654, Eva Scott, 1905

'God Save the King'

Souvenirs de la Marquise de Créquy, Maurice Cousin de Courchamps, 1842

French Colonies in Canada, North America and India

Acadian-cajun.com
Histoire de la colonisation française, Henri Blet, 1946
Cyberacadie.com
Cod, Mark Kurlansky, 1997
History of the French in India, from the Founding of Pondicherry in 1674 to the Capture of That Place in 1761, G. B. Malleson, 1893
Pioneers of France in the New World, Francis Parkman, 1865

Eighteenth-Century Explorers

Voyage autour du monde par la frégate La Boudeuse et la flûte L'Étoile, Louis-Antoine de Bougainville, 1771
The Journals of Captain Cook, James Cook, 1955, 1961 & 1967

The South Sea Bubble

John Law: The Projector, William Harrison Ainsworth, 1864
Memoirs of Extraordinary Popular Delusions, Charles Mackay, 1841

Eighteenth-Century France and the Revolution

Reflections on the Revolution in France, Edmund Burke, 1790

Histoire générale des émigrés pendant la Révolution française,
Henri Forneron, 1884
Lettres philosophiques (originally published as *Lettres écrites
de Londres sur les Anglois et autres sujets*), Voltaire, 1734

French Tourists in England
Londres, Pierre Jean Grosley, 1774

Napoleon
Code civil, Napoleon Bonaparte et al., 1804
Napoleon, Vincent Cronin, 1971
The Life of Nelson, A. T. Mahan, 1898

Shakespeare and the Romantics
Shakespeare Goes to Paris, John Pemble, 2005

Louis-Philippe
Histoire de la vie politique et privée de Louis-Philippe,
Alexandre Dumas, 1852

Death of Napoleon IV
The Washing of the Spears, Donald R. Morris, 1959

Edward VII
Gay Monarch: The Life and Pleasures of Edward VII, Virginia
Cowls, 1956
Edward VII, Man and King, H. E. Wortham, 1931

World War One
Over the Top, Arthur Guy Empey, 1917
Goodbye to All That, Robert Graves, 1929
Tommy Atkins at War, James A. Kilpatrick, 1914
Les Silences du Colonel Bramble, André Maurois, 1921
The Last Fighting Tommy: The Life of Harry Patch, Harry
Patch and Richard van Emden, 2007

World War Two

Allies at War, Simon Berthon, 2001

Marthe Richard: L'aventurière des maisons closes, Natacha Henry, 2006

The British Channel Islands under German Occupation, 1940–1945, Paul Sanders, 2005

Instructions for British Servicemen in France, Herbert Ziman, 1944

Post-War

Talk to the Snail, Stephen Clarke, 2006

Les Carnets du Major W. Marmaduke Thompson, Pierre Daninos, 1954

Loi n° 94-665 du 4 août 1994 relative à l'emploi de la langue française, Jacques Toubon, 1994

Illustration Credits

p.30 Bayeux tapestry facsimile: detail 'hic fecerunt prandium' © Mary Evans Picture Library/Alamy.

p.104 Battle of Crécy: illumination from a fourteenth-century manuscript of Froissart's *Chronicles* © Roger-Viollet.

p.143 Joan of Arc at the stake: illumination from 'Les Vigiles de Charles VII' by Martial d'Auvergne, 1484. Ms Fr 5054 f.71, Bibliothèque nationale de France, Paris /Bridgeman Art Library.

p.187 Execution of Mary Queen of Scots: woodcut © Bettmann/Corbis.

p.239 Exploding Champagne bottle, from *Facts about Champagne* . . ., 1879.

p.246 Louis XIV as Apollo: anonymous seventeenth-century watercolour design for the ballet 'La Nuit', Bibliothèque nationale de France, Paris, © RMN/Agence Bulloz.

p.369 *The Guillotine*, anonymous eighteenth-century engraving, private collection/Bridgeman Art Library.

p.396 *Un Petit Souper à la Parisienne, or A Family of Sans-Culottes Refreshing after the Fatigues of the Day*, hand-coloured etching by James Gillray, 1792, © the Warden and Scholars of New College, Oxford/Bridgeman Art Library.

Index

740

749

752

759

A Year in the Merde
Stephen Clarke

'Edgier than Bryson, hits harder than Mayle'
THE TIMES

Paul West, a young Englishman, arrives in Paris to start a new job – and finds out what the French are really like.

They do eat a lot of cheese, some of which smells like pigs' droppings. They don't wash their armpits with garlic soap. Going on strike really is the second national participation sport after pétanque. And, yes, they do use suppositories.

In his first novel, Stephen Clarke gives a laugh-out-loud account of the pleasures and perils of being a Brit in France. Less quaint than *A Year in Provence*, less chocolatey than *Chocolat*, *A Year in the Merde* will tell you how to get served by the grumpiest Parisian waiter; how to make perfect vinaigrette every time; how to make amour – not war; and how not to buy a house in the French countryside.

'This is the season's word-of-mouth must-have book for Francophiles and Francophobes alike . . . this comedy of errors has almost certainly done more for the *entente cordiale* than any of our politicians'
DAILY MAIL

'Must-have comedy-of-errors diary about being a brit abroad'
MIRROR

Dial M for Merde

Stephen Clarke

In the South of France, Paul West has a licence to thrill.

He has just received an offer he can't refuse: two weeks in the sun, all expenses paid, with a beautiful blonde called Gloria Monday.

But it soon becomes obvious that M, as Gloria likes to be known, is not really interested in holidaying with Paul. She has bigger fish to fry.

Meanwhile Paul's best friend Elodie is getting married, and Paul has been asked to do the catering. Cooking for the French is a risky assignment at the best of times, but Paul assures Elodie that nothing can go wrong.

Or can it?

When Paul discovers that M's real target is France's biggest fish of all – the new President – and that he's coming to Elodie's wedding, he realizes that the merde is about to hit the fan . . .

'Clarke brings off his story with panache'
Sunday Telegraph

'Combines the gaffes of Bridget Jones with the boldness of James Bond'
Publishers Weekly

A Brief History of the Future
Stephen Clarke

Englishman Richie Fisher and his wife Clara have won a weekend in New York in a newspaper competition.

While Clara is off blowing their spending money, Richie wanders aimlessly, chewing on a veggie-burger, ending up in a gift-shop where he finds himself standing in front of an instant transporter machine. It looks nothing like the open-plan teleporter on Captain Kirk's Starship Enterprise; in fact, it seems more like a glorified microwave oven.

Richie places his burger inside, hits the return key on the linked-up computer – and the burger disappears. But if he can teleport a half-eaten veggie-burger, what else could you do with the machine? The possibilities are endless.

Richie buys a teleporter and takes it back to England. Where the chaos begins . . .

Talk to the Snail

Ten Commandments for Understanding the French

Stephen Clarke

The **only** book you'll need to understand what the French **really** think, how to get on with them and, and **most importantly**, how to get the best out of them.

With useful sections on:

- Making sure you get **served in a café**
- Harassing French **estate agents**
- Living with **bacteria**
- Pronouncing French **swear-words**
- Surviving the French **driving** experience
- Falling in **amour**, Paris-style

And beaucoup beaucoup more!

DON'T GO TO FRANCE WITHOUT
READING THIS BOOK!

Stephen Clarke lives in Paris, where he divides his time between writing and not writing. His first novel, *A Year in the Merde*, originally became a word-of-mouth hit in 2004, and is now published all over the world. Since then he has published four more bestselling *Merde* novels, as well as *Talk to the Snail*, an indispensable guide to understanding the French, *Paris Revealed*, an insider's guide to the secret life of his home city, and *Dirty Bertie: an English King Made in France*, the true story of the young Edward VII's transformation from playboy prince into world-class diplomat, all thanks to Parisian *femmes fatales*. His most recent history book is *How the French Won Waterloo (or Think They Did)*.

Research for Stephen's books has taken him all over France and America. For *1000 Years of Annoying the French*, he spent two years breathing the chill air of ruined castles and deserted battlefields, leafing through dusty chronicles, brushing up the medieval French he studied at university and generally losing himself in the mists of history.

He has now returned to present-day Paris, where he is doing his best to live the Entente Cordiale.

For further information on Stephen Clarke and his books, you can follow him on Twitter @sclarkewriter or consult his website: www.stephenclarkewriter.com

Praise for *1000 Years of Annoying the French*:

'Tremendously entertaining'   *Sunday Times*

'Relentlessly and energetically rude about almost every aspect of French history and culture'   *Mail on Sunday*

'Guaranteed to infuriate the French . . . anyone who's ever encountered a snooty Parisian waiter or found themselves driving on the Boulevard Péripherique during August will enjoy this book'   *Daily Mail*

Also by Stephen Clarke

A YEAR IN THE MERDE
MERDE ACTUALLY
MERDE HAPPENS
DIAL M FOR MERDE
THE MERDE FACTOR

A BRIEF HISTORY OF THE FUTURE

TALK TO THE SNAIL: TEN COMMANDMENTS
FOR UNDERSTANDING THE FRENCH

PARIS REVEALED: THE SECRET LIFE OF A CITY

DIRTY BERTIE: AN ENGLISH KING MADE IN FRANCE

HOW THE FRENCH WON WATERLOO
(OR THINK THEY DID)